DIFFERENTIAL DIAGNOSIS IN CLINICAL PSYCHIATRY

DIFFERENTIAL DIAGNOSIS IN CLINICAL PSYCHIATRY

The Lectures of Paul H. Hoch, M.D.

edited by
Margaret O. Strahl, M.D.
and
Nolan D. C. Lewis, M.D.

Jason Aronson, Inc.
New York, N.Y.

Library of Congress Catalog Card Number: 72–76812
Standard Book Number: 87668–053–8

Manufactured in the United States of America

Table of Contents

Preface

This volume represents a lecture series presented by Dr. Paul H. Hoch to a group of physicians taking residency training in psychoanalysis and psychosomatic medicine at the Columbia Psychoanalytic Clinic for Training and Research. Dr. Hoch died in 1964. Publication has been delayed because the original presentations—taken from disc recordings—were predominately informal and required considerable editing. Particular care was taken to give Dr. Hoch's intended meaning and structure while at the same time preserving his inimitable "paprika" conversational style.

In the opinions of several contemporary psychiatrists these lectures are the most instructive since Emil Kraepelin and Eugen Bleuler wrote their books many years ago. It is not, however, a complete textbook of psychiatry, but concentrates on symptoms, differential diagnosis, and the evolution of mental disorders for the purpose of reviewing and orienting the material for the instruction of advanced students.

Since Dr. Hoch was presenting the important factors in differential diagnosis, the material, naturally, focuses on accurate, detailed observation and evaluation of the symptoms and behavioral expressions of mental patients. Because the skills of differential diagnosis are too often neglected in the training of psychiatric students, these lectures are of special value; we know of no other single source that affords such a wealth of information in this particular area of psychiatry, to which little, if anything, has been added to the literature since these lectures were given.

The general neglect of differential diagnosis is, probably, due to a number of reasons. One of them may be the usual psychoanalytic tendency to study and interpret individual mental symptoms psychodynamically rather than in terms of a total pattern to be named. Another reason could be that the remarkable advances in psychopharmacology have encouraged more and more physicians to rely on drugs to ameliorate the presenting symptoms, thus frequently blurring the diagnostic picture. Improvements may occur regardless of the type of therapeutic procedure a physician prefers, but long-term follow-up studies indicate that Dr. Hoch was correct in emphasizing that accurate diagnosis is of paramount importance for prognosis and for the selection of appropriate therapy for any psychiatric disorder.

In these lectures a holistic viewpoint is presented. Psychodynamic processes have not been neglected; they are freely discussed among the current theories of the dynamics of mental disorders. Somatic factors are given due consideration along with those components that in our present state of knowledge can be described only in terms of the patient's biological makeup, a combination that attempts to understand the human organism in its struggle to cope with a serious, handicapping condition.

10

In several of the lectures this coverage, of all the known factors entering the picture, is in considerable detail. As examples, those discussions of the schizophrenias and of various forms of alcoholism are extensive and also inclusive, with the exception of some of the most recent biochemical findings.

Changes in therapeutic procedures are occurring continuously in psychiatric practice; in most instances, therefore, Dr. Hoch referred to therapy only briefly and in terms of basic approach. He did not make it a prime topic of discussion, but often discussed it as it related to etiological and diagnostic factors.

One is impressed by the fact that these lectures were based on scientific principles without forcing the observations and ideas into any given "system" of thought. One is further impressed by Dr. Hoch's repeated pleas for additional research on those obscure issues that lend themselves to controversial discussions and interpretations.

Dr. Hoch had the well-deserved respect, admiration, and affection of his students and collaborators, and to them these lectures obviously will be most welcome. They will also be in broad demand because they serve to complete the syndromic pictures for those physicians who have had the opportunity to be orientated only in psychodynamics or, in fact, for professionals orientated in any of the other fields of medicine.

The editors are greatly indebted to Dr. Abel Lajtha, Director of the New York State Research Institute for Neurochemistry (founded by Dr. Hoch), for graciously and gallantly inviting us into his Institute and providing office space to edit these lectures.

Former students of Dr. Hoch—Dr. Louise Coleman, Dr. Elizabeth Davis, and Dr. James L. Curtis—cooperated by making available some of their lecture notes, which served as guidelines when problems arose in deciphering the disc recordings.

Dr. Hoch's secretary, Miss Helen Anderberg, deserves credit for the lengthy task of transcribing most of the original lectures from the discs and for initial advice and assistance in editing several. Mrs. Louise Mussolini, secretary to the late Dr. Heinrich Waelsch, eagerly gave us her support by transcribing many lectures, devotedly aware that Dr. Waelsch had been the prime mover in publishing this, as well as other, important works of his close friend, Paul Hoch.

Miss Sally Shroyer has been indispensable; she is remarkable both for her expert skill in typing the drafts and the entire final manuscript and for her generosity in donating the countless hours required—all given out of her personal admiration for Dr. Hoch. And, the woman who helped us all in so many ways of encouragement is our friend, Mrs. Paul H. Hoch. The publication of her husband's lectures has been her liveliest interest.

Margaret O. Strahl, M.D.
Nolan D. C. Lewis, M.D.
Eds.

THE AUTHOR

Dr. Paul H. Hoch was born in Budapest, Hungary, in 1902. For the nine years prior to his death, he was Commissioner of the New York State Department of Mental Hygiene and had created "The Master Plan" for the treatment of mental disability. His professional history includes substantial achievements in research, clinical work, teaching, and administration. His creative talents ranged from the microscopic to the macroscopic aspects of psychiatric medicine.

Paul Hoch's medical training, received at the University of Göttingen in Germany, was completed in 1926. Following his internship, he was assigned First Assistant Physician at its Neuropsychiatric Clinic and was placed in charge of the University Hospital Brain Research Division of the Clinic. He had also been assigned Assistant Physician at the Psychiatric Clinic in Zürich, Switzerland, at which time he became strongly influenced by Eugen Bleuler's work in schizophrenia. From then on, Dr. Hoch was ardently engaged in research in the biological and clinical aspects of schizophrenia. He came to contribute beyond Bleuler to the knowledge in this field and was acclaimed the leading authority. An example of this was his thorough study of what he termed the "pseudoneurotic form of schizophrenia." In his lectures he discussed the diagnostic methods of appraising that extremely prevalent disorder, a procedure that was one of his most important contributions to the techniques of differential diagnosis.

After arriving in the United States in 1933, Dr. Hoch soon became recognized for his remarkable talents and was offered a succession of research and clinical positions. In 1943, after surmounting many bureaucratic problems, Dr. Nolan D. C. Lewis, then Director of the New York State Psychiatric Institute and founder of the Psychoanalytic Clinic for Training and Research, secured the appointment of Dr. Hoch to his staff at the Institute and in the Clinic. Dr. Hoch became Senior Clinical Psychiatrist in 1946, and Director of the Department of Experimental Psychiatry in 1948.

Besides being admired internationally for his research abilities and clinical acumen, Dr. Hoch attracted wide attention as a competent therapist, consultant, and as an outstanding teacher. He possessed rare leadership qualities and was in constant demand as a speaker by various professional societies, agencies, and institutions. His bibliography includes more than 300 publications *(Lewis and Strahl, 1968).*

In all areas, Dr. Hoch was noted for the care and solid judgment he displayed in reaching decisions, his ability to grasp the essential issues of problems, and for his resolute maintenance of high standards. As a teacher, too, his mind always focused on the basic questions in psychiatry. This attitude of perceiving and emphasizing fundamental issues while dealing lightly with superficial matters, and his ability to point out the doubtful, the unproved, the unanswered elements in current theories always impressed his students. Tireless in professional honesty, with deep concern regarding human problems, he gave selflessly of his talents to all who sought to learn from him. Although his energy was prodigious, he gave beyond his strength.

Editors' Note

In consideration of Dr. Hoch's conversational style, the editors have not overburdened the readers with references.

Bibliographic references are of two kinds: specific references to works which are neither well known or readily accessible, and general references to men and topics the reader may wish to explore further. The specific references are indicated by the author's name and/or the date of publication in italics, *e.g., (Haslam, 1798)*; complete bibliographic information may be found in the References on page 797. General references are indicated in the text by italicized numerals, *e.g., (4)*, which refer to works listed under General Readings in Psychiatry and Neurology on page 801.

We hope this method of notation will not impede the flow of Dr. Hoch's delivery, while at the same time providing documentation for those who require it.

Part I

Introduction to Clinical Psychiatry

1

HISTORY TAKING AND
INTERVIEW TECHNIQUE

Preliminary to my discussion of clinical psychiatry, I want
to take up—very much in general—the history taking of
psychiatric patients. How, for example, should examinations be executed, and how should descriptive and psychodynamic material be handled in interviews? What I have to
say will not be new. Nevertheless, I would like to stress a few
basic points because it is often obvious that certain things
are not done as well as they should be; in fact, sometimes it
is rather shocking how histories are done.

At first we must realize that, unfortunately, we do not
have such a thing as a model for psychiatric history applicable for all patients. We take different types of histories for
different kinds of patients and actually we are not able to
use the same type for every kind of psychiatric case. For
instance, a somewhat different history is required for psychotic patients than for neurotic patients; a different history

is required for mental defectives and retardates, for psycho-somatic patients, and also for patients who are cooperative and those who are uncooperative; different forms of histories are required for adults and different forms for children. Therefore, for anyone taking psychiatric histories, it is essential to size up the patient with whom he is dealing, and to some extent adapt the interview to the patient. If not, we will obtain rather peculiar histories. For instance, it is not rare for an inexperienced physician to examine all psychiatric patients from the point of view that he is dealing with a psychotic; the examiner asks all those questions which would document whether or not the patient is psychotic. In other words, the entire history is organized around this decision, but none of the neurotic or other pathology in the patient is looked into sufficiently. Conversely, very often the patient is simply examined from the point of view that he is suffering with a psychoneurosis. If the examiner is actually dealing with a so-called psychosomatic disorder, in addition to examining the patient for neurosis some very special questions should be included to gain particular information, the patient being a certain form of neurotic in which somatization will be in the foreground.

In some cases the average psychiatric interview is not sufficient for special purposes. For instance, if the psychiatric patient examined as a clinical case suddenly becomes a legal case, the physician may be embarrassed when he appears in court, particularly if a clever lawyer asks questions the physician cannot answer simply because he has not obtained the information from the patient. Therefore, if a patient becomes a legal case or a compensation case, again the history will have to be adapted to that particular purpose. Now this all indicates that even though we have a basic form of history taking, nevertheless, we occasionally must adapt our examination of the patient to fit some special purpose.

The basic principle for examining psychiatric patients has evolved rather slowly. Even a few decades ago, history taking in clinical psychiatry was entirely different from that of the present time. Very possibly several years from now history taking will be further modified, although probably some of the basic issues will remain unchanged. A complete fusion of the different aspects of history taking, which I will present in detail, is as yet not fully achieved in psychiatry; therefore it lacks such a completely organized form as, for instance, exists in medical school on medical services as such.

Today three aspects are especially stressed in the history taking of a psychiatric patient. First, there are the *hereditary, constitutional,* and *physical* factors which should be, and are, covered. The extent to which we probe into a patient's heredity, constitution, and physical status will be taken up in more detail later on. Second, there are the environmentally related so-called *individual experience* factors which must be taken into consideration. Third, there are the *socioeconomic* factors in which the patient's mental condition moves. These also have to be evaluated.

Every psychiatric interview today covers these three areas more or less. It is obvious, however, that in viewing psychiatric histories from different clinics or by different psychiatrists, the three aspects just mentioned are each stressed in different ways. There are clinics where the first area is nearly completely neglected, and only the individual experience factors are taken into consideration. In other clinics, the reverse can be seen; great stress is given to the patient's heredity, constitution, and physical factors, but the second area is neglected. There are still a number of clinics who pay attention to the first and second aspects, but completely neglect the third, the socioeconomic factors.

Actually an unbiased evaluation of all these factors should be done in any interview. When you have gathered the facts, their importance will then, naturally, have to be reorganized and deciphered. But, please remember that all the *facts* must be gathered! In other words, no history is complete when the psychiatrist who has examined the patient is unable to explain the patient's present physical condition, what physical diseases he has had, any mental or nervous diseases that have occurred in the family, the nature of the patient's life experiences during certain periods of his life, and the patient's socioeconomic condition in relationship to the civilization and culture in which he lives. All of these three different aspects must be taken into consideration.

Historically speaking, history taking in psychiatry was originally done in the same way as it is done in other fields of medicine. This is understandable because when psychiatry emerged as a department of medicine, mental conditions were treated strictly as diseases, the disease concept here being very similar to the disease concept in internal medicine. The medical student learned how to take an anamnesis from a patient suffering, for example, from paresis or from tuberculosis, and he strictly applied the same principles and obtained an anamnesis in a similar way on the patient's mental condition. Although these anamneses at first closely resembled a medical history, as the relationship of neurology to psychiatry later became apparent the anamneses then resembled those of neurological patients. Not so long ago, the psychiatric interview placed stress on the neurological aspects of some cases—for instance, in paretic or in encephalitic patients—and the history was mainly organized around these factors.

Following the establishment of this so-called medical history procedure, we entered a second phase in psychiatric history taking: psychological questions were asked. However, the psychological questions were not asked in the same way as is done today, namely, from a dynamic point of view. The questions were based mainly on some knowledge of academic psychology which was essentially experimental psychology or that dealing with physiology of the sense organs. Therefore, questions were introduced into the medical anamnesis for testing the patient's memory, his thinking, and some of his psychophysiological functioning. Later on, when methods were developed to test the intellectual patterns of the individual, questions began to appear concerning intellectual functioning and capacity. These questions, however, were usually not directed in a way that would disclose the dynamic factors underlying the patient's thinking or feeling disorder because, naturally, psychodynamic concepts did not exist at that time. At first they were mainly academic questions, and later they perhaps became more practical questions to determine whether or not there was an existent memory disturbance or an intellectual impairment.

Following this, psychiatry entered a descriptive era; the patient's symptoms were described in detail, and the history included descriptions of his gross pathological behavior—his delusions and hallucinations, obsessions, depressions, and so forth.

In a more recent phase of the evolution of psychiatric examination, questions were introduced which had something to do with the personality organization of the patient. Some knowledge about personality structure was based partly on constitutional research and partly on studies of emotional organization, and all of these findings were then correlated to indicate the personality makeup of the patient. At first the different types of constitutions were mainly stressed from the somatic point of view. Then, however, aspects of the personality organization were explored and the so-called reaction formations to the environment were studied. Questions in this respect were then introduced in attempting to determine how, and in what way, the patient reacted to the environment. For example, it was questioned: "Did he show a tendency to withdraw? Did he show a tendency to break through? Did he show a tendency to be sensitive?" and so forth. In other words, questions were introduced in attempts to find out on what matrix the patient's mental disorder developed.

At the present time quite a number of such questions are introduced in trying to ascertain not only in what way the patient is functioning mentally, but also what type of personality he showed at the time he was considered to be functioning relatively normally. This is done not only to be able to formulate some idea on what matrix the mental disorder developed, but also—which is of great importance when formulating some prognostic interpretation of the patient's mental disorder—to ascertain what the base line is for this patient to return to when the present mental disorder is over.

In time, questions began to be posed to the patient regarding what has come to be termed dynamic material. Now, dynamic material mainly contains so-called interaction behavior patterns with the environment, and this was especially strongly organized around the relationship of the patient to his parents during early childhood. It was later expanded, naturally, to also include his reactions in adulthood. But, especially under the influence of the psychoanalytic schools, childhood experiences were stressed regarding the patient's relationship to his immediate family. Later on, questions appeared taking into consideration his interrelationship with his enlarged family, friends, and other people. Every psychiatric inventory elucidated the patient's behavior on this so-called dynamic material.

By this time, more and more questions were introduced into the psychiatric interview to try to discern the motives of the patient's actions. This so-called environmental interaction as seen from the point of view of patient's motivation is a part of every psychiatric interview. I may immediately add here that those questions seemingly concerned with motivation covered, naturally, only the conscious motivation of the patient or his own interpretation on the subject. It would not necessarily be a true one; often, as one sees in many neurotics or psychotics, it is actually the patient's rationalization. Nevertheless, it is extremely important to be aware of just how the patient interprets to the physician and to himself his motivations for his own action, regardless of whether or not it is later found to be the true state of affairs or the working of unconscious neurotic mechanisms.

The tendency of some psychiatrists to introduce immediately their own interpretations and their own motives, in practically the same way the patient projects some of his ideas into other people, is naturally not a good practice. Therefore, obtaining the patient's own ideas and own motives for his actions is an essential part of any well-conducted psychiatric interview today.

Finally, questions began to appear, based especially on some investigations in anthropology and in sociology, in recognition of the fact that no mental disorder occurs in a vacuum, regardless of the origin of the mental disorder. The person afflicted naturally moves in society, moves in a certain civilization, and obviously this civilization with its own social organization, set of mores, permissions, and inhibitions will influence the patient's behavior and reactions up to a point. Therefore, it is important to know in what environment he moves, how he responds to this environment, and especially what restrictions the environment imposes on him. Naturally the economic status and economic atmosphere in which the patient moves are also of great importance. This is obvious to the examiner, and it is always so intimate to the patient that it need not be stressed. Therefore, the social background, the social adaptability and, furthermore, the social restrictions to which the patient is, and has been, exposed must be ascertained in a well-conducted psychiatric interview.

Today we try to fuse all the various aspects of history taking, and in our approach we refer back to the basic three factors mentioned. In interviewing the patient we attempt to ascertain the heredito-constitutional and physical factors, the psychodynamic factors, and the socioeconomic factors. In different clinics and in private practice, sometimes certain modifications of this basic interviewing technique occur. For instance, the psychiatrist might give certain emphasis to one or the other of these main aspects in the psychiatric interview. This is permissible provided the psychiatrist doing it knows for certain that he is dealing with rather consistent material. If not, or if he has yet to establish some form of a diagnosis, it is a dangerous habit to examine the patient only from a psychodynamic, or only from an organic, or only from a sociological point of view because quite often diagnostic and, quite naturally, therapeutic mistakes are made as a result of a somewhat one-sided psychiatric interview.

There are psychiatrists who do not often deal with psychotic material, but it does not prevent a psychotic individual from appearing in their office and being promptly misdiagnosed as a psychoneurotic. Vice versa, there are psychiatrists (mostly hospital psychiatrists) who deal mainly with psychotic patients, and then the reverse occurs; they are not very apt to find neurotic disturbances and, therefore, are rather rigid in their diagnosing. These are the two main mistakes usually made. It is also not uncommon for psychiatrists who are not trained in an all-round way to overlook an organic condition in those patients who are at the same time showing neurotic or psychotic manifestations. Actually, 40 to 50 percent of all admissions in mental hospitals move on an organic level. Therefore, in quite a number of patients an organic disorder is present which expresses itself in disturbances of the mind. These cases are so extremely common that every psychiatrist has to be equipped to recognize and diagnose them, even should he specialize in some other forms of mental disorders and not want to treat them. Unfortunately, even in large metropolitan medical centers false diagnoses—because of limited facts—are frequently made by examiners who simply do not think about the probability of an organic disorder. Again the reverse mistake is commonly made; in some so-called functional psychoses or in the neuroses the psychodynamic factors are not properly elucidated, and inexperienced psychiatrists who simply view the patient from some organic or otherwise biased attitude sometimes overlook fundamental issues which would have clarified the patient's condition quite well had the patient been interviewed properly.

INTERVIEW TECHNIQUES

In discussing methods for conducting interviews, there are two techniques which must first be considered: one approach is the so-called classical interview, which consists of simply questioning the patient; the other approach is through questionnaires, these being used in quite a number of places. Both techniques may be used; the pros and cons of each will be discussed.

In addition to the so-called classical and the questionnaire interview techniques, several other methods of interviewing were subsequently introduced. One, for instance, is the use of projective techniques such as personality inventories or outright psychological tests—the Rorschach and so forth. These are not in themselves actually interviewing the patient in a psychiatric sense. Still another technique is the so-called associative anamnesis whereby the psychiatrist does not ask questions, but immediately uses free association from the patient. Then again, there are psychiatrists who immediately inject the patient with some form of drug, such as sodium amytal, for interviewing purposes. My position on any of these methods of questioning is that, discarding exceptional situations, they should not be used as a primary approach to the patient. In other words, for diagnostic purposes a patient should always have a classical psychiatric interview.

If one wishes to use some projective techniques to elucidate the personality structure or some diagnostic problems in the patient, he is fully entitled to do so, but it should be as an auxiliary to the psychiatric interview. A pernicious habit is developing rather rapidly among some psychiatrists: they see a patient for only a few minutes, practically asking only his name and age, and they then send him somewhere for a projective test for diagnosis. This is not the way psychiatric interviewing for psychiatric diagnosis should be conducted because it is grossly incomplete (not to mention that an absolute correlation does not exist between psychiatric knowledge arrived at by interviewing the patient and psychiatric data from projective techniques). It is obvious that any psychiatrist who wants to treat a patient will have to familiarize himself with the patient's troubles first-hand and not simply read the report of a psychologist that this-or-that was found from the projective techniques. No responsible internist would send his patient for a laboratory test or an x-ray without first examining him; similarly, immediate referral for psychological tests is not the responsible policy to follow with a psychiatric patient. Projective techniques are valuable only as an auxiliary aid to psychiatric diagnosis.

The so-called associative interviewing method misses obtaining a tremendous amount of valuable material about the patient. Free association interviewing should not be done except in very exceptional cases, and should be used only as a treatment technique after the patient has been so thoroughly examined psychiatrically that the psychiatrist has derived a good idea of the type of patient he is dealing with. It often happens that a patient can be treated for two or three weeks who then suddenly makes a suicide attempt or becomes violently psychotic—quite to the psychiatrist's surprise—simply because very simple questions were not asked and very simple examinations were not done. The patient had been immediately laid on the couch and asked to free associate. Free association as an interview technique should be used only in the framework of therapy along with all that it implies. Also, the import of free association techniques on the transference situation, especially, should be understood by the therapist and utilized in the therapeutic framework. It is a poor policy to conduct free associative interviews before formally examining the patient to arrive at some idea of the type of therapy this particular patient should actually have.

The introduction of drugs immediately into the interview situation is also not permissible, with the exception of cases who are very uncooperative or mute. It is only on such patients that this technique might be applied in order to make the patient accessible for psychiatric interview. To immediately use drugs routinely on any patient is not good policy. As with projective techniques, drugs are an auxiliary procedure which can be very important as a diagnostic aid, but only after the patient has been psychiatrically examined in a general way.

Returning to the so-called classical interviewing technique, I shall first discuss it in terms of the form of the interview, and then its content.

FORM: The form of the interview does not need much explanation. Nevertheless, I would like to review some very simple matters which are so very often violated.

For one thing, the psychiatric interview should be done with *complete privacy* of the patient with his psychiatrist. Even today in Grade-A hospitals, especially general hospitals, one will see a ward psychiatrist asking psychiatric questions in the presence of other patients or nurses. With the exception of a very grossly psychotic patient, this is very bad practice—it is bad even when done simply to ascertain therapeutic disposition for the patient. Psychiatric sickness, especially when the patient is quite aware of it, is a form of sickness that has a profound emotional connotation to him, and I think that the most primitive requirement of a patient is to confide in someone, and we should give him the privilege of doing so in privacy. A psychiatric interview in public is not a psychiatric interview! We all, to some extent, violate this rule with patients when we speak with them in conferences. We have to for teaching purposes. Questions put to patients in a conference, however, are selective, and because it is a conference we are often inhibited in asking certain questions. Questions regarding issues which would embarrass the patient will not be asked, simply to avoid embarrassing the patient and pushing him into a situation whereby he will refuse to answer. Conferences aside, the first rule of the psychiatric interview is to be alone with the patient and not examine him publicly.

A second rule concerns the length of time of a formal interview; it should not be longer than *about an hour*. There are psychiatrists who indulge in marathon interviews—two or three hours or more. The patient usually is unable to follow along or will become fatigued in this length of time. I believe that an hour is probably the maximum amount of time a patient is able to tolerate. Naturally, I do not say that this rule cannot be violated in exceptional cases, but that it should not be done routinely with the idea in mind that a very interesting case is now on hand, such as a patient with a lot of interesting psychodynamic material who talks on and on, and as he keeps on pouring material out the therapist goes on thinking, "Now I will listen to this stuff for three or four hours." That is not good policy. Every interview should be organized on a one-hour basis.

Thirdly, if you use a questionnaire, it *should not be read* from in the presence of the patient. It is a rather bad procedure to pick up a book and, while reading from it, ask the patient: "Now, how do you feel?" "Are you depressed?" "Are you elated?" The patient cannot help but receive the impression that you do not know anything yourself and need a book to guide you. This, of course, impairs the patient's confidence in you. If you use a questionnaire (and at first they are useful in order not to forget things) to enable you to cover an interview rather completely, then memorize some of the material or write it out on a piece of paper. By this means you can avoid allowing the patient to feel that you need a guide, or that you have a mere form with printed data that must be taken care of, thus making him feel that as an individual he is being neglected and being treated as some number and classified accordingly.

The fourth rule in the formal part of interviewing is to *cover the whole field*, if possible, in this one-hour initial interview. This needs some experience and probably for the first few times you will not be able to do so. Nevertheless, you should aim for the ability to examine a patient in one hour in such a way that at least you have a general idea as to the personality and condition of the patient with whom you are dealing. Now, with some very complicated cases this probably cannot be done and a great deal more observation of the patient is needed, but even there it is a good idea to note this rule. You will be asked, for instance, for consultations on the general wards of hospitals. You will sometimes interview a private patient and be required to formulate some advice in the first hour. It is bad policy, therefore, to examine the patient and spend an hour on the family history, giving yourself no time to examine the patient in other areas. Surely a great many patients will need more than one interview, most likely five or six, before you are satisfied that every area has been well covered. But in the first interview the patient should be examined in a general way in order to give yourself a general idea as to what is going on; then the details can be fitted in later with much less difficulty.

It is not rare in my experience to find that in the first interview the patient brings up some rather interesting issue—and the psychiatrist concentrates on it. He then omits touching upon the patient's intellectual capacity to determine whether he is dealing with someone of normal intelligence or sub-normal intelligence. Or, the psychiatrist forgets to ask the patient obvious questions regarding his physical status and so forth. Then a completely distorted first impression is gained. First impressions are rather important, and later on these impressions are not easily corrected. Therefore, it is very important to examine the patient all around, and when this is done you can fill in the details at a later time.

You must always safeguard yourself against another difficulty that often arises, namely, conducting a *stereotyped* interview. Stereotyped interviewing leads to stereotyped case histories, and it is especially conspicuous among doctors who somehow can never free themselves from using a questionnaire. As I have mentioned, good questionnaires cover a lot of material, and in the beginning every psychiatrist uses them because otherwise he will omit things. But in conducting such an interview the psychiatrist must keep in mind that he is dealing with an individual, and that this individual has individual experiences, very often unique experiences which cannot be fitted into a mold. Therefore, always pay attention to individual features even though much of the material must be covered in a general way.

One or two things should be mentioned regarding something which a great many examiners violate: The proper *timing of questions.* This is particularly important when using a questionnaire. The therapist usually goes through it in a very methodical way; he begins by asking the patient questions about the family history, goes over to the personal history, then comes to the patient's illness, and so on, ending up with questions to appraise insight and judgment. From a methodical point of view this is acceptable, but from the patient's point of view it is quite often wrong. For instance, one must never begin by asking the patient the family history. The basic rule should be to *ask the patient his complaint,* or why did he come to the hospital, or why did he consult us. That is logical, because he is coming as a patient. He would naturally first like to pour out his emotional tension, his difficulties, and try to inform us as to what is important to him. Furthermore, a certain empathic contact—or what can already be called a certain amount of transference relationship with the patient—is obviously much better established through the substance of the patient's complaints and your reaction to them rather than through the family history. A great many patients do not know why they are being asked questions regarding their family history or what significance it has, and such questioning might easily arouse a negative reaction in a patient whereupon he will not give you some important fact he would otherwise have given had you first gained his confidence. Therefore, the interview starts with the patient's complaints.

It is incredible how certain persons, who call themselves psychiatrists, will, in the first few moments of the interview, immediately throw questions at a patient, usually of a sexual nature, from which the patient recoils and which he cannot even answer. Questions concerning intimate relationships with members of the family, sexual relationships and such, should always be asked after the more indifferent material has been disposed of and when the patient is, up to a point, "in your hands." In other words, the more intimate questions can be asked once the therapist has established a good transference relationship with the patient. This rule can be violated only when occasionally dealing with, for instance, a schizophrenic patient who is so dominated by his sexual thoughts and at the same time so indifferent to social defenses organized around this that he immediately blurts out some of his sexual difficulties and offers them to his therapist on a platter. As will be seen when I discuss some of the psychodynamic factors in schizophrenia, such offerings are quite often of diagnostic importance. In the average patient, however, you cannot question concerning sex in the initial interview because he employs some social defenses around this area and he is naturally quite perturbed if he sees the psychiatrist immediately trying to hit this spot first of all.

In immediately questioning the average patient about his sexual life, one may also do another wrong thing. Many patients are informed on psychiatric matters—sometimes better informed than the psychiatrist—and they know some psychiatric theory or psychiatric schools of thought. They watch very carefully just how the psychiatrist approaches them and deals with them and I have heard, and not rarely, that the patient later questions: "Does this doctor devote all of his time to sex?" "Will he talk about other things, too?" "My problem is not primarily sexual." In other words, when the psychiatrist's questions are not completely relevant, the patient feels it. It is obvious to him when the interview is narrowed down to one aspect of his life. Questions that probe into areas around which a great deal of anxiety is generated should ordinarily be asked of the patient only at the proper time. The timing is very important, not only in initial interviewing but also throughout the treatment.

Finally, when interviewing a patient, always take into consideration two factors: (1) the *intellectual capacity*; and (2) the *emotional status*. Violation of the first point is unlikely because the psychiatrist usually realizes when he is dealing with a person who is not very intelligent. The matter of intelligence is important, nevertheless, because the therapist will question a patient who is of above-average intelligence differently than a person who is feeble-minded. Overlooking the second point—emotional status—is, however, all too common. Disregard of the patient's emotional state in an interview relationship should never happen. For instance, it is not satisfactory to interview a patient who is paranoid, or a patient who is depressed, or a patient who is flighty, all in the same manner. The psychiatrist must adapt himself to the mood of the individual patient. He should adapt himself quite differently to the person who is elated than to the person who is depressed, or suspicious, or paranoid. To conduct a satisfactory interview, certain variations in technique have to be employed to elicit facts from patients regarding their particular state of emotion.

CONTENT: How should an interview be conducted? Quite a number of mistakes are made here; I would say they go in two directions. One interviewer lets the patient ramble on while he remains completely passive. On the other hand, another interviewer questions the patient in a manner and form that prohibits the patient from expressing some of his own ideas and feelings on subjects. Considerable experimentation has gone on in the last few years to determine the best way for the psychiatrist to approach the patient:

should he let the patient talk freely and act only as some form of a catalyst or enzyme that makes the patient talk more, or should he follow a fairly rigid scheme of questioning the patient? Today we try to combine both methods.

The best policy to follow at the start of the interview is to allow the patient to speak freely. For instance, start out with his complaints and ask him to describe just how he feels and what he thinks about these complaints. Incidentally, the patient's interpretations of his own complaints are very valuable, so always ask him what he thinks is the origin of his symptoms. It is here the patient will give some hint that he has a more or less preconceived idea, or that he is following a sort of scheme he has worked out for himself or acquired from some other person in whom he temporarily believes. Some patients are markedly "hipped" on an organic explanation of their symptoms, or perhaps some ideological explanation. Listen for a while to acquire a certain feeling of how the patient thinks and feels about his symptoms. This is a very important strategic point in the beginning of therapy for determining what measures to take to help him overcome some of his prejudicial ideas.

Patients who are able to verbalize and who are intelligent enough to formulate their ideas, and those who are introspective enough to have given some thought to their own symptoms, are the type which usually present the least difficulty. These patients can usually be attended to by means of a free-flowing interview without its requiring very much interference on the part of the therapist. With a great many other patients, however, this technique will not be satisfactory because, if allowed to talk freely, these patients will simply talk about things that are unimportant, or will be circumstantial, or will be unable to verbalize and, probably what is most important, they will omit many of the essential issues. In such cases the patient must be questioned.

How to question a patient must be learned. Initially, it would probably be advisable to follow one of the interviewing guides. After having gained some experience you can modify it in any way you wish. It is very important that the questioning should not appear to the patient as a form of probing. A great many neurotic patients resent that. They are appreciative when questioned intelligently, but they usually become irritated if they feel the questions have nothing to do with their troubles and that you are on a soul-searching expedition which they are unable to follow.

In questioning the patient it is also important, especially from a diagnostic point of view, that the questioning be unbiased—unbiased in the sense that it covers all the pertinent facts concerning the dynamic, organic, and social status of the individual. A large number of psychiatrists like to use short cuts. Many others are fascinated by certain schools of thought, and, by listening to them questioning a patient, one can actually label their school by the way in which they group and interpret the facts elicited. It is a very bad form of questioning to simply single out one psychodynamic factor in the patient. For instance, a patient reveals a very marked attachment to his mother, and the examiner immediately concludes that this or that is the basis of the patient's disorder and from there on directs all questions toward proving this specific type of dynamic or clinical point.

Quite a number of case histories are tailored to fit a particular approach or a particular psychiatric trend of thought. These case histories are valueless because whoever reads them later on will naturally ask questions which had not been asked because the interviewer simply did not get around to them, having been so fascinated by one or another dynamic formulation. Therefore, questioning should be an unbiased fact-finding, and sufficient facts should be gathered so that not only the interviewer but anyone else who reads the case history at a later date should be able to form an equally unbiased opinion of the patient's mental status. To summarize this point, the best approach today is to let the patient speak and then intersperse questions in order to elucidate those things the patient had not mentioned. If the patient wishes to explain or enlarge upon some of the morbid feelings he has, this naturally should be granted him.

I have touched upon the associative form of interview and stated that I do not use this in history taking because I believe that it is too cumbersome and usually fails to reveal many things which are important to the diagnosis. I feel that associative interviews belong to therapy, not to initial interviews per se. You have probably read or heard about the therapeutic interview which was expressly advocated by Felix Deutsch in Boston (1949). This is a valuable addition to psychiatric interviewing and also to psychiatric treatment when it is considered on the level of short-term treatment. This therapeutic interviewing, however, can be done only by someone who both knows how to interview, and who also has had a considerable amount of experience as a therapist. The technique is organized around the idea that, as soon as the patient reveals certain material, the material is to be picked up and used for directing the patient's attention to certain problems, or even for actually interpreting the patient's behavior. In other words, it is a combination of an interviewing and interpretive session which obviously requires a psychiatrist skilled in doing both. It is used today in a number of veterans' clinics in order to shorten the therapeutic time by injecting psychotherapy immediately in the first interview.

Actually, in large mental hospital situations (not so much in out-patient clinics where the patient material is voluntary) the psychiatrist has to overcome the hostility of many of the patients in the first interview. Most of these patients are psychotic, and in a number of them the commitment procedure and knowledge that they are committed reactively produce a great deal of hostility toward the person interviewing them. This is only natural. It must be taken into consideration in the interview, and the therapist's attitude and behavior will have to be such as to overcome this patient's hostility. I mention this because it is not rare that in some such situations the interviewer gets very little material from the patient, often much less than the referring psychiatrist received, and sometimes false diagnostic notions crop up simply because the patient was not thoroughly examined due to his rejecting and hostile attitude which the interviewer was unable to overcome.

Another common mistake made by interviewers is to argue with the patient about his symptoms. Now that may sound rather silly to mention, but I do mention it because it occurs so often. The patient brings up some form of imagination, some form of delusion, or some very peculiar phobic or obsessive idea which, for one reason or another, irritates the interviewer. Then the argument starts. The doctor tries to persuade the patient that he does not hear voices, that he is a fool to believe he is followed on the street, and so forth; he simply tries to convince the patient that these things are not true. This, of course, is the worst therapeutic policy and it becomes doubly bad if done in the framework of the initial interview because it will obviously destroy any possibility of establishing a good transference situation from the very beginning. Unfortunately, it will not only destroy the transference relationship between the interviewer and the patient, but will probably block for a considerable time any possibility that interviews with other psychiatrists will benefit the patient. Therefore, argument with the patient should be strictly avoided.

There are patients who try to lure a psychiatrist into arguments and this should also be watched. There are patients who will try to argue that you also hear the voices, or, "Don't you think that you are followed on the street, too?" "Don't you believe that this plot against me is going on against you?" In other words, they try to put you on the spot, asking for confirmation, because naturally if you also hear the voices, they must be normal. They realize they are actually trying to get reassurance that some of their complaints are not severe symptomatology. In such a situation you naturally do not agree that you yourself hear these voices or that you also are followed on the street (as some psychiatrists do), but you explain to the patient that you do not have these experiences because they are uniquely confined to the patient himself. You do not tell the patient he is wrong or "crazy" in having such ideas, but say that you are very willing to go into every point with him to elucidate why he has these ideas and feelings.

To move to an entirely different branch of psychiatric interviewing, I would like to mention another issue that one meets in connection with neurotic-type somatic symptoms. Quite a lot of patients will present complaints which are organized around somatic symptoms. In interviewing such a patient, if he had perhaps already been examined by fifteen specialists in other branches of medicine, one can probably concentrate essentially on the psychiatric angle. You will encounter, however, an increasing number of psychosomatic patients in an anxiety state who have not gone through the mill but have been seen by a general practitioner or perhaps one specialist, and then referred on the supposition that they are psychiatric cases. It is in such cases that some psychiatrists relate wrongly to the patient. They assume from the beginning that the patient's symptomatology is purely mental and this assumption is conveyed to the patient—conveyed before sufficient physical examinations have been executed! This mistake is made especially by psychiatrists who, when the patient describes his symptoms in detail, brush them aside and say that this is completely unimportant. For instance, if a patient complains of a burning sensation in his stomach, or that his bladder contracts fifteen times a day, he would be told: "We have to discuss your real problems which are on a different level"; "We have to discuss your relationship to your father and your mother"; "We have to discuss how you behaved in your early childhood"; and so on. This attitude usually ruins the chances for successful treatment from the very beginning because the patient actually believes the psychiatrist has a one-track mind, that he does not want to go into the patient's somatic complaints, and, furthermore, that should some organic disorder occur in his stomach or bladder, the psychiatrist would never be able to recognize the fact. Naturally, this blocks the patient's emotional attitude and further interferes with the transference situation.

When beginning treatment of a patient with neurotic-type somatic complaints, the basic rule should be to pay as much attention to the somatic as to the other manifestations and to reliably and conclusively ascertain whether or not somatic deviations are present. When this is done, the patient can be confronted with the evidence, then gradually helped to work through the somatic part of the problem, and eventually maneuvered into treatment of the emotional part. There is nothing so disastrous in the treatment of a patient as when the psychiatrist interrupts or disregards the so-called psychosomatic complaints without any elucidation, and after about twenty or twenty-five sessions must give in to the patient because an x-ray or some complicated examination should be done. He has thereby admitted to the patient that the symptoms are not merely on a psychogenic level; he has admitted to the patient that the initial examination was not conducted well, and insofar as any of his interpretations go, he has finished himself as a therapist.

Only after it has been clarified that the patient has no actual somatic problems can the therapist call a halt to the patient's hypochondriacal preoccupation as such. If the patient does have somatic deviations, a very thorough check of these deviations should be arranged. The patient should feel that you are paying attention to every aspect of the treatment.

Many patients, particularly those with neurotic or somatic complaints, have a definite feeling about the origin of their symptoms. They will say, "I know that I have a mother fixation," or "I know that my trouble is due to inferiority feelings," or they will say that their "libido" is misdirected. Such explanations come mainly from patients who have read quite a bit or have had some previous psy-

chotherapy. Therefore, instead of relating the original complaint or its sequence of development, the patient tries to
embroil you in an intellectual argument on this level: "Do
you think that it is due to a mother fixation? Dr. X said
that." "Do you think that 'this' or 'that' was so?" This is
usually done in the first interview and most likely within
the first fifteen or twenty minutes. It is a bad policy, of
course, to enter into this type of discussion. First of all, no
therapist is equipped to do it after merely fifteen or twenty
minutes. Secondly, this would immediately intellectualize
the whole treatment situation and would not allow sufficient
attention to be paid to the patient's emotional grasp of the
situation. Therefore, such questions should be parried and
the patient told that this will be taken up in the treatment
in due time, that at present you would like to pay attention
to the basic symptomatology rather than interpretations of it.

It is very important in interviewing to size up the intellectual level of the individual patient. It is here that quite
often fundamental mistakes are made by the interviewer.
There are those who constantly talk down to patients, and
there are those who constantly talk up to patients. Both are
wrong. To talk down obviously creates a feeling of resentment in many patients. In other words, the interviewer is
then simply a person who lectures to them, or who puts
questions in such a way as to constantly demonstrate his
superiority over them. This may be the very situation which
has caused much of the neurotic disorder in the patient; he
may harbor a lot of resentment and a lot of hostility because
a particular teacher, a particular brother, or his father
behaved exactly the same way and, naturally, he has
developed all kinds of reaction formations in relation to it.
Therefore, do not talk down to the patient.

Talking up to the patient is probably less often recognized
today than talking down, especially in connection with that
group of highly intelligent neurotic patients who have had
great accomplishments or great attainments in their fields.
Competent writers, journalists, actors, and so forth, very

often belong in this group. These people usually have excellent insight into some of their emotional problems. Very often they are well read and have picked up quite a lot of psychiatric jargon. These individuals will begin by testing you to find out whether or not you are competent to treat them. Therefore, from the very beginning, if you do not pay attention to the fact that you are dealing with a highly intelligent individual and handle the interviews in an adroit manner, the patient will form the opinion that you are less intelligent and less capable than he and therefore will not be able to help him. Thus, it is very important to pay attention to the intelligence level of the patient and evaluate it immediately in relation to the interview.

In this connection it is also important to have some knowledge about the social and ethnological background of each patient. Not knowing, for instance, something of the religious and social attitudes in the culture from which the patient comes can naturally lead to an interview, and later to a treatment, which is not propitious simply because the patient feels he is dealing with a therapist too narrow in his views to have the ability to understand him. Therefore, in dealing with a person from some ethnic group that is unusual or unfamiliar, it is a good idea to familiarize yourself with it or, if the discrepancy is very great, to refer the patient to someone else who is qualified to deal with it.

I would also like to offer one or two specific points in connection with some psychotic patients. Paranoid patients are especially difficult to interview. I am not referring to just those patients actually suffering from an overt paranoid psychosis but, in a broader sense, to patients who have a paranoid personality structure. It is a fairly common personality type, and you will deal with a lot of paranoid schizophrenic, paranoid neurotic, paranoid sociopathic, and, one might even say, paranoid "normal" individuals. A large number of people use this particular form of defense in which a mixture of inferiority and superiority is present in their approach to other people. Obviously the highly suspicious paranoid psychotic picture would be more than the paranoid variant seen in a neurosis; nevertheless, all have some very similar basic behavior patterns. And all of them are difficult to interview.

A paranoid patient is one who is especially able to provoke aggression in you. Therefore, you will have to guard yourself against this so-called aggression reaction which usually takes one of two forms: that of brushing aside the patient's complaints, or that of trying to convince him that the complaints are not justified. Paranoid patients should always be listened to in the same way and manner as one listens to those who relate a stomach ache or an anxiety experience. If the patient is delusional, here again, the delusions—even if bizarre—should be treated as though they are real experiences, not as something which is incomprehensible or as something which simply must be brushed aside.

Interestingly enough, quite a number of paranoid patients do not answer questions when approached directly, but will answer questions if you approach them in an oblique manner. Getting material from schizophrenic patients with paranoid manifestations usually can be done only in an indirect manner.

In dealing with a patient who is hostile or negativistic, many psychiatrists avoid asking certain questions. The omission of certain questions can very often lead to false diagnostic impressions. For instance, a patient comes into the office and is rather belligerent and hostile; the psychiatrist then omits asking questions to the point, "Does this patient have hallucinations? Does this patient have delusions?" Some benign diagnosis is then made, and, although the therapist knows he is dealing with a patient who is rather hostile, somewhat belligerent, and paranoid, he feels that there is no psychosis present. Then, upon seeing the patient for examination and after proper preparation (obviously not in the first minute), when the patient is asked, "Well, do you hear voices?" the answer is a simple, "Yes." Obviously the fundamental diagnosis had been missed because the patient's attitude was such that the psychiatrist who examined him did not want to annoy or provoke him and so questions which he thought might upset the patient were not asked. Therefore, questions concerning delusional material and hallucinations should be asked the patient whenever suspicion is present that he is not a case of straight neurosis. Naturally, when to ask these questions is up to interviewing skill and timing, but they must be asked and gone into. Otherwise, a correct diagnostic judgment cannot be made.

One further point in interviewing concerns talking with the relatives as well as the patient. In other branches of medicine it is usually fully sufficient to talk only with the patient himself, provided he is able to relate his troubles. In psychiatry, it would be the ideal situation in any and every case (whether the patient is psychotic, sociopathic, neurotic, or something else) to be able to talk with the relatives, friends, or collaborators of the patient. It is amazing how much information can be gathered by talking to other people involved. Regardless of what etiological ideas the psychiatrist has as to the origin of the psychosis or neurosis, one fact is outstanding—the disturbance of the patient manifests itself particularly in interrelationships with other people. Therefore, an interrelationship anamnesis on these individuals is highly significant and very important. I usually follow the general rule of speaking to at least one relative of the patient, regardless of whether the patient is neurotic, psychotic, or whatever. Some psychiatrists may not want to follow this rule generally, but I strongly advise it when it is uncertain whether or not the patient is psychotic. It is rather interesting how many times the diagnosis of a psychosis is missed because this very simple expediency is not followed. The patient is examined in the psychiatrist's office (and I have seen certificates given to such persons that they are perfectly sane, which is much more difficult than to certify that a person is not sane), and after one interview the psychiatrist fully relies on his own omnipotency and does not speak to the relatives. Then when somebody does talk with the relatives they provide him with bizarre material in regard to the psychotic individual.

There are many psychotic individuals who are perfectly able to present an excellent front. This so-called dissimulation is also referred to as a form of "covering" of psychotic symptoms. Paranoid individuals are especially capable of dissimulating; in an hour interview, they can convince you that everything is fundamentally all right, that they are fine. Therefore, not knowing certain facts, naturally you are unable to confront the patient with them. The patient will certainly not divulge them, and you will have the impression that you are dealing with a perfectly normal individual. For example, a patient will present a primarily psychosomatic disorder, perhaps migraine with other somatic complaints, and will logically relate his symptoms organized around those complaints. You do not speak to the relatives. You make the diagnosis of a psychosomatic disorder with some anxiety reactions in the framework of a neurosis. Then you meet the father of the patient two weeks later and he says that the patient is suffering from colitis, spends all day in bed, is completely withdrawn from the environment, has hallucinations, and so forth.

Keep in mind that the patient should be interviewed privately and the relatives interviewed at a completely separate time. It is not a very good technique to talk to the patient, then send the patient out of the room and then speak to the relatives, or vice versa. This is an especially bad procedure if the patient is psychotic because the patient will think his therapist is concocting something. Make a separate arrangement to contact the relatives and, depending upon the mental state of the patient, he is told about it then, or it is postponed until the time when the relatives will be seen. Quite a number of patients who do not actually have delusions involving their own relatives will nevertheless resent it if the therapist circumvents them in contacting their relatives. You must respect the patient's sensitivities by expressly mentioning to the patient your wish to speak to one or more of his relatives. It should be arranged so that it is not in any way disagreeable to the patient, and in 99 percent of the cases this can be done without difficulty.

Part II

Alterations of Consciousness, Perception, and Conception

2

ALTERATIONS OF CONSCIOUSNESS

Consciousness is a phenomenon that is poorly understood and difficult to define. William James arrived at the conclusion that everybody understands what consciousness means—until somebody tries to explain it. In attempting to define the state of consciousness we run into a great deal of difficulty with past errors that developed in trying to discern just what it is or is not. To give a working definition for the purpose of further investigation, we might regard *consciousness* as: *the sum total of mental functions dealing with the awareness of self and the environment.* Actually, that contains practically everything taking place in the mind of the individual in terms of awareness of what operates in his mind and awareness of his environment.

Consciousness is a part of the ego functioning of the individual. The "ego" has two parts: (1) that which we designate *the conscious part* of the self, and (2) that which

49

we refer to as *the unconscious part* of the person's mind. There is not a clear-cut demarcation between conscious awareness and the unconscious part of a person's mind because actually most of the material we consider to be unconscious was originally perceived consciously by the self and after some time turned into the unconscious where it exists in a different state of awareness on a different level than the conscious part of the mind. There is a borderline between these two states and, although they are regarded as being different, on that borderline level neither the unconscious part nor the conscious part has ever been clearly defined and fluctuations are in continual process. Furthermore, Freud referred to the "preconscious" mind as that which is actually accessible to the conscious self and enters the level of consciousness whenever the adaptive needs require the information. Here, also, there is no sharp differentiation between conscious and preconscious, however defined.

The self-awareness, or consciousness of that which is going on in the individual, is a shifting continuum; when a person is perceiving practically everything going on around him, his awareness of his feelings, his ideas and bodily sensations will be different than if he was mainly perceiving his own self rather than the external environment. The shifting of conscious perception is a functioning part of the ego, and if the conscious part of the person's mind is not disturbed or impaired, or the part that is unconscious does not markedly intrude, there is no interference with his consciousness.

Certain disturbances in the unconscious part of the self can interfere with the state of consciousness, and there is also a reciprocity between the preconscious part of the self and alteration of consciousness. In the reverse, states of consciousness can be altered by some of the experiences of the conscious part of the self—such as some special strong affectivity, or certain physical disorders. Actually, therefore, consciousness can be altered as a result of conditions affecting any part of the total functioning of the self. Alterations can occur in many organic states, in schizophrenia, or in so-called psychoneuroses. Even in the "normal" individual, a strong affective state—such as fear or rage—can disturb the state of consciousness.

DESCRIPTION OF MANIFESTATIONS

To describe consciousness we usually differentiate between two issues: the *field* of consciousness, and the *clarity* of consciousness. As we presently define consciousness, it is the person's awareness of many events occurring around him and within him. This awareness has variations of intensities, or clarities. It also has variations in field range. Consciousness can be impaired in two respects: the field narrows in that his area of consciousness becomes reduced, and the person's awareness becomes less lucid. Although these two phenomena are independent, very often both impairments are present in the individual; the awareness field becomes limited, or narrower, and at the same time the lucidity, or clarity, of the awareness is impaired.

I will mention a few of the conditions under which seemingly one or the other of these functions is impaired. For instance, it is frequently observed, especially in some cases of schizophrenia, that the clarity or lucidity is impaired, but the field range of awareness remains unaltered. In organic states a narrowing of the awareness field and impairment of lucidity usually occur concomitantly; this can be observed most clearly in cases of delirium. Particularly in cases of emotionally based alteration of consciousness, we at times observe that the field of consciousness is narrowed but the lucidity is not impaired.

In *depressions* (and this is probably the best example), very often the field is narrowed but the awareness is not hazy. There are patients who are so severely depressed they are dominated by the depressive component and an actual narrowing of the field of awareness takes place, and many of these individuals could impress one as persons whose consciousness is interfered with to some extent but, in contrast to schizophrenic and organic states, there is much less of a decrease in lucidity associated with whatever narrowing of consciousness does occur. Especially in patients manifesting so-called depressive semi-stupor (stuporous depressions are extremely rare, unless in the framework of schizophrenia, but half-stuporous states can occur in severe depressions), the patient seemingly perceives everything rather clearly. In other words, the haziness, the cloudiness encountered in organic cases and some cases of schizophrenia, is not present but the field of awareness becomes markedly narrowed. In these cases we observe quite clearly the difference between these two consciousness functions.

Stupor is a form of interference of consciousness but is not usually included as a pure example of alteration of consciousness because many of the mechanisms are not quite clear. In *schizophrenia,* stupor is perceived as being an unconscious refusal to accept (exclusion of) environmental stimuli. As is known, consciousness can be altered by the cutting off of sensory perception. If exclusion of environmental stimuli is very marked, it is followed by an alteration of awareness. An individual entering into a stuporous state, either from emotional or organic causes, begins to exclude or prevent the reception of stimulation from the environment, and here, also, an interference of consciousness occurs. It is not clear, however, whether or not the change of consciousness is secondary to the stupor. Is the person prevented from receiving stimuli by the narrowing of consciousness, or does alteration of consciousness in stupor run simultaneously with, or as a result of, the exclusion of sensory stimuli? Despite these questions, many psychiatrists include this type of stupor among disorders of altered consciousness.

Regarding schizophrenia several situations can occur. We observe schizophrenic patients behaving like depressive patients, in that their field of awareness is narrowed but their clarity is not impaired. Then again, we observe schizophrenic patients in whom the field of awareness is not so much interfered with but in whom the clarity of awareness is impaired. We also observe acute schizophrenic cases that behave very similarly to acute organic cases inasmuch as their clarity and their field of awareness are both impaired; such are the acute catatonic states. Insofar as consciousness is concerned, these cases are very impressive. Their awareness is hazy, or cloudy, they are unable to present a good report of what is occurring within them or around them, and simultaneously the linked functions, namely, the anamnestic orientative functions, are also impaired, as is similarly observed in the acute organic cases. This is important to note: In schizophrenic stupor, as in organic stupor, the alterations in consciousness may not be limited to changes in field and lucidity, but may also extend to secondary alterations in orientation and memory. Insufficient attention to this fact is responsible for many misdiagnoses. (In discussing catatonic schizophrenia, it will be pointed out that many patients in a stuporous state are quite keenly aware of all that occurs around them and later recount it, but the difficulty was in their inability to report it at the time.)

It has been stated that if alterations of consciousness occur they are invariably in either organic or psychotic individuals. That is not true. I would like to make a few comments about alteration of consciousness occurring as situational responses in the *psychoneuroses* and in some of the sociopathic states. In the psychoneuroses, per se, alteration of consciousness does not occur. It does not occur, the one exception being at the height of an anxiety reaction. Anxiety and rage, even in a normal individual—I say "normal," if such a state exists, in the sense that there is no psychoneurosis present—are able to narrow the field of consciousness and are also able to interfere with the clarity of awareness. These are well-known facts that have often been demonstrated clinically in psychological test situations, as well as forensically. Normal individuals do not like to be made aware of this fact, even less accept it because our whole education is geared to the idea that we are masters of the environment and, up to a point, masters of our destiny. Any concept indicating we are not creates in many people a certain amount of anxiety and is rejected. Therefore, ideas that consciousness can actually be interfered with at the height of an emotional state or storm are not very well-liked and, as you will know if you read books on forensic psychiatry, the representatives of criminal law strenuously object to such a concept.[1] Nevertheless, it can be clinically demonstrated again and again that when an individual is at the height of a strong anxiety bout or in a state of rage, interference of consciousness occurs. The question remains: Is the individual who manifests this type of reaction normal or not?

In individuals suffering from either anxiety neurosis [an anxiety reaction in which anxiety is manifested freely and appears in an undisguised form] or anxiety hysteria [a particularly channelized and displaced form of anxiety appearing often in the form of specific phobias], anxiety reactions are particularly capable of influencing consciousness. At the height of an anxiety attack, or when a phobic patient is thrown into a panic because he is unable to avoid or fails in his attempt to cope with his phobias, we occasionally observe anxiety becoming so intense that the patient is suddenly not clearly aware of his surroundings. This phenomenon is well-known in the case of rage. A person in a state of rage can experience a narrowing of consciousness. Often such states are either not investigated, or cannot be investigater easily, because they are too fleeting; usually after a few minutes or perhaps a little longer (but surely not very long) following the emotional peak of anxiety or rage, all alterations of consciousness that had appeared are no longer

---

[1] As New York State's Commissioner of Mental Hygiene, Dr. Hoch implemented the overriding of McNaghten's rule. Since it is no longer the only basis in New York for judging whether or not an individual is legally responsible for his acts, this statement is no longer valid.—*Eds.*

present. Incidentally, many of the linked functions, the anamnestic orientative functions, can also be interfered with in these individuals, and it is not rare that after a state of rage the person does not remember what had occurred during that period, or at least his recollections are hazy. This does not refer to haziness regarding his own actions necessarily, but to actions and happenings in the environment which he does not register.

The most common nonpsychotic state in which alterations in consciousness occur is hysteria. Hysteric patients *dissociate*. They are able to cut off stimuli from consciousness; they not only cut off bodily sensations but also environmental stimuli and memory recall. They may enter stuporous states resembling psychotic stupors. These may appear as the so-called *twilight states,* or *dream states,* in which consciousness is altered and awareness is markedly decreased. In such a state the patient may be able to act out certain ideas, feelings, and impulses which he had been unable to release when in a state of normal awareness; and, we maintain that the patient enters into those states *in order* to be able to perform in an automatized manner actions otherwise prohibited. Similar states occur in certain sociopathic individuals who perform automatized acts without relation to the environment when under severe emotional stress. Dream states occur also in organic disorders such as epilepsy. All those dream states give a very similar appearance and it is often not easy to determine whether we are dealing with a dream state in an organic, in an hysterical, or in a sociopathic setting. Efforts to differentiate dissociative states due to schizophrenia from those due to organic conditions by use of hypnosis, sodium amytal, and so forth, have not been fully satisfactory because in many schizophrenic individuals the dissociation is not reconverted, while with many organic cases these techniques may lead to marked improvements in the state of consciousness.

Dream, or twilight states can be compared superficially with normal states of dreaming in the sleeping person; both phenomena have a latent and a manifest content, and both can be understood in terms of condensations, displacements, and so forth. Although many people consider them identical states, actually there is a basic difference between a sleeping individual who is dreaming and an individual in a twilight state. This important difference is that the sleeper can be awakened from the dream with external stimuli, whereas one cannot awaken a person in a state of altered consciousness by ordinary means. Reconnecting such a person with reality is a longer and less clearly bordered affair. Also, unlike twilight and dream states in which the individual is usually disorientated for time and place and sometimes also for person, orientation is not disturbed in a dream during ordinary sleep.

Pathological dream states, incidentally, all demonstrate an interference in anamnestic orientative functions. Actually, such states occur in which the consciousness of the individual is so narrowed that he is not aware, or only very hazily and very partially aware, of what is occurring around him. Many of these functions are automatic. In other words, much of the "will" control is removed or markedly reduced. Usually such an individual is disoriented for time, place, and, at times, also for person. The *sociopathic person* is very likely to commit acts of violence when in such a state under certain conditions. It usually occurs if some strongly provoking emotional pattern is present and often under the influence of some pathological intoxication. Spontaneous occurrence is rare. In other words, the sociopath does not go into this state very often, but it is fairly likely to occur when he is in a state of marked emotional upheaval, as, for example, when being arrested or confronted with some other emotional aggravation, or when under the influence of some intoxicant, which is frequently the case. When we discuss the different alcoholic disorders, I shall call your attention especially to the clinical entity of pathological intoxication which consists of a sociopathic background plus an intoxicant and usually results in a particular dream-like, or twilight-like, state rather characteristic of these individuals.

Although the twilight state or dream state manifests alterations of consciousness as well as impairment (usually) of the anamnestic orientative functions, the quantity of interference in these linked mental functions varies with different individuals. In some textbooks one may read that every so-called dream state, or twilight state, is followed by a complete amnesia. In other words, when the patient awakens, he does not know what occurred during the state. That is incorrect. There surely are individuals who are not at all aware of what occurred; their conscious registration of the environment was completely suspended. In others, however, a varying degree of awareness was present, in much the same manner as the person who dreamed is often able to recall what he dreamed, to a varying degree. Therefore, it cannot necessarily be assumed that a person in a twilight state or in a dream state always has a complete amnesia for what had gone on. He might have only a partial amnesia. On the other hand, it never happens that he remains so completely lucid as to remember every detail of just what he did and what happened around him while he was in the twilight or dream state. If complete lucidity was present and there was no interference with the state of consciousness, we would not be entitled to call such a condition a twilight state or a dream state; the prerequisite for the diagnosis is the establishment of the fact that narrowing or impairment of consciousness took place.

I have mentioned that impairment of consciousness also occurs in hysteria. The older literature is filled with descriptions of hysterical twilight and dream states. In recent times we rarely observe these states; it is more usual for hysteria to occur in the form of amnesias—usually circumscribed amnesias. The basis of these states, as in dream states, is dissociation of a certain part of the memory material from the general flow or general availability of consciousness. In other words, this is a peculiar repressive, dissociative mechanism by which the person suddenly blots

out certain memory material of emotional importance to
him. As an hysterical patient is able to dissociate an organ
or a part of the body from general body awareness and
functioning, he is also able to dissociate or cut off a part of
the memory material and functioning from his general consciousness. Hysterical patients suffering from amnesia are
usually in a state of impairment of consciousness to a varying degree. There are cases of hysterical amnesia in which
patients manifest only circumscribed impairment of memory
and no apparent impairment of consciousness. There are
other cases of hysterical amnesia which have a true dream
or twilight state in addition to the hysterical amnesia. In
such cases, the patient's awareness appears to be somewhat
hazy; he performs automatically and at a later time is
unable, or only partially able, to give a report of what he
was doing. At the same time, anamnestic orientative functions are quite impaired.

I would like to emphasize here that if you encounter a
marked so-called hysterical twilight state, it will occur in
relationship to an acute and massive emotional experience,
such as a disaster or a combat situation, which is capable of
producing in the individual an acute emotional upheaval
due to the basic flight reaction pattern leading to a dissociation reaction—in other words, a cutting off of stimulation or
cutting off of the memory material painful to the individual.
If, however, twilight states occur spontaneously, such a
patient in our present civilization must be carefully
examined to determine if he is in a dream state or experiencing an hysterical dissociative reaction in the framework
of schizophrenia. In any case, these massive hysterical
amnesic states, as well as the massive bodily reactions so
prevalent many years ago, very rarely occur spontaneously
in our civilization. They are common to cultures in which
fear and anxiety are handled more openly than in our culture. We can still observe it in certain so-called primitive
groups. These conditions are occasionally observed in our
civilization as a reaction to a great emotional experience, as

I have mentioned, but more and more cases in which gross hysterical mechanisms are spontaneously demonstrated later reveal the early signs of psychosis, indicating that much deeper ramifications are present than in an ordinary hysterical dissociative reaction.

To the two provoking factors, namely, combat situation or disaster situation, I may also add one other in which these reactions may be observed. This is the situation in which a great deal of secondary gain is involved. For instance, certain compensation cases may also manifest gross hysterical reactions. Those numerous hysterical reactions, however, which filled the clinic of Charcot at the end of the last century, on the basis of which Freud and many others first described the great hysterical manifestations, are increasingly rare, although we cannot explain why. Moreover, the gross hysterical reactions in the war neuroses, interestingly enough, have also changed. During World War I there were an enormous number of gross hysterical reactions, whereas in World War II those reactions were not so marked and were replaced by many somaticized reactions, or so-called psychosomatic symptomatology, which had rarely occurred formerly. So, while gross hysterical alterations of consciousness occurring spontaneously without any great external provocation can surely happen, the patient should nevertheless be carefully examined to determine if he is in a true state of hysteria.

METHODS OF EXAMINATION

Practically speaking, methods for ascertaining alterations of consciousness can be separated into two categories. Alterations can be ascertained partially by the *direct method,* and partially by the *indirect method* of examination. By the direct method you simply observe how the patient appears—how he is influenced by stimuli, how sensitive are his reactions, and how he handles the situations he is in. The indirect method depends on your observations of other mental impairments present in the individual, because alterations of consciousness are often associated with impairments of other functions.

DIRECT METHOD OF EXAMINATION: There are four components of consciousness which can be impaired, and usually all of these components are affected, not merely one. To some extent, these can be examined by talking directly with the patient. Among the different organic disorders that can alter the state of consciousness, usually the four components of consciousness are nearly equally affected. In other words, organic disorders much more commonly influence all four components of consciousness than do those disorders not based on organic factors. On the other hand, there are variations in component alterations occurring in the so-called psychogenically based alteration of consciousness, or in the psychoses, which (as we observe in schizophrenia, for instance) are an intermediary group between organic reactions and straight psychogenic reactions. The four components of consciousness to be examined are usually broken down to include the following:

The first. *Intact awareness of inner life experience* is present if the person is able to give a coherent, lucid, clear account of what is going on in his mind at the moment. The person is able to describe his inner experience. For instance, when you ask the patient how he feels, where he is, and what he is doing, he is able to describe it coherently and clearly. However, if you talk to a patient who is in a state of delirium, his consciousness is narrowed and clouded and he is not able to give you a clear-cut account of what is going on in him. In that case, usually his account is fragmentary, unclear, and very often jumbled. In short, the person is unable to report on his inner experiences in a lucid and logical manner.

The second: *The subject-object differentiation is intact in the patient* if his consciousness is not interfered with, but is impaired when there is interference with his consciousness.

This means that an individual in an intact state of consciousness is able to differentiate clearly between subject and object, while the person whose consciousness is narrowed, or markedly interfered with, begins to treat subject and object alike or interchangeably. He is confusing them. Actually, one of the basic definitions of confusion rests on the fact that the patient is not only confused as to time localization and as to spatial localization, but is also confused between subject and object. He may be unable to differentiate between inanimate and animate objects. For example, he may look at you and say, "You are a chair." Looking at a table, he may say, "A person is over there."

The third: *Ego boundaries are sustained* if there is no interference with consciousness. When consciousness is impaired, ego boundaries become substandard and rather hazy. As is the case with the first two components, maintenance of ego boundaries is an ego function and it is the ego function which becomes impaired. Here, again, the relationship between the person and his environment tends to become confused. Occasionally the ego boundaries become markedly altered, particularly when the person is under the influence of some toxins or drugs. For example, a patient will say that his arms or legs do not belong to him. Or, he will state that everything external to him is fused within him. You observe this occasionally in organic cases and most particularly in schizophrenic patients. In other words, the ego boundaries are unclear; the environment and even the self are not clearly differentiated. As you know, with people of "primitive" cultures and with young children, that is a patterned normal experience. The ego's ability to differentiate between environment and self develops gradually. An infant reacts as though his oral-self and the mother's breast are all one unit and a small child is unable to clearly differentiate between what is "he" and what is the outer environment. In adults of primitive cultures, similar tendencies can be observed with regard to "incorporation fantasies" and certain rituals, but if such a person's development had taken place in our civilization he would likely be able to discern very clearly his ego boundaries. It is rather interesting that the ego boundary erected in the normal individual and even maintained in a state of anxiety becomes disturbed when consciousness is narrowed or altered. Actually, if a person becomes unable to clearly differentiate between himself and the environment it indicates that interference with ego boundaries is very definitely a component feature of the state of impaired consciousness.

The fourth: *Clear awareness of body image*; a person normally has a clear-cut awareness about his body and its performance, and it becomes *markedly* confused in persons when consciousness becomes impaired. This was especially obvious in some studies made of persons whose state of consciousness was influenced by certain drugs.

All these observations can be summarized as follows: Consciousness is impaired when a person's clear awareness of his body image becomes confused; when awareness of his position in relationship to the environment becomes altered, becomes hazy, and he is unable to clearly differentiate his ego boundaries as well as he had been able to do formerly. In other words, clear awareness of the "I," and clear awareness of that which is the environment, become disturbed when there is narrowing of consciousness.

Here one has to emphasize that the awareness of ego boundaries is quite varied among normal individuals. In other words, not every individual's ego boundaries are as sharply established as they are in others, but if the person's consciousness is altered, usually the disturbance of his ego boundaries is furthered. Otherwise, these individual variations of ego boundaries are not so great as to interfere very much with a clear-cut perception of the body image, with one or two exceptions. One might encounter difficulties in determining whether consciousness is interfered with in the case of so-called primitive persons. Or, more especially, this difficulty may be encountered in the case of certain feebleminded persons because a developmental lag obviously already exists in differentiating the self from the environment. Here, because marked difficulty already exists on a physiological level, when mental pathology then enters the picture, it is not so easy to judge the person's state of consciousness. Ordinarily, however, the individual variations of sharpness of ego awareness in relationship to the environment are not, I would say, very disrupting to adaptive functioning.

The direct method of examination is insufficient for several reasons. With the direct scheme we can employ only three approaches, these all relying on talking with the patient. (1) asking the patient to give an account, if he is able, about his inner life at the *moment*; or (2) asking the patient *after* a psychotic episode what he experienced in the process of the episode; and (3) utilizing the rapport that develops between you and the patient. Naturally, we cannot rely on these approaches alone to judge whether or not the patient is in a state of altered consciousness. It cannot be determined, obviously, on the basis of what the patient may or may not be able to tell you during his actual experience. Furthermore, we cannot rely on what the patient reports after the psychotic experience is nearly over because by that time it is too late. Now, the third approach—how the patient relates himself to you during an interview—is, naturally, of very great importance, but with many patients one is quite unable to establish a sufficient rapport, and accurate judgment as to the presence of alteration of consciousness actually depends to some extent on the rapport established. Therefore, if one does not also utilize other observations, but completely relies on what the patient says, one could be guilty of a false diagnosis in either direction. Therefore, we do not rely entirely on how the patient relates himself to us when examining him to determine his state of consciousness, but in addition, as I have mentioned, we employ indirect approaches.

INDIRECT METHOD OF EXAMINATION: By this method we

examine the patient's *sensorium* in relation to his anamnestic orientative functions. In other words, we determine the extent to which the patient's thoughts, feelings, perceptions, and so forth are altered as manifested by his *stream of consciousness,* or continuum of consciousness. We appraise the patient's (1) *attentiveness,* his (2) *ability to grasp and assimilate* stimuli, and his (3) *capacity for learning and recall.* The indirect approach gives us the added advantage that those functions can be investigated not alone from simply what the patient tells us, but we are able to apply it, up to a point, during a disturbed episode and when a patient is in somewhat fluctuating consciousness states.

First of all, in relation to the patient's sensorium, one of the most important indirect examinations is to determine to what extent the patient's stream of consciousness is disturbed in terms of his ability to maintain *attentiveness.* We observe that this part of consciousness is often the first one affected, there being a falling off of the patient's attentiveness whenever there is any disturbance of consciousness. The stream of consciousness, which is a function of awareness of surroundings, of awareness of what is going on in the person, and especially of what is going on in the person in relationship to his environment, is considered to be very intimately related to attentiveness, because the function of attention is actually a prerequisite for keeping aware of anything.

A person who is unable to focus his attention on anything, a person who is unable to turn toward ideas similar to those of others, or especially a person who is unable to concentrate or assimilate and organize stimuli, is obviously impaired in his mental function of awareness. Therefore, the awareness function and the attention function, although not considered psychologically identical, are very closely related. Actually, changes in attention, changes in the ability to concentrate, and most of all, changes in the patient's ability or inability to sustain attention and to maintain concentration are probably the most important features relating to alteration of consciousness. We are not so much referring here to the marked alteration of consciousness when the patient is stuporous or when the patient is nonrelating or nonverbal, because in such cases it is easy to make the diagnosis. It is much more difficult, however, when seemingly the patient's consciousness appears cleared, or when the patient occasionally appears to give full attention, but at the same time, however, he does not.

Now, how does attention present itself in a patient having no alteration of consciousness? For a normal individual, attention is usually manifested in the way we described: If related ideas are introduced in discussion, for instance, the person recognizes them; he clearly grasps their meaning and could give a clear and logical response. However, there are normal variations in attentiveness. One normal person may be more attentive than another and will be more fully responsive than will another who may be less attentive. Actually, the normal individual differences between those who are more or less attentive are not very clear-cut, but there are no great deviations. It is very rarely observed that a normal individual responds by being very attentive for five minutes and not at all attentive for the next five. If such is encountered occurring in a normal individual, it is not normal unless he is in a special state which would explain this condition such as, for instance, being sleepy, being exhausted, and so forth. With these exceptions, a marked variation, whereby a person is not at all able to focus or maintain his attention, never occurs in a normal individual.

You can, however, observe—in speaking to persons who are under the influence of certain toxins or drugs or who have some other organic impairment which so markedly alters the state of consciousness that they are delirious or somewhat stuporous—that the attention wanders very markedly. Perhaps you are able to keep his attention for a few minutes and then suddenly you are no longer able to do so. Even if one tries repeatedly during this particular refractory period, the patient's attention cannot be regained. Such very marked wandering of attention is usually present in persons manifesting an organic impairment, or manifesting a psychosis, such as schizophrenia. (In schizophrenia, naturally, to some extent an organic impairment plays a role and you may observe affective components also playing a role.) In many patients the attention is impaired in such a way that the patient is able to respond to you at times, and at other times not. The so-called lucid intervals are a particularly common occurrence in organic cases and are quite interesting.

Secondly, when a patient is unable to be attentive and to focus himself by turning toward stimuli, that patient would, in addition, be unable to mentally *grasp and assimilate*. For example, if you give such a patient two or three written sentences and ask him to memorize these and to repeat what is written, he is unable to do so. Most of the organically disturbed patients will only grasp in a rather faulty way what had been written. In other words, the patient being inattentive would be unable to concentrate, he would also be unable to grasp meanings, and therefore he would be unable to assimilate, or to *learn*.

Thirdly, attention and concentration, grasp, and learning ability are all very intimately linked together. Therefore, when consciousness is impaired in a person we observe a fluctuation in attention, a lack of concentration, an inability of the person to grasp ideas, and we also observe the inability for recent *memory-recall*. When you ask such an organically disturbed person, during a lucid interval, to recall his experiences when in the state of altered consciousness, he may tell you, "I do not remember what went on during that time, but I only remember that everything seemed hazy, that nothing seemed clear." The feeling of vagueness, the feeling of being unable to think clearly is the substance of his observations.

Combined direct and indirect examination of the patient's sensorium can often be employed. When the level of consciousness is definitely interfered with, we are faced with both the *subjective* reporting and the *objective* evidence of impairment in most instances, particularly in the acute organic reactions. In other words, the patient will say that everything seems hazy; the patient will say that things are not clear; the patient will say that he is drowsy. And, the fact that we can at the same time demonstrate an impairment of attention and of focus and concentration indicates there is interference with consciousness. If such alterations of attention and concentration are observed on a subjective and an objective level concomitantly, usually an alteration of the level of consciousness is present.

A patient is giving a subjective evaluation when, during the lucid interval following an altered state of consciousness, he says that he felt as though nothing was clear in his mind during his confused state. It is not rare to find a subjective feeling of altered consciousness occurring in psychoneurotic persons—particularly cases of anxiety neurosis and obsessive-compulsive neurosis—even though objective tests do not demonstrate any impairment. The reverse also occurs; objective evidence of gross defects of consciousness can be demonstrated in patients having no subjective feeling of impairment. This occurs in many organic states. When we encounter such a phenomenon we should go further and examine the patient very carefully to determine whether the objective findings of impairment in the patient—this lack of concentration, this lack of attentive focus—are actually due to impairment of consciousness. Impairments of thought processes, and so forth, that can occur, for instance, in organic psychoses such as atherosclerosis, may or may not be in connection with an actual impairment of consciousness.

In normal individuals alterations of consciousness can be observed under two effecting conditions: (1) Some *physiological disturbance* occurring in a person, such as when influenced by some drug or some toxin. A person becomes abnormal when under the influence of a drug or under the influence of a toxin because he is then, naturally, in a state of acute organic disorder of the mind; and (2) under the impact of a certain *strong affective charge,* psychotic reaction states and alterations of consciousness may occur. Temporary alterations of consciousness occur—and I would like to underscore strongly that they are always very temporary—in certain normal individuals under the impact of an extraordinary emotional experience. Under the influence of *fear,* or of *rage,* we observe alterations of consciousness to follow the lines of organic patterns so closely that some psychiatrists even use the term "affective delirium," or "affective confusion." These states are usually, however, very short-lived, lasting for a few hours or, at most, a day. If they are not brief, one must question the validity of the diagnosis; alterations of consciousness running a longer course, as are those due to toxic causes, never occur in a normal individual. Such an individual is one usually manifesting a neurotic or a psychotic reaction, the alteration of consciousness occurring in the framework of, for instance, an hysterical state, or an underlying psychotic state. It is not normal, naturally.

In a circumscribed way, however, strong emotions, especially fear and rage or a combination of both, are able to produce temporary narrowing of consciousness in normal individuals. For example, at some place there could occur an accident involving many people, and a number of individuals could become very frightened during this accident. Then, when questioned at a later time, they would be unable to give you an accurate account of what had happened. In other words, a narrowing of consciousness took place which would probably be justifiably termed an abnormal reaction and yet we surely could not label those individuals psychotic. What the actual relationship is between an abnormal reaction and a psychosis has not been solved but the reaction could be an hysterical one. Actually, we do not consider it psychotic because many of the abnormal mechanisms of true psychosis are not present in these states. However, of course, there are psychiatrists who would say that such reactions are nothing other than a form of psychosis, although I would wager they can also be found in every normal individual, provided security is severely threatened. This phenomenon is not to be confused with catathymia; that is something else again. Catathymia is an emotional state produced by an unconscious wish. Furthermore, when a schizophrenic patient is in a catathymic state, it lasts longer than a few hours or a day or two. And, the so-called hysterical alteration of consciousness I have mentioned rarely lasts for as much as a single day.

In summary, then, the patient's inability to concentrate, to think clearly, to grasp meanings, and to assimilate and recall experiences, can be observed indirectly when examining the sensorium. These observations, along with your direct observations when he attempts to describe to you his inner experiences in relation to these functions, all indicate an impairment of consciousness in the patient. Furthermore, when there is very marked interference in consciousness, we not only observe more marked impairment of memory but also find *disorientation.* All this indicates that consciousness is linked very strongly to the so-called anamnestic orientative functions, and that often the diagnosis of impairment, or interference, in the state of consciousness is deducted not so much by direct observation as to the extent of alteration of consciousness, but the extent to which associative, or linked, mental impairments are present.

Alterations in consciousness can occur in pure culture without impairment of orientation, memory, or attention. For all practical purposes, however, if interference occurs in the state of consciousness we usually, but not invariably, also perceive some impairment of the anamnestic orientative functions, particularly in those states we will now enumerate, although it is not always the case. For instance, very interesting alterations of consciousness can be observed in schizophrenia in which the anamnestic orientative functions are nevertheless not impaired. Once in a great while, similar observations have also been made in patients suffering from hysteria, although in hysteria the anamnestic orientative functions are quite often impaired in connection with narrowing of consciousness. We also encounter states similar to, or identical with, some hypnotic states having interference in consciousness without impairment of anamnestic orientative functions. In a few depression states also, alterations in consciousness occur without changes in attention, memory, and orientation. On the other hand, in the large group of organic psychoses in which narrowing or alteration of consciousness commonly plays a role, changes in consciousness are almost invariably linked with changes in the anamnestic orientative functions as well.

3

ALTERATIONS OF PERCEPTION

Many different types of perceptual alterations can be experienced, some of which are not always indicative of pathological conditions although, naturally, certain ones are. Before defining, describing, and differentiating these various perceptual alterations, I would first like to comment on the problem of the theoretical bases of both perceptual and conceptual disorders.

A number of investigators have felt that the clue to an understanding of how illusions, hallucinations, and, to some extent, delusions are formed could probably be approached through detailed study of the acute organic syndrome cases to determine what the factors are and how they play a role in producing those manifestations. Hallucinatory or illusionary experiences are observed frequently in delirium and their form and content are manifold. There are many different theories floating around regarding the origin of these phenomena. Although I shall mention a few of the different theories, at this point we do not know actually how these

71

experiences originate. If we were able to understand some of the manifestations occurring in an acute organic hallucinatory episode or delusionary episode, we would probably also be able to understand these manifestations to some extent when they occur in the other psychoses which are, I consider, even less well understood, regardless of the many theories proposed.

Considerable progress has been made in understanding a few of the *motives* underlying the content of illusions, hallucinations, and delusions. We are also much better able to link these phenomena with some of the individual psychodynamic manifestations. However, that still does not give us any explanation as to *why* the person hallucinates or *why* the person has a delusion. Just what are the changes that take place in the mental apparatus of the individual so that ideas suddenly become distorted or that perception or concepts are handled differently than in a normal individual? To take up the matter in a definitive way first, we usually differentiate between illusions, hallucinations, and pseudohallucinations.

DEFINITIONS

We usually speak of *illusions* as experiences based on actual perceptions. In other words, some external stimulus is perceived, but the perception is falsely interpreted, or is misinterpreted. For example, if the person perceives a curtain moving and believes it is a man entering the room, this person has an optic perception but the optic perception is distorted. Here I must point out that—with the exception of so-called elementary perceptions, whereby the person perceives fairly simple percepts such as figures or colors—all the higher perceptions are mixed with concepts. They are not perceived purely as percepts but are mixed with whatever concepts the person has of that particular subject or object on which he bases the perception. Misconstruing a curtain to be a man is possible only if the person injects concepts into the perception, which involves conceptual transmutations of the perception, indicating the very close relationship between the sensory (perceptual) sphere and the ideological (conceptual) sphere.

Attempts have been made, especially in experimental psychology, to separate these functions in order to operate with pure sensory perceptions and with pure conceptions. While it is not fully possible to do this, as one can nevertheless observe, differentiation on these levels is possible to some extent. For instance, visual hallucinations are often very much on a perceptual level and auditory hallucinations are very much on a conceptual level. A clear-cut division between a percept and a concept is not fully possible, as is clearly demonstrated in the illusionary experiences of patients where it is possible to understand how a perception is misconstrued or misinterpreted only when we assume that the person has already injected some amount of conceptual material into his perception.

Although in experiencing an illusion the patient has an actual perception and then distorts that perception, an *hallucination* is an imaginary experience; the person has absolutely no perception on which to base it. *No* external stimulus is involved. The hallucination, therefore, is a purely endogenous issue. This specifically means that the end organs of the sensory apparatus in which much of the hallucinatory material appears, especially those of sight, hearing, touch, and so forth, do not receive any stimulus that might then produce the hallucinations.

Pseudohallucinations are experiences considered to be in between illusions and hallucinations, but are closer to actual hallucinatory experiences. In the literature many subdivisions have been made of these phenomena; but, although they are very important from a theoretical point of view, they have practically no importance from a clinical point of view. They are termed pseudohallucinations because the person does not actually perceive these experiences with the same vividity and with the same plasticity as he perceives hallucinations. You will encounter a patient, particularly a schizophrenic patient, who might tell you, "Some of my ideas are becoming loud!" or, "I am having a very peculiar experience but I am unable to describe it; it remains shadowy, it remains in no way vivid." Such experiences are actually not treated by the patient himself as being true perceptual experiences; they appear more as ideas, more as thoughts, more as concepts having more intensity than ordinary thoughts. They are probably also more obsessive and dominant than are ordinary thoughts, meaning that the patient is unable to shut those ideas out of his mind. They dominate him and he is unable to interfere. In a passive way, he feels forced to accept such experiences. However, they are not as vivid, not as colorful, not as clear-cut as true hallucinations, and he is aware that they are the product of his imagination and not reality.

Ordinarily, unless we are in a state of dreaming or of daydreaming, our ideas or thoughts are usually very shadowy issues; even in attempting to recall certain experiences that were originally very vivid, very clear, very lucid, and even very colorful, our recollections appear rather shadowy and surely lack the clearness of a perception. There is a marked difference, for instance, between actually perceiving a table and attempting at a later time to recall that table. The first experience is very vivid, lucid, clear and is stimulus bound; the second is a rather shadowy issue. That is also the reason why a great many individuals are not at all able, when recalling a perception, to describe it very much in detail. It lacks vividity and it lacks, I would say, the actual bodily pattern of the percept.

Interestingly enough, there are also normal individuals endowed with a special ability—*eidetic* individuals. Eidetic individuals are able to recall percepts which then become as vivid, or nearly as vivid, as were the actual perceptions. In other words, they are able to review an experience with the approximate clarity of the original perceptual experience. This phenomenon is in no way related to hallucinations; it actually concerns only the ability to vividly recall original perceptions. Many artists have eidetic imagery. The plasticity and the vividity of an eidetic experience, while approximating the original perceptual experience, is not identical to it, the original experience being still clearer and stronger.

Incidentally, eidetic individuals are normally able to clearly differentiate between an original perception and the image they recall. However, if one observes an eidetic individual who has become very tired or exhausted, or if he is given a drug which narrows his consciousness, one can observe interesting transitions between a so-called eidetic image and an hallucination. In such a state, the person can at times have an intrusion of eidetic images which he will treat as though they are real percepts, and at times he might even react to them as percepts taken in at that time rather than in the past. In other words, during stress he approximates individuals who actually hallucinate, because an hallucinating individual believes the perceptual experience he is undergoing at the moment actually is taking place at that time; he hears the voice *now*, he sees the figures *now*, he experiences the tactile sensations *now*. Because we know that eidetic individuals exist and because we know that sometimes such individuals under the influence of a drug (including the influence of alcohol) have vivid experiences which approximate hallucinations, we gained the first clue to the understanding of hallucinatory experiences. Ordinarily, however, when an eidetic individual is not in a state of exhaustion, is not under the influence of an intoxicant, or is not under the influence of a great emotional upheaval which can also produce something similar by narrowing the conscious awareness, he is always able to clearly differentiate between an eidetic image and a percept, on the one hand, or an hallucination on the other.

Keep in mind that the eidetic faculty is a variation of the norm. It has no pathological implication whatsoever. If you examine a hundred normal individuals you will find all types and degrees of eidetic abilities and, even when very marked in a person, it is a normal trait just as are many other unusual traits. In the area of motor behavior, some people—dancers, for example—are very capable in fusing different bodily movements while others are not. In these issues we are dealing with a normal characteristic, although we do not know its origin. Apparently it rests on some particular organization of that particular nervous system; it is an unusual ability. One person has unusual musical ability, another person has none. Unusual abilities cannot be considered in any way abnormal; their only relationship to pathology is that if an individual possessing them becomes exposed to something which decorticates him or interferes with the higher organization of his nervous functioning, he is probably more apt to have related symptoms than is an ordinary person, but even that is not fully determined.

Many children have strong eidetic imagery; most of them gradually lose it as they grow older, with the exception of a few individuals who remain eidetic. Attempts have been made to link eidetic imagery to different metabolic processes. An interesting relationship between persons who had a tendency toward hyperthyroidism and eidetic phenomenon was found, and at one time they were even given a term, the Basedow type (which is the name for hyperthyroidism in Continental literature). Many people believed that the eidetic phenomenon could even involve relationships with other metabolic types. While none of these ideas has given a successful explanation, it is interesting that among some patients who develop hyperthyroidism, the eidetic phenomenon can be definitely discerned. Such patients have a great ability to recall perceptions very vividly, very much in detail, and very colorfully. They are able, for example, to recall in great detail paintings they have seen.

DESCRIPTIVE SYMPTOMATOLOGY

HALLUCINATIONS: They are usually subdivided into

so-called elementary and complex. *Elementary* hallucinations are those that concern a simple perception, such as seeing a light or hearing a sound. *Complex* hallucinations are those concerning a person's perception of a complex issue; he sees figures, he has visions, or he has auditory experiences such as hearing someone speaking. In a number of patients both elementary and complex hallucinations are mixed, while in others only elementary or only complex hallucinations occur. Elementary hallucinations are often mixed with delusions in organic cases. Occasionally this also occurs in schizophrenia. In schizophrenia, however, the complex hallucinatory experience is more prevalent than the elementary one. This is easy to understand because hallucinatory experiences of a schizophrenic individual are mainly based on concept formation, whereas the hallucinatory experiences in most organic mental disorders are based mainly on percept formation.

In describing several of the attributes of hallucinations I would like to start by discussing the basic features of these phenomena. That hallucinations *cannot be resisted* is a basic issue. In other words, hallucinations *cannot be suppressed or repressed.* Hallucinations may be to some extent ignored or shunted aside, a process which, however, should not be confused with repression or even with suppression. Ignoring the hallucination or living with the hallucination, as some schizophrenic patients do, does not indicate that the hallucinations are not present. It indicates that the patient has the ability to ignore their existence, or at least not respond to them. Naturally, this very interesting phenomenon of ignoring, or seemingly not perceiving hallucinations, is illuminated by patients who have undergone lobotomy: the hallucinations still occur, but the patients do not react to them.

The basic attributes—that an hallucination cannot be suppressed, or repressed, and that the patient is unable to resist it—are especially marked in organic cases where you can observe that the person is completely powerless. With certain drugs, hallucinations can be easily produced in non-psychotic individuals; you can then ask such an individual to attempt to do something about his hallucinations—to influence them, to modify them, to suppress them, to repress them, or whatever you want him to try to do—and the end of the story will be that he is completely unable to do anything about them. This is an important feature of mental experience; the person's "will" is unable to have any control over these elementary experiences.

The irresistibility of hallucinations is connected with another feature of these experiences, namely, their *obsessiveness* or their *dominance*. Hallucinations compel attention. The compelling force of hallucinations gives them a special note. Hallucinations intrude into the mental life of the patient in exactly the same way as, for instance, anxieties (especially phobic anxieties) or obsessive-compulsive manifestations intrude into an individual's mental functioning. Probably the only difference is that the patient experiencing hallucinations is actually not aware of this intrusion because he believes in their reality. The obsessive or the dominance force, however, can be clearly demonstrated in those patients who zig-zag across the reality line, patients who occasionally have the feeling that what they experience is actually not real. For instance, in some cases of delirium, in some schizophrenic experiences, or in some experimentally produced hallucinations, the patients are actually aware of the fact that the experiences are strange to them in the same manner as when you are aware—up to a point—that you are dreaming and that it is not reality. In many of these patients, naturally, this feeling or insight later becomes lost. Those patients who still have an ability to differentiate will definitely state that, although they realize these are strange experiences, they are not able to influence them. They are dominated by them. It is interesting to mention that the old idea that the patient was "possessed by evil spirits," or that the person was "possessed" by some other force outside of himself actually has its roots in this dominance phenomenon; the person feels he is obliged to experience certain things, that such an experience is thrust upon him, and that he is completely powerless to do anything about it. The fact that the hallucination compels attention or that it is an obsessive and a dominant phenomenon has been long recognized and, as I have mentioned, these features can be studied in persons who are only mildly intoxicated, or persons in whom emotional tension leads to an hallucinatory experience such as occurs in many schizophrenic patients; the experience is not so strong that they do not zig-zag over the reality line. In other words, so some extent they are still able to believe that those experiences are most likely unreal, but they are nevertheless unable to divert their attention from them.

Incidentally, the preoccupation and self-absorption of patients who are in a state of hallucinating are also partially based on the presence of what is practically a process of double-attention: The patient is compelled to listen, or to look, or to pay attention to somatic or other hallucinatory experiences, and therefore is unable to fully externalize his attention and direct it to stimuli coming from the outside. Naturally, this double-attention—attention to internal as well as external stimuli—considerably impairs the mental functioning of the individual. Thus, the patient's preoccupation and self-absorption (especially in cases of schizophrenia) are probably not due solely to any narrowing of consciousness but are due to the fact that the patient's inner experiences so definitely compel him to divide his attention, or have so nearly completely absorbed his attention, that he no longer has any ability to contact the environment. In such a case the patient is usually dominated by hallucinatory experiences, as is observed quite often in catatonic patients. Some have even believed that many of the stuporous states occurring in organic and schizophrenic patients can be explained psychologically on this basis. Others, however, maintain that the narrowing of consciousness is on another basis and is actually a primary phenomenon. Regardless of any hypothesis we follow, the fact remains that hallucinations intrude to the same extent into the patient's mental functioning as does pain. Pain is also a dominant experience, or an obsessive experience, and compels the patient to pay attention to it regardless of whether he wants to or not.

It is an interesting observation that most hallucinatory experiences, similar to most obsessive (as well as phobic) experiences, are *disagreeable.* There are, however, quite a number of patients who have what are considered to be agreeable hallucinations—those peculiar experiences which are generally termed ecstatic states. The disturbing and disagreeable nature of most hallucinations is particularly true of those experiences which occur in a clear setting. Those hallucinatory experiences which occur in a clouded state, or those which occur in the framework of a dream state—when in this narrowed state of consciousness the patient may experience all varieties of scenes recapitulating everyday experiences—probably do not have a disagreeable element as prominent as do those hallucinations which occur in a clear conscious setting. But, even in delirious states, particularly those based on toxins having a specific effect on the nervous system, we quite often observe disagreeable experiences. For example, in the state of alcoholic delirium (which I will describe when discussing alcoholic mental disorders), it is a common experience for the patient to hallucinate rather disagreeable things that produce a great amount of fear and anxiety in him. Only about one in twelve patients suffering from delirium tremens experiences hallucinations which could possibly be classified as agreeable.

Complex hallucinations especially, and those occurring when consciousness is not very clouded, appear to the patient as *organized.* The patient does not experience them as fragments but as organized themes and events, in which he sees figures acting or he hears people speaking. They can be very elaborate. What is important, furthermore, is that they are *sustained.* They are very persistent and they are also consistent. A great many patients having these markedly dominating sensory perceptual (to him) experiences do not remain passive. The dominance and sustaining quality provokes the patient into action; since his total mentality reacts to these experiences in a systematic manner, he usually attempts to participate in the vivid events he perceives occurring around him. Concerning the elements of such hallucinations, a synthesis takes place in the mind of the patient similar to an actual perception or concept formation. In other words, with rare exceptions, there is no difference between a reality experience and an hallucinatory experience so far as the patient is concerned; the patient actually experiences it in the same organized way as one experiences reality. This can be easily demonstrated with experiments, such as the psychogalvanic, in which the patient never gives a lie response when asked about his hallucinatory experience, but behaves in exactly the same way as he normally would in an experience, and the same way he would if the experience were a reality. That is extremely important, because people have doubted the elemental nature of these experiences, believing that the patient actually has a certain control over them and is able to modify them. When hallucinations reach such a degree that the patient does not operate with the expression, "It is as *if* it were so," but definitely states, "It *is* so—I hear the voice," or "I see the figure," or "I smell the thing," it is as real to the patient as are any of the reality perception experiences.

I must also emphasize the fact that the occurrence of hallucinations is *spontaneous*. They appear spontaneously and do not evolve out of fantasy, which means that the patient is not able to bring on or shut off hallucinations as he is able to bring on and shut off fantasy. A person can decide when he will start to daydream about something and he is then able to shut off that material. He is also able to relive the fantasy material and frequently does, and is to some extent able to play with it. Hallucinations, however, cannot be brought on by the patient's own efforts, and you might as well not ask a recovered schizophrenic patient or a recovered delirious patient to reactivate his hallucinations. Only by using hypnosis, chemicals, or other special methods can you have the patient relive the experience. This ability is never in the patient's control; he cannot willfully shut them off, or keep his attention on something else, or modify them. After the patient has recovered he may be able to recall a few of these experiences and tell you that he was dominated completely by them and was unable to do anything at all about it.

It has also been maintained that hallucinations do not correlate with the configuration of the conscious sphere, which is true, especially concerning those hallucinations which occur in a clear setting. Here again, it means that *ideas, concepts, or percepts* intrude into the mental life of the patient which are *incongruous with the conscious configuration* taking place at that time. The patient may be talking to you and suddenly a voice remarks to him that he is "no good," or he may suddenly see a figure. Neither the voice nor the figure has anything objectively to do with what is taking place at the moment and apparently has nothing to do with what is going on in the patient's conscious mind at the time. In other words, it does not correlate with the conscious configurative field. Naturally, however, this does not apply to the unconscious field where the experiences can actually correlate very well.

I will discuss in more detail a few of the dynamic mechanisms of the content in hallucinatory experiences that are present in persons who are intoxicated. An intoxicated person does not hallucinate purely at random. To some extent he appears to do so, but in those random experiences there are intimately linked elements having dynamic meaning for that particular individual. He thinks, for example, that he is being followed by two men, after which he behaves as though he were going to be attacked by those two men. You will quite likely be able to link this hallucinatory experience to some demonstrable unconscious motivational content in the individual, but this still will not explain why the person is hallucinating under the influence of alcohol.

The patient's hallucination itself and the content of the hallucination are not identical. This can be observed especially in the case of intoxicated persons; while the content of the hallucination is constantly changing, the fact that the patient hallucinates, that the patient has unreal, imaginary experiences, remains. It is almost as though something peculiar and unknown makes the patient hallucinatory, and then that hallucinatory something selects one particular content or channels the hallucination into some other content realm. I would like to emphasize that the content of an hallucination is, therefore, not the mechanism of the hallucination itself. Although to a large extent we are able to understand the motives behind the person's hallucinatory content and are, to some extent, able to understand and analyze what is taking place in that content, we still do not know what an hallucination is. The two should not be confused; by understanding the content, you still do not know *why* the patient hallucinates. These two issues have constantly been confused in the literature and confused clinically and, obviously, this has also led to a number of misconceptions.

The situation is very similar with delusions, and here the issue is even more complicated. The content of a delusion can be understood, but nevertheless, why one individual evolves a system of false beliefs which he does not give up and from which you cannot shake him, and why another individual having the same dynamic constellation does not, we do not understand.

PSEUDOHALLUCINATIONS : These phenomena belong in a group of experiences falling somewhere in between illusions and true hallucinations, but they are actually closer to the latter. And as I have discussed, hallucinations cannot be produced voluntarily; they may be produced voluntarily only if the person is in a special state—for example, if he is intoxicated, if he is exhausted, or if he is sleepy—when cortical control is lowered. If that is not the case, the patient has no such facility and is even unable to autosuggest himself into experiencing hallucinations or delusions. But when a person's cortical control is lowered, such phenomena as eidetic imagery and fantasies can act as forerunners of true hallucinatory experiences. Also, if a person's cortical control is lowered there are experiences, the so-called *pseudohallucinations,* which are not identical with true hallucinatory experiences but which can occur as forerunners of them. These pseudohallucinations are the so-called *oneiroid* experiences and the so-called *hypnagogic* experiences.

Both the oneiroid and hypnagogic experiences are intimately related to experiences in dreams and are usually vivid *fantasy pictures* that very *fleetingly assume reality value* to the person, their reality value becoming modified in the next instant. They are rarely sustained; they are variable; they shift; and furthermore, the person has certain insight that they are not reality experiences. At times, however, the feeling that the experiences are unreal can slip away, and the person might temporarily believe and even act upon some of those oneiroid or hypnagogic experiences as if they were really true.

Hypnagogic experiences are not rare, particularly for eidetic individuals if their conscious cortical control over their mental flow is lowered. For instance, before falling asleep, or when being roughly awakened from sleep, the person could experience hearing a voice, or seeing some figure, or experience somebody touching him, while nothing of the sort was actually happening. These experiences, furthermore, can be linked with scenic experiences and have the vividity of an hallucinatory experience. But, as I have mentioned, they are very fleeting, their configuration is constantly changing, and after a second or two the person usually realizes they are not real. It is not essential for the person to have a real perception and then distort it, such as picking up certain percepts—seeing a curtain, seeing a chair, a table—and basing an illusionary experience on it. In other words, it could be that the person is lying down and begins to weave a fantasy around a scene he experienced during the day, perhaps selecting a somewhat emotionally loaded scene on which to build his fantasy, until suddenly aspects of the fantasy reach such a vividity that he gets up from bed because he has the impression somebody is in the room. The next moment, however, he corrects this experience. Actually, he behaves as many people do who in a dream have a very vivid and reality-like experience. In other words, it is not simply an illusionary experience; it is based on fantasy concept rather than on real perceptions from the external environment. Hypnagogic experiences are more closely on an hallucinatory level, but can in some cases be based on delusions also. These hypnagogic experiences are very interesting because they lead to some understanding of the more sustained form of experiences in which the person loses reality awareness.

Hypnagogic states are not fully synonymous with oneiroid states. Oneiroid states usually occur in the framework of pathologically narrowed consciousness, as in some schizophrenic persons or in individuals under the influence of alcohol. They can also occur nontoxically, particularly in exhaustion states. They may last for a rather long period of time. The oneiroid experiences are mainly confined to the optic sphere. Hypnagogic experiences are also preeminently optic, but occasionally other sensory experiences press in. One thing is very interesting: All these pseudo-hallucinatory, or near-hallucinatory, experiences such as the hypnagogic and oneiroid states are preeminently, or as some would even say, exclusively, in the optic realm. In this respect they resemble dreams. Discussions in a dream, or a dream in which a person is talking to somebody, occasionally occur, but very infrequently compared to visual dream experiences. Actually, they are all "seeing" experiences. It is also interesting that hallucinations produced experimentally by drugs are also preeminently in the visual field. Moreover, it has been practically impossible to reconstruct, in experimentally produced conceptual hallucinations, the auditory hallucinations as they are observed, for instance, in schizophrenic individuals; they occur only occasionally and probably *only* in predisposed people. Here again, intoxicants ordinarily produce preeminently optic manifestations.

Incidentally, even blind people dream visually. Congenitally blind people have, however, an extremely shadowy configuration in their optic experiences. Although their dreams have no color and no vividness, they do have dream experiences which can be termed optic. One might ask how they can experience such things since actually they have no idea of how their surroundings appear in an optic sense. One answer is that certain optic "pictures" of objects in the environment are implanted by touching those things. They are not transmitted in the form of figures, but what they feel through touch is then associated with certain concepts they had picked up from the environment. Their dreams recapitulate or reconstruct some of those experiences. Furthermore, it is also interesting that if blind persons rub their eyes or are hit over the eyes, they apparently have elementary optic experiences very similar to ours. In the same manner, some congenitally deaf people have experiences in dreams, or in a delirium, that have something to do with sound, but here again they are secondarily implanted concept formations about sound experiences, not primary ones. They lack the vividness, they lack the clearness, and they are more a theory of how sounds should be experienced than the actual sounds themselves.

We do not know very much about the mental propensities of persons for experiences in the olfactory, the tactile, or the other sensory fields. Actually, only the eidetic field has been investigated and, up to a point, the auditory. However, eidetic individuals are markedly predisposed to pseudo-hallucinatory experiences because optic recall of pictures or utilization of vivid optic fantasy pictures is much easier for eidetic individuals than for persons who are not. Incidentally, there are individuals with the ability to have unusually vivid recall not in the optic field but in the auditory field. For instance, a person who has very good musical ability can actually hear a known melody; he can turn on its recall and realize that the melody is not occurring outside of himself. However, if his cortical control is lowered, as when falling asleep, temporarily the melody could sound as though it were really being played; it then is an hypnagogic type of experience.

There are persons who, while falling asleep, have vivid experiences and they know that those experiences are not real. Occasionally, however, in such a person it happens that a scene (or a sound) becomes so vivid, so intense, that for a second or two he does not know whether it is real or not. Then it resembles a very fleeting, a very temporary hallucination. But hypnagogic or oneiroid experiences are not as dominating or as disagreeable as true hallucinations, and the patient does not react to them in the same way. They are near to being the same but are not actually. It is important, by the way, when you examine mental patients to differentiate between hypnagogic or oneiroid experiences and real hallucinatory experiences. In many individuals under the influence of a drug such as alcohol or the barbiturates, and in many persons under the impact of a very strong emotional factor, particularly anxiety, experiences can emerge which are *not* really hallucinatory but are experiences of the hypnagogic or oneiroid type. But those hypnagogic or oneiroid experiences in predisposed persons can then slip over the border and become the basis of some hallucinatory experiences. At first the patient is still able to tell that the pseudohallucinatory experiences are not actually true perceptions—he introduces an "if," stating it is "as if a voice were talking to me, but I'm not certain." When the experience becomes more intense, he leaves out the "if" and states, "I am hearing the voices talking to me." From then on, naturally, the predisposed patient becomes dominated by those voices and is unable to do anything about it. In the "if" stage, he is probably still able to say, "Well, I don't want to listen to the voices, I don't want to hear them, I'll shut them off." But when they become dominant, he is unable to do so. This obsessive dominating quality of the hallucinatory experiences is very interesting.

DIFFERENTIAL SYMPTOMATOLOGY

In comparing *hallucinatory experience and fantasy*, it had been thought that a person can, in fantasy, produce experiences or recall experiences which become so very vivid that he simply thinks they are actual present perceptual experiences. This question was never fully settled. It is probably possible that fantasies can actually be so vivid as to appear to merge into hallucinatory experiences. On the other hand, the majority of such fantasies we encounter in most persons usually lack the vividity, the dominance, and the obsessiveness of an hallucinatory experience. I would like to stress this factor; there are many individuals who have very vivid imagery experiences but somehow these individuals have the ability to shut these off and to bring them on. Furthermore, usually the person knows that it is fantasy and states it as such. Retrograde falsification of memories concerning fantasy, where later on the person believes he lived through a certain experience which had actually been only in fantasy, is a phenomenon we occasionally observe. But that is not identical to believing the fantasy of the moment to be an actual present experience. In retrograde falsification, the person had a fantasy and later believed the fantasy events to have actually happened, but *while* he was experiencing his fantasy he was able to differentiate—it was a fantasy and not an hallucination.

Many patients who have fantasies also have hallucinations, but that does not negate the statements just made. Naturally, both can occur, in a mixed form. That occasionally their fantasies give an appearance of merging into hallucinations is also correct. In this regard we are dealing with two processes which are linked, but they are not processes which are identical to each other.

Comparisons have been made between *hallucinations and dreams.* Now that we have described the phenomena of fantasies, of pseudohallucinations, of illusions, of some persons being able under certain circumstances to experience very vivid imagery, and so forth, we must establish another link going from the normal over to the abnormal. At this point we come to the issue of so-called normal dream experiences. As you know, in dreams perceptual experiences are recalled; actually the whole dream is nothing other than a perceptual experience, a perceptual experience during sleep, however, which is usually fragmented and usually distorted. The vivacity of the dream differs markedly in different individuals and can also differ in the same individual depending on the various constellations of stimuli, organic or emotional. Illusionary misinterpretations, pseudohallucinatory experiences, and hallucinatory experiences have often been compared to the dream experiences of the normal individual. Any relationship, however, is merely superficial because hallucinatory experiences differ to a great extent from experiences in the dream. There are, however, a few *elements in common.*

The element which has always fascinated people who investigated patients who are hallucinating and who investigated patients who were dreaming is the common element of the *impairment of consciousness.* However, this narrowing of consciousness, or the obliteration of the higher mental functions, this partial decortication of the individual, is also similar in experience and in behavior in a dream state and in a state of, for instance, delirium. Many delirious patients complain of being sleepy, exhausted, and appear "clouded," a few at times behaving as though dream-walking. Nevertheless, there are *marked* differences between such organically provoked dream states and hallucinatory experiences. And, you should not be fascinated unduly by our use of the term "dream state" as an expression for some of those organic reactions, thereby assuming that a complete analogy exists between a dream of a normal individual and an hallucinatory episode of a patient who is suffering from an acute organic reaction. It can be stated, however, that there is one similarity, namely, the clouding of consciousness.

There is another similarity which interests us considerably. The *psychodynamic content* of hallucinatory and delusionary episodes and that of normal dreams are very closely allied. Actually, Freud's descriptions concerning the latent and manifest components—described by him as being condensations, displacements, fragmentations, dissociations, distortions, and so forth—in the normal dream can definitely be established in the same manner in the hallucinatory entity. Freud later worked out the concept that dream mechanisms are based on the mechanism of repression; that certain of the unconscious material present in the individual leads to the dream processes.

From those assumptions it was only a step further to assume that in hallucinatory experiences, also, the repressive mechanism is actually at work; that because dissociation, condensation, projection, and so forth can be demonstrated in many hallucinatory experiences, the common denominator of both is an alteration of the repressive mechanism. From this point of view, hallucinations or hallucinatory experiences are nothing other than experiences coming to the fore which the individual had at one time repressed. Although the point of view was also expressed that many hallucinatory experiences are the original experiences themselves which now dominate the person's mental function, others had the view that they are not the original experiences, per se, but a distortion, or a displacement, or some other alteration of a previous and repressed experience which appears in a disguised form as hallucinatory content. Those who stressed this point of view then went a step further, stating that the same symbolisms observed and interpreted in dreams could be applied equally well for explaining hallucinatory experiences, that actually there is not much difference between the two.

A few investigators even went so far that, in reading some of their explanations, you are given the impression hallucinatory experiences are perfectly normal experiences —that some people are awake-while-dreaming—and that is all. In other words, the *gravity* of the mental alteration, the gravity of the distortion of the individual's mental life was not accepted, and the individual became so normalized in the eyes of those investigators that actually the whole concept of the hallucinating person suffering from a psychosis was more or less disregarded; hallucinations became regarded as one part in the variety of experiences which can occur in fairly normal individuals.

Obviously, I do not share this view and, naturally, in dealing with hallucinating persons as patients, regardless of what philosophical concepts you may form, you will very quickly discover that we cannot assume hallucinatory experiences to be variations of normal experiences, even though on rare occasions you might encounter a so-called normal individual who had had hallucinatory experiences. Here, I might add that any hallucinatory experiences are so very dependent upon specific constellations of factors that they are practically nonexistent in normal people. Therefore, we should be rather rigid in our criteria for assuming a normal individual has hallucinatory experiences. Usually what he experiences are not hallucinations at all, but are either pseudohallucinations or they are concepts which become so vividly endowed with substance that the person actually experiences them as perceptions although he is aware they are not true percepts. As I shall discuss, tendencies to normalize patients have also been expressed on the basis of a few psychodynamic ideas concerning delusions as well. There is much more difficulty in drawing a line, and much more difficulty in accepting or refusing some of those ideas concerning normalization of delusional material than those concerning false perceptions, dreams, and hallucinations.

At most, then, we are aware of two similarities of hallucinations and dreams—the clouding of consciousness being one, the other being that, to some extent, the content of the hallucinatory manifestations follows the observations made on a normal person's dreams, both having been regarded as analogous by some observers. At this point the similarity ends.

Now we approach the issue of the *dissimilarities* between the normal dream and the hallucination. I have alluded to the fact that hallucinations, illusions, and pseudo-hallucinations have two qualities: (1) they are *dominant*; and (2) they are experienced by persons in whom consciousness is not so much clouded as it is *being obsessed*.

The dominance aspect of these experiences is of great importance. The matter of dominance of ideation is not alone present in hallucinatory experiences but also occurs in a very great many other mental mechanisms (obsessive phenomena, phobias, anxiety experiences). The patient must submit to those experiences and is actually unable to do anything about them. In addition to their dominance they are fully incorporated into the patient's mentation. In other words, for the patient, *it is so!* You cannot argue with an hallucinating patient that his hallucinations are not experienced percepts at all. He refuses to accept that because his hallucinations have the vividity and acuteness of an actual perceptual experience.

It is obvious that during an hallucinatory experience, the patient *cannot be aroused* from this state by external stimuli, although, naturally a person can be quite easily aroused from a sleeping state and the dream experience is then viewed by the patient as an imaginary, even though "involuntary," event. He would not confuse the dream with the reality he observes when he is awakened. In other words, usually when awakened he can "turn off" the dream experience rather quickly.

The domination of the patient by an hallucinatory experience is usually *sustained*. Hallucinations are rarely as fleeting as is a dream experience; usually they are very persistent. In particular, those hallucinatory experiences occurring when the person's consciousness is not very clouded have the tendency to be quite persistent. In an hallucinatory experience, furthermore, those sustained perceptions are usually *organized* in a much more *elaborate* form and in a much more *consistent* form than occurs in dreams. Therefore, although the hallucinatory experiences probably share the perceptual recollection or reactivation of the dream, they are usually much more intense, as well as more sustained, than in dream experience.

With the exception of a certain group of individuals— for example, cases of coordinated, and even complex, acts of sleepwalking—a person who dreams rarely *acts* upon his dream experience. No action is provoked because the mentality of the person, *in toto,* does not react to such fleeting experiences in a systematic way. It is quite different in the case of patients having an hallucinatory episode. There are, naturally, patients who remain passive and in whom the hallucinatory experiences are probably as fleeting as in a dream, but a great many patients are so very markedly dominated by sustained and usually very disagreeable hallucinatory experiences that they very often try to participate in them.

Keeping in mind that most hallucinations, especially those occurring when consciousness is not very clouded, are *disagreeable* experiences, we observe that dreams of the wish-fulfilling variety usually are not unpleasant. Although they may include disguised anxiety and "riddance" configurations, for the most part they do not have a persistently disagreeable quality but are often rather bland or even pleasant experiences. (I am not including here the so-called anxiety dream, or "nightmare.")

Whether the difference between the hallucinatory experience and the dream is quantitative only, or is also qualitative, has never been fully decided. There are those who believe the difference is only quantitative. There are those who believe the dream experience and the hallucinatory experience are also qualitatively different. In any case, I would like to emphasize that a few psychiatrists may still believe that hallucinations are actually dreams taking place during the person's waking state. Although to some extent a comparison can occasionally be made, one cannot assume them to be identical. Much more work has actually been done to point out the similarities than the dissimilarities from a psychopathological point of view, although the dissimilarities between the two are quietly assumed by those who attempt to establish an analogy.

Attempts to compare *hallucinations in children* with their dreams or fantasies have led to quite some confusion. To discuss for a moment the subject of hallucinatory experiences in children, some observers have suggested that very young children normally hallucinate in a wish-fulfilling way. In this regard, we encounter the following difficulties. First, children imitate older people, long before their ego is as strongly delineated as that of an adult, at a time when reality and fantasy boundaries are not as sharply drawn as in an adult. In an immature individual, hallucinatory experiences are more prevalent. Secondly, there is probably not only some psychological but also some physiological background. Interestingly enough, it is easier for a child to produce hallucinatory experiences when under the influence of some toxin or during a fever than it is for an adult. Many people even maintain that the adults in whom hallucinations are very easily provoked under the influence of an infectious or other toxic agent, are actually individuals who have retained a particular infantile physiology and in addition, I might suggest, an infantile psychology. Both factors play a role in children. Their physiological apparatus can more easily become disturbed, which may lead to hallucinatory experiences since hallucinatory experiences have, of course, a physical substrata. Also, the unclear delineation of their ego boundaries with the unclear ability of the person to differentiate between reality and fantasy are very important factors. An additional factor which has never been fully investigated is that eidetic imagery is stronger in children. Therefore, their fantasy pictures are much more vivid than those of most adults.

It is obvious, therefore, that hallucinatory experiences are more easily provoked in children. But again, the so-called fantasy productions in children are usually not true hallucinations. A child will make believe that when he runs around on a stick the stick is a horse, but actually he *knows* that it is not a horse. Now, some factor might wash the reality boundary away, but that would be only very fleeting, very temporary, and the child would never handle the experience in the same manner as he would an hallucinatory experience. I do not know if you have ever seen a child who is delirious, or if you have ever seen a schizophrenic child who is hallucinating. In such cases what you observe is entirely different, despite *all* the similarities, from those interesting fantasy pictures experienced by normal children. However, there probably are bridges between the two; the one could possibly pass into the other. Nevertheless, in dealing with an hallucinatory experience we are dealing with something basically different from a fantasy experience.

It had been assumed by a few classical psychoanalysts that all children have hallucinations. Fenichel (*1963*) was one of the psychoanalysts who had a very strong normalization tendency, with the idea that hallucinatory experiences in children can originate normally. He was among those observers who were very inclined to reason on one basic tenet: *All* mental manifestations in an adult are actually remnants, or reactivations, of infantile mechanisms. Therefore, it was assumed that practically every phenomenon encountered in an adult has been observed as a manifestation in a child, and, in addition, that any pathological manifestation observed in an adult can be encountered as a normal manifestation in a child. It was assumed, in other words, that in all those manifestations we are actually dealing with reactivation, or regression phenomena; that an adult resumes or returns to a lower level of mental and emotional adaptation, and on that lower level of adaptation he naturally utilizes mechanisms which were normal at that particular age level. From this point of view a great many ideas were introduced into the literature which have since become very questionable as to their validity. It is my feeling that, among the views I have just mentioned, here again, facts were introduced to support a theory, a preconceived notion about the organization of the psyche.

Children do *not* normally hallucinate. Anyone who has served in the pediatric service of a hospital, or served on a children's division of a psychiatric hospital, will know that children do not normally hallucinate, even though they have vivid experiences. They have fantasies and they often tell you about those fantasies as though they have really happened. It is the same, as you will observe, in some psychotic patients who actually *know* that what they tell you did not happen, and yet they will insist that it *is* so. This is the so-called double-bookkeeping of the psychotic, which occurs especially in the schizophrenic person. You will also observe the interesting emotional coloring and the convincing ability of many sociopathic liars and acting-out psychoneurotic individuals. You will find that those individuals treat what they tell you as though the fantasy events actually happened, while at the same time there is that double-bookkeeping. They know that it is not true. The complete incorporation of the experience as his own, the complete conviction that the events are actually happening in the environment and are reality events, are lacking in those experiences. Therefore, if you want to be very generous you can say that the fantasies, the vivid fantasy pictures, the enlivenment of an idea or a thought, and the pseudohallucinatory experiences are related to each other. But they are not the same as hallucinations. It is quite possible that it will finally be concluded that there is a fairly sharp difference between these two phenomena when we learn a little more about their origin.

Naturally, it is not so easy to discover just what is going on in the mind of a very young child; he may be too young to communicate it. How would one interrogate a one-year-old child regarding his fantasy or hallucinatory experience? It would be similar to asking what is going on in the mind of an unconscious person; he cannot tell you what is going on. If a very young child does not *behave* as though he is hallucinating, you are not able to actually determine how vivid his fantasy experiences are; and, therefore, it would only be an assumption to state that this child hallucinates. His experiences are probably so weighted by the fact that the reality boundaries are not laid down, that everything going on in his mind is still a mixture of fact and fantasy. However, if you study two- or three-year-old children who suffer with meningitis or encephalitis and are hallucinating—then you see the difference. Incidentally, the same thing is true with regard to animals. Up to a point, say two years of age, when the ego development is as yet not very strong, a child may be compared to certain other mammals. If you intoxicate a monkey or a dog with certain drugs, it will hallucinate. They behave as if they are. They do not behave the same way when not intoxicated. Everything considered, we should be careful not to extend ourselves to conclusions. We should always be aware of the fact that we are dealing with similarities in these comparisons, and we are probably working only with analogies. Although we must very frequently work with analogies, in psychiatry more so than in any other branch of medicine, we should keep aware of the fact that they are merely analogies rather than identical phenomena. Such theories are very tempting from a theoretical point of view, but they are not based on facts.

I would like to emphasize that one is able to clinically determine whether or not a dog or a monkey hallucinates, and whether or not a child is hallucinating. When an hallucinatory experience occurs in a child there is something different about it which probably cannot be clearly defined, but it *is* different from a vivid imagery or fantasy experience; the two are not the same. The question is, are the differences only quantitative or are they qualitative? It is my personal feeling that it is not a purely quantitative issue; something qualitative is involved which makes it different.

There is another matter which I would like to clarify. There are behavior patterns in very young children which you must not assume to be based on either fantasies or hallucinations. For instance, when a baby puts whatever he picks up into his mouth, something more complex than merely response to fantasy is occurring, just as it is more complex than a so-called reality-testing function. It has several functions: first, a part of it is surely reality testing; actually the child or the animal tests reality with the senses that are available to him, not alone by putting things in his mouth, but touching things, picking things up, releasing things, and even looking or smiling at certain things. Secondly, putting things in his mouth has a sensory function. Naturally, the oral organ system has a very high sensory endowment; the child constantly stimulates this organ system because it gives him a certain amount of satisfaction. Thirdly, as one can quite clearly observe in animals, the mouth seems to be also utilized as a tension discharge apparatus. It is an early focus of tension discharge which later becomes broadened to include many other areas—the skin, the anal region, the legs, the arms, and so forth are definitely tension discharge foci in the child. That has nothing to do with reality testing as a whole. Therefore, reality testing, sensory pleasure, and tension discharge functions merge, and so one cannot actually assume that reality testing is the only function involved.

I would like to comment on a statement of Fenichel that food is fantasied, and then the child puts objects into his mouth. This suggestion rests on an assumption for which we have no verification. The only supports that have emerged for this assumption are in some of the papers by Ferenczi and by Abraham *(Arieti 1959)*. They broadened the concept of infantile experiences to include the idea that in the first phase of the child's omnipotence he attempts to incorporate the whole world by means of the mouth, and in the second phase (later interpreted as oral-sadistic or cannibalistic) the child's biting and chewing are attempts to destroy by means of the mouth. These are retrograde verifications, not direct verifications. One must be careful about building any theory on retrograde verifications. However, even should I assume that some of Abraham's interpretations are correct—and basically I think they are correct, in the sense that tension discharge in infants actually is organized around the oral feature—I am much less convinced about the correctness of the elaboration of this theory. I still doubt that when a child picks things up and puts them in his mouth the child also fantasies anything. Because this act is performed by so many animals and adult people in a semiconscious state, I believe we are dealing here with primitive reflex mechanisms. In response to stimulation at that early age level the motor manifestation is such that the very young child picks up an object and, naturally, puts it into his mouth. This phenomenon can be observed also in markedly regressed schizophrenic patients, and you will not find that there are any fantasies or ideations connected with it. The only definite feelings they will verbalize are of certain motor tensions. They release tension orally. I would not go so far as to say that it is not possible for a child to fantasy during his oral activity, but I would object to assuming that each time he acts in such a manner the ideation of food, or oral libidinization, occurs and is the primary factor to which the execution of the act is secondary. In my opinion, any food fantasies are secondary. Those theoretical constructs mentioned are not supported by much factual evidence and I do not believe they have much factual basis.

There are so-called hallucinatory experiences that occur

in various *culturally determined settings*. I will discuss this subject in more detail in connection with culturally determined false ideas and false judgments as those, for instance, occurring in a delusion; they are intimately linked with hallucinatory phenomena. If we investigate the so-called culturally determined hallucinations, two phenomena will be revealed. (1) Most of them are experienced when an individual or a group is in a special mental and emotional state. In other words, the individuals do not have hallucinations on their own; they usually hallucinate in the framework of a group setting, such as certain religious or ritual ceremonies during which times the involved individuals hallucinate. Quite often, incidentally, those culturally organized hallucinations are actually provoked by certain intoxicants or drugs. Therefore, many of those experiences cannot actually be termed pure hallucinations in the sense of being produced in an individual whose consciousness and mental functioning were not impaired by, for instance, some drug or by some intoxicant. Furthermore, (2) many of those so-called cultural hallucinations are actually not true hallucinations. Here again, in most cases they are vivid conceptual experiences rather than actual hallucinations, although I do grant that there are descriptions of people experiencing, for instance, sessions of group ecstasy, or sessions of group visual and auditory experiences. However, an investigation would demonstrate them to be concepts which had become very vivid, rather than true hallucinations. Even though the person believes the happening to be real, it does not have the vividity and does not have the clarity of the hallucinatory experiences. This is not true, however, if the person is under the influence of drugs, and other toxins. In such cases he may actually have hallucinatory experiences; and those experiences are as real as any other true hallucinations.

In connection with the *influence of drugs,* if one is dealing with a schizophrenic patient who is hallucinating and that patient is then intoxicated with one of the drugs capable of producing hallucinations, such as mescaline, that drug will intensify the original hallucinations of the patient. In addition, however, it will produce typical organic hallucinations. For example: A schizophrenic patient hears voices; they are telling him what to do and what not to do; under the influence of the drug his hallucinations become more intense; he hears his voices more intensively; the voices tell him in a much more urgent manner what to do and what not to do; they make comments on his behavior and so on. In addition, that patient begins to have visual experiences which are characteristic of mescaline intoxication; he sees geometric figures, color distortions, alterations of things in space, distortions of body image, and so forth. Now, the interesting thing is that the schizophrenic patient is able to clearly differentiate between those hallucinations which are his own and those which are produced by the drug. In other words, he has a certain feeling, or certain knowledge of that which is "out of tune" with his own spontaneous experiences.

In summary then, the hallucinatory (as well as the delusional) experience contains elements that have not yet been fully explained physiologically or psychologically. It has a certain, I would say, "experience quality" of its own which does not appear in any of the other phenomena resembling it—such as fantasy pictures, eidetic imagery, and dreams—even though an intimate relationship exists. Again I would emphasize, the content of an hallucination actually is very similar to the content of a dream, but that still does not explain the actual mechanism of an hallucination. This is, in my opinion, the greatest difficulty with which we are struggling. The same difficulty applies concerning delusions. We are able to understand, for instance, the reasons for a person's having expansive ideas, and we can understand the reasons for a person's organizing his emotional difficulties in the form of ideas of reference; but what we do not understand is *why* the person develops the conviction with its inflexibility and *why* he has the inability to change it. In other words, why is it he develops that particular symptom process rather than one of many other symptom processes? What a delusion is and, in the same way, what an hallucination is—we do not know, even though we are often able to explain the content.

Finally, hallucinations are intimately *linked* with delusional formations. It is false to state, however, that they always occur together, or one is the prerequisite of the other, as you can read in some textbooks. An hallucination is *not* the prerequisite for a delusion, and a delusion is not a prerequisite for an hallucination. But they occur very often together, and they are very often linked. Optic hallucinations are much *less* apt to be used as a basis for, or are less linked with, delusional formation than are the auditory ones. This would indicate that there are differences between the two. I mentioned that the visual hallucinatory experience is very similar to a perceptual experience. In other words, that is very similar to the person's actually perceiving something, and any ideas formed around it are secondary. The person will perceive a figure and then will probably form ideas around the figure—that the figure is threatening, or the figure will do this, or the figure will do that. If you want to put it very crudely, you could say that in a visual hallucination the ideation, the concept, *follows* the percept. In an hallucinatory manner a person first perceives something and then begins to organize his concepts around it. On the other hand, in hallucinations of the auditory field usually concept formation is primary and it is then projected onto the environment as if it were a perception. (That is an oversimplification I use only to contrast the two experiences.) For example, a schizophrenic patient at first has an idea, and this idea becomes then so very intense that the person hears somebody telling it to him; the concept reaches a perceptual vividness.

Actually, from a clinical point of view, these matters are not very important to consider, but from a theoretical point of view they are very important because they lead to different hypotheses and different speculations as to the role of perceptual and conceptual thinking in the various disorders. There are many theories regarding the origin of hallucinations and delusions. None of them are fully satisfactory and not one of them explains any of the variety of observations made and the experiences had in this field. To understand some of the theories and also to be able to criticize the merits and demerits of those different theories, you must distinguish more than is usually done between an hallucinatory experience per se and the content of the hallucination.

4

CONCEPTUAL DISORDERS (OVERVALUED IDEAS)

Having discussed the main aspects of the hallucinatory experiences, I now want to consider a second, extremely important, mental manifestation which plays a tremendous role not only in a psychosis but also in many neurotic disturbances. This is the subject of overvalued ideas, with its subdivision known as the real delusions. Just as with hallucinatory experiences, quite a number of psychiatrists have tried to establish a continuum and attempted to trace the vagaries of an idea from the normal, through the slightly abnormal, to the more abnormal, and then to the most abnormal.

What happens to an idea when it becomes endowed with a special significance to the person? One can read a great many papers which maintain that there is a continuous chain of manifestations extending from the normal idea to a so-called overvalued idea, and then to an incorrigible conviction—which would be another term for a delusion. Again, others have stressed the point with regard to delusional experiences, similarly as with hallucinatory experiences, that although undeniably a relationship exists between a normal idea, conviction, or judgment and an overvalued idea, conviction, or judgment and finally a so-called incorrigible conviction, nevertheless the delusional experience has a certain not too well-defined quality which gives them a somewhat special note, thus placing a normal idea or a normal conviction apart from an overvalued idea and an overvalued conviction.

As I now try to trace the development of the whole issue, it will become apparent that the matter is not fully settled. You will realize how very difficult it is to really differentiate between normal and abnormal—for instance, how very often the abnormality of ideation does not rest on the phenomenon alone but on a great many auxiliary factors, or the "setting" in which it occurs. In delusions, cultural prejudices or cultural mores intrude much more markedly than in the case of hallucinatory experiences. Although it is not very difficult for a psychiatrist to state that a particular person is delusional, and probably not even difficult for many laymen to recognize that this particular person is delusional, one will encounter difficulty the very moment the matter is discussed in terms of the structure and basis of delusions in their relationship to ideation or thought processes in general. It will be realized immediately that the moment one leaves the clinical—the moment one leaves the empirical and becomes theoretical—the issue becomes extremely complicated and difficult. In this sphere the delineation between normal and abnormal is, naturally, a difficult task.

The definition of a delusion itself is not very easy to establish. Different textbooks present the definition of delusions differently. This lack of unanimity is probably due to the fact that all which we term delusions are not actually the same. It is possible that certain mental aberrations that could be termed delusions are not etiologically, or even psychopathologically, identical. The designation "delusion" probably covers somewhat different psychopathological factors. The most common definition of delusion, which is rather old but yet maintained in the psychiatric literature, is that the *delusion* is (1) *a conviction of extraordinary strength.* This feature is stressed by a great many observers and it is obvious that whenever dealing with a delusional patient one is able to demonstrate the extraordinary strength of his convictions quite convincingly. Nevertheless, when discussing it in detail we shall observe that the point where strong conviction leaves off and extraordinary sense of conviction starts is naturally rather difficult to determine. People who have had extraordinarily strong convictions about certain things have sometimes been adjudged by others to have delusions while actually they did not. On the other hand, it is true that the delusional patient usually insists that his ideation on a particular issue *is so,* and furthermore he usually does not deviate from that conviction.

In addition to the extraordinary sense of conviction, it is usually mentioned that (2) *the ideation is not influenced by experience to the contrary.* This is important. Usually persons who have a strong conviction can be argued out of it, or at least be convinced intellectually of the reasons why the idea which they put forward is not correct, or why it should be revised. On the other hand, as you will observe, not every conviction or every idea which you cannot argue away from somebody is necessarily a delusion. In addition, I should mention that quite a number of persons, especially a certain group of psychotic persons usually included in the paranoid group, are able to marshal excellent facts, or what are actually pseudofacts, establishing seeming validity to their conviction. So, it is difficult to demonstrate that a so-called conviction which is uninfluenced by a contrary experience is a delusion. For instance, many paranoid patients who are quite able to organize, or to marshal, a great many facts to support their own ideas are very successful in marketing these ideas; they even convince people who have no delusions that their conviction is fact, while basically the whole phenomenon actually moves on a delusional level.

In defining delusions, most textbooks usually mention (3) *the improbability of content*. The three features—the extraordinary strength of conviction, not being influenced by experience to the contrary, and the improbability of the contents of such an ideation—are usually described as characteristics of a delusion. The third feature must be more seriously questioned than even the first two. It is true that we encounter quite a number of delusions in which the content is so bizarre, so fantastic, so out of order, and so far away from reality as to be immediately obvious that the idea the patient holds is completely improbable. A schizophrenic, for example, will tell you that some rays are coming from another planet and these rays influence his thinking or influence him to now behave this or that way. Naturally, this is quite improbable and would be recognized as a fantastic idea, and from the way it evolved there would be no great difficulty in maintaining that idea as delusional.

The situation becomes much more complicated in the case of a patient who begins to complain that he is being mistreated and presents a large number of arguments about how at his place of employment other persons are against him, and explains rather convincingly why those persons are mistreating him. In such a case the delusion, which in time one can most likely establish as a delusion rather than being true, is *handled* by the patient in such a manner that unless you are able to investigate the situation carefully it cannot be verified as being a delusion. It could be a fact. In such an instance the so-called improbability of content does not help at all in deciding whether you are dealing with a set of facts or are dealing with delusions.

Furthermore, a rather common feature in delusion formation must be mentioned which is often overlooked, even by able psychiatrists: Delusional ideas can be entertained that are based on actual facts. In other words, that an idea is a fact does not mean the patient cannot be delusional about it. If you treat patients who have paranoid ideas about infidelity, for example, you very often will find that many of their ideas are justified, and therefore the facts are probably true, just as the person expressing those ideas suspected. Nevertheless, the *intensity* with which the idea is maintained, how the person constantly *elaborates* on it, and how he constantly builds on it and tries to utilize all varieties of other factors to support that idea can yet be delusional. The following example will clarify this point. Assume that you are treating a female patient who expresses ideas that her husband is unfaithful; these ideas are expressed with a great deal of vehemence; these ideas are expressed in such a way that the counterarguments are not accepted. In other words, a strongly patterned conviction is present. You then speak to the husband; he will most likely reveal (as in a particular case I have in mind) that actually what she suspects is true. Therefore, you could assume that because the facts are there this patient is probably very upset emotionally and very vehement about it, but she does not have any delusions. Examining the patient further, it develops that even though the facts are there, she handles the idea in the following way: "I was home yesterday and I saw somebody out in the street, winking while holding a handkerchief to her eye. This winking was a sign that my husband was receiving a signal that in an hour he will meet another woman somewhere else." A great many paranoid patients interpret incidental events in terms of their delusions.

In this regard, one has to be always very careful not to fall into misinterpreting the whole matter. That a patient is delusional about something does not mean that some factual evidence for the delusion cannot be present. The patient is delusional nevertheless, and the way in which the patient handles the evidence, how he elaborates on it, how he indulges in argumentation, how he in actuality responds emotionally to the set of facts put forward, are all very important. In consultations I have occasionally heard psychiatrists argue that the patient is perfectly well because the factual evidence *is* really there. Here is another example. Once I saw a patient who became very depressed, very upset, and very agitated, expressing the idea that he had done some tampering with his books for income tax purposes. Since it was not known to the environment, everybody could put it down as a delusion. He was depressed and had an unrealistic self-accusatory idea. I discussed this matter with him, and I somehow became suspicious that maybe his idea was true. He sent his accountant to me to confirm that it was true; the tampering had happened. When the family psychiatrist on the case was informed about it, he immediately reversed his stand, stating that the depression of the patient was fully justified and his ideas were not delusional at all. Then the patient started in to explain that he had become excessively agitated and upset because the room was wired, because the district attorney was listening to every thought of his, and therefore knew that he tampered with his books. So, we can see here that two things coincide: the ideational content can actually be based on facts and still be handled in a delusional way. When evaluating a delusional idea we must be especially careful, *not* labeling as a delusion only that which is so fantastic or so bizarre or so incredible that every layman would be able to recognize it as such.

Actually there is a rather subtle differentiation between delusions and the set ideas of a neurotic individual (one encounters neurotic individuals who have very set ideas). A neurotic person usually immediately tries to convince you as to the why and how of his convictions. The delusional person is so convinced he is right that he usually does not argue it—it simply is so. In general, you could use this as a kind of differentiation, although there are exceptions to the rule. For instance, some paranoid litigants may behave very similarly to neurotic persons. They may try hard to convince you with a great deal of argument, sometimes bringing volumes of arguments, to show why they have those ideas.

One has to realize another important point, that just as hallucinations fluctuate, so do delusions. When I discuss the basis on which delusions develop, you will see that there are quite a number of individuals who have an "if" relationship to their delusions. In other words, they are not at all times fully convinced that their ideas are correct, and sometimes they even make revisions. However, when the emotional charge behind the matter again arises, suddenly they again state that "it *is* so." We observe fluctuation quite often, especially in some acute schizophrenic patients.

Actually the three points of the definition of a delusion briefly discussed could be debated for hours. They do not fully distinguish a delusion from a conviction. It is really very difficult to decide at what point an idea stops being a conviction and a delusion starts. There is marked variability in psychiatrists' evaluations of the content of a patient's ideas. And I am convinced there are quite a number of people who have certain delusional ideas which to one psychiatrist appear to be emotionally charged ideation but understandable in that you can see yourself in it, whereas another psychiatrist would say that these are clear-cut delusional ideas. That is not a rare occurrence, particularly in the case of some paranoid patients. I have here in mind especially paranoid litigants who convince the court, convince the lawyers, even convince some psychiatrists, that they are really right; it is only after they have continued with such procedure for about ten or fifteen years, having popped up in different courts, that finally everyone realizes something must be wrong. Then the whole matter is investigated to find that much of the litigant's ideation was actually delusional. There is no fixed rule for delineating delusions.

Another thing has to be taken into consideration: One must recognize in what civilization or culture the person moves. I would not deny that there are probably such things as delusions recognizable as delusions everywhere. A patient who is in a grossly organic state and quite disorganized, expressing all varieties of peculiar mixed-up delusional ideas, probably would be as recognizably delusional in one environment as another. But, subtleties at times can mislead you; a person from a different cultural organization may maintain that certain ideas which here would definitely be called delusional are, in his home environment, a part of that particular civilization. Incidentally, on this point mistakes are made by psychiatrists in both directions. For instance, one may encounter a patient from central Europe who expresses certain superstitions in a certain way. This was quite often argued as being a part of his culture; therefore, it is normal; and in this case we are not dealing with delusional patterns. On the other hand, it could later develop that although this person used that particular set of ideas in his culture, he nevertheless handled it in a delusional way. In reverse, observations can also be made in that, for instance, delusional individuals within their cultural environment can be regarded as perfectly normal and not as suffering from any mental aberration simply because their ideation belongs to their particular cultural setting.

I once had an interesting experience with a Chinese patient who had been in New York for only a very short time. He arrived by ship and had never been in a Western community. He came from a remote part of China, and while still in China he passed through cities which were organized in a pattern of culture differing from that of his province. In his travels he began to behave very strangely. He evolved ideas that people were following him, trying to kill him, and he expressed all kinds of ideas that turned out to be his religious ideas and beliefs. He was picked up in New York for observation because of his strange behavior. One psychiatrist argued that the patient's set of ideas were perfectly logical, if the man had never been confronted with our civilization. The patient was rather fearful and upset about it, he did not know how to handle it, and he employed, furthermore, primitive ideas about it which were all quite understandable based on his culture. His examining psychiatrist, by the way, once had been in China and therefore purportedly carried a great deal of authority on anything Chinese. Because he stated that the patient's particular ideation was naturally quite characteristic for his particular province, it was acceptable as normal behavior. However, within a few days the patient began to behave in a catatonic manner and wound up in a typical catatonic state, expressing in addition many delusional ideas which were, of course, definitely couched in the language of his civilization. Therefore, when dealing with a person of a different civilization, we must always be careful to not misdiagnose the behavior.

It could still be fully true that a person may express ideas, superstitions, behavior patterns, and so forth, and, although we do not share such things with him or we may even think they are probably silly, we should not immediately label that person psychotic on the basis of such ideas. On the other hand, we also have to be extremely aware of the fact that a person coming from a so-called primitive civilization and expressing certain mental aberrations in a rather primitive language could be as psychotic as any other individual we encounter, and thus only the structural analysis of the entire case will be likely to reveal the whole matter. Actually, in my opinion, mistakes are made in this respect if the psychiatrist concentrates on simply evaluating an idea and does not evaluate the person who is conveying the idea. If an idea is put forward by a schizophrenic patient, one can argue quite often: Is this idea understandable and is this idea true, or is this idea improbable and is this idea false? Actually, this is not the decisive issue. The decisive issue is the way in which the person actually handles his ideations and the way in which the person actually behaves, *in toto*.

DESCRIPTIVE SYMPTOMATOLOGY

We usually differentiate between *primary* and *secondary* delusional formations. This differentiation is not employed clinically, but is used from a psychopathological point of view. *Primary delusions* are those encountered in patients suffering, for instance, from the paranoid form of schizophrenia (or "paranoia," or "paranoiac states," which are the same thing). There, the ideational distortions are the primary mental aberrations expressed by the patient; they dominate the whole field and, furthermore, give one the feeling that ideational distortion is actually the main issue. This was especially stressed in former years because many people then believed that the patients actually suffered from an intellectual disorder. We now know that even in those individuals, where it appears to be an intellectual disorder, very profound emotional changes are present which actually force the individual to think in a particular way. Nevertheless, the old observation of the individual is still correct, that seemingly the intellectual aberration—that peculiar *ideational aberration*—is *in the foreground*. There is a marked difference between talking to a patient who is fully lucid and well oriented, who does not hallucinate, who seemingly conducts himself perfectly normally, and who yet discloses a great many paranoid delusional ideas, and—in contrast—talking to a patient who expresses delusions while in a state of narrowed consciousness, who is hallucinating, and who is manifesting marked emotional and behavioral deviations. Primary delusions, therefore, usually occur in a clear setting in those patients in whom other psychiatric abnormalities are not readily detected. They are present but inconspicuous.

Secondary delusions usually form upon some other mental aberration and are secondary to it. For instance, an organic patient who is confused, or who is disoriented, or whose memory is impaired will then misinterpret people in his environment and pour out some ideation about those people. Such delusional formations are secondary, not primary, ones. Moreover, they are secondary delusional formations if the patient has illusions or hallucinations, and then begins to erect on them some form of an *interpretive structure.* From a psychopathological point of view, they are all secondary delusional formations. The same applies to delusions in the type of depressive patient, for instance, who at first expresses a marked feeling of exhaustion and inertia, then complains that he is unable to cope with certain situations because he has lost his "pep" and is unable to do anything about it, and then begins to elaborate on some organ function in his body in a markedly hypochondriacal manner, perhaps believing that he is not well because he has cancer of the liver and therefore is unable to function. Or, because he is markedly depressed, he may begin to evolve some self-accusatory ideas and blame himself, saying that he is in such a miserable state because he committed a certain sin, and his suffering is now some form of atonement for his sin. These are secondary elaborations and being secondary elaborations, naturally are understood in the framework of other underlying mental pathology.

Clinically we do not differentiate very strictly between primary and secondary delusional formations, as it was formerly considered so important to do, because we feel that dynamically even in the so-called primary delusional formation there is some underlying emotional factor; the delusional formation there, too, is most likely secondary to some form of an emotional state in the person. Nevertheless, one may say that the difference is probably not an etiological one but a formal difference between these two delusional patterns. Delusion occurring in a clear setting, elaborated by a person with a high intelligence, without overt display of emotional changes, and by one who has no hallucinations and no sensory defects indicates a phenomenon quite different (at least in its technical execution) from a delusion which grows out of hallucinations, which grows out of marked and obvious emotional distortions, or which grows on the base of sensory impairment in the patient.

THEORY

Whether the ideational disturbance is primary or the

emotional disturbance is primary has never actually been settled. At one time many psychiatric schools interpreted delusions as being primarily based on ideation; that the ideation developed first and the emotional changes second. Then views were reversed and it was thought the emotional changes developed first, and the ideational second. There was never full agreement on this issue because one can quote patients in whom apparently the ideation developed first, and others in whom the emotional change came first.

A somewhat more complicated theory has since evolved, based on the general opinion (and it does not necessarily mean that it is the right one but it is the idea mainly expressed) that emotional change occurs first and the ideation actually follows it. The issue is not that simple because actually there are two layers of processes in delusions. It is very true that an emotional matrix is prepared, and then the idea which crops up can reinforce it as feedback into the original emotional state. But there are different psychiatric theories regarding that, especially in cases of some paranoid conditions. The condition once termed "paranoia," in particular, was first used as an example of so-called pure ideational development of a delusion. However, the underlying emotional factors as to *why* a paranoid individual evolves his system, and *why* his delusional system is necessary for bolstering his ego, and so forth, was completely overlooked. But one can read very interesting discussions on the intellectual elaboration and the type of intellectual impairment present in those persons. No present-day school of psychiatry thinks that these intellectual impairments are etiological. Nevertheless, a great many interesting observations have been made on the argumentations of these patients, which is worthwhile considering.

This leads us to the discussion of some of the ideas expressed concerning the actual basis of delusional formations. The three psychiatric schools which attempted to cope with the problem of delusional formations took different stands. One school maintained that such a thing as delusions does not exist. That makes everything very simple, naturally. This psychiatric school maintained that the differences are *only quantitative,* that no qualitative differences between a conviction and a delusion exist. I would like to stress this point, because these ideas will again crop up when I discuss the relationship of psychosis to psychoneurosis. As you know, two views were expressed concerning that relationship. One assumed that there is a continuum from the normal, through the neurotic, to the psychotic and, here again, that there is no qualitative difference but only a quantitative difference. To use the classical Freudian scheme, there is only a difference in terms of level of regression: the normal individual is on a fully genitalized level, the neurotic individual manifests regressive symptoms but not to the narcissitic or oral levels, and in the psychotic individual there is regression back to the autoerotic or narcissitic level of psychosexual development. And so, many psychiatrists have maintained that there is a true continuum ranging from normal to psychotic. Exactly among those members who maintained that such a continuum exists were those who also maintained that a continuum from ideas to convictions and then delusions has only some quantitative but no qualitative differences.

Other psychiatrists, however, maintained that there is not just a quantitative but also a qualitative difference present between a psychotic and a neurotic individual; they also attempted to draw a sharper line of demarcation between a delusion and a conviction. The issue is not settled and you can continue to read papers that support one or the other point of view. The issue is completely in flux; it depends on the person's preconceptions, training, and I-don't-know-what ideas on psychiatry whether he will join one or the other group.

Therefore, although one school of thought maintains that such a thing as delusions in their qualitative connotation do not exist, that a delusion is simply an over-valued idea, an over-valued conviction, it also maintains—which is logical to some extent—that because such a thing as delusions does not exist, every so-called delusional idea expressed by a psychotic individual can naturally be broken down into its understandable components, and can be understood, explained, and filed away. Others are a little less optimistic that this can be fully done.

The second school of thought, being particularly the school of Wernicke in Germany, maintained that delusions are due to *impaired intelligence*. Actually, they place the patient's lack of judgment and the lack of criticism of certain reality factors in the foreground in their understanding of a delusional process. For this school, the essential point was that they are intellectual disorders. Incidentally, this view was actually preceded by Viosin. When one reads the old psychiatric literature one constantly runs into designations such as "demented." What was formerly assumed to be dementia was not at all what later came to be understood as dementia; it did not refer to the circumscribed range of intellectual deterioration in an organic state, but every person who deviated more or less from the norm was termed "demented." The basis of the idea—which was believed, by the way, for many, many hundreds of years— was that something happened to the person's mind in terms of a purely intellectual impairment. Therefore, the formulation of Viosin, who put it into slightly more scientific language, cannot be considered very new; it was simply the crystallization of an age-old idea that in those people suffering from "false" ideation, the "false" ideation is actually due to an impairment of intellect. They were all lumped together in the category of mental defectives. This also infers to some extent why (since people were treated rather contemptuously because they were imbeciles or because they were idiots) the same contemptuous approach was taken toward people suffering from mental disease. A psychotic individual was actually regarded as an intellectual imbecile; he was assumed to have an impairment of his intellect, and that was why he expressed strange, peculiar, and outlandish ideas.

The idea that delusional persons were intellectually impaired was maintained until practically the end of the nineteenth century, and some reformulations then began to appear. As you will observe, certain of these issues are not yet fully settled. For instance, in schizophrenia, we will again meet the question: Is schizophrenia an emotional disorder, is schizophrenia an organic disorder, or is schizophrenia a disorder of both? There are, naturally, a few factors which would indicate that in schizophrenia there are intellectual impairments of a special kind which cannot be fully explained on the basis of emotional distortions simultaneously present in these individuals. However, we no longer believe that delusional formations are actually primarily intellectual.

According to the third—more recent—school of psychiatry, delusional formations are considered to be usually *based* on very *strong emotional demands* of the individual, most often unconsciously motivated. The delusion fulfills the inner need for that particular individual to think in that particular way. Unfortunately, here again, as in the hallucination phenomenon, this does not explain *how* the person becomes delusional. It probably explains some of the content of the delusions, but does not explain the basic etiology of the delusions. Again I stress this particular point, because this is quite often confused in the literature, the explanation of the content of a delusion very often being taken as the explanation of its basic etiology.

The third school of psychiatry therefore stresses the basis of the emotional experience to be very important in delusional formation. Naturally, it includes remnants of the other schools of thought also, but the general consensus grew that along with the delusional experience of the patient the emotional experience is very important. These patients manifest no intellectual impairments and their formal intelligence is actually intact, particularly the patients whose delusions interest us most, those who manifest so-called primary delusional formations. Regarding these delusional experiences, the idea was introduced, based on observations of a great many patients, that they were in a condition which could probably be translated (there is no English word for it) as a so-called readiness to be delusional; the German term is *"wahnbereitschaft,"* which means "readiness-to-evolve-delusion." In other words, a delusion can develop upon the person's peculiar emotional state. These observations were made especially on patients who had "situational" delusions, certain mood alterations preceding the evolution of their delusion. For example, a depressed patient goes about in a suspicious frame of mind and then because of something that happens in his environment, suddenly a paranoid delusion will begin to crystallize. But when the person is *not* in a particularly strong mood, when he is not particularly suspicious and tense or paranoid in attitude, then the delusion does not occur. There are individuals in whom this matrix on which the delusion occurs is seemingly always present; in other individuals, however, it is present only at times. In some patients it is rather interesting to observe the development; at first they have somewhat peculiar feelings toward the environment and begin to express such ideas as "Well, I have the feeling that people around me don't like me"; then there is a somewhat stronger idea, "They try to avoid me . . . they do not want to establish any contact with me"; the next idea is "They will try to do something to me"; then finally, they express the fully-developed idea, "They plan to do this terrible thing to me."

The evolution of a delusion cannot be followed in many patients very clearly, but in some it can. It is interesting that in certain patients having fluctuating disorders, such as some schizophrenic or some epileptic patients, this peculiar mood "readiness" to evolve a delusion, this "readiness" frame of mind, grows first and is demonstrable, and then it very suddenly crystallizes into a delusional idea. Furthermore, it is interesting to note that some of those ideas are changeable.

In other words, the basic mood level could produce and attach itself to different ideations which are apparently secondary to the mood alteration in the patient.

DYNAMIC OBSERVATIONS

As I have mentioned, there are different psychiatric schools of thought in relationship to delusions. One group does not acknowledge that we are actually dealing with a very special psychic abnormality, and tries with every means to establish a bridge between emotionally emphasized normal thinking and delusional thinking. There are others who believe a delusion is a special form of thinking disorder in the sense that it is purely an intellectual disorder having no connotations other than that the person's associative apparatus is altered or changed in a specific way—although it was never stated clearly in what respect altered or changed—which leads to delusional thinking.

The third approach emphasizes the emotional basis of delusional formation, and I tend to agree with this prevalent concept. This school of thought points out that if the person developed a delusion, usually an emotional alteration is present which preceded it. The emotional alteration preceding the delusional formation was expressed in terms of a so-called *readiness* to form delusions based on that emotional state. For example, a hypomanic individual is, naturally, ready to form delusions based on his hypomanic state; the depressive individual based on his depressive state; the paranoid individual based on his suspicious, hostile, and projective state of mind. This implies the presence of some form of a primary emotional organization which makes the person ready to form delusions. It also assumes that many of these individuals develop delusions partly on the basis of their emotional state of mind and frequently certain added experiences, some of which come from the environment, suddenly or slowly reinforcing that basic emotional pattern.

I might add, first of all, that although this theory has

been prevalent, it does not explain very well why it is delusions actually form, even though it does give a clue as to the content of the delusions. Secondly, there are delusional formations which occur that are actually not primarily due to the emotional state of the individual but in some cases due to impairment of the integrity of his mental functioning. It can be observed, for instance, that in many an organic patient probably an interaction is present between his emotional state and a loosening of his mental integration; the delusional formations and misinterpretations are based on the person's disorientation or memory impairments *in addition to* his emotional alterations. Therefore, mechanisms other than the emotional must surely be considered. In the purely delusional disorders such as the paranoid form of schizophrenia, which is probably the clearest form of a delusional psychosis, it is likely, however, that a certain emotional organization of the individual, a certain emotional readiness to react to environmental situations by means of delusional formations, is probably the only understandable mechanism recognized so far. Just how this is actually accomplished is unknown. Many theoretical investigations are under way, partly on a phenomenological, and partly on an experimental, basis to discover what factors can produce delusions in individuals, how delusions can be obliterated, and so forth.

Those who assume that the emotional organization of the individual gives us a clue to the formation of a delusional thought will usually point out that, with the exception of some schizophrenic individuals, the delusional formation is usually congruent with the underlying emotional state. In other words, a depressive patient will have delusions which are basically pessimistic and basically have something to do with a negative elaboration of things; the manic patient will do the opposite, and obviously he will not have delusional formations that would be contradictory or inappropriate to his basic emotional tone. Interestingly enough, contradictory, disharmonious, or inappropriate delusional formations, however, do occur in schizophrenic persons with the exception of the paranoid form. An inappropriate or disharmonious delusional formation in the paranoid form of schizophrenia, or in related paranoid states, does not occur. In those individuals the emotion which feeds the paranoid elaborations is usually in harmony with the delusions he produces.

In many other forms of schizophrenia, preeminently in the hebephrenic and catatonic forms, this congruence is not seen. Especially in the hebephrenic form, markedly incongruent delusional formations may be observed which are often rather hard to explain in terms of the underlying affect of the individual. Moreover, investigations demonstrate that in these individuals in whom the affect appears to be inappropriate, the basic emotional tone seems not only unrelated but even contradictory to the delusional formation that he admits. For example, when the hebephrenic person relates with great glee a delusional formation in which he is involved in a negative sense, he may laughingly tell you that last night somebody tried to torture him, tried to take out his brain, or tried to cut off his genitals. In these individuals it can even very often be demonstrated that many of their delusions have very ambivalent connotations, and the patient actually expresses only the incongruent part of the affect in relationship to his delusions, whereas the true affect with which it is connected is repressed.

It was quite logical, for those assuming that the emotional organization of the individual's personality is a clue to the delusional formation, to hold that the *content* of his delusion has meaning to the patient. That the content of the delusions became scrutinized more carefully is comparatively recent, added mainly since dynamic interpretations entered into psychiatry. Formerly, delusional contents were merely described and it was simply noted that the patient had delusions, in which case a diagnosis that the patient was psychotic, and very often even in what way psychotic, could be established. But the meaning of his delusions was not considered specific; they indicated only a "mental breakdown." Then, under the influence of the dynamics, the content of delusions as well as hallucinations was investigated and discovered to have a meaning for the patient in most cases. Again, I would like to emphasize that even though the content often has meaning for the patient, the reason why the patient forms delusions to express his emotional difficulties is not illuminated. In other words, the meaning of a patient's delusional content can often be understood, but how and why they are formed is still obscure.

The content of the delusions, from a dynamic point of view, usually can be organized around two main contentional themes, the so-called catathymic delusions. One being the direct wish; the other being the negative of the wish, namely, fear. In other words, delusions, as such, express either the wishful thinking of the patient or the opposite, those of fear. In going further and scrutinizing these two main groups, we then find the following subgroups. Wishful delusions occur usually in two particular forms: (1) delusions of *self-aggrandizement,* and (2) delusions of *persecution.* Aggrandizement of the ego is especially prominent in some paranoid patients with well-developed delusions, as are also grandiose ideations often observed in manic patients who have a paranoid "fringe." Such a patient consistently expresses delusional ideas as to how powerful he is, how capable, how rich, how beautiful he is. The paranoid patient employs many similar compensatory ego mechanisms for underlying feelings of inferiority and quite a number of paranoid delusions also have some degree of grandiose content. For instance, they feel they are victims persecuted by the environment *because* they have something to contribute, or *because* they are quite capable, or *because* they are very gifted, and so forth—all such delusional formations expressing positive compensatory attitudes concerning the patient's relationship to the environment. It is interesting that (except for cases commonly observed in state hospitals) delusions of self-aggrandizement or delusions of grandeur are comparatively rare, while delusions organized around persecutory ideation are very prevalent.

The *relationship* of a person *to his environment* and the evaluation of that relationship preoccupies human beings considerably. Actually, if one studies "sensitive" individuals (and there are many), a great many so-called *precursors* of a delusional formation will be discovered—the so-called *overvalued ideas,* or overemphasized ideas, where the person continually expresses difficulties in evaluating his relationship with the environment. This preoccupation may be markedly intense in a great many people who are by no means psychotic, and in many schizophrenic patients before they become overtly psychotic. That peculiar feeling of "inferiority" (which was a term stressed by Adler, although I do not like to use it because it has so many different connotations in different minds) would simply mean that the person feels his relationship with the environment is such that he does not perform up to expected standards. These ideas are prevalent in the minds of a great many people, and prevalent in many neuroses as well as psychoses (especially in schizophrenia), often being the core around which the contents of persecutory delusions are organized.

The contents of persecutory delusions and delusions of grandeur or self-aggrandizement are usually concerned with the two main spheres of human life: (1) preoccupation with the extent to which the person establishes his personality in his society—his ideas being based on his performance and self-expression or on his achievements—and (2) preoccupation of the individual with his adequacy in sexual achievement. Actually, if you scrutinize the delusions in these individuals, they usually can be traced back to such ideas as "They are talking about me because I am no good"; "They are talking about me because I am no good sexually"; "They are observing me because I am unable to perform the simplest duties"; or "They observe me because they consider me sexually abnormal." The theme has a great many variations. It may be expressed either in a very primitive way or in a very elaborate way; it can be expressed either in a simpleminded way or in a very sophisticated way. However, the basis of the content is nevertheless the same; the individual usually feels nonperforming or inadequately performing in comparison to others.

The question was ventilated—and from an academic point of view it is a very interesting question which nobody has been able to answer—would these patients express delusions of this kind if they were not concerned with their social relationship? In other words, would the disorder from which they suffer produce delusional formations per se, as would a toxic disorder for example, or are these delusional formations actually present only because of very intense emotional preoccupation of the person with his relationship to the environment? It is obvious that since nobody lives in a vacuum this question cannot be settled. However, arguments are stacked up on both sides, particularly in connection with schizophrenia, some maintaining that the schizophrenic individual would have delusions anyhow because it often gives the appearance of being a toxic process. Others maintain that if the person did not have a very strong awareness of his social inferiority in relationship to others, most likely those aggressive or productive delusional formations would not develop. As I have stated, these interesting and, from a theoretical point of view, important speculations have not as yet indicated an answer. Are delusional formations (especially in the psychoses in which the person's sensorium remains clear, as in the paranoid form of schizophrenia) specific disorders on the level of what might be termed an "emotional toxemia" (in other words, produced by an intrinsic process occurring in that person) or are they really simply social interrelation phenomena of great intensity and produced only because of the particular relationship of that particular person with his environment?

Even though the factor of the environment plays a very great role, most likely *multiple intrinsic mechanisms* are involved. Supporting evidence is seen in the fact that delusional elaborations are very similar in cultures which are very markedly different from each other. That is really very interesting! In schizophrenia especially, although a symptom pattern varies in different cultures, it varies only superficially, and basically the process is very similar in every culture, which is a strong argument in favor of the intrinsic determining factors. The evidence of similarities of delusions in different cultures would very definitely indicate that in delusional individuals some intrinsic mechanism is lighted up by a particular environmental relationship, and if that would not release it, then probably some other relationship factors would, or at least would keep it activated.

Incidentally, the fact that delusions are refractory to psychotherapy adds no support to the argument that an intrinsic mechanism is involved, because why somebody does not respond to something is then open to question. In other words, we know the characteristics of habits and how difficult it is to change certain acquired habits; the fact that one is unable to change a thinking habit does not necessarily mean that it is not acquired.

To return to the subject of delusional content being based on wish and fear, the wish and the fear are usually organized around the person's concern for *self-preservation*. It is not concern for actual life preservation, especially not in our civilization, but self-preservation in a very interpretive and broad sense. In our civilization, so-called self-preservation has many refined connotations. In a so-called primitive culture, self-preservation most likely means simply self-preservation of the individual. As the particular culture or civilization became more sophisticated and in many ways more abstract, a great many symbols changed in terms of what is connoted by self-preservation. In our culture, being unable to perform, or losing face or being condemned on moral or other issues, definitely has in many minds—especially in sensitive minds—the connotation of threat to self-preservation. In other words, when lacking some particular attribute, people feel they are not accepted or acknowledged by the society in which they live, and they may attempt suicide or annihilate themselves, indicating that this attribute has very great value to them, a value as important as that directly attached to survival. Therefore, survival of the individual in a complex culture is actually social survival on a very high and a very abstract level. Delusional formations clearly express the patients' feelings of failure. Many of these patients, first of all, express delusions based on their feeling unsuccessful in intellectual and social achievements. Of second importance is the extent to which they feel unsuccessful sexually, and the sexual delusional formations are, naturally, very common. Here again, we are probably dealing with the interesting mixture of intrinsic and extrinsic phenomena.

When I discuss alcoholic hallucinosis and the paranoid form of schizophrenia, I will examine in detail the assumed relationship of paranoid delusional formations to homosexuality. Incidentally, it has been interesting to observe that homosexual delusional ideas occur very frequently in the male; in the female they occur only in occasional cases. A paranoid or paraphrenic female usually has paranoid ideas in reference to men; she fears heterosexual attack. On the other hand, men usually fear homosexual attack. This was clinically observed for a long time without any dynamic interpretations. Then differing interpretations were formulated. One of the main arguments put forward was that, due to the social pressure against male homosexuality, men naturally have much more preoccupation with this type of delusional formation than do women. It was maintained that especially in cultures in which homosexuality is under very strong social condemnation, such as in Anglo-Saxon countries, the prevalence of this particular form of delusional expression in the paranoid or in the alcoholic hallucinosis forms of schizophrenia is extremely common. When cases were investigated and examined in various cultures it was interesting to observe that in many other cultures the individual suffering with the same disorder also expressed a great many paranoid delusions but the homosexual tinge was not present. This indicates that in each of those individuals some intrinsic mechanism operates to express many conflicts in the form of a delusion but that the actual content of the delusional formation adapts itself to certain inferiority feelings in relationship to the particular culture in which he lives. In many Latin countries, homosexuality is under much less pressure; it is tolerated much more, it is not under the penal code, and, therefore, the preoccupation of the people with it is far less than in some of the Anglo-Saxon countries and cultures. Paranoid schizophrenic patients or any patients suffering from alcoholic hallucinosis also express plenty of paranoid delusions but, interestingly enough, the paranoid content is somewhat dissimilar in different cultures. These observations have led to the reexamination of the tenet of Freud, and especially those of Ferenczi, who actually attempted to delineate a paranoid delusion as always an expression of repressed homosexuality, which is plain nonsense. Incidentally, I would like to call some attention to the fact that quite a number of homosexual males view homosexuality not simply on the basis of their being homosexual but because it has connotations of weakness, of something which is debasing, of something which is condemned, and of something which is a tabu in their culture. With the female, promiscuity with men holds the same connotations.

Concerning delusional content, therefore, we are dealing with a fusion of some intrinsic mechanisms and certain extrinsic mechanisms, the basis of this observation being that the individual usually expresses in his delusions some form of a mental or emotional handicap and an incapacity to cope with the situation in relationship to the environment, and this failure to cope is then expressed in the language of the culture in which he lives.

In the closely knit, well-elaborated, and well-organized delusional system of a paranoid patient, intrinsic and extrinsic components are fairly clearly discernible. If one carefully investigates such a patient over a long period of time, one is usually able to discover his feelings of personality inferiorities around which his delusional system is crystallized. It is much more difficult to understand some of the delusional experiences and expressions wherein the delusional system is fantastic, bizarre, and loosely organized, such as, for instance, those of schizophrenic patients. Other rather interesting mechanisms enter into these delusions, and I shall mention them in passing.

As I have already said, in certain organic cases delusional formations occur because of some basic disorganization of the psyche, and whatever it is that integrates psychic functioning in that individual is either loosened or is absent. What that mechanism actually is, we do not know. Such a mechanism exists, however; it is one that actually coordinates the different mental functions operating within the individual into a compact and well-functioning whole. Impairment of memory, impairment of orientation, the feeling that "I cannot associate well," feelings of impediment in thinking, such as retardation or blocking, are all mental phenomena which are not only objectively apparent, but which also have subjective connotations for the patient.

To the patient, the subjective connotations of these mental phenomena are sensations he feels but which he nevertheless cannot explain. Quite often delusional formations, especially in depressed or schizophrenic patients, begin to evolve based on the experience of some feeling which the person is somehow unable to classify or unable to understand, and not rarely delusional formations are then also used to explain that particular sensation. For instance, a schizophrenic patient's first complaint will be that he feels very tired, that he cannot sleep well, that he feels listless, and he feels dopey. In a number of cases of early schizophrenia, these are their chief complaints. A few days later the same patient will state, "I don't know why it is, but I feel dopey . . . I'm doped . . . Somebody is doping me . . .

Somebody is hypnotizing me . . . Somebody is taking my thoughts away . . . Somebody is preventing me from moving my arms and legs properly." Especially the feelings of passivity, the feelings of being influenced, the feelings of inability to concentrate and inability to function with definite lucidity or clarity are often used by these patients to explain through delusional formations that "Somebody is doing that to me . . . Somebody put poison in my coffee and this is why I feel so doped, this is why I cannot function."

It is also interesting that the moment you are able to lift some of those patients out of these basic sensations their delusional interpretations promptly disappear. Please do not misunderstand me; I do not imply that the somatic sensations which the patients acquired, and the feelings of passivity or the feelings of depersonalization and unreality, are the sole basis for their delusional formations. Many other mechanisms, including some of those we have so far discussed, must surely enter concomitantly. But, that the patient *utilizes* those experiences which he is unable to explain, utilizes those very strange experiences—and, interestingly enough, the expression "strange experience" returns again and again into the patient's interpretation—is really very important. Very often schizophrenic individuals also utilize the peculiar distortions of bodily sensations for delusional formations. In other words, they are ready to pick up all types of sensations from within as well as sensations coming from the environment, and begin then to weave explanatory delusions around the sensations, usually based on the other dynamic factors such as nonperformance.

Now, are the so-called depersonalization mechanisms as well as the sensory somatic mechanisms *primary* to the delusion which then follows, *or* are they already a *part* of the delusion, also being the psychogenic expression of the person's inability to perform? That has not been clarified. The fact remains, however, that a great many delusions, especially those of depressed and schizophrenic patients, develop on the basis of nonperformance plus explanatory ideations for those sensations they experience within themselves which very often are mixed with a great many bodily sensations. Some observers believe that the bodily sensations in these individuals are secondary and already a form of handling the conflicts; that they are actually what one might term peculiar tension manifestations of repression or regression mechanisms. Others, however, believe that the bodily sensory experiences are organic and primary, and that the patient's elaborations on them are then secondary; that they are psychogenic elaborations on actual experiences and sensations which are so strange as to be inexplicable to the patient. I would say that both ideas are fully tenable but we simply do not know which one is actually valid.

From a purely experimental point of view, it is very interesting that if we are able to somewhat alter the basic mood level of the patient and if we are able to alter his somatic and psychic sensations (especially depersonalization and feeling of unreality), then the actual delusional formation he had erected upon those experiences disappears. For example, you may deal with a depressed patient who is markedly preoccupied with his feeling of depression, or with his feeling of lassitude and inability to move quickly (which we term retardation), who constantly complains to you that the whole world is very strange around him and that everything is somehow altered. He might then begin to express such ideas as, "It is due to the fact that my bowels are rotting away" or "I have no heart any more and that is the reason why all these things are actually happening." If you then inject into this patient, for instance, an amphetamine or Pervitin and stimulate him into action, you remove his feeling of lassitude and ennui and ten minutes later, when the patient is confronted with his previous ideas, he will state "It isn't so . . . I feel perfectly well . . . That was all a bunch of foolishness . . . There is nothing wrong." In other words, alteration of the basic level of mood can oftentimes alter the delusions in certain patients.

I may add that this type of experiment does not alter

some of the delusional formations of paranoid schizophrenic patients; for them delusions move on a level different from that pertaining to their bodily sensations and the so-called secondary elaborations or secondary explanations. Their delusional formations are really primary. Therefore, when dealing with a delusional patient we should always ask ourselves, are we dealing with a primary or with a secondary delusional formation? Are we dealing with a person who elaborates on matters in a delusional way with apparently no other abnormal mental mechanisms discernible, or are the delusions really secondary elaborations on some other underlying process? There is a very marked difference in the prognosis of those patients who have primary delusional formations rather than only secondary delusional formations. This is particularly obvious regarding manic-depressive patients, in whom all the delusional ideations are very definitely secondary to the underlying depressive process and usually vanish when depression lifts.

In concluding this topic I would like to reemphasize: Delusional formation is no longer considered to be an impairment of intelligence. How a person *uses* his intelligence, however, and how his intelligence is used, I would say, selectively at the service of his emotional distortions, is important. Furthermore, the only disorder into which the issue of intelligence enters, as a formal psychological issue, is schizophrenia! Many of those conceptual alterations and distortions of the schizophrenic patient that are much more than simple emotional distortions of the individual could probably also enter into the so-called mechanisms of delusional formation. Many of the bizarre and fantastic delusional formations occurring in a schizophrenic individual are not explained alone on the basis of his emotional difficulties; they are also due to his difficulty with concept formation and the relationship of his concept formation to his perception of reality on the ego level. Fantastic delusional elaborations always indicate an impairment of the person's relationship to reality. Those types of delusions occur only in patients in whom the reality perception, or the reality awareness, of the person is distorted or altered. Usually it is altered either in organic cases (at times even suspended, particularly in acute cases with delirium), or in schizophrenic patients, where it is peculiarly distorted and impaired since distortions of concept formation are also present.

Part III
Organic Reaction States

5

ORGANIC REACTION STATES:
HISTORY AND CLASSIFICATION

The organic disorders in psychiatry are presently subdivided into the acute and the chronic forms. These comprise a very large clinical group. Actually, probably 40 or 50 percent of all psychoses are known to be of organic origin. We do not know the exact percentage, however, one of the reasons being that a considerable number of individuals who develop transitory emotional or mental states do not enter mental hospitals. Furthermore, a great many individuals develop mental alterations that may reach the height of a psychosis but are not documented because they occur in the framework of some somatic disease.

HISTORICAL BACKGROUND AND DEFINITION

Organic conditions which lead to psychiatric disorders have been studied for a long time, and were investigated very intensively in the nineteenth century, it then being believed that a great deal was known about them. More recently it came to be realized that much of our knowledge about these disorders needed revision. Originally, patients who suffered from organic brain disease having mental changes were studied mainly along the lines of medical and neuropathological investigations, which led to the idea that each organic entity evolved its own separate etiology, anatomical findings, and thereby its own prognosis and therapy. Kraepelin, who delineated the organic group of psychoses in detail in the same manner as he did the functional psychoses, defined the organic group as those mental disorders in which specific etiological factors are present that lead to an organic impairment of the brain, which, in turn, leads to mental changes. Since Kraepelin, the basic definition of organic psychoses has remained unchanged; it is understood that patients in this group of psychoses are those suffering from some organic brain disease which in turn produces mental symptoms.

Organic mental disorders have been understood to be those in which definite structural pathology can actually be demonstrated in the nervous system itself. This concept was later broadened to include not only pathology in the nervous system but in other parts of the body as well. To give an example: in patients suffering from a psychosis due to hyperthyroidism, histological changes in the brain are very rarely demonstrated but pathological deviations can be found in the thyroid and other organs. The same also applies to cases of hyperinsulinism; there again, in many instances, no anatomical changes were demonstrated in the brain but anatomical changes were demonstrated in other parts of the body. Therefore, the definition can include those conditions in which actual pathology is not necessarily in the brain, but is in some other part of the body causing chemical alterations which affect the brain. However, the majority of the organic mental conditions which I shall discuss are those having actual pathological tissue changes in the brain.

The second issue that broadened the definition was the awareness that, although a number of disorders were discovered in which apparently no anatomical changes were demonstrated, they nevertheless had to be termed organic because a significant amount of physico-chemical deviations were demonstrated which were recognized to be based on alteration of structure. Here, again, I would like to mention that in certain cases of hyperinsulinism, in cases of reactions to ACTH and cortisone, and in certain cases of mental disorders due to anoxemia, a period of time must elapse before anatomical changes can be demonstrated. *Before* anatomical changes are demonstrated, however, patients can manifest marked mental deviations. These groups of disorders, however, are not always included in the organic group because unequivocal tissue changes are not demonstrable. To clarify the issue, we must continue to assume the term organic to mean that tissue changes are present in the nervous system, or that physico-chemical changes are present which can be linked to the etiology of the disorder despite the absence of any clear-cut anatomical changes.

It is obvious that designating a disease organic or non-organic depends on our present knowledge of tissue changes and depends entirely on the subtlety of our investigative methods. As occurred in the past, a great many so-called "functional" or "nonorganic" conditions could suddenly turn out to be organic if methods were devised to demonstrate the presence of either tissue changes or physico-chemical changes. Therefore, it is very important, in any psychiatric approach, never to consider it completely out of the realm of possibility for cases having no demonstrable organic pathology to have organic changes demonstrated at some future time. It is rather illogical to assume that our somewhat crude staining techniques and our other rather crude physical and chemical methods of investigating the nervous system have so sufficiently added to our knowledge that we can treat the whole issue as though every organic state has been discovered. Just because the presence of anatomical changes has been demonstrated in some cases and not in others, those cases in which anatomical changes are not demonstrated cannot logically be labeled nonorganic and the others organic.

The organic states should not be diagnosed purely from the standpoint of whether or not anatomical changes are present, but must also be diagnosed on the basis of certain clinical criteria quite often found linked to the organic process present which are usually (but not always) absent in those disorders lacking tissue pathology. I shall later describe, when discussing the differential diagnosis, many disorders having clinical criteria so overlapping that it is very difficult to determine whether the patient is really suffering from an organic disorder or a so-called psychogenic, or "functional," disorder. It is possible to make a diagnostic delineation on a clinical basis in clear-cut cases, but it is not so easy when mixed symptomatology is present.

Originally, as I have indicated, the basic aim in psychiatry was to describe in detail the pathology of each organic disorder and the etiology of each disorder. Kraepelin, who made the first clinical descriptions, described them so very minutely that it was possible to evolve for each organic condition not only a specific anatomy and a specific etiology but also a specific psychological picture. To put the matter rather simply, his idea was that one could describe a psychosis based on typhoid fever, a psychosis based on malaria, or a mental disorder due to syphilis, a mental disorder due to tuberculosis, and so forth, whereby the actual clinical symptoms described in the patient are significant for, or indicative of, the underlying etiology of the disease. His idea that it is possible to link a mental pathology in detail to a somatic pathology in detail, and that the mental examination of the patient will give a clue to the etiology of the disease producing the mental change, was prevalent for a very long time. In many of the old records of patients, there are descriptions in minute detail of the clinical symptomatology of innumerable organic disorders, each designated by its etiological name: typhus delirium, pneumonia delirium, or specified delirium in one of innumerable other conditions. Not only the acute, but also the chronic organic mental conditions were dealt with in exactly the same manner: a specific clinical picture for general paresis, a specific clinical picture for arteriosclerosis, one for senility, one for carbon monoxide poisoning, one for alcoholic disorders, and so forth.

When reinvestigating those detailed clinical reports on a patient's mental condition, it was very quickly recognized that an actual etiological diagnosis in those cases was very rarely established on the basis of mental symptomatology alone. However, by examining each patient and getting a great deal of neurological, medical, and laboratory data in addition to his clinical mental symptomatology, it was possible to detect the etiology in many of the cases. If, however, the examining psychiatrist was restricted to examining a patient's mental performance alone, discarding all somatic evidence and discarding all the laboratory evidence, it became very quickly apparent that *the form of the mental reaction in a human being responds to a large variety of organic impairments in a very similar manner, regardless of the etiology.* Although a few of the organic psychoses manifest features which might be termed pathognomonic for the disorder—and there are very few such disorders—it became obvious that all the different reactions occurring under the impact of any organic disease follow a very particular and, I must say, a very stereotyped pattern. Therefore, around the first part of this century, the idea that each of these organic disorders has specific psychiatric symptomatology was discarded. More and more the idea evolved that here we are dealing with a specific form of reaction of the human nervous system having very similar manifestations in each of the various etiological disorders. From a psychiatric point of view, the symptomatology is specific with regard to organic disorders as a whole but is not specific for any particular one. In other words, the human mind manifests a particular reaction pattern which is similar in any of the organic impairments regardless of the etiology of the impairment.

We recognize very similar situations in many of the basic neuropathological disorders in the brain. And, in neuropsychiatric research we are attempting to differentiate one organic process from another anatomically and chemically, but very often we are unable to do so; an inflammation caused by etiology "a" could resemble that caused by etiology "b," and very often only the localization of brain involvement taken into consideration permits an etiological clue. Naturally, there are a few forms of involvement from which an etiological conclusion can probably be drawn. There are also some forms in which a careful psychiatric examination alone enables an experienced psychiatrist to gain a clue that the reaction in the patient is, for instance, an alcoholic intoxication or some other intoxication. But basically, what we have said stands: The reactions are so similar that great mistakes can be made if we limit ourselves purely to the psychiatric examination of the patient.

From a psychiatric point of view, therefore, instead of describing a delirium in pneumonia, in malaria, in typhus, in encephalitis, or in any of the other infectious toxic disorders, we now describe it as an acute organic reaction if the organic agent affects the nervous system in an acute way, and a chronic organic reaction if the organic disorder develops slowly and insidiously and affects the nervous system in a chronic way. This very important distinction brought about a fundamental change in the psychiatric classification of these disorders. A number of psychiatrists gave up the idea of linking psychiatric pictures to some etiology or to some specific organic processes; the idea was introduced that we are dealing here with so-called *reactions*. Apparently, just as the physical organism responds somatically with an inflammation to all sorts of etiological agents, so does the human mind respond to organic impairment with either an acute reaction or a chronic reaction; it does not respond in any special way to each of the different etiological agents, with a few limited exceptions which I shall mention. And so, a new concept was formulated and has become generally shared: the concept of the *organic reaction type* of mental disorder, as it was termed by Adolf Meyer in 1910 *(3)*.[1]

CLASSIFICATION

Regardless of etiology, then, the so-called organic reactions are subdivided into two groups: *acute organic reactions* and *chronic organic reactions*. Together they form a very large clinical entity. When I discuss a few of these organic conditions, the similarity of many of the basic mechanisms will be convincingly indicated. Before discussing these disorders by etiological groupings as was formerly customary—for instance, all the disorders caused by syphilis, or the mental disorders caused by some other entity—I should like to discuss the basic organic reactions. We can then observe that actually all those conditions manifest varying degrees of the same form of response, at times with some individual twists added.

In psychiatry, the acute organic state has for a very long time also been known as the delirious form of reaction; the term delirium, in turn, means what Meyer termed "acute hallucinatory reaction." Incidentally, adequate descriptions of delirious states are to be found in ancient Greek literature. The chronic organic reaction is also termed the Korsakoff syndrome. The Korsakoff syndrome should not be confused with Korsakoff psychosis, which is of alcoholic origin. However, Korsakoff's observations and descriptions of the alcoholic psychosis were later applied as the basic symptomatology for the whole syndrome covering all chronic organic mental reactions.

---

[1] For an explanation of our reference system, see the Editors' Note, p. 15.—*Eds.*

Whether the form of organic reaction is acute or chronic, here again, does not necessarily give a hint to the etiology. In some cases, it does. For example, we know that certain disorders, such as atherosclerosis or senility, are pre-eminently in the chronic reaction group. Syphilis, however, can produce acute reactions or can produce chronic reactions. Tuberculosis can produce acute or chronic reactions. Many of the acute infectious diseases, in contrast to atherosclerosis or senility, are more apt to produce acute reactions than chronic reactions, although many individuals do have an acute reaction to certain infectious processes, such as encephalitis, which later develops into a chronic reaction. Also, drugs and other intoxicants, such as alcohol, can produce both acute and chronic reactions.

6

ACUTE ORGANIC REACTIONS

The so-called acute organic reactions (also termed confusional states, or delirious states) are important in that they are actually the states in which impairment of consciousness most frequently occurs. Delirious states occur especially in acute infectious disorders and other toxic disorders. They also occur after injuries, such as head trauma, or they may occur in certain metabolic or deficiency or allergic disorders.

CLINICAL COURSE

The acute organic reactions, or delirious reactions, are usually subdivided into three phases: (1) the *initial delirium reaction,* also termed preconfusional or predelirious state, or prefebrile psychosis; then (2) the *acute delirium reaction,* during the toxic or infectious state, referred to as the fever delirium, or toxic delirium; then (3) the *postdelirium reaction,* or postfebrile, or posttoxic state. This subdivision is, naturally, arbitrary but has some advantages in that an acute organic reaction gives a somewhat different appearance in each of these three phases, although, of course, the phases often overlap. The main symptomatology evolves when the patient is actually in the state of a delirium, but we very often see quite significant mental manifestations before and after it.

Before the actual delirium, the mental manifestations are usually unspecific. It is interesting that in quite a number of toxic infectious reactions, during the so-called *initial delirium* the patient will make general complaints about feelings of lack of well-being and usually a feeling of malaise, headache, fatigue, irritability, and so forth, but actually a delirious reaction is not yet present. Changes in personality pattern and alterations of mood with states of depression or states of excitement not infrequently occur, but these pre-delirious mental manifestations have no specificity. Therefore, it is not in any way possible to assume the person will or will not develop a delirium, provided you do not find symptoms indicating a narrowing of consciousness which would, naturally, immediately focus attention on the possibility that the person will develop an organic reaction. The symptoms are as unspecific as those in the psychoneuroses or in other psychoses. I would also like to mention that occasionally psychodynamic features appear in the framework of these prefebrile manifestations. Here, again, the psychodynamic content is nonspecific and does not give any clue as to whether the patient is suffering from an organic reaction or a psychogenic reaction, not to mention that an acute organic reaction can and does occur in a number of individuals already suffering from a psychogenic disorder such as, for instance, a psychoneurosis.

In delirious states in general, and in prefebrile or initial delirious states in particular, I must call attention to the fluctuations in the state of consciousness. Even in a normal individual consciousness is not a static issue, quite often there being interference in clarity or field of consciousness and therefore in the awareness of either. Fatigue, for instance, in a normal individual, interferes. In initial delirium, however, fluctuation is quite marked, and in some toxic disorders or infectious disorders mild confusional states can occur. These fluctuations are very important because occasionally an individual is judged psychiatrically sound if he is examined at a time during a lucid interval, and then a few minutes later his consciousness could be quite clouded. Therefore, when examining such a patient one must always take into consideration the fact that fluctuation in consciousness occurs quite frequently and only one examination of the patient does not disclose whether or not there is any interference.

In the state of initial delirium you will find, however, interference with some of the linked symptoms. For instance, a person will not be able to concentrate as well as he normally could. Most likely he is subjectively aware of it; if not, it can be demonstrated objectively. His attention usually wavers markedly, and attention span—the ability to maintain attention for a certain period of time, the persistence in maintaining interest in a particular issue—is impaired. That, again, can be objectively demonstrated. Retention ability is also impaired and this can be very easily tested; if the person is given a few lines to read and asked to memorize them, very likely during this initial state his ability to do so will already be impaired. Orientation in other respects, and memory in a gross sense, are usually well preserved. However, if the patient should become confused, these functions may also show impairment. The diagnostic term "confusion" or "delirium" should be applied only if, in addition to impairment of anamnestic orientative function, such actual impairment is present that the patient is not fully oriented and not able to handle memory material adequately.

When the patient moves from the initial phase into the main phase of the delirium, the phase of actual *acute delirium* or confusion, all the symptoms are, naturally, much more marked. The symptomatology being well developed, diagnosis can usually be made without any great difficulty in the majority of cases. However, considerable difficulty may arise in those few individuals in whom the delirious state is a part of some other psychotic picture, or when the delirium acts to release an underlying psychosis.

In the acute delirious reaction, the basic and outstanding impairment consists of oscillating and varying degrees of alterations in the state of consciousness. There is disorientation for time and place or even for person. Often there are many secondary impairments, both intellectual and emotional. The intellectual impairments may be in the form of dream states or hallucinations and delusions. The main emotional impairment is a marked "emotional incontinence," the patient shifting moods rapidly and in an exaggerated manner under even the slightest provocation.

If the acute organic reaction was pure and not complicated by other entities, during the *postdelirium reaction* all the symptoms present during the height of the main phase of delirium diminish and then disappear. Moreover, they usually fade away in a rather harmonious manner.

SYMPTOMATOLOGY (PRIMARY)

In the acute delirious reaction the first and basic outstanding symptom is an *alteration in the state of consciousness*. Alterations of consciousness are invariably a part of the fully developed acute organic reaction picture. If an alteration of consciousness is not present, that does not mean the patient cannot be having some organic reaction but the possibility that it is complicated by another condition must be very carefully investigated. If a patient, for instance, should develop an acute hallucinatory episode in a clear setting—in other words, without impaired or altered consciousness—one must carefully investigate whether or not it is really a toxic, infectious, or some other such organic state. Because alteration of consciousness does occur in most acute organic reactions, if it is seemingly absent, we must suspect that we are not dealing with a clear-cut case.

At this point I wish to emphasize that *variations in the degree* of alteration of consciousness occur in acute organic reactions, ranging from the patient's having slight haziness or slight impairment of ability to contact the environment to the extreme of his being markedly out of contact with the environment. Some delirious patients may be semicomatose, and other semistuporous. In still other patients a mixed symptomatology of coma and stupor occurs. Coma and stupor are not identical phenomena. Coma indicates an organic impairment of consciousness into gradations of unconsciousness. Stupor connotes the patient's attempts to ward off external stimuli; this condition could be mild, or could be profound as, for instance, in the case of catatonic stupors. Organic stupor can also be profound. In milder cases, particularly those due to some sort of an intoxication, the patient experiences only slight drowsiness or slight haziness; you have the feeling that somehow it is more difficult to contact the patient, that his cerebration is rather slow and he is not fully alert in picking up stimuli coming from the environment but appears to be somewhat preoccupied. As I have pointed out before, occasionally it is difficult to evaluate the state of the individual's consciousness. It is obviously easy to determine if the patient is in a state of coma and it is also easy if the patient is fully delirious, but not in those patients having only a mild alteration of consciousness.

There is an additional fact which is often overlooked. In the acute organic reactions especially, there are very marked *oscillations* in degrees of haziness or drowsiness, and at times even of the more profound impairment of consciousness. If you follow a delirious patient along from hour to hour, you observe the patient at times to be quite lucid, quite in contact with the environment. Perhaps only fifteen minutes later, the patient can be in a fairly deep stupor, or in a fairly deep coma, and out of contact with the environment. The oscillations in degrees of lucidity or degrees of impairment of consciousness are very often not taken sufficiently into consideration in mental examinations or in the care of such patients. Quite a number of suicides and pseudosuicides occur whereby the patient swings into a confused state and, for example, jumps or falls out of a window due to the fact that safety measures had been withdrawn when the patient was examined moments before and found to be completely lucid. Delirious patients very often have repeated fluctuations of consciousness occurring over a long period of time. Interestingly enough, partly due to physiological and partly due to psychological factors, fluctuations are especially common during the night; if a patient has established some sort of contacts with the environment during the day and if these are then withdrawn at night by his being in a quiet and dark room, the mind turns back onto its own inner stimuli. Thus, his already impaired ability to contact the environment becomes even more impaired.

When a patient is in the delirious state with markedly narrowed and yet fluctuating consciousness, his awareness is hazy or clouded and he is not consistently clear about what is going on around him. Therefore, his ability to associate and his ability to obtain new material from the environment are markedly impaired. The patient seems a dumbbell. This associative and retentive impairment is usually linked with incomplete orientation and if the patient becomes very sick it progresses to complete *disorientation*. Disorientation, similar to memory impairment, follows a special stratification in the human being; it is always initially disorientation for *time,* then disorientation for *space,* and, finally, for *person.* The disorientation stratification follows the youngest, or the latest (phylogenetically and ontogenetically) acquired function. Although the organic (circadian) time sense is the earliest phylogenetic function, the latest acquired is the "time clock" function in the central nervous system which is influenced by environmental stimuli. Other mammals as well as man appear to have quite a good space sense, but very few show indication of having much cortical time sense. This "time clock" is not very markedly developed;

people wear watches to determine what time it is, yet nobody needs to carry instruments for orientation in space.

The "time clock" function governed by the central nervous system is, naturally, the most vulnerable and the first to be affected in brain disorders. It is often observed that many patients in an acute organic reaction state are confused about time while their orientation concerning place and person nevertheless appears to be fairly well preserved. In more profound delirium, however, the patient usually becomes very confused not only about time but also about place, and finally about person. The orientation for person, due to the strong interpersonal environmental relationships present in the human being, is interfered with the least; patients will be observed who are disoriented as to place and time but who still retain their orientation for persons. When their orientation for person then becomes impaired, the patients' ability to distinguish persons in their environment becomes impaired first. Misinterpretation or misidentification of the people around them is a common occurrence even while they retain their ability for self-identification. In other words, a certain amount of orientation regarding themselves remains. Only in very profound delirious states is the ego-identification so completely lost that the person does not know who he is, where he is, or what he is doing. Such disorientation regarding his own person very rarely happens; even markedly disturbed and delirious patients are usually able to tell you who they are, because, naturally, the identification of themselves as persons is the most strongly ingrained (due to repetition it is the most conditioned orientation).

Impairment of orientation goes hand in hand with *impairment of memory* because orientation and memory functions are intimately linked. Memory impairment also shows a stratification: learning ability, or retention, is impaired first; recent memory material is impaired next, and remote memory material is the last to be impaired. Recent memory consists of that which the patient experienced and memorized in the recent past. If you ask an acute delirious patient to read a newspaper and to then tell you what it is he has just read, he will tell you he is unable to recall it or he will give you a completely confused and garbled account. The same patient, however, may be sufficiently oriented so that less recent memory is not impaired and he could tell you how he came to the hospital, what he did on the previous day, and so forth. But, the more markedly disoriented and acutely disturbed patient would not be able to tell you about recent experiences, although he could tell you quite adequately where he was born, where he went to school, or what he had read in a book several years ago. In other words, the inability to focus on new material, the inability to assimilate, the inability to retain and then to recall any newly attained material is marked in a patient suffering with an acute organic reaction.

You will observe that in delirious states, in contrast to chronic organic reactions, impairment of recent memory retention is much more predominant; a patient's remote memory usually remains much better preserved and he is able to give a fairly adequate account of his past. This stratification of memory impairment, however, is apparent only in cases when delirium is not very profound. When delirium becomes profound, the remote segment of the memory also becomes impaired and the patient usually jumbles up everything. As it is with consciousness and attention, this orientative function also undergoes very marked fluctuations; many patients who are able to recall persons and are in contact with the environment will be completely unable to do so within a few minutes.

SYMPTOMATOLOGY (SECONDARY)

As I mentioned, the essential, or basic, deviations in acute organic reaction states are: impairment of consciousness, impairment of orientation, and impairment of memory. All symptoms that follow are secondary to these reactions. Many patients suffering from an acute organic reaction do not have secondary symptoms. It is not necessary, for instance, for the patient to have hallucinations, delusions, marked fragmentation of mental functioning, and other intellectual impairments, or the number of emotional changes that can appear, in order to demonstrate that he has some form of acute organic impairment. In a great many patients, however, these very characteristic manifestations do occur in addition to impairments of consciousness.

Intellectual impairments may appear in these individuals as hallucinatory, illusional, and delusional experiences. Actually, the term "delirium" means "hallucinatory confusion." Many psychiatrists have used the designations "confusional state" and "delirious state" interchangeably, although it would be better if the term "confusional state" were applied only to the patient who is confused—in other words, having an anamnestic-orientative impairment present but no hallucinations—and the term "delirious state" applied only to the patient who also manifests illusionary or hallucinatory content in addition to disorientation and memory impairment. Until the other manifestations were more closely analyzed, particularly the disorientative and anamnestic impairments, practically all the early descriptions of the acute organic syndrome were organized around the hallucinatory and delusionary experiences of these patients.

Of these secondary impairments, I must also include the occurrence of the so-called dream states, or dream-like states. Dream states may occur in patients suffering from so-called psychogenic disorders, but occur more especially in patients who are in a state of acute organic reaction. They are very interesting from a psychopathological point of view because they actually demonstrate an impairment of consciousness in which the patient has quite a number of illusions and hallucinations. Dream-like, or nightmare-like, states have, furthermore, another significant feature: The patient is usually fully or partially amnestic for that experience. If you should ask delirious patients what it is they experienced in their delirium, most of them will tell you they do not remember at all and may state, "There is a complete gap; I do not know how I came to the hospital, I do not know what has happened to me here, I do not know who visited me, I do not know who treated me," and so forth. In some patients, however, there is not a full memory gap, but some fragments are recalled rather similarly as dreams are ordinarily recalled by a person.

It is obvious that in the delirious dream-like state, especially when the patient's orientative functions are impaired, the tendency to misinterpret perceptions is very great and the next thing observed is that the patient has many illusions. In addition to the illusions, many patients have hallucinations. Illusions and hallucinations can occur in any perceptual sensory field. The patient may have illusions about body perceptions, and may have hallucinations or even delusions concerning every sense organ. By far the most prevalent are, however, illusions or hallucinations of sight. The relationship which optic illusions or optic hallucinations have to specific organic states and specific acute organic reactions is unclear. Why the intoxicated or delirious individual should show preference to illusions and hallucinations of sight rather than hearing, taste, touch, or any of the other perceptual possibilities, is not clear. Experimental investigations bear these observations out: Experimental drug intoxication of persons usually first produces alteration in the optic apparatus, and only secondly in the auditory apparatus. Therefore, the optic apparatus in the occipital lobe probably has some affinity for toxins.

Another very interesting thing, however, is that the optic phenomenon is not only demonstrated in an hallucinating patient; even a patient barely in a state of narrowed consciousness experiences essentially a pictorial involvement. Furthermore, when a normal person dreams, here again, he is not so likely to hear things in his dreams as to visualize them. Actually, most dream reports are pictorial reports.

Therefore, the optic apparatus seems to be markedly involved in any reduction of consciousness. As is the case normally, with reduction of consciousness the dream-like experiences are pictorial and the same is true in the case of delirium.

Naturally, in all these states the starting point of the illusion or the starting point of the optic hallucination is seemingly perceptual, whereas in the auditory hallucination the primary issue is the concept which then becomes perceptualized. Auditory hallucinations are largely based on ideas, on concepts, which become so concretized by the patient that he finally hears them; here, somewhat different psychological mechanisms are involved than those observed in patients suffering from optic illusions. Many patients, however, experience both visual and auditory hallucinations. How important the issue of conceptualizing mechanisms becomes diagnostically, however, is recognized by the following fact: If you examine a number of patients suffering with acute delirium, you will find in follow-up studies that many of those patients who experienced preeminently auditory hallucinations during what had surely been an acute delirium will later manifest a schizophrenic process, therefore indicating that some "release" mechanism was present in a so-called "schizoid" individual. The prevalence of auditory hallucinations in any acute intoxication or in any other acute organic reaction must arouse your suspicions and be studied further. A mixture of visual and auditory hallucinations occurs quite often, but auditory hallucinations rarely occur alone. I shall take up this issue later in the example of zooscopic and Lilliputian hallucinations occurring in alcohol hallucinosis. Although once described as a special entity, it has been demonstrated that alcohol hallucinosis occurs in schizophrenic individuals.

When speaking about the presence of hallucinations or illusions in a patient, obviously the next question is, do these patients have delusions in an acute organic reaction? The two are so intimately related that we very rarely encounter a person having vivid hallucinations who then does not, naturally, formulate some ideas based on his hallucinations which are usually misconceptions and in the realm of delusions. This holds true for persons who formulate their hallucinations essentially on a conceptual basis. For instance, you would very rarely encounter a patient suffering from schizophrenia who is dominated by hallucinations and yet does not have delusions.

It is interesting that quite a number of patients suffering from acute delirium have hallucinations, and vivid hallucinations, but nevertheless delusional material is not elicited. There are, however, patients in whom delusional material is elicited and these delusions—in contrast to the usually rather elaborate and rather more or less persistent delusions that occur in the conceptual form of this system, as in schizophrenia—are characterized by the fact that they are fleeting, they are completely unelaborated, they are primitive, and they are very closely linked with the patient's hallucinatory experiences. Some of these hallucinatory experiences are then utilized in a rather primitive, archaic manner to express the person's relationship to the environment. Therefore, delusional ideas such as being killed, such as being threatened, such as being raped, and many other ideas relating to the body integrity of the person, very quickly appear in many of these delirious states, particularly if the patient has a strongly apprehensive or anxious form of delirium. However, the delusional formations are never elaborated; they usually come and go with the hallucinatory experience and, except when the hallucinatory experiences are at a high pitch, the patient actually pays very little attention to them. Therefore, delusions in an acute organic state are fleeting, are unsystematized, are usually illogical or logical only if understood in relation to the hallucinatory experiences. They could take any form, naturally; they could be ideas of grandeur or they could be ideas connected with a depressive state, but the most common ideation is always, in every psychiatric disturbance, the projective type.

Up to this point I have described intellectual impairments in the acute organic reaction: They mainly consist of the ego-functioning of the individual toward the environment, his ability to contact it, his ability to evaluate the contact, and his memory and orientation ability. In addition to this impairment of intellectual functioning of the ego, there are quite a number of other impairments present in delirious states that were never very carefully studied. They were neglected because they are not so conspicuous as are the intellectual changes. I am referring to the considerable amount of emotional alteration present in patients suffering from an acute delirious state.

Among the *emotional alterations* present, in any organic patient there is always an impairment of regulation of affect. The person becomes emotionally labile. This lability of affect should not be confused, descriptively or psychodynamically, with emotional instability. (Sociopathic, psychoneurotic, and schizophrenic individuals are emotionally unstable.) In the acute organic reaction we are dealing with emotional lability, meaning that the patient displays a quick change from one emotional state to another under very slight provocation. The provocation, by the way, very often does not come to these patients from the outside environment, but emerges from within due to their hallucinatory experiences. These patients often laugh and cry in turn, depending either upon how they interpret certain attitudes of the environment toward them or, for instance, upon how the hallucinations or delusions influence them from within. The lability of affect has long been described. In some patients it is very conspicuous during the acute delirious state; the patient continually displays an affect that shifts rapidly from one mood to another. This does not occur in a normal individual, nor does it occur in an unstable individual who, although unstable, is usually able to maintain an affect level for a considerable period of time.

Another issue (which is more common in the chronic organic state, although the lability is present in the acute state also) is that the affect shift can be provoked rather easily. If you tell the patient a joke, or tell the patient something sad which would probably provoke some comment or slight emotional response in a normal person, the patient will react with a markedly exaggerated, uncontrolled response. This removal of emotional regulation, this "emotional incontinence," is rather characteristic of many organic states.

It is interesting to study the emotional alterations of these patients and observe that, although the affect is labile with the tendency for rapid shifts, nevertheless the shifts are usually manifested in line with an altered basic mood. In other words, the patient is, in general, apprehensive or anxious or euphoric, but, in the framework of this general mood, he is emotionally very labile. It is also interesting that very few delirious patients feel basically "agreeable." The vast majority of them demonstrate an affect having a disagreeable connotation. The patient is usually anxious, apprehensive, or paranoid. In a comparatively small number of cases, however, we encounter euphoria, the patient feeling rather contented and even happy.

As we shall observe, different drugs and different toxins can provoke different reactions, but, in addition to the particular property of drugs and toxins, which are themselves interesting from a psychopathological point of view, the emotional level on which the patient moves is very often determined by his personality and is determined by conflictual experiences which were never "digested." During a delirious state the patient is, to some extent, decorticated, so to speak, as when under the influence of sodium amytal or any of the other decorticating drugs. Obviously he is "loosened up," and obviously a great many things that had been stirring within his personality will emerge and will color the picture. Naturally, some of these experiences are agreeable and some are not. Therefore, the affect displayed by the patient in such a drugged state, whether euphoria or anxiety, is not all due to the drug, nor is it always the direct organic effect of the drug on the brain. In a number of instances, the personality speaks its voice, too. On the other hand, we should not go so far, as some people have done, and state that the content of a delirium or the content of an hallucination is determined purely by psychogenic factors and that it is incidental whether the patient is intoxicated by alcohol or by opium or by an endotoxin or a bacillus. Because, even though the personality plays a role in shaping and coloring the manifestations of a delirium, it is still undeniable that many drugs and toxins have specific properties which seemingly have some specific way of altering perception, altering mood levels and, naturally, altering the metabolic functioning of the brain in general.

ETIOLOGICAL AGENTS

I now want to discuss the main symptomatology of the acute organic reaction in the setting of the various diseases in which it occurs, and immediately following that, I will discuss the chronic reaction symptoms, because occasionally the acute and the chronic occur based on the same etiology. The acute organic reaction occurs in innumerable diseases. Actually, a disorder of any kind which affects the nervous system, directly and sometimes even indirectly, is capable of producing an acute organic reaction. Therefore, the acute organic reactions are rather well-known and have been for a long time in terms of symptomatology and, to some extent, how the etiological agents act and in what ways the nervous system is affected. However, there is a gap in our knowledge: we do not know the details of the tissue changes or physico-chemical alterations which take place in the nervous system, nor just how they are linked with the mental changes manifested by the patient. In this regard, much of our knowledge is hypothetical.

Acute organic reactions were first recognized and described in relationship to certain *intoxicants:* alcohol, opium, then later the barbiturates, bromides, and more recently the psychotomimetic drugs, and so forth. There are quite a number of drugs—intoxicants, sedatives, and stimulants—all over the world which produce acute reactions in some individuals. Acute reactions can occur in certain persons following a single dose of one or more types of drugs or intoxicants. For example, the "pathological intoxication" occurring in alcoholism is often an acute organic reaction in predisposed individuals; such pathological intoxication, usually accompanied by an outburst of rage or fear mixed with disorientation and hallucinatory experiences, can occur after one dose of alcohol in seemingly nonalcoholic persons. The same holds true for many other drugs; there are persons who develop acute delirious reactions after one dose of opium, or one dose of marijuana *(cannabis indica)*, or one dose of a great many of the stimulants and intoxicants used all over the world. The varieties of drugs used in different civilizations to stimulate mental action, or to retard mental action, or preeminently to alter emotional states, are innumerable. Many are used in our civilization and the comparative study of those intoxicants is of great importance, not only from a pharmacological but from a psychological and psychiatric point of view as well. So one must be aware that even a single dose, in predisposed individuals, is capable of occasionally provoking an acute organic reaction. With the synthetic drugs such as barbiturates or the different bromide preparations, one no longer observes many acute organic reactions although occasionally you will observe persons sensitive to barbiturates who go into an acute delirious state following a comparatively small dose.[1]

In addition to those patients having an acute reaction after a single dose, many patients having acute reactions are chronic users of certain drugs or intoxicating substances.

---

[1] Since these lectures were delivered, Dr. Hoch went on to become one of the pioneers in research on the clinical reactions of a great many toxic drugs: LSD_{25}, Mescaline, Pervitin, and others. Some of his essential observations can be read in Lewis and Strahl, 1968.—*Eds.*

We are accustomed to assume that if a person takes an intoxicant or a certain drug for a long time, the mental symptomatology resulting from such chronic intoxication is always that of a chronic organic reaction. That is incorrect. For example, chronic alcoholics who have taken alcohol for a long time may nevertheless manifest an acute psychiatric syndrome with a picture of delirium tremens; it is an acute reaction in the framework of a chronic base. Delirium tremens occurs only in chronic alcoholics. It cannot result from a single dose of alcohol, and yet the symptomatology, the prognosis, and the whole reaction of the person in a state of delirium tremens is that of an acute reaction and not that of a chronic reaction.

Therefore, many persons who take drugs or intoxicants for a considerable period of time, persons who are chronic "habitués" (or chronic "addicts," as the case may be), may nevertheless have psychiatric *reactions* which are sometimes quite acute and sometimes chronic in nature. Alcohol is an excellent example to demonstrate that the same etiological agent can lead to very different clinical pictures. One chronic alcoholic develops delirium tremens with an acute picture lasting for a week or ten days and then a restitution takes place. Another chronic alcoholic slowly and insidiously develops a chronic organic reaction, the Korsakoff syndrome, and never manifests a delirious phase. Again another chronic alcoholic suddenly develops delirium tremens, does not recover, and progresses to an alcoholic Korsakoff syndrome. Therefore, acute reactions and chronic reactions are not so sharply divided as was formerly assumed; there are many conditional phases between the two. What is very important, and must be again emphasized, is that the same etiological agent can for unknown reasons produce in some individuals an acute reaction and in others a chronic reaction.

A very large group of acute organic reactions includes those occurring in the framework of *infections.* This, again, is a group that has been recognized for a long time. Delirious states in connection with infectious diseases having high fever were already described quite accurately in ancient times. We do not wish to enumerate all the different bacteriological and viral agents that can produce deliria because it would take many pages to simply list all those infections with which a delirium can occur. Actually, any generalized infection affecting the nervous system is capable of producing a delirium. Again, please, do not assume that in every such instance you will be able to demonstrate specific and localized histological changes in the brain. In many cases, although often the histological changes are not at all marked, very subtle changes might be present. There are cases known of persons who died from an infectious disease which produced a delirious reaction state, and histological examination did not disclose any pathology, or at least very little. However, gross edema of the brain is practically always present in autopsy. Of course, some physicochemical alterations were surely present which were not demonstrated.

Acute organic reactions induced by infections almost always occur during a very high fever. However, there are infectious diseases that produce delirium states without fever. Therefore, you should not make the mistake, as some psychiatrists do, of diagnosing the condition as an acute organic reaction or delirious state only if the person has a high temperature. High temperature delirium cases were the first to have been described simply because they were the most conspicuous and therefore the easiest to diagnose. Just to mention it, some time ago false diagnosis was given to quite a number of patients who suffered from Bang's disease, which was then rather prevalent in certain parts of the country. Brucella infections can manifest rather marked variations in the clinical picture; although often accompanied by only a slight rise in temperature, some patients can nevertheless have a delirious reaction. Invariably their delirious reactions were diagnosed as being psychogenic confusion.

In times past, the most prevalent fever delirium was in connection with pneumonia. It is rarely observed today. Knowledge of chemotherapy has developed to the extent that fever delirium does not occur in bacterial pneumonia. Cases of delirium in the virus pneumonias can still be encountered, however. Here again, occasionally a patient suffering from virus pneumonia in whom the temperature is actually not very elevated will nevertheless manifest a delirious state which is, naturally, essentially toxic in origin due to some metabolic process.

In the United States, delirium is commonly observed in connection with infectious diseases. It can occur in patients suffering from typhoid fever or typhus; these cases are no longer common, occurring only sporadically. Typhus delirium, by the way, was used for a long time in psychiatric case demonstrations as the prototype for the classical description of delirium. We naturally are no longer able to demonstrate these cases because they so rarely occur, yet a case of typhus delirium demonstrates all the criteria of an acute organic reaction. Typhus patients usually have a high temperature and display all the symptoms I have described including visual hallucinations and misinterpretations of the environment.

Malaria is another disorder capable of producing acute organic reactions. However, malaria also can cause a chronic organic reaction, and at times mixed reactions occur. The delirium in malaria is occasionally based simply on the high temperature or, to put it another way, on the defensive measures taken by the organism against the plasmodium. In other cases, however, a typical meningo-encephalitis is present; cases with the inflammation of the meninges and the brain are naturally much more serious, and some later manifest a mild chronic organic syndrome.

Another group of acute organic reactions occurs in states of *avitaminosis*. Knowledge about those cases is comparatively recent and, until we knew about the vitamins and understood their role, mental conditions linked to any form of avitaminosis were invariably diagnosed in the category of some other disorder. The acute reactions, for example, were often attributed to some intercurrent infections; and the chronic reactions were all diagnosed as organic polyneuritis on some other basis. Cases of pellagra, formerly very prevalent, especially in the southern part of the United States, at one time comprised 10 percent of all the admissions in mental institutions—a considerable number, not to mention those that were not admitted but who nevertheless manifested mental symptoms—and they were all diagnosed in other categories, such as "toxic reaction" caused by ingesting "diseased corn," until it was recognized that various types of avitaminosis are capable of producing mental reactions.

Although the majority of reactions due to avitaminosis are chronic and in the Korsakoff group, occasionally an acute avitaminotic state develops with a delirious reaction very similar in appearance to any other delirium. Cases of pellagra manifest a chronic reaction but acute reactions can occur within the chronic setting. At one time it was not rare to observe patients admitted to a hospital in an acute delirious state which was later discovered to have been produced by pellagra. However, the great majority of mental patients in whom the origin of the disease is pellagra belong in the chronic reaction group. Avitaminotic acute delirious states are known to occur in patients suffering from diabetes; by the time the polyneuritis develops in connection with the diabetes, some patients manifest an acute delirious reaction. It rarely occurs initially, however, and most of the reactions in diabetic patients continue in the chronic form.

In relation to psychiatric disorders, two forms of avitaminosis have been studied rather intensively: vitamin B-1 deficiency and deficiency of nicotinic acid. Both disorders can produce acute confusional states, even in individuals not actually suffering from clinical pellagra but suffering from a subclinical, or so-called pellagroid, form of pellagra. When I discuss the senile psychoses, I shall point out that in many cases the psychosis is not entirely based on atherosclerosis, or at least not the whole clinical picture can be so explained. In quite a number of senile patients, it is explained on the basis of secondary nutritional changes due to some actual vitamin B deficiency, and when that is corrected a marked clinical improvement frequently takes place. Therefore, many atherosclerotic patients and many senile patients may manifest an acute organic reaction, a sudden delirious reaction which at times is surely based on a sudden circulatory change but often is based—especially in patients who did not eat well, who were neglected, and who were neglecting themselves—on an avitaminotic condition, and their acute delirious reaction clears up after the condition is corrected.

Another group of the acute organic reactions is caused by *metabolic disorders.* Conditions such as diabetes, uremia, and what was formerly described as "toxic exhaustive states" belong in this group. Acute organic reactions in the framework of diabetes and uremia, although still observed, are no longer prevalent due to better control of those disorders. The so-called toxic exhaustive state has become an uncommon diagnostic term because the specific etiology of many such states has been clarified. A few psychiatric hospitals for some time continued to use the diagnostic term "delirium due to toxic exhaustive state" in reference to two conditions: (1) the acute reaction following childbirth, and (2) the reaction to war combat or stress. The latter condition referred to service personnel who, lacking food or sleep and so forth, developed an acute so-called toxic exhaustive state. For example, among navy or merchant seamen rescued after having been in a lifeboat for many days or weeks, with very little nourishment or water and probably exposed to the sun, acute organic reactions occurred which in many cases were delirious. This was termed "toxic exhaustion delirium," and such cases are observed during war or during special stress situations. In ordinary civilian practice we encounter very few patients falling into this group.

The so-called toxic exhaustive state following childbirth was a very common and favorite diagnosis made by both obstetricians and psychiatrists, but as an entity it slowly dissolved due to better knowledge of postpartum psychotic states. Many psychiatrists do not go so far as to abolish this as a diagnostic entity because occasionally they encounter patients in whom some metabolic alterations are present concomitantly with the delirious states. Nevertheless, the majority of psychiatrists are wary about this being termed a toxic exhaustive state following childbirth because follow-up studies of many such patients indicate that actually their psychotic reaction is not so often toxic exhaustive but belongs in another psychotic category. For instance, the majority of patients who develop acute psychosis after childbirth are cases of schizophrenia. Follow-up studies have indicated that many patients who manifested an acute delirious postpartum reaction and recovered, at some later time developed a typical schizophrenic psychotic picture. I will discuss later how this can be differentiated from schizophrenia.

Among the metabolic disorders which can produce an acute organic reaction, one other disease should be mentioned because it is occasionally encountered. Hyperthyroidism is capable of producing acute delirious reaction and many times these cases are not recognized diagnostically. They are not picked up especially if the patient had been drugged down to alleviate the symptoms of nervousness or anxiety which are, naturally, present prior to the actual delirium, or if the psychiatrist was so fascinated by the patient's display of marked anxiety that he declared the symptoms to be simply anxiety reactions. It is true that the majority of cases assumed to be hyperthyroidism, especially cases in which the basic metabolic rate and all other symptoms usually associated with hyperthyroidism are not unequivocally present, are in fact anxiety states and anxiety

reactions. Nevertheless, occasionally you observe the opposite. The case is diagnosed as an anxiety reaction, but you
are actually dealing with a quite marked case of hyperthyroidism in the framework of which the patient displays an
acute delirious reaction.

There is also the group of acute organic reactions due
to *trauma*. When we speak in psychiatry about trauma, we
actually mean, with very few exceptions, a head trauma. It
is interesting that following trauma to other parts of the
body—unless some circulatory complications are present,
such as fat embolism, or complications due to other factors,
or if the patient is not excessively drugged—one really
rarely observes an acute organic delirium reaction. Delirium,
however, is not rare as a sequel following return of con-
scousness from head injuries. A delirium directly following
a head injury may occur at the time of the trauma. The
person suffers head injury and immediately enters into an
acute delirious state. Such cases are rare, however. The
much more common sequence is that of a patient having a
concussion or contusion; he is then unconscious; upon
returning to the state of consciousness, instead of recovering,
as do the majority of patients following concussion, he has
a delirious reaction that may last for hours and in some
cases lasts for weeks. On the average, the delirium lasts
only a few days. Here again, these deliria are quite typical
and indistinguishable in their structure and symptomatology
from those deliria due to other causes.

Finally, there is that group of delirious states occurring
in connection with *organic disease of the brain*. Again, I
will state that most organic diseases of the brain are of a
chronic nature, if we omit the generalized acute infectious
diseases. Nevertheless, chronic organic brain diseases are
capable of producing acute organic reactions also, even
though the majority produce the Korsakoff syndrome.
Syphilis of the brain, which in general paresis produces one
of the most typical chronic organic reactions, is also capable
of producing an acute delirious reaction, referred to as

"galloping paresis," in the secondary or tertiary stage of the disease. In many cases of encephalitis, the disease is ushered in by a delirious reaction, particularly encephalitis of the epidemic, or Economo, type which does not so often occur as in former years. Tumor of the brain, which is by nature a chronic disease, is nevertheless capable of producing acute delirious reactions in individuals, and such cases are often difficult to diagnose. Acute delirium can occur in frontal lobe tumors especially. In cases of temporal lobe tumors, there may be a period during which the mental symptomatology is so marked as to overshadow the neurological and other symptoms; these cases are then usually diagnosed as cases of delirium but the fact that they are caused by a brain tumor is not recognized. Pressure or vascular changes due to the tumor are made responsible, rightly or wrongly, for this delirious symptomatology. From the practical point of view, it is important to know that such cases occur; not all mental changes in connection with brain tumor fall into the chronic organic reaction group.

Incidentally, the matter of etiology also brings up a very important question, namely, *the role of emotional experiences.* Work started in England, and then picked up in this country, regarded the emotional experience as a toxin. Now, that may sound ridiculous. Nevertheless, you have to realize that in a great many so-called psychosomatic cases under the influence of a strong emotional tension histamine is liberated, and through histamine liberation all sorts of organ changes are produced, such as urticaria and other symptoms due to vegetative innervation alterations of skin. It is believed that some similar phenomenon is also possible in many individuals—for instance, schizophrenic individuals under great emotional tension—in that some of the experiences they have, those so-called additional experiences, are mediated through some chemical substance released under the impact of an emotional experience. Of course, these phenomena are not as yet clarified.

At this point I should like to discuss in brief detail *certain forms* of acute organic reactions, emphasizing their *relationship to other psychotic reactions.*

It has generally been assumed that under a major physiological or psychological stress everybody is capable of developing an acute organic mental reaction. However, if you investigate this statement, and contrast it with findings in follow-up studies on a very large number of patients, you will realize that this is not true. It is not true even when the stress is actually so great that it cannot fail to produce some form of reaction—as when a person is actually confronted with the threat of extinction—and even then it is quite interesting to note that a very large number of persons do not develop psychotic reactions.

If you examine many of those patients who suffered acute organic reactions you will find that although theoretically it is probably true that when a person receives a massive dose of toxin or poison or rather massive brain injury some organic reaction is produced, actually those who develop the acute delirious reaction have a very strong predisposition for it. Persons who develop a delirious state under the influence of a toxic agent, fever, anoxia, and so forth, usually have a more labile physiological organization of the nervous system than does the average person. Naturally, that does not obviate the generally observed assertion that if the damage is very massive most likely some form of organic reaction can be produced in everybody, but some people respond more on a physical and others more on an emotional level.

The amount of the toxins or drugs involved must always be taken into consideration. Many people develop an acute organic reaction only under the influence of extremely massive doses, in which case this can probably be assumed to be in the framework of a reaction generally occurring in normal or fairly normal individuals. In most instances, however, it is found that those persons responding with delirium to moderate or even low doses of intoxicants are somehow predisposed to respond to toxins in that manner. Many individuals, for instance, display an acute organic "pathological intoxication" reaction under the influence of alcohol; actually they are even unable to tolerate comparatively small amounts of alcohol without having massive acute reactions appear under the influence of this drug.

It is interesting, furthermore, that many patients who respond with a delirious reaction to a particular causative agent display this reaction again and again whenever exposed to the same or to a similar agent. Those who develop delirium under the influence of, for instance, influenza will often respond with a delirious reaction each time they contract the disease. Persons who as children developed a delirious state due to some infectious agent are known to retain a lifelong tendency to respond with a delirious reaction when in that same situation, although it must be admitted that children are usually even more predisposed to respond with delirium to toxins or infections than are adults.

With regard to toxic reactions, we actually are able to differentiate people into two main groups (there probably being several subgroups): those who show a simple toxic picture, and those who show an elaborate symptom picture. For instance, even though many different kinds of drugs are used, the response in an individual remains the same. In other words, the individual who tends to respond to a drug with a simple intoxication reaction will respond similarly to drugs of different chemical constituency, while one who responds with a more elaborate toxic reaction will again enter a very similar state when under the influence of different drugs. The individual propensity issue is still under investigation, and as yet we are unable to make very positive statements about it.

I cannot discuss all the possible agents which could produce delirium but will discuss one or two of those producing important clinical pictures. A very fine study of this was made by Karl Menninger (1919) on a large number of influenza patients who developed all types of acute organic reactions. Many of the interesting points that emerged from his study have been more or less confirmed by other investigators. He found the following types of reactions occurring in patients. (1) The inflammatory toxin produces a straight acute organic reaction—a *delirium*. Many patients belong in this straight acute reaction group. In some other individuals, however, the same type of influenza does not produce a straight delirium but, (2) the toxin *precipitates a psychotic reaction,* usually manic-depressive, schizophrenic, or pictures very similar to that of a psychoneurosis. In another group of patients, (3) the influenza produces an acute organic reaction which *alters the clinical picture of an already existing psychosis.* For instance, if the patient suffering from schizophrenia develops influenza, an acute organic reaction then occurs and an alteration appears in the schizophrenic process. And finally, (4) the influenza produces an acute organic reaction which *aggravates and accelerates an underlying chronic organic process.* As I have mentioned, when a paretic patient develops an acute organic reaction, very often the underlying chronic organic process is markedly aggravated.

Therefore, whenever examining a patient who manifests an acute organic reaction, one must consider all of these reaction possibilities: First, are we dealing with a straight acute organic reaction occurring in an otherwise relatively normal or a predisposed individual? Secondly, is the acute organic reaction only a part of the story, in that actually we have on hand the precipitation of another psychosis? Thirdly, if an acute organic reaction develops in a person already suffering from a so-called functional psychosis, what alterations of the psychotic picture occur under the influence of the superimposed acute delirium? Fourthly, is there an admixture of acute and chronic organic reactions present, and does the acute organic process aggravate the underlying chronic one?

The first two—the straight acute organic reaction, and the acute organic reaction which releases or precipitates a so-called functional psychosis—are, naturally, of diagnostic, prognostic, and therapeutic importance. The prognosis and treatment of an acute organic reaction depend entirely upon the etiological agent plus certain features in the individual's personality organization. The more you are given the impression that the acute organic reaction is mixed with manic-depressive or schizophrenic features the more cautious you will have to be, first of all, in making a prognosis, and secondly, the more you will have to combine treatments in order to help the patient. You will have to combine treatments directed against the etiological agent with those used to combat attacks of manic-depressive or schizophrenic psychosis.

When I discuss differential diagnosis, especially that of schizophrenia in relation to many other disorders, this issue will repeatedly arise. It is by no means rare, particularly in a general hospital, that a psychiatrist is called in as consultant to examine a delirious patient and the patient is simply written off as a case of acute delirium, especially if the etiological agent is fairly well determined. For instance, the internist diagnoses influenza, malaria, or whatever, depending upon the demonstrable etiological agent; the psychiatrist is therefore called in to verify the presenting mental picture or advise on therapy. If the examining psychiatrist then finds the patient delirious but does not study the delirium carefully, he simply puts down a note on the chart, "Patient suffering from an acute delirium," adding that he should be treated by the internist. The psychiatrist then simply stands by or treats the delirium only as far as is necessary from a psychiatric supportive point of view. Then, three to five days elapse and still the delirium does not clear up; the patient remains psychotic. When the psychiatrist is then confronted by the internist with the question, "What happened?" he must admit that the patient did not actually suffer from only a straight acute delirium but is also schizophrenic, the schizophrenia having been released, precipitated, or activated by the particular organic stress involved.

If the fact of a released psychosis is overlooked, the psychiatrist may diagnose a case of "prolonged delirium." This is a diagnosis I would warn against. It was a designation quite often applied to patients in whom the delirium fails to clear up within a week or ten days or so. It can surely occur as such, but it is rather rare—and actually the majority of these patients usually die. Usually cases of prolonged delirium are those in which the acute organic reaction is slowly becoming chronic (as in the slow transition from an alcoholic delirium to a Korsakoff syndrome) or else they are actually cases in which a so-called functional psychosis was precipitated and, under the diagnosis of prolonged delirium, a manic or a schizophrenic or some other process is at work.

The third and fourth reactions mentioned—the alteration of an existing functional psychosis, and the mixture of acute and chronic organic psychosis—are of interest more from a theoretical and therapeutic point of view, but do not offer any specific diagnostic pitfalls. When discussing schizophrenia, I shall point out in detail that this disorder responds to a great variety of external influences.

One observation is extremely old: A schizophrenic patient under the influence of an organic disease may manifest, provided the organic influence is not very severe, an interesting remission of his psychotic symptoms. The person often then appears to be fairly normal; he is in better contact with his environment than usual and many of the secondary symptoms of the disorder, such as hallucinations, delusions, and regression symptoms, vanish. Therefore, under organic stress a schizophrenic patient may reintegrate. In other instances, however, a schizophrenic patient may manifest an exacerbation of his psychosis; he may suffer a disintegration. Which type of organic process disintegrates a schizophrenic person, and which reintegrates him, is not known. But both observations, however, are valid. In some cases if the schizophrenic patient is infected with influenza you will observe that the psychotic clinical picture becomes aggravated; in quite a number of schizophrenic patients, however, you will observe that the typical schizophrenic disorganization is replaced by fairly normal integrated behavior. This usually lasts for only the duration of the acute organic episode and then the patient slumps back to his former psychotic state. Nevertheless, in very rare instances these patients maintain their clinical improvement and remain well. Incidentally, the same courses may be observed in cases of depression.

A few instances have also been observed of the schizophrenic patient's clinical symptomatology changing from one subgroup to that of another—for example, from catatonic to projective types—under the influence of an acute organic disease. Similar phenomena are also observed in relationship to manic-depressive psychosis, although not so often as in schizophrenia. This reaction, however, is of lesser importance than the other two reactions mentioned, namely, the aggravation or the remission of an existing picture under the influence of an acute organic reaction.

In the acute organic reaction, furthermore, we must observe several other transitional features when an acute delirium merges into a Korsakoff syndrome. These transitions most frequently occur in cases of alcohol toxicity but they occasionally occur in cases of infectious diseases. Such a patient manifests a typical delirium, the delirium does not clear up completely within a short time, and slowly a chronic organic syndrome emerges. When this happens, usually the disorientation and memory impairments remain. Although in an uncomplicated case of delirium the disorientation and memory impairment, and any hallucinations or delusions present, usually all disappear simultaneously and rather harmoniously, in patients undergoing a transition certain dissociations occur, meaning that the four symptoms mentioned do not disappear simultaneously; they actually take separate courses. Patients whose hallucinations and delusions disappear but whose disorientation and memory impairment remain are often those who gradually develop so-called simple dementia following the delirious state. The opposite course, whereby a patient's memory defects and disorientation disappear but hallucinations and delusions remain, is very often indicative of schizophrenia. This should definitely be kept in mind. Therefore, the resolution of the delirious picture in terms of the *extent* and the *manner* of symptom resolution are the two important issues to be kept in mind. In other words, the thoroughness and the harmony of symptom disappearance should be observed. First of all, does the memory impairment and the disorientation disappear, or not? Secondly, if those symptoms do disappear, do they disappear simultaneously along with any hallucinations and delusions present in the patient, or not?

Following an acute organic reaction many patients resolve the delirium but yet another very interesting picture then begins to emerge, namely, the syndrome which was first termed "postdelirious emotional weakness." Actually, the syndrome includes a few organic residual symptoms mixed with additional symptoms resembling those of a psychoneurosis. To what extent these pictures are organic and to what extent they are release manifestations in persons having an underlying psychoneurosis will be discussed in detail in connection with head injury syndromes. The symptom pictures are extremely common following concussion and the reactions are similar to those of persons who are recovering from an acute delirious state. You will encounter, for instance, a person who suffers with influenza or pneumonia and has a delirium for about three or four days; the delirium resolves itself; and the patient then begins to complain of fatigue, a slight headache, apathy, a lessening of his usual desire for work or for sexual activity, and so forth. He complains he does not feel his usual self. His many vague symptoms are somewhat difficult to interpret. In some of these patients there are psychodynamic clues to indicate the person's integration was not quite adequate, but the syndrome develops in many patients without such clues being present. There then develops what was formerly termed a "postfebrile exhaustion" state, more recently termed the "postdelirious pseudoneurotic" syndrome. This reaction must be given your attention because it contains a great deal of psychiatric inference and treatment is really necessary after the organic disorder is resolved.

In connection with the acute organic syndrome, I would like to mention a few additional issues, particularly in regard to those patients who develop an acute organic reaction in the setting of an acute infectious disease. The delirium is usually described as a "febrile" delirium, indicating that it was assumed to occur invariably at the height of the temperature rise and was intimately linked with the high fever. This is true in a number of patients but not true in every case. Actually, all the so-called toxic-infectious deliria have been subdivided into three groups: (1) the prefebrile delirium, (2) the delirium occurring with the height of the fever, and (3) the postfebrile delirium. These three headings indicate that there must be a number of patients who develop delirium before the onset of fever and a number of patients in whom delirium develops after they are actually on the road to recovery from the infectious disease. These prefebrile and postfebrile cases of delirium are of great interest, and many theoretical questions are involved concerning what produces them. Their origin is usually due to a toxin or its elaboration.

The prefebrile cases are of great diagnostic importance because when the patient suddenly develops a delirium nobody understands why or how it happens; then a day or two later there follow symptoms of the infectious disease that produced it. Prefebrile delirium is observed, for instance, in typhus, in smallpox, in influenza, and in quite a number of other infectious diseases. Therefore, in many cases the possibility arises that the patient has a delirious reaction before actual medical and laboratory signs of the disease itself become manifest. So, one must be aware that such a phenomenon occurs.

In the majority of patients the delirium occurs at the

height of the fever. It is especially evident in malaria, usually the main delirium and its hallucinatory manifestations appearing at the height of the fever and disappearing when the temperature sinks.

Postfebrile patients sometimes display delirium, but this incidence is the least common. We must be particularly guarded in diagnosing postfebrile delirium because it was discovered that the majority of patients belonging into this group were cases where another psychosis had been precipitated. Postfebrile delirium has often been observed in postpartum patients, the delirium having often been attributed to an infection, especially before the discovery of the antibiotic drugs when infections were fairly prevalent following childbirth. At present time, however, if a postpartum patient has some fever, and then two or three days after the fever subsides an acute delirious reaction occurs, that patient is usually suspected to be suffering from an underlying psychosis which was precipitated by the organic disorder, unless it can really be demonstrated that some protracted infection or intoxication is present.

7

TRAUMATIC
MENTAL DISORDERS

Traumatic mental disorders are those in which mental changes occur as an aftermath of concussion, contusion, or compression (and the phenomenon of fat embolism) of the brain. Mental manifestations following head trauma are commonly observed; they range from predominantly organic brain syndromes to psychogenic syndromes. In other words, in some cases all the mental symptomatology consist of organic changes which are etiologically based on the trauma. These are rather rare. And there are many cases in which the mental symptoms are precipitated by the trauma but mainly psychogenic in etiology. Frequently the symptomatology is a mixture of both. It is important that the etiology of the symptoms be differentiated in each case. Differentiation is usually difficult.

The *traumatic psychoses* should be so labeled only if they are organic in etiology. Many posttraumatic psychoses are actually "release" phenomena, an underlying psychosis already being present which is then precipitated by the trauma. These should not be diagnosed as true traumatic psychoses. In other cases, psychogenic reactions occur which appear to be psychoses—such as hysterical reactions in the form of twilight states, and so forth—but which perhaps belong in the category of the so-called traumatic neuroses. In describing the *traumatic neuroses,* here again we are confronted with a loose use of the term. Some psychiatrists regard them as being the "postconcussional syndrome" characterized by headache, dizziness, "neurasthenia," and so forth. Others consider traumatic neuroses as pertaining only to emotional changes following head trauma. Therefore, in the present flux of definition, it would be well to label a syndrome postcontusional only if you really think it is based on organic change. In a large number of cases the symptomatology is a mixture of both organic and psychogenic features, and should be regarded as such.

There is a third group of traumatic mental disorders: the *posttraumatic amentia.* This is also referred to as the secondary form of mental deficiency. Actually, about 5 percent of all cases of amentia are etiologically based on head trauma.

Incidentally, head injury occurs rarely *in utero*; when it occurs, it is usually due to injury inflicted on the abdominal wall of the pregnant woman. Head injury to infants occurs more commonly during parturition, naturally, especially in connection with problematic forceps delivery. These infants can suffer injuries to the meninges or even to the brain substance. Some of the parturition injuries produce mental defects which are seemingly purely on the intellectual level. In other cases, the children do not show very much of that, but show an impairment of emotional control; many develop sociopathic behavioral patterns which often resemble the postencephalitic sociopathic type of emotionally disorganized behavior. The majority of cases, however, show both intellectual as well as emotional deterioration as a result of head injury, but it should be kept in mind that the emotional deterioration can be present alone. Many of the birth-injured children are cases of *spastic paralysis* (Little's disease) and this disorder is usually, but not always, associated with some mental defect. The degree of brain damage varies; in some cases there is complete plegia, and in others there is merely poor coordination and timing of motor activity. Speech functioning in spastic children is very often impaired, and they are frequently erroneously diagnosed as being feebleminded. Quite a number of cases of spastic plegias are normal intellectually, but the majority are also intellectually impaired.

TRAUMATIC PSYCHOSES

There are organic reactions caused by a disturbance of brain functioning due to a force directly or indirectly inflicted on the head. Traumatic psychoses may occur following concussion, contusion, compression, or other trauma affecting the brain. Each of those traumatic conditions has its particular pathological background and its different manifestations, but this differentiation is difficult to make.

Concussion is the most common cause of traumatic psychoses. In the case of concussion the central nervous system is, you might say, "shaken up," but there are no observable anatomical changes found to take place. It is questionable, however, whether a simple concussion can occur without some amount of contusion or some bleeding occurring in the brain matter. In the case of contusion, the quantity of clinical symptomatology is, naturally, much greater than that observed following concussion. Most cases of concussion and contusion recover insofar as acute symptoms are concerned.

The clinical picture of true traumatic psychosis is, as I have mentioned, that of an organic reaction, but the symptomatology and course of the disorder vary from patient to patient, as do organic reactions regardless of the cause.

This depends on many factors, a few of which I will discuss briefly. In the majority of cases the symptomatology develops in the following general way: Immediately after concussion has occurred the patient is unconscious. He may remain in that state for only a few minutes, or it may continue for many days. The duration of loss of consciousness is in direct proportion to the severity of the injury suffered. Therefore, a trauma is probably mild if the patient does not lose consciousness at all. However, there are exceptions to this rule: Occasionally there are patients who suffer a surprisingly light injury to the head and yet after a few weeks, or even a few years, begin to manifest organic symptoms which are actually the result of the head injury. The severity of a head trauma also cannot be determined by the extent of the external injury on the head. For instance, a person can suffer a severe head trauma, due to direct or indirect causes, without there being any injury to the skull itself. (In all these respects, head trauma can be as much a diagnostic problem as asymptomatic, or "quiet," brain tumors.)

As the patient is regaining consciousness the mental symptoms usually begin to appear: the patient complains of headache, dizziness, and perhaps nausea, a feeling of fogginess, and an inability to concentrate. Persons who have suffered head trauma are extremely sensitive to noises; just ordinary noises make them very irritable—a condition which continues until the other symptomatology disappears. Probably it is largely organically based, although it could be related to psychogenic irritability as well. Most patients do not develop psychotic manifestations and the patient either recovers completely, or displays the postconcussional syndrome or a posttraumatic neurotic syndrome, or both. A small number of patients, however, do develop a psychosis specifically caused by the trauma. Nobody knows why this so rarely occurs; it is so rare that some observers believe there is no such entity.

If a true traumatic psychosis does develop, it usually occurs in the following manner: Immediately following the trauma to the head, the patient is in a coma; as consciousness returns the patient enters into a state of delirium with hallucinations and perhaps delusions; these hallucinations and delusions then fade away and the patient experiences simple confusion with disorientation and memory impairment. Now, all of these events merge one into the other. These are the acute organic reactions. The patient usually recovers. In a few cases, however, after the delirium subsides and is followed by the confusional state, the subacute reactions of the Korsakoff type develop. This does not commonly occur. When it does occur, occasionally the symptoms will progress until finally the end point reached is the chronic Korsakoff syndrome. These are the cases of so-called posttraumatic dementia, or posttraumatic personality disorder.

Further studies should attempt to delineate the many factors that influence the clinical picture of the traumatic psychoses. Attempts have been made to correlate the visual or auditory hallucinations with pathological changes in the occipital and parietal lobes, respectively. However, irritation in the ventricular gray matter of the diencephalon or mesencephalon can also produce hallucinations as well as delusions. It is very difficult to establish the localization clinically even in those cases in which the head trauma was circumscribed. For example, localization of injury to the cerebellum cannot be definitely determined in the course of the ordinary clinical examination since a section of the brain remote from the site of the trauma may be involved as in contrecoup. The electroencephalogram is an important aid in the diagnosis of locality of traumatic lesions to some extent, but it does not usually disclose the more minute circumscribed lesions. In many cases of traumatic psychosis the hallucinations and delusions present were not accompanied by neurological signs characteristic of cortical or subcortical lesions. In the absence of neurological signs, naturally, attempts to localize these psychic manifestations become very difficult.

A number of posttraumatic syndromes can develop other than the more clear-cut psychosis I have described: the acute, subacute, and chronic organic reactions. There are syndromes which are acute reactions due to the trauma but are not actually psychoses. There are others which are actual psychotic reactions but their etiologies are not based on the trauma per se. Furthermore, the symptomatology in all traumatic psychoses may be markedly influenced by the basic personality structure of the patient, or influenced by other complicating factors, such as the presence of unrelated disorders existing in the individual previous to the head trauma.

Occasionally, for example, patients are encountered who, following a head trauma, manifest the twilight state syndrome so frequently observed in cases of psychomotor epilepsy. I am not referring here to the patients who develop posttraumatic epilepsy, but I am talking about those patients who, while in the stage of narrowed consciousness following a head trauma, enter into a twilight state and perform some kind of complicated ritual that is abnormal for them to do. During these states a patient, naturally, is capable of performing almost any type of act. In some instances the patient who has received a blow on the head will get up, will appear to be perfectly normal, but actually he will be wandering about in one of the dreamlike states. Then after a few hours or days have elapsed, the situation clears up and the patient is recovered. There is usually complete retrograde amnesia for the acts performed during these states.

Interestingly enough, reactions occur that appear to be psychotic which are not based on organic trauma but are based on a fright reaction occurring simultaneously with the presumed trauma. These patients believe that they had suffered a head injury and their anxiety generates such tremendous tension that it leads to the development of seemingly psychotic symptoms. In the majority of such cases, however, the reaction is a mixture: An hysterical twilight state due to a fright reaction and an organic reaction are combined. But the occurrence of a purely hysterical psychosis following a head trauma is very, very rare! Often they turn out to include something more—such as subdural hemorrhage or contusion and so forth.

The clinical pictures of actual traumatic psychoses usually do not differ in detail from those of other organic impairments of brain functioning. But in quite a number of cases a trauma acts to "release" psychotic pictures that have elements of schizophrenia, or elements of manic-depressive psychosis. They are not rare! When this occurs, it leads to diagnostic confusion: Is it a true case of schizophrenia or manic-depressive psychosis released by the head trauma, or is it a direct result of the trauma? This is a debatable question. Some psychiatrists claim there is no such thing as a true traumatic psychosis; others claim that a "released" psychosis is directly a result of the trauma. Regardless of whether or not either of the above hypotheses is correct, the fact remains that there are a great many patients showing mixed symptomatology which makes classification difficult.

There is a general basic principle applicable for classifying every organic psychosis presenting a mixed psychotic picture. If the patient manifests auditory hallucinations and delusions, as well as memory impairment, confusion, and other signs of acute organic reactions, the final diagnosis depends on how harmoniously the symptoms clear up. This is a very important point! For instance, if the feeling of haziness, the memory defect, the disorientation, and the other organic symptoms all clear up within three or four days, but the patient still continues to have hallucinations and delusions, then you are not dealing with a severe organic problem. Follow-up observations show many of these patients to become overtly schizophrenic. There is a question concerning the importance of the trauma in such cases. On the other hand, if the patient shows the two different psychopathological aspects of the disorder moving up and down in a rather interlocked manner, and shows a harmonious disappearance of both aspects of the psychotic picture simultaneously, then you are probably dealing mainly with an organic problem.

The peculiarities and duration of the hallucinations and delusions in patients who suffer traumatic psychosis are considerably influenced by many factors other than the organic trauma. The basic personality organization of the individual is an important factor. For instance, if a patient experiences a paranoid form of posttraumatic hallucinatory episode, it is not simply due to irritation or inhibition of certain foci in the brain. The personality makeup of the individual is also contributing to the clinical picture. And, if hallucinatory experiences continue after the organic psychotic features have disappeared, the individual should be evaluated as to his previous schizoid personality structure. Of the many factors which combine to influence the clinical picture in the more protracted cases, the personality structure of the patient is of great importance. It should be mentioned that environmental stress factors—social, sexual, financial, occupational, and so forth—surely can influence the symptomatology and the course of a traumatic psychosis to some extent, but more attention should be focused on the *way* in which the patient *handles* these stress situations; this gives a clue as to how his personality organization acts to influence his particular symptom reactions to the traumatic situation. Any number of clinical variations are possible on this basis alone.

In addition to psychological factors such as an individual's schizoid personality makeup, complicating factors stemming from external sources can influence the clinical picture following head trauma. Naturally, drugs and toxins very often aggravate posttraumatic symptomatology. For instance, the intake of alcohol usually markedly heightens a patient's reactions to head trauma. The following situation can occur: An individual receives a blow on the head and becomes unconscious; he regains consciousness and then manifests a mild postconcussional syndrome—perhaps complains of slight headache, dizziness, and so forth—but you do not observe him to have any particularly abnormal behavior pattern. Then, suddenly, after taking a drink of alcohol, he goes berserk. Of course, another patient suffering a similar head trauma will display some other behavior pattern when he takes alcohol, depending on his particular personality structure. In other words, whatever reaction pattern is characteristic of a particular individual will be displayed to a more heightened degree when he is under the influence of alcohol or some other drug or toxin. This is similarly observed, for instance, in epilepsy. Epileptic individuals are notoriously susceptible to alcohol, and drinking can actually precipitate a seizure, or a psychomotor episode, or whatever manifestations the particular epileptic patient is prone to have.

The *prognosis* in traumatic psychoses depends on many factors. In other words, the presence of complicating disorders, psychological or organic, in persons who suffer head trauma are not only of etiological and clinical significance, but are also of great importance prognostically. In uncomplicated head trauma the prognosis for the traumatic psychosis is usually favorable, but it becomes much more serious when complications also exist. *Psychological* complications can include inadequacy of the patient's personality organization, or the presence of an underlying psychosis unrelated to the head trauma, and can also include emotional stresses in the patient's life situation, as I have discussed. *Organic* complications can include any among a number of existing somatic disorders unrelated to the head trauma. Several complications, naturally, may exist in combination to alter the prognostic picture.

First of all, individuals having a schizoid, or "introverted," personality organization have a relatively poor prognosis. They have less ability than others to cope with organic or any other stress situation. The so-called "extraverted" personality types have twice as good a chance for recovery. The same observations have been made regarding the prognosis of patients suffering from a drug-induced psychosis. In other words, the schizoid type of individual seemingly has a poor adaptive ability; just what the "lack" is in his constitutional endowment is not delineated; it might be related to some adrenal cortical dysfunction, or to some constellation of metabolic dyscrasias. At any rate, when under any kind of stress these people do not have adequate adaptive reserve and vegetative stamina. They attempt to protect themselves by means of withdrawal; their energy is discharged inward, you might say. Many of these people select to capitalize on physical illness as an excuse for their withdrawal. On the whole, their tendency to recover from trauma is poor. Furthermore, should the patient who suffered a head trauma actually have an already existing psychosis, such as schizophrenia in a very mild form, the traumatic psychosis is likely to be complicated by the symptoms of a full-blown schizophrenic psychosis probably "released" by the head trauma and, naturally, the prognosis is usually poor.

As has been pointed out by Adolf Meyer *(3)*, an impressive number of so-called traumatic psychoses are not psychoses purely due to the trauma alone but are associated with other somatic disorders. In one study *(Hoch and Davidoff, 1939)* 47 percent of the total number of cases were complicated (in order of frequency) by alcoholism, cerebral arteriosclerosis, senility, neurosyphilis, and other miscellaneous conditions such as primary mental deficiency, epilepsy, and so forth. Whenever any of these complications are present in a patient who suffered head trauma, the prognosis is much worse than that in an uncomplicated head trauma. As in any other field of medicine, the prognosis of a disorder is made more serious when complications are present, particularly when the complications involve the cardiovascular system, an example being the influence of vascular disorder in diabetes which retards the healing of wounds. Incidentally, that traumatic psychosis has a relatively poor prognosis in schizoid individuals may be somehow related to the fact that they usually have a hypoplasia of their vascular apparatus.

TRAUMATIC NEUROSES

"Traumatic neuroses" are an ill-defined group and many classifications have been suggested. At the present time, so-called traumatic neuroses are usually divided into two subgroups: (1) the postconcussional *organic reaction* syndrome in which the symptoms of encephalopathy are organic sequellae directly caused by the physical trauma; and (2) the posttraumatic *neurotic reaction* syndrome in which there are no organic sequellae and the symptoms are independent of any physical or structural alterations in the brain except to the extent that they are precipitated by the trauma and then utilized by the patient for primary or secondary gains.

It is difficult to differentiate these two subgroups because in the majority of cases the clinical picture is a mixture of both, the organic and neurotic symptoms appearing simultaneously. In fact, we are actually dealing with symptoms having two separate but linked etiologies. There is no absolute method for clearly differentiating between the organic and the psychological origins of the symptoms, and in appraising cases mistakes are made in both directions.

The clinical course in the postconcussional *organic reaction* group of traumatic neuroses varies. The patient may or may not become unconscious for a brief period of time immediately following the injury. In either case, when conscious the first complaint is that of headache in about 95 percent of the patients. This postconcussional headache may be diffuse or may be localized around the site of injury. It is a continuous headache, with intermittent exaggeration in relation to physical or emotional causative situations. Another common symptom complaint is that of dizziness; it is not usually a true vertigo but rather a feeling of lack of balance with giddiness and lightheadedness. Actual vertigo with nystagmus does occasionally occur because the concussional "shaking up" of the brain is capable of increasing the irritability of the labyrinths. However, the presence of vertigo is not a diagnostic feature since many neurotic individuals already have labyrinth hyperirritability reactions without benefit of any head trauma. The patient is also likely to complain of some mental symptomatology. He may state that he is unable to concentrate since the trauma occurred. He may manifest circumscribed memory impairments, and often there is a retrograde or an anterograde amnesia for the traumatic event. He may complain of fatigue, a feeling of faintness, or other signs of vasomotor instability may be present. Then, depending on his previous personality organization and dynamic patterns, various neurotic symptoms may or may not emerge, but the other symptoms mentioned are the most common complaints made by the postconcussional group of patients. Examination rarely discloses neurological changes. Neurological signs are found only in cases of contusion, but not in concussion.

The posttraumatic *neurotic reaction* group of patients usually complain of a few above-described symptoms, such as slight headache and dizziness, but mainly they then complain of neurotic symptoms, particularly those which were formerly designated "neurasthenic." Many of these individuals were seemingly within the limits of normal prior to the head trauma. Therefore, since their complaints occurred subsequent to the trauma it was usually assumed that organic changes within the organism (such as alterations of vasomotor and spinal fluid balance) were the actual cause of the symptoms of irritability, impairment of concentration, withdrawal from the environment, and so forth. On the other hand, a considerable number of patients examined gave the impression by their behavior that their complaints were on a psychogenic basis and were being utilized for primary and secondary gains. To finalize this assumption, the symptoms could often be removed by means of hypnosis. This matter of secondary gains should probably be taken into consideration in many cases, particularly when the compensations involved are quite obvious. Keep in mind, moreover, that for many patients the secondary gains are not financial, but rather a convenient opportunity to withdraw from sexual, social, professional, or other responsibilities with which the patient feels unable to cope. Many individuals practically anticipate some accident in order to utilize it for some such gain.

Differentiation between organic and psychogenic symtomatology in the traumatic neuroses is difficult to determine because: (1) we have to rely on the patient's description of his subjective manifestations and take his word for it, and (2) the laboratory tests at our disposal are inconclusive. There is, however, one test which is rather reliable: If you are doubtful about the basis of a patient's symptoms, submit him to a sodium amytal interview. This will remove the patient's inhibitions and the true nature of his symptoms may be disclosed. For instance, psychogenic amnesias usually clear up during the interview. Many cases of amnesia are assumed to be on an organic basis which are not actual organic amnesias; often they are psychogenic and part of a fright syndrome. Organic amnesias are not influenced by sodium amytal injection. The Rorschach test has also been employed to differentiate between organic and psychogenic symptomatology but this test, in my opinion, is completely unreliable. There is another differentiation point that should be taken into consideration when examining posttraumatic patients. In organic cases there is usually evidence of decreased cerebration; the patient's thinking is slower than it had been prior to the trauma.

Long-term follow-up evaluations of posttraumatic symptoms should be made. Some patients complain of headache for years following a head trauma but, in practically all such cases, if the patient continues to display psychogenic symptoms as well, the differentiation is difficult to determine. In other words, instead of the patient's concussion being cured in three days or perhaps three months, it is not cured even after a period of three years. In such cases we are dealing with symptomatology of mixed etiology, and this is the reason why we are unable to differentiate the organic from the psychological features in these cases.

8

CHRONIC ORGANIC REACTIONS

The chronic organic reaction, or Korsakoff syndrome[1], is characterized by chronicity, as the name implies. The organic reactions are now subdivided into acute and chronic. Formerly they were subdivided into over a hundred different entities because it was believed each form of organic disorder had its specific mental expression; that, for instance, there was typhoid delirium, delirium in connection with pneumonia, and a syndrome for general paresis or for senile dementia as well as for the many other chronic organic reactions. Each was considered specific for that particular etiological agent. This view is no longer maintained, with a very few exceptions. It is now accepted that there is an acute type of reaction and a chronic type of reaction, regardless of etiology.

---

[1] This should not be confused with the Korsakoff psychosis, the form of chronic organic reaction due to alcohol.—*Eds.*

That certain pathogenic agents can color the acute or chronic reaction no one denies, and occasionally this coloring can be so significant that, based on the clinical symptomatology, one is able to at least make a good guess as to the etiology. For example, in some patients who have an acute delirium due, for instance, to cocaine or bromide, the delirious reaction is colored in such a specific manner that if a physician has already had experience with the clinical picture he could readily recognize it without any great difficulty. Nevertheless, that which is only a coloring is not some form of specificity of the mental picture itself in relationship to the etiological agent. Very often the same etiological agent produces clinical pictures in which the etiology cannot be readily recognized. Actually, to be accurate, in most organic reactions the patient's mental picture alone rarely discloses the etiology. It is rare, for instance, that psychiatrists diagnose general paresis based purely on the mental picture without serological, neurological, and other diagnostic aids which usually clinch the diagnosis etiologically. Before having those aids, false diagnoses were rather frequent—only later to be corrected in autopsy by microscopic study of the brain cortex. By simply basing diagnoses on the mental pictures many organic conditions were either not diagnosed or were falsely diagnosed which are now more or less routinely diagnosed by means of diagnostic aids. This is valid not only for general paresis but applies equally to practically all the organic conditions which we meet clinically.

Some psychiatrists differentiated a subacute reaction as one in between the acute and the chronic organic reactions. This is not fully justified because we are unable to diagnose a subacute organic reaction clinically, there being no characteristic clinical symptomatology attached to it other than that probably the syndrome develops neither slowly nor acutely but somewhere in between. Therefore, I think the division between acute and chronic is sufficient. I may add, however, it is an occasional contingency when both acute and chronic reactions occur simultaneously in an individual. A patient can develop an acute reaction which does not subside but progresses into a chronic reaction. This can be observed in some cases following head injuries. For example, following a concussion the patient may at first manifest a delirious syndrome; the delirium then disappears but slowly the patient develops a chronic organic syndrome. This development is rare, but it occurs. Similarly, occasionally a patient develops an acute delirious reaction such as delirium tremens based on alcohol; the delirium tremens subsides but the patient develops a Korsakoff psychosis, which is the chronic organic reaction. Therefore, it is possible for a patient to start off with an acute reaction which goes through some subacute phase, and then becomes chronic.

The reverse is also possible. A patient may suffer from a chronic organic reaction and in that framework develop an acute reaction. For example, a patient may suffer from a senile dementia and then, perhaps due to some physical, emotional, or metabolic upset, he may suddenly develop a delirium. This is not at all rare. Or, similarly, persons who are senile or atherosclerotic may suddenly experience an acute delirious reaction; and when it subsides, the underlying chronically developed disease may then become manifest. Such combinations are occasionally diagnostic problems. Naturally, with regard to the management of these patients one must always consider whether he is dealing with an acute or a chronic organic reaction or the combination of the two, because in each situation the management is somewhat different and obviously the prognosis is also different.

As I have mentioned, the essential and outstanding features of the acute reaction—the so-called delirious reaction, which could be produced by any among innumerable etiological agents—are acute onset, disorientation, impairment of intellectual functioning, hallucinations as well as delusions, and rather short duration of the reaction. Furthermore, usually no personality changes are sequellae of the acute reaction; after the patient recovers he usual reintegrates on the same level as before the attack. Occasionally personality changes do occur following acute delirium, particularly in cases of encephalitis, but such cases are exceptions. Usually the acute delirious reaction is favorable in that after the patient recovers any personality alterations are only temporary.

In contrast to the acute organic reaction, the chronic organic reaction shows, naturally, a somewhat different symptomatology. The onset is extremely slow; it progresses insidiously, and usually takes a comparatively long time before the full clinical picture unfolds. The clinical symptoms are mainly progressive intellectual deterioration, emotional changes, and marked alterations of the personality of the patient. Meanwhile, considerable pathology, or considerable damage, is already present in the nervous system before the psychiatric symptoms emerge. Histological changes in the brain are usually much more massive in the chronic than in the acute organic disorders, and there are very few chronic organic disorders in which anatomical pathology cannot be demonstrated.

If these abbreviated designations of the symptomatology of the acute and the chronic organic reactions are compared, you will recognize immediately that one important issue was not mentioned: namely, alteration of consciousness. Alteration of consciousness (which plays such a marked role in the symptomatology of the acute delirious reaction) is not conspicuous in the Korsakoff syndrome. To express it differently, most of the chronic organic reaction impairments occur in a clear setting, consciousness rarely being impaired. That is not true for all chronic organic cases, there being those in which alteration of consciousness does occur. Nevertheless, the basic rule is that the chronic organic syndrome occurs in a clear setting. The chronic patient manifests impairment of his intellect: memory defects, perhaps disorientation, and a gradual dementia, but these symptoms are demonstrated in a setting in which the person's consciousness is unimpaired or interfered with to a much less extent than is customary for the acute organic state.

In those cases, however, in which clouding of consciousness does occur, both acute and chronic reactions may be present, one superimposed on the other. For example, a patient suffering from general paresis who manifests a gradual diminution of intellectual faculties, an impairment of memory with disorientation, and who yet has clear consciousness with fairly good contact with his environment can suddenly become completely confused and appear to be dreaming or appear to be in an acute delirious state. In such a case the acute reaction has become superimposed on the chronic reaction, an issue which occurs in a number of organic disorders, as I have mentioned. These cases are interesting because the symptomatology of the acute and chronic appears to be mixed for a period of time before the acute reaction subsides, leaving only the chronic reaction.

CLINICAL SYMPTOMATOLOGY

The chronic organic syndrome is essentially characterized by slow and insidious: (1) *reduction of intellectual abilities,* (2) *alterations of the affective state,* and (3) *changes in the personality* of the individual. There are marked variations in these main features, especially when profound symptoms develop.

Reduction of intellectual abilities is the most outstanding feature occurring in the chronic organic disorders. This decline of intellect develops very gradually, although the time involved varies. There are persons, for instance, in whom the intellectual decline culminates within a year or two. Persons who develop early atherosclerosis, or others who develop presenile psychosis, and those having certain forms of general paresis can develop a senile dementia very quickly. Usually, however, it takes many years before the full clinical picture unfolds.

This decline of the intellect is termed *organic dementia.* The original concept of dementia holds at the present time: it is irreversible. Actually, dementia has always meant *irreversible deterioration* of the intellectual faculties of the patient. This idea is based on clinical observations of the chronic organic diseases, dementia occurring in them most frequently. For example, in senile dementia the patient's progressive *and* irreversible intellectual deterioration can be demonstrated very easily. At one time a very similar point of view was also expressed concerning general paresis and a number of other organic diseases. But, when fever treatment was introduced in general paresis it was a surprise to observe that some patients who were considered deteriorated manifested considerable return of their intelligence. Then for the first time the question was raised: Is it really truly correct that intellectual deterioration is always irreversible? This has since been observed in a few other disorders in which a so-called intellectually deteriorated patient would actually stage a comeback. Apparently there are a considerable number of such exceptions. For the majority of patients, however, the basic idea that in chronic organic diseases the intellectual deterioration is insidious, progressive, and irreversible is essentially correct. This is valid concerning those diseases still virtually uninfluenced by present therapies, such as senile dementia.[1] Be aware of the fact that the basic psychiatric concept of intellectual deterioration's being really irreversible depends to a large extent upon the efficacy of therapies at our disposal. It is quite possible that many disorders now diagnosed as cases of dementia, meaning irreversible deterioration, may at some future time prove to be otherwise.

---

[1] Before his death, D. Ewen Cameron was investigating drugs which seemingly reverse apparent mental senility.—*Eds.*

Although the terms dementia and deterioration have often been used interchangeably, many psychiatrists restrict the term dementia to mean progressive irreversible intellectual deterioration on an organic basis, and define deterioration as progressive mental loss without making any assumption as to its cause or permanency. However, in referring to intellectual deterioration which is assumed to be reversible, the term *regression* is now preferred.

Here again, however, a controversy in the literature must be pointed out. Originally, Hughlings Jackson *(5, 6)* perceived regression as a neurological concept indicating that in any impairment of the nervous system the latest ontogenetically and phylogenetically acquired functions disintegrate first and the individual regresses to a lower level of neural functioning. However, Jackson's theory of regression was elaborated from observations of lower nervous system functions—motor function, sensory function, coordinating function, and so forth—and mental functioning was only touched upon without elaborations.

Freud, influenced by the work of Jackson, then introduced the idea of applying regression to behavior; that a patient steps back to more infantile forms of behavioral organization. He then expanded the idea of regression to include a stepping back to more infantile emotional organization. Finally he expanded this to include stepping back to, or being fixated on, lower levels of "libidinal" developmental organization. Actually, therefore, Freud's concept of regression involved essentially emotional developmental phenomena in reference to the patient's emotionally stepping down or stepping backward to a lower or infantile level of emotional organization. Originally his concept did not include regression in reference to intellectual impairment.

After it became apparent (especially in connection with schizophrenia, and later with some of the organic cases in which anatomical changes could be demonstrated) that so-called intellectual deterioration is not always permanent, in some cases fluctuating and even being reversible, psychiatrists began to also apply the term regression to intellectual impairments. And so, they spoke of intellectual regression, they spoke of emotional regression, and of course they spoke of the specifically Freudian conception of libidinal regression. Therefore, three expressions evolved concerning intellectual and emotional impairment of a person: *dementia,* which is confined purely to intellectual spheres (nobody refers to emotional dementia); *deterioration,* which applies to intellectual and emotional functioning; and *regression* of the intellect or the emotions.

If dealing with a case in which you are not certain whether the patient's intellectual impairment is really mainly due to a permanent damage, and if you have the feeling that probably emotional or other factors are present which influence the patient's mental performance, you might simplify matters as follows: If, for instance, it is a case of an acute organic reaction or an early and mild chronic reaction, it might be permissible to speak of the patient manifesting intellectual regression to a certain level. That leaves open any idea that this patient is intellectually completely doomed, or that regardless of anything done the person will become demented. The designation of intellectual deterioration or dementia should be reserved for those patients in whom the disease process has reached a completed or nearly completed stage and there is no hope for any great improvement. At the present time the best policy probably would be to use the terms deterioration and dementia interchangeably, but for dementia the emphasis should be on irreversibility, and for deterioration this issue should be left open.

Now, intellectual deterioration in the Korsakoff syndrome usually develops so slowly that it is imperceptible. It is interesting how long it takes before it is recognized that the person is demented. It is unbelievable how many people carry on in routine performance jobs while their intellectual capacities are actually in many ways "shot to pieces." This indicates that those in the patient's environment do not notice the change. Moreover, the majority of patients are also not aware of their intellectual impairment, although a considerable minority are. This has a certain significance from a therapeutic and prognostic point of view insofar as quite a number of these patients can adjust even on their lower level of intellectual performance because in some occupations or organizational groups apparently considerable mental defect is tolerated in an individual before he is recognized as being unable to perform at all.

Often (and this is very important) before one is actually able to demonstrate a definitive decline of the formal intelligence of the patient clinically or in tests, for quite a while impairments are already present of what are termed the *operational intelligence.* The efficiency level of the person's intellectual performance shows impairment before gross clinical examinations or tests can actually disclose any intellectual impairment. For instance, the patient, or those in his environment, will report that he is unable to *concentrate* as well as formerly; that he is unable to *conduct* his business as well as formerly; that he is not as *alert;* that his *memory* occasionally fails, and that his *judgment* is somewhat impaired. *Planning,* and particularly well-organized planning, is often impaired in these individuals long before interference of his formal intelligence can be demonstrated.

Such complaints arise quite often in middle-aged or older individuals. At times it is very difficult to discern whether the complaints represent premonitory signs of an oncoming organic process or whether they are actually due to emotional alterations in these individuals. Mild, and sometimes even severe, operational impairments of intelligence can occur which are not due to impairment of the intellect alone but which are also due to emotional interferences, and frequently the patient must be observed for a considerable time before one can decide which is the main factor present. Errors are made both ways. I have known patients to be diagnosed as having organic disease when actually they did not. For example, a fifty-year-old patient was diagnosed as suffering from atherosclerotic dementia but actually no signs of an atherosclerotic dementia were present, and the patient was in a state of an involutional depression which responded to treatment promptly. You can imagine what it means to the patient or to his relatives when it is disclosed that he is suffering from an atherosclerotic dementia when he is not! On the other hand, in comparatively young individuals in their late thirties or early forties the diagnosis is often assumed to be that of a functional disorder although all the symptoms of chronic organic disorder—impairment of planning, lack of concentration, inability to perform as well as formerly—are overlooked at the expense of some emotional alterations. Emotional alterations are present in chronic organic disorders as well as in functional disorders. A patient may be diagnosed as suffering from psychoneurosis or from some form of a mild involutional disorder when he is already suffering from a chronic organic disease, not infrequently an organic disease which could be expected to respond to therapy. For instance, the number of false diagnoses in cases of brain tumor is appalling! Brain tumor must always be carefully considered, particularly if an individual is middle-aged and begins to make complaints which could be interpreted as indicating decline of operational intelligence. The case should be scrutinized both ways. Are you really dealing with an organic impairment and are the symptoms actually the first signs of a serious organic disease emerging, or are you dealing with a psychogenic disturbance for which, obviously, management, treatment, and prognosis would be entirely different?

Unfortunately, in the early phase of chronic organic reactions—sometimes a few months, occasionally up to a year—the formal intelligence is not impaired and tests for operational impairment are as yet not very reliable. Therefore, sometimes a patient must be observed for a considerable time and explored by means of various physical and psychological examinations before arriving at a basis for diagnostic decision. However, although methods at our disposal enabling us to differentiate are not very satisfactory, we are nevertheless able to do much more than simply rely on impressions. At any rate, the gradual decline of intelligence is the most important aspect of a chronic organic disorder.

As the clinical picture unfolds over a period of time, impairment of the operational intelligence will progress to also include an impairment of the patient's *formal intelligence*. This can then be quite convincingly demonstrated clinically, and even with any of the many psychological tests for indicating organic decline of intellect. When the patient reaches the level of impaired formal intelligence, everything characteristic of intellectual deterioration is present.

The first intellectual impairment noticed is *impairment of memory*. The memory defects are stratified. Recent memory is more impaired than remote memory and is usually manifested first. As the organic process develops, remote memory also becomes invaded. For example, at first the patient does not know where he is or how he came to the hospital, but he is able to give you a fairly accurate account of where he went to school and even the names of his classmates, although it had been forty or fifty years ago. Disorientation sometimes occurs in connection with more recent memory impairment. However, its occurrence is not mandatory and it is never so conspicuous as that observed in acute organic cases. There are chronically demented persons who do know approximately where they are, what date it is or what time it is, although their orientation is not fully reliable. Other patients, however, are noticed to become profoundly disorientated for time, place, or person, and usually in that order of stratification. With temporal disorientation often there is also misidentification of the place and persons around them.

Gradually, more and more remote memory also

becomes impaired and many patients, particularly senile and paretic patients, become deteriorated to such an extent they actually have no memory and practically vegetate on a more or less animal-like memory level of existence. Formerly some investigators reserved the designation of a case as demented only when the patient demonstrated marked remote as well as recent memory impairment. This is not correct. A person may already manifest dementia without having very great interference with his remote memory. By observing persons who have marked interference with recent memory one can understand that when left with only remote memory many people cannot really perform except by confining themselves to purely manual tasks, because in our civilization recent memory has a very important function to fill.

Memory defects are particularly interesting in chronic organic patients in connection with the so-called *confabulatory syndrome*. A number of patients, particularly the alcoholic Korsakoff patients, fill in memory gaps with their own fabrications, or confabulations. You will encounter many organic patients demonstrating this phenomenon, but you will also encounter quite a few who do not. The presence of confabulation, therefore, is not essential for diagnosing a chronic organic reaction. Furthermore, the presence of confabulation is not pathognomonic for the alcoholic Korsakoff case, as was formerly assumed; it occurs in the framework of all chronic organic reactions. It is not rare in senile dementia, it is not rare in some forms of general paresis, and it is even questionable that it is so much more prevalent in the alcoholic Korsakoff patient than in many other chronic organic disorders.

Confabulation, or fabrication, occurs in mental disorders other than the clearly organic, but there they are not utilized to fill in memory gaps. That is the main difference. Actually, the confabulations of a sociopathic or a schizophrenic patient should be designated by another term but unfortunately the same term has been used. It must be kept in mind, however, that true confabulation is utilized in chronic organic patients to breach memory gaps and for no other reason, even though many underlying basic dynamics might be the same. That the patient attempts to overcome a feeling of handicap and lift his ego by attempting to convince others, and even himself, that he is functioning better than he actually is, does not detract from the basic phenomenon that confabulation in organic cases is employed only to fill memory gaps. On the other hand, in schizophrenia and in sociopathic personalities there are no memory gaps, and the patient employs confabulation for other dynamic reasons.

Patients in whom intellectual impairment is marked can confabulate on what you might call a "pay as you go" basis; a new confabulation appears in each situation and the whole phenomenon is fleeting, unorganized, and actually made up in your presence. In those still retaining a better preserved intellectual organization and probably also a somewhat different emotional structure, confabulation could very well become a more or less organized issue, it occurring more or less along with over-valued ideas or even a delusional process. For example, a Korsakoff patient could begin by telling you that he has been outdoors and, if questioned, that he went shopping although, naturally, he had not even left the institution. Then, that could congeal into the idea that he goes out shopping and visiting every afternoon, even though he actually never leaves the institution. This confabulation is not the same as conscious falsifying; the organic patient believes he is telling the truth and is often surprised when you question or correct his statements. But, in many chronic organic patients you will find confabulations are made up on the spur of the moment; they are fleeting and probably within an hour the patient no longer knows what he has confabulated and will then offer an entirely different story without perceiving any conflict between the different versions.

In connection with memory impairment, another initial

phenomenon noticed when a patient's intellect begins to fail is an *impairment of learning ability,* or ability to assimilate new material. Although he retains a certain amount of knowledge and utilizes it fairly well, the patient is unable to add to that knowledge because his ability to recall newly acquired facts is markedly impaired. (In older individuals this is a physiological issue and you must be watchful, naturally, not to confuse some amount of physiological impairment with that which is pathological. People's efficiency obviously gradually declines with age, individuals in a senile age group very often losing their ability to learn new things, but this physiological aging process usually never progresses as far as does that observed in persons suffering with pathological intellectual impairment.)

Needless to say, the finer intellectual functions, the patient's *retention of knowledge* and ability to manipulate his knowledge (which can be measured, for instance, by intelligence tests) become markedly impaired as the organic disease progresses. There is increasing impairment of the patient's ability to form any new associations or to even activate old ones. Eventually he is unable to answer even very simple questions taken from an elementary school book although his intelligence quotient may at one time have been average or far above average.

There are chronic organic diseases which first manifest interference in the personality organization on the emotional level or on the behavioral level while the intellect is still functioning quite well. We do not know, however, a single case of a chronic organic disease of several years' duration in which the intellect eventually does not become involved and intellectual deterioration does not occur. Therefore, before making the diagnosis of any chronic organic reaction, the patient must show intellectual impairments by the time the clinical symptomatology is full-fledged.

It is obvious that with this decline of formal intelligence there is also marked decline in the patient's personality functioning on the operational intellectual level. There is conspicuous impairment of planning and judgment and anticipation of events or needs. The person becomes unable to plan logically or in terms of the future. The entire planning process becomes reduced to planning from one day to another, and eventually instead of planning it becomes improvisation. Judgment becomes impaired in that the person who at one time handled tasks efficiently and well now begins to fumble and to perform those tasks in a rather inefficient, slipshod, and at times not quite logical manner.

Because intellectual impairment in a Korsakoff patient is so much more in the foreground when the patient has been sick for so long as to have reached a state of deterioration or dementia, it took considerable time before other changes in these patients came to be as carefully investigated as the intellectual impairment. Many of these patients, however, display quite marked emotional changes, and many display quite marked personality changes which are, naturally, measured mainly in relationship to the behavioral patterns of the society in which the persons live.

Alterations of the affective state—the second characteristic of the chronic organic syndrome—basically consist of *impairments* of *emotional regulation,* or emotional homeostasis. As in the acute mental disorder, emotional incontinence is an outstanding feature. These patients are unable to control their emotions as well as they could formerly, and under the slightest provocation they react with explosive emotional discharge.

In all this the patient *overreacts* to stimuli. If told a joke, he may carry on in a very hilarious manner and may laugh for a long time even though the joke should appropriately have provoked only a smile. In reverse, the patient becomes depressed and cries if told, for example, that an old friend of his died twenty years ago. Patients may become markedly sentimental or, in rare cases, very callous upon slight provocation. They overreact, the relationship between the provoking stimulus and the response being altered. Some patients are aware of emotional lability and even comment on it, stating that formerly they never responded emotionally in such an exaggerated fashion. Similar reactions are observed in infants, which is one reason why chronic organic patients, especially senile persons, are referred to as being "in second childhood." These exaggerated emotional responses usually *fluctuate very rapidly*; they emerge quickly and they die down quickly, all in response to internal or external stimuli. In the rapid emotional fluctuations a patient quite often displays a variety of affects; for instance, he commences to laugh, a few moments later he cries, then becomes angry, and so forth. A certain steadiness, a certain maintenance on an emotional level, is no longer present. Normal individuals, depending on their personality organization, have a certain affective equilibrium. When responding to external or internal stimuli with change of affective tone the changes are usually not very swift, provided the provoking factor is not great, and the person maintains a certain emotional equilibrium characteristic for his emotional personality organization. In organic cases the marked volatility in the emotional display is sometimes due to a specific environmental stimulation or event, but in some cases the patient is unable to offer any psychological explanation. In such cases we are dealing with emotional display phenomena which are, up to a point, on a neurological level.

The form of emotional incontinence which is usually somewhat motivated should not be confused with the very similar form of emotional incontinence in which peculiar emotional displays occur in the chronic organic patient without any volition on his part. This form is observed, for instance, in some atherosclerotic patients who have lesion patches bilaterally in the cerebral white matter. It is a neurological syndrome also observed in some thalamic disorders and quite often in persons suffering with pseudobulbar palsy. It moves on a neurological level. The patient cries or laughs involuntarily and without any apparent motivation. It is not considered a psychological disturbance, as are those cases of emotional incontinence due to impairment of the psychic emotional regulation, but the patient displays a forced laughing alternating with a forced crying without any psychological, or at least any obvious psychological, release factors being present. A patient simply states, "I have to do it." Bilateral white matter lesions may not be so extensive as to cause a fully developed pseudobulbar neurological syndrome, but in many chronic organic patients motor innervation is partially impaired. The patient may experience difficulty swallowing or perhaps some interference with his speech apparatus along with this rather forced emotional display of laughing or crying, indicating he lacks any influence over it whatsoever. The whole reaction simply runs its course as a release mechanism.

In some thalamic disorders, not only does emotional display appear without volition or motivation but the emotional experience is not present either. Such patients are aware of laughing or crying but do not experience doing so for any reason. They are considered release mechanisms due to removal of a neurological control function. It is a form of hyperpathy, similar to the hyperpathy of sensory pseudobulbar disturbance. Naturally, thalamic disturbances are very complicated in that there might be some motive factors there also. A few psychiatrists actually believe that the so-called forced emotional changes in Korsakoff patients are not true emotional changes, but are actually only released motor expressions as in a thalamic syndrome. It is very difficult to distinguish which is the fact because the patient actually does display a certain emotion even though he may disclaim feeling it. Here a peculiar dissociation mechanism is present, the origin of which has not been fully clarified. But, we must understand and assume that emotional regulation in most Korsakoff patients is somehow impaired. Whatever may be the cause, the clinical fact remains that these patients are emotionally incontinent in that they overreact and show sudden change in emotional display.

Another factor believed partially responsible for the swift changes in emotional display is the marked memory defect present in chronic organic patients. The stimulus which provoked the emotional response is forgotten very quickly and, naturally, the patient shifts to another emotional tone when confronted with another stimulus. This is particularly observed in Altzheimer's disease. The presenile patient will listen to a joke and laugh in an exaggerated manner. Then if you tell the patient something else, suddenly his whole jocular mood vanishes and his mood shifts. Then if you ask the patient, "What did I tell you that made you laugh a moment ago?" the patient will state, "I don't know." The patient's ability to retain newly acquired material is so impaired he cannot recall anything that happened only a few minutes before and so obviously the corresponding affect is no longer displayed.

In connection with these emotional changes, I would like to call attention to the fact that in chronic organic patients the affective responses are in harmony with the provoking stimuli. They are *stimulus-bound*. Paradoxical emotional responses do not occur. If you tell a chronic organic patient a joke, he will laugh; he will not cry. If you tell him something that should enrage him, he will be enraged. If you tell him something sad, he will be sad. An uncomplicated chronic organic case will display appropriate affect in relationship to the provoking stimulus, but two complicating factors can lead to exceptions to this rule. The first: If certain areas of the brain of chronic organic patients are injured, paradoxical emotional responses can occur, as, for instance, in patients having certain areas of the temporal lobe affected. Secondly (which is very common): If under the impact of the chronic organic process, schizophrenic features or even a full schizophrenic release can occur in a person with a so-called schizoid make-up. Highly mixed psychotic pictures are observed; all the attributes of the chronic organic process become mixed with other symptoms which, by our present knowledge, can be regarded only as schizophrenic, or at least schizophrenic-like, symptoms. In such cases one observes the paradoxical, inappropriate, disharmonic affective responses to stimuli so often observed in straight schizophrenia.

In many patients the emotional lack of regulation reaches such a degree that they display emotional outbursts formerly not displayed. These emotional outbursts are of great interest because they are somewhat different, dynamically and phenomenologically, from emotional outbursts observed in either schizophrenic or neurotic individuals. They often resemble, however, the emotional outbursts observed in sociopathic patients. It is not rare for a young individual suffering from an organic disease to be diagnosed as having a sociopathic personality simply because of his emotional outbursts. The outbursts are impulse reactions usually discharged under very slight provocation, and at times one even gets the impression that the patient pins the emotion onto some provoking factor as an excuse to discharge it. In other words, the provoking agent is not the true precipitating agent but is simply used as a tool for the patient to manipulate his emotional outbursts. It is undeniable that when frustrated or when somebody has put an obstacle before them, many organic patients have a very exaggerated emotional outburst. One of the most classical examples to demonstrate how such a person handles a situation is that of a patient suffering from motor aphasia. If you press him to speak and then begin to scold or ridicule him—it not even being necessary to do it excessively—the patient will suddenly fly into a state of rage to express his frustrations. Many organic Korsakoff patients display a similar tendency for rage outbursts and impulsive acts. Often, naturally, this is preceded by an irritability. These explosive outbursts are rather primitive reactions in the majority of cases. They are uncomplicated, simple, emotional discharges. The person may become noisy and shout and yell; occasionally he might even attack people. Sometimes, however, more complicated acts are committed in such a state, such as complex criminal acts, but generally speaking in an organic case (with the exception of special organic cases, as in epidemic encephalitis) a certain primitivity characterizes even such actions, for instance, as setting fires, committing burglary, and so forth. The act is badly thought out; it is usually poorly organized intellectually and is carried out in a rather impulsive manner. Special exceptions to this rule are cases in the early stage of organic disorder in which planning, good execution, and an organized attempt to discharge the emotional tension are made. Such cases are at times difficult to diagnose. However, in a demented or a deteriorated patient, the impulsive acts and emotional outbursts are definitely on a rather primitive and simple level, intellectually and emotionally.

I have discussed the lack of emotional regulation and the volatility of the emotional organization in patients suffering from chronic organic mental disease. This develops in the majority group, which is usually designated the simple deteriorating, or simple dementing, group. There are, however, quite a number of chronic organic patients who develop certain definite complicated emotional pictures as the intellectual deterioration progresses. These are persons in whom the emotions become "tilted" to one side, and remain so. In other words, besides having impaired emotional homeostasis, there is a *sustained emotional deviation* in one direction or another. For instance, quite a number of chronic organic patients constantly display a depressed affect, and others constantly display a rather manic or euphoric affect. Again, there are patients who display a paranoid attitude, or an angry irascible form of emotional reaction. This indicates that not all organic patients manifest simply a bland state subject to swift change of emotions; many of them display sustained emotional alterations very similar to those observed in many of the so-called functional psychoses. It is not rare to observe an atherosclerotic patient who is quite depressed, or to observe an atherosclerotic or paretic one who is quite manic, or again, to encounter one who is quite paranoid, all regardless of the organic etiology.

Therefore, be aware that you will encounter chronic organic patients with very marked, sustained emotional deviations. This emotional alteration can be so marked, especially in the early stages of the illness, that it obscures the intellectual changes present. Moreover, in a small minority (fortunately) of patients suffering from chronic organic mental disease, the symptoms of the disease are ushered in by these emotional changes and no intellectual impairment can be demonstrated, or can be demonstrated only by subtle methods, until considerable time has elapsed. These are usually the patients, especially if they fall into the younger age group, whose symptoms mislead so many psychiatrists. Such patients usually sail for a considerable time under the diagnosis of a functional psychosis or psychoneurosis until it is discovered they are actually suffering with an organic illness. The number of these patients is rather great and, I must say, they are not very flattering to the diagnostic acumen of many psychiatrists. It is obvious that because considerable psychic material can be obtained and the dynamics can to some extent be worked out, it is very easy to be trapped when diagnosing this type of patient if an all-round investigation is not done—particularly if the patients are deeply depressed, markedly manic, or display a markedly paranoid attitude. When any of these three particular states is profound, it is difficult to conduct a proper psychiatric examination because the emotional coloring of the picture and the emotional interference with the person's intellectual functioning are so great that it is very difficult to determine whether intellectual deterioration is present, whether intellectual regression is present, or whether simply an emotional interference is present which prevents the depressed, manic, or very paranoid person from functioning properly intellectually.

Why this emotional tilting occurs in these patients is not clearly understood. It does not occur in those simple dementing forms of chronic organic reaction in which the only emotional impairment is that of dysregulation. This group of emotionally "tilted" organic patients is very interesting not only from a clinical point of view but also from a theoretical point of view. There is actually very little factual evidence as to why, for instance, one patient suffering from general paresis displays his former emotional state simply with emotional incontinence thrown in, while another paretic patient gradually develops such a manic picture that he is diagnosed manic, and yet another patient develops paranoid or schizophrenic symptomatology. At least three or four *hypotheses* have been voiced in attempts to explain the emotional deviation phenomena, each offering some explanation without resolving the issue satisfactorily.

One hypothesis related it to the *rapidity of the organic process*. It was maintained that these different clinical pictures—manic, depressive, schizophrenic, and so forth—depend to some extent upon the rapidity with which the organic process moves. It is generally correct that slow-moving chronic organic pictures usually manifest a simple symptomatological picture, complicated pictures occurring more frequently in the so-called subacute forms. There are so very many exceptions to this assumption that this hypothesis is considered the least valid for explaining the different affective, or different so-called psychotic, colorings in the chronic organic reactions.

A second, the oldest hypothesis, attempted to explain that the *localization of the organic process* is responsible for the different emotional displays. It was maintained that impairment of certain frontal or temporal lobe regions leads to this or that picture. For instance, the manic picture was often described as a "frontal lobe syndrome," although we now know this is not correct. Along with the parietal lobe, the temporal lobe was also often accused of being the region which produces schizophrenic-like pictures. Usually such hypotheses are maintained for as long as some surgical operations have not been performed on the lobe in question; then they usually evaporate. However, it is presently recog-

214 DIFFERENTIAL DIAGNOSIS

nized that certain hypothalamic lesions and certain other lesions in the midbrain can produce affective changes, and therefore some possibility remains that localization of an organic process is capable of producing some forms of emotional change. As yet there is no conclusive data, but there are strong hints from mammalian brain research that probably localization of certain organic processes is connected to some extent with the emotional display in chronic organic reactions.

A third hypothesis attempted to explain that the *personality make-up* of the individual could also play a part in the emotional deviation. Arguments were put forward that the affective reactions occurring in the framework of an organic psychosis are actually based on the psychodynamic development of the individual's personality. According to this idea, the personality make-up lends a particular coloring to the organic picture; that although the patient is suffering from an organic psychosis alone, an additive paranoid, or manic, or depressive coloring is present. This hypothesis is rather suggestive and material can surely be demonstrated to support it. Again, however, there are many exceptions and therefore we cannot state that the hypothesis sufficiently indicates that the display of a particular affective picture is actually sequential to the previous personality make-up. (This must not be confused with the fact that an individual may be suffering at the moment with a so-called functional psychosis even in addition to the chronic organic psychosis present.) The question of the extent to which personality make-up influences the picture in chronic organic psychoses is of therapeutic importance. It is being investigated further in our experimentally produced psychoses studies *(Hoch, 1960, Hoch et al., 1952, 1953)*. Both the organic and the personality factors should be considered together in treatment procedures. For example, alcoholic hallucinosis should be treated as partly an alcoholic disorder and partly a schizophrenic disorder, there otherwise being absolutely no therapeutic results, most cases becoming chronic.

One controversial idea advanced to explain the origin of the emotional changes attempted to tie it to the particular *mental trend* reaction present during the psychosis. For instance, if the patient had delusions and hallucinations necessitating his being upset with depressive, paranoid, or whichever emotion was linked with them, those delusions and hallucinations had caused him to react emotionally as he did. This would imply that the delusional or hallucinatory mechanism actually originated on an intellectual level first and then produced a concomitant emotional change in the patient which corresponds with it. In other words, if a senile patient believes somebody stole her pocketbook, she becomes very upset and angry about it; the idea that she had been robbed originated first and then produced the emotion. This concept is to some extent feasible, particularly in patients suffering memory impairment or marked intellectual deterioration. On the other hand, observational evidence indicates that in most cases delusions and hallucinations originate on the emotional level and precede the ideations formed by the patient. Therefore, this hypothesis is acceptable only up to a point.

A fourth idea is termed the *release* hypothesis, indicating that the organic process releases in these individuals a manic-depressive, or a schizophrenic, or some other so-called functional psychosis to which the individual is hereditarily predisposed. This, again, naturally, is very open to discussion. Incidentally, this phenomenon of an underlying so-called functional psychosis being released by the organic disorder is not exactly the same as the phenomenon of the personality make-up lending emotional color to the organic picture—unless one should assume a functional psychosis to be nothing other than an exaggeration of the patient's personality make-up which is, naturally, an assumption not shared by all specialists. The phenomenon of organic release of an underlying psychosis is one of the most frequent sources of diagnostic error, particularly with regard to schizophrenia. When a schizophrenic episode appears in connection with another disorder, physicians do not wish to diagnose it as such; they attempt to avoid it by emphasizing the role of the organic releasing factors. One can do that, but should at least keep aware of the possibility of some underlying disorder. I will give you an example. Several years ago I was called upon to attend a doctor because he had suddenly threatened to kill his office nurse. At the time I arrived he was confused and somewhat disorientated. I also learned that he had been taking one of the sulfa-antibiotic drugs. After talking with him for a while, I observed that he expressed paranoid delusions and was having auditory hallucinations. It was a typical picture of the drug toxicity. My diagnosis was that of a toxic reaction with, naturally, the possibility of a released schizophrenic psychosis. The patient soon recovered and appeared to be well. A year later the patient's brother developed a full-fledged schizophrenic psychosis. Now, although we may see certain interrelationships present, nothing can be proven. Actually, the patient's episode could have been toxic; it could have been schizophrenic; it could have been a toxic reaction colored by his personality make-up. However, with the added factor of a schizophrenic brother I would not be surprised if the patient had a similar personality organization and that the drug had released a short-lived schizophrenic episode.

Of the many hypotheses which have attempted to explain why in some patients the chronic organic syndrome is colored by manic, depressive, or paranoid clinical manifestations, most observers preferred to assume that they were dealing with phenomena whereby either the different emotional pictures were due to the personality organization of the individual or, as has been especially maintained, that they were actually "release" manifestations.

I would like to stress the issue of these release manifestations because it is not only important concerning just one or another of the organic psychoses but also very probably has a general validity concerning all the organic psychoses. Organic psychoses were originally considered due purely to toxic-infectious, or to degenerative agents or to whichever agents commonly produced them. And, all the mental manifestations were attributed purely to the exogenic agent itself, particularly in those cases suffering from a toxic-infectious psychosis, or even from a metabolic or degenerative psychosis such as the atherosclerotic psychosis. More recent observations have indicated this to be only partially true. Quite a number of persons becoming sick with an organic psychosis actually become sick not alone due to the toxic-infectious agent, or not alone due to any degenerative or metabolic process, but because they are also actually predisposed to one of the functional psychoses. In other words, the organic process simply releases a dispositional psychotic mechanism which is already present. In what percentage of the organic psychoses this is true, we do not know. The fact, however, is important from a prognostic and from a therapeutic point of view.

To give a few examples, I have mentioned, for instance, general paresis patients whose intellect is only mildly affected may develop in addition to the dementing picture— or in some cases not even added onto the dementing picture but practically replacing it—a rather involved paranoid or paranoid-hallucinatory picture very similar to that observed in schizophrenia. Such patients are now considered "release" cases. Their prognosis and their response to therapy are usually far worse than that of the patients without such complications. Generally speaking, those release reactions in the more chronic rather than acute form have a worse prognosis, and the therapeutic endeavors are considerably more difficult.

In connection with alcohol toxicity, most psychiatrists have come to consider the alcoholic hallucinosis reaction an expression of schizophrenia. There is no discussion at all with regard to chronic hallucinosis; it is no longer considered by anybody as due to alcohol alone. Acute hallucinosis, also, has become more and more recognized as being a specific response to a toxin in those individuals dispositioned to develop that particular type of reaction. Ordinarily an alcoholic does not develop hallucinosis.

The postpartum psychosis is probably the best example to indicate changes of diagnostic opinion. Originally every postpartum psychotic reaction was attributed to either a toxic-infectious agent or to exhaustion. As toxic-infectious processes become less and less prevalent because of newer, more effective methods of treatment, fewer and fewer cases of acute so-called "toxic-infectious" postpartum psychosis are encountered. So-called "exhaustion psychosis" never was very well understood as an entity and, although a few cases may yet be diagnosed as such, I personally think it simply a "cover" diagnosis to hide our ignorance of what is occurring in these particular patients. What is meant by exhaustion? Most of the cases encountered are acute episodes of depression or schizophrenia which light up postpartum. Some occur as acute episodes only; others, however, become chronic. Here again, in postpartum psychoses you will very often encounter mixtures. The person may manifest delirious features which, however, will very soon assume perhaps a depressive or a schizophrenic coloring. Therefore, the ideas that every postpartum case is a very benign affair and that postpartum psychosis will always resolve very quickly are simply not correct. Many of these psychotic episodes are indeed serious. Furthermore, quite a number of them later display a full-fledged schizophrenic course and outcome.

Regarding head injuries, it was at one time assumed that if a patient suffers a concussion or a contusion and develops a psychosis in connection with it, this could really be considered a strictly organic psychosis. We now know that psychosis due to head injuries is extremely rare. Actually, the mental pictures observed have indicated that a considerable number of psychotic episodes following head injuries, especially those colored by other than simple dementing features, are, here again, release psychoses whereby the organic process lights up or touches off a process already present.

All this does not mean, of course, that an organic psychosis does not exist in the situations we have mentioned; organic psychosis exists in quite a number of those patients. It does mean that whenever dealing with an organic psychosis we must scrutinize its structure and organization very carefully, and we should not be satisfied in stating that simply because an organic process is present the psychosis is thereby purely organic. You will encounter quite a number of individuals in different organic situations who will, in time, impress you as having an organic psychosis which is not clear-cut but which is a mixture of an organic with some schizophrenic coloring, for instance, or later even becoming frankly schizophrenic. Therefore, the release reactions are important phenomena. Just how the release is accomplished nobody knows. Nobody knows the etiology of schizophrenia, and therefore nobody knows how the organic process can release it. Empirically, however, we have to assume that the released pictures are similar to schizophrenia. That these cases can really be considered cases of schizophrenia rather than simply cases symptomatically resembling schizophrenia can be assumed partly based on the fact that the personality structure, the dynamics, and many of the psychological responses of these individuals are very similar to those in people suffering from schizophrenia. In addition, a number of patients studied had one or more relatives suffering with full-fledged schizophrenia, although the patients themselves began to develop the schizophrenic psychosis only when it was triggered by an organic process—infectious, degenerative, metabolic, and so forth.

Despite all the hypotheses advanced to explain the origin of the emotional changes in chronic organic patients, we actually know very little about these phenomena. In this respect I wish to make only one final remark. When we study the marked emotional variations that can occur in chronic organic patients, and observe the tremendous lability of the emotional changes in response to stimuli, as is peculiar to these patients, one thing is learned: Because our study in psychiatry is still mainly based on phenomenology— since we know so little about etiologies, particularly of the so-called functional psychoses—analysis of symptomatologies indicates that seemingly the same etiology in mental disease can lead to different pictures and different etiologies can lead to the same pictures. This indicates that as long as the etiology of a disorder is not fully known it is often futile to speculate as to why or how a particular mental syndrome originates. For instance, patients suffering from general paresis are encountered with features so resembling schizophrenia, not only clinically but in response to complicated intellectual performance tests, that only a serology test determines the correct diagnosis. Another patient having the same disease may present a bland euphoric picture; a third patient might present a depressed picture; the fourth a manic picture, and so on. This all indicates that the various symptomatological pictures depend not on the etiology of the disease alone but that there are other factors involved which are as yet only partially known.

The third characteristic of the chronic organic syndrome is *change in the personality*. Varying in degree, these changes are prevalent in persons suffering from a Korsakoff syndrome. Very often they are the logical sequence to the intellectual impairment and the emotional changes, but occasionally they are the first conspicuous signs of an organic psychosis. There are persons who maintain their previous personality organization fairly well, and once in a while it is surprising to note that a person who is quite demented intellectually nevertheless maintains an excellent preservation of the presenting or superficial aspects of the personality and is even able to carry out many of the usually required social gestures. There are, however, persons who undergo marked personality impairment, particularly on the social level, and signs of behavioral regression appear. The person, for instance, becomes less inhibited than formerly, he displays behavior which appears to be incongruous to his previous personality make-up, he becomes sloppy, he fails more and more in carrying out routine matters, he becomes rude or obscene in public, and so forth. The control of the sexual drive is also markedly impaired in Korsakoff patients. They display erotic interests in public quite openly or try to carry out their sexual desires, of any kind, publicly. This represents a loss of restraint in addition to a lack of judgment.

These personality changes, in toto, have long been recognized. They usually are in keeping with the patient's previous personality organization, although they are often observed in persons who never had shown any inclination at all to any such type of behavior prior to their sickness. Therefore, an organic sickness can transform anybody into a regressed individual whose behavior can be socially unacceptable. These behavior changes are of great importance from a legal point of view as well as from a medical point of view. Incidentally, practically every day individuals are apprehended on criminal, including sexual, charges who are later discovered to be suffering from some form of an organic process.

In the majority of chronic organic cases the behavioral changes (similar to the emotional changes) are either concomitant with the intellectual impairment or else they follow it. In the latter case they usually do not offer diagnostic difficulties. But, they do offer diagnostic difficulties (as also do emotional changes such as irritability and emotional outbursts) when they precede the intellectual impairment, as is sometimes the case. The behavior is then usually explained in psychodynamic terms or quite often diagnosed and treated in some form of sociopathic or even psychoneurotic category, although actually it is the first sign of a serious organic disease. There are two disorders especially which manifest behavioral changes without simultaneously showing intellectual impairments: one is tumor of the frontal lobe; the second is cerebral arteriosclerosis.

On rare occasions a presenile psychotic patient manifests behavioral changes prior to intellectual impairments, but in most cases these symptoms either go hand in hand or else intellectual impairments precede the behavioral changes.

In common practice cerebral atherosclerosis and frontal lobe tumors often lead to false diagnoses when behavioral changes are the first signs to appear. The diagnosis usually made is that the person is suffering from a neurosis or is displaying sociopathic behavior. We all know about the celebrated case of Gershwin, who was psychoanalyzed for two years before a frontal lobe tumor was discovered and by then it was too late to do anything about it. Therefore the frontal lobe pictures are often misleading. The patient appears quite well with no intellectual impairments present, until suddenly he begins to display peculiar emotional changes, a disinhibition, or he slips up in some form of social behavior. The same type of phenomenon occurs in cases of cerebral arteriosclerosis, and early cases with atherosclerosis are occasionally characterized by behavioral and emotional changes at a time when intellectual changes are not as yet very marked.

General paresis, also, played havoc with many diagnosticians in former years. Since routine use of serological tests and effective early treatment have led to a rapid decline in the incidence of syphilitic processes in the brain (at least in the United States), it is no longer so conspicuous as a differential diagnostic entity. However, due to carelessness there will be an increase in the number of individuals suffering from general paresis, and therefore it must always be considered in persons who suddenly manifest gross personality changes, particularly middle-aged persons with a past history of being rather normal.

Although atherosclerosis, frontal lobe tumor, and

general paresis are the usual diagnostic pitfalls that can arise, there are a few others, naturally, but they are comparatively rare. It should be a standing rule, whenever a middle-aged or older person displays a change in personality, especially a change incongruent with his former personality organizational make-up, to first rule out the presence of any organic disease, because many disturbances of organic origin have remained for a considerable time under all types of functional designations. The diagnosis of a sociopathic personality, especially, should be avoided in persons in their late forties or fifties, because it never exists; not a single patient correctly diagnosed as being sociopathic would show onset of such behavior in middle age. It always reveals itself much earlier. The same rule applies to a number of neurotic patterns, with some reservations, naturally. We occasionally hear about well-integrated persons who, particularly under the impact of environmental stress, begin to develop a few neurotic reactions. But, if any patient who previously manifested no neurotic disturbances should then begin to display them at the age of fifty or so, be on guard, because quite often you have on hand a "pseudoneurosis" that represents a certain amount of decortication, disinhibition, and a lowering of integration in mental functioning which is usually the first sign of an organic disorder.

It is interesting to note that when an organic disorder arrives in a rather massive manner, insofar as the disintegration process in the patient is rather rapid, the so-called pseudoneurotic features are not usually observed. This holds true for the Korsakoff syndrome as well as for other organic disorders. Pseudoneurotic features do, however, appear quite often in patients when the organic process creeps along very slowly and when signs of organic impairment are subtle. This is also the reason why quite a number of organic disorders in which neurological signs are absent or not detected (for instance, multiple sclerosis, dystonia, and a number of others) are invariably diagnosed as cases of psychoneurosis; it later being discovered, naturally, that the patient is suffering from an organic sickness. Any type of gradual disintegration in a person frequently leads to clinical pictures similar to those observed in functional disorders. They are similar to those observed in individuals who would otherwise be diagnosed as psychoneurotic or sociopathic personalities. Or, occasionally the clinical pictures simulate a functional psychosis. Therefore, these behavioral pattern changes in chronic organic cases are of great importance.

This alteration and impairment of a personality pattern becomes more and more marked as the person's intellect deteriorates. He can lose all his social values as the disease progresses, which is frequently the case in paretic patients, in senile patients, and in any of the other chronic progressive organic processes which we are unable to influence.

In addition to the psychiatric picture, actually the great majority of patients suffering from a chronic organic psychosis have demonstrable *impairment* on a *neurological* and a *medical level*. Very often these patients voice certain subjective complaints. The subjective complaints are not necessarily present in all patients; those few organic patients who are euphoric usually do not complain of subjective symptoms. However, many Korsakoff patients complain of headache, dizziness, fatigue, sleep disturbances, impairments of appetite, and loss of sexual drive and potency—these are quite frequently the complaints. Here again, should such symptoms appear in middle-aged individuals with a fairly adequate history and past performance, it must never be immediately concluded that they are suffering from a psychogenic disorder. These patients must always be examined on all levels, otherwise very obvious mistakes can be made. Just as atherosclerosis and brain tumor can simulate so-called functional disorders, so can general paresis, and before serological tests were discovered it was appalling how many of these patients were diagnosed as suffering from some functional disorder. Obviously, this disorder can be picked up not only serologically but also on the basis of neurological signs usually long before psychotic symptomatology becomes so massive as to be labeled impressive.

Lesions in the Korsakoff syndrome (as in acute organic reactions) can be caused by any of a large number of *etiological agents*. I cannot enumerate them all and shall discuss only the most prevalent ones. General paresis, although at the present time of diminished importance, could actually be termed the classical form of chronic organic disease on which all the diagnostic and other problems can be studied very clearly. The second most important clinical group of chronic disorders is the arteriosclerotic and senile group. Presenile dementia, however, is not rare. There is also a small number of epileptic patients who have a deteriorating course culminating in a so-called epileptic dementia. Of the very large group of toxic disorders the most prominent toxin is alcohol. Actually, the alcoholic Korsakoff syndrome was the clinical prototype on which the chronic organic syndrome was erected, but many other toxins also produce this condition. To mention only one, carbon monoxide poisoning quite often produces not only extra-pyramidal system impairment but also Korsakoff-like pictures. Cases due to other toxins have also been described, such as the so-called bromide Korsakoff picture, which is usually reversible. It is rare, but nevertheless occurs. As in the rare cases of psychotic manifestations due to head injuries and a few other rare entities, disorders due to alcohol contain not only psychotic but also neurotic pictures.

In contrast to the *prognosis* of the acute organic reaction, which is favorable, generally speaking, the prognosis of the so-called Korsakoff reaction is usually poor. The chronic organic reaction mainly occurs in diseases that are progressive and that follow a deteriorating course which in many patients cannot be reversed. Actually, the prognosis in many of these cases was until recently considered quite hopeless. The situation changed considerably when effective treatment was introduced for general paresis, which to some extent reversed the course of that disease in many patients. However, particularly if we include the large number of senile dementia cases for which there is as yet no established therapy, the future for a patient belonging in the chronic organic group is not too bright. The alcoholic Korsakoff group, once considered a hopeless proposition, has recently become more "treatable," but we are still very far from having a very effective treatment for many of these patients. Nevertheless, for quite a number of patients something can be accomplished whereas formerly we were unable to do anything.

Having given this general outline of the acute organic and chronic organic syndromes, and before going into more detail with a few of the diseases mentioned, I would like to repeat that in some patients a combination of both an acute and a chronic reaction is displayed simultaneously. These cases are rare, but they nevertheless occur. The most prevalent so-called *combination reaction* is that of a patient suffering from a chronic organic disease—such as general paresis, or senile dementia, or atherosclerosis—who develops a superimposed acute process and enters into a delirious reaction. In some cases the acute process is produced by an entirely different etiological agent than that of the chronic organic process. For instance, when a senile patient develops pneumonia, he can develop a delirium on top of the chronic organic syndrome. In many cases, however, the acute and chronic reactions are both caused by the same agent, and the pathogenesis of the processes is not fully understood. It is not rare, for example, in cases of general paresis for a paretic patient to develop an attack of delirium in addition to the Korsakoff syndrome that he displays. This was attributed to acute intoxication due to a sudden destruction of a large number of spirochetes; it was attributed to an allergic reaction to the spirochetes or their by-products; and some observers actually blamed the arsphenamine treatment for this "Herxheimer" reaction, it being believed the drug suddenly liberated toxic products which produced a delirious reaction. Actually, this issue is not clear. It is the clinical observation, however, that sometimes delirious reactions occur in patients who suffer from an underlying chronic organic process. Similar phenomena can be observed in patients suffering from cerebral athero-sclerosis whereby a sudden change in the circulation due to intermittent claudications of the cerebral blood vessels can produce acute confusional and delirious states along with the chronic organic reaction in those persons. These cases are of interest and at times diagnostically difficult when the patient has this rather mixed-up symptomatology. The delirium can be so messy that you cannot wade through it unless you know beforehand that actually much more is present in the patient than an acute delirious reaction. Delirious reactions, furthermore, are generally very often precipitated in many truly organic patients due to some somatic or occasionally due to some psychic stress. Organic patients are much more susceptible to it than are ordinary individuals, and one frequently encounters patients in a senile, or atherosclerotic, or paretic state who develop some form of delirious reaction under the influence of an inter-current disease. Occasionally atherosclerotic persons under the influence of an emotional or other form of distress sud-denly develop some form of impairment of the cerebral cir-culation, and then a delirious reaction follows. Anoxia due to any cause, but particularly anoxia in older people due to circulatory impairment, often leads to delirious reactions that are then superimposed on the chronic organic picture already present.

9

GENERAL PARESIS

General paresis was at one time a common and very important entity. This disorder is generally considered a classical example of the chronic organic reaction type showing that which I have already discussed in a general way—the Korsakoff syndrome. I would like to mention some historical data concerning general paresis before discussing the clinical data.

HISTORICAL BACKGROUND

The first clear-cut description of general paresis was published in 1798 by John Haslam. Before this time occasional reference was made to it in the older literature, especially the Latin and Greek, but it did not contain any description of general paresis. The general idea was that syphilis, and that general paresis, which is a form of syphilitic disorder, did not exist at that time. The literature on syphilis is controversial. One school of thought believes that syphilis existed in ancient times, but was not diagnosed. Others maintain that syphilis did not exist in Europe and was "imported" later on. One thing is certain: If syphilitic disorders, which became so very conspicuous, had existed in ancient times they would most likely not have escaped the observations of early Greek and Roman physicians. Another possibility is that it had occurred only in a sporadic and fulminating way and was therefore not recognized until, as it happened over the years, it became epidemic and endemic, thus coming naturally to the foreground of attention.

For all practical purposes, general paresis was not described before Haslam *(6)*. Obviously, before the discovery of the spirochete it was not emphatically stated that all these conditions were due to syphilis, because that was not known. But the suspicion was nevertheless expressed that some of these mental disorders were due to syphilis and, particularly in the 19th century, a few astute clinicians demonstrated the fact that some mental disorders developed after syphilis infections, although they knew nothing about serology and did not know the pathology. Esquirol *(4)*, the outstanding French psychiatrist and follower of Pinel *(4)*, published in 1826 a rather good clinical and pathological study on general paresis. At the same time in England, Bayle *(4)* also described the clinical manifestations of general paresis in detail and at some length. Esmark *(4)*, a German physician, first expressed clearly from observations of clinical data on patients that the disorder was of syphilitic origin. This is of importance because, even though all the previous observers described some of the clinical symptomatology and also—in a crude way—the pathology in these disorders, they nevertheless did not express the view that these disorders are of syphilitic etiology. They stated them as "possibly" syphilitic, and in addition to syphilis they mentioned a lot of other etiologies. Even until the year 1910, textbooks on psychiatry contained statements that this disorder was "possibly" caused by syphilis. However, alco-

230 DIFFERENTIAL DIAGNOSIS

hol, sexual excesses, masturbation, worry, and many other things were listed also as possible causes. Therefore, the etiology was unclear. It became clear when the origin of the disease was discovered.

Next came the interesting experiments of Krafft-Ebing *(3, 4)* at the end of the 19th century. Krafft-Ebing, the Viennese psychiatrist and the predecessor of Wagner-Jauregg *(3)*, suspected general paresis to be of syphilitic origin; he attempted to infect patients suffering from general paresis with syphilis to demonstrate that it was impossible to do so. Based on this experiment he concluded that general paresis was syphilitic in origin.

Neuropathological studies at the end of the 19th century, particularly those of Nissl *(3, 4)* and also Alzheimer *(3, 4)*, demonstrated that we are dealing with a meningo-encephalitis. Even though they described certain features—such as the assimilation of plasma cells, a special glial reaction and ganglion degeneration—these observations were also made in some cases of meningo-encephalitis probably not of syphilitic origin, and thus they could not demonstrate conclusively that this disorder was syphilitic. However, their histological observations contributed sufficient neuropathological evidence, linked with some clinical observations, to indicate the presence of general paresis—which, in turn, meant syphilis. Nissl and Alzheimer worked in close collaboration with Kraepelin *(3)*; they were the neuropathologists in his clinic. Therefore, it is not surprising that their neuropathological studies were published at the same time Kraepelin published his clinical studies which describe general paresis in quite some detail.

The etiology of syphilis then became supported by two discoveries, namely, the Wassermann reaction in the blood in 1906 and in the spinal fluid in 1908 *(4, 7)*. This, of course, was prefaced by the discovery of the spirochete by Schaudinn and Hoffmann in 1905 *(3, 4)*. The discovery of the spirochete, however, did not immediately show the origin of general paresis because it was not easy to demonstrate the spirochete in a paretic brain with the older techniques. After a time, the discovery of the spirochete and the serological reactions, particularly the strong positive Wassermann reaction in the serum spinal fluid, indicated to most clinicians that they were dealing with a disorder of syphilitic origin. Finally the etiological chain was cinched in 1913 when Noguchi and Moore *(3, 4)* demonstrated the presence of spirochetes in the paralytic brain.

A treatment for general paresis did not exist. Many methods were tried without success. The introduction of the fever treatment was an important historical step. This revolutionized the treatment of general paresis and was the first great discovery in treating the psychoses on an organic level. In 1917, Wagner-Jauregg *(3, 7)*, the successor of Kraft-Ebbing at his University in Vienna, demonstrated conclusively that fever influences the outcome of general paresis.

These are the main historical data concerning general paresis. We are now able to add to this the discovery of penicillin; since studied extensively during World War II by Moore and Cutler *(1952)*, it has obtained paramount importance for the treatment of primary and secondary syphilis, although in general paresis it is of much less value.

INCIDENCE

A few general points should be mentioned concerning general paresis in civilized countries. In former years approximately 10 percent of all admissions to mental hospitals in the United States were persons suffering from general paresis. There were countries where the number of patients hospitalized with general paresis was much higher; yet, in others general paresis was so rare that it would be very difficult to demonstrate a case to medical students. This was due not only to improved treatment of general paresis, but also to the fact that syphilis was more reliably controlled and treated in its primary phase. In addition, many states instituted social hygiene programs which cut the incidence rate of syphilis considerably. Actually, in certain countries, such as the Scandinavias, syphilis was almost completely eradicated, and therefore any late manifestations such as general paresis did not appear. General paresis has slowly declined in the United States. Recent hospital census would probably show an admission rate of these cases no higher than 5 to 6 percent; it is conceivable that in about twenty years it would be as difficult here as, for instance, in Sweden to show a case of general paresis except for the fact that during wars syphilis again shows an increase in incidence.[1] Therefore, it is quite possible that a new crop of paretic patients will appear after their incubation period, provided newer treatments do not demonstrate the ability to prevent the occurrence of late manifestations of syphilis.

ETIOLOGY

General paresis is caused by the Spirochaeta pallida and nothing else. You may think this statement made today is very naïve, but it is worth mentioning that, as recently as 1948, some psychiatrists applying for specialty boards in psychiatry who were asked to name the etiology of general paresis replied it could occur based on masturbation or on alcohol.

The idea that alcohol or certain substances can produce general paresis should be discussed. There is an entity, termed the so-called alcoholic paresis; there is also an entity in which carbon-monoxide or manganese poisoning produces clinical pictures resembling general paresis. But there the similarity ends. In other words, chronic organic impairments can all appear alike, but be unrelated. For instance, if a person manifests an alcoholic pseudoparesis, he is an

[1] Since 1964 there has been a rising curve of syphilis; the U.S. Public Health Service has noted carelessness in prophylaxis on the part of the people and laxity on the part of doctors in diagnosis.—*Eds.*

alcoholic who has developed a chronic organic reaction. That alcoholism confused the diagnostic issue in a time when serological findings were not known and neuropathological techniques were only crude is, furthermore, even more understandable because so very many paretic persons drank heavily and so many alcoholics acquired syphilis. Mixed cases are not uncommon: There are alcoholics who develop paresis and there are paretic individuals who begin drinking heavily under the influence of their organically caused disinhibition, and then you have quite a combination on your hands. However, all this has nothing to do with the etiology of general paresis. General paresis is based on syphilis.

PATHOLOGY

As you know, in a very high percentage of persons the spirochete invades the nervous system during the second stage of infection. However, the majority of syphilitic persons are able to handle this invasion and only about 5 percent actually develop neurosyphilis. Two percent of those infected develop general paresis, which is a late tertiary or early quaternary stage of infection. In this form of syphilis the main involvement is in the parenchyma of the cortex, especially in the frontal and temporal lobes. The ganglian cells are severely diseased and diminished in number, there is a dense growth of glial fibers, perivascular infiltration of cortical vessels, and disturbance of cellular polarity giving a "windblown" appearance to the cortex. Degeneration of cells diffusely over the cortex, basal ganglia, and in fact over the entire brain, naturally causes marked generalized brain atrophy. In some types of paresis the diffuse degeneration includes the brain stem and occipital lobe with all the focal signs (Lissaur's type). In general paresis the meninges are also involved to some extent, but the characteristic mental impairment present is mainly due to the marked involvement of the parenchyma. Meningo-vascular lues is a tertiary form and differs from general paresis in many respects, except in etiology; luetic pathology is generalized over the meninges and lining of the ventricles, ganglion cells and blood vessels. It is an interstitial form of syphilis and the main involvement is vascular. This meningo-vascular form of syphilis occasionally may also lead to psychiatric pictures, but neurological disturbances are more commonly observed.

IMMUNOLOGY

Why some individuals develop general paresis and others do not, is not known. At one time this was one of the favorite subjects of speculation. However, even though we do not know the mechanisms leading to the development of paresis, treatment has become so increasingly effective that seemingly the question is of little focal interest. Actually, all the theories are reduced to two main concepts. One concept maintains that individuals suffering from general paresis have been infected by a special form of spirochete, a particular so-called neurotropic spirochete which produces general paresis. This idea has been generally abandoned. Another explanation for the development of general paresis is based on the idea that immunological manifestations in these individuals are different, and it appears that a person develops paresis because he has no power of immunity against the spirochete. This view was supported by quite a number of investigations and experiments and, although the nature of the particular immunity is not understood in detail, this is probably the theory shared by most syphilologists at the present time. In other words, it is generally assumed that patients who develop general paresis have a different kind of immunity against various spirochetes than those who do not.

If you consider that in the so-called secondary stage of syphilis 25 percent of the persons who have syphilis show not only an invasion of the central nervous system, but that the central nervous system is actually affected as well,

whereas only 5 percent develop neurosyphilitic manifestations, it is most likely that some immunological factors
play a role. Any variation in different races or in different
individuals in relationship to development of neurosyphilis
is handled today on the basis of immunity in general or on
special immunization of the general nervous system. That
such special immunities exist is surely correct. Seemingly,
some persons succumb to a syphilitic infection quickly, yet
others do not; whereas in some persons one form of syphilis
develops, and in other persons another form develops.
Although correct, we do not know how it happens. It is
probable, however, that it is linked with immunological
processes and not linked with different types of spirochetes.

It was also put forward that if you examine a large
number of patients suffering from neurosyphilis, you would
find that the skin reaction to the primary and secondary
form of syphilis had been weak, but in individuals in whom
the skin reaction had been rather marked, usually no neurosyphilis developed. This theory of the so-called "reciprocal
putting-in" of ectodermal tissues, of "the skin protecting the
nervous system," has quite often been apparent, although it
was never fully proven. The interesting fact remains that if
one examines a large number of patients suffering from
neurosyphilis, they protest convincingly that they had
never been aware of any primary manifestations nor
observed any secondary manifestations in themselves. Formerly it was assumed they were lying. Of course, many
patients do lie because they do not want to admit they were
infected with syphilis, but we now realize that not all are
necessarily lying, that many actually did not know they
were infected because the course of their infection was so
insidious and produced such slight reaction. Keep in mind
that both skin and nervous system are ectodermal structures
and show a strong relationship: From an immunological
point of view, most likely there is some connection between
this fact and the immunity reaction.

It has been assumed that those patients who are to

develop general paresis are usually sero-positive in the secondary stage and never lose their sero-positiveness after that. There are exceptions, however, to this rule. It is interesting that a number of patients who were treated in the secondary phase and who became sero-negative nevertheless developed general paresis. It is not even absolutely true that the majority of patients show an uninterrupted positive serology in blood and spinal fluid until the time general paresis develops. Many patients are refractory to antisyphilitic treatment insofar as their serology is concerned, but there are a number of exceptions. There are persons who were adequately treated, became sero-negative, remained sero-negative for a while, and later again became sero-positive and developed general paresis. Persons falling into this group are usually sero-positive for a considerable period of time before the psychosis appears. The serology of general paresis is very interesting and I will touch upon some of the highlights.

INCUBATION PERIOD

As you know, general paresis has a long incubation period and as a rule it takes ten to fifteen or even twenty years after infection before the disorder manifests itself. These figures are simply averages, and it does not mean that one will not run into patients who show upward or downward deviations from the mean. An occasional case arises in which general paresis develops two, three, or four years after infection. This is the minimal incubation period, and such rapidly developing cases are a rarity. It has never been determined, however, why some people develop paresis in two or three years and in others it is delayed for as much as thirty years. The so-called incubation period (probably "incubation" is not even the correct term) refers to the number of years that elapse before the psychosis manifests itself. During all this time the patient, naturally, has syphilis and changes are slowly taking place in the central nervous system until they eventually reach a severity that results in psychiatric manifestations.

EPIDEMIOLOGY

That paresis is much more common in males than in females is more a social phenomenon than a biological one. Many more males acquire syphilis than females. It usually manifests itself between the ages of twenty and sixty, most commonly developing in the forties.

This is not including so-called juvenile paresis, which is a special group composed of children or young adolescents who were infected *in utero* by a syphilitic mother, and then their syphilitic infection slowly progresses. They are congenital cases. (Formerly these were incorrectly termed "inherited" cases of paresis.) Incidentally, juvenile paresis is becoming very rare due to marked improvement in prenatal care given mothers; routine Wassermann tests are done and anti-syphilitic treatments are given to the syphilitic pregnant woman. Nevertheless, in any institution for the feebleminded or any mental institution, one always finds a few patients who begin to develop paresis around the age of fourteen; these juvenile cases were invariably infected during their embryonic life.

There are very interesting connections between general paresis and certain races which, if fully investigated, would probably lead to interesting immunological concepts. For instance, it was claimed that Mongolian races do not have general paresis. Similar statements were made about the Japanese, that at least they had much less general paresis than do Caucasians, even though syphilis was as widespread in Japan as elsewhere. However, that the Mongol groups do not have general paresis at all is a false observation. It has even been claimed that the Siberian-Mongolian tribes have no neurosyphilis, and a great deal was made out of this until the League of Nations sent a large commission to study these populations. They returned and stated that it was untrue that they had no neurosyphilis; in fact, general paresis was quite prevalent. However, some of these people showed a type of slow and insidious mental deterioration that did not become conspicuous, particularly because these people did not live on a very complex level of civilization and cases were not easily detected. About 10,000 serological specimens, along with neurological and psychiatic examinations on these patients, also demonstrated that they have quite a number of cases of general paresis, but it is possible that some Mongolian races, and the Japanese, do have a lesser incidence.

It has been stated that North American Indians show very little affinity for general paresis. Syphilis in its primary and secondary stages is prevalent, and it was therefore assumed they have a special immunity against paresis. The interesting thing is that other Indians in the Western Hemisphere have shown a rather fair incidence of paresis. The explanation for this has never been fully determined.

Quite a number of investigations were made on Negro populations both here and abroad. Neurosyphilis of the meningo-vascular form is much more common in the Negro race than in the white. General paresis is also more prevalent among Negro than white people. On the other hand, tabes is very rarely encountered in the Negro and is much more common among white people, which is rather interesting. There is no explanation for this, but there may be some special immunological factor involved. Although apparently some races have a different reaction to syphilis than others, you have to be very careful about making any sweeping statements because many of these findings can be explained by factors other than immunological.

General paresis becomes a social issue when we realize it is more prevalent in urban than in rural areas. Again on a social level, there are certain occupations which show greater than average susceptibility. Paresis is rather prevalent among seamen; it is rather prevalent among traveling salesmen; naturally, it is rather prevalent among prostitutes. Social factors are here involved, not immunological.

SYMPTOMATOLOGY

Three clinical phases can usually be discerned in general paresis: (1) the onset phase, (2) the full-blown picture, and (3) the terminal stage.

The onset phase presents two types of clinical pictures: the slow and insidious, which occurs in the majority of cases; and the sudden, which occurs in the minority of cases.

The *insidious* onset is characterized by alterations in intellect, behavior, and mood. Many patients display "pseudoneurasthenia" for a number of months or years. This pseudoneurasthenic stage is of special interest and is probably more important in many ways than the full-blown picture in that diagnosis of the full-blown picture is very rarely missed today because it is rather characteristic. The person suffers from a chronic organic disorder, and naturally the routine employment of serological and neurological investigative methods discloses the diagnosis quickly. On the other hand, within this so-called pseudoneurasthenic stage, the preliminary stage before the patient develops a full-fledged psychosis, quite a number of mistakes are still being made in diagnosis. Interestingly enough, these mistakes are made not so much by the hospitals as by the private practitioners. Hospitals perform a routine Wassermann (or at least they should), but private psychiatrists usually do not and here you occasionally run into the peculiar situation whereby the patient is treated for quite some time as a psychoneurotic.

Only recently I interviewed a patient who had been analyzed for two years. The analysis ended when she went into a full-blown paretic picture, which was naturally a little embarrassing to the analyst. This situation is duplicated frequently. Such cases are not good testimonials for the clinical ability of the analysts. Disregarding clinical ability, which all of us can slip up on occasionally, there were indications in the case mentioned which would have definitely necessitated the carrying out of a Wassermann, thus disclosing the whole thing. To mention, as another example, an analyst could be treating a person who had typical pupillary disturbances: The analyst sat always behind the patient, naturally, and not until he looked at the patient for the first time—I don't know when that would be—might he observe a definite mydriasis of one eye. It should have been observed clinically in the first five minutes of treatment. The complaints of such a paretic patient are not characteristic; symptoms are diffuse and, if there is no other supportive evidence, could very well be mistaken for those of a psychogenic disorder.

In the pseudoneurasthenic picture, the symptoms are based on luetic infection of the brain and the mental symptomatology is insidious. Very often the patient's initial complaints are not on a mental but on a physical level. These patients will complain about headache, pressure of the head, shifting aches and pains, easy fatigability, decrease in sex drive and potency, lack of stamina, insomnia, poor appetite, disturbance of sleep, loss of weight, and that their equilibrium is not as good as formerly. And then, vague mental complaints emerge such as loss of interest, inability to concentrate, irritability, and moodiness. They sound like neurotic complaints; and sometimes, especially in younger persons in whom paresis is not immediately suspected, they are even accepted as neurotic complaints.

Thus, a rich symptomatology can develop which superficially appears very much like a psychogenic disorder. In this stage patients do not usually show marked intellectual impairment and the emotional changes are in the realm of some type of psychogenic disorder. Therefore, if a middle-aged individual begins to complain of neurotic-like symptoms for the first time, it certainly could be an involutional process, it could be a psychoneurosis, or it could be one of a number of disorders. But we have to think about it! These vague symptoms could very well be signs of some developing organic disturbance, among which general paresis could be one—and one which is very easily clarified by means of a serology test. Furthermore, you must realize that even though the organic process can in itself produce so-called pseudoneurotic manifestations, a considerable number of neurotic individuals will also develop general paresis, and then naturally you observe a quantity of neurotic material emerging under the impact of the organic disintegration.

In addition to the pseudoneurotic symptoms mentioned, the patient may begin to complain about failing memory, inability to concentrate, and diminution of his judgment acuity. But many patients are not subjectively aware of this intellectual impairment and will attempt to prove to you that it is not so. In some patients there is a depression of mood, or a slight euphoria, a certain form of *laissez-faire,* and a careless attitude toward things. Many show a peculiar lack of foresight and impaired judgment in family affairs. Others suffer with apprehensiveness and brooding about the future. It is a frontal lobe syndrome. (We have evidence for this from frontal lobotomy performed on individuals with these symptoms.) Sometimes these finer functions are impaired before gross memory defects or other impairment of intellect occur.

The emotional drive in some of these patients becomes less and less. This is also a frontal lobe symptom. It can lead to frontal akinesis and occur in an impaired emotional state, but often there is merely a certain slumping of emotional "push." The patient and his family may report this as a sign of being "overworked" or "in the climacteric." Gross emotional changes also develop in that the patient is no longer able to control or organize his emotions. Some of these patients show an increase in suggestibility, just as is observed in many other organic disorders, and, combined with their lack of judgment, they are easily persuaded to get entangled socially, sexually, professionally, and so forth.

At first all these alterations are slight. They do not all

appear at the same time. The clinical picture varies with each individual. In some cases the emotional alterations occur first and intellectual defects develop later; in other cases it is the reverse. Or, there are those patients who manifest behavioral changes first; they may show a sudden loss of judgment, temper displays, decreased moral organization—such as the fifty-year-old man who will suddenly have the irresistible urge to attack children. Sometimes a heterosexual man of this age will suddenly begin to have homosexual relationships, or an individual who had always been honest will suddenly begin to embezzle.

The phase of onset described usually progresses into the second phase of paretic symptomatology—the full-blown psychosis—and this then goes over into the terminal stage of the disorder. The so-called pseudoneurasthenic, or pseudo-neurotic, form of insidious onset is the most common, but there are other types of onset that you should know about. Some psychiatrists have been so impressed by the slow and insidious development of a chronic organic reaction that they overlooked the fact there are numerous exceptions to the rule. In other words, symptoms in general paresis may have a sudden onset.

A *sudden onset* of psychiatric manifestations may be such that the patient actually impresses you as suffering from some acute organic reaction. In these cases the diagnosis is usually missed, particularly when the outbreak is precipitated by factors other than syphilis such as drugs, head injury, infection, and so forth. Usually the sudden type of onset occurs five to thirty years after the luetic infection, the average period of time being about fifteen years. Onset occurring in less than five years is rare, and often it is tertiary lues instead of paresis.

The sudden onset can show a number of different psychiatric pictures. Some cases show symptomatology of a delirium, others appear as an acute manic attack. The onset can also appear in the form of acute neurological manifestations. For instance, an apoplectic form of attack or paralysis of certain eye muscles can occur, which are only temporary. These are more common in the meningo-vascular form of syphilis but can also occur in general paresis, in which case they usually appear together with, or slightly before, the psychiatric manifestations.

By the time the patient shows either the sudden or the insidious development of psychiatric symptoms, neurological manifestations are usually present and can be detected upon examination. (And, naturally, it is obvious that the sero-logical manifestation is present before any of these psychi-atric or neurological symptoms—if only someone would think to look for it.) When present, the neurological mani-festations feed the outlet of the mental symptomatology, and therefore that would also probably be disclosed if the patient were examined neurologically. This examination does not necessitate any involved or great neurological knowledge and can be done in five minutes flat.

Neurological manifestations usually observed are an involvement of the pupils. It is present in practically all patients. Most common is the nonresponse to light and accommodation. Next common is the so-called Argyll-Robertson pupil: the patient's pupil is stunned and does not respond normally to light, but only to accommodation. Whenever a patient's pupils are small, unequal, irregular in outline, and respond sluggishly to light, this observation should always automatically provoke an immediate sero-logical examination. These pupillary signs occur in other disorders too, but they are most common in general paresis where the pupils are rarely normal. Other impairments usually found are exaggerations of knee and ankle jerks, or quite often the opposite, namely, the absence of them. These findings are not rare, especially when the paresis is com-bined with tabes. Taboparesis is a rather common entity and usually the tabes foreruns the paresis. Naturally, everything found in a tabetic individual—the absence of knee and ankle jerks, ataxia, the impairment of deep sensitivity, and many of the other sensory disturbances which appear in tabes—

are present in a paretic individual. Later on, paretic patients also show other neurological signs such as a peculiar tremor in the muscles of the face, tongue, and hands, and an impairment of coordination that is quite clearly discernible in the finger-nose or in the knee-heel test. Speech becomes impaired in the form of slurring, and usually words or syllables are transposed, mixed up, or duplicated. Writing also becomes sloppy and shows manifestations similar to those in the speech. Haptic atrophy is also not uncommon.

Along with psychiatric and neurological manifestations, in early paresis many patients show medical disorders, a few of which I shall mention in passing because they are important in connection with treatment. For instance, syphilitic involvement of the cardiovascular system, including peripheral blood vessels, is not uncommon. Blood pressure is often increased. There are often transient focal cortical signs of vascular damage. Quite a number of older patients already show evidence of cerebral arteriosclerosis and, as we know, arteriosclerosis and syphilis are closely allied as vascular disorders; they both damage the vessels. Syphilis can damage the vessel walls, making them easily prone to becoming sclerotic.

In the second phase of general paresis, the *full-blown phase,* the clinical picture is easy to diagnose, even should the etiology not be clinically offered. When the disorder has progressed into this phase, we usually observe that which I have described as the chronic organic reaction—the Korsakoff syndrome. Along with the common features, the paretic individual may show a variety of typical paretic features. Intellectual impairment is obvious, but occasionally the emotional changes are so strong as to confuse the picture for a short time. Intellectual impairment usually consists of disorientation, memory defects, lack of insight, and lack of judgment. There is one small group where it is hard to demonstrate this, namely, the paranoid group. In these patients the clinical symptomatology is so similar to that of paranoid schizophrenia and the intellect seems so well preserved that diagnosis is made only by means of serology.

There is progressive dementia. It is in a different emotional setting in different individuals and there are many variations. The spirochete can produce clinical pictures which everybody would label as definitely psychotic, and the organic nature of it could be overlooked unless one actually knew the etiology. In discussing the intellectual deterioration, we must take into consideration the various types of symptom pictures: the simple deteriorating form, the expansive form, and others.

The so-called *simple* deterioration, or simple dementia, is quite characteristic of a number of paretic patients. To be exact, 40 percent of them show this simple deteriorating form. The term "simple" means nonproductive; there is a slow, bland intellectual decline. There is a poverty of ideas, memory defect, lack of intellectual capacity and performance, and a shortening of associative ability. A display of carelessness and a slow deterioration of the whole performance of the person are the outstanding features. Usually the person shows no gross emotional disturbance except perhaps euphoria and diminished emotional regulation, but no expansive psychotic picture. Memory defects, especially those in the realm of recent memory, are common and progress to include the more remote memory realm. Initially, the person has some impairment of orientation but it is not marked; it is patchy. Later on, when the dementia becomes profound, naturally the disorientation is of some magnitude.

Therefore, the mental picture is that of a typical Korsakoff syndrome whereby the person shows an intellectual dementia which becomes more and more progressive if he is not treated. These simple cases of paresis show only a simple form of dementia which ends in nearly complete decerebration. The person actually loses his whole intellect and sinks to a simple vegetative level at which every form of thinking, memory, ability to speak and deal with even the simplest tasks is eliminated. Naturally, emotional changes are a progression of those observed in the early phase of paresis; there is marked emotional lability and emotional incontinence. Formerly these pictures were common, but due to present-day treatments given in the early phase we do not see them very often.

In addition to these so-called simple dementia pictures, there are forms of paresis which remind us of manic, depressive, and various types of schizophrenic disorders. The grandiose and *expansive* symptomatology was formerly very common and considered the classical picture of general paresis, but at the present time it comprises only about 15 percent of paretic cases. In this manic-like form, the individual shows intellectual impairment accompanied by exuberance, manic flight of ideas, motor restlessness, grandiose ideas which are stupid and badly organized. Very often the delusions of grandeur are somehow connected to a vaguely felt underlying sense of inferiority. As examples of this grandiosity connected with the feelings of inferiority, there are the impotent men who have delusions of sexual prowess, the obscure men who have the so-called Napoleon complex, and so forth. However, in many cases, perhaps the elevated mood swing is sufficient dynamic explanation for many of the grandiose ideas. Be on guard in patients around fifty to fifty-five years of age who suddenly develop a manic picture. If it first occurs in the early forties it can be simply manic-depressive psychosis, but not necessarily so in the fifties. This expansive picture with intellectual speeding up is sometimes so great that the intellectual deterioration behind it is overlooked; the factor of intellectual deterioration differentiates it from the manic-depressive psychosis. Paretic delusions are outright primitive and stupid—too stupid to be on a psychogenic basis. (Occasionally schizophrenic delusions are of this order but better logic is displayed.) Many of the delusions are obviously contradictory and they shift in content. There is a lack of perseverance and the contradictions are openly stupid. There is no display of ambivalence and it is usually an organic picture.

Why the clinical picture in paresis has changed so that the expansive form is no longer common, nobody knows. Nobody knows if these expansive pictures actually were more prevalent at one time or were simply emphasized and favored in psychiatric literature and lectures because they offered such nice conspicuous descriptions of delusions and other entertaining symptoms. It was at a time when psychiatry in medical schools was considered more a circus, and naturally an expansive paretic patient afforded a very interesting demonstration. However, some psychiatrists maintained that this was not the issue, but that the clinical picture of paresis actually has changed. (As you know, changes have taken place in the clinical pictures of the psychoneuroses over the years, but nobody knows just why and how these changes came about.) Some physicians also put forward the idea that those individuals who would ordinarily have developed the expansive form of paresis were the ones who responded very well to anti-syphilitic therapy, and therefore these pictures develop less frequently.

In the *depressive* group of paretic psychosis many patients show a straight picture of depression. Sometimes the depression is so deep that, there again, it covers the signs of intellectual deterioration. Patients have delusions and hallucinations in accordance with their mood; the delusions are not of grandeur unless in an inverted form, such as "I have no nerve, and therefore I can't live." Again, these are much more stupid and less organized than in patients suffering from a nonorganic depression. Many somatic delusions are often quite bizarre. For instance, a paretic patient will tell you he believes he has no bowels, or that he has no lungs, no heart, or no brain—nihilistic delusions which can also occur in a straight depressive picture. If, however, you ask the paretic patient to elaborate, he will not be able to do so or else his arguments will begin to be childlike and not the arguments of a depressed patient who would be able to marshal a rather logical interpretation for these things, provided he is not too retarded by his depression to be able to think clearly. In other words, there is a difference in the way these delusions are handled, even though there may be similarity in content. A nonparetic depressed patient will tell you, for instance, that he has no "guts" because something has happened to his body; he will be able to give you a fairly elaborate picture of how his "guts" were eliminated. However, a paretic depressed patient will tell you, "My guts have rotted away," and if you ask him how this was accomplished, he will shrug his shoulders and say, "I don't know—but it is so." *Hypochondriacal* preoccupations are also common in depressed paretic patients, and again the ideas are put forward with a not very great intellectual ability, obviously corresponding to the mental deterioration picture in these patients.

In the *paranoid* form of paresis, delusions are expressed in the same way as in other paranoid states: They are being followed; they are being poisoned; they will be killed, or similar ideas. Here again, the elaboration of these ideas is not very good. Usually the stupidity and non-organization, the elasticity and lack of "set," are characteristics of this, an organic psychosis. However, some paretic patients falling into this paranoid group will surprise you by the fact that they are intellectually fairly well-preserved. An inverse relationship exists between paranoid response and the tendency toward deterioration. As you will also observe in schizophrenia, the more organized the paranoid elements that enter into a psychotic picture, the less the intellectual impairment. However, the emphasis is on *organized* paranoid material, not on fleeting paranoid ideas. Fleeting paranoid ideas can occur in a very deteriorated person, but to put forward an organized and logically elaborated paranoid system requires an intellect.

Some of the paranoid elaborations are naturally the work of good intellect, but wrongly applied. Here too, there is an inverse relationship. The more organized the paranoid picture, regardless of the psychotic setting, the less the person shows deterioration and the less prone he is to deterioration. In schizophrenia this is quite clearly observed; fleeting paranoid ideas can occur in any form of schizophrenia—catatonic, hebephrenic, and so forth—but the organized, well-elaborated, and fairly logical delusional systems of the paranoid schizophrenic patient occur only in schizophrenic individuals whose intellect is not impaired and who usually, if they deteriorate, do so very slowly and rather late in the disorder. Interestingly enough, a somewhat similar relationship also exists in the organic psychoses. If one has observed a patient suffering from general paresis who shows organized paranoid pictures—again emphasizing organization—one finds this paretic patient to have a surprisingly good intellectual faculty and intellectual impairments are not very marked. If such patients are not examined fully—meaning neurologically and serologically in addition to the psychiatric examination—they are often diagnosed "paranoid schizophrenia" or "paranoia," and the fact that they are actually paretic individuals is overlooked. Surely they do show intellectual impairment when examined, but it is usually not so marked as is customarily observed in the simple form or in the other forms of general paresis.

In addition to delusions, sometimes hallucinations develop in the full-blown paretic picture. These hallucinations are often very much in the background in general paresis. Naturally, any form of hallucination may develop—visual, auditory, tactile, somatic, and so forth. Auditory hallucinations usually occur with the paranoid picture. Visual hallucinations occur sometimes in the expansive depressive picture. The simple form usually does not have hallucinations. Actually, in general paresis hallucinations are comparatively rare. However, massive hallucinatory and delusional episodes occasionally do occur in patients suffering from general paresis similarly as in other organic disorders.

I have mentioned that occasionally *delirious* or *confusional states* are superimposed on the chronic organic reaction picture. This is not rare in general paresis; the patient who progresses in the simple deteriorating form of impairment may suddenly become markedly disoriented, markedly confused. This superimposed confusional picture sometimes remains. Most often, however, it disappears. In other words, suddenly a massive picture appears which impresses you as a delirium with disorientation and hallucinations—visual, auditory, and so forth—and usually after a while it will pass. These delirium states sometimes appear spontaneously ("spontaneously," because we have no clue why they come on). Sometimes, however, they are in relationship to physical, or even emotional, happenings in the patient. It is not rare, for instance, that when a paretic patient develops pneumonia, or drinks, or fractures his leg, suddenly an overlying delirious picture develops which later subsides.

In the past when anti-syphilitic drugs were used extensively in the treatment of general paresis (although they had very limited value) sometimes similar secondary phenomena were observed. The so-called Herxheimer reaction was also observed in some of the paretic patients. It was assumed that a sudden liberation of toxin was achieved due to changes in the immune balance between the spirochete and the organism and that this produced the delirious state. How true this theoretical explanation is, we do not know. With the more modern treatments it is not observed. However, I would like to call attention to the fact that during the fever treatment of some of the paretic patients such delirious reactions could occur.

Excitement states are also common in general paresis. They are massive outbursts which may or may not occur in relationship to a paranoid hallucinatory episode. Catatonic manifestations have also occasionally been observed and described. The precipitating factors for these states are not fully clear. Some observers believe they are release manifestations. Others, however, believe they are actually manifestations of frontal lobe or extrapyramidal impairment. In other words, some consider them psychiatric pictures and others consider them neurological pictures.

Finally, I would like to call attention to the so-called *paralytic attacks*. These paralytic attacks are frequently observed. "Paralytic attack" is an overall term for various neurological manifestations that sometimes occur either simultaneously or as individual phenomena. Some patients, for instance, suddenly throw an epileptic fit which is due to cortical or subcortical irritation. Instead of a fit, some paretic patients have a sudden apoplectic attack, usually a monoplesia, a hemiplesia, a paralysis of the eye muscles (most commonly the oculomotor nerve is involved), or a facial paralysis. The characteristic thing is that these neurological impairments are usually fleeting and disappear fairly quickly. They sometimes occur in connection with epileptic manifestations and sometimes alone. They can occur when the patient's consciousness is unimpaired or, similarly as in any apoplectic attack, when the person loses consciousness. Occasionally, either alone or in relationship to apoplectic attacks, we see the development of agnosia, apraxia, and aphasia. Agnosias are often overlooked because the patients are not examined very carefully. Apraxia is completely obvious when you see the person fumbling around. Aphasia is also readily detected; it is more massive and could be of a motor, sensory, or combined type.

Usually these neurological impairments are fleeting. However, they may remain permanent, particularly after the patient has had one or two such attacks. This is a form of general paresis, described by Lissauer, showing permanent focal neurological impairments that are not mainly localized in the frontal lobes (which are usually the most affected parts of the brain in general paresis). The Lissauer form of general paresis is mainly characterized by focal signs of aphasia due to involvement of the temporal, apraxia due to involvement of the parietal, and agnosia due to involvement of the occipital lobe. Sometimes these focal manifestations develop first, and naturally they can raise questions diagnostically unless someone thinks to examine the patient carefully neurologically and serologically.

The final diagnosis rests with the serology; in most cases all the tests are positive. Usually there is increased flocculine and pleocytosis in the spinal fluid, and the colloidal gold test shows the paretic curve. But the paretic curve appears in other conditions, too, and this test alone should not be considered valid. Occasionally the serology is negative, but this is extremely rare. Occasionally only the spinal fluid serology is positive and the blood serology is negative, but this also is very rare. The serology is usually strongly positive in both the spinal fluid and blood.

Before penicillin treatment was introduced, in 99.9 percent of the cases the general paresis progressed, and after about two or three years these persons died. They usually died in the third phase of general paresis, the so-called *terminal stage,* whereby almost a complete decerebration was achieved; the person's intellect was practically gone, his speech dulled and—as the term paralysis indicates—the motor function of the extremities was also largely impoverished. We do not see these pictures today, but I remember observing several cases in the past in which the deterioration was incredible; such individuals showed practically complete decortication, whereby the person was practically unable to tell his own name and would only be simply lolling a few syllables whenever approached. They usually lie in bed curled up like embryos, with stiff arms and legs, practically paralyzed, incontinent, showing all primitive reflexes such as sucking, grasping, and so forth, as is observed only in decorticated individuals. In this condition they usually die of inanition because they are unable to take food, of pneumonia, or of some other intercurrent disease.

I would like to mention that in addition to brain impairment these patients naturally show many other changes in the body which we do not have time to fully enumerate. For instance, the bones are affected; they are usually quite brittle. Vegetative metabolic changes are profound and syphilitic fibrosis of the internal organs sometimes develops. The cardiovascular system is quite often involved; syphilitic aortitis is present in the majority of cases, and arteritis of the smaller vessels is usually present. Therefore, general paresis is a very serious disorder of the total individual, with brain involvement playing a large role.

DIFFERENTIAL DIAGNOSIS

General paresis may clinically resemble many other disorders including frontal lobe tumor, presenile psychoses, chronic metallic poisoning, multiple sclerosis, cerebral arteriosclerosis, chronic alcoholism, schizophrenia, neuroses, and so forth. Serological tests usually rule out these other disorders unless, of course, they should occur concomitantly. For instance, the clinical picture in paresis sometimes resembles that of arteriosclerosis, and in many cases the two disorders are present in combination. After all, both alcoholic and syphilitic individuals have a predilection for secondary development of arteriosclerosis. As has been mentioned, paresis can also be confused with certain other syphilitic disorders, especially tabes and meningo-vascular syphilis. These I shall discuss briefly.

Tabes was considered to be a special entity in the past, but so-called "tabetic psychosis" is no longer recognized as such. Often there are psychotic manifestations in which tabetic and paretic signs occur together—so-called tabo-paresis. Occasionally an individual shows only tabetic neurological manifestations along with neurasthenic symptomatology. This gives rise to the question, are these psychological symptoms only a reaction of the patient to his having tabes or are they signs of oncoming paresis? Very often oncoming manifestations of paresis slowly develop, but it happens just as often that the tabetic individual develops all sorts of neurotic symptoms and years go by without these symptoms being followed by those of general paresis. We now know that these are individuals showing the early signs of general paresis.

On the other hand, in some cases the neurotic symptoms are simply a reaction to the impact of the tabes on the mind of the individual and indicate his attempts to cope with the fact. Each individual psychologically reacts in his own way; this is a secondary reaction to the tabetic disorder. For instance, if he feels a social condemnation for having syphilis, he may react with a paranoid picture; he will tell you he is discriminated against, or he may project his own ideas onto the environment. This is rarely linked with the presence of any schizophrenia in the individual. Usually the delusions in tabetic patients are not expansive, but are logical and center around the sensory symptoms which the organic disorder presents. To label this a "tabes psychosis" is not warranted because actually it is just the person's psychological inability to cope with his organic disorder.

Every now and then one encounters a syphilitic patient who manifests a "syphilophobia." If a tabo-paretic individual wants to remain ignorant of the fact that he has syphilis or wants to hide the possibility from others, he might express a fear of contracting, or having contracted, syphilis. Do not be misled into assuming that this is merely a phobia and therefore rule out the fact that he may have syphilis. He may very well have it.

Meningo-vascular syphilis is a tertiary form, whereas general paresis is quaternary. Symptomatology in these two forms may overlap, depending upon which nervous system structures are involved and the individual's immunological reaction to the spirochete (as expressed in the serology). Meningo-vascular syphilis can be differentiated from general paresis by the following factors: First, symptoms in meningo-vascular syphilis usually develop within four to six years after the initial lesion. In general paresis the symptoms usually do not appear for about fifteen years. Second, the meningo-vascular picture is preeminently neurological and few individuals develop psychiatric manifestations. Third, when psychiatric manifestations do appear, they are mild; they generally consist of irritability, diminished judgment, poor memory, and complaints about organic symptoms. There are cases of meningo-vascular syphilis which show a paretic picture of simple dementia in the absence of neurological signs, and yet these individuals are not suffering from general paresis; their serology is not so intensely positive and the patient responds well to anti-luetic treatment, which is not the case in general paresis.

TREATMENT

Since the advent of penicillin, therapy for general paresis has changed markedly.[1] Formerly, chemical agents and fever therapy were inadequate and prognosis was very bad. As you know, penicillin is a highly effective drug in primary, secondary, as well as early tertiary syphilis. In the primary and secondary stages, treatment is nearly exclusively done with penicillin, thus replacing all other antisyphilitic agents formerly used. If the person suffering from syphilis is rendered sero-negative with penicillin treatment, the possibility of a late syphilitic development is probably greatly diminished. However, quite a number of reliable physicians contradict this view and state it requires further proof.

There are conflicting opinions regarding treatment of general paresis with penicillin. Many syphilologists and psychiatrists who use this treatment extensively maintain that equally good results are reached with penicillin alone, without support from fever or antisyphilitic drugs, as was accomplished by means of fever therapy. The trick is, however, to give much higher doses of penicillin than is usually required in other disorders. Originally, paretic patients received five

---

[1] Since Dr. Hoch made these comments on treatment, not much change of view has occurred, according to the 1969 U.S. Public Health Service reports.—*Eds.*

to eight million units; today they receive twenty million units, and probably this dose will go even higher.[1] Furthermore, despite higher penicillin concentration in newer preparations, it must also be taken into consideration that a resistant spirochete is likely to evolve.

PROGNOSIS

At the present time, the results with fever and penicillin treatment of general paresis show that roughly one-third of the patients treated have good remission in that they seemingly recover or are much improved; one-third show slight improvement; one-third remain unimproved or die. Evaluation of prognosis from a psychiatric point of view—disregarding the presence or absence of any physical manifestations in other parts of the body—is based on two important criteria. One, the *duration* of time that the patient has manifested psychotic symptomatology. The earlier a patient having psychotic symptoms is treated, the better the results. Therefore, patients who are caught serologically before they develop any, or only slight, mental symptoms have a very good chance prognostically. However, if the paralytic mental process has progressed for a considerable time, the chance of recovery is not good and such patients are cured only insofar as further progression of symptomatology is concerned. Nevertheless, you are unable to restore the person's mental faculties because a great deal of brain tissue is already destroyed.

The second prognostic criterion is based on the *clinical picture*. The simple and expansive forms of paresis usually respond much better to treatment than do the hypochondriacal and paranoid forms. Schizophrenic "tinge" in the clinical picture makes the prognosis much worse. Schizophrenic "tinge" should here be interpreted as schizophrenic-

---

[1] By 1965, 30 million units was the usual accepted dose of penicillin given syphilitic patients.—*Eds.*

like symptomatology that is a persistent manifestation in the patient, not just fleeting reactions which might resemble schizophrenia. Furthermore, the schizophrenic picture must be fairly clear-cut. And then, if there is the peculiar paranoid hallucinatory organization—usually with a fairly well-preserved intellect—along with the many other schizophrenic-like manifestations in persons who previously showed a schizoid personality make-up, this alters the prognosis considerably. As you will see, we meet a very similar situation in all organic psychoses: Actually it is a very interesting observation that usually the more paranoid or more schizophrenic the psychotic picture, the less it will respond to any treatment given and the more unsatisfactory is the prognosis.

Combined use of electro-convulsive and insulin coma therapy has been attempted in paretic patients who show these paranoid and schizophrenic pictures. I must admit the results are not very good. A few patients respond to it; many, however, do not. Nevertheless, when dealing with such a patient it is extremely important to begin therapy as quickly as possible. If the patient fails to respond to anti-syphilitic and antiparetic treatments, or even if you have the impression that although you have arrested the patient serologically, he still shows no improvement mentally, the patient should be exposed to electro-convulsive therapy as is done in treating a schizophrenic patient. This treatment approach is indicated provided the paretic patient's physical condition is such that he is able to endure it. How much will be accomplished with this is questionable because, as I have stated, quite a number of these patients do not even respond to such a combination treatment.[1]

---

[1] Psychopharmacology has by now (1972) largely replaced, but not completely, the use of somatic therapy for this disorder.—*Eds.*

10

ALCOHOLIC PSYCHOSES

Alcoholism is one of the major psychiatric problems and therefore merits more intensive discussion than it is usually awarded in textbooks. There are two major groups of alcoholic disorders: *chronic alcoholism,* and various *alcoholic psychoses.* Chronic alcoholism is not a psychosis but has been either classified as sickness resembling a form of neurosis, or as a separate entity. Although in many of its manifestations it does resemble certain neuroses, there are differences, as we shall discuss. The alcoholic psychoses, however, are problems secondary to the much broader basic problem of alcoholism. Practically all the basic psychiatric issues—organic, psychodynamic, social, and so forth— appear in the group of alcoholic psychotic disorders.

Chronic alcoholism is a prerequisite for the development of an alcoholic psychosis. This fact must be emphasized and re-emphasized! The old notion that any person is capable of developing an alcoholic psychosis after simply drinking a huge amount of alcohol is incorrect. Only chronic alcoholic persons develop an alcoholic psychosis, with the exception of one entity—the so-called pathological intoxication—which is rather prevalent among individuals who are not actually chronic drinkers. But to diagnose Korsakoff psychosis, or delirium tremens, or alcoholic hallucinosis in a person who is not a chronic alcoholic is nonsense. However, erroneous diagnosis, particularly that of alcoholic hallucinosis, is often made. For instance, a person, who is not a chronic drinker, drinks a few glasses of beer and develops an hallucinatory reaction. The doctor is informed that the patient had some beer, and then the patient is listed on the chart as "Acute alcoholic hallucinosis." Now, the physician making such a mistake either had not taken an accurate history or simply did not know that the diagnosis of acute alcoholic hallucinosis is valid only for chronic alcoholic persons. The term "acute" does not imply here that in acute alcoholic hallucinosis the patient developed hallucinosis following an acute episode of drinking, but simply refers to the fact the hallucinations appeared in an acute setting as opposed to a chronic setting. In other words, after having been drinking a great deal over a long period of time the person develops a so-called acute hallucinatory reaction which in many patients terminates in recovery but in others terminates in a picture formerly termed "chronic hallucinosis." Therefore, it is always important to investigate whether a patient who manifests an alcoholic psychoses is a chronic drinker of alcohol or not, because, I repeat, with the exception of so-called pathological intoxication—which readily develops in certain individuals under the influence of a small amount of liquor and is actually more an intolerance psychosis than an alcoholic psychosis—all other mental disorders classified as alcoholic psychoses, such as delirium tremens, alcoholic hallucinosis, and Korsakoff psychosis, develop only in chronic alcoholic persons.

Chronic alcoholism is therefore the actual basis for the understanding of the entire problem of alcoholic disorders, and the entire problem depends on both the physiological and psychological factors involved in the extensive use of alcohol. Why it is that some persons drink alcohol to excess and others do not, and why some persons who drink alcohol to an excess develop mental disorders and others do not, we only partially understand. I will discuss some of the etiological considerations when discussing the problem of chronic alcoholism.

Because chronic alcoholism is a prerequisite to the alcoholic psychoses, it probably should be discussed first. However, I shall first discuss the alcoholic psychoses because, as you will see, some of the problems in these psychoses will give us a few hints as to how they are linked to the much broader problem of chronic alcoholism. Therefore, I shall now give a general outline of the alcoholic psychoses in terms of symptomatology, organic pathology, and what little is understood about the psychodynamic factors. Then, finally, I will discuss the actual underlying chronic alcoholism that occurs in quite a number of individuals who do not develop a psychosis.

The main groups of alcoholic psychoses may be classified as (1) *pathological intoxication,* (2) *delirium tremens,* (3) *Korsakoff psychosis,* (4) *alcoholic hallucinosis,* and (5) *polio-encephalitis hemorrhagica superior* (Wernicke's disease). With the exception of the pathological intoxication, all of these psychoses are based on chronic alcoholism; they all occur in patients who have been heavy drinkers for a number of years before they developed a psychotic tendency. The chronic heavy drinker who drinks continually is much more predisposed to an alcoholic psychosis than is the "dipsomaniac." (Dipsomania is only a descriptive term for the chronic alcoholic—whether neurotic, sociopathic, schizophrenic, or any other diagnostic category—who drinks very heavily but periodically. He drinks heavily and is very drunk for a few weeks, then he somehow emerges and is "on the wagon" for several days or weeks before resuming his drinking cycle.) Intermittent drinkers are also capable of developing an alcoholic psychosis but, most likely because they interrupt the drinking and return to a state of normalcy, they are not so prone to it as are those who drink steadily, heavily, and continually.

INCIDENCE: Alcoholic psychoses occur in every country and civilization where alcohol is consumed. It comprises a considerable number of mental patients; in this country about 10 percent of all admissions into mental hospitals are due to alcoholic psychosis, which is an impressive number. Its prevalence varies from country to country depending upon drinking and social habits. It also depends to some extent on the type of alcohol consumed; all statistics agree that "hard" liquor produces many more cases of alcoholic psychoses than does beer, for instance, or wine. Incidence of alcoholic psychoses in countries where "hard" liquor is not preferred, or not consumed perhaps for economic reasons, is far less than in those countries having hard liquor in the foreground of consumption. The incidence of alcoholic psychoses in the United States is very high; the incidence in France is considered very low.

Actually, however, any type of alcoholic beverage is capable of producing chronic alcoholism and subsequently, with the addition of complicating factors, a psychosis can be produced. But, that persons who develop an alcoholic psychosis are mainly those who drink hard liquor is not too surprising, naturally, since hard liquor drinkers consume a much larger amount of alcohol than do persons who drink only wine or beer in which the alcoholic content is considerably less. It is true, however, that heavy beer drinkers can develop an alcoholic psychosis; and of course they are more predisposed if they "chase" their beer with hard liquor.

CLINICAL PICTURES: The alcoholic psychoses may present acute, subacute, or chronic pictures, and in fact all variations of organic reaction syndromes can be encountered in the alcoholic psychoses. For unknown reasons, some chronic alcoholic persons develop more acute reaction pictures, such as delirium tremens; others develop more subacute, or chronic organic pictures, the so-called Korsakoff psychosis; yet again others manifest organic pictures mixed in with "released" symptoms of another psychosis, the acute and so-called chronic forms of alcoholic hallucinosis falling into this group. Thus, the same agent is able to produce different clinical pictures in different alcoholic individuals.

PREDISPOSING FACTORS : It has come to be realized that the alcoholic psychoses contain many more etiological elements than simply alcohol. Practically all the basic psychiatric issues—organic, psychodynamic, social, and so forth—are involved. On the organic level, avitaminosis and related organic issues play one role in these conditions. Probably the so-called constitutional predisposition of the individual and his early acquired emotional organization play other roles in these psychoses. Many persons are recognized to be allergic to alcohol, but the extent to which allergy plays a role is not fully known. The alcoholic psychotic pictures are surely much more complex than had been realized during the 19th century when these mental disorders were simply labeled "state due to alcohol." That alcohol itself is the most important organic factor is undeniable, but many other organic factors are involved, particularly the tendency for addiction to alcohol.

An alcoholic psychosis can be really understood only by analyzing two of its aspects: the *psychotic picture,* and, when the psychotic episode disappears, the *personality of the individual* who had the psychosis. In fact, the prepsychotic personality organization of an alcoholic individual is of extreme importance. It is just as important as the clinical picture of the psychosis itself. Until this became recognized, practically every person treated for an alcoholic psychosis was discharged as "recovered" after his psychotic symptoms subsided. In most old hospital records are such statements as, "Patient suffered from delirium tremens; recovered"; or,

"Patient suffered from acute alcoholic hallucinosis; recovered"; or, "Patient suffered from Korsakoff psychosis; recovered" (although only a very limited number of those patients improved). Upon that, naturally, each case was closed. An extremely high percentage of those individuals, however, began to drink again the day they were discharged from the hospital, and in some hospitals many of the delirium tremens patients were readmitted every few months or every few years, each time being then discharged as "recovered." "Recovered" meant simply recovery from the psychotic reaction; it did not mean recovery from the underlying chronic alcoholism or from the underlying craving or habituation which had only made the psychosis possible.

PATHOLOGICAL INTOXICATION

The only clinical picture known in the framework of alcoholic psychosis which is not based on chronic alcoholism is so-called pathological intoxication. All the other main psychotic pictures—the acute in the form of delirium tremens, the subacute and chronic form of Korsakoff psychosis, and the release pictures in the form of alcoholic hallucinosis—occur only in chronic alcoholic persons.

INCIDENCE: Generally speaking, pathological intoxication is a reaction occurring in certain susceptible individuals whenever they drink a small or a large amount of alcohol. The interesting thing is that the full-fledged pathological intoxication can be produced in persons who do not drink especially much or often. It is known to occur in persons after drinking two whiskeys or a few glasses of beer. These susceptible individuals have a certain intolerance to alcohol, an intolerance which fairly recently was discussed in terms of an allergy. This matter of alcohol tolerance and intolerance is not a purely social and psychological issue; a great many physiological processes are involved, naturally, of which only a few have been determined experimentally. Alcohol tolerance and intolerance are definitely linked to the metabolic organization of the individual. There are individuals who are so highly susceptible to alcohol that even a small amount produces a state of intoxication. Of course, if it just produces a state of intoxication we usually do not encounter these persons in the office; they are recognized by everybody as persons who, after only one or two drinks at a party, begin to show marked signs of intoxication, but usually they do not become more conspicuous than that. However, persons suffering with pathological intoxication become very conspicuous because they actually become psychotic under the influence of a small amount of alcohol.

SYMPTOMATOLOGY: Pathological intoxication is characterized by a typical acute confusional state, or a state of acute intense excitement with fury and rage mixed in with hallucinations and delusions. The hallucinations are usually visual and auditory, and the delusions are usually of a paranoid nature. Actually, these are acute confusional hallucinatory and delusional episodes in individuals who also display very marked emotion. The emotion is sometimes that of depression but most often, however, is that of excitement with marked violence. This excitement usually becomes a wild, maniacal frenzy, and in such a state the patient is definitely homicidal. Or, when the emotional undertone suddenly shifts, the patient becomes depressed and a suicidal risk. During such attacks the person's consciousness is narrowed and the behavior of many of these patients very closely resembles that of a patient having an epileptic equivalent, an epileptic discharge state.

When very drunk they usually become relatively harmless because their coordination is so impaired they often lack the stance required to fight. But occasionally their coordination is perfect and they are able to carry out complicated actions under the influence of their emotional excitement; many are known to have committed very serious criminal offenses during such a state of pathological intoxication. In this condition they are often provoked by some minor incident. For instance, the person becomes drunk, misinterprets someone's gestures, has an altercation, suddenly goes berserk, becomes extremely aggressive, and tries to harm those around him. Or, the opposite can occur and he directs his aggression against himself, impulsively attempting to commit suicide.

Usually these aggressive acts are unplanned, impulsive, short-circuited actions. Nevertheless, in some cases consciousness is not so clouded that they are unable to comprehend the situation to some extent and to perform in a way that would appear to be fairly planful. I mention this because from a medico-legal view it is quite often claimed, "Well, the person was actually able to pick up a weapon—"; or, "He was able to run around and pick up a bottle and hit somebody over the head; therefore he planned it." This is not fully a planfulness in such patients; naturally, they are dimly aware of their position and dimly aware of how to organize their attack or defense, but that is a very far cry from planful behavior. However, these alcoholic persons are much feared because they cause an awful lot of trouble and are so very violently aggressive as to be dangerous to themselves and to others.

COURSE: An episode of pathological intoxication may last for only a few minutes but usually continues for several hours and in some cases for a day or two. Following the episode the patient will fall asleep. Upon awakening he most likely has complete amnesia for what had happened during the state. If amnesia is incomplete, any recollection of where he had been and how he behaved is very hazy, blurred, and spotty. Very often he even has a retrograde amnesia in that he does not remember what events actually preceded his drinking.

Because episodes of pathological intoxication are short-lived and patients usually sober up rather quickly, the psychiatrist ordinarily does not observe them in the acute state but rather in the restored state of apparent normalcy that quite often follows such an attack. Since the psychiatrist is least likely to encounter patients during their attack, unless he works on admissions at a large hospital, he is considered to have a false impression concerning the frequency of this disorder. Actually, it is not very prevalent but these cases are well-known to large psychiatric hospitals, and well-known to the police.

DIAGNOSIS: This disorder is sufficiently common to warrant attention to the diagnostic grouping of these patients. Besides occurring in individuals particularly susceptible to alcohol and not chronic drinkers, the relationship between their personality and their environment is of importance. They are usually persons who use alcohol in occasional attempts to normalize themselves by lowering their tension states. Many suffer from periodically mounting tensions. Already prior to drinking they feel tense and aggressive toward the environment, or have all kinds of peculiar paranoid notions, feel depressed, or feel anhedonic. It is at such times that they decide alcohol will change those feelings and so they start to drink. And then after a few drinks, the acute episode occurs.

Empirical clinical observation disclosed that two or three groups of patients usually fall into this reaction category described. The first group consists of those individuals having a tendency to act impulsively anyhow, without benefit of alcohol; they tend to short-circuit all emotional discharges, in a dysregulated manner. These are the sociopathic individuals. A second group is comprised of persons having sustained either a traumatic or surgical brain damage, and also includes certain types of epilepsy. A third group consists of schizophrenic individuals in whom short-lived psychotic episodes are released. Possibly there is another group, the so-called acting-out neurotic type, but those patients usually fall into the category of the socio-

pathic personalities and often have underlying schizophrenia.

Now, pathological intoxication is a reaction occurring
in the first, the sociopathic, group of patients. In examining
their personality organization, it is surprising how many of
these patients have the characteristic emotional immaturity
and inability to control or regulate emotional tensions. It
has been known for a long time that a certain group of
sociopathic persons does not tolerate alcohol very well;
many of their underlying tendencies for emotional discharge
and impulsive actions become so markedly heightened
under the influence of alcohol that they then become irresponsible. From a legal point of view, however, such patients
suffer from a true psychosis in the sense that they manifest
all the signs and symptoms of an acute organic reaction.

Concerning the second group, it is well known that
persons who have suffered organic brain damage often
become markedly intolerant to alcohol. Although they may
have been able to drink considerably before sustaining the
brain damage, after the trauma they are unable to do so.
This is particularly true of persons having had focal brain
damage due to surgical or other causes, but is true also of
persons who sustained a more generalized concussion or contusion. Quite a number of patients who suffered head injury
fall into this group. In such patients the symptoms
resembling pathological intoxication are mixed in with all
kinds of confusional or acute organic reactions. Following
the head trauma a person might feel quite well or complain
of only mild postconcussional symptoms, such as slight
headache and dizziness and so forth, but show no particular
behavior pattern changes. Then suddenly, under the influence of alcohol, the patient might go berserk. Naturally, in
certain individuals who manifest a great number of
behavioral changes following head injury, those changes
become heightened under the influence of alcohol. In all
these cases, however, the reactions should be diagnosed as
acute confusional states, or amnestic states due to head

trauma, even though the clinical picture may appear to be that of pathological intoxication.

Since a number of persons behave in an epileptic manner during an attack of pathological intoxication, in several quarters the suspicion was voiced that they are probably epileptic individuals. That cannot be generally assumed. A few of them may have latent epilepsy, although very few show electroencephalographic patterns which would indicate its presence. Differentiation must be made. Epileptic individuals are notoriously susceptible to alcohol; they may throw fits or, instead of that, they may demonstrate the picture of pathological intoxication following which they simply enter into a fugue state. But if such a reaction occurs in an epileptic person, we usually do not diagnose it as pathological intoxication, but diagnose it as an epileptic equivalent or so-called psychomotor epilepsy even though clinically these pictures are extremely similar, if not identical, to pathological intoxication pictures observed in persons having a sociopathic personality structure.

There is a third group of patients, furthermore, who do not manifest overt schizophrenia but have a so-called schizoid character structure. Many of them drink in order to alleviate the symptoms of their schizophrenia. They are quite aware that they do not function as well as others normally do, and it is not rare for these individuals to drink in order to disinhibit themselves to some extent in attempting to establish better interpersonal relationships socially and sexually. It so happens that many of these individuals also have an intolerance to alcohol and when they drink suddenly manifest pictures of pathological intoxication. They are then usually classified as alcoholic, although actually their experiences were short-lived schizophrenic episodes "released" under the influence of alcohol.

It is interesting to note that posttraumatic, epileptic, and schizophrenic disorders on the one hand, and the sociopathic personality organization on the other hand, all predispose the patients to a pathological intoxication type of reaction; they all have one phenomenon in common—an intolerance to alcohol. (Many observers believe these psychotic reactions to occur in people who are allergic to alcohol, and instances have been described of alcoholic psychotic reactions occurring in persons who do have such an allergy. The extent to which allergy plays a role in these individuals, however, is not fully known.)

The diagnosis of pathological intoxication, however, should be made *only* in those persons showing that acute reaction *without* any other mental conditions being involved. Therefore, the diagnosis is not made in patients suffering from epilepsy, or from head trauma or from schizophrenia. But, it surely is made in those persons having a sociopathic personality background. This could possibly include a select few patients suffering from a special form of neurosis with tendency for acting-out under disinhibitory situations, as when drinking alcohol. Their personality organization, however, very closely resembles that of the sociopathic individual who also has the tendency to react to alcohol with pathological intoxication.

It should not be underestimated that in some cases the pathological intoxication reaction is constellative. In other words, there is more than one component present to release such an attack: alcohol intake is one; the individual's intolerance to alcohol is another; others include a sociopathic personality organization, environmental provocations, and, finally, the emotional state provoked. It is not rare for sociopathic individuals, particularly those with underlying schizophrenia, to be in a state of rage because of some real or imagined slight or action against them. These people are highly sensitive to all that is going on around them and upon hearing a casual remark can become enraged, take three or four drinks, and then suddenly "blow up" with a violent reaction. All constellative components must be analyzed and recognized as contributing to such an attack.

Unfortunately, in many individuals this phenomenon is not constellative, but automatic. In other words, each time they drink they undergo a similar type of reaction regardless of other circumstances. Nevertheless, there actually are a number of individuals in this group whereby a certain constellation definitely must be present before they fly into such a reaction. In this group we occasionally encounter people who are seemingly not very intolerant to alcohol and do not have the reaction following only one or two drinks but only after a bout of heavy alcohol consumption.

To repeat, pathological intoxication is the only form of alcoholic psychosis known to occur in persons who are neither regular nor intermittent chronic drinkers. The difference between this alcoholic psychosis and the chronic forms is not so much in terms of the clinical picture—for sure, a chronic alcoholic person can become delirious and react with aggression or depression—but the main difference is that pathological intoxication occurs in individuals who have a certain intolerance to alcohol. It occurs in a person who does not drink for months or perhaps a year and then suddenly, for one reason or another, sits down and drinks five whiskeys and at that point flies into this state. I might add that one does not encounter the same amount of violence and excitement in the other forms of alcoholic psychotic reactions.

DELIRIUM TREMENS

This very important alcoholic psychosis has been recognized for a great many centuries; the earliest historical documents of India, China, Egypt, and then Greece all mentioned delirium tremens (5). Seemingly, in ancient times people had indulged in alcohol, and indulged very freely, and many good clinical descriptions were made of delirium tremens. According to the observations of ancient Egyptian physicians, apparently the symptomatology in those times is exactly the same as that observed today.

INCIDENCE: Although there is no fixed minimal time

period for drinking before symptoms can develop, it is generally assumed that a patient suffering from delirium tremens had been drinking for at least several years. Therefore, it occurs rarely in young people. It usually occurs during the fourth or fifth decade of life. It is not very prevalent in women; that is not because women are incapable of developing delirium tremens—they can display as dramatic symptomatology as do men—but it is related to the drinking habits in most countries. Chronic alcoholism is not yet so widespread among women as among men, although in the past few decades women have been making great progress and very likely we will encounter an increasing number of delirium tremens pictures in women. This is somewhat counterbalanced, however, by the fact that alcoholic women seem to place much more emphasis on internal beautification than do men, and counteract the development of this disorder by their reliable intake of vitamins. It is interesting to note the difference between men and women who are chronically alcoholic. Alcoholic males usually become extremely careless about their eating habits as well as their habits in general. Alcoholic females, although their other habits may be as markedly altered as those of men, interestingly enough retain slightly better attention to their nutritional hygiene.

Delirium tremens develops only in the chronic alcoholic person. It never develops in a person who drinks occasionally, regardless of the quantity of alcohol he may consume at a given period of time. An alcoholic bout might result in other symptoms of alcoholic intoxication, but never delirium tremens. In other words, the chronic drinker apparently undergoes a metabolic alteration, and that alteration must occur before the person is predisposed to the development of any true alcoholic psychosis (with the exception of pathological intoxication). In the majority of patients who develop delirium tremens, there is a prodromal interval between an abstention from alcohol and the delirious attack.

PRECIPITATING FACTORS: The early observation that a prodromal state precedes the delirium tremens led to considerable discussion which is not yet fully settled. The question was asked, is a sudden withdrawal of alcohol in these individuals a precipitating factor? For instance, it was observed that when alcoholic persons were taken to jail and suddenly cut off from alcohol, they developed the delirium. Cases having very similar reactions were observed in certain hospitals. This was noted in the medical literature and statements then appeared that actually delirium tremens was precipitated by withdrawal from alcohol and it could have been avoided had these patients been given moderate amounts of alcohol. Many interesting medical practices followed this false assumption. Private institutions for alcoholic patients utilized this observation by giving their patients gradually reduced amounts of alcohol. This so-called slow-withdrawal practice made the institutions very popular.

Sufficient observations have since been made to disprove the theory; sudden withdrawal of alcohol does *not* precipitate the delirium. Sudden withdrawal of alcohol from chronic alcoholic patients could precipitate a cardiovascular collapse, however, and in that sense the old practice of giving the patients small amounts of alcohol is valid. But such support is no longer necessary because we now have other more effective methods to support the circulatory system. Naturally, such precautionary measures must be taken with persons suspected of having circulatory impairment which, by the way, is prevalent among chronic alcoholic individuals.

Therefore the question of gradual-versus-sudden withdrawal from alcohol appears settled, provided future observations do not reopen the issue. On the other hand, in those cases in which the precipitations were originally ascribed to abstinence, other precipitating factors entered into the clinical picture which were far more important than the abstinence. For instance, it is commonly observed that alcoholic patients become delirious after the onset of an infectious disease, such as pneumonia, to which they are very susceptible. Or, that they suffer a fracture or head injury and when hospitalized suddenly become delirious. In other words, aside from abstinence, seemingly many other factors, which are capable of further disorganizing the function of the nervous system and the metabolic homeostasis of the individual, contribute to produce the delirium. Why it is that an infection should precipitate a delirium, or why a fracture should precipitate a delirium, or why also a marked emotional excitement should precipitate a delirium, we do not know. It is common knowledge empirically, but we do not know what the intimate mechanisms are that translate this phenomenon into action. The person's abstinence has been blamed but, I repeat, the abstinence is most likely far secondary to the other factors which were introduced into the clinical picture.

The phase of nondrinking that often precedes the delirium is usually the patient's own doing. Such patients often stop drinking alcohol because of the symptoms they feel of nausea and revulsion for alcohol. The situation is comparable to the person who loves to indulge in large amounts of food, eats to great excess, experiences an upset stomach, and then has distaste for the food he formerly craved. But it cannot be assumed that his resulting food abstinence precipitated his abdominal seizures. And so, when the alcoholic patient cuts himself off from alcohol during the prodromal stage of the oncoming delirium, it is as much a part of the clinical symptom picture as his feeling cold, anorexic, tremorous, and so forth.

ONSET: Prior to the acute psychotic episode, the chronic alcoholic person usually drinks regularly. Then he may enter into a very impressive and prolonged debauch. During the prolonged drunken state he most likely does not eat and has very little rest. He begins to feel weak. Suddenly he becomes very nauseated and experiences a revulsion for alcohol. He then stops drinking. There is a prodromal period. During this period there are a few patients who switch to another type of liquor or to barbiturates or tranquilizers, but most patients become total abstainers and for a day or two consider themselves "on the wagon." Then, suddenly, the acute delirium occurs.

There is a small minority group of patients, however, in which a prodromal period does not occur but, while drinking steadily, the patients slowly and imperceptibly enter into a delirious state. They are observed to shake, they describe seeing spots before their eyes, and then visual hallucinations slowly begin to appear. Such undramatic onsets are rare and probably occur in those patients who have continued to eat, while those patients who neglected food are most likely to go through a prodromal period and have a dramatic onset of symptomatology.

SYMPTOMATOLOGY: The clinical picture of delirium tremens is that of a typical acute organic reaction which occurs in a person suffering from acute alcoholism. In many ways the symptomatology resembles the delirious pictures that we described occurring, for instance, under the influence of an infection or toxin, although alcoholic delirium tremens has certain special features, partly psychiatric and partly neurological, not appearing in the other deliria.

The *intellectual alterations* occurring in delirium tremens are dramatic. Delirium tremens is basically an acute hallucinatory confusion state, with complete disorientation on the psychiatric level, and with marked tremor and impaired coordination on the neurological level. There are, of course, many additional psychiatric and neurological symptoms but this is the essential picture. The patient is confused and disorientated as to time, place, and occasionally even for persons. Misidentification of other persons is quite common but he usually is not so confused as to lose a sense of his own identity. The patient's attention fluctuates, memory is impaired, and intellectual functioning is clouded. In the framework of disorientation, the patient appears to be in a dreamlike state and acts as though in such a state. The dreamlike state is interspersed with illusions and hallucinations.

There are cases of delirium tremens reported in which confusion is present without any hallucinatory experiences. Some observers detached this form of alcoholic psychosis from the category of delirium tremens and termed it an acute confusional state. Actually, these cases differ very little from delirium tremens; the only difference in delirium tremens is the addition of hallucinatory experiences on the psychological level and somatic manifestations, such as tremor, on the neurological level. Actually, there are various gradations and transitions from the acute confusional state to the state of delirium tremens.

Illusional experiences occur rather commonly and are usually mixed with hallucinatory experiences. Some patients experience only illusions, others only hallucinations, but in most cases there is a mixture of both experiences. Illusionary experiences are usually misinterpretations of perceptions; the patient perceives forms as being things other than what he actually views. For instance, he may interpret a moving curtain as being someone climbing through the window. Identity of persons is often misinterpreted, although the figures are recognized. Illusional misinterpretations are manifold. Sometimes they move along without the patient's being very affectively impressed by them. At other times, however, they become fused with delusional elements and utilized with considerable affect, usually in a paranoid manner. For instance, based on a misinterpreted perception of a moving curtain, the patient may believe he sees a man climbing through the window who will try to kill him. Hallucinatory experiences are also manifold. They are usually in the visual field. Auditory, tactile, and other types of hallucinations do occur, but the hallucinations in delirium tremens are predominantly visual. They may be crude and unorganized hallucinations, in that the patient sees stars or simple patterns. Much more often, however, they are

276 DIFFERENTIAL DIAGNOSIS

organized hallucinations and the patient sees complicated sequences rolling off as on a movie screen. The hallucinated pictures are often very archaic, such as horrible animals, objects, or people.

Most textbooks have stated that hallucinations in delirium tremens usually center around animals. That is not correct. The visual hallucinations can take any form. Some patients do hallucinate bugs crawling around, mice moving about, or pink elephants, but, against popular and even psychiatric belief, such experiences are decidedly in the minority. It is also not necessarily so that delirium tremens patients usually hallucinate small objects, because there is still the matter of pink elephants. As is often the case, a few notions crept in such as the idea that micropsia occurs. It does occur in a few patients under the influence of alcohol, but it also occurs with the use of other drugs. Actually, in many delirium tremens patients the hallucinated object is not distorted, not reduced in size, but is hallucinated in its proper size. I will discuss later the matter of optic alterations that definitely occur on a neurological level in patients suffering from alcoholic encephalopathy, such as Wernicke's disease, but as a rule these do not occur in an uncomplicated case of delirium tremens. In other words, there are delirium tremens patients who do not hallucinate animals or small objects, and furthermore, there are patients whose psychosis is not alcoholic who do hallucinate animals or small objects.

Although cultural elements prevail in the patient's selection of hallucinatory content—and I have observed patients in many countries, including Germany, where my patients tended to hallucinate what it was the policy to see—we must also take into consideration what type of substance the patient drank. That factor colors the picture to some extent. There are a number of physiological as well as psychological elements involved. Basically, the hallucinations have two components: a physiological component, in that certain parts of the brain are most likely irritated in a toxic way; also, a psychological component, in that some of the hallucinatory experiences are linked to the patient's psychodynamic configurations.

Another interesting thing is that the content of the hallucinations can have a two-fold reaction on the patient. (1) There is the alcoholic patient who experiences the illusions and hallucinations passively, similar to the intoxication reactions of many drugs, such as marijuana or hashish or mescaline, at certain dose levels. The hallucinated pictures experienced are similar to what is observed in a moving picture reel. The patient is not particularly impressed by the phenomenon and experiences them without feeling very emotionally involved. In the more commonly occurring form, (2) the patient definitely participates in his hallucinatory experiences. His visual hallucinations envelop and influence him; for instance, he thinks animals are chasing him, or peculiar figures are following him, and that these terrible creatures will do harm to him. The patient usually goes through all kinds of motions to ward the creatures off, or tries to flee from them. The illusions and hallucinations are usually linked to the patient's rather vague, ill-defined but nevertheless well-expressed delusional interpretations concerning his surroundings.

The symbolization of the hallucinated figures may be utilized in what can be termed the delirious interpretations, following along the line of interpretations of dream symbols of psychoneurotic or psychotic patients. Interpretations disclose that some of the archaic figure material hallucinated is not produced by the toxin alone but in many patients reveals very deep-seated underlying conflicts which are then expressed in the delirious experiences. For instance, they frequently indicate feelings of guilt with regard to drinking as well as other matters.

It is known that Freud originally concluded that dream content, particularly latent content which also may translate itself into manifest content, is based on a wish. This concept was later broadened; it is not only a positive form of wish that the individual expresses in the dream, but also a negative form of wish, namely, the wish to be safe. In other words, the wish is not only that of striving for something but there can be the wish to avoid something threatening, to be secure. It is simpler to formulate these issues as being basically that of (1) a wish, and (2) anxiety. The sexual element also occurs similarly in both deliria and dreaming; it can be linked either to wish or to fear. The sexual element can be treated somewhat separately from that of wish or fear, however, because it is not a simple wish or fear but very often pathological elements are present in the alcoholic deliria to an even larger extent than that found in dreams of non-alcoholic neurotic or psychotic individuals. Marked anxiety about their sexual integrity is very often expressed by these patients in their deliria.

Homosexual conflict material, to which the patient reacts strongly, also appears very often in the delirious experiences. For instance, the patient fears the hallucinated persons following him are trying to mutilate him, or kill him. That can throw him into a state of anxiety, and in his panic reaction and frenzy he may struggle to hide in a corner to save himself. Quite often he hears voices in connection with these experiences; they call him a homosexual, or an s.o.b., and so forth, always alluding to the patient's sexual conflicts. Hallucinations regarding homosexuality occur mainly in male alcoholic patients. The female delirium tremens patient hallucinates heterosexual conflicts, often hearing voices telling her she is a whore or a slut, and so forth. As I will discuss in connection with the paranoid mechanisms, a considerable amount of cultural emphasis is involved in these experiences. In many cultures women would consider the greatest accusation that people can make of them is the label of prostitute, and men would consider it the label of homosexual.

Naturally, in many delirium tremens patients sexual conflict does not appear. Hallucinatory experiences are often organized around the delusion of a plot against the person as a whole. Or, the experiences are often not fully hallucinatory but rather more illusionary distortions of things and events occurring around them. Therefore, delirium tremens experiences can range from those of superficial illusionary distortions, through social attitude and behavior patterns expressed in hallucinatory experiences, to very deep-seated intrapsychic conflicts expressed in hallucinations linked with delusions which are very often paranoid.

Another feature was at one time stressed, because it was thought to be interesting and believed to be somewhat pathognomonic for delirium tremens: the marked suggestibility of patients who are in a state of delirium tremens. One of several tests for this phenomenon is to give the patient a piece of blank paper and ask him what he sees on it. Most patients suffering from delirium tremens describe figures of people, animals, or other objects on the paper. To demonstrate the presence of suggestibility, you then give the patient a piece of blank paper and remark, "Look, here is a bear on this paper"; or, "Here is a tree"; or, "A gorilla is on this paper"; and so forth. On each occasion the patient will see on the paper whatever you mentioned and can describe it in detail. In other words, you are actually able to implant this experience into the patient. Another test is to have the patient close his eyes and then press over his eyeballs as you suggest various illusions and hallucinations. The patient will promptly accept them and elaborate upon them. Of course, this form of suggestibility is not pathognomonic for an alcoholic delirium; it can occur in quite a number of other types of deliria, in hypnosis and to some extent in so-called hysteria, although it is interesting to note that it is much more prevalent in delirious states produced by certain drugs.

Naturally, *emotional changes* occur in patients suffering from delirium tremens. There is the marked emotional lability characteristic for patients in an acute organic reaction. Quite a number of these patients are excited, many are depressed, but the most prevalent feeling is that of anxiety. They are extremely fearful! Very often paranoid delusions aggravate their anxiety. Despite a misconception that the delirium tremens person has a happy experience, only an extremely small percentage of them experience a so-called ecstatic form of delirium which might be regarded as happy. It is very rare that a patient experiences some rather exhilarating pleasant hallucination for a few moments. Most delirium tremens patients are frightfully anxious and very far from happy.

Psychomotor hyperactivity usually occurs in the delirium tremens patient. He continually moves about. He is restless. He is often picking at his clothes, or tries to flick off insects (which, by the way, are often hallucinated in delirium tremens). He may try to hide from the animals or people he sees pursuing him. He may climb up on chairs or tables, and even finds it possible to climb walls provided he is not so weak as to be unable to move. The explanation for this continual psychomotor discharge is not quite clear. Some observers believe it is based on the hallucinatory experiences, but I do not think that is correct because it occurs even in cases in which hallucinations are actually very much in the background. If hallucinations are in the foreground, however, they may have a directional influence on the patient's behavior.

Many patients display the so-called occupational delirium in that they recapitulate the routine behavior of their everyday occupations—for instance, a chauffeur drives a car, a farmer drives his tractor, or a bartender mixes drinks—and each patient reenacts all the motions entailed in his occupation. These occupational deliria are well known.

Incessant talking is characteristic for these patients. Usually they have a running commentary with their voices, or they express their fears to others and seek reassurance. Because of their confusion and misinterpretations of environmental situations they often act aggressively and many patients are quite assaultive. However, unless they are very strong to begin with, they usually do not accomplish much harm because they are in a rather weakened state.

From the somatic whole view of the patient, there are many major organ systems influenced by alcohol, naturally. Alcohol does not attack the nervous system alone but also has a strong influence on metabolic functioning of particularly the cardiovascular system and the vegetative system. I shall briefly mention three extremely important areas of change observed in delirium tremens patients: (1) *neurological* impairments, (2) *cardiovascular* impairments, and (3) *vegetative* impairments.

First, the symptomatology added to the classical delirium picture is not so much in the psychiatric field as in the *neurological* field. All the patients display a marked tremor. In fact, the designation "delirium tremens" stems from these two outstanding clinical features: the delirium, in the psychiatric field; the tremor, in the neurological field. The tremor has long been recognized by the layman under the popular term "the shakes." It is a marked gross tremor and is particularly noticeable in the patient's extremities. It is usually so conspicuous that the patient need not be put through any formal tests, such as finger-nose or knee-heel tests, in order to demonstrate its presence. A complete neurological examination points out not only impairments of coordination in the patient, but also adiadokokinesis and other indications of fronto-ponto-cerebellar tract impairments, as well as impairments of many other tracts dealing with regulation of neuromuscular activity. Reflexes are usually unaltered unless the patient suffers a polyneuritis along with his alcoholism, in which case reflexes may be exaggerated or absent. Manipulative difficulties, such as are observed when the patient attempts to button or unbutton his coat, accompany the gross tremor. The tremor is very often more than just a tremor; it is actually an ataxia, and a symptom of pyramidal tract involvement. The equilibrium of these patients is often disturbed; they usually walk with a broad base in order to maintain their equilibrium. Although the tremor is noticeable in the lower extremities, usually it is much more marked in the upper extremities and even in the head, face, and tongue. The tongue tremor is usually retained for a longer time than any of the other tremors and in former years was utilized to diagnose delirium tremens.

Secondly, alcohol has a particularly strong influence on the *cardiovascular* system. Metabolic changes occur which lead to impairment of the peripheral circulation. Many patients develop early arteriosclerosis and then, of course, all of the functional difficulties that arise in persons suffering sclerosis of their blood vessels. Quite a number of delirium tremens patients are found to have some amount of myocardial damage, as is often demonstrated on the electrocardiograph.

Thirdly, many *vegetative* functions become impaired. As delirium tremens develops, surface manifestations of vegetative impairment include profuse perspiration which accompanies the fever, rapid pulse, anorexia, nausea, weakness, and dehydration. One very important impairment (especially in terms of future research for the understanding of this particular form of intoxication) is that occurring in the liver. In all probability, many of the phenomena observed in these patients are due to impairment of liver metabolism. Of all the liver functions, the carbohydrate metabolism is the most impaired, as is indicated, for instance, in the sugar tolerance test, but usually this impairment is transitory and the changes are reversed after the delirious state has subsided.

COURSE AND PROGNOSIS: The delirious state usually lasts five to seven days. In a few patients the period of attack is shorter, and others are occasionally encountered in whom it continues for about ten days. The attack terminates in one of three ways: (1) death, (2) recovery from the psychotic state, or (3) the Korsakoff psychosis.

In former years especially, quite a number of these patients died. Death was usually directly due to pneumonia, to which these patients are highly susceptible, or due to cardiovascular collapse. Very few patients died of what could be termed a so-called cerebral death, the death due to central nervous system changes. The problem of deaths due to cardiovascular impairments is of particular importance because the majority of patients suffering from delirium tremens are middle-aged individuals. It is more likely to develop in middle-aged persons because they have had ample time in life to "tank up" and predispose themselves to the psychotic state. It occurs rather rarely in younger individuals, although there are heavy drinkers encountered who already developed the psychosis in their twenties or thirties. However, the majority of delirium tremens patients are at an age when their cardiovascular apparatus is no longer exactly in best condition and, furthermore, many of these alcoholic persons already manifest cardiovascular changes due to long use of alcohol.

In former years, the mortality rate was very high; in many clinics it was as high as 30 percent. The mortality rate dropped considerably since the development of more effective treatments and by the fifties it ranged from 5 to 10 percent. It remains high, however, in those cases improperly handled medically and, I must say, that even in many good hospitals there are still cases being improperly handled.

Following the five- or ten-day period of delirium, a number of patients enter a period of very profuse perspiration, and then they fall asleep for about twenty-four to forty-eight hours or so. When they awaken, the delirium is gone. Then they feel rather well, although weak. They are largely amnestic for the psychotic episode. The tremor is probably present, but only slightly, and it usually disappears rapidly. They are able to take food, and within a comparatively short time they recover sufficiently to begin drinking alcohol all over again.

There are some delirium tremens patients who recover from the delirium, but recover only partially. These are the patients in whom the Korsakoff psychosis, the subacute form of alcoholic psychosis, develops following the episode of acute delirium tremens.

A delirium tremens patient may therefore follow one of the three common clinical courses. In one group, the patient dies. Those in a second group recover rather quickly from the acute psychotic state. These are the two extremes. In a third group, the patients graduate from the acute to the subacute Korsakoff psychosis, and many of these patients then progress into the chronic Korsakoff syndrome. In some cases—in fact in quite a few—the delirium precipitates an underlying schizophrenia which becomes chronic and permanent.

KORSAKOFF PSYCHOSIS

The Korsakoff psychosis belongs in the category of chronic organic reactions. It develops in persons who are chronic drinkers; nobody can develop the Korsakoff psychosis who drinks only occasionally, who is not a heavy drinker, and who has not indulged in alcohol for a considerable period of time. The Russian psychiatrist Korsakoff was the first to devote a great deal of time studying this alcoholic psychosis and gave one of the best descriptions of it; in fact, he based his later descriptions of the Korsakoff syndrome on the main symptomatology of this psychosis (6).

ONSET: The Korsakoff psychosis develops in one of two ways: (1) following an acute alcoholic psychotic state, or (2) slowly and insidiously from the state of chronic alcoholism. In the first instance, the patient develops the Korsakoff psychosis after having been in an alcoholic delirium, usually delirium tremens. For instance, following an attack of delirium tremens the patient's delirium subsides, but not completely; his sensorium becomes clear and he no longer hallucinates, but his intellectual defects, memory impairment, disorientation, emotional lability, and so forth, do not disappear. Along with these residual symptoms some signs of delirium may oscillate for a while. After a few weeks, however, the person marches on to become a chronic case of Korsakoff psychosis. Korsakoff psychosis also can emerge following an attack of acute alcoholic hallucinosis, but that occurs very rarely. In the majority of cases one or more attacks of delirium tremens have occurred before the final attack which does not clear up entirely.

Although in many cases the onset of Korsakoff psychosis follows an attack of delirium tremens, a large majority of the chronic alcoholic patients who never develop an acute alcoholic psychosis eventually do develop Korsakoff psychosis. These are the cases in which the psychosis develops slowly, insidiously, and without any apparent clouding of consciousness. In other words, there are some chronic alcoholic persons who develop the Korsakoff psychosis following an acute alcoholic delirium, and there are others who develop the Korsakoff psychosis gradually, without a preceding delirium. Why it is one person develops this chronic psychosis following a delirium and another does not, nobody knows.

Incidentally, many cases of acute alcoholic intoxication are mistakenly diagnosed as Korsakoff psychosis, although I will never know why. Once in a while a person is picked up in a state of stupor due to alcoholic intoxication and diagnosed as suffering from Korsakoff psychosis. Of course, many of the clinical manifestations might be similar since the various organic reactions can appear the same. Nevertheless, the so-called alcoholic stupor pictures should not be confused with Korsakoff psychosis. Acute alcoholic stupor pictures can occur, naturally, in an occasional drinker who consumes such a large amount of alcohol at one time that he actually suffers an acute alcoholic poisoning, with one of its manifestations being stupor. Korsakoff psychosis, on the other hand, has a slow onset and belongs in the category of chronic organic reactions.

SYMPTOMATOLOGY: The clinical picture in the Korsakoff psychosis is in no way specific. It is a typical chronic organic mental disorder and in many ways similar to the basic symptomatology of general paresis. At one time, "pseudoparesis" (a term no longer used) referred to a group of patients who manifested the psychiatric symptomatology of a paretic and the neurological symptomatology of a tabes patient; these were actually cases of Korsakoff psychosis.

The psychosis develops very gradually as the chronic alcoholic person drinks and drinks. The first noticeable sign, as in any chronic organic mental reaction, is impairment of the person's intellect. His operational intellect diminishes progressively; he is less able to think as clearly as formerly and he becomes more and more simpleminded in his mental conduct. The familiar impairments of memory are observed; recent memory becomes lost and, gradually, increasingly remote memory defects appear. Disorientation occurs which is often at first oscillating, the patient appearing disoriented at times and at other times not.

When the psychosis has reached its height there is less and less reversal of symptoms, and they are all very severe. The patient continues to drink and becomes more and more slovenly and sloppy in his personal appearance as well as in his behavior and entire attitude toward the environment. Memory impairment is marked. There is disorientation for time, place, and (in rare cases) even for persons. He misidentifies people around him; he does not know where he is; he does not know what time it is. He is functioning on a very low mental level. Extremely severe deteriorative manifestations, however, are not observed in the Korsakoff psychosis per se. They occur only in those patients who do not recover from the Korsakoff psychosis but progress to another psychotic group, which is termed alcoholic deterioration, the end product of the Korsakoff psychosis, the intellectual deterioration then being similar to that of any of the other chronic organic mental disorders such as general paresis, atherosclerosis, or senile dementia. Consciousness is usually unimpaired in a clear-cut case of Korsakoff psychosis.

There are, however, patients in whom the Korsakoff psychosis is combined with an encephalopathy, and delirium is superimposed on the existing chronic organic reaction.

Interestingly enough, many Korsakoff patients are able to maintain fairly good contact with the environment and the superficial shell of the personality is often somehow retained. At times such a patient makes a better impression, in the sense of perfunctory relationships with people, than he does in a psychiatric interview. On the wards in every state hospital there are Korsakoff patients who might be engaged in some small tasks and who greet the doctor very pleasantly as he makes his rounds. They are able to exchange a few friendly comments with him about the weather and other such matters, and the doctor may assume the patient to be functioning fairly well. Should the doctor, however, ask such a patient, "How much is two times three?" he may be surprised to learn that the patient is unable to give the answer. In other words, these patients often have profound intellectual impairments behind the façade of superficially maintained interpersonal relationships.

Many Korsakoff patients display another façade of great importance, namely, that of confabulation, or fabrication. This symptom was originally believed by Korsakoff and others to be pathognomonic for the Korsakoff psychosis. We now know that not to be the case; confabulation occurs in many organic settings and can be observed in every chronic organic disorder; it is encountered in patients suffering from general paresis, cerebral atherosclerosis, senility, brain tumor, and so forth. Therefore, although it is not a characteristic specific for Korsakoff psychosis, it is undeniably most prevalent in patients suffering from this psychosis.

The Korsakoff patient utilizes confabulation mainly in order to fill memory gaps for the specific purpose of convincing the listener that no memory gaps exist. He usually relates to people by filling out his memory gaps in great detail with apparent sincerity and emotional conviction.

The fabrications are at times quite convincing to others, particularly if the patient is not very deteriorated. He can talk in a clear, intelligible manner, and in case demonstrations the examiner usually does not recognize that the patient is actually fabricating. The stories are often put forward so well that, unless they are checked with real facts, they impress others as being true. Naturally, when the patient becomes intellectually deteriorated, all the confabulations become primitive, simple, and childish. But, early in the disorder, I must admit the fairly well-elaborated and organized confabulations do credit to the person fabricating them.

Confabulations utilized to fill memory gaps should not be confused with "superlogia fantastica," or the "tall stories" of which the patient himself often becomes convinced. Usually the stories are ego-elation, or ego-expansion, measures to reassure the patient he has mastered some unique situation. These occur in sociopathic or so-called neurotic acting-out types of individuals, and tendencies for such stories are occasionally observed in some Korsakoff patients. Why this occurs, we do not know. Perhaps it is due to the fact that many Korsakoff patients have a euphoric and often even mild hypomanic coloring that drives them to spinning out all kinds of yarns. Many chronic alcoholic persons appear to have a rather cycloid make-up, and when euphorized by alcohol, they often maintain that mood level and then tend to confabulate even without having memory impairment. Therefore, it is quite possible that some temperamental factors in the personality touch off this mechanism when such a person develops a Korsakoff psychosis. This, however, cannot be proven or disproven until further investigation determines whether or not this type of confabulation is most often observed in Korsakoff patients who have a cyclothymic personality make-up.

The confabulations of Korsakoff patients may merge into the category of grandiose delusions, similar to those of general paresis patients. They may have a compensatory delusion of being very powerful and very capable. The difference between superlogia fantastica and delusion is this: Superlogia fantastica is only momentarily believed by the patient who fabricated it but, if confronted with evidence that it is not so, it collapses and the patient accepts that it was a lie. The grandiose delusion, naturally, is not accepted by the patient as being untrue when he is confronted by the fact. Psychologically, these catathymic mechanisms are basically related but cannot be considered identical. Actually, delusions and hallucinations do not primarily belong in the Korsakoff picture and are not essential to the diagnosis. Any delusions are either grandiose or paranoid in nature and are poorly elaborated. A considerable number of Korsakoff patients, however, have been known to experience visual or auditory hallucinations that are usually poorly organized and rather childishly simple.

The Korsakoff patient, therefore, is capable of manifesting all three types of confabulatory phenomena. He can utilize them (1) to fill in memory gaps because he is perturbed by them and also would like to appear well-functioning to others. Catathymic wish elements are probably present, so (2) the fabrications can serve as ego-expansion attempts indulged in to impress himself and others with his adequacy. And (3) confabulations can be utilized in delusions of grandeur for the same purpose. Psychodynamically, all three mechanisms seem to indicate the patient utilizes confabulations as a compensatory mechanism for whatever deficiency he feels, whether solely that of memory impairment or some other intellectual, emotional, and functional deficiencies.

In addition to the intellectual changes, emotional changes also occur in the Korsakoff psychosis. There is emotional lability and emotional incontinence. Various stimuli easily provoke exaggerated emotional reactions. Patients are usually somewhat childish emotionally; their emotions change quickly from moment to moment but they forget what it was that provoked one emotion and why it was they switched to another emotion. The psychosis often follows along the lines of the patient's basic personality pattern. For instance, the schizothymic patients may become even more morose, irritable, or withdrawn than formerly. Patients tending to be cyclothymic may become depressed; others may become euphoric and even hypomanic. In the Korsakoff psychosis the depressive mood is not so prevalent as is euphoria. A euphoric form of decortication seems to occur and Korsakoff patients are usually rather happy, not wanting to be made very aware of their mental impairment.

All kinds of neurological manifestations can occur in the Korsakoff psychosis. Korsakoff's first description of this psychosis was in connection with polyneuritis, and in many textbooks Korsakoff psychosis is described as an intellectual deterioration plus polyneuritis. Polyneuritis is prevalent in Korsakoff psychosis and in many patients is so full-fledged that there is very little difficulty diagnosing it. These patients usually develop a foot-drop and often a wrist-drop; the peroneal nerve is mainly involved but the radial, the median nerve, and perhaps other peripheral nerves may also become involved. The polyneuritis is usually typical; there is an absence of reflexes and an impairment of motor function with subsequent muscular atrophy. Sensory impairments are also typical; all qualities of sensory perception are diminished to varying degrees, including pain, tactile, kinesthetic, proprioceptive, and vibration, the latter being one of the first impaired and the last to return. In some patients the sensory impairment is more marked, in others the motor. Actually, motor impairment is more conspicuous and therefore is usually more often described, especially because many patients are unable to express their sensory symptoms very well, while an inability to elevate a foot or wrist is, naturally, quite obvious.

The detailed neuropathology of Korsakoff psychosis is very impressive and I would at least like to remark that in these cases there is much more present than simply a peripheral form of neuritis. The entire neuron is actually involved. Not only are the peripheral neurons involved but also the spinal cord and, in quite a number of instances, the brain is also involved. For instance, many patients manifest some amount of ataxia due to impairment of the pyramidal tracts in addition to the peripheral motor impairments. Actually we are dealing with an encephalomyeloneuropathy, that being a more expressive description than neuritis because the neural involvement is really not an inflammation but is a degenerative disorder.

At the time Korsakoff psychosis was first described it was incorrectly believed that the so-called polyneuritis was invariably part of the Korsakoff picture. Although it is prevalent in a more or less severe form, full-fledged Korsakoff cases are encountered which have no polyneuritis or have it in such a mild form that it is very much in the symptom background. Therefore, the presence or absence of polyneuritis is not a diagnostic criterion. It is important when present, however, because the patient may require practical specific treatment for his polyneuritis along with treatment of his Korsakoff psychosis.

COURSE AND PROGNOSIS: Korsakoff psychosis can perhaps be regarded as a subacute form of alcoholic psychosis. Delirium tremens would be the acute form, the subacute Korsakoff the second to develop, and alcoholic dementia the chronic and final form of alcoholic psychosis. A number of alcoholic patients travel down the whole road: they begin with the state of chronic alcoholism; they may then develop delirium tremens; they reach the stage of Korsakoff psychosis; finally the Korsakoff psychotic state does not lift, and the patient then progresses to become a case of alcoholic dementia or deterioration, the end product of the disease.

The clinical picture of alcoholic deterioration and dementia is very similar to that of general paresis. In former times the medical literature frequently described them as "alcoholic pseudoparesis" because they so resembled general paresis. Furthermore, the chronic polyneuritis, absent reflexes, impairment of the peroneal nerve, ataxia, and so forth present in the Korsakoff patient reminded many observers of tabo-paresis, and therefore those patients were described as "alcoholic tabes" or "pseudotabes." These designations should not be applied because they are only misleading; they merely indicate that the end product of an alcoholic psychosis can closely resemble the end products of patients having general paresis or some other form of luetic involvement, but it is not necessarily the same in both disorders.

In central nervous system syphilis, the patient's intellect usually remains impaired. The patient does not recover but remains for years, or for life, in an institution. He is able to perform very simple tasks, but is otherwise fragmented intellectually, emotionally, and in terms of maintaining himself independently. However, if I should quote the statistics (which are unreliable) I could show that a fair percentage of patients suffering from Korsakoff psychosis recover; not all of them progress to the state of alcoholic dementia or deterioration. Despite improved treatment methods, however, Korsakoff psychosis continues to be regarded as a very serious mental disorder and the recovery rate is far from gratifying. I believe approximately 50 percent of the patients recover and the other 50 percent progress to a state of dementia. And those who recover do not recover fully. A certain amount of intellectual and emotional weakness and a certain inability to function on exactly the same level as formerly remain.

The Korsakoff patient who does not recover then progresses to the state of alcoholic dementia. Deterioration is actual in that the condition is irreversible; as yet no means have been found to reverse the process. We do have certain means of treatment for Korsakoff psychosis, but if a patient reaches the state of dementia he will not respond to present therapeutic methods and usually is simply a case for custodial care.

The older the individual, the more guarded should be

the prognosis. This psychosis usually occurs in middle-aged or older persons, since one must drink for a considerable period of time before graduating to the Korsakoff class. And the older-aged person is, naturally, also likely to have other complicating disorders. Atherosclerosis is, of course, the most common complication. Therefore, it is not very rare to find a number of patients to be suffering from a combination of Korsakoff psychosis plus atherosclerosis which, as we well know, does not improve their prognosis. In former years, before the treatment for syphilis became effective, physicians also encountered many cases of Korsakoff psychosis combined with syphilis. In some instances it became a rather frustrating neuropsychiatric game trying to determine, for example, whether the dementia in a fifty-five-year-old patient was a form of syphilis, atherosclerosis, or alcoholic Korsakoff psychosis. If he suffered from all three disorders, it would be very difficult to apportion the basis for the dementia because of the multiple etiological factors present. Naturally, the existence of combined disorders considerably impairs not only the prognosis but the therapeutic procedure as well. Furthermore, in many Korsakoff cases there is frequently an additional complication: During an alcoholic debauch, for example, the patient falls and sustains some head trauma, such as a skull fracture or concussion. The clinical picture of the head trauma may eclipse the pictures of the other disorders present. It often, I would even say, overshadows them completely.

ALCOHOLIC HALLUCINOSIS

This interesting group of patients presents a clinical picture which demonstrates every factor entering into a psychosis. The peculiar experiences of these patients are, obviously, partly organic due to intoxication and its metabolic alterations in the individual, but partly the experiences have psychodynamic implication.

This disorder occurs only in chronic alcoholic persons,

the hallucinosis developing after they have imbibed for a number of years. It is fairly prevalent, making up roughly perhaps 3 percent of hospital admissions of chronic alcoholic patients. For some unknown reason, it occurs preeminently in males. That is not explained on an organic basis, nor from the viewpoint of so-called constitution, nor in psycho-dynamic terms. There have been a few unconvincing reports of alcoholic hallucinosis in females, but I have never encountered a true case. All this may be partially explained through the observation that many more cases of alcoholic psychosis occur in males. On the other hand, there are a sufficient number of cases of delirium tremens in females to make us wonder why they do not also manifest alcoholic hallucinosis. Pictures of delirium tremens mixed with hal-lucinations surely occur in the female, but those well-organized hallucinatory and delusional experiences that occur in a clear setting in acute alcoholic hallucinosis patients are comparatively rare in women.

Characteristic for this disorder, the patient's halluci-nations are nearly exclusively auditory. This is more or less in contrast to delirium tremens in which the patient has preeminently perceptual and visual hallucinations. It is also in contrast to other alcoholic disorders in which halluci-nations are of a visual or combined nature. Visual hallucina-tions are extremely rare in alcoholic hallucinosis, and I have never encountered such a case. Occasionally, however, tactile hallucinations are also present.

ONSET of acute alcoholic hallucinosis rarely is slow and insidious. The auditory hallucinations appear rather sud-denly, within a day or two, without any preliminary signs of a major mental disorder having been present. (In that respect, the onset resembles those described as due to sudden withdrawal from alcohol, or that of pathological intoxica-tion.) The person's auditory hallucinatory experiences may at first be those of just noises or sounds. Within a short time he hears voices talking to him; they could be male or female voices but are usually male voices. The hallucinations soon become increasingly organized so that the patient hears voices making remarks about him, most likely calling him every insulting name in the books.

SYMPTOMATOLOGY: It is extremely important to keep in mind that in acute alcoholic hallucinosis all hallucinatory and delusional experiences occur in a clear setting. The sensorium is not involved. Therefore, the patient does not manifest intellectual impairments such as disorientation or any other signs of alteration of consciousness characteristic of acute organic reactions. He is not deteriorated. His knowledge is well preserved and there are no memory defects. Although by no means intellectually well, he nevertheless functions fairly well, for all practical purposes. He is lucid and in good contact with the environment. But, in this apparent clear setting, he has auditory hallucinations and he has delusions. Aside from that, the individual shows no personality impairment.

In this group of patients, one can observe quite clearly the very intimate relationship between auditory hallucinations and delusions. Auditory hallucinations and delusions are more closely linked than in any other sensory sphere, so that often it is very difficult to discern at what point delusion begins or hallucination ends, and vice versa. Auditory hallucinations are essentially conceptual hallucinations, and the other types of hallucinations are essentially perceptual. In a great many cases it is actually that the patient's concept is organized into a delusion and it becomes so intense that it spills over into an auditory experience. But it starts on a conceptual basis of a thought, an idea, which is then projected into the auditory sphere.

To illustrate this by contrast, visual hallucinations are often purely perceptual; the person sees figures or scenes as in a moving picture reel, and these hallucinations are not necessarily connected with very much conceptual material. It is interesting that when visual hallucinations are produced experimentally with certain drugs or intoxicants, the patient's conceptual manifestations often are not linked to his visual field perceptual experiences. In the auditory field the hallucinatory situation is different: the phenomenon is rarely on a perceptual level. The person rarely hears just noises, or music or something equivalent to a moving picture sound reel. In most cases he hears voices and the voices are actually expressing whatever ideational content is intimately linked with the thought processes of that particular patient. This is a probable explanation for the interesting fact that, although it has been possible to produce visual hallucinations experimentally, it has not been possible to experimentally produce auditory hallucinations in a reliable manner because seemingly the conceptual background on which the entire auditory experience grows probably cannot be constructed with any drug or intoxicant. (This is an important point in terms of how we should assess cases of alcoholic hallucinosis.)

The content of the alcoholic hallucinosis patient's delusions is essentially paranoid, his hallucinatory-delusional experiences usually moving along on two main themes: (1) the patient feels there is a threat to his bodily integrity: he is being chased, being persecuted, being annihilated; and (2) the patient feels concern regarding his sexual conduct, attitudes, and inclinations; he hears voices accusing him of impotence, of being weird or perverted, and, in a great many cases, accusing him of being homosexual.

Since alcoholic hallucinosis is extremely rare in women, a few psychiatrists expressed the idea that it is because males and females probably handle their preoccupation with homosexuality dynamically somewhat differently. This is no real explanation. Others have mentioned the idea that the alcoholic hallucinosis syndrome is nothing other than "homosexuality soaked in alcohol." Naturally, that is not true either, because there are many cases in which homosexuality does not play a role, particularly in those societies lacking any sentiment regarding homosexuality. Alcoholic hallucinosis occurs there, also, but then the patient hears voices accusing him of sexual issues other than homosexual. In this disorder we are actually dealing with very intricate problems which require further research. We often tend to assume that the content of these hallucinations and delusions is probably the sole clue to explaining the phenomenon, but apparently that is not always the case. In many of these individuals the dynamic pattern seems to be secondary to some basic processes which are as yet unknown.

COURSE: Alcoholic hallucinosis usually runs a much longer course than that of delirium tremens. Acute delirium tremens usually clears up within a week or ten days. Acute alcoholic hallucinosis—if it clears up at all—usually does not clear up for several weeks. There have been cases known to last for only a few days, and there have been cases known to last many weeks and run an intermittent course. In the latter case, the person has the experience for a few days, then suddenly it disappears and the person appears to be well; but a week or so later the hallucinosis again occurs for a day or two. At any rate, the course to recovery is usually slower than that of delirium tremens.

PROGNOSIS: It has been estimated that about two-thirds of the patients who manifest alcoholic hallucinosis recover from the psychotic episode. The remaining one-third of these patients progress further, in that the acute clinical picture becomes chronic. Their chronic hallucinatory and delusional content assumes, for all practical purposes, a typical schizophrenic picture. Many of these patients fail to respond to the therapeutic measures currently employed for this chronic condition, continue to be overtly psychotic, and are institutionalized for the remainder of their lives.

Incidentally, post-mortem brain studies disclose too many secondary pathological changes to be specific for this disorder, but a few of the patients who died during an acute state were described as having brain alterations similar to post-mortem findings in delirium tremens cases.

DIAGNOSIS: Now we come to the big question: What are the basic processes occurring in alcoholic hallucinosis patients? They are not fully known. Are the clinical symptoms based on an actual toxic reaction to alcohol? Or, are they actually symptoms of another psychosis which is released under the toxic influence of alcohol? Are they due to some already present metabolic disturbance which is then influenced by chronic alcohol consumption? Actually, as I have mentioned, it is probable that in this disorder we are dealing with a multi-factorial issue. There are organic factors, there are psychodynamic implications, and there *is the factor of schizophrenia.*

Many of these questions remain open in the minds of a few psychiatrists. Actually, the person suffering from acute alcoholic hallucinosis has a nervous system so organized as to be neurologically predisposed to react to stress situations, organic or psychic, with what appears to be a schizophrenic reaction. It is my own feeling that the acute cases as well as the chronic are, for all practical purposes, schizophrenic. But it cannot be denied that there are facts which considerably support the view that it is a toxic reaction. For instance, occasionally acute hallucinosis pictures are combined with those symptoms occurring in cases of delirium tremens. Furthermore, one cannot deny the fact that these patients have imbibed alcohol for a long period of time. And it is not explained why it is that, should they suddenly develop the acute hallucinosis episode lasting for a week or so, it often clears up very rapidly and quite spontaneously after the alcohol is withdrawn. Quite a number of these patients do show recovery, moreover, although recovery is slower and far less satisfactory than that of patients suffering with delirium tremens. Also, several of the detoxication treatments have been effective in treating acute alcoholic hallucinosis. Therefore, there is a certain hesitancy on the part of a few psychiatrists to label these cases schizophrenic, because the relationship of the symptoms to the alcohol is rather close in many instances.

None of these arguments is very valid, however, because it is known that attacks of schizophrenia often do occur under stress, without any exogenous toxic precipitating agents present whatsoever, in which the duration is short and the individual reintegrates fairly well regardless of the type of organic or psychotherapy applied or—to be very frank about it—without any therapeutic attempts whatever. It must also be taken into consideration that acute alcoholic hallucinosis patients often show only gradual and limited improvement when given specific detoxication treatments and nevertheless respond well to certain treatment methods which are advantageous to schizophrenic patients. We should be alert to the fact that often it is not sufficient (as it may be in the other alcoholic psychoses) to confine ourselves to treating the toxic component in these individuals. We must also consider that psychotherapy and other treatment methods must be introduced to specifically deal with the schizophrenic matrix on which this disorder grows. Many of the dynamic factors must be appreciated in the therapeutic approach to such persons. The dynamics of the hallucinations and delusions more closely resemble those of schizophrenia than of the simple organic psychoses. The tendency to recover is also in many ways similar to that of schizophrenia, and, furthermore, in their response to treatment they may also behave more as schizophrenic than organic cases, especially those patients who march on to develop a so-called chronic alcoholic hallucinosis picture.

In terms of prognosis we must also recognize factors other than the toxic because otherwise the psychiatrist treating the patient can be unduly optimistic. He may tell the relatives that the patient's disorder is only toxic and can blow over in a few days or weeks; then six weeks or six years pass and the patient continues to be psychotic and in an institution. Follow-up studies of such a patient demonstrate that a typical chronic schizophrenic psychosis had evolved following the acute episode of alcoholic hallucinosis.

The term chronic alcoholic hallucinosis has in fact been discarded. Those investigators who continued to maintain that patients suffering from acute alcoholic hallucinosis were essentially suffering from a toxic psychosis gave up the idea that so-called chronic alcoholic hallucinosis is a toxic psychosis. Such cases are now universally diagnosed as schizophrenic because it is assumed that if the toxic factor is removed and the patient continues hallucinating, expressing paranoid delusions, and in other ways manifesting a psychotic organization similar to that prevalent in schizophrenia, the patient is schizophrenic. Most likely we are dealing with the "release" phenomena. All the patients I have examined were invariably schizoid in their personality make-up, and schizoid features were obvious on psychiatric examination and often in psychological tests.

Those who lack sufficient courage—as some assume is required—to diagnose acute alcoholic hallucinosis patients as being schizophrenic, overlook this point: that it develops only in schizoid individuals. Patients suffering with the acute alcoholic hallucinosis as well as those with the so-called chronic form are invariably schizoid in their personality background. The question only arises, why do not all schizoid persons react to alcohol in such an acute manner? Probably it is a matter of predisposition. A certain group of schizoid individuals most likely has a specific metabolic organization which, in addition to their schizoid dynamic organization, predisposes them to have an acute psychotic reaction released under the impact of alcohol. We do not know just how the metabolic factors are responsible. In comparison, it is interesting to note that not all delirium tremens patients necessarily have a schizoid personality make-up. However, if one closely investigates acute alcoholic hallucinosis patients he will frequently discover that, even during their nondrinking periods, they often expressed vague feelings of fear and had preoccupations pertaining to certain areas of their lives which, when they are under the influence of alcohol, then become the hallucinatory and delusional danger zones.

In conclusion, before diagnosing any patient a case of acute alcoholic hallucinosis or so-called chronic alcoholic hallucinosis, we should be aware of the fact that a large number of schizoid and even outright schizophrenic individuals attempt to regulate their emotional tensions by drinking alcohol. Many of these patients are clear-cut and manifest cases of schizophrenia at the time they were admitted to the hospital but were diagnosed only in the alcoholic category on the basis of the presenting toxic symptoms and history of heavy drinking. Only if the alcoholic picture is further investigated can it be discovered that the diagnosis was wrong, that from the very beginning the patient was suffering an acute schizophrenic psychotic episode which was released by the toxic factor of alcohol the patient had taken as medication in attempting to cope with the great tension and anxiety provoked by stresses.

POLIO-ENCEPHALITIS HEMORRHAGICA SUPERIOR

This entity was first described in 1881 by Wernicke *(6, 8)* and is also referred to as the encephalopathy of Wernicke. Initially it was considered a rare neurological entity but it became of great importance for two main reasons. First, it is not a rarity; it is a much more prevalent neurological and psychiatric entity than had once been believed. Secondly, it has given us the first real clue as to the localization and clinical aspects of the neuropathological processes in the alcoholic psychoses, which has added much etiological and therapeutic knowledge concerning these psychoses. Therefore, it merits more discussion than that usually afforded a rare disease. Wernicke's original descriptions were based on a fairly small number of patients of special interest due to the neurological signs and peculiar mental symptomatology they displayed. He described the symptomatology not so much from the psychiatric viewpoint as from the neurological. Actually, psychiatric interest in this disorder was aroused at a later time when intensive studies were made of the clinical pictures.

ONSET: This disorder may develop rather suddenly in chronic alcoholic persons. In other cases, however, it develops in patients already manifesting signs of Korsakoff psychosis, this more acute clinical picture becoming superimposed on the already existing rather chronic picture.

SYMPTOMATOLOGY AND NEUROPATHOLOGY: Wernicke described patients who manifested delirium with a peculiar mixed symptomatology: The delirium was without tremor, unlike delirium tremens, but the patients seemed to be dreaming, confused, and memory defective as in an ordinary fever delirium except that in these patients delirium was often very profound. Naturally, all the other intellectual impairments of an acute organic reaction were also present. Rather vivid auditory and visual hallucinations occurred in the delirium. Occasionally there were delusions, although usually the patients hallucinated to such an extent and were so confused that no organized delusional formation was possible; they simply reported in a confused and dreamlike manner the images they perceived in their peculiar dreamstate. They would sleep, but usually could be aroused. Occasionally they were stuporous.

The delirium-like picture with oscillating impairment of consciousness and impaired sleep regulation are all indicative of a somewhat more acute process than that observed in a Korsakoff psychosis. Actually, the entire incident is a peculiar mixture of an acute and a chronic organic reaction with neurological manifestations included.

From a neurological point of view, in contrast to Korsakoff psychosis patients who manifested polyneuritis,

Wernicke's patients manifested symptoms that indicated involvement of the brain stem. The neurological manifestations were manifold. The main involvements were those of the optic and the oculomotor nerves. Optic neuritis was present. All branches of the oculomotor nerve were involved: For instance, the various forms of ophthalmoplegias and the many pupillary disturbances, such as Argyll-Robertson pupil and typical anisocoria, were described. Additional cranial nerves were also involved in this disorder.

Neurological symptoms further indicated major involvements in the area of the corpora quadrigemina, especially the superior colliculi. There would be paresis of the vertical gaze, or symptoms indicating involvement of the vestibulo-cerebellar tracts, mainly nystagmus and occasionally conjugate deviation disturbances. Patients displayed impairments of coordination, the ataxia indicating involvement of the cortico-ponto-cerebellar tracts. Impairment of eye coordination resulted from involvement of the longitudinal fasciculus. The cerebellar signs were not due to actual involvement of the cerebellum but due to the impaired connections of the cerebellum with the midbrain.

Incidentally, a psychiatrist by the name of Gamper, in 1927, collected a large number of anatomical specimens from patients who died of this type of disorder, and he pointed out that quite possibly there is a correlation between the delirium and the lesions in the corpora mammillaria, because that area closely approximates the anterior sleep-regulating centers, the reticular bundle, dorsal to it (6). He went even further to postulate that in many cases the memory impairment is not due to cortical impairment but due to impairment in this region. The latter idea was not very popular, but the idea that these patients who become delirious probably do have some involvement in the sleep-regulating centers around the corpora mammillaria has been given considerable attention.

COURSE AND PROGNOSIS: Patients suffering with

polio-encephalitis hemorrhagica superior usually remain in a delirious and dreamlike condition for several days. Quite a number of them then progress to develop a Korsakoff type of syndrome. In former years, the mortality rate was extremely high. Since the discovery of relatively effective treatments, the mortality is no longer so great as in the past although the disorder is obviously very serious.

In this connection, some investigators who examined quite a number of cases of Korsakoff psychosis made a statement that appears to be correct: No patient suffering from Korsakoff psychosis has died of a directly cerebral death (not meaning to infer they died of pneumonia or other complications) if a picture of Wernicke's encephalopathy is not demonstrated on autopsy. In other words, this encephalopathy picture is seemingly very severe and patients displaying it are very severely sick, while other alcoholic patients probably have mild brain changes of a similar nature but do not have such a severe disorder.

Most of Wernicke's patients died, and autopsies disclosed a peculiar vascularization and a peculiar parenchymous degeneration around the corpora mammillaria in the hypothalamus. The fornix and the grey matter around the cerebral aqueduct and the superior colliculi were especially involved. In some cases there was also involvement of the corpus striatum and the substantia nigra. However, involvements of the mesencephalic regions and the region of the pons were usually more marked. In the first cases described by Wernicke, anatomical changes in the cortex and the basal ganglia were overlooked, but the fact remains that apparently the main areas of impairment in animals and man are the grey matter of the midbrain.

Originally, it was believed that polio-encephalitis hemorrhagica superior was some specific atypical type of alcoholic disorder. The term was derived from Wernicke's early descriptions; "polio," meaning involvement of the grey matter, "encephalitis," meaning brain inflammation, "hemorrhagica," meaning hemorrhages due to congestion and vascular impairment with diffusion into the tissues, perivascular cellular infiltration becoming organized and followed by reparative gliosis, "superior," meaning the main involvement was in the superior part of the brain stem, not the inferior.

Following Wernicke's descriptions of this alcoholic encephalopathy, a great many autopsies were performed by others. It was further discovered that very similar anatomical changes occurred in alcoholic patients in which the entire brain was involved, even though many alcoholic patients showed the peculiar predilection for mesencephalic involvement. Nevertheless, it was recognized that there is nothing very specific about this disorder. Then the broader term, alcoholic encephalopathy, was applied. Such an alcoholic encephalopathy was found present in many alcoholic cases. Many investigators believe that some form of encephalopathy is present in all alcoholic psychoses to a varying degree. In cases of delirium tremens or Korsakoff psychosis it is not always easy to gather pathological material because many of those patients recover, but sufficient evidence on a pathological level has been obtained to indicate that anatomical changes are present in all the alcoholic psychoses, and that in this particular metabolic disorder of the nervous system the psychotic symptomatology is secondary to the encephalopathy present. Why it is that some patients have more of a cortical distribution and others have more of a mesencephalic distribution or a polyneuritic distribution was not determined.

It was then suddenly discovered, by Russell and Campbell, that very similar anatomical changes occur, and even in the same distribution, in a number of disorders other than alcoholic (8). For instance, the identical clinical and anatomical pictures described in polio-encephalitis hemorrhagica superior were observed in persons having died with a thyroid condition, gastric carcinoma, pernicious anemia, and a number of other disorders. Upon investigation, all those disorders were found to have one feature in common: B-group avitaminosis. Naturally, with this observation the so-called specific anatomical pictures once assumed to be characteristic for Wernicke's encephalopathy became recognized as neither characteristic for these nor for other alcoholic encephalopathies alone, but characteristic for disorders complicated by deficiency of thiamine hydrochloride and nicotinic acid. This was later proven by Alexander *(1940)* in animal experiments. Further work in experimental avitaminosis in animals produced very similar clinical and anatomical pictures of hemorrhagic encephalitis, the findings being also similar to those in patients suffering from beri-beri and pellagra. Therefore, whenever such vitamin B deficiency reaches a very severe degree, it is most likely capable of producing characteristic vascular changes over the entire brain but having a particular predilection for the upper part of the brain stem.

This observation, added to the observed anatomical changes, greatly enlarged our knowledge concerning the etiology and treatment of these disorders. It is now known that the pathology present in polio-encephalitis hemorrhagica superior and the other types of severe alcoholic encephalopathy is not specific for alcoholic disorders. Whenever encountering such clinical pictures, one must keep in mind not only the alcoholic disorders but also all the other disorders capable of producing marked vitamin B deficiencies. And so it is that polio-encephalitis hemorrhagica superior, a comparitively rare and rather obscure disorder, was one which led to much of our understanding of the alcoholic psychoses.

COMMENTS ON THERAPY

Many investigators believe that a certain amount of encephalopathy is present, in varying degrees, in all the alcoholic psychoses. Naturally, it is not always easy to gather anatomical material from cases of delirium tremens or Korsakoff psychosis because many such patients recover.

However, sufficient neuropathological evidence has been obtained to indicate the presence of anatomical changes in all alcoholic psychoses, and that actually the clinical psychotic symptomatology is secondary to a particular metabolic derangement of the nervous system. Any discussion of specific therapies in dealing with these alcoholic disorders could be outdated within ten days, due to ongoing metabolic research and rapid advances in neuropsychopharmacology. However, I shall briefly mention therapeutic factors that are important to consider in that they point up the complex medical problem underlying the psychotic symptomatology.

Needless to say, there was no organized treatment for the alcoholic psychoses before it was discovered that the clinical pictures are very similar to other encephalopathies that were clinically and experimentally observed to be caused by avitaminosis. Before the link between alcoholic psychoses and these nutritional deficiences was recognized, treatment consisted of administration of ample fluids to support the circulation. This was somewhat effective in treating delirium tremens but not in the treatment of Korsakoff psychosis or alcoholic hallucinosis; those patients were simply institutionalized and alcohol was withdrawn. As a result of our growing knowledge concerning the metabolic disorders present in these psychoses, increasingly effective treatments are introduced. As yet there are no treatments yielding spectacular results for many of these psychoses, but treatments are becoming more and more effective for delirium tremens and even for the alcoholic encephalopathy of Wernicke's type.

Treatment for each of the alcoholic psychoses is quite similar and has become organized around three basic medical approaches, utilized independently or in combination: (1) detoxication, (2) treatment of the nutritional deficiencies, and (3) interruption of the excitement states. Actually, the alcoholic psychoses, being manifestations of encephalopathy due to toxic and nutritional derangement of the nervous system, are extremely serious disorders. And, until methods were developed to quickly detoxicate the patient, to terminate the acute excitement states, and then to correct the marked nutritional deficiencies, the mortality rate was extremely high.

Detoxication methods vary, depending on the views of different therapists, but essentially the same drugs are utilized in all the alcoholic psychoses to overcome the state of alcohol intoxication. The amphetamines, as well as other ephedrine derivatives, have been very useful as a sobering influence. However, in our experience amphetamine drugs have been more effective in sobering chronic alcoholic individuals than influencing the clinical picture of an alcoholic psychosis per se. Therefore, this drug should be more or less reserved to detoxicate persons who simply suffered an acute debauch, since this measure is much less effective in patients suffering from acute hallucinosis, or Korsakoff psychosis. If administered to alcoholic psychotic patients, it should be kept in mind that amphetamine does not eliminate the nutritional difficulty, naturally, and vitamins should immediately be included in therapy.

When a state of excitement is present in an alcoholic psychosis, emergency sedation measures are obviously necessary. Often, excitement becomes very pronounced and taxes the patient's circulatory functioning considerably. Without sedation many patients have died in a state of cardiac decompensation or circulatory collapse. Formerly, patients were given huge amounts of paraldehyde, barbiturates, chloral hydrate, scopolamine, and so forth. At one time paraldehyde was popular because it seemed to resemble alcohol in its effects and there was the hope that it could be used as a substitute. The same hope is seemingly arising with regard to the use of various tranquilizers, but (as I shall discuss) searching for an alcohol-substitute is complicated, particularly because alcoholism is multifactorial in etiology. Sedation has come to be used on a much more reduced scale than formerly and other forms of dealing with alcohol excitement states have become preferable. This is partly because, due to faulty medication, many patients developed a psychotic drug reaction superimposed on the alcoholic psychosis; an iatrogenic issue developed when therapists did not sufficiently know about the effects of the various sedatives on different alcoholic patients. Drug tolerance in alcoholic patients, by the way, is quite different from that of a normal person. Many alcoholic patients respond very rapidly to some of the sedatives and require extremely small doses; others are extremely refractory to certain sedatives and when given large doses of drugs to which they are less refractory can develop manifestations of confusion states and a drug psychosis superimposed on the psychotic effects of the alcohol. Therefore, sedatives, per se, are utilized sparingly.

Excitement states can be aborted in all alcoholic psychoses by shock therapy. I personally prefer to treat these patients by other means, however, since there is already an organic impairment present in alcoholic psychosis and, naturally, shock will set off another chain of organic impairment. This is true in the case of Korsakoff psychosis, and also, for that disorder, shock therapy is of no advantage. However, shock therapy is indicated for delirium tremens provided the excitement state is so pronounced as to endanger the patient's life and, for some reason, other sedation methods have proved ineffective. But I do not advocate treating delirium tremens with shock therapy routinely if the excitement state can be controlled by other means.

A special form of treatment then evolved for dealing with delirium tremens which corrected the nutritional deficiencies in the patient as well as detoxicating and somewhat sedating him. It was introduced at the Philadelphia Institute and termed the "Philadelphia cocktail." It was highly effective and the rationale continues to be utilized, with some modifications. There are three basic ingredients —vitamin B complex, hypertonic glucose solution, and insulin—mixed according to your preference and given to the patient by slow intravenous infusion. These ingredients are logically based on knowledge of the metabolic problems of these patients.

The first ingredient is vitamin B complex, which is deficient in alcoholic patients. Thiamine chloride is particularly required in high doses to restore the proper metabolic functioning of their nervous system. As I have mentioned, subclinical or actual pellagra-like states are present in many of these patients, and the findings in the nervous system are similar to those observed in patients suffering from pellagra or beri-beri. It is important that the high doses of vitamins be given by injection because many alcoholic people suffer from an alcoholic gastritis and therefore the oral absorption of vitamins is not so effective as when given parenterally, at least in the first phase of treatment.

The second ingredient, hypertonic glucose solution, is included for several reasons. The disturbed water metabolism in these patients results in "wet-brain," or increased intracranial pressure, and hypertonic glucose solution reduces intracranial pressure. Glucose, furthermore, has a high nutritional value and acts as a substitute for glycogen which, in these patients, is usually not converted into glucose due to impairment of liver metabolism. Of course, many chronic alcoholic patients only drink and do not eat, and alcohol has high caloric value but has the difficulty in that it contains no vitamins. Then, when alcohol is withdrawn, due to the gastritis present and the patient's aversion to food, he is placed into even further nutritional difficulty which the infusion of glucose combats.

The third ingredient, insulin, is not only a very potent sedative but also has a marked quieting effect on the vegetative nervous system which is disturbed in connection with the avitaminosis and the derangement of hormonal interactions. (Incidentally, it has been claimed that insufficiency of adrenal cortical hormone accounts for some of the psychotic symptoms, although some observers do not consider that it plays a prominent role in the alcoholic psychoses.) Insulin also serves to improve the utilization of the injected glucose, and it is quite clear that insulin has enzymatic influences on brain metabolism.

Before such an organized treatment was introduced, delirium tremens patients would remain in a delirious state for six or eight days, and usually in a state of great excitement, fear, and tremulousness. They frequently suffered complications: many of these patients repeatedly fell and would sustain all types of injuries; many contracted pneumonia and died. The mortality rate was greater than 30 percent. Since the introduction of effective treatment measures, the mortality figures are small and the acute delirium will subside in about twenty-four hours.

The measures so effective in treating delirium tremens are much less effective when applied to Korsakoff psychosis, and are actually ineffective for treating alcoholic hallucinosis. This indicates that in these disorders we are probably dealing with somewhat different mechanisms which require more complicated treatments. Attempts have been made to treat patients suffering from alcoholic hallucinosis as one treats schizophrenic patients who are in acute excitement states, namely, to administer some form of shock therapy. In the case of Korsakoff psychosis it only adds to the organic impairment in the patient, but it is quite a different proposition in the case of alcoholic hallucinosis. In my opinion, alcoholic hallucinosis patients have a specific schizophrenic organization and, although it is important that therapy should consider the toxic factors which release the schizophrenic psychosis, the underlying personality organization is seemingly equally important.

It has been demonstrated that the more schizoid the patient, the less possibility for his recovery from any form of organic psychosis, including alcoholic. I believe this to be a very important point! Therefore, whenever a patient's history and clinical picture indicate the presence of schizophrenia, he should not be treated as suffering from a toxic process alone. The schizophrenia should be taken into consideration also. A case of alcoholic hallucinosis is properly treated by administering the vitamins required, employing all detoxication measures, and then without delay, treating the hallucinosis episode in the same manner as one treats an acute schizophrenic episode. The response of schizophrenia to shock therapy is less effective than is the response of affective disorders, but it is quite possible that very early treatment of alcoholic hallucinosis with shock will prevent many of these patients from progressing to, and remaining in, a chronic hallucinatory psychotic state. It remains to be proven whether or not a greater percentage of patients treated in this manner will recover from alcoholic hallucinosis but, because of the schizophrenic organization in these patients, I think such a treatment method should be attempted.

11

CHRONIC ALCOHOLISM

Chronic alcoholism is a major problem from psychiatric, medical, and social points of view. It is at the basis of the alcoholic psychoses. In itself chronic alcoholism is quite a large psychiatric problem; and the alcoholic psychoses comprise only a comparatively small number of those patients who have difficulties through alcohol. At one time alcoholism was considered only in the light of the alcoholic psychoses, but in time it became increasingly evident that the major problem underlying the alcoholic psychoses is that of chronic alcoholism. It is recognized as a very great problem to psychiatrists and to the community in many countries.

Chronic alcoholism is defined not so much in terms of the length of time that a person has been drinking, or to what extent the person drinks or how drunk he becomes, but is actually defined in terms of the extent to which the person has a craving for and is dependent upon alcohol. It is an extremely involved problem having physiological, sociological, psychodynamic, and many other unsolved aspects. That it is a very involved problem should be emphasized, because there continues to be a great tendency for over-simplification on every level in attempts to interpret this complex and interlocking issue in simple sociological, in simple psychodynamic, and often in simple etiological terms. This is not permissible in the light of all the presenting available material. The confusion is to some extent due to the fact that investigators working in this field approach it from entirely different backgrounds. Moreover, they also encounter different types of people nominally afflicted with chronic alcoholism: Psychiatrists observe a certain group of drinkers; people in social organizations working to prevent alcoholism observe an entirely different type of alcoholic individual; prison physicians and psychiatrists observe yet another type of individual; and so it goes. Each observer has his own pet concept and theory which are then generalized and applied as valid for every alcoholic person.

For instance, the physiologist might point out that the metabolic factors involved indicate why it is one person who drinks becomes addicted to alcohol and another does not, even though the social and psychodynamic factors are similar in both. The sociologist might be preoccupied with factors relating to social habit-formation and might consider the chronic alcoholic simply a social drinker who demonstrates to an extreme a liberal social attitude toward drinking, and that drinking habits can be induced or reduced by altering the habits of an individual and a social community. Such a sociological argument carried to its conclusion would mean that an entire community could develop chronic alcoholism simply by means of habit formation, an assumption which is not shared by most of those who approach the issue from a physiological or from a psychiatric point of view. The psychiatrist, naturally, might approach the problem from yet another extreme because he is usually the one who indulges in the psychiatric treatment of chronic alcoholic patients. So, he believes that the primary basis for alcoholism is in the individual's psycho-pathology and not alone in his social setting, that problem drinking is always a syndrome in the framework of a psychoneurosis, of a psychosis, of a sociopathic configuration, or of whatever other diagnosis the psychiatrist may prefer, through which the individual expresses his problems by drinking.

Actually, alcoholism basically depends on three factors mentioned, none of which are fully investigated: (1) the *physiological* organization of the individual, (2) the *psycho-logical* organization of the individual, and (3) the *social* organization in which the individual lives. These three factors contribute in varying degrees to the understanding of the problem of alcoholism. For instance, it is obvious that if the social setting is one that prohibits alcohol consumption, even those individuals having a physiological and psycho-logical urge to satisfy their craving for alcohol will attempt to deal with the craving by means other than alcohol. To the contrary, in countries where no ostracism is attached to alcoholic indulgence, or, as in our society, where drinking alcohol is socially encouraged and even considered a positive feature, obviously the social factor considerably influences persons who, for physiological or psychological reasons, drink alcohol.

In terms of background, I would like to mention the physiological aspect of alcoholism before discussing the psychological and social aspects. In the 19th century the alcoholic psychoses were interpreted as disorders based on a "constitutional" inadequacy of an individual to resist alcohol. This fitted in with the general concept of mental disorders of that time and, as you will see, although rather crude and badly elaborated it did contain a grain of truth, in that most likely only certain types of individuals have the tendency to become alcoholic although it could not be proven that a tendency is in any way inherited. Alcoholism was once assumed to be a hereditary disorder, especially on the basis of accounts published of family trees in which a large number of family members were demonstrated to be alcoholic. Actually, alcoholism itself is not transmitted as a hereditary trait. What can be transmitted, however, are hereditarily determined emotional constellations which can lead to alcoholism. The most important of these are the hereditary traits with which we are familiar in connection with such so-called functional psychoses as schizophrenia or manic-depressive psychosis. When I discuss the so-called functional group of psychoses it will be seen that certain emotional dispositions, or constellations, are definitely transmitted and that some of these transmitted constellations predispose the individual to handle emotional disturbances by means of alcohol. Of course, if that individual also observed other members of his family doing the same, there would obviously be the additional factor of his copying them. Alcoholism per se, therefore, is acquired. But in certain individuals, acquiring alcoholism is made much easier by a predisposition in terms of his emotional organization and his imitation of those with whom he lives.

When a little more became known about alcoholism, the entire concept of a constitutional alcoholic factor was completely abandoned, and for a period of time alcoholism was explained almost purely in terms of social factors. This was done particularly because until more recently it was not possible to demonstrate the physiological basis for the craving mechanisms for alcohol.

That alcoholism, or drug addiction, or any dependency on an external agent in order to function, is connected with a craving which the person is unable to overcome was recognized, but the mechanisms for this craving were not known and are as yet known to only a very limited extent. For a long time this craving was actually assumed to be purely on a psychological basis; in other words, if the psychological background of the craving was altered, the craving would then disappear. This is now known to be true for certain individuals, up to a point, but in other individuals seemingly a metabolic formula is present in the body which facilitates the craving and to some extent makes it necessary.

Animal experimentations are of interest in this regard. Various animals have been experimentally addicted to alcohol, as well as to other drugs. This indicates that when animals, including man, use one of these drugs over a period of time it seems to become incorporated into the metabolic functioning of his nervous system and his body in general. However, for reasons as yet unknown, some animals and some individuals do not metabolically incorporate a given drug: such individuals could never develop significant addiction to the drug. Experimental addiction produced in animals apparently moves predominantly on the physiological level. In these animals one cannot extrapolate concerning a form of superego structure, or even ego structure, in the same sense as that operating in man. And in referring to a bunch of animals one cannot assume psychologically introduced anxiety, phobic, or compulsive mechanisms, are the same; their brain organization, educational processes, and social environment are not comparable to man's. Therefore, further investigations are required before it can be demonstrated to what extent addiction in the human individual moves on a psychological level, whether or not it is predominantly on a physiological level, and what metabolic mechanisms definitely play a role.

Williams *(1947)* wrote about the physiological craving in alcoholism and brought up a few very important points regarding the metabolism of individuals who become alcoholic. This was the first significant amount of scientific material accumulated to indicate that in alcoholism we are not dealing with a psychological disorder alone, but definitely with a physiological disorder, and one which actually predisposes these individuals to the use of alcohol. Interestingly enough, these physiological changes are very similar to those also observed in individuals who suffer from anxiety and tension states whereby apparently a certain metabolic organization —whether constitutional or acquired has not been decided—

definitely predisposes these individuals to attempt to alter the regulation of their metabolism by taking some drug, such as alcohol or barbiturates. These physiological mechanisms are essentially based on the individual's carbohydrate metabolism which is, of course, regulated hormonally by quite a number of the major endocrine glands, the adrenal cortex being one of the most important. The liver metabolism plays a great role in the alcoholic psychoses, and seemingly it also plays a considerable role in chronic alcoholic manifestations in those individuals craving alcohol. It is primarily through these physiological findings that we begin to somewhat understand why a tremendous craving for alcohol is present in some individuals and why it is we are not very well able to break that craving without first altering this metabolic process. The problem remains, but because there is as yet no definitive metabolic formula to explain addiction, the physiological role in alcoholism tends to be ignored.

When studying alcoholic patients from a physiological point of view it becomes apparent—and becomes even more apparent as psychological studies continue—that chronic alcoholism is not a single etiological entity. It has always been treated as such. This is a generalization that can be permitted only from an administrative or a social approach, but actually, in speaking about chronic alcoholism, one simply indicates that the group of people who use alcohol to excess differ, that they use it for different purposes, and that there is no unified formula to explain its excessive use. This is an extremely important point because, as one will discover in therapeutic attempts to cope with alcoholism, unless this point of view is taken, the therapist will very soon be quite confused as to why it is one type of alcoholic individual responds to one measure, another type responds to another measure, and yet another type will not respond to any currently employed measure.

From the physiological and from the psychological points of view, alcoholic individuals may be classified as so-called *social drinkers* or as *problem drinkers*. The vast number of problem drinkers is usually differentiated into the following etiological groups: the *psychotic,* the so-called *borderline schizophrenic* or schizoid, the *sociopathic,* and the *psychoneurotic* drinkers. In each group there are many subgroups, many of which I will not discuss in detail. Nevertheless, I would like to give you some inkling of the problems confronting us in each group.

First, there is the so-called *social drinker.* The term usually refers to the individual who, due to his social milieu and the general use of alcohol as a socializing agent, drinks; and he drinks to excess, particularly under the influence of the environment. Emphasis is here placed on the environment rather than the pathology of the individual. In other words, the social drinker is actually the representative of a social malady, of a group malady whereby the group morbidity is in the foreground and the individual morbidity is more in the background, although naturally it plays a certain role. These drinkers are not uncommon to certain professions in which alcohol is utilized as a socializing agent. If you investigate these persons you will discover that quite a number of them who overindulge in alcohol are actually fairly well-adjusted individuals who do not have a very great craving for alcohol. They are able to abstain. They usually do not abstain because drinking alcohol is continually being reinforced by their environment. They drink as a social custom rather than for self-medication, similarly as a growing number indulge in other drugs, such as marijuana, simply to be accepted in the social group promoting its use, but who could easily accept a substitute drug if socially influenced.

A few among those who drink excessively become a social problem. Occasionally a psychiatric problem develops, but not the severe type of psychiatric problem with which we struggle when treating problem drinkers. However, it may be that after a period of time certain physiological and certain psychological craving mechanisms also develop in these individuals. The group of social drinkers responds more effectively to current treatment approaches than do any of the other alcoholic groups and are often manipulated quite well by nonpsychiatrists, often even better than by psychiatrists.

All other groups of chronic drinkers are the so-called *problem drinkers*. In these people, the social environment definitely plays a role by being permissive, encouraging, or even provoking in the use of alcohol, but the problem is not seemingly that of the social group. The problem belongs to the individual in his relationship to the social group. Now, different publications have described problem drinkers differently in terms of etiological mechanisms. The fact that some are sociopathic, some are psychoneurotic, some are borderline schizophrenic, and some are psychotic would already indicate that there is no single psychological common denominator for problem drinkers. Furthermore, if one investigates the psychodynamic structure of each of these individuals in each of the diagnostic groups, it will be found that although common dynamic features can be demonstrated, nevertheless we are faced with many individual problems which stand alone and cannot be understood in the framework of the generalizations prescribed in textbooks. We should not fall into the rather prevalent trend of thinking that by understanding a few of the generalities known about persons who use alcohol or drugs we thereby understand the whole problem, because very often the etiology of the drinking is different in each individual of a group, and sometimes even the trigger mechanisms which are set up, physiologically or psychologically, are different in different individuals. This most likely also accounts for differences in prognoses and differences in response to the various treatment attempts. Actually, treatment attempts have all been based on the generalizations; they were always global attempts to solve the problem of alcoholism, and all global attempts failed, with the exception of one: dispensing with the use of alcohol. But if the use of alcohol is permitted, different groups of problem drinkers will respond differently to treatment methods simply because the underlying etiological mechanisms are different. These issues will become obvious as I now describe, in general, the main groups of problem drinkers that I have mentioned.

The *psychotic* groups include problem drinkers suffering from organic and so-called functional psychoses (naturally, this does not include the alcoholic psychoses). In the first instance, the *organic psychoses,* it often occurs that under the influence of disinhibitory mechanisms produced by the organic psychosis, the individual drinks to excess. This is prevalent among cases of general paresis; a huge number of paretic patients become heavy drinkers. Aside from the factor of organic disinhibition, it should also be emphasized that often the same constitutional and emotional backgrounds lead to both the patient's paresis and his drinking. The large majority of paretic individuals having a so-called cyclothymic temperament were rather sociable, went about and drank a great deal, indulged in a great deal of sexual activity, became infected with syphilis, and later developed paresis. Then, partly due to the continued habit of drinking and partly under the influence of the organic psychosis which further disinhibited them, they became problem drinkers. A minority of paretic individuals were schizoid individuals who had not been in the habit of drinking and who developed alcoholism, if they developed it at all, when symptoms began to appear which they were unable to handle—such as tension, insomnia, depression, and other symptoms—symptoms common to organic and functional psychoses and neuroses and which could lead to self-medication with alcohol.

Arteriosclerotic and, occasionally, senile persons also begin to rely on alcohol. Here again, it is partly because they have become disinhibited, and partly because some of the mental manifestations—such as tension, anxiety, and other symptoms—creep up on them, and they begin to dose themselves with alcohol, at first in small amounts and later in increasingly large amounts, in order to function or to eliminate symptoms.

The medicinal use of alcohol is tremendous! Its medicinal use to regulate tension is particularly great. One could write a book on alcohol problems from two viewpoints: How detrimental alcohol is in so many individuals who use it to regulate their tensions and anxiety, or, how beneficial alcohol is in saving many people from suicide, because it can be a very anti-depressant drug. It is very interesting that in our society there is an increasing tendency to use alcohol, and a growing variety of other drugs, to control the widely prevalent symptoms of tension, anxiety, and depression.

In addition to those suffering from the organic psychoses, persons diagnosed in the category of so-called *functional psychosis* quite often indulge in alcohol. In the manic-depressive psychosis, manic patients obviously indulge in alcohol; they are exuberant and drinking usually reinforces their euphoria. They are sociable and friends pour alcohol into them. Therefore, it is not very rare to observe a manic and alcoholic admixture in these patients. In such cases it is important to diagnostically differentiate whether one is dealing with a chronic alcoholic individual taking a "jolly flight," or a hypomanic manic-depressive individual. If they are actual hypomanic individuals they are not dependent upon alcohol.

Among the depressive patients there is the group of self-medicating individuals who attempt to influence their depression by drinking. The number of depressive individuals who drink is very great. They are not often encountered in psychiatric hospitals because either they are able to navigate about somehow or else they are treated in general hospitals, many under the diagnosis "chronic alcoholism." Incidentally, it is quite often forgotten that chronic alcoholism is not a diagnostic entity but a description of a state of being, that underneath the chronic alcoholism there is usually another disorder, and that the underlying disorder should always be defined. Often a patient suffering with a so-called masked depression is simply diagnosed as being alcoholic and it is overlooked that actually he is a depressed individual. There are depressive persons who drink only periodically whenever they are depressed. And there are depressive persons who drink continually, partly in order to remove the existing depression, and partly because they think the depression will recur and the thought of having to again endure the agony of a depressive phase is so disturbing that they euphorize themselves beforehand.

By far the largest group of drinkers in the psychotic range are the *schizophrenic* and so-called *schizoid* individuals. Full-fledged schizophrenic persons usually become quite conspicuous and are less likely to be diagnosed as alcoholic. They are labeled alcoholic only during a remission when their psychotic manifestations are not clear-cut, or only in the event the psychotic symptoms are confused with those of an alcoholic psychosis. However, among schizophrenic patients whose psychotic symptoms are not very dominant, and especially among the borderline schizophrenic patients—the pseudoneurotic, latent, abortive, or whatever term is used—alcoholism is extremely prevalent.

I would particularly like to emphasize that the *schizoid personality make-up* has a special affinity for the use of alcohol and other drugs, an affinity present in schizoid individuals ranging from those with psychotic to those with neurotic symptomatology. Whether this affinity has some physiological underpinning or is purely psychological has not been determined. The schizoid individual has homeostatic disturbances in the mental as well as the physiological spheres. The homeostatic disturbance is actually the core of the disorder, it being a disorder of the total personality! This disorder is encountered in the so-called abortive cases of schizophrenia as well as in neurotic individuals having schizoid tendencies. In fact, most major so-called functional disorders have preference for persons having a schizoid temperamental disorganization. This includes the serious, the severe, neuroses which most readily occur in individuals who have a schizoid or so-called narcissistic emotional personality organization. For instance, the serious phobic states and the serious obsessive-compulsive states have a very intimate relationship with the schizophrenic group of disorders. The relationship is so intimate that many of us consider the term neurosis a misnomer in that these individuals are not neurotic at all; they are individuals with a "diluted" psychosis in that their schizophrenic manifestations are not so clear-cut as those of a fully psychotic individual. Even when these patients are treated as purely neurotic individuals, it is very often discovered that their emotional organizational configuration is such that they handle reality situations in exactly the same manner as do schizophrenic individuals. This relationship has long been recognized and interpreted by many observers. What is of great interest in connection with alcoholism is that these individuals often have a strong desire to regulate their tensions by drinking.

Generally speaking, all individuals with schizoid manifestations—ranging from so-called borderline to pseudoneurotic schizophrenic individuals—have several clinical features in common. One of the features in common is their *intolerance to tension*. They feel determined to rid themselves of tension by every possible means and to return to a comparatively tension-free, or tranquil, state. In addition, they usually suffer from two other features: the *lack of self-esteem* and the *inability to handle interpersonal relationships*, both of which create a great deal of anxiety and mounting tension. All these features are much more marked than can be observed in neurotic patients who drink, and these schizoid patients are usually very anxious individuals, individuals who are unable to adequately cope with reality situations, individuals who have a so-called inferiority complex in relationships to other persons and feel a great need to rid themselves of mounting tensions. Such an individual finds it extremely easy to turn to a drug, such as alcohol, to rid himself of such symptoms. Alcohol temporarily does that quite effectively. Under the influence of alcohol, the individual feels less tense, less anxious, less inhibited, and thereby more able to cope with social or sexual situations which he is otherwise unable to do. And, under the influence of alcohol, he behaves—so far as he himself is concerned, introspectively and subjectively—as he thinks a normal person behaves. The desire for this so-called normalization is, naturally, very great and some of these individuals obtain it by means of alcohol.

Many dynamic theories have been proposed to explain alcoholism. Why some individuals use alcohol and others do not, why some use it to excess and others with the same psychological constellation do not, may be due to some of the physiological factors mentioned or due to factors as yet unknown. Obviously, not all persons observed to have a schizoid makeup, nor all persons suffering from this peculiar form of anxiety and intolerance to tension, and so forth and so on, are able to relieve their symptoms by means of alcohol. Many people do not derive any pleasure from alcohol and many who are intolerant to alcohol do not use it; others, however, do. But the empirical fact remains that the use of alcohol is prevalent among schizophrenic and schizoid individuals and the number who are alcoholic is extremely great.

Incidentally, there is a special component in the schizoid personalities that must be considered. Many schizoid individuals who drink to excess are very ambivalent toward any medicines they select to take for self-regulation, and quite a number of these persons periodically abstain from alcohol. This so-called self-cure is observed in schizophrenic alcoholic persons and also in schizophrenic drug addicts. Many, however, are unable to cut themselves off from the drug and some then even slip over the border and develop a frank psychosis.

To demonstrate how views have changed, I would like to call to your attention that until very recently the drinking man was actually described in the scientific and popular literature as being a rather jovial, extroverted, sociable fellow. However, practically all the large alcohol studies indicate that such personalities are rarely observed among problem drinkers; most problem drinkers are schizoid, introverted, unsociable, and not very reality-bound individuals. This shows a complete reversal of opinion. If you treat alcoholic individuals, your clinical impression will be that most of the problem drinkers encountered are tense, anxious, and withdrawn individuals who have difficulties in social relationships. Often they are able to socialize only while drinking or when drunk; many of them are even solitary drinkers. This observation indicates that the very jovial, congenial, and sociable fellow is not the usual type encountered among the problem drinkers. This is in contrast to the so-called social drinkers, those who usually drink for pleasure and not for medicinal reasons and very often are really extroverted individuals.

Among the group of so-called *sociopathic* drinkers, alcoholism is so prevalent that in former years, both home and abroad, certain psychiatric textbooks listed excessive drinking under the diagnostic category of "psychopathic state," automatically appointing every alcoholic individual "psychopathic." Even though the definition of sociopathic personality is not very clear-cut (as is apparent in some court trials whereby psychiatrists are practically labeled sociopathic while those persons on trial are cleared of the label), we are nevertheless cognizant that it is so sufficiently defined that it cannot be stated that every problem drinker has a sociopathic personality. But it is also true that among sociopathic individuals there are quite a number of problem drinkers.

Here, again, many sociopathic drinkers are tension-sociopaths, sociopathic individuals who fall into the schizoid range in terms of tension, sociopathic individuals who are emotionally compelled to rid themselves of tension or at least regulate tension through the use of alcohol. Many of them commit criminal acts under the tension-releasing influence of alcohol; this is where alcohol and crime meet. If you should read case records in the psychiatric division of a large prison, you would there see, rather monotonously repeated, the diagnosis "psychopathic personality, chronic alcoholism," "sociopathic personality, chronic alcoholism," and so on. In other words, it is a common diagnostic combination. Sociopathic personality and drug addiction are another common diagnostic combination. Here again, not every drug addict is a sociopathic type by any means, and the same holds true with regard to alcohol. There are many excessive drinkers who have no sociopathic traits and do not have the sociopathic type of emotional organization, and therefore only some of them belong into that group.

The largest group of chronic alcoholic individuals is thought to be suffering from a type of *psychoneurosis*. It does not usually include the psychoneurotic problem drinker whose drinking is in the framework of mild or moderate neurotic disorder, who drinks to escape his neurotic symptoms but does not have a strong dependency craving for alcohol *per se*. He drinks in order to function, socially and sexually, without his usual inhibitions. Although alcohol is a cortical depressant, it releases the individual from inhibitory forces and provides a feeling of emotional stimulation as well as a subjective sense of intellectual stimulation. These individuals can be cured of their problem drinking provided they are cured of their neurosis or are given a substitute means for relief of symptoms. They often switch from alcohol to barbiturates or other drugs.

The psychoneurotic individual, on the other hand, who craves alcohol and becomes dependent upon it, suffers from a type of psychoneurosis having certain differences from the other psychoneuroses. So far, unfortunately, the psychodynamics of those differences can be expressed only in phenomenological terms—in other words, how the patients behave, how they react—and *not* in etiological terms. It is very interesting that the great deal of research expended to discern just what the specific psychodynamic mechanisms are in alcoholic individuals has disclosed practically nothing. The same holds true with regard to criminal behavior. In criminality we are also dealing with the problem that many criminals are sociopathic and many others are probably acting-out psychoneurotic individuals, but nobody has ever offered an explanation as to why it is that one individual having a certain emotional and psychodynamic constellation is an inhibited psychoneurotic who, on the analytic couch, produces the most complicated criminal fantasies but never does anything about it, or even becomes very scared if the notion pops into his head that he might do something about it, and yet another individual having the very same constellation goes forth and acts out his criminal fantasies.

All currently offered explanations for criminal behavior are inconclusive and we are dealing with exactly the same situation concerning drug addiction or alcoholism. The same psychodynamic constellations encountered in psychoneurotic patients who do not drink alcohol are met with in patients who do drink, and no specific explanation has been conclusively offered as to why one of these persons drinks and another person having apparently the same conflictual constellation does not.

At this point, I would like to mention a few of those generalizations which have been elaborated relating to the use of alcohol among the problem drinkers (not including the so-called social drinkers) actually suffering from alcoholism. Again and again it has been observed that these generalizations, which were widely used in the theater, in literature, and even in psychiatric publications to explain all cases of alcoholism, *do not* explain all cases of alcoholism. They are features which emerge only in a certain group of alcoholic individuals. And they are also found in a group of alcoholic individuals who belong in the category of so-called problem drinkers—psychoneurotic, sociopathic, schizophrenic, and so forth.

As I have mentioned, there are individuals in whom the essential feature is that of a very great craving for security and unusually low self-confidence, self-assertion, and self-esteem. Now, upon hearing these four symptoms, I am fairly certain you will quickly discover that you have encountered many psychoneurotic patients who had all of these symptoms, but that this had nothing to do with alcoholism. Incidentally, in one of the best-known psychoanalytic books on the structure of the psychoneuroses *(Fenichel, 1945)*, persons having these symptoms were described and then the very illuminating sentence was added to indicate that, in addition, "a subtle and imperative craving for alcohol" is present in these individuals. Although this "subtle and imperative craving for alcohol" is in fact correct, naturally it is nothing other than a description; it gives no clue as to how the subtle and imperative craving is actually brought about.

I have mentioned that in addition to these four features, which are present in many alcoholic persons, they are also intolerant to tension. This is a very important point. I would like to add a fact that was not mentioned: These patients are found to have a peculiar combination of a *craving for tension* and, at the same time, an *intolerance for tension*. I have directly observed this combination present in a number of pseudoneurotic schizophrenic patients who drank. Having investigated the pseudoneurotic group more thoughly than other groups, I cannot state if such a symptom combination is present in other diagnostic groups, but it is a common feature of many schizoid or schizophrenic individuals. They display the same combination: a craving for tension and an intolerance for tension. A patient will complain to you, "I have no ability to maintain a sustained effort toward anything; everything soon bores me and then I feel that I have to find something to relieve this boredom." In markedly introspective schizoid or schizophrenic individuals you may have the statement, "I must see to it that something is constantly going on and that reinforces my relationship to reality."

This so-called reality reinforcement symptom, as a

secondary mechanism of defense against a feeling of detachment, is quite often the case in schizophrenia. In other words, some amount of tension must be present: Some unique sexual excitement must be had; some new idea must be explored, always something to drag the individual back from his deep feeling of detachment and reconnect him with the environment. At the same time, however, when the individual does seek this reality reinforcement and does strive to again become in better contact with the environment, all kinds of inhibitory barriers crop up because he is very sensitive, because he is very anxious, and because he lacks confidence in handling situations. So, these persons are continually swinging, in an ambivalent manner, between an attempt to reinforce reality contact and a simultaneous withdrawal from it because they cannot tolerate the situation. Exactly this process is present in a number of alcoholic individuals who attempt to regulate these ambivalent efforts to solve the problem—by drinking alcohol.

It is already apparent that these few basic mechanisms to which I have just alluded are rather vague, so omission of their detail will not be a great loss. The same applies to some further generalizations which I shall now mention briefly.

First of all, several attempts were made to interpret alcoholic phenomena as a special form of *obsessive-compulsive* manifestation. Basically, there is no objection to that, provided obsessive-compulsive phenomena are interpreted more in a very broad psychopathological sense rather than a narrow clinical sense. (This, by the way, is part of the confusion present in psychoanalytic literature.) Psychopathologically speaking, most repetition-compulsion phenomena as described by Freud actually can be interpreted as being obsessive-compulsive in the sense that the patient is dominated by them, and because he is unable to throw them off there is a tendency toward repetition, or perseveration, of those symptoms. But that does not mean that all such patients have an obsessive-compulsive dynamic structure as it is presently defined. You will encounter alcoholism in persons who actually are obsessive-compulsive individuals in that they manifest an obsessive-compulsive structure dynamically as well as descriptively. However, many alcoholic persons do not have that dynamic structure and are obsessive-compulsive only in the broad descriptive sense that, naturally, they are obsessed by the craving that compels them to take alcohol.

Tausk and others who also investigated alcoholism pointed out another mechanism which they observed in their patients: Alcoholic individuals usually introject guilt, and this *introjection* mechanism is rather obvious in them. That is true of those alcoholic individuals who drink in order to rid themselves of depression. It is not true of the many alcoholic individuals whereby guilt is manifested through alcoholism as the substitute for introjection, and depression in *not* present. Therefore, the alcoholic mechanism is not always similar to that observed in depressions.

According to another interpretation, which was obviously more to the point, in many alcoholic individuals a very strong *oral longing* is present. Orthodox Freudian interpretation placed it into the primary oral phase. It was termed the so-called archaic oral longing and it was mentioned that it was connected to the person's need for security and being fed. This need was later somewhat reinterpreted as being the patient's continual striving to regain an infantile state of passive-protection. At the same time, he is in great need of ego-strength and tends to feed it into himself with a drug. The difficulty with this interpretation is that such phenomena as oral-aggression, feeling of dependency, striving for security, and so forth are rather general dynamic terms and, as you know, cannot be applied as a specific mechanism to explain any particular disorder because they occur so often in such different constellations. For instance, this same constellation described by several investigators in connection with alcohol is also observed in neurotic persons who do not drink to excess or who are even total abstainers, and we have no explanation as to why one person drinks and another person having a quite similar dynamic constellation does not.

Some observers mentioned that in alcoholic patients there are weak primitive drives moving on a pregenital level, and some believe on an even lower level—an oral or anal "narcissistic" level. Actually, this would simply be interpreting alcoholism as a *regressive* neurosis whereby the great degree of narcissism present would place these patients close to the obsessive-compulsive or to the psychotic group. Incidentally, the alcoholic person under the influence of alcohol is likely to do much of his thinking out loud, after the fashion of small children. This may be interpreted as regression to childhood in this one respect. Here again, the difficulty is that although some alcoholic patients do show these features, others do not.

Robert Knight *(1937)* gathered data with which he attempted to interpret the alcoholism as a manifestation of a *fixation* that occurs in the following manner: Specific oral frustrations in early childhood were demonstrated, and there followed a strong turning away from the mother and turning toward the father. On this assumption, Knight tried to link the craving for alcohol with the homosexuality that was considered the sequel. This brings up the constantly discussed point with regard to alcoholism, namely, the relationship between alcoholism and homosexuality. A great many dynamic formulations on alcoholism view it on the level of homosexuality and many books and papers have treated the two phenomena as being practically interchangeable, at times giving the impression that homosexuality is a prerequisite to alcoholism, or that alcoholism occurs only in individuals who had latent or manifest homosexual tendencies. The latter assumption could stem from the fact that many overt homosexual individuals do develop an increased tolerance for alcohol; although not actually "alcoholic" they belong in the group of "social drinkers" who drink to ease their tension, frustration, and anxiety in certain social situations. In my opinion, this type of interpretation of alcoholism is incorrect, incorrect insofar that it makes generalizations from specific mechanisms that are, of course, demonstrable in a few cases. This is based on rather circumscribed logic. You must keep in mind that the number of fully analyzed alcoholic patients is comparatively very small; that this material has actually been used as a generalization to explain the whole complex pattern of alcoholism.

The issue is not a clear-cut matter of homosexuality's being a factor in alcoholism. It is undeniable that quite a number of chronic alcoholic males, and chronic alcoholic psychotic males, manifest *disintegration* of their sexual organization. This disintegration feature is rather complex: (1) In many individuals it is definitely true that their sexual organization never became well genitalized. Quite often individuals remain in a state of somewhat diffused sexuality, that in their different phases of sexual development, including the homosexual phase, they show certain fixation points. Some of these individuals actually drink in order to, I would say, genitalize themselves. These are the persons who are potent under the influence of alcohol and impotent without alcohol. They seemingly gain a feeling of security; they become more aggressive; they become, you might say, more masculine under the influence of alcohol and their so-called feminine strivings are subdued so long as they are under the influence of alcohol. Another group (2) of alcoholic individuals, interestingly enough, manifests the reverse phenomena: Individuals who were apparently fairly well integrated sexually begin to regress under the influence of alcohol. In other words, alcohol does not normalize but does just the opposite. It releases certain strivings or drives which, without alcohol, the individual is unaware of and would not display. This occurs in every adult age group but, interestingly enough, it is more prevalent in individuals of the higher age group. One finds a number of older persons who have, at least by all appearances, a fairly adequate sexual organization and in whom homosexual, exhibitionist, sado-masochistic, and many other strivings become apparent under the influence of alcohol.

Therefore, it might be stated that in some individuals alcohol has a normalizing effect; in other individuals, however, it has definitely a regressive effect. We do not know for certain which individuals fall into the first group and which fall into the second group. I personally feel that the group of patients described by Knight, consisting of only a few cases, is too narrow a sampling to explain all alcoholic cases in terms of specific oral frustration or some oedipal difficulty within the family, a turning away from the mother and turning toward the father. That family difficulties are prevalent among alcoholic individuals is obvious; they occur in all varieties of combinations and constellations and any specific mechanism remains to be defined.

I would also like to mention that all the dynamic mechanisms which were elaborated on the male alcoholic, especially those relating or attributing alcoholism to homosexuality, are invalid for the alcoholic female. The dynamic mechanisms of alcoholism in the female are much less well understood and, as you know, sexual disturbances in general are less understood in women than in men. That is based partly on biological phenomena, in that sexuality in the male is less diffused than in the female, and partly on a social phenomenon, in that it is easier to obtain reliable material on the sexuality of men than of women. Furthermore, research, which was to some extent based on Freud's empirical concepts of sexuality, was all worked out on men and investigations of female sexuality actually were later added as an afterthought. So, all three of these components played a role in interpreting the relationship between alcoholism and homosexuality. There are quite a number of alcoholic females in which homosexuality seemingly plays no role in connection with alcoholism; at the very most, it plays a much lesser role in females than in males.

Incidentally, paranoid mechanisms may also in some instances be connected with alcoholism. Although I would prefer to discuss paranoid mechanisms in detail in the framework of schizophrenia, I might now mention that alcoholic individuals resemble those addicted to any other drugs in that many of them become sensitized in relation to their environment and continually watch others for indications that it is discovered they are addicts. In other words, a forthright paranoid feeling develops which is at times possibly aggravated during a withdrawal period when their symptoms are especially conspicuous. In such situations, any homosexuality factors and any schizoid factors present are not the main issues.

I would also like to call your attention to the fact that quite a number of chronic alcoholic individuals, whether or not they develop an alcoholic psychosis, are markedly schizoid, probably many being attenuated schizophrenic individuals. And actually, if you study the sexuality of these alcoholic patients, you will find that it is incorrect to interpret their sexual manifestations as being homosexual. It is incorrect because in addition to the homosexual component, which is surely correctly observed, a number of other sexual strivings are present also. Actually, the expression "chaotic sexuality" is a much more accurate term in that homosexuality is only one component but many other sexual strivings can be demonstrated as well. It is due only to the social interest in homosexuality and to whatever social tabu is attached to it that only this particular fragment of the person's sexual organization was selected. If you examine these patients carefully, and particularly if you treat them carefully, you will be astonished how many pregenital sexual drives appear. Individuals who attempt gratification by homosexual means will also have exhibitionistic, voyeuristic or sado-masochistic strivings, and so forth. You can read through the entire textbook of *Psychopathia Sexualis* (Krafft-Ebing) and discover many of the strivings present in a parallel form in these individuals. Homosexuality is only one among them. I would like to emphasize that, because in the research and treatment appraisal of these patients it was forgotten that seemingly we are dealing with a more profound sexual disorganization than simple homosexuality would imply. These individuals quite often manifest a sexual structure which is encountered in schizophrenic individuals; actually, nonmaturation of sexuality is present on all its levels.

It is interesting, furthermore, that sexual gratification of these individuals is seemingly linked with experimentation on all levels. However, the majority remain anhedonic on all levels and are frustrated on all levels, which is a quite important fact. We therefore see these individuals constantly trying to force sexual realization by all ways and means, not being gratified by any one method and then trying something else. But in this realm of different sexual experimentation, homosexuality produces, naturally, probably the g eatest anxiety in the patient and the greatest repercussions in our particular culture. It is understandable because this is the form of sexual activity which the person perceives as being the most condemned of all and so most likely links it with the idea that he is not functioning normally. In many cultures, including ours, homosexuality is regarded as synonymous with being an incomplete or a nonfunctioning individual and, therefore, it has considerable secondary connotation for the patient.

But I would again like to emphasize that in schizoid drinkers, along with the so-called homosexuality present, there is much more sexual pathology. We actually are dealing with an immature and chaotic personality who is unable to integrate, to fuse, sexual impulses realistically and appropriately but leaves-and-plays with the various diffused fragments present. Many of these individuals drink and some drink in order to accomplish fusion of their sexual drives by means of alcohol. Or, which is even more common, the fusion is not accomplished with alcohol but while drinking the person simply does not care that he is unable to achieve sexual gratification on any level. The number of such alcoholic patients is great.

Naturally, alcohol can serve all varieties of functions in the sexual, social, and other areas of the person's life performance: (1) he drinks because he becomes normalized by alcohol, (2) he drinks because he wants to forget that he cannot function, (3) he drinks and then manifests regression phenomena under the influence of alcohol. I have mentioned these issues—using the area of sexuality somewhat in detail, as an example—to call attention to the complexity of the whole multifactorial matter of chronic alcoholism and how difficult it is to find a common denominator for all the different observations available in terms of etiology and dynamic mechanisms. Therefore, chronic alcoholic disorders continue to be an intricate and unsolved problem in terms of all therapeutic approaches attempted.

TREATMENT RATIONALES

Treatment of chronic alcoholism is a very sad chapter in psychiatric medicine. Individual psychiatrists and hospitals are able to point to a fair number of recoveries which appear very impressive—until there are follow-up studies. Alcoholism is a clear example to show why psychiatrists are so reluctant to make follow-up studies. Reluctance is fully justified because the rather dramatic number of improvements or recoveries reported has not stood up under the scrutiny of the few follow-up studies made; the studies demonstrate that the rate of relapse is very high. If the relapsed patient does not return to his former therapist or hospital, naturally it is not even known that he suffered a relapse. Patients often do not return to their former therapist because their feelings of guilt or shame can be so great that, rather than recontacting and disappointing the therapist, many patients proceed elsewhere. They also wish to avoid exposing themselves to the accusations and ridicule they anticipate when the therapist who had discharged them as recovered then realizes they are again in the same alcoholic condition as when having commenced therapy. Nevertheless, treatment for alcoholism is not a completely hopeless matter and approximately 20 or 25 percent of treated patients remain well.

Therapy consists mainly of measures attempting to *diminish the patient's craving for alcohol,* and for this there are three approaches: (1) the *physiological,* or *medical,* (2) the *sociological,* and (3) the *psychiatric.* These three approaches are, naturally, interlocked. They are combined in various ways, more or less happily or unhappily dependent on the points of view of different therapists.

Before discussing these treatment measures, preliminary medical treatment should be mentioned because in many cases the organic toxic effects of alcohol are the first problem confronting the therapist. When dealing with an acutely intoxicated patient or one who has engaged in a prolonged alcoholic debauch, obviously medical treatment is required to remove the organic effects of the alcohol before actual treatment of the patient's main underlying problem can begin. As I discussed in connection with the alcoholic psychoses, various drugs can be used to detoxicate the patient; treatment for any secondary metabolic problem, including avitaminosis, can be applied; if the patient is agitated, certain sedative measures can be included, keeping in mind that some patients are prone to iatrogenic effects from certain sedative drugs. Those cases who arrive for treatment without any toxic physical or psychotic reactions may not require these medical treatments.

The next procedure would be to determine what treatment measures should be employed to combat the patient's craving for alcohol. It must be realized that even those patients who responded to medical treatments continue to have the basic problem of alcoholism. Quite a number of them appear to be well; and, after a short time, they go forth and begin the whole drinking pattern all over again. Treatment of the toxic effects of alcohol removed only the secondary problem. The primary issue, the individual's desire to make use of the drug, must be dealt with.

Medical treatment, per se, for chronic alcoholism does not exist. For centuries attempts were made to find some medicinal substance which, when taken by the patient, would cure him of his craving for alcohol. Drugs have been found which to some extent allay the quantity of a person's anxiety response to stimulation coming from social sources, but the quality of anxiety response, as expressed in a craving for alcohol, is not affected. One must realize that the human mind is peculiarly organized so as to be stimulated in two ways: It is stimulated by physiological intraorganismic changes, and it is stimulated by sources external to the organism—not alone by physical, but by social and other means. External stimuli then fuse with the existing physiological stimuli. It is obvious that insofar as its source is social, the craving cannot be influenced physiologically; but what can be influenced physiologically is the quantity of a response of the organism to any form of stimulation. The problem next to be solved is how to reduce the intraorganismic stimulation. This has been attempted on a psychological and on a physiological level. Theoretically, a drug which could reduce anxiety by reducing the intraorganismic stimuli producing it (in the same way as barbiturates reduce all stimuli from any source which produce insomnia) would then prevent the subsequent events in the organism, both physiological and psychological, from being put into operation. The reduced stimulation within the patient would be sufficient.

In the 19th century, when more and more insight was gained in certain pharmacological issues, efforts were made to influence alcoholic individuals with sedatives such as bromides, then barbiturates. With the exception of very few patients, these attempts failed. Sedation rarely influences the craving for alcohol. However, the issue did emerge that seemingly many patients are able to function normally when brain functioning is reduced somehow, because then they are at least enabled to cope with their internal and external stimuli. Naturally, this does not solve the problem and in some cases barbiturate addiction is even exchanged for alcohol addiction, depending on the patient's preference, or the two are even combined.

Renewed attempts to treat craving for alcohol by means of drugs were made when the ephedrine derivatives were introduced as detoxicating agents. It was found that the amphetamines could reduce hangover effects in a patient and many patients discovered they could drink more and regret it less. A small minority of the schizophrenic alcoholic individuals who used amphetamines ceased drinking; their craving for alcohol seemed to be diminished or eliminated, but how that was brought about is a matter of speculation. Actually, when a psychiatrist treats an alcoholic patient psychotherapeutically and attempts to include the regular use of amphetamines, it usually leads only to the patient's drinking more alcohol, but because the effects of the drinking are less apparent to the psychiatrist, he begins to be very relaxed about his patient and satisfied in thinking he is accomplishing a great deal. Meanwhile, the patient's consumption of alcohol may increase perhaps 50 or 100 percent.

Therefore, sedative or stimulant drugs do not diminish the craving for alcohol, with one rare exception: a small percentage of certain schizoid individuals who use alcohol as a normalizing agent—to overcome hypochondriacal fears, obsessions, phobic symptomatology, or, to overcome depression—respond beneficially to sedatives, or to stimulants, or to one of the various so-called tranquilizing agents, or sometimes to combinations of these drugs. Their craving for alcohol seems diminished.

Some therapists medicate the patient with vitamins. This may be done in the course of therapy but all the same the patient should be told that the vitamins will in no way prevent his drinking alcohol, because some patients might assume they were prescribed for that purpose. Misconceptions about the role of vitamins went to such an extent that a few decades ago a large liquor concern advocated mixing vitamins into marketed liquor with the idea that then all dangers of alcoholism would be avoided and therefore it would give green lights for more people to drink. Fortunately, the idea did not materialize because the Food and Drug Administration feared it would convey the notion that drinking is a safe procedure and would cause alcoholism to increase by leaps and bounds. Actually, although vitamins may be beneficial, many alcoholic patients suffer with gastritis and when the stomach mucus membranes are hit with a big dose of liquor it is doubtful that any vitamins are very readily absorbed into the body.

Incidentally, a procedure referred to as "sham drinking" has been tried. In the minds of some patients drinking is associated with the labeled bottle and with the social surroundings. It was therefore proposed that by reproducing the entire setting with the omission of one thing— alcoholic content of the drink put into the bottle—the person would become reconditioned. Temporary cures have been made by this conditioning, but usually only in cases of the so-called social drinker who does not have a craving for alcohol based on physiological factors or a severe personality disorder which had required him to drink. That brings us to the matter of the so-called conditioned reflex therapies formulated during the early part of this century.

Combined medical and psychological approaches were derived based on Pavlov's simple observations that an unpleasurable association suppresses a particular reflex. Actually, in practically all forms of therapy, conditioning plays a role in both the acquiring of habits and the discontinuing of habits, as has been observed in the production of so-called experimental neuroses. From Watson's basic theory that environmental influence is exclusively important emerged the idea of utilizing a drug which would influence the alcoholic person to develop a distaste for alcohol. The drug apomorphine, originally used in the so-called aversion treatment to condition patients suffering from so-called hysteria, was then used to condition patients suffering from chronic alcoholism. The feeling of nausea and the feeling of sickness produced by this drug are rather dreadful ones. In other words, it did not serve as a superficial stimulus but inflicted a great physio-psychological wallop to the patient. The drug's use was based on the concept that a punishing stimulus would put the patient in a disagreeable frame of mind in association with his particular symptom and this would persuade him to relinquish it. The method was later refined and pilocarpine or ephedrine was injected or given orally; because it would take a time for it to act, the patient would then be seated in a chair and suggested, or hypnotized, to expect all the symptoms of nausea, malaise, sweating, trembling, weakness, and so forth. Then he would be told that, naturally, whenever he began to express his neurosis—or, in the case of the alcoholic patient, whenever he would drink his whiskey—these same symptoms would again occur. In that manner, the primitive conditioning took place. This form of conditioning therapy carried out without psychotherapy was effective in about 25 percent of the patients, and when psychotherapy reinforced the conditioning therapy approximately 35 or 40 percent of the patients improved or recovered.

At first, marked claims were made for this method and it was believed by several investigators and others to be the cure for alcoholism, that the country would be freed from alcoholism by means of a few gallons of a conditioning drug. The method, naturally, was successful for treating the so-called social drinkers, but in treating actual problem drinkers or patients with marked psychiatric problems it was not so effective. After ten years or so, the original enthusiasm faded. One of its shortcomings was that if conditioning did not take hold after one, two, or three sessions, the patient promptly returned to his drinking pattern. Furthermore, since the drugs used for the conditioning did not alter the alcohol metabolism in the patient, they did not influence the underlying craving for alcohol.

In the 1940's, conditioning treatment improved when "antabuse" was introduced in Denmark. Its use has many drawbacks and certainly is not a total treatment in itself. The method consists of giving the patient one or more daily oral doses of the drug; if the patient follows that with a drink of alcohol, the antabuse interferes with the metabolism of the alcohol, acetaldehyde forms in the stomach and is distributed through the circulation to all parts of the body including the nervous system and produces many subjective symptoms such as nausea, vomiting, marked feelings of malaise, sweating, and so forth. The subjective feelings are supposedly so disagreeable as to condition the patient against taking alcohol. It differs from the former conditioned reflex treatments which required conditioning to take hold after a few applications in that antabuse can be taken indefinitely and each time the patient drinks, conditioning is automatically produced.

Two seemingly valid objections arose in connection with antabuse in treatment. The first objection was on the physical level. This drug is not completely safe. Persons suffering from heart disease or metabolic disorders such as mild diabetes may have violent reactions to the drug. Marked retching could tax the cardiovascular system. The production of acetaldehyde further interferes with the already disturbed keto-metabolism in diabetic individuals. It has been reported that several patients died while using the drug. It is not clear exactly what caused the fatalities but they occurred when the following happened: The patient first drank alcohol; upon reconsidering his indulgence he then took antabuse; upon further reconsideration he countermoved by drinking again. So, there were several layers of psychological and physiological actions on the part of the patient. The sequence of alcohol, antabuse, then alcohol again, produces a violent reaction in many patients.

The safest procedure in prescribing antabuse is to hospitalize and detoxicate the alcoholic patient and then, as if in a controlled conditioned reflex experiment, give him antabuse followed by a measured amount of alcohol and observe his response. If the adverse reaction is quite marked, next give the patient antabuse followed by a smaller amount of alcohol. After continuing this pattern, the patient is discharged from the hospital already in a somewhat conditioned state, the conditioning having been processed under observation rather than being left up to the patient. It is a poor policy to simply give the patient a prescription for antabuse and tell him, "You take that, and when you drink some alcohol afterwards you will become very sick and will stop drinking." Even those patients who did not drink before taking a dose of antabuse can have a violent reaction when they follow it by drinking an amount of alcohol not regulated in proportion to the drug.

The second objection to the use of antabuse was that this procedure is obviously dependent on the patient's cooperation. Nothing can be achieved unless the patient takes the medication and it is frequently a psychotherapeutic problem to bring him to that point. Many clinics have made it a policy to hospitalize the patient for a few days, determine his personality structure, then expose him to the antabuse and study his reactions to it. Meanwhile, relatives living with the patient are instructed to exert a certain amount of supervision of the person taking the antabuse; the hospital social service worker visits the patient and his relatives periodically and insists upon a report of the patient's behavior to determine whether or not he has been drinking while taking antabuse.

The rate of relapse was found to be fairly high during the first few weeks of antabuse therapy, especially in chronic alcoholic individuals already quite conditioned to alcohol and having a very marked craving for it. But even in the relapsed group a considerable number were rehabilitated by eventually becoming accustomed to avoiding alcohol.

Statistics have not been extensive but they indicate that antabuse combined with psychotherapy can rehabilitate about 40 percent of alcoholic patients; however, it was not determined how many patients remained well. Despite warranted skepticism, this therapeutic attempt which has long been ridiculed as a primitive and somatic method to treat a supposedly predominantly mental sickness was more successful than all previous treatment methods.

It is extremely interesting that the compound itself (tetraethylthiuram disulphide) was first used in factories for vulcanizing rubber and there it was first discovered that persons inhaling it reacted to alcohol with vomiting, malaise, and so forth. A Danish doctor was impressed by the fact, and, as a logical sequence, animal experiments were worked out. It was found that by developing alcoholism in a monkey, which is easy to do, and then feeding him antabuse and alcohol, exactly the same physical reactions occur. This very primitive mechanism seems sufficient to lead some individuals away from drinking alcohol.

One very interesting problem emerges which should be tackled from a psychiatric point of view. Assuming antabuse is successful and the patient discontinues drinking alcohol, what then happens to the patient? From the psychiatric view, the patient's drinking is surely in connection with some conflictual problem: he drinks because he wants to obliterate certain conflicts from his mind, he drinks to escape from certain feelings and ideas, he drinks to bolster his sexual performance, or he drinks to override some other dynamic mechanisms observed in his culture. Assuming he then responds to antabuse, is he now cured because his alcoholism is cured or will he switch to other symptoms? This very important question emerges, naturally, in the psychiatric treatment of many disorders. If you block certain discharge mechanisms utilized by the patient to solve his conflict—for instance, blocking somatic channelizations of tension—what happens to the particular conflict and to the patient? This important question should be further investigated. Many psychiatrists feel that when the mechanisms of alcoholism are blocked the alcoholic patient only demonstrates a palliative cure in terms of his alcoholism, but remains a sick person—neurotic, or psychotic, or whatever. The interesting thing is that many individuals when blocked in utilizing the alcoholic mechanism to express their neurotic conflicts continue to function. Naturally, the conflict in the neurosis is not the sickness; it is the inability to cope with the conflict that is the sickness. Therefore, the individual probably remains a conflicted individual but if given the possibility of mastering that conflict caused by his alcoholism, he will probably function. However, this question remains completely open and will be very interesting to investigate.

Social treatment of alcoholism, the second therapeutic approach, is largely on a nonpsychiatric and nonmedical level. Although its effectivity is not very great, at the present time the social approach is probably the most effective form of therapy. Because of their background and training, psychiatrists tend to forget the value of social manipulation in treating emotional disorders, but it has actually been much more successful for more alcoholic individuals than have all other individual psychotherapeutic attempts. This finding is based on observations of patients who had no success with individual psychotherapy and whose alcoholism was then successfully controlled with the social form of treatment. That the reverse also occurs is obvious, but we must keep in mind that the social attempt to manipulate alcoholism is a very important one.

The social handling of an alcoholic person has been attempted many times, in many ways, in many different countries. The so-called "Blue Cross" movement was inaugurated by a Swiss psychiatrist, Forel *(3)*, in the latter part of the 19th century and was similar in its organization to that of the more recent "Alcoholics Anonymous" (AA). The Blue Cross differed from the AA movement mainly in that the members were largely nondrinkers who were simply against alcoholism for moral or other reasons. As you know, the AA members are themselves alcoholic and therefore their insights into the alcoholic patient are based on experience, not on intuition alone. Their psychological appraisal of the drinker can be far superior to that of a non-alcoholic psychiatrist, and AA members often are well able to manipulate the alcoholic person.

In the AA and similar social therapy movements, two elements should be considered: first, the *social element*, which operates rather consistently throughout therapy, and secondly, the *suggestive element,* which is not consistently effective. The suggestive element in treating alcoholism, as in treating any disorder, is modified by time. All organized movements and therapies carry a certain suggestive value initially. It is enhanced by propaganda, by literature on the subject, and particularly by a certain group spirit that evolves. After a period of time, somehow the suggestive powers attached to the phenomenon begin to wane and then the therapy, which had initially been greeted with a great deal of enthusiasm, loses its effectivity. Ross, in his book on treatment of the common neuroses *(1937)*, wrote an interesting chapter on how a person's conviction of one or another therapeutic methods carries a therapy along successfully—until he begins to doubt it. This is valid with regard to individual therapies and also very much valid with regard to group movements having a formula for treating alcoholism. The Swiss Blue Cross movement was highly effective for a few years but then the number of persons "cured" of alcoholism dwindled considerably. The AA movement has increased in popularity but it remains to be seen how long its suggestive powers will continue to influence alcoholic persons.

Not an organized form of psychotherapy, AA is conducted simply by means of social implications and by examples. In other words, it is a morale-building form of psychotherapy. The therapists are former drinkers having no training in psychiatry; they usually do nothing to investigate any dynamic reasons why a person drinks beyond applying a few clichés, such as "escape," or "relief from depression," or some other small item picked from the popular literature. Although no attempt is made to actually investigate the source of the alcoholic disorder, a therapist in such a group competes very successfully with those trained to know the function of the mind, probably due in large part to his experience, good intuition, and in part to his not being inhibited by psychotherapeutic concepts. He applies all those primitive treatment approaches utilized in good psychotherapy. But he appeals to the conscious mind of the person. Of course, a great many unconscious elements are unwittingly involved, but what the worker accomplishes with the drinker is mainly through ego influence. As you know, the whole first phase of the psychoanalytic movement consisted of analysis of the so-called id, attempting to discover just how these different drives become influenced and modified. Because the original idea was that some form of cathartic experience should release these dammed-up id drives, psychoanalysis concentrated on that procedure and the ego and ego forces were largely ignored until much later. But, a better balance has been gained since the ego has also been taken into consideration. Influencing the ego, "lifting" the ego, and ego "infusion," became an increasingly important part of all forms of psychotherapy due to the recognition of the role played by the ego in the patient's analysis of his unconscious motivating forces. In other words, if a soldier cannot march on an empty stomach, neither can a patient deal with his dynamic conflicts on an empty self-esteem.

It must be kept in mind, however, that should a non-alcoholic therapist attempt to influence or convert alcoholic patients with ego-supportive measures, these patients will not drink less; they will drink more because they will definitely feel that the therapist is talking down to them. All their existing hostilities and resentments of certain rules and regulations are reinforced. But if the therapist is a former drinker, if they regard him as being socially as degraded as they feel themselves to be, it gives them some basis for identification.

In all group movements and in all organizations, the ability of the person to identify himself with the group, both in positive and negative evaluations, plays a very significant role. Naturally, a person more easily relates to, believes in, and leans upon people who have been through similar experiences. Therefore, by means of identification with an alcoholic group, the alcoholic person is surrounded by an atmosphere in which he feels understood, in which he feels that the others in the group have the same difficulty as his, and their ability to overcome it spurs him on in feeling he will also be able to overcome it. This pattern of identification is often activated and can remain indefinitely.

You will observe that in any organization, whether it advocates scientific, artistic, social, religious, or any other form of change, there will be a few among the followers who are rather paranoid and manipulate their identification by projecting their own thinking into the particular ideation of the organization; this is then maintained with a great degree of conviction and often the conviction actually reaches a delusional level. Occasionally these paranoid problem drinkers, even though severely disturbed, actually benefit from the social approach because they are able to utilize the organization as a vehicle to absorb some of their paranoid symptomatology. For example, after recovering from an overt psychotic episode, one of my schizophrenic patients related the intimate details concerning the alcoholic peregrinations of his brother, a severely alcoholic person who resented and had rejected any form of psychotherapy. One nice day my patient came to me and remarked, "You know, because my brother was dead drunk and in a terrible state I was able to persuade him to join AA. At first he did not want to go but then he went, and in about two weeks he transformed himself from a severe alcoholic into a total abstainer with the help of AA."

Now, the interesting thing was that the brother's transformation actually involved another mechanism in addition to that prescribed by the AA scheme: he quickly became an AA organizer. He became a very effective organizer but a very aggressive, a very domineering, and a very sadistic organizer. Many of the paranoid mechanisms which had once led to his alcoholism he now utilized constructively in the framework of the organization. As in the case mentioned and one or two similar ones I have encountered, the individual gave up drinking simply because suddenly he was enabled to redirect his paranoid trend and proselytize other people. That played a very great role. The so-called conversion experience is a very potent therapeutic factor which we, as psychiatrists, do not or, perhaps because of our training, cannot utilize. We should never underestimate, particularly in schizoid individuals, the ability to hitch some of their difficulties onto a concrete idea and then manipulate that idea. However, I would not go so far as to state that the therapeutic influence of an organization, such as AA, is purely based on some form of fanatic fervor, because the majority of alcoholic individuals are not fanatic but are actually persons who, having been drinkers, are able to handle many alcoholic people quite well.

Criticism of social organizations formed to manipulate alcoholic individuals rests on two points. First, social manipulation succeeds preeminently with those individuals who do not suffer severe personality disorders. With the exception of a few schizoid patients with a paranoid trend who may benefit from the social approach, the majority of members of social organizations who actually succeed in giving up alcohol are the so-called social drinkers or the problem drinkers who are not seriously disturbed by their neurotic or psychotic disorder. Secondly, the social approach itself does not employ those reinforcements made available by other treatment approaches, such as drugs and psychodynamic insights. In other words, the problem drinker who suffers from severe phobic or obsessive neurotic symptomatology, or the problem drinker who is a withdrawn person with a complex and involved schizoid personality structure, is usually much less benefited by the social approach than is the drinker who has a rather well-organized personality structure. Naturally, the social treatment fails in many cases, as the AA admits. Many AA groups therefore try to treat these individuals in collaboration with psychiatrists.

Psychiatric treatment of chronic alcoholic patients— the third therapeutic approach—is very difficult without adjuncts of any medicinal or social measures to reinforce the value of the treatment. This is especially so because the therapist is confronted with the patient alone, without any extraneous supports which could to some extent curb the patient's acting-out tendencies. Results with all forms of psychotherapy, analytical or nonanalytical, have been uniformly disappointing. Results with psychoanalysis have been so disappointing that the majority of analysts do not accept alcoholic patients for analytic treatment because it is somehow a foregone conclusion that the outcome would be poor or, if the psychiatrist is an optimist, very dubious, but never good. The few available statistics on other forms of psychotherapeutic approaches with alcoholic persons have indicated that apparently this group's response to treatment is in many ways very similar to that in the group of neurotic patients bordering on psychosis, the patients who demonstrate a high degree of so-called narcissism. The most optimistic statistics on the psychotherapy of alcoholic patients does not rate more than 25 percent cures, and of those cures very few demonstrate a five-year period of abstinence.

Alcoholic people tend to cope with their tensions and anxieties by acting-out in the form of drinking, and progress in psychotherapy of acting-out patients is always dubious. They pose the same difficulty as sociopathic personalities, which is one of the reasons why alcoholism was at one time categorized, together with the group demonstrating criminal or sexual anti-social behavior, in the so-called sociopathic group. Many clinics have automatically labeled alcoholic persons as sociopathic personalities, which is, of course, not correct. One thing is correct: Acting-out individuals, persons who put their abnormal dynamic mechanisms into action, or employ remedial measures by taking alcohol or stealing or some other acts, seem to respond to therapy less favorably than do persons having similar emotions and impulses present but in whom somehow their abnormal adaptation is based on inhibition or over-inhibition. Or, to put it very plainly, it is easier to treat a patient who has too many "brakes" than to put "brakes" into a person who has none. This is a universal observation: All persons who manifest the tendency for acting-out behavior, including those who act-out with alcohol, do not respond favorably to psychotherapeutic attempts.

Comparable statistics on psychotherapy, psychoanalysis, and group therapy are insufficient to indicate which is the best to apply in treating the alcoholic group—or treating any other group of psychiatric disorders—and, more important, which form of therapy is appropriate for which type of alcoholic personality. Alcoholic patients who had failed to respond with psychoanalysis were reportedly treated successfully with rather superficial group therapy. Patients were reported who received group therapy or psychotherapy without success but who responded very well when psychoanalyzed. Relationship of the form of psychotherapy to the different approaches for treating individual cases is unclear; there are more assumptions and theories about it than actual facts.

Regardless of the psychotherapeutic approach, the alcoholic patient attempts to gain dynamic insight into reasons for his drinking. In many cases, a patient is able to "work through" the underlying dynamic mechanisms for his craving and the therapist may convincingly demonstrate the reasons for the patient's craving, but, nevertheless, the craving does not subside. This is not an unusual occurrence in the treatment of all the neuroses, as we know. Why it is the elucidation of the underlying mechanism leads to a cure in one person, and in another it does nothing or leads to little improvement, is not quite clear. We have a few notions about it but nobody has yet fully explained it. We must face the fact that many patients who have been for years in formal psychoanalysis gain insight into the dynamics of their problems and they could even give a lecture on their insights, but they are unable to alter their emotional constellations or to alter anything of the basic pattern. This is a fact that we must face. It is because none of the various forms of psychotherapy have reliably cured alcoholic patients that many other much more primitive forms of therapy flourish. Each alone, as we have mentioned, also failed to provide the answer.

It is my present opinion that the best procedure in dealing with an alcoholic patient is the following: (1) Try to size up the patient—is he a social drinker or a problem drinker? (2) If the patient is obviously in an alcoholic state, apply appropriate medical procedures for detoxication and further restore the patient to good physical condition. (3) When psychotherapy is commenced, it would be best to hook the patient up with one or the other social organizations designed to treat alcoholic persons (provided you are not investigating the efficacy of your therapy). It helps the patient very much if he is in a working relationship with, for instance, the AA, while his underlying psychoneurotic, sociopathic, or psychotic structures are for the psychiatrist to treat.

This form of combination treatment, if the patient is one of the many who can be exposed to it, can be quite effective provided the psychiatrist is able to establish a successful liaison with the AA group which accepted the patient. If this liaison is not established, all sorts of difficulties will quickly arise and soon all the work will be at cross purposes. But if a liaison is established between the group and the psychiatrist, I would recommend this as being probably the best therapeutic approach for the alcoholic patient who does not require intramural treatment.

If you are dealing with a highly morbid specimen, a patient having a very ramified and deep psychoneurotic or psychotic structure, and especially if he is a sociopathic patient having an acting-out mechanism present, it is always preferable to treat the patient intramurally during the first few months. I have observed a great deal of energy and money wasted by psychiatrists who, if I may say so, degraded themselves by treating such patients on an office basis from the beginning. Naturally, a psychiatrist should have a good sense of smell; that is essential equipment for deciding whether the patient should be treated in the office or the hospital. Many psychiatrists have feelings of omnipotence and believe they can handle any alcoholic patient immediately by tackling the problem in the office. Then, naturally, within two days or so, the police phone the psychiatrist: "Mr. X. tells us that you are his psychiatrist; you are obliged to go to such-and-such a drinking dive and get your patient out." This is not exactly pleasant because the police are very skeptical about psychiatrists. Then, perhaps three days later, the patient makes a disturbance and is admitted to the municipal hospital. The hospital then phones the psychiatrist: "Your patient is under treatment and is nice and cooperative; won't you take the patient home, won't you take over?" This is the spectacle that goes on, and, of course, it does not improve the standing of the psychiatrist and psychiatry with either the patient or the community.

Therefore, in dealing with a very morbid case of alcoholism it is safer for the patient and for the psychiatrist to tell the patient, "You must undergo hospital treatment for a few months of withdrawal, and when you are able to handle the situation there, therapy can be continued on the outside." Unfortunately, few state or private hospitals are equipped to give appropriate treatment to alcoholic patients other than those suffering with overt psychosis. This is one reason many psychiatrists would rather go through all the difficulties just outlined than send the patient to a hospital. Specially designed institutions are probably required to treat chronic alcoholic patients, particularly if they are not psychotic. Special colonies or special farms or institutions where these patients would receive specific supervision and therapy would be much more effective than are most state or private hospitals.

The treatment of *dipsomania* is a special problem and more involved than that of the simple form of chronic alcoholism. Rather than being social drinkers, the majority of dipsomaniac individuals are problem drinkers; they drink periodically and between times they abstain or drink only moderately. The term dipsomania does not refer to the person who occasionally goes on a binge and gets drunk, but refers to those people who have prolonged debauches, who imbibe very heavily, without any restraint, and usually to such an extent that they regress to the lowest possible level of functioning. There are dipsomaniac patients who for three months or so do not drink at all; they then go out and within a week will "get lost" and fully compensate for the three months of abstinence. In many patients the attacks actually resemble epilepsy in that they are preceded by mounting tension and restlessness. When observed during treatment, they actually give the impression that many women give when a menstrual cycle is approaching, with all the emotional tensions and all the paradoxical responses. Then suddenly, at the height of the tension cycle the dipsomaniac patients go out, get drunk, and continue drinking until they are completely senseless, and then a gradual recuperation takes place and they return to a sober life routine.

Treatment of these patients essentially focuses on trying to determine what triggers off the attacks. Occasionally the trigger factors can be dealt with psychotherapeutically, often in combination with social therapy. I have found that the dipsomaniac individual is much more refractory to therapy than are other chronic alcoholic people, probably because there are the intervals during which the patient abstains and seems to recover. Also, when the patient does not drink for three, four, or five months you are likely to be lulled into the security of thinking the patient is responding to your treatment, while probably the only thing accomplished is that you have deranged his schedule. Instead of having a drinking episode after three months, he now has a drinking episode after four. I advise intramural treatment for these patients, although it is difficult to suggest it to them because during their periods of nondrinking they do not see the necessity of hospitalization for alcohol withdrawal; they claim they can withdraw themselves. Despite this, intramural treatment is essential for those patients, particularly if a very strong morbid structure is discovered because it is often much easier to investigate the tension and trigger mechanisms that release the drinking episodes while the patient is hospitalized and free from certain environmental stresses.

I would also suggest that in dealing with any dipsomaniac patient you obtain his electroencephalogram. Latent epilepsy was discovered present in approximately 5 percent of all dipsomaniac patients—every twentieth patient—and because in such cases therapy must be handled somewhat differently, it would be most wise to investigate every case.

Why some people are able to cut themselves off from alcohol apparently spontaneously and others are not is a very interesting question. A certain group of schizophrenic patients is able to withdraw from alcohol, particularly those falling into the pseudoneurotic group. These are persons who suffer with tremendous tension and anxiety practically all of the time and will attempt every means to master the symptoms. Some take barbiturates or tranquilizers, some take alcohol, and some take both. They function much better under the influence of a drug such as alcohol. Soon a craving for it develops. For this group of people, alcohol is actually medicine, in a sense. It relieves their tensions, reduces their anxieties, and somehow they become able to face realities while under the influence of alcohol which they were otherwise unable to do. However, these people also have a very strong hypochondriacal structure, and any palliating substance introduced from an external source they look upon with suspicion and fear it will damage them. They need it; at the same time they are afraid of it. With this ambivalent attitude they develop further anxiety and tension. When they do attempt to relieve the anxiety and tension by drinking, a feeling of guilt and self-reproach for self-damage arises. This is reinforced in many patients by the presence of latent suicidal drives; their taking alcohol is perceived unconsciously as a partial suicide, then such a person is maneuvered into a vicious cycle: he begins to drink heavily to relieve himself of anxieties, suddenly he arrives to the conclusion that he cannot drink any more because that would be the end of him, then he cuts it off! These people do so suddenly, quickly. This is rarely observed in other types of chronic alcoholic individuals; usually they are able to taper off or give up drinking under the gradual influence of treatment. However, I do not state that the sudden giving up of alcohol from one day to the next does not occur in other alcoholic types, but it is quite prevalent in the alcoholic person who has a pronounced schizoid structure or even a schizophrenic psychosis present. We should pay attention to the manner in which persons having multiple morbid manifestations, especially those having many phobic-obsessive mechanisms present, handle their withdrawal from alcohol.

In concluding, I would like to restate some of the problems regarding the craving for alcohol in chronic alcoholic individuals. Psychiatrists are mainly preoccupied with the so-called psychological craving, meaning that a person takes a drug because it has euphorizing properties or because it relieves such symptoms as depression, anxiety, and tension. Physiological craving means something else; it means that the organism has a need for a certain chemical compound, which originally was not required, in order to function. Both psychological and physiological cravings can appear combined, but they can also occur somewhat independently.

Many of the chemical compounds that lead to physiological addiction in man can be produced in a variety of other animals. In them, we surely do not presuppose superego-ego conflicts or that the animals are anxiety-ridden or incapacitated by tension. Nevertheless, addiction to certain compounds can be achieved, which would indicate that, aside from psychological functions, a physiological adaptation takes place. In other words, the nervous system incorporates these compounds in its metabolism and utilizes them. Alcohol, as well as many other compounds, seemingly has some form of an "enzymatic" action on the nervous system. Therefore, we must continue to ask ourselves what the specific issues are in the metabolism of the nervous system which play a role in the craving for alcohol or other addictive drugs. As you know, one of the main areas of investigation has been that of carbohydrate metabolism. Although it is quite possible that the explanation for the physiological craving for alcohol may be found in an entirely different area, observations have so far indicated that there is a relationship between the craving and disturbed carbohydrate metabolism. But, despite their validity the many observations have not as yet led to any explanations for the physiological craving phenomenon. To state that disturbed carbohydrate metabolism explains the craving for alcohol, would be highly speculative. But, these metabolic disturbances occur so very often in combination with alcoholism that probably it is one of the predisposing factors. It is also recognized that there are persons having similar carbohydrate disturbances who do not crave alcohol and who are not even very tolerant of alcohol. Therefore, some as yet unknown factors remain to be included before the craving can be explained.

Incidentally, more and more evidence has accumulated to support the observation that in certain emotional states, such as anxiety, an alteration of carbohydrate uptake in the nervous system of the individual occurs. That the regulation of carbohydrate metabolism is disturbed in schizophrenia is known. And, due to the presence of anxiety and tension many individuals have disturbances of their carbohydrate metabolism occurring secondarily to certain psychosomatic alterations. For instance, constant tension interferes with stomach functioning and hyperacidity may lead to gastritis or ulceration, which then leads to certain assimilative disturbances. In such patients the constant tension leads to hypoglycemia. Now hypoglycemic persons have a tolerance to alcohol. Chronic alcoholic individuals invariably demonstrate a disturbance of carbohydrate metabolism even though it may not appear on a simple routine examination. That obviously does not explain their craving for alcohol because even though many individuals drink alcohol in order to relieve themselves of great tension or of anxiety states, quite a number of individuals who have similar metabolic alterations based on their emotional states are not alcoholic. So, further investigation is required on the chemistry of the nervous system, and the understanding of the metabolic disorders in relationship to emotional states and alcoholism is still vague. Obviously, in dealing with psychosomatic problems such as chronic alcoholism, we must become more orientated toward the physiological aspects of these phenomena rather than just the psychological.

Great progress was made when it became recognized that emotion is as much an organic force as are other physiological manifestations. For instance, emotional experiences and anxiety can create tension; tension subjectively perceived is expressed in psychological terms, and objectively it is expressed in physiological terms: they are one and the same function, expressed on different hierarchies. This fact is important in dealing with the psychoneuroses. Alcoholism is an even more difficult problem than that of the neuroses, however, because we are dealing with interorganismic situations which naturally can be expressed only in psychotherapeutic terms. It should not be overlooked that the interorganismic conflict—the conflict of the person in relation to his environment—which is anxiety-creating, translates itself into physiological function terms in the organism. This is very often forgotten. Some therapists think only in terms of what is going on within the organism physiologically and disregard anything and everything relating to the person's environment. Others do just the opposite; they stress only the interorganismic situations and do not perceive them in their relationship to the physiological events occurring within the person.

Despite all the shortcomings in our knowledge concerning alcoholism, it has at least been demonstrated that stimuli coming from the social environment are as important as the physical ones. How these environmental stimuli translate themselves into organismic responses remains unclear, but it is apparent that emotion works as an organic force, as does a toxin. The role played by intraorganismic stimuli is also unclear. However, it is apparent that in the chronic alcoholic individual the craving for alcohol somehow involves all these interacting forces.

12

SENILE AND PRESENILE PSYCHOSES

Now I shall discuss in general the group of mental disorders comprised under the headings of *senile psychosis, atherosclerotic psychosis,* and *presenile psychosis.* Also included here will be mention of those patients showing emotional or intellectual impairments of functioning due to aging who are not actually psychotic but who show manifestations that might be termed neurotic. I must also point up the relationship of all these so-called organic, structurally destructive disorders causing a psychosis to the involutional psychosis which, although occurring at an earlier age, nevertheless overlaps to some extent, especially when arteriosclerosis is involved.

The number of patients belonging to the senile, atherosclerotic, and presenile groups is very large. In some institutions they comprise about one-third of the number of patients in treatment. A considerable number of these individuals are never institutionalized, although that does not by any means imply that their mental functioning is normal. People are living to an older age now than in the past, and the number of aged people in the general population is markedly increasing. Probably within a few decades a fairly large proportion of the general population will live to develop senile and arteriosclerotic disorders. And, an increasing number of presenile mental disorders will be observed, even though they are not so commonly or reliably diagnosed as are those in the senile and atherosclerotic group.

All three groups—the atherosclerotic, the senile, and the presenile—are organic psychoses, organic in the sense that structural damage exists in the brain which is responsible for the mental deterioration in these persons. I shall discuss the relationship between the structural changes on the one hand and the mental changes on the other when discussing the etiology, prognosis, and treatment of these disorders, but I would first like to mention one fact: The old idea that if an atherosclerotic, senile, or presenile change is demonstrable in the brain it is automatically responsible for the patient's mental condition is definitely incorrect. Quite a number of patients have such anatomical changes —in some instances even rather marked structural changes —and yet show no mental impairment. One also observes patients who show mental impairment even though the changes in their nervous system are not at all impressive. Therefore, some demonstrable structural damage is probably prerequisite to the development of these types of mental disorder, but the roles played by additional factors must also be considered before it can be assumed that the actual mental changes are due to the structural changes observed. A number of metabolic (particularly nutritional), neurophysiological, and psychodynamic factors enter in to produce in persons a psychosis resembling that of the presence of a structural change in the brain.

Classification: Now, of these psychoses—presenile,

atherosclerotic, and senile—the *senile psychosis* is the most prevalent. This mental disorder occurs late in life, usually after the age of seventy. Different textbooks fix the age range of senile psychosis somewhat differently. A few mention that sixty is already the lower age limit, which is slightly too low. There are senile patients aged sixty or sixty-five, but the vast majority who develop this psychosis are over seventy years of age. We should be cautious about diagnosing a sixty-year-old patient in the category of senile psychosis. Such patients are encountered, but are actually much more likely to be suffering from an arteriosclerotic or a presenile form of disorder. Senile psychosis develops in both men and women, although it is more prevalent in females, in contrast to atherosclerotic psychosis, which is more common in males.

The age at which *atherosclerotic psychosis* develops is loosely delineated as between about sixty and seventy years, thereby usually occurring at a younger age than senile psychosis. From that, however, it should not be assumed, as many physicians tend to do automatically, that if the patient is younger than seventy the psychosis is due to atherosclerosis and if over seventy it is due to senile psychosis, because there are exceptions to this rule. For instance, you will encounter patients younger than seventy suffering from a senile psychosis, and you will encounter patients in their seventies suffering from an atherosclerotic psychosis.

For so long as no etiological treatment exists for these disorders, it is probably of not very great importance whether they are diagnosed as senile, or atherosclerotic, or senile and arteriosclerotic combined, which many clinicians do to avoid diagnostic quibbling. Nevertheless, as new methods of treatment emerge it will become important to determine the diagnosis—as it is in any other field of medicine—and whether the patient is really suffering from a senile or from an arteriosclerotic disorder. Although there are structural and clinical similarities in both, there are nevertheless significant anatomical and clinical differences which indicate (as will be observed when I discuss etiologies of psychotic groups) that possibly the prognosis and treatment of the arteriosclerotic psychosis will change considerably, while that of the senile psychosis must, at least for the time being, be considered rather poor. Manifestations in the senile brain are very closely linked with physiological changes and the senile psychosis is therefore more or less the *cessation* of certain physiological performance. On the other hand, arteriosclerosis is much more that of a sickness, much more a *metabolic disorder*, and, even though it is linked to aging, the linkage between the two is not absolute. Because the processes of arteriosclerosis are influenced to some extent by treatment methods, prevention of atherosclerotic psychosis seems closer at hand than for senile psychosis. Naturally, however, that does not mean that research will not eventually enable us to interrupt the development of senile psychotic processes as well.

With regard to diagnosis of the psychosis being related to cerebral arteriosclerosis, a further fact should be mentioned: There are increasing numbers of people suffering from arteriosclerotic mental disturbances at a comparatively early age. I have encountered such patients between the ages of thirty and forty, and a few not much older than forty. Therefore, here again, that a patient is diagnosed as suffering from cerebral atherosclerotic psychosis only if he is sixty or more years of age is not always correct. It is valid only in the majority of cases. Evaluation of the clinical symptomatology and all the etiological factors in the disorder is of much more importance than chronological age in determining the presence of atherosclerosis. For instance, an individual may be advanced for his years in his specific protein enzyme age level; he may initially develop an essential hypertension or any of the other arterial degenerative and metabolic disorders somehow combined; this could then merge into the development of arteriosclerosis involving the individual's nervous system; and he could eventually wind up having true cerebral atherosclerosis with all the neuro-

logical and psychiatric sequentia associated with this condition. Therefore, you will encounter patients who are
suffering at a comparatively early age from psychotic manifestations due to atherosclerosis.

The *presenile psychosis,* as the term indicates, occurs at
a presenile age level. Most cases are in the category of
Alzheimer's disease and Pick's disease, these being not extremely rare but difficult to diagnose in vivo. At this point
I would like to correct a rather widespread fallacious
assumption that presenile psychosis, with all its anatomical
changes, occurs only at the presenile age level. That is
incorrect! Alzheimer's disease, for example, with all its
anatomical changes, occurs also in the senile age period.
You will also hear mention of a special senile group, the
so-called presbyophrenic subgroup of the senile psychosis,
in which persons actually show, anatomically, many of the
characteristics otherwise attributed to Alzheimer's disease—
the argentophilic "Alzheimer plaques," neurofibrillary
changes, marked degeneration of the ganglion cells, glial
proliferation, and so forth and so on—except that in these
cases the so-called Alzheimer anatomical picture occurs at
the senile age level. Actually, Alzheimer's disease is probably a senile psychosis occurring in certain individuals at a
very early age; instead of being in their seventies, such
persons are in only the fourth or fifth or sixth decade of life.
Pick's disease also occasionally occurs at an age level of
about sixty years. In the majority of cases, however,
Alzheimer's disease and Pick's disease (whether regarded as
separate diseases or two variations of the same metabolic
disorder under the heading of presenile psychosis) usually
occur when the person is between forty and sixty years of
age.

The symptomatology of all three of these chronic
organic disorders basically follows the outline of the so-
called Korsakoff syndrome. There are, however, variations
of the general clinical picture, a few of which we shall
discuss.

SENILE AND ATHEROSCLEROTIC PSYCHOSES

CLINICAL SYMPTOMATOLOGY: The senile psychosis is generally characterized by a gradual progressive mental enfeeblement manifested especially by memory failure; there is forgetfulness and inability to recall a recent occurrence. In diagnosing somebody as suffering from a senile psychosis, one must take into consideration not only qualitative changes but also quantitative changes. A great many symptoms shown by a senile patient appear in a normal individual who has a few signs of senility. For instance, there is a certain rigidity in thinking, a certain inability to learn new material, and a certain inability to recall recent events, which is termed "senile forgetfulness." And, as we shall observe later, quite a number of emotional and behavioral pattern characteristics are observed in a senile patient as well as in an individual who is simply aged but lacks marked mental impairments. Actually, one could view it as a continuous chain of changes ranging from a normal aged person to a fairly normal aged person with some emotional and intellectual impairment, through to the senile psychotic person. Usually, we diagnose a person as suffering from senile psychosis only when the changes are so massive that the intellectual impairment or emotional change is really markedly conspicuous.

In diagnosing senile psychosis, the patient must show the following clinical signs: First, a loss of comprehension of their environment; this could be permanent, or it could be changeable in that, as in other chronic organic reactions, the patient is at times orientated and at times disorientated. Secondly, the patient should show a loss of memory, at least for recent events. A normal aged person, even though his memory is somewhat faulty, does not have a generalized impairment of recent memory functions and, despite some difficulty in recalling recent events, he is able to function quite well. A senile psychotic patient, however, usually shows a marked impairment of recent memory and, as the psychosis progresses, there is also a progressive loss of remote memory. In some cases these memory defects become so profound that the patient remembers practically nothing. By then, the intellectual functioning of the person—forming associations, recalling associations, and so forth—is much more than just somewhat impaired. All these impairments mentioned are generalized and irreversible in senile dementia; that is important to note because in cerebral atherosclerosis, especially in the early phase of the disorder, these impairments are usually fluctuating and patchy.

As these generalized impairments progress, quite a large number of senile patients then manifest more complicated clinical pictures such as hallucinations and delusions. Behavioral and emotional changes are prevalent; there is irritability, and emotional incontinence with sudden outbursts of temper. This, again, is characteristic for chronic organic reactions and is no different from those described, for instance, in general paresis.

Judgment and insight are markedly impaired in many senile psychotic patients, which is clinically important for establishing the proper diagnosis. It is also important legally because quite a number of these patients run into all kinds of difficulty due to their impaired judgment. In some respects, however, this impaired judgment might occur in a person simply in connection with being aged. In addition to the impaired judgment, many senile patients manifest so-called hyper-suggestibility. This is very often exploited by people who try to manipulate the senile person to do such things as draw up and sign a will favoring them. Although hyper-suggestibility and impairment of judgment are only moderately present in an average person who is aged, in senile psychotic patients these are usually quite marked. In other words, the judgment of senile psychotic patients is very markedly enfeebled with a regression to an unusually immature level; often their intellectual functioning in judgment issues is really below that of a small child.

Along with the emotional changes, personality characteristics sometimes appear in senile psychotic patients which could be considered an accentuation of their previous personality traits; and, I must admit, it is usually the undesirable traits that become accentuated. Occasionally, however, one observes an improvement in personality traits. For instance, a person who was rather disagreeable, paranoid, and aggressive appears somehow more mellow than he had formerly been. Such a change is, for certain, in the minority of cases. The majority of patients usually display an exaggeration, or accentuation, of those personality traits which were never especially well received by the environment. The eccentricities, the personality peculiarities, and the emotional rigidity of an average senile person are common knowledge, and have been described quite well in the psychiatric textbooks as well as in the literature. However, in the senile psychotic person these features are often even more marked; in addition to lacking judgment and having really very impaired intellectual function, he is quite often belligerent, disagreeable, nasty, quarrelsome, and misomanic. Some amount of this, as I have mentioned, seems to be an underscoring of a normal aging process. Seemingly, the integration of the personality becomes somewhat loosened as the person ages, insofar as the organic process taking place in the brain must be considered a form of stress on the individual personality organization so that the person is no longer able to respond with his compensatory resources as well as he formerly could.

A certain obsessiveness is also characteristic of quite a number of senile patients. For instance, a patient shows the phenomenon known as *misoneism*; he insists that certain things have to be done always in the same way at exactly the same time, day after day. To indulge in a mention of dynamics, quite a number of senile patients develop compulsive manifestations even though such traits had formerly not been very conspicuous. In many patients this compulsory trait also expresses itself in stereotyped behavior, or in stereotyped handling of situations. This tendency for stereotypy, along with the tendency for emotional rigidity and, in addition, a memory impairment, usually then leads to the following behavioral pattern: The person, for instance, continually indulges in reminiscing, and because the material which he relates is always mainly the same it is usually incredibly boring to those in the environment. But the patient does not take particular notice of that and insists on relating always the same story of the same experience of his past life, again and again, as on a gramophone record. This is quite characteristic. Most likely, the gradual memory impairment very much fosters this pattern. For example, there was the patient who was given only one book. She read the book, and after she finished reading it the book was withdrawn from her. The next morning it was presented to her as a new book; she reread it with the same initial enthusiasm and was even able to report on the content of the book, provided she was asked about it within an hour after she had read it. If more than an hour elapsed, she no longer remembered anything about what she had read. But she was very happy with this one book for a few years without ever realizing she was always reading the same book. This is a common type of phenomenon in those senile persons who have a marked memory impairment. I also think that the security feeling of senile persons is markedly enhanced by their always revolving around that which is familiar to them. Actually, their turning back to the past is a usual and general psychological pattern observed in old-aged persons. This is explained partly by the fact that the future, naturally, is not very promising for these people and therefore they turn back to the past, but partly also because new engrams are no longer very readily established in these patients and, therefore, they have to draw on whatever is in their mental bank account. They can no longer add very much to it.

The delusions and hallucinations of a simple senile person are not very colorful; the content is usually pointless and simple. The elaborations are poor and both form and content of the delusions are usually organized around mis-representations or misidentifications of everyday matters. The hallucinatory as well as the delusional content is mainly arranged around their memory defect and disorientive functions. For instance, one of the most common delusional ideas in simple senile persons is that they are being robbed, that somebody is taking away their property. Usually the ideation evolves in the following manner: They have a package containing something to which they are attached; and then they place it somewhere, and a few minutes later they do not remember where they put it. Then, however, instead of having insight into that and searching for it, they immediately accept the idea that somebody took the thing away from them. In their uneasiness about the loss, they project onto the environment, and the idea is then born that they were robbed. A very common occurrence in senile patients is their feeling that somebody is taking things away from them, that somebody is taking advantage of them.

Even the ordinary nonpsychotic senile person will usually have a much more marked sense of possessiveness than will younger individuals. This becomes quite further exaggerated in some patients who suffer from senile psychosis. Their memory defects and occasional periods of confusion rob them of those orientative landmarks that we all employ in formulating judgments about the environment, it then becoming very easy for these people to misinterpret situations in which they find themselves. So complaints that they are robbed, that somebody has taken advantage of them, that somebody has taken away their property, that somebody is mistreating them are fairly common. It should be emphasized that this occurs even in those senile patients who had no previous paranoid tendencies. Therefore, such form of behavior should not necessarily lead to the assumption that one is dealing with a paranoid individual whose paranoid attitude toward the environment was simply released by the organic process. This rather mild, unelaborated, and usually fleeting paranoid ideation of a senile patient should not be confused with the clinical picture of the so-called paranoid senile (which I shall discuss in slightly more detail) in whom the paranoid picture is actually in the foreground. In these senile patients who express ideas that they were robbed or mistreated, however, the simple dementia is usually in the foreground and, as I have stated before, the paranoid ideas are usually organized around the patient's inability to mentally grasp certain issues, or due to disorientation, all in connection with memory impairment. Naturally, many of these mechanisms will require further study in order to explain why it is that some other person suffering from any sort of simple dementia accepts the memory defect and disorientation—and does not organize any paranoid or other defense mechanism around it.

The hallucinations arranged around memory defect and disorientation could be visual, auditory, or somatic. They occur rather rarely in the senile patient and are, as are the delusional ideas, usually fragmentary and poorly elaborated. In most cases they are fleeting. In other words, at times the patients have hallucinations and at other times not, just as at times they have delusional ideas and then a short time later forget having previously expressed such ideas.

Occasionally, for one reason or another, some simple senile patients enter into a state of delirium. It is sometimes due to a somatic disorder, such as an intercurrent infection, and is sometimes due to some emotional upheaval, as when the patient is confronted with increased emotional stress. It should be included under the heading of emotional stress that senile patients, when confronted with transplantation to an unknown environment, develop what are termed senile delirious states. This senile delirium is actually a mixture of the acute and the chronic organic types of reaction combined, the delirious reaction being secondary and superimposed upon the chronic organic reaction. These patients will invariably show memory impairment, enfeebled intellectual performance, and disorientation; but, on top of that, they will develop, for some reason or other, rather vivid hallucinatory experiences. The confusion in these patients is usually much more marked than is observed in an ordinary senile person. Quite important is the fact that their consciousness is usually narrowed or impaired as in a delirium, while ordinarily in senile dementia an alteration of consciousness is not observed. Such a senile delirium may run a course of a few hours or a few days but there are cases of this type that continue several weeks or months. As I have stated, senile delirium is often precipitated by certain stress situations, physical or emotional, but occasionally we will observe it without being able to actually state the reason why the patient should suddenly develop the delirious reaction.

Similarly as in general paresis, all types of symptom colorings can appear in senile psychosis. In addition to the simple dementia picture most commonly observed, patients can develop manic pictures, depressive pictures, paranoid pictures, schizophrenic pictures, and so forth. The depressed pictures and paranoid pictures are especially important because they are quite common, because they often lead to diagnostic difficulties, and because the handling and prognosis of these patients are, in many respects, somewhat different from that of uncomplicated senile pictures.

Depression is a very common symptom, and these depressed senile patients suffer considerably. They are very hypochondriacal, often expressing nihilistic and somatic delusions. This delusional material is usually not well elaborated but remains rather simple because of the mental enfeeblement. Occasionally, however, you will encounter a patient in whom the depressive mechanisms appear very marked, and the deteriorative mechanisms are more in the background. These patients naturally suffer the most. Suicide can occur, provided they are intellectually able to carry out the suicidal plan.

The paranoid form of senile psychosis is particularly

serious, not only because the environment suffers very much from it, but also because the treatment of such patients is much more difficult than that of a simple demented senile patient for whom care is actually uncomplicated. But the paranoid senile person, being aggressive, disagreeable, suspicious, and noisy, is usually very much of an institutional problem. In these paranoid senile patients one observes a clinical fact which is practically universal in all individuals who manifest a paranoid psychotic picture : The personality of these psychotic patients usually remains preserved far longer than in other types of psychotic patients. You will find this to be so in paresis, in arteriosclerosis, and in schizo-phrenia : Even though you are dealing with disorders having a strong tendency to deterioration or dementia, the person-ality in those patients who develop a paranoid picture remains well preserved for a long period of time; deteriora-tion is usually gradual and their intellectual impairments are not so marked as in other patients. It must be empha-sized that this applies to those patients who show a clinical picture in which the paranoid manifestations are in the foreground with full-blown paranoid delusional and halluci-natory experiences. It does not apply to patients who have only a few paranoid ideas occasionally embroidering the dementia.

DIFFERENTIAL DIAGNOSIS : Having described the main symptomatology of the senile psychosis, by way of general review I would like to stress a few points in the differential diagnosis of the *senile psychosis* and the *atherosclerotic psychosis.* This differential diagnosis seems somewhat academic because as yet we have no etiological treatment for senility; and, as a matter of fact, we have no etiological treatment for arteriosclerosis. Nevertheless, with so much research in progress with regard to atherosclerosis, and with so many advances being made in the understanding of arteriosclerosis as a metabolic disorder, the possibility is given that, in contrast to senility, atherosclerosis will also eventually come to be understood as a metabolic disturbance, and then most likely some specific form of treatment will be made available for it. Although it is a possibility that arteriosclerosis in conjunction with atherosclerotic disorders, will eventually be diagnosed chemically rather than clinically, nevertheless the clinical aspects of symptoms and the clinical evaluation of treatment of these cases will still remain important. Therefore, a certain amount of clinical acumen will still be necessary to differentiate the atherosclerotic from the senile disorders. No absolute clinical diagnostic criteria exist from which we can make such a differential diagnosis, and the criteria that are described can at best be considered only relative ones. In this regard, I shall enumerate some important points that must be considered in order to make the diagnosis.

AGE FACTOR: As I have mentioned, senile psychosis is not diagnosed clinically in persons who are less than sixty-five years of age, nor even safely before the age of seventy. Should a person manifest a senile picture at an earlier age, he is more likely to be suffering from presenile psychosis rather than psychosis due to cerebral atherosclerosis.

THE PRESENCE OF CLINICAL SIGNS OF ATHEROSCLEROSIS: Clinical signs often employed as diagnostic criteria are sclerosis of retinal vessels, sclerosis of peritherial tissues, and sclerosis of the arteries in general. However, this could be present in both atherosclerotic patients and senile patients who, besides senile changes, usually have arteriosclerotic changes. Moreover, these signs will be present in quite a number of presenile cases, as we will see. Therefore, the old idea that atherosclerosis can be diagnosed simply by examining the patient physically and finding the presence of hypertension, or finding retinal atherosclerosis, or finding a few other such signs, is insufficient. If these findings are present in a very massive or very conspicuous form, that would naturally speak more for atherosclerosis than for senility or presenile psychosis, because in the latter conditions the atherosclerotic changes usually are in the background. But, their mere presence does not prove that the patient is atherosclerotic.

SUDDEN NEUROLOGICAL CHANGES: A sudden occurrence of an apoplectic insult, paresis, or paralysis is obviously more suggestive of the presence of atherosclerosis than of senility. Temporary monoplegias, temporary hemiplegias, temporary paralysis, or paresis of the motor innervation of the eyes, can also occur in a senile psychosis but it is usually fleeting, rarely permanent. If prior to such an apoplectic insult the patient showed no conspicuous mental changes, the disorder would most likely be an atherosclerotic one, provided the sudden change appeared subsequent to apoplexy. This holds true not only for the lower age group, but also for the higher age group. In this connection, you should remember that a person over the age of seventy can also develop an atherosclerotic mental disorder, and just because he reached the age of seventy it does not necessarily follow that his disorder must invariably be senile. Age predilection is relative, although in some medical circles it is employed as absolute.

EPILEPTOID OR EPILEPTIC MANIFESTATIONS: Seizures are always suggestive more for an atherosclerotic process than a senile one. It is surprising that with brains so markedly deteriorated as those observed in many senile patients, so few senile patients actually suffer from convulsions, whereas quite a number of cerebral atherosclerotic patients do suffer from convulsions. No explanation for this has yet been offered; there are all sorts of hypotheses but none are conclusive. Why it is that vascular disorders seem to have a marked tendency to provoke epilepsy, whereas those disorders associated with diffuse ganglion cell degeneration do not, is not known.

THE COURSE OF THE DISORDER: This is a matter of

considerable importance. The atherosclerotic disorders usually follow a fluctuating course, whereas the senile course is steady, progressive, downhill. No pronounced fluctuations are noted in senile psychosis; occasional fluctuations that do occur are usually fugal fluctuations. As already mentioned, in senile psychosis we occasionally observe a combination of an acute organic reaction superimposed on a chronic organic reaction—in other words, a delirious state in the setting of a senile psychosis. Now, whenever such a delirium is present, obviously the senile patient's condition appears to be, and most likely is, worse. But, when the delirium disappears and the simple chronic organic reaction remains, the patient's condition appears improved. These changes should not be confused with what is considered a fluctuating course. As we understand it, in the fluctuating course it is the patient's essential and basic symptoms which show temporary recession whereby the patient appears to be much improved, not just that the patient's mental symptomatology is occasionally more marked or less marked.

Now, in atherosclerotic psychosis marked fluctuations are sometimes observed. For instance, the patient becomes confused, disorientated, shows memory impairment or emotional instability, and he may even manifest delusions or hallucinations for a period of time. Suddenly he appears to be quite normal again and even seems able to function quite normally; then the disorder again occurs and the symptoms reappear. At times the fluctuation is so slight that the patient cannot be labeled recovered, but many atherosclerotic patients do show considerable improvement, especially during the early phase of the disorder. Naturally, when they reach a state of deterioration, fluctuation no longer occurs. At any rate, a fluctuating course is much more prevalent in atherosclerotic than in senile patients.

THE PATIENT'S INSIGHT INTO HIS CONDITION: Insight is also an important differential point, namely, that the atherosclerotic patient usually retains insight whereas the senile patient has no insight and no judgment whatsoever concerning his condition. The senile patient very rarely consults a medical doctor or a psychiatrist because he is upset by the senility disturbance. On the other hand, the vast majority of patients suffering from an atherosclerotic mental disorder do consult a physician or psychiatrist because they are very aware that something is wrong with their mentality. In fact, the atherosclerotic patient usually consults a physician or psychiatrist not only with complaints that he is unable to perform as well intellectually as formerly, that he has become forgetful, that he is unable to gather his thoughts together, and that his associations span is shortened—all being phenomena of which many of these patients are aware—but because of subjective complaints in addition.

SUBJECTIVE PHYSICAL COMPLAINTS: These complaints may develop early and become marked in many atherosclerotic patients. The patients may complain of headaches, loss of libido, a general feeling of weakness, a general feeling of unsteadiness, and so forth. Senile patients rarely complain about physical symptoms. They do not belong in the hypochondriacal group, or at least not so persistently and continually as do atherosclerotic patients.

MEMORY FAILURE: The course of this psychiatric symptom is a further differential point. The onset in atherosclerotic patients is usually characterized by a failure in remembering material, particularly names. The memory failure is mainly for recent events, but even for recent events the impairment is patchy. I would like to underscore this: At times the recall mechanism functions properly and at other times the same recall mechanism does not. Or the patient's recent memory is impaired only in certain circumscribed areas. In contrast to atherosclerotic patients, the memory disturbance in senile patients is distributed diffusely;

it is not patchy, it is not circumscribed. In both conditions memory impairment first involves recent events; eventually it involves remote events as well.

THE TENDENCY FOR INTELLECTUAL DETERIORATION: Although it occurs in both disorders, deterioration in a senile patient is usually accomplished much more quickly and is much more generalized and much more diffuse than that observed in an atherosclerotic patient. Usually, intellectual deterioration in an atherosclerotic patient is reached only at the end of the course. Such profound deterioration as is ordinarily observed in senile patients is rarely observed in atherosclerotic patients, mainly due to the fact that seemingly the atherosclerotic patient dies before achieving such marked deterioration as that ordinarily observed in senile patients; and, furthermore, in senile patients the progress of deterioration is much more rapid.

EMOTIONAL CHANGES: Lability, irritability, outbursts of temper, and so forth, are usually observed in both disorders, being part and parcel of the chronic type of organic reaction (which I have described). Nevertheless, in atherosclerotic patients the presence of irritability, emotional outbursts, and faulty regulation of the emotional life is so preeminent as to be characteristic more for the atherosclerotic than for the senile disorder.

PERSONALITY CHANGES: The patient's personality, in general, and particularly concerning social and other habits, is much more impaired in a senile psychosis than in an atherosclerotic psychosis. Delusions and hallucinations are not particularly characteristic for either psychosis because they are similar in both, with only one notable difference: the so-called miseristic attitudes or delusional formations, meaning that as the person in many respects tends to withdraw within himself he becomes rather acquisitive and rather retentive of everything that in any way relates to himself; this is much more characteristic in a senile than in an atherosclerotic condition.

The points mentioned would generally differentiate between the senile and the atherosclerotic psychosis. Now, I would like to mention one or two supplementary points. As you know, different *psychotic colorings*—manic, depressive, paranoid, and so forth—occur in any type of organic psychosis; therefore, they occur also in the atherosclerotic and the senile psychoses. Whenever such a coloring occurs, it must be taken into consideration because the treatment of the patient is influenced considerably by these factors. The most important psychotic colorings are the paranoid and the depressive pictures.

The *depressive* pictures should be particularly emphasized because they are not only prevalent, but are therapeutically more accessible than other pictures. Whenever depression is present in an organic psychosis, particularly in atherosclerosis at an age level suggestive for either atherosclerosis or senility, one must first make this decision: Is the depression in the patient a part of the mental deterioration and therefore merely a coloring in that disease, or is the person preeminently depressed without any actual intellectual deterioration disorder being present? I believe I mentioned that quite a number of patients who suffer from so-called involutional depression do not develop this type of psychosis in their forties or fifties but develop it when sixty or more years of age. Furthermore, in a number of manic-depressive patients it is possible for the depressive attacks to occur when the patient is over seventy or even eighty years of age, and then, because the patient is so old, automatically the diagnosis made is senile psychosis, depressed type, or atherosclerosis, depressed type. The case is then usually closed instead of the very important differentiation being made as to whether the seventy- or eighty-year-old patient is a person suffering from depression or is a person suffering from an atherosclerotic psychosis or a senile psychosis with depressive coloring.

Why has it become so important to mention differentiation? It is important because the involutional depression, or depression in any patient in whom no marked deterioration has taken place, can be influenced rather well by measures such as antidepressant drugs or electro-convulsive therapy and so forth. On the other hand, the depressive coloring of an atherosclerotic psychosis or the depressive coloring of a senile psychosis cannot be easily influenced; and, in fact, electro-convulsive treatment is contraindicated in such individuals. If a patient suffers from a deteriorating senile or atherosclerotic psychosis whereby his intellect is already considerably impaired, we hesitate to inflict any treatment on him which would disorganize intellectual functioning even further—not to mention that we would gain nothing by it because in a severe atherosclerotic or senile patient such treatment rarely produces much effect.

On the other hand, if the patient shows no, or only mild, intellectual impairment, we then dare employ a type of therapy which would otherwise impair organic brain functioning because sometimes these patients respond excellently to this treatment. In fact, quite a number of patients over seventy or eighty years of age who had been written off as absolutely incurable were successfully so treated. I might thus treat a patient who had been institutionalized for six, seven, or eight years and completely given up therapeutically, who then, after five or more electroconvulsive treatments, recovers—a very startling response—because all along he probably did not suffer from an atherosclerotic or a senile psychosis but suffered from an involutional depression, or he perhaps suffered from an atherosclerotic psychosis whereby the depressive or other affective components were very much in the foreground and the intellectual impairment was in the background. On the other hand, I have observed patients so treated who were outrightly senile and already deteriorated, or outrightly atherosclerotic and also deteriorated, and they responded to the treatment with an aggravation or an acceleration of the deteriorative process. Therefore, I advocate electro-convulsive therapy only for patients in whom the intellectual deterioration is not marked and in whom the depressive component is the predominant symptom. For these patients this form of treatment is definitely a progress. Whereas formerly these individuals were diagnosed, written off as inaccessible to treatment, and simply placed in a care ward, they can now not only be treated and improved, but quite a number of them actually recover as well.

It is permissible to consider electro-convulsive therapy if the deteriorating patient is in an agitated state, or even to save the patient's life if he is exhausted by this state. The therapy cuts the agitation, but it does not improve the psychotic condition. In such a case, electro-convulsions can serve as a symptom-palliative measure in the place of sedation. It is probably superior to heavy sedation since these patients do not tolerate sedatives at all well and often develop drug deliria from any type of drug. In my opinion, even though electro-convulsive therapy further impairs the patient's memory and intellectual performance, it could be preferable to his developing an abrupt psychosis. However, in giving this treatment to such patients it should be applied only in blocks, never in continuous succession. In other words, the patient in an excited state should receive one or two electro-convulsive treatments, then a few weeks should elapse, then he again could receive a few more, if necessary. But if these patients are given ten or twenty such treatments in continuous succession they become awfully deteriorated and go downhill very, very rapidly.

The second group of patients showing psychotic coloring is the *paranoid* group. The paranoid group is extremely problematic, problematic in many respects; they cause a great deal of trouble at home and a great deal of trouble legally. They usually remain fairly well preserved intellectually for a long time. Paranoid attitudes seemingly have a preserving influence on the person's intellect and personality. Deterioration is not so rapid as occurs in other psychotic patients. In these patients, electro-convulsive treatment can also be applied although the results are not so favorable as in the case of depression.

TREATMENT APPROACHES : This brings us to two other points I would like to stress. One is that the treatment of atherosclerotic psychosis per se continues to be completely neglected, chiefly in psychiatric hospitals, the assumption being that nothing can be done to influence atherosclerosis. Cleckley and Sydenstricker *(1939)* made an interesting study on atherosclerotic and early senile patients and discovered that in about 10 or 15 percent of these patients a marked improvement can be achieved if their *metabolism is altered* by treating them with vitamins. Since this treatment's introduction into many hospitals both here and abroad, it was discovered that approximately 10 or 15 percent of atherosclerotic and senile patients suffer from a special form of pellagra. Their pellagra was explained on the basis that a great many of these patients do not eat properly, or do not assimilate vitamins properly, and therefore develop a vitamin deficiency which leads to all sorts of secondary mental complications. It was found, for instance, that in these patients nicotinic acid has a very marked influence on brain metabolism. However, keep in mind that nicotinic acid is also a respiratory as well as a circulatory stimulant and is used quite extensively for those purposes. And actually, treatment of these patients with massive doses of vitamin B, often in the form of coramine in addition to massive doses of vitamin B_1, became a widely used procedure. A further observation made was that intravenous sodium iodide seemed to influence the circulation in quite a number of these patients. Although this and other metabolic theories are inconclusive, the empirical fact remains that many patients are therapeutically responsive to it. Therefore, we must request that every patient in whom the diagnosis of atherosclerotic psychosis is made should at least be exposed to a few weeks of such a treatment before being written off therapeutically because, although the yield is only about 10 to 15 percent, for the individual who falls into the responsive percentile group this is rather important! For that reason, it should be done. Meanwhile, further improvements in the treatment of atherosclerotic psychosis may in time be devised.

The additional point concerns the *psychotherapy* in the senile and atherosclerotic groups. The general attitude is that formal, organized, or deep psychotherapy is ineffective in these groups. How valid this is is difficult to state because very few patients have actually been so treated. It is obvious, however, that if a patient shows marked intellectual impairment, based on that fact alone and not so much on the age factor, no organized form of psychotherapy, analytical or otherwise, can be given. Attempts were made with various analytical approaches in a few of the only mildly impaired patients. That did not succeed very well because apparently the intellectual capacity of one of these patients was such that he was unable to follow along mentally, and, because of that, instead of improving, he became more and more upset. In applying any of the available psychotherapeutic approaches to this group of patients, it is very important to take into consideration the extent to which their intellect is damaged.

If the intellect is at all damaged, even though it is not so very marked, and the patient has difficulty in memorizing, in associating, and in recalling, it is quite obvious that only a *supportive* form of psychotherapy can be given him. It is important that the psychotherapy be supportive because, in addition to the intellectual difficulties, many of these patients suffer from considerable emotional difficulty for which they need support. Anxieties are frequently activated in these patients. Quite a number of them, furthermore, have a previous neurotic structure which becomes loosened under the impact of the slow decortication process that takes place in the atherosclerotic or the senile patient and, naturally, this also requires some attention. The main psychotherapeutic issues usually involve the extent to which the patient is able to maintain himself and to conduct, for instance, his profession or business affairs. The second issue concerns his home adjustments; many of these patients develop difficulties in their family relationships.

Most essential in the psychotherapeutic situation is that attempts are made to avoid introducing much that is new to the patient. Everything that is new, everything that requires new adaptation, anything introduced which might create anticipatory anxiety in the patient, should never be touched upon. There are some enthusiastic psychiatrists who think the patient would improve if the environment were completely changed or if the patient were to acquire new attitudes and "develop this" or "acquire that" outlook, and so forth. Because of actual incapacitation, the patient is really unable to assimilate very much that is new and you will only aggravate the situation if you attempt to humor a patient by introducing new issues to him. Some psychiatrists try, for instance, to divert the patient's attention by encouraging him to learn new hobbies or acquiring new interests. It usually fails. It creates considerable anxiety and considerable resentment because the patient feels, naturally, that he is constantly being tested on the extent of his ability or inability to perform. The patient should be occupied, of course, but should not be made to feel he must "perform."

All atherosclerotic and senile persons are, furthermore, highly sensitive to any removal of emotional landmarks. It is interesting to note that many atherosclerotic patients go into a state of panic when they are moved from one house to another, or from one environment to another. Because of failing intellectual performance, a patient looks to all sorts of supportive signs in the environment, and if these are removed he becomes unable to orientate himself appropriately, that then creating problems and difficulties.

PRESENILE PSYCHOSES

With regard to the presenile psychoses, I cannot discuss treatment; it does not exist at the present time. The presenile psychoses, which include *Alzheimer's disease* and *Pick's disease,* often present difficulty in terms of differential diagnosis. Differentiation between Alzheimer's and Pick's diseases may be difficult clinically, especially in the early phase and in the terminal phase when symptoms are similar in both. In the middle phase, however, clinical differentiation is often readily made. At times these presenile diseases offer difficulty in their differentiation from other organic psychoses of various etiologies. These include such conditions as senile dementia and cerebral atherosclerosis which develop in the older age group, and general paresis, brain tumors, and certain forms of schizophrenia developing in any age group.

DIFFERENTIATION FROM VARIOUS ORGANIC PSYCHOSES: The differentiation from *senile dementia* becomes an issue only when the clinical picture of Alzheimer's or Pick's disease occurs in the senile age period, as occasionally happens.

The differentiation from a psychosis based on *cerebral atherosclerosis* is a much more frequent issue and often quite difficult, especially in the early stages of Pick's disease. As one of the distinguishing differential features, the atherosclerotic patient usually has subjective complaints: headaches, vertigo, poor concentration, and general feelings of being ill. These manifestations occur infrequently in presenile psychosis. It should be stressed that memory impairment is more patchy in cerebral atherosclerosis, whereas in presenile psychosis it is much more diffuse, following more the characteristic pattern of senile psychosis. Of equal diagnostic importance is the manner in which the focal neurological signs make their appearance. They may occur in atherosclerotic as well as presenile psychosis, but present themselves differently in each. In the presenile psychoses these signs develop slowly and progress in an orderly manner, whereas in atherosclerosis they usually make sudden apoplectic appearances with subsequent recessions, and if not so sudden are surely not orderly. At this point I might mention that, although moderate arteriosclerosis of the brain and other parts of the body may occur in a presenile psychotic individual, this is not grounds for making a diagnosis of psychosis due to cerebral atherosclerosis.

General paresis is easily distinguished by its characteristic serological findings in the blood and spinal fluid. In a few presenile patients, however, the serology is found to be mildly positive and many of these cases have been diagnosed as having general paresis. Therefore, the serological findings must be relatively massive before you could insist that the patient is suffering from cerebrospinal syphilis or general paresis. In the so-called Lissauer form of general paresis where, in addition to the dementia there are many focal neurological signs present—particularly those alluding to the parieto-occipital lobes as well as the frontal and temporal —a striking resemblance to Alzheimer's disease is observed clinically. However, the serological examination provides the differentiation.

When the patient's neurological signs are more prevalent on one side of the body than on the other in presenile psychosis, confusion with *brain tumor* has occasionally been made. Obviously, other neurological findings—electroencephalogram, air-encephalogram, spinal fluid pressure readings, changes in the fundi, and so forth—can differentiate these cases. From the point of view of mental impairment, the dementia observed in a presenile psychosis is generally much more profound than occurs in a frontal or temporal lobe brain tumor.

DIFFERENTIATION BETWEEN ALZHEIMER'S AND PICK'S DISEASES : Once the diagnosis of presenile psychosis is established, it is of more or less academic interest (rather than practical, therapeutic interest) to differentiate between Alzheimer's and Pick's diseases. This is not always possible because the differentiating signs are only relative, not absolute. In fact, some investigators regard these two diseases as being merely clinical variations of the same metabolic disturbance in the brain. Nevertheless, I shall enumerate a few of the signs that may make differentiation possible.

In terms of *pathology*, Alzheimer's disease usually affects the brain diffusely; impairment is not lobar. Pick's disease impairment is lobar, those mainly affected being the frontal and temporal lobes. Therefore, in Alzheimer's disease one observes many symptoms in addition to those of the frontal or temporal lobe impairment observed in Pick's disease.

The *age of onset* of both diseases is about the same (usually between forty and sixty years of age), although a few authors claimed that Alzheimer's disease often appears at an earlier age. The *sex* distribution, as in senile psychosis, shows preference for females in both presenile diseases. An *insidious onset* with slow progress is common to both, although acute forms of Pick's disease have been described.

The *course* of the illness is progressively downhill and generally more rapid in Alzheimer's disease, deterioration being completed in four to six years. Pick's disease often runs a longer course, ranging from six to ten years except for occasional acute forms having a duration of two years from onset. Death is most likely due to impairment of some of the vegetative functions controlled in the brain, but occasionally death is due to some intercurrent disease.

The *clinical symptomatology* in both of these disorders is markedly similar in the early stage of the illness before all signs and symptoms become manifest, and also in the final stages when marked deterioration is present. Usually, however, differences are apparent which are not always conclusive. The differentiation can be grouped under three headings: (1) mental changes, (2) aphasic-apraxic disturbances, and (3) certain other neurological manifestations.

Mental changes occur early in both presenile disorders. First, memory impairment develops, then other intellectual impairments and disorientation. These mental changes usually appear earlier, are more widespread and progress more rapidly in Alzheimer's disease. In Pick's disease, memory disintegrates more gradually and usually is fairly well retained for remote events. It is more generalized in Alzheimer's disease. Confabulations (of the Korsakoff type) are prominent in Alzheimer's disease but rare in Pick's disease. Emotional changes occur early in both disorders and follow the typical range of organic impairment, including irritability and emotional instability. Affect changes, such as depression or euphoria, are more pronounced in Pick's disease.

Pick's disease is very often characterized by a dullness, inactivity, lack of initiative, and a peculiar slowing down of mental functioning—the so-called bradyphrenia—and, in fact, there is a general mental and often even a motor akinesis. In contrast, many Alzheimer cases present a rather characteristic state of hyperactivity. The patient is restless and continually "on the go" for prolonged periods, often engaging in senseless activity, the so-called occupational delirium whereby he play-acts his former occupation in a manner similar to patients suffering with delirium tremens. If hyperactivity is present in a middle-aged person who manifests mental and emotional deterioration, it is probably the most significant feature pointing to an Alzheimer's disease, because Pick's cases rarely show hyperactivity. It is in direct contrast to the underactive akinetic patient with Pick's disease who becomes increasingly dull, increasingly inactive, and sits around without any initiative. This mental akinesis, or bradyphrenia, is a frontal lobe syndrome which Korsakoff described occurring in brain tumors. It has also been described in patients suffering from atherosclerosis of the frontal lobes and in many lobotomized patients.

Emotional and especially habit deterioration occurs

more frequently and progresses more rapidly in Pick's disease, here again being frontal lobe involvement. Asocial and immoral conduct is rare in Alzheimer's disease; the outward behavior of the patient is usually very well preserved in contrast to his marked intellectual deterioration. In other words, the Alzheimer patient is shallow but retains social amenities and may continue to behave in a rather polite and nice manner. Psychotic symptoms such as hallucinations, delusions, and other so-called productive symptoms are a great deal more common in Alzheimer's than in Pick's disease, which is usually characterized by a meagerness and impoverishment of mental performance.

Neuropsychic manifestations such as aphasia, apraxia, and agnosia may occur in both disorders. The aphasias in Alzheimer's disease are difficult to classify, often falling into the group of amnestic aphasias, while the aphasia in Pick's disease, if present, is of the sensorimotor type. The presence of apraxia and agnosia is characteristic of Alzheimer's disease because it is a parietal and occipital lobe syndrome and these lobes are especially involved. Apraxia and agnosia, in the true form, occur very rarely in Pick's disease because the involvement is mainly in the frontal or temporal lobes. Actually, neurological changes in Alzheimer's disease indicate a diffuse disorder of the brain, while in Pick's the neuropathology is more localized.

Focal neurological signs occur in both disorders. The pyramidal tract may also be involved in both diseases but the involvement is usually very mild. Extrapyramidal manifestations are more frequently observed in Pick's disease. For instance, athetosis, cogwheel phenomenon, rigidity, loss of associated movements, and other symptoms similar to those observed in Parkinson patients or postencephalitic patients, are often observed in Pick's disease. These signs practically never appear in Alzheimer's disease. Typical frontal lobe signs such as forced grasping, sucking, mastication, and so forth are characteristic of Pick's disease and rarely occur in Alzheimer's.

Finally, I would like to mention that epileptic attacks are very prevalent in Alzheimer's disease, while very rare in Pick's. Vasomotor syncopes are common in Alzheimer's disease. The electroencephalogram indicates that cortical degeneration is diffuse in Alzheimer's disease, and that it is more localized in Pick's.

In conclusion, patients with presenile psychosis do not often present themselves, and the diagnosis is frequently overlooked. However, these disorders are more prevalent than was formerly believed. The few presenile psychotic patients I observed have indicated that with careful clinical evaluation the diagnosis can be recognized much more frequently than has been the case in the past.

13

EPILEPSIES AND CONVULSIVE STATES

The term epilepsy is derived from the Greek verb meaning "to seize upon." Since ancient times it has been referred to as "the falling sickness" or "the sacred sickness." Many superstitions arose in connection with epilepsy and the epileptic person was even considered by ancient man to be either divine or possessed by evil spirits. Actually, the general term epilepsy, or convulsive states, does not designate a specific disease; epileptic, or convulsive, symptomatology may develop in a large number of pathological conditions involving the brain.

Epilepsy is an important topic having a great many neurological and psychiatric as well as analytic ramifications, but I will have to confine myself to only a few of the psychiatric aspects of epilepsy in the short space allotted for this subject. Epilepsy is of interest to the psychiatrist for several reasons. First of all, some investigators have claimed

that the epileptic attacks themselves occur in those individuals who have a special *constitutional character structure;*
other investigators believed that they have a special *psychodynamic structure.* This is the first issue confronting us: Do
persons suffering from epilepsy have any such special structure? Secondly, we are interested in the *emotional changes*
observed in patients suffering from fits: A person's awareness of his being epileptic and his awareness of having fits
obviously produces an emotional reaction in that person.
Thirdly, we are interested in more *gross alterations* of the
psychic structure itself in epileptic individuals who, for
instance, suffer from a gross mental picture termed epileptic
deterioration, and persons in whom the epileptic manifestations are essentially on the mental level—the type of epilepsy
termed psychomotor, epileptic equivalents, or epileptic
fugue states—and these cases are very important from a
clinical, dynamic, and also from a medico-legal point of
view. In addition, we are interested in epileptic individuals
in whom seemingly the trigger mechanism which releases
epileptic attacks is psychogenic. So, all these problems must
be discussed briefly, and I shall begin by defining epilepsy
and mentioning the physiological background for the psychiatric aspects of this disorder.

DEFINITION

Epilepsy in general may be defined as an organic disorder characterized by a paroxysmal and transitory occurrence of excessive neural discharges in the brain; they occur
suddenly, disappear spontaneously, and have a tendency to
recur. Epilepsy may be differentiated into two main types:
(1) *symptomatic* and (2) *idiopathic.* In *symptomatic
epilepsies* the convulsions are due to specific causes such as
brain impairment resulting from injury, tumor, cerebro-
vascular disorder—such as arteriosclerosis, hemorrhage,
emboli, and so forth—congenital cerebral anomaly, toxic,
and metabolic disorders, acute infectious disease, and many

others. The term *idiopathic epilepsy* simply means that no specific etiological factors have yet been determined. No unequivocal anatomical pathological process has been found in the nervous system. What was at one time described as specific for epilepsy, namely the sclerosis of the cornu ammonis (hippocampal area), is not specific and most likely is secondary to the vasoconstriction produced by the fits. Some disarrangement of the psychoarchitectonic scheme in the brain and mild gliosis have also been reported but these findings are not characteristic. Actually, idiopathic epilepsy is recognized as an organic disorder mainly on the basis of our knowledge of some of the electroencephalographic and physico-chemical relationships, but not on the basis of anatomy. Naturally, anatomical changes may be found in those epileptic persons in whom the epilepsy is secondary to definite brain changes, but these are the cases of symptomatic epilepsy. For example, if a child has a porencephaly or an agenesis of any portion of the nervous system and has frequent fits or if the child has tuberosclerosis and has frequent fits, or if in later life the child develops some organic brain disease in which the brain tissue is destroyed and has fits, in all such cases pathology is present but the pathology is not really specific for epilepsy but rather for the particular disorder in connection with which the epilepsy appears.

The only electroencephalographic patterns actually pathognomic for epilepsy are the grand mal patterns showing the big spike discharges, and the petit mal patterns showing the typical spike-and-dome discharges. These two patterns are grossly characteristic for epilepsy. The petit mal pattern is particularly clear-cut. The grand mal spike discharge pattern is not always pronounced, but is especially so when real epileptic discharge periods are imminent.

There are two other patterns suggestive of epilepsy although not characteristic for epilepsy alone. In one pattern there is a slow alpha rhythm; instead of eight or ten waves per second the rate slows down to five or four. These so-called slow alpha patterns occur, however, in many organic diseases other than epilepsy. The other pattern, the so-called psychomotor pattern, had originally been described as characteristic for epilepsy but is now recognized to be suggestive only of epilepsy, particularly if there are clinical findings which support it.

The psychomotor pattern consists of unusually slow waves having a flat so-called "table top" pattern interspersed with an average normal rhythm or perhaps with a so-called dysrhythmic wave pattern. In other words, there are some alterations of the wave pattern; the patient does not maintain eight to ten waves per second consistently but there are marked variations in the pattern. This so-called psychomotor pattern occurs in a rather large number of other disorders. For example, approximately 40 percent of schizophrenic patients will show a psychomotor wave pattern. Behavior disorder in children is occasionally connected with the presence of this wave pattern. It is sometimes present in sociopathic personalities. So, it has come to be realized that the psychomotor dysrhythmic pattern is not fully characteristic for epilepsy. However, should a patient be encountered who experiences fugue states and also shows this pattern, one can be quite certain that he is epileptic.

Incidentally, about 10 percent of persons who are clinically epileptic show wave patterns that are normal. The converse is also true, that about 10 to 15 percent of persons who are seemingly normal show abnormal wave patterns, these abnormal wave patterns usually being the so-called psychomotor type but never the petit mal or grand mal type.

DETERMINING FACTORS

Idiopathic epilepsy is an *organic* disorder. I emphasize that because investigations of the trigger mechanisms, investigations of the psychodynamic configurations, and also investigations of the mental alterations observed in epileptic individuals sometimes convey the idea that epilepsy is merely some form of an emotional reaction. That is incorrect. All confronting evidence indicates that epilepsy is really an organic disorder, despite the fact that its final etiology is as yet unknown. The introduction of electro-encephalography has demonstrated that epilepsy is an organic state. It became conclusively demonstrated further by family studies wherein members who suffered overt epilepsy showed demonstrable electroencephalographic changes, and other members of the same family who were not clinically epileptic also had electroencephalographic changes closely related to those observed in the epileptic member of the family. A considerable amount of available material demonstrates that persons who have this particular discharge picture in the brain which shows up in the electro-encephalogram become overtly epileptic if there is the added factor of trigger mechanisms.

Therefore, there remains very little doubt that idio-pathic epilepsy is really an organic disorder. The disorder is based on some metabolic disturbance in the nervous system, the expression of this disturbance being the peculiar electrical discharge picture demonstrable in these patients. And individuals classified as epileptic, regardless which variant of epilepsy is present—grand mal, petit mal, psycho-motor, or psychic equivalent, or other subgroup forms of epilepsy described, such as the narcoleptic, the pyknoleptic, and so forth—have a special metabolic formula of their nervous system. Apparently the symptoms may remain latent unless some additional mechanism becomes involved to act as a trigger. The trigger factor could be chemical, toxic, mechanical, emotional, or some other type, and many in idiopathic epilepsy are as yet not fully recognized. Thus, in approaching an epileptic patient we are aware of the fact that we are dealing with an individual having a special organic formula, and not only must the patient be examined from the viewpoint that such a formula is present but also examined for subtle or conspicuous trigger mechanisms.

Investigation of *trigger mechanisms* that precipitate

attacks in epilepsy is an important function to be carried out on the organic as well as the psychodynamic level. In some cases, trigger mechanisms are organic as well as psychological. For example, when an epileptic person who is a heavy drinker becomes depressed or in a state of rage, he may sit down and drink; alcohol then temporarily depresses the cortex by reducing its electrical or other discharges. Then, as the person becomes sober, he suddenly has an epileptic seizure. A similar phenomenon could occur with the use of barbiturates. For instance, an individual disposed to epilepsy who takes doses of a barbiturate may suddenly throw a fit upon withdrawal of the drug. Drugs which somewhat reduce brain responses to whatever stimulation is present definitely have a suppressing effect on the organization of the cortical portion of the nervous system and disinhibit the lower portion. In other words, any person under the influence of a cortical depressant such as alcohol becomes freer insofar as his subcortical mechanisms are concerned. (Incidentally, it is on this basis that many people have a feeling of well-being when they drink; they are freed from their cortically controlled inhibitions.) Now, epileptic individuals are notoriously susceptible to alcohol, and often throw fits either during or following its toxic influence. Moreover, patients who suffer the psychomotor type of epilepsy often enter into a fugue state precipitated simply by the alcohol. A number of them suddenly have an epileptic seizure while drinking; and, following the fit, they then enter into a fugue state or a frenzy. Sometimes these patients have another seizure during the sobering-up period. Many such variations of this theme can occur. Several components are involved: the organic trigger mechanisms include disturbances of fluid balance, carbohydrate, and other metabolic functions; the psychological trigger mechanisms include the emotional background of the epileptic person that prompted his drinking.

As yet, no reliable statistics indicate in how many epileptic individuals psychogenic trigger mechanisms do, or do not, play a role. Sufficient material is on hand, however, to demonstrate that in quite a large number of epileptic individuals, psychogenic factors play a role insofar as psychic conflict in the person produces tension and anxiety which promotes the release of an epileptic attack. Should that emotional trigger in the individual be removed, his number of attacks is diminished but, naturally, he does not thereby become a nonepileptic individual. Nobody is able to cure an epileptic person of his epilepsy by means of psychotherapy —or by any other methods presently known. We are only able to eliminate many of the patient's epileptic manifestations, partly by organic and partly by psychotherapeutic means.

Now, it has been claimed that in those persons who have an epileptic disposition a special mental organization is also present; it has been described as *epileptic character*. In the psychiatric literature, some authors *(6)* have claimed this epileptic character to be present in patients who had already shown epileptic manifestations for many years, and that therefore the so-called epileptic character formation was a sequella of the patient's epileptic manifestations and it should not properly be classified as epileptic character but regarded as mental manifestations (with either neurotic or psychotic coloring) resulting from the epilepsy. Other authors *(6)*, however, quite correctly interpreted these mental changes as being apparent even before the patient manifested epilepsy. Several studies indicated that epilepsy occurred in persons having this so-called epileptoid, or epileptic, character formation. Of course, such reportings are very few because very few investigators studied epileptic patients intensively from a characterological point of view before those patients manifested epilepsy. Actually, much of the material on the so-called epileptic personality, or epileptoid character, was accumulated from epileptic patients' relatives who had no epileptic manifestations themselves but displayed character traits similar to those of the person who had epilepsy.

The so-called epileptic character was described as a person who is hypersensitive, stubborn, unsociable, markedly egocentric, and having strong narcissistic manifestations with hypochondriacal fears. Epileptic characters have also been described as being very pious, religiously speaking. Some observers described their mentality as being rather slow-moving, narrow-gauged, and inflexible. We now realize that none of these character descriptions are actually specific for epilepsy. All these so-called traits are observed frequently in individuals suffering from an organic disorder of the brain, therefore also an organic disorder of the mind. They are all mild signs of alterations in the person's organic integrative functioning. They are observed in quite a number of individuals who have some form of an organic brain damage without having epilepsy. But it must be admitted that these combined traits, which have come to be interpreted as organic signs, are rather prevalent in epileptic individuals. To this, it can be added that projective techniques such as the Rorschach were also employed to demonstrate epileptic personality and epileptic character. Piotrowsky and others found that the Rorschach, similar to the clinical material, is nonspecific in most epileptic individuals. Actually, many of the Rorschach responses in epilepsy only demonstrated the presence of organic changes and followed along the pattern of responses found in cases of organic brain damage —not cases of gross organic brain damage, but the more subtle forms. A few psychiatrists, however, continued to hold onto the idea that there is such a thing as a specific epileptic character.

Now, the so-called epileptic character in those patients who, for instance, have been sick for many years with quite a number of epileptic attacks is, of course, a sequella of their epileptic manifestations and not simply pre-epileptic character manifestations. In the patient whose character formation is due to the epileptic disorder present, three factors must be considered: (1) the organic disorder per se, (2) the reaction of both the patient and his environment to the disorder, and (3) the patient's compensatory efforts to cope with his handicap.

The *organic disorder* per se manifests itself as a total organismic affair. On the intellectual level, the slowness of cerebration, the difficulty in forming new associations, the narrowness of interests, and the "sticky" rigidity in the thinking of the epileptic individual are due to the fact that the rate of cerebration is interfered with and so often abruptly interrupted by the convulsions. After each convulsion, naturally, recuperation takes place, but each convulsion entails a tremendous neural discharge which considerably disrupts the functioning of the nervous system, as can be observed in any person having an epileptic attack or having convulsions provoked artificially. These mental changes can be attributed to the organic changes in the brain per se. On the emotional level, lability of affect, irritability, an easily provoked emotional discharge, and the tremendous intensity of emotional outbursts released in an epileptic person are, here again, on an organic basis and are also observed in quite a number of nonepileptic patients who have organic brain changes.

Concerning the *reactions of the patient and his environment,* certain other rather common manifestations have been observed in epileptic patients—for instance, seclusiveness, hypersensitivity, and many such features described as schizoid—but they are difficult to interpret. Some observers believe them to be reactions secondary to the fact that epileptic individuals usually grow up in an environment which is partly overprotective toward them and partly rejecting of them because they have a disorder which still, in the minds of many, carries a rather bad connotation. In other words, on the one hand epileptic persons are socially stigmatized and their participation in social activities is restricted, not alone because they are sick in the physical sense but because they are afflicted with this particular disorder. On the other hand, at home they are usually treated in an overprotective manner, but often along with the overprotection there is strong hostility toward them because their affliction is not only disabling but, until rather recently (and probably even today in some segments of the population), also very disagreeable.

There is no doubt that emotional changes which could in general be described as schizoid, such as emotional with-drawal and self-enmeshed seclusiveness, are very prevalent in epileptic individuals. Their distorted appraisal of reality is a logical sequence to the emotional withdrawal; and, in turn, suspiciousness develops in connection with their inability to adapt. In other words, all the secondary mani-festations that are observed in schizophrenia can develop based on the autistic attitude of the epileptic individual toward the environment. This issue is especially important to recognize when attempting to treat and socially rehabili-tate epileptic individuals because autism could, in many cases, lead to secondary elaborations.

Epileptic individuals are, furthermore, considered to be very moody and difficult to get along with. They are continually undergoing an increasing or decreasing emo-tional tension-flow; sometimes it is present in relationship to attacks and at other times independent of them. It is very interesting to observe that in many epileptic individuals the mounting up and discharge of tension takes place without fits occurring, and seemingly in some patients it even replaces fits. In any case, we pay attention to all these secondary mental phenomena in epileptic patients, but do not believe them to be specific for epilepsy. They should be interpreted as being due partly to the organic process itself and partly as a secondary reaction to the patient's awareness of his epileptic disorder.

Compensatory efforts to cope with their handicap are obvious in a great many epileptics, particularly in those unable to handle environmental situations very well. All types of compensatory neurotic reaction formations occur. One observes anxiety, phobic, obsessive, and other pictures rather frequently in epileptic individuals. The neurotic clinical manifestations are usually *more* marked in those patients who have very few epileptic manifestations, and are *less* marked in patients having very pronounced epileptic manifestations. That sounds paradoxical. Nevertheless, there is an inverse relationship between severity of organic brain disorder and neurotic symptom formation. Neurotic reactions which are essentially reactions developed by individuals due to inability to cope with environmental situations occur much more commonly in persons suffering from an organic disease which only partially handicaps them, and are rarely observed in persons suffering from a very serious organic disorder.

When psychodynamic investigations were made, it was also claimed that epilepsy had a specific *psychodynamic structure*. Actually, all the dynamic formulations are those which can also be applied to the neuroses or applied to the psychoses—especially in schizophrenia, there being an interesting relationship existing between epilepsy and schizophrenia. It was found that epileptic individuals do not show any dynamic structures that differ from those that can be observed in any of the neuroses or the other psychoses. Therefore, any claim that a specific epileptic dynamic pattern has been found is completely groundless, regardless of one or two such claims having been made on exactly this basis.

Many investigators who have made psychodynamic studies of epilepsy were struck by the marked psychosexual infantilism of many epileptic patients. It was pointed out that oral, anal, passive-aggressive, and pregenital manifestations in general are very prevalent in epileptic persons, particularly aggression on an oral and anal level. Some investigators also pointed out that many epileptic persons have unresolved oedipal relationships. Here again, however, on close examination these dynamic structures are not really so very different from those observed in other psychotic structures and even in many psychoneuroses. Whether this is a matter of psychosexual underdevelopment (or psychosexual regression in those who develop epilepsy in later life), or whether it is based on the organic process per se, on the fact that the epileptic person is raised in a peculiar way, or on the person's reaction formation to an early awareness that he has epilepsy, has not been verified. The observations, however, are valid; detailed studies show these psychosexual dynamic structures to be extremely prevalent in epileptic individuals. In many epileptic patients this may go to the extent of presenting a picture of undifferentiated sexuality: Some epileptic patients, for instance, have the same difficulties in differentiating between maleness and femaleness as schizophrenic individuals do.

There is another issue which formerly tended to be overlooked. Many psychoneurotic structures, many pre-psychotic, or psychotic schizophrenic structures, occur combined with epilepsy in some individuals. Schizophrenia is an extremely prevalent disorder; schizoid character formation is also extremely prevalent; psychoneuroses are very prevalent; and epilepsy is also prevalent. It would be rather peculiar if they were not found occurring together in some individuals. The issue is thus complicated even further because in many cases of epilepsy we do not know whether we are dealing with coincidental manifestations of a neurotic or psychotic nature, or with mental reactions on an organic level which are due to the epilepsy itself. This is a rather complex question and at the present time it can only be stated that many epileptic individuals have a marked psychosexual deviation present which is similar to that observed in schizophrenic individuals, or similar to that observed in persons suffering from a deep and markedly ramified neurosis such as the obsessive-compulsive. Obsessive-compulsive manifestations, by the way, are not rare in epilepsy and in some patients assume the form of epileptic equivalents.

There is only one claim, from a dynamic point of view, that can be considered fairly specific for epilepsy: the phenomenon of so-called *rebirth fantasies.* However, although rebirth fantasies are observed much more frequently in epilepsy than in any other disorder investigated psychodynamically, similar dynamic structures have been observed in catatonic schizophrenic patients, but not often. But in epilepsy it is a very recurring theme. Thus, the fantasies of rebirth in an epileptic patient are intimately linked with the catastrophic anxiety connected with a feeling of imminent annihilation that ushers in the attacks. You will find it occurring particularly in those epileptic patients who experience a so-called anxiety aura. Upon very close examination it is quite often found that these patients interpret the aura as the premonition of dying, the fit as death, and the postconvulsive feeling as the rebirth.

It is interesting that in a few epileptic patients an aura may actually be recalled in their dreams. In such dreams the patient is preoccupied with the same sensation as that felt during the aura itself. Some epileptic individuals experience psychotic states, or near psychotic states, which were formerly termed epileptic ecstasies. In these states, too, the patient is preoccupied with the idea of death and rebirth.

A few observers went to the extent of arranging a psychodynamic formulation of epilepsy around this one factor alone, which is of course not tenable because quite a number of epileptic individuals—in fact, the majority—do not experience the rebirth fantasy phenomenon. But if it does appear, and if one is able to detect it in the patient, it can be regarded as fairly specific and the only specific dynamic experience that can be assigned to epilepsy.

CLINICAL VARIANT FORMS

In terms of clinical manifestations, there are many variant forms of epilepsy. The most commonly observed are: (1) major, or *grand mal,* attacks, (2) minor, or *petit mal,* attacks, and (3) *psychomotor,* or epileptic equivalent states, in which the predominant clinical manifestations are the psychic alterations. Grand mal and petit mal attacks are predominantly manifested by organic features, but psychological elements are also involved.

In many cases, *grand mal* convulsions are ushered in by an aura; in quite a number of others an aura does not exist, or it is very brief. There are, however, epileptic individuals who experience a prolonged aura and these prodromal symptoms may precede the attack by many hours. The aura is usually specific for each individual experiencing it. All varieties of subjective perceptual distortions and emotions as well as objective motor and vasomotor phenomena may occur. For instance, the person may experience peculiar sensations in his stomach, an unpleasant odor, or color perceptions. He may experience momentary rages, running spells, yawning, flushing, pallor, and so on. Furthermore, as I have mentioned, many epileptic persons experience very strong prodromal feelings of anxiety or depression. These may include feelings of impending death, or a sensation of oppression, or sensations of being choked, and with any of these sensations a catastrophic anxiety fills the patient.

To mention the organic features briefly, the grand mal seizure itself develops suddenly; suddenly the patient becomes unconscious, drops to the ground and may or may not injure himself in the process. There first occurs the tonic phase of the convulsion: the body is rigid, the arms and legs are extended, the jaws are tightly clenched, the eyeballs roll upward and the head jerks from side to side. Eye pupils are at first contracted and then dilate and remain fixed. Respirations cease, the face becomes livid and there is usually incontinence of urine and feces. This tonic phase may last from a few seconds to half a minute. The clonic phase suddenly follows. The jerking of the head increases; there is rolling of the eyeballs; the limbs thrash about violently, alternately flexing and extending. There is frothy salivation, noisy breathing, and perfuse perspiration. The patient's pulse is rapid and weak. This clonic phase may last from one to five minutes. Then all motor manifestations cease, and the patient appears to be stuporous and exhausted. Often he appears bewildered and in this state performs some automatic act. He may fall into a deep sleep for several hours. He awakens with complete amnesia for the attack. Occasionally following the attack the patient may have a frenzy of excitement, the so-called epileptic furor, and in such a state can severely injure himself or others. A furor state indicates the possibility, which is demonstrated in the patient's dreams and other psychodynamic productions, of a strong underlying sadistic tendency in his personality organization. The epileptic is therefore considered by many psychiatrists to be the most dangerous of all psychiatric patients.

Petit mal episodes usually are not preceded by an aura. The patient suddenly becomes unconscious; he ceases all activity, such as eating or walking or talking, and is momentarily "absent" but does not fall and does not have convulsions. The episode is of only a few seconds' duration, following which the patient resumes his activity as though it had not been interrupted. He usually has amnesia for the episode. Many such attacks may occur during the day. Petit mal usually first appears in childhood and may be the only manifestations of epilepsy, but in some patients they alternate with grand mal attacks. In many cases, petit mal disappears with maturation; in others, grand mal seizures may eventually develop.

Before describing the clinical manifestations of the psychomotor form of epilepsy, which is characterized mainly by psychic rather than organic features, we should concern ourselves with two *gross mental pictures in* epilepsy: (1) so-called epileptic *deterioration,* which is usually in connection with grand mal epilepsy, and (2) the full *psychotic pictures,* either in the form of psychomotor epilepsy or the actual epileptic psychoses.

Epileptic deterioration is actually nothing other than an intellectual and emotional dementia following along the lines of an organic reaction. It differs in no way from the chronic organic reaction pattern which, as I discussed extensively, culminates in deterioration. Intellectual functioning is, of course, somewhat impaired in a number of epileptic persons and some of them show remissions, but at present I am referring only to those who actually develop gross deterioration pictures more parallel with the Korsakoff syndrome, general paresis, or any of the other organic dementias.

There is a relationship between frequency of epileptic attacks and deterioration. Epileptic deterioration is rarely observed in a person who does not have frequent attacks—usually grand mal attacks. It is interesting that patients suffering mainly from petit mal attacks display very little tendency to deterioration. Those who suffer frequent grand mal attacks run the greatest risk of falling into the deterioration group.

Naturally, epileptic patients who show marked intellectual and emotional impairments are very often hospitalized; and, in former years, the number of deteriorated epileptic persons was markedly overestimated simply because the epileptic population described generally counted only those patients who were in mental institutions. Fortunately, however, the number of epileptic persons who deteriorate markedly is actually not very great. Another confusion arose regarding so-called epileptic deterioration. Epilepsy is very frequently a complication in persons suffering an agenesis of the nervous system, which often occurs together with feeblemindedness of some form. And epilepsy is a frequent complication of organic brain damage or brain atrophy diseases. Now, these persons are mentally enfeebled, and those who have frequent fits naturally become even more mentally enfeebled. Formerly, such cases were also counted among the patients suffering from epileptic deterioration. They obviously do not belong in the category of epileptic deterioration because most of the patients are already feebleminded to begin with. A certain percentage of epileptic persons deteriorate. There is no question about that. But the percentage is small; it is probably no higher than 3 to 5 percent.

The second of the gross mental pictures occurring in epilepsy are the *psychotic pictures.* These gross psychotic pictures can be subdivided into two types: (1) *psychomotor epilepsy* (the so-called epileptic equivalents), and (2) actual *epileptic psychoses.*

Psychomotor epilepsy has also been termed epileptic equivalents because it was thought that these states replace convulsions, that they appear instead of convulsions. The designation is rather unfortunate because nobody really knows that they actually do occur instead of convulsions. Many epileptic persons suffering from this type of disorder have convulsions also, but there are others who have no convulsions, only the so-called equivalent manifestations. In any case, the terms epileptic dream states, epileptic automatic states, or psychomotor epilepsy have come to be preferred for this type of epilepsy.

Clinical manifestations of psychomotor epilepsy are extremely varied. The core of the clinical picture usually consists of the person committing automatic acts. There are many types of automatic acts committed: For instance, the person wanders away from home in a so-called epileptic fugue state; he flies into a state of rage; he has a delusional hallucinatory episode; or he commits some complicated act. In some instances the complicated act is harmless, but in others it is antisocial and he kills somebody; he sets fire to property; or he goes into some form of sexual frenzy. Following the episodes, the person has absolutely no recollection for the acts. The automatic acts are very often performed in a stereotyped manner, meaning that the behavior is the same, again and again, in every attack. For example, during each attack the patient runs away from home, and this pattern never varies. In some patients, however, the psychomotor manifestations vary in pattern with each attack.

Quite a number of epileptic patients perform rather brutal crimes during a psychomotor epileptic state. These brutal crimes are usually executed crudely; it is obvious they are not premeditated. Nevertheless, they may be executed fairly efficiently. Furthermore, you should not forget that, although premeditation cannot actually be legally claimed for these acts because they were not consciously premeditated, a number of the acts do express the individual's unconscious premeditation with certain strivings or wishes and, naturally, are executed accordingly. Unconscious premeditation may erupt in the form of exhibitionism, destructiveness, sexual assaults on others, and so forth. Aggression in the form of damaging others or damaging property is also fairly common. Very often aggression is fused with erotic manifestations. The structure of this phenomenon is interesting: aggression and sexuality are fused in the form of exhibitionism. In other words, very often the aggression is exhibited in the framework of sexual assaults. The criminal acts of epileptic persons have long been feared. They are usually so extremely brutal and backed by such a tremendous discharge of aggression that during these states patients are very, very difficult to handle. I reiterate that these patients have complete amnesia for their committed acts; legally they are not responsible for them.

In many cases, epileptic psychomotor states occur without any other manifestations of epilepsy. Formerly, such patients were very difficult to diagnose, it naturally being easier to make the diagnosis when the patient also has full-fledged grand mal or petit mal attacks. Electroencephalography has simplified the diagnosing of psychomotor epilepsy because many patients show rather typical brain wave patterns, although these patterns are merely suggestive of psychomotor epilepsy but not pathognomic, as I have mentioned.

In a medico-legal case, the presence alone of such electroencephalographic patterns would not substantiate the diagnosis of psychomotor epilepsy. In such a case, or in the case of a patient who shows no abnormality of electro-encephalographic pattern and has no history of grand mal or petit mal attacks, one would have to more or less rely on the overall clinical description of the epileptic psychomotor picture. For instance, your psychiatric testimony would stress that the patient was amnestic for the events in question. Naturally, you should substantiate that whenever possible. Then, you should point out the manner in which the event in question was executed; for instance, that the lack of planning, the impulsiveness, the crudeness, and the brutality of the whole act are characteristic of an automatic discharge phenomenon. Then, you could probably gather together some information indicating the person had periodically had such experiences in the past. That would, of course, be the most convincing argument of all. Despite all evidence, however, you can guarantee that quite a number of persons who really were suffering from epilepsy will be adjudged "insane," and vice versa.

The second type of psychotic picture that occurs in epilepsy includes the *epileptic psychoses.* Ordinarily there are two forms of epileptic psychoses that may appear: (1) the *organic psychosis,* and (2) the *schizophrenic psychosis.*

The *organic psychosis* has all the attributes and all the elements of a typical organic psychosis. Sometimes it takes the form of an acute delirious confusional state showing many hallucinatory and paranoid elements. It usually follows an attack—a grand mal attack, or a so-called psychomotor attack in the sense that the attack suddenly begins with some automatic behavior pattern and then merges imperceptibly into a psychosis. In other patients, we observe the chronic organic syndrome developing in the form of a Korsakoff picture or a picture of epileptic dementia. These cases are readily diagnosed. More complicated to diagnose are those cases of organic psychosis which, in addition to some of the organic features, manifest so-called functional symptoms. Depression is one which can occur.

The most common psychotic pictures in connection

with epilepsy, however, are those of a *schizophrenic psychosis*. There has been considerable discussion about the interpretation of these schizophrenic pictures and as yet there is no general agreement on the issue. The empirical fact remains that quite a number of epileptic individuals manifest schizophrenic symptomatology when they become psychotic. In many cases the schizophrenic symptomatology is so clear-cut that they are diagnosed as actually suffering from schizophrenia. Some psychiatrists classify them as true cases of schizophrenia with epileptic attacks. Others classify them as cases of symptomatic schizophrenia, indicating that the patient is suffering from epilepsy and the psychosis merely resembles schizophrenia symptomatically, or that the organic process of epilepsy precipitated or released a schizophrenic process in a predisposed individual on a symptomatic level. Some French psychiatrists even attempted to establish a special entity termed "schizolepsy." Thus, there are many rather interesting variations in theoretical views as to how these cases should be interpreted and classified. This empirical issue is extremely important because one observes quite a number of epileptic individuals who, when psychotic, manifest schizophrenic or schizophrenic-like clinical symptomatology.

Several attempts have been made to establish an etiological relationship between epilepsy and schizophrenia. Two attempts, in particular, were made in this respect. One claimed that the two disorders are strictly antagonistic to each other. Some of the shock treatments—especially metrazol treatment—were introduced on the basis of the fallacious theoretical assumption that these two disorders never appear together, that they are antagonistic to each other. That is not correct; there are schizophrenic individuals who have epileptic attacks and, as I have mentioned, there are many chronic epileptic psychotic individuals who show a schizophrenic picture. Therefore, that the two conditions are antagonistic to each other cannot be stated.

Secondly, when electroencephalography was introduced, Lennox and Gibbs maintained that the psychomotor epileptic pattern is very common in epilepsy and rather common in schizophrenia. Mainly on the basis of the electrical discharge pattern in the brain, they initially postulated that there is an etiological connection between the two disorders. This, again, was a wrong assumption which they themselves, after considerable criticism, corrected. So, the idea is also buried that schizophrenia and epilepsy are etiologically related simply because the encephalographic pattern appeared to be similar, the similarity being more phenomenological than etiological.

TREATMENT RATIONALE

To mention briefly the *treatment* of epileptic states in general, the approach is three-fold: *Organic treatment,* mainly based on special medication; *psychotherapy* on those cases in which it can be demonstrated that the attacks are set off by a psychogenic trigger; and *social rehabilitation,* or social readjustment: Attempting to determine the most fitting place for the epileptic individual in the community with regard to occupational and other community resources; and attempting to diminish the social implications of the affliction, which naturally, can also be construed as part of the psychotherapy given the patient.

Without discussing all the possible pharmacological approaches in treating epilepsy, certain general principles should be mentioned. Quite a number of anticonvulsant drugs are available, different drugs influencing different types of epilepsy in different ways. Therefore, it is important to know which drug to use in which type of epilepsy. Often the treatment of an epileptic patient fails on a pharmacological level because the appropriate drug was not selected for the particular case. Another matter wherein a great deal of difficulty arises is that seemingly many physicians who treat epileptic individuals give the appropriate drug for a particular epileptic condition but do not test out *the adequate drug dosage.* It is sometimes rather impressive to observe that raising or reducing the amount of a particular drug, or combining different types of drugs in adequate amounts, suddenly benefits a patient who was formerly not benefited by exactly the same drugs. Therefore, the proper dosage must always be worked out for each patient, and sometimes it is necessary to experiment with dosages by testing them empirically on the patient. But schematic prescriptions—t.i.d. one capsule of dilantin, t.i.d. so much tridione, so much phenobarbital, or whatever—are rarely sufficient in the treatment of epileptic individuals.

Every year, more antiepileptic drug substances become available which are known to have anticonvulsive properties and at the same time lack the property of making the patient sleepy. In other words, the sedative property of the newer compounds is circumscribed around their anticonvulsive affects without causing the diffused cerebral or cortical inhibition as did the bromides. The influence of phenobarbital was also such that it is now relegated to a minor role. Dilantin and related drugs became preferable, even though still in combination with small amounts of phenobarbital.

In prescribing the various drugs, it is important to know that some drugs affect only the grand mal conditions, some affect petit mal, and others affect the psychomotor or epileptic equivalent states. The psychomotor states are those most difficult to treat. At the present time, in fact, patients manifesting epileptic equivalent states, those suffering from narcolepsy, or from one of the other variants of epilepsy are more difficult to treat than those suffering from grand mal or petit mal attacks.

In treating grand mal epilepsy, dilantin has continued to be the usual drug of choice. The dosage of dilantin must be established for each patient experimentally. This is preferably done by raising the dilantin level up to the point at which the patient ceases to have convulsions. Some neurologists go so far as to push the level of dilantin up until the patient shows very slight signs of dilantin toxicity and then reduce the dose to the patient's level of tolerance for the drug. In my opinion, it is not important to push the dilantin up to a toxic level but it certainly should be raised up to the level on which convulsions cease to occur in the patient. In approximately 70 percent of the cases, dilantin will eliminate or considerably reduce the number of convulsions. It is also advisable to give very small doses of phenobarbital in addition because phenobarbital reinforces and enhances the influence of dilantin. Drugs such as mesantoin, phenytoin sodium, or all the derivatives of dilantin can be used just as well and usually in the same dosage, the minimum dose for adults being approximately $1\frac{1}{2}$ grains of dilantin three times a day.

In the petit mal form of epilepsy, tridione has been the drug of choice in doses from 0.3 to 1.5 grams three or four times daily. Some patients use that drug alone; some use it in combination with phenobarbital and some in combination with dilantin. This drug combination treatment is particularly important for those patients suffering from both grand mal and petit mal epilepsies, but in some cases it is necessary to combine medications even though the patient suffers from petit mal only. The response of petit mal to pharmacological treatment is usually less favorable than that of grand mal epilepsy although tridione has afforded considerable progress in treatment of petit mal epilepsy. Glutamic acid has also been tested in the treatment of petit mal but found to be less effective than tridione. However, a trial with glutamic acid should be made before using tridione because tridione is toxic and some patients do not tolerate it very well, while glutamic acid rarely produces side effects.

The dietary treatment of epilepsy—such as the ketogenic diet, low carbohydrate intake, dehydration, and similar procedures to prevent alkalosis—were considerably in vogue a number of years ago but are practically all discarded as being rather ineffective and very cumbersome to apply. Surgical procedure is indicated only for those epileptic individuals in whom the attacks are symptomatically produced by some pathology in the brain which is circumscribed and therefore accessible to surgery. Operations which were at one time performed to relieve symptoms in idiopathic epilepsy are no longer employed other than experimentally.

Patients suffering from epileptic equivalent states, or epilepsy dream states, usually receive the same treatment as that given patients suffering from ordinary forms of epilepsy. In addition, however, in quite a number of cases electroconvulsive therapy is applied to break up the patient's dream state. It is interesting that the artificially produced convulsion effectively cuts or eliminates the dream state or equivalent state, the patient usually requiring only one or two treatments. At one time, electro-convulsive therapy was also applied in cases of grand mal epilepsy, the assumption being that if the patient received artificially produced convulsions, his ability to produce a convulsion within himself would be lessened because the so-called epileptic threshold will have been raised. These experiments did not pan out very successfully. In some cases of epilepsy, of course, it was possible to prevent the occurrence of the spontaneous attack by giving the patient an artificial attack in advance. On the other hand, however, although the epileptic mechanisms in the genuine epileptic attack and those in the artificial attack produced by electro-convulsive shock are phenomenologically very similar, seemingly etiologically and neurophysiologically they are nevertheless differently founded. They are, in short, not identical.

There is as yet no special form of treatment for the organic form of epileptic psychosis other than that employed for treating epilepsy in general. For most cases of epileptic patients who do not respond to medication, who have frequent attacks regardless of antiepileptic measures, or who slowly deteriorate—who develop a Korsakoff syndrome or a chronic epileptic deterioration picture—there is as yet no treatment. Fortunately, these conditions are rather rare. Considering the large number of individuals who are epileptic, they do not occur very frequently. As I have mentioned, this does not include those so-called demented epileptic cases once reported from many institutions which often were combination affairs in the sense that they were patients suffering some form of organic brain disease or mental deficiency who developed epileptic attacks in addition. While only part of the populations of those particular institutions was evaluated for statistical purposes, the large number of epileptic individuals treated elsewhere and the large number ambulating without receiving any treatment are considerable. The fact remains that there are patients who fit in the category of epileptic individuals who became deteriorated or demented due to straight idiopathic epilepsy, but the number of such patients is far less than had originally been assumed.

Those patients manifesting schizophrenic or depressive symptomatology are usually treated with the same anti-epileptic measures I described, namely, with medications plus psychotherapy applicable to the particular patient's epileptic condition. Actually, both these treatment measures are rather ineffective for this group of patients. If the psychotic state is episodic it usually clears up anyhow. If it is not episodic, the patient then remains in that psychotic state. Attempts were made to treat these patients as one would approach patients suffering from combined disorders: partly as epileptic patients and partly as cases of depression or schizophrenia. In some of these patients so treated, however, it is difficult to state whether or not this combination approach was superior to that of treating them simply as cases of epilepsy. Further attempts should be made in this respect because antiepileptic measures are usually not sufficient to gauge the efficacy of treatment for these patients. It could happen that, although the number of

attacks is reduced by the antiepileptic medication, it nevertheless does not affect the patient's mental manifestations,
or affects them only slightly.

Treatment of the many atypical forms of epilepsy
(many of which will not be discussed here) is, naturally,
organized around these typical epileptic situations. Atypical
forms of epileptic attacks are prevalent, and the prevailing
attitude in psychiatric literature and clinical practice is that
many of these attacks are actually psychogenic. Naturally,
the reverse stand was also taken, but, since psychogenicity
of attacks became increasingly stressed in appraising attacks,
it became more common to diagnose the patient as suffering
from psychogenic rather than organic attacks. I also wish
to call attention to the fact that a number of individuals
have attacks which came to be described as so-called vegetative discharges, or so-called vaso-vagal attacks; these were
formerly considered to be purely psychogenic. However,
considerable evidence indicates that many of these patients
are actually epileptic; they show epileptic brain-wave
patterns and also respond to antiepileptic medication. These
cases are of especially great interest psychiatrically because
many of them demonstrate definite psychogenic trigger
mechanisms—psychogenic release mechanisms which,
naturally, must be dealt with by means of psychotherapy in
addition to the organic treatment, exactly as in cases of
typical epilepsy.

Narcolepsy, another subgroup of epilepsy which is also
atypical, and pyknolepsy which occurs in children, are
borderland disorders. On the one hand, they display organic
features relating them to epilepsy, and on the other hand
they also display a great many psychogenic features—often
psychodynamic features of hysteria, or those that remind one
of psychosomatic disorders—and this is a very broad borderland where organic and psychogenic mechanisms appear
so intertwined in these patients that at times it is very difficult to differentiate them. At the present time, the safest
procedure is to attempt to treat them along both lines and

give them the benefits of both organic and psychiatric approaches. One should not be dogmatic by stating, "I treat such a patient this way only." Treating these patients with just one or the other approach is justified only when doing it for research purposes; naturally, one then does not wish to clutter up the field with multiple approaches. But, clinically speaking, quite a number of these patients do require the benefit of both approaches if something is to be accomplished with them therapeutically. They are very difficult cases to treat, and in looking over the medical literature one can read that the number of these patients circulating around is so considerable that practically everyone encounters them, and yet very little is reported statistically of how effective therapeutic results are on these patients.

In narcolepsy, treatment does not entirely follow those measures just outlined for epilepsy. Usually the treatment of narcolepsy is carried out with amphetamines such as desoxyn or benzedrine. In other words, treatment consists of stimulating the diencephalon. Sometimes this is done with, and sometimes without, the combined use of dilantin or phenobarbital. In every case of narcolepsy a very intensive inventory should be made as to psychogenic trigger mechanisms. One encounters patients, however, in whom the narcolepsy episode is actually produced on a purely organic level; in others the attacks are precipitated, or probably even determined in part, by psychodynamic mechanisms in the patient whereby narcolepsy is the particular means for expressing conflicts.

Pyknolepsy occurs only in children. It was formerly considered purely psychogenic, which definitely is not the case. Pyknolepsy is a form of epilepsy in which the patient has innumerable little attacks of so-called absences, sometimes up to several hundred every day. They are actually very small, short-lived petit mal attacks. These attacks had been assumed to be psychogenic because occasionally environmental influences modify them, and especially because the child never shows any degree of mental deterioration despite having had innumerable such attacks. In most cases, the intelligence of children suffering from pyknolepsy remains equivalent, in marked contrast to any expectations of persons having as many as several hundred attacks each day. Nevertheless, the electroencephalographic evidence indicates that these children really are epileptic. Then, again, psychogenic trigger mechanisms in pyknolepsy are very common; therefore, a few observers believe that pyknolepsy, also, is in a borderland between psychogenic disorders and epilepsy.

It is obvious that discharges of the brain can be facilitated by emotional factors as well as by organic, and etiologically different mechanisms are able to utilize common neural pathways in an individual. One observes quite clearly in epilepsy, especially in research on the borderland cases, that the nervous system is able to respond in exactly the same way to an organic as to a psychogenic stimulus, and that actually there is no difference between the two responses, provided the concept is broadened to the level of assuming that an organism responds to a given stimulus in whatever particular manner its metabolic organization directs.

Introduction
"Functional" (Idiopathic) Mental Disorders

14

DIAGNOSTIC APPROACH TO "FUNCTIONAL" MENTAL DISORDERS

Up to this point I have dealt with essentially organic disorders. Now I want to discuss disorders in which the etiology is not clear: manic-depressive psychosis, involutional psychosis, the group of schizophrenias, the sociopathic states, and the psychoneuroses. In these illnesses no pathological anatomical substrata have as yet been determined, while in organic disorders they have been, at least to some extent.

Psychiatric diagnosis is based on etiology only in the organic psychoses. In the organic psychoses there is a close relationship between an etiological agent and a mental disorder, even though the relationship of the mental pathology resulting from the underlying structural pathology is not fully clear in each instance. For example, in the case of general paresis, when one investigates the phenomenological picture of several patients in detail, he finds there are many varied symptomatologies present caused by the same etiology.

In most areas of medicine which are not psychiatric, there are many fairly well-defined etiological entities. This holds true in psychiatry, up to a point (the organic psychoses, so far as structural changes are concerned). The emotional changes, however, are not so clearly understood, but at least one can say that conditions such as general paresis and cerebral atherosclerosis are disease entities which can produce different psychotic reactions in the organism.

The situation becomes even more complicated in the so-called nonorganic psychoses where all data about the patient in the past and in the present are purely phenomenological. In other words, a patient is diagnosed a depressive because he appears depressed, a manic because he appears manic. This does not give us any clue regarding the etiology and we usually juggle diagnosis in descriptive terms. As will be explained later, psychodynamic interpretations do not help here because they are not etiological but are symptomalogical from another framework of reference. Some psychiatrists argue differently, but they have not as yet been able to give us any etiological clues. Therefore, our diagnostic approach in so-called nonorganic psychoses, and in most of the psychopathic states and even in some of the psychoneuroses, is purely phenomenological.

We cannot say that such conditions as manic-depressive psychosis or schizophrenia are disease entities because we do not know the underlying etiology; we see only the second part—the reactions. In fact, when diagnosing a patient as having schizophrenia, for example, a psychiatrist is being no more and no less specific than would be an internist's stating the patient is suffering from a fever. In internal medicine there was a time when patients were diagnosed as suffering from a fever but that did not give any clue as to the etiology—the etiology, such as a particular microorganism for instance, had to be discovered. In psychiatry it can be recognized that a given symptom can probably have different etiologies even though there is one common reaction involved which produces that symptom.

In medicine many different bacteria can produce inflammatory reactions strikingly similar to those produced by the pneumococcus. Etiology of the reactions may thus be different in each case. Even though these reactions may respond to a single drug it does not mean the etiology must be the same. In psychiatry it is also true that certain symptom reactions may be more or less responsive to one or another therapeutic approach. Furthermore, when it was recognized that disorders having different etiologies can frequently produce similar manifestations of mental distress, it was also recognized that disorders having the same etiology can produce different manifestations of mental distress. All these findings merely indicate there are great difficulties in diagnosing and treating the so-called functional psychoses because we have no clear idea of their etiologies.

In the psychoses now to be discussed, anatomical, chemical, or other structural alterations have not been reliably shown. There are an increasing number of reports, on schizophrenia especially, which indicate that probably such changes are present, but they have not been convincingly demonstrated. Because the designation of an organic disorder is usually interpreted in terms of structural change, and because this structural change has not been demonstrated in all the psychoses, all kinds of other designations were introduced, such as "functional psychoses," indicating they are actually functional disorders. Some psychiatrists have gone so far as to state that these disorders are psychogenic. Again others were impressed by the hereditary influences; due to the multiple occurrence of certain disorders in some families, they believed that these disorders were constitutionally inherited. There are a number of other designations for these psychoses of unknown etiology which will be considered when I discuss the different etiological concepts. At present I think the simplest and the most honest approach is to assume that the etiologies of the so-called functional psychotic disorders are unknown. There are theories about their origins and probably ongoing research will show a few of these theories to be correct and prove many others incorrect. However, we have only theories and no convincing proof regarding the bases of these disorders.

Realizing that, from the prognostic view of therapy, we perceive why some fixed factors become established, such as the presence or absence of deterioration or factors worked out partly on a constitutional and partly on a psychodynamic level. These naturally make the physician observing the patient more secure in appraising which forms of therapeutic process he wants to use. Actually it is not that all these differentiations give us any insight into what is going on in the patient, but they do serve as empirical landmarks for us to follow. They at least give some idea what will become of a patient and how he will respond to certain therapeutic measures even though these measures are also empirical. For this reason, Kraepelin's classifications made great progress even though his formulations were not fully correct and have been supplanted in many ways by other approaches (4). Before his contributions the trend in psychiatry and in many other fields of medicine (particularly dermatology, which continues to suffer from the same classificatory difficulty) had been to accept phenomenological observations as though they were etiological. Phenomenological observations were actually considered basic.

Kraepelin's differentiation in psychiatry was organized around the so-called deterioration concept. With the help of his pupils, Alzheimer and Nissl (3, 4), he established a rule for differential diagnosis of the psychoses: (1) Psychoses in patients who remained without deterioration were diagnosed functional psychoses. (2) Psychoses in patients with deterioration and without definite organic brain changes were diagnosed dementia praecox. (3) Psychoses in patients with deterioration and with organic brain changes were diagnosed organic psychoses. This etiological outlook was the first stabilizing influence in psychiatry from a diagnostic point of view. Actually, he subdivided mental disorders into two groups: The patients who did not show deterioration, the so-called functional psychoses, and the patients who did show deterioration, the organic psychoses. He considered schizophrenia organic because of deterioration.

Kraepelin paid much more attention to the presence or absence of deterioration than to the presence or absence of other clinical symptoms or other psychological and psychodynamic factors which were later used for evaluation. He often subordinated clinical judgment and symptom picture to this theory of etiology. For example, he included some depressed paranoid patients in the same category with manic-depressive patients. More recently less emphasis has been placed on the factor of deterioration, and we usually diagnose mental disorders phenomenologically in terms of the clinical picture presented and psychodynamic factors that can be unearthed. We have been paying much more attention to symptomatology than to outcome because it has become recognized that many patients who are definitely schizophrenic do not become obviously deteriorated. Kraepelin based diagnosis on outcome because, in the first place, he found the outcome was easy to determine by follow-up studies. Secondly, at the time of his investigations, the idea of "dementia" was important; it was thought to occur in all mentally ill patients. Kraepelin wanted to point out that such a conclusion was not right. He was the first investigator to believe that emotional derangement could still be present without intellectual derangement in a person considered "insane."

One might think that Kraepelin's differentiation of a large group of individuals into two groups—deteriorated and nondeteriorated—is a rather crude division to make. Nevertheless, in that large "mess," during the 19th century and before, when all kinds of clinical pictures were described, and all kinds of fantastic explanations were given of how these clinical pictures originated, his was actually the first attempt to introduce some kind of scientific explanation or organization into the chaos. That chaos had consisted of nothing other than describing each patient's many clinical symptoms, connecting and systematizing the symptoms into syndromes, which were then intermixed with loose explanations of how those symptoms originated. These explanations were largely based on the liberal exercise of the imagination rather than on any scientific facts. Kraepelin's great contribution was that he tried to instigate a certain order into classification of mental disorders. Although his classification immediately produced objections concerning its rigidity and questionable general validity, we have not markedly changed our clinical system of diagnosis since his time. No other psychiatric classification has been able to entirely replace it. Even investigators who tried to replace the diagnoses of the functional psychoses by psychodynamic observations, or by simply pointing out what assets or liabilities a psychotic individual has, were, in the final analysis, constantly falling back upon Kraepelinian terminology and interpretation in their prognostication and therapeutic suggestions. In my personal opinion, regardless of what is thought concerning Kraepelin's theory, the important issues were, first of all, his tenacity in attempting to introduce scientific methods into the psychiatric appraisal of mental illness and, secondly, his careful evaluations in the light of follow-up observations on patients.

Kraepelin was a master of follow-up studies. This part of his approach continues to be as valid as ever before, and is as often violated as before. Unfortunately, psychiatry is extremely shy of doing follow-up work compared to other fields of medicine. This shyness is understandable if we analyze the therapeutic results; they have not been very impressive regardless of all methods used, ranging from organic to psychoanalytic approach. In fact, follow-up studies of patients over a period of five or ten years after development of the symptomatology or after treatment, have been remarkably few. The few reported have revealed astonishing mistakes in appraisal of the patient's original symptomatology, in prognostication, and in application of therapy. A large number of follow-up studies of the clinical symptomatology in psychoneurotic or psychotic individuals after a five- or ten-year period are as seriously needed as ever before. A great many preconceptions, theories, and formulations could be disregarded if such studies would be appraised systematically and compared with original diagnostic, prognostic, and treatment evaluations. Follow-up studies had enabled Kraepelin to discern that mental pictures which often appear alike are nevertheless not always indicators of the same disorder; and, by careful analysis of the outcome of a disease, he was able to very convincingly demonstrate the changes in the clinical picture. On the basis of his deterioration concept, he had been able to observe, for example, that depressions occur in a great many disorders other than manic-depressive psychosis. In fact, he recognized that there are certain symptoms which, although regarded as characteristic for a particular mental disorder, may be observed in many psychopathological entities.

Clinical investigations have since proven that in every mentally disturbed human being three cardinal psychopathological phenomena can occur: depressive patterns, paranoid patterns, and anxiety patterns. Actually these three clinical manifestations describe most of the symptomatology in the so-called functional mental disorders and to some extent these symptom patterns also occur in the organic psychoses. It is also a valid observation that depressive, paranoid, and anxiety reactions are uniformly identical in phenomenological appearance in each and every cultural group without exceptions. However, in different cultural groups these reactions vary in their content—the content being influenced and modified by the beliefs, opinions, and attitudes of the particular ethnic group in which they occur. This all indicates that these human reactions are very deep-rooted; they are not produced by cultural influences alone, as had been stressed in former years.

It must always be kept in mind that most mental disorders are disturbing, depressing, and difficult for the patient to bear. These facts about a patient are not only of theoretical importance but also, to some extent, of practical importance. In psychiatry a great many statements have been made about the patient's "flight into sickness," implying that the patient "tenaciously clings" to his particular symptomatology because he likes it. In the minds of some psychiatrists, a psychotic state may appear to be a pleasant experience for a patient. Many of these assumptions originated from observations of patients who displayed some euphoia, who displayed some memory defect due to organic lesions, or who displayed some manic exuberance such as may occur in manic-depressive patients, all indicating they were very well satisfied with the mental disorder. Now, I do not state that this never occurs; and I do not even state that in some patients, particularly schizophrenic patients, we do not see a certain complacency or even a certain liking for the psychotic picture, but the vast majority of psychotic patients suffer from their mental disorders. This is particularly true of the patient experiencing anxiety; there the symptomatology is very painful and will always impress people as such. The idea that psychosis is something pleasant is one of the basic misconceptions in psychiatry. Many of the depressed patients who suffer—and some of them suffer incredibly—do not seem to want help, or may actually repulse help. This is not due to the fact they do not want it, but is often due to the fact that they believe they should not have it.

The methods of treatment of the so-called functional disorders vary to some extent depending on the diagnosis, the severity of the disorder, and pattern of the symptomatology. Generally speaking, treatment is organized around psychotherapy, pharmacotherapy, or other forms of somatic therapy with one or another method predominating at certain points in the course of therapy. Several methods of approach may be combined. Usually more than one method is indicated, especially in the treatment of the psychoses.

Part IV
Affective Disorders

15

MANIC-DEPRESSIVE PSYCHOSIS

The manic-depressive psychosis is an affective disorder of unknown etiology, characterized by clinical pictures which are conventionally divided into three subentities in the manic group and three subentities in the depressive group. The manic subentities are designated: *hypomania, acute mania, delirious mania.* The depressive subentities are designated: *simple retardation* or *simple depression* (corresponding to hypomania), *acute depression* (corresponding to acute mania), *depressive stupor* (corresponding to delirious mania).

Referring to the manic and the depressive pictures as "corresponding" implies that the subgroups within each syndrome differ only in degree; they are designated on the basis of quantitative differences. In other words, although the basic clinical syndromes are mania and depression and those two differences are evaluated qualitatively, the subgroupings of each are then designated according to the

431

quantitative elevation or the quantitative depression of affect. In contrast, the clinical syndromes in the subgroups of the schizophrenias are designated on the basis of qualitative differences, each subgroup being characterized by special clinical features which the other subgroups do not manifest, or do not manifest clearly, and then the quantitative prefix—mild, medium, or severe—is added. For example, the catatonic subgroup of schizophrenia manifests catatonic features predominantly and these features do not occur in the paranoid or the simple subgroups of schizophrenia.

In the manic-depressive psychosis, it would probably be better if the historically determined designations—hypomania, acute mania, and delirious mania—were replaced by the expressions mild, medium, or severe mania, the corresponding quantitative expressions also being applied in describing the depressions. Psychiatric diagnostics are often found to be very confusing. Diagnostic confusion is present in other branches of medicine, also, wherever the designating terms are the results of historical developments rather than logic.

Most of the Kraepelinian clinical subgroups of the manic-depressive psychosis are of only historical interest. The few subgroups generally retained in clinical use are the so-called manic-depressive manic type, manic-depressive depressed type, and manic-depressive circular type.

HISTORY

The manic-depressive psychosis is interesting not only from the clinical but also from an historical point of view because actually many psychiatric concepts concerning this psychosis have been tried and discarded. The assumption that Kraepelin was the first to describe the manic-depressive psychosis is not quite correct. Manic-depressive psychosis had already been described long before Kraepelin. In fact, Egyptian and Greek physicians described the symptomatology rather well and put forth etiological speculations which are strikingly similar to those of recent times. From the 16th century on, descriptions of manic and depressive states were mixed with a great deal of religion and philosophy which distorted the descriptive pictures. Much later, in 1896, Kraepelin (4) organized the knowledge into a whole and developed a classificatory scheme for manic and depressive conditions, although he was by no means the first to have attempted it.

Before Kraepelin, it had been known that manic episodes occurred several times in a person's life. It had even been known that this affliction occurred in many members of certain families. Descriptions were mainly of depressive or of manic manifestations; only a very few publications described the so-called cyclic psychosis indicating the same individual could have both manifestations. Therefore, the so-called cyclic manifestations had been described before Kraepelin, and therefore those observations cannot be first ascribed to him. Kahlbaum (4, 6) had described them and coined the term "cyclothymic disorder." However, Kraepelin formulated the concept of "manic-depressive psychosis" by clearly defining the cyclic manifestations as being different phases of the same reaction pattern or entity (4, 6). In other words, he formulated that a certain group of patients showing this clinical symptomatology belong together, even though at different times the clinical pictures appear dissimilar. Furthermore, he described in detail the depressive and the manic manifestations of the disorder.

Although Hecker (2, 4, 6) had pointed out that no dementia occurs in these patients, Kraepelin made the actual differentiation between persons suffering from this type of disorder and persons showing an array of similar symptom manifestations who deteriorated. He was the first to demonstrate that, in the true case of manic-depressive psychosis, no emotional and no intellectual deterioration developed regardless of how long attacks lasted or how often they occurred. (Nevertheless, Kraepelin continued believing that all psychoses are basically organic disorders and always looked for evidence indicating organic pathology even in the clear-cut manic-depressive psychosis.) Kraepelin pointed out that manic-depressive psychosis is primarily an emotional disorder rather than an intellectual one, and that the difference between normal and pathological elation or depression is a matter of degree. Intellectual changes do, of course, appear in the manic or the depressive individual, but it remains valid that these intellectual changes are invariably secondary to the emotional changes present. It can always be observed that they last only as long as the emotional changes persist in the patient. Therefore, there is no such diagnostic entity as a deteriorated manic-depressive patient. If a physician makes that diagnosis in a deteriorated patient it indicates he is not familiar with the concept of manic-depressive psychosis. When Kraepelin observed that the great majority of patients with manic-depressive symptomatology actually do manifest rapid or slow intellectual deterioration, he reclassified them in the diagnostic group he termed "dementia praecox" (later named "schizophrenia" by Bleuler).

The observation that manic or depressive symptomatology also occurs in individuals other than those suffering from the so-called manic-depressive psychosis has become more and more recognized as the result of clinical investigations since the time of Kraepelin. Keeping clearly in mind the fact that depressions occur in all psychotic individuals and in all types of psychoses, depressions will obviously be encountered in the manic-depressive psychosis. Kraepelin placed a great many patients in the manic-depressive diagnostic group who would no longer be considered in that group, but he did so because at the time of examination they did not show deterioration. Later, after regarding other diagnostically important factors, a great many of those patients have been placed in other diagnostic groups.

A few decades ago many psychiatrists, especially those abroad, raised the question of whether or not manic-depressive psychosis actually is an entity. Some considered manic-depressive psychosis only a mild form of schizophrenia because they observed so many of these patients either emerging from, or entering into, a schizophrenic state. A few psychiatrists believed that, from a psychodynamic point of view, much of the dynamics observed in manic-depressive psychosis are also observed in schizophrenias and actually also observed in certain psychoneuroses—in the obsessive-compulsive neurosis, for instance. On the basis of psychodynamic investigations, effort was made to abolish the concept of manic-depressive psychosis as being a separate entity.

Those who followed the line of approach proposed by Kretschmer (3, 6) and others found that Kretschmer's idea of a liaison between the physical and temperamental constitution—so-called pyknic physical type and the cyclothymic temperament—can be demonstrated in many individuals who develop manic-depressive psychosis. Nevertheless, many patients having depressive and manic features do not have a pyknic physical make-up and do not manifest a cyclothymic temperamental background. This is especially apparent in the so-called involutional depression group; usually these individuals do not demonstrate pyknic or cyclothymic configuration; they are more inclined to show physical and temperamental features which are often considered characteristic of certain types of schizophrenics. Here again, the question was introduced as to whether or not the original designation of manic-depressive psychosis as a definite entity is justified. Many observers describe manic-depressive psychosis as an entity in those individuals showing certain hereditary, certain "constitutional," certain psychodynamic and certain reactive features and who are recognized to be individuals behaving similarly in a given constellation of circumstances. The whole issue remains in flux. From the standpoint of present knowledge the matter cannot be proven one way or another. We should realize that the classification of this disorder is most likely temporary and will naturally yield to a corrected classification when the etiology is known.

The manic-depressive group as described by Kraepelin and his school is much smaller than it was at the end of the 19th century and the early part of the 20th. This reduction has been interestingly reflected in the admission rates at different state hospitals. In reviewing these admission records it was found that during the early part of the 20th century the admission rate of patients suffering with manic-depressive psychosis was approximately 25 percent, and about double the admission rate of patients diagnosed as being schizophrenic. Later, a complete reversal of these figures occurred in most hospitals and for a while the admission figures for manic-depressive psychosis were between 6 and 10 percent.

DIAGNOSTIC CONCEPTS

It has gradually come to be recognized that the true manic-depressive psychosis is a comparatively rare disorder—comparatively rare in that individuals suffering with this disorder are not very often observed, particularly in mental hospitals. They are much more likely to be encountered in private practice.

The large majority of patients formerly diagnosed manic-depressive psychotic have fallen more and more into the schizophrenic diagnostic group. Many have been placed in the organic group or other diagnostic categories. These had formerly been overlooked because diagnosis had been made merely on a phenomenological basis, most patients showing manic or depressive symptomatology having been placed in the manic-depressive group. For example, in many hospitals the diagnosis of general paresis had been missed in a large number of individuals before the time of routine serology and some of these elated paralytic patients remained with the diagnosis of manic psychosis. Also, many other conditions, such as frontal lobe impairment on an atherosclerotic level or brain tumor, were diagnosed as manic-depressive psychosis, especially because many of the neurological and other diagnostic facilities had not yet become available. The reduction in number of manic-depressive patients is, therefore, partially due to better diagnostic knowledge about the organic categories. It is also partially due to the change in our attitudes toward the relationship of manic-depressive psychosis to schizophrenia. Many psychotic patients phenomenologically diagnosed as being manic-depressive later became diagnosed as schizophrenic because, although acknowledging the phenomenological part of the diagnosis, we now go further and try to investigate the dynamic implications and also try to perceive how each patient copes with reality situations. Furthermore, follow-up studies on patients' progress are done in a much more efficient way than formerly.

All these issues indicate the following: A patient may first manifest manic-depressive symptoms and show no signs of deterioration. Therefore, by simply applying the Kraepelinian approach, the patient should logically be diagnosed manic-depressive psychotic. However, later on he may manifest schizophrenic symptoms. By carefully following the symptom changes and paying attention to the psychic organization of the patient, correct diagnosis can be made before any signs of deterioration appear. A few of the psychological tests may aid in formulating the differential diagnosis and may point in the direction of schizophrenia.

Depressions are so extremely common in the schizophrenias that most psychiatrists are of the opinion that there are many more schizophrenic depressions than true manic-depressive depressions. It is obvious that depression is a very common symptom in involutional psychoses. Depressions are also encountered in the organic psychoses, as mentioned before; there occurs a depressive form of general paresis, a depressive form of arteriosclerosis, and so forth. Depressions may even be seen in a few types of so-called sociopathic individuals. Moreover, depressions are commonly encountered in the psychoneuroses, where they differ to some extent in their organization and structure. There are the reactive depressions in patients encountering strong precipitating factors, depressions are observed in phobic individuals and depressions are particularly common in obsessive-compulsive individuals. A great many cases will be puzzling; you will wonder if you are dealing with a neurotic or a psychotic depression. This decision, in my opinion, is of importance secondarily; it is first important to perceive whether or not the patient is actually depressed and to then take the individual's full depressive mechanism into consideration.

It should be emphasized again that although you will see a large number of patients who phenomenologically fit into the manic-depressive group, it does not mean all patients showing manic or depressive symptomatology are automatically manic-depressive psychotics. As has been pointed out, depression occurs in a great many psychiatric categories and, naturally, the diagnosis has to be determined. Regardless from which frame of reference it is approached, even the psychiatrist avoiding the use of exact psychiatric diagnosis is forced to face the diagnostic problem from the point of view of therapy and prognosis because he has to formulate some idea about which type of patient he is dealing with. Actually, the psychiatrist who does not believe in diagnosis merely uses some other frame of reference which simply replaces one diagnostic approach with another. In any case, he has to form a point of view concerning the particular disorder in the patient, the treatment appropriate for the disorder, and the prognosis. Patients and their relatives are certain to confront the doctor on these issues.

INCIDENCE

Many statistical reports have been published regarding the incidence of manic-depressive psychosis. When appraising statistical figures it should always be realized that in many an acutely depressed patient the depression may be secondary to one or more other complaints, such as anxiety, which is frequently the underlying problem in schizophrenia and other psychiatric disorders. Conversely, another thing is very clear: If a manic-depressive patient, particularly one who is only moderately depressed, complains about other symptoms, especially vegetative symptoms, and then is diagnosed on a somatic level belonging to internal medicine, he is hospitalized under a medical rather than a psychiatric diagnosis. These cases do not appear in any statistics under the heading of manic-depressive psychosis.

A few of the statistical reports concerning the relative incidence of manic-depressive psychosis among males as compared to females indicate that manic-depressive psychosis is much more common among females, others indicate it is probably twice as frequent among males. One state hospital's statistics indicated a similar male and female ratio of incidence. However, in the clinical experience of every physician dealing with manic-depressive patients, the psychosis seems to occur more frequently among women than among men (as opposed to schizophrenia, where the distribution is approximately equal).

Other differentials have been described. For example, a few studies demonstrated that the socio-economic status of the patient has some bearing on the psychosis, indicating that manic-depressive psychosis occurs more frequently in the upper social and upper financial groups than in the underprivileged ones. This is true to some extent. Many more manic-depressive individuals have been observed among the well-to-do than among the patients who are not well-to-do. However, the illness is not *due* to the socio-economic status of the patients. The high level of socio-economic status has some relationship to the drive in manic-depressive patients. When they are in a manic phase, naturally, by being self-driving and by driving others they usually obtain more. The whole phenomenon then appears to occur in the higher socio-economic group. Also, because the disorder is prevalent in a few families who have obtained a higher social or a higher economic level, the statistics are further influenced.

The reverse trend has been claimed for schizophrenia, particularly by a Chicago group of sociologists *(Faris and Dunham, 1939)*, who reported that while manic-depressive psychosis occurs more frequently in the upper socio-economic strata, schizophrenia occurs more frequently in the lower strata. Statistics were compiled and convincingly presented which indicated that certain slum districts in Chicago had a very large ratio of schizophrenia compared to the better residential districts. A great deal of credence was given to this study. In one college where normal psychology and sociology are taught, these studies were actually used as a basis to indicate the relationship of socio-economic patterns in schizophrenia. It even went so far as to be interpreted, purely on a sociological basis, that frustrations, broken homes, and very adverse environmental background are difficulties responsible for the production of schizophrenia. In other words, an etiological reference was made through this study. It is amazing how people who must have had a certain amount of authoritative training could miss a most obvious factor. The most obvious factor, to which any psychiatrist can testify, is that schizophrenic individuals who are lacking in drive and who are unable to cope with the environment are protected and, naturally, often sink down to a much lower scale of adaptability and performance. When this occurs it appears as though the schizophrenia is due to the unfavorable environment. Here again, a lift up the socio-economic ladder is obviously not possible for families in which schizophrenia runs to a considerable extent. In other words, studies have to be taken with a grain of salt if they try to establish a pattern of relationship between etiology and socio-economic status for psychoses.

The socio-economic status of the person plays a role in the personal dynamics of a particular psychosis as a contributory factor but obviously it is not a primary etiological factor.

There have been several studies on the occurrence of manic-depressive psychoses in different cultures and different races. All of these are interesting but have never offered anything conclusive although it appears that in some ethnic groups manic-depressive psychosis is more prevalent than in other groups. However, many of the studies regarding the occurrence of manic-depressive psychosis in ethnic groups was done around the time when Kraepelin's concepts of the disease entity were rather rigidly formed and many of the factors which loosened these concepts had not yet been discovered. Therefore, all these statistical evaluations must be scrutinized very carefully because, if reevaluated at a future time, markedly different conclusions could probably be drawn.

There are a few observations which might be of interest from an ethnic point of view. In Scandinavian countries, for instance, the incidence of manic-depressive psychosis is probably not so very prevalent; most of the functional psychoses in those countries manifest clinical features of schizophrenia. Manic-depressive psychosis has been assumed to be much more prevalent in the southern part of Germany, and it has been considered fairly common in ethnic groups of Italy and southern France. It has been considered to be more frequent among Jews than gentiles. There have been reports that manic-depressive psychosis is not very prevalent in so-called primitive cultures and that psychotic manifestations in those cultures usually resemble schizophrenia. However, there is very little information regarding the occurrence of manic-depressive psychosis in the "less advanced" cultures; such studies would prove very interesting.

Varying and conflicting reports on racial differences in the incidence of manic-depressive psychosis have been described even in our culture. For example, it was pointed out that among Negro people in New York State, manic-

depressive psychosis occurs one and a half times more frequently than among white people. A few of the other states
offered similar statistics. On the other hand, comparing
these statistics with those from other countries having Negro
populations, there is considerable contradiction; and, furthermore, none of the statistics were very well compiled. For
instance, many manic-depressive patients were not admitted
to public hospitals or were treated outside of hospitals,
which probably distorts the statistical picture to a considerable extent.

Entirely new studies with more refined methodology
should be instituted if investigators desire a demographical
picture of the distribution of psychosis among ethnic and
racial groups. At the present time we can only state that
different ethnic and racial groups appear to have different
incidence of the manic-depressive disorder. It should be
questioned to what extent this difference is related to some
"constitutional" constellation and to what extent it is manifested in relation to ethnic factors in the social and socio-
psychological organization in each particular group. Sufficient data regarding this have not been established. Furthermore, it must be kept in mind that there is considerable
difficulty regarding differential diagnosis of depressive
reactions. For instance, it is not known how many of the
depressions observed in the so-called primitive cultures are
actually manic-depressive psychosis or only resemble it
because the individuals are depressed. We do not know how
many of these depressions are schizophrenic depressions,
so-called "primitive reactive" depressions, psychoneurotic
depressions, or whatever.

An important factor to take into consideration when
diagnosing patients is the age group in which manic-
depressive psychosis occurs. Interestingly enough, although
much has been written regarding this, a great deal of ignorance is present among psychiatrists. For example, it is frequently observed that a seventeen- or eighteen-year-old
patient is diagnosed a manic-depressive psychotic. This

diagnosis indicates that the doctor is not familiar with psychiatric concepts; he merely sees a patient who is depressed, or sees a patient who is manic, and assumes that the patient is suffering from manic-depressive psychosis. It is as though a patient complaining that something fell on his head fifteen years ago is diagnosed suffering with traumatic psychosis, or as though a patient who happens to be seventy years old is therefore suffering from senile psychosis or arteriosclerotic psychosis. Such assumptions are not psychiatry! Manic-depressive psychosis does not occur in adolescence, and any doctor diagnosing an adolescent person as being manic-depressive does not know psychiatry.

Manic-depressive psychosis is generally first manifested in individuals who are at least thirty or forty years of age. Adolescent persons with a psychotic depressive or manic symptomatology are usually either schizophrenic or are suffering with an organic disorder. The rare exception to this rule can be observed in certain families in which manic-depressive psychosis is rampant; it is an interesting phenomenon that the psychotic manifestation prevalent in a family appears at an earlier age in each subsequent generation. Occasionally, a patient of such a family states that the grandparent had a manic attack at the age of forty, the parent at thirty, and the child at eighteen, nineteen, or twenty. However, these cases are very rare and a doctor should be particularly careful before diagnosing an adolescent individual as suffering from manic-depressive psychosis since eventually the patient almost invariably is found belonging in another diagnostic category as the disorder progresses.

VARIATION IN MANIFESTATIONS

When dealing with a manic-depressive patient it is not possible to foretell how long an attack will last, how often the attack will be repeated, or how long the interval will be between attacks. Statistical prediction has been attempted but has not been convincing above the level of a guess. Foretelling the future is, of course, a part of medical practice. The patient and relatives obviously think it is an important function of the physician, and it would be an important function if the physician were able to fulfill it. In psychiatry, although the physician may feel very uncomfortable, the fact remains that the patient cannot be given an answer to questions about prediction because an answer can be given only by a psychiatrist who has had a few drinks. Actually, the manic-depressive psychosis can manifest tremendous variations in its manic, depressive, or cyclical course.

Kraepelin originally diagnosed patients as being manic-depressive only when the psychosis appeared in repeated attacks, and at that time it was assumed every manic-depressive patient had repeated attacks. Later it was discovered that about 30 or 40 percent of all patients suffering from this disorder had only one attack in their lives. This fact came to light only when follow-up studies were made. Certain patients having only one severe attack in their lives probably belong in the manic-depressive diagnostic group; others, however, may belong in other psychiatric categories. If it is not kept in mind that more than 30 percent of manic-depressive patients have only one attack, the diagnosis can easily be missed. When a psychiatrist is dealing with a patient who has had five attacks, naturally he can feel much more secure about the diagnosis than when the first attack is all the patient had. Furthermore, this first and only attack occurs in a few of the patients during middle age; it is already the equivocal age from a differential diagnostic point of view because involutional factors can complicate the picture. It has to be qualified that this one attack means an attack sufficiently severe to require hospitalization or an attack with the basic symptomatology so marked as to be obviously psychotic.

Very possibly, many patients classified in the non-repetitive manic-depressive group actually do have more than one attack, but the attacks may be so mild and inconspicuous that those patients need not be hospitalized. If they go to a physician it is usually observed that they retain good contact with the environment and both the physician and the patient do not realize the problem is a mental illness. Many of these patients undoubtedly have mild attacks, perhaps lasting for a few weeks. (If lasting only a few days, they are probably micro-schizophrenic attacks.) This would appear to be true not only for the depressive but also, to some extent, for the manic phase. The manic phase is usually difficult to recognize because the attacks cannot always be regarded as full-fledged. Nevertheless, if there are very clear descriptions from patients or their relatives, it is not very difficult to demonstrate which of these patients had had several mild attacks.

The remaining 60 or 70 percent of manic-depressive psychotic patients have repeated attacks. The classical description of the psychosis is the so-called circular form of manic-depressive psychosis, namely, alternating manic and depressive attacks. Again, however, no fixed rule has been established. Depressive attacks are much more common in occurrence than manic attacks; the ratio was never clearly demonstrated but it would not be surprising to learn that depressive attacks occur ten times more frequently than manic attacks. A few patients experience repeated attacks which are always of the same type in that they are always either manic or depressive, or they may alternate from a manic to a depressive phase or in the reverse order. A few individuals experience a certain uniformity of reactions in the framework of the recurring manic or depressive episodes; occasionally even the contents of the ideation or the expressions of the anxiety appear exactly as they had occurred in former attacks.

Observers in several hospitals have described a condition diagnosed manic-depressive "mixed type" in patients who manifest changes from depressive to manic phase, or vice versa, without interval. In the transition, overlapping of the symptoms occurs; the patients do not remain clearly in either phase as they would in the circular form of manic-depressive psychosis. When overlapping of symptoms occurs, one can usually detect other symptoms indicating that those patients are not manic-depressive but schizophrenic individuals. Doctors in many hospitals, however, do not want to diagnose patients as being schizophrenic so they simply put in the records "manic-depressive, mixed type." If we ask them "Mixed with what?" or "Mixed how?" they usually can only answer that the symptomatology does not appear to be clear-cut.

The number of attacks of the disorder is unpredictable: Besides there being patients having a great many attacks as well as patients having only one or two attacks, there are those patients who have an attack every year. In patients who have repeated attacks, it is sometimes felt that prognostication is somewhat easier to make. If a patient, for instance, had the first attack when about thirty-four years of age, and the following year had another attack—as a matter of fact, two attacks, being depressed four months, feeling well for an interval, and then manic two months—and every single year since repeated the entire cycle, what is likely to occur from now on? Although there are patients who have two attacks, who have five attacks, and those who have ten, when a patient develops such a regular cycle it is fair to assume it will continue and you can practically prognosticate that he will most likely have another attack next year.

When the patient does not manifest a regular cycle of attacks, recurrence cannot be predicted. If there is a very long interval between attacks, it is particularly difficult to predict whether or not they will recur. It is wise to tell the patient frankly that you do not know and cannot predict recurrence; simply reassure him that there are adequate means to deal with the attack.

A few observers have claimed that when manic-depressive patients grow older they have less tendency for attacks; others have claimed just the opposite. There are contradictory statements in the literature on this point. It has been my clinical observation, aside from statistics, that although many patients had fewer attacks as they became older, many others had more frequent attacks during old age.

Several observers have pointed out that the intensity of attacks is mitigated with age. Although this may be a fact for a few patients, many other patients have attacks as intensely, and sometimes more intensely, in old age. It is usually not possible to foretell the intensity of future attacks. There are patients who have a mild attack of depression one time and the next time a very severe attack of depression. The intensity of the psychosis is an individual issue and can occur with equal severity in an old person or a younger person.

The duration of each attack is also a matter of discussion for a patient, who frequently asks, "Will it last for a week?" "Will it last a month?" or "How long will it last?" Realize the fact that an average attack in manic-depressive patients is one year in duration. I would like to emphasize that this is the average duration and, please keep in mind, this means without treatment. These are patients who are in a hospital, exposed to the usual hospital facilities, but who have been given no course of specific antidepressive or antimanic drugs, no electro-convulsive therapy, or any other form of intensive therapy. The statistics for this finding have been compiled from patients having had so-called spontaneous recoveries. There are patients in whom the attacks run much longer than one year and there are patients in whom attacks are much shorter.

Occasionally a patient is observed who has a depressive or a manic attack lasting a week or even less. The more short-lived the attack which has not been interrupted therapeutically, the more suspicious one must be regarding the diagnosis. This is especially so if there is no history of previous attacks to be studied for clearly establishing whether or not one is actually dealing with a manic-depressive patient who has very short-lived depressive or manic attacks. A large majority of such patients will prove to be suffering with organic problems, schizophrenia, or perhaps even psychoneurosis. Very short-lived manic or depressive attacks can occur in schizophrenic individuals, particularly in the younger age group: A patient may suddenly develop severe mania or fall into a depression and a few days later snaps out of it, saying, "I am all right." Symptoms of such extremely short duration are often the "three-day catatonic" schizophrenic reactions, which more commonly occur than three-day manic-depressive reactions. Manic-depressive symptoms may develop gradually or rather rapidly, but true manic-depressive attacks usually take a longer time than a few days before swinging into full force and before finally abating. Rare exceptions are the manic-depressive individuals who respond to environmental stress with manic or depressive reactions. However, these "reactive manias," or "reactive depressions," are ill-defined as a group and similar reactions can also, of course, occur in psychoneurotic individuals.

Although the duration of the attacks is not predictable, younger people usually have attacks of somewhat shorter duration and in the older age group it is occasionally observed that the attacks become more prolonged. In many of the older patients, moreover, it is possible to discern the presence of arteriosclerosis and this additional pathology aggravates the disorder. Therefore, when a patient in whom some cerebral arteriosclerosis is present has a manic or depressive attack, the prognosis is considered to be, I would say, a little more unfavorable than when attacks occurred in the patient twenty years earlier. On the other hand, keep in mind that many patients suffering with involutional depression or manic-depressive manifestations late in life are diagnosed as having an arteriosclerotic psychosis, occasionally even senile psychosis, and treated as such. This means they are written off therapeutically, and yet these patients would often respond very well to the treatments appropriate for manic-depressive patients and recover promptly. Therefore, whenever you see manic-depressive symptomatology in the older age group, carefully evaluate these patients for indications of arteriosclerosis and other conditions.

From the point of view of therapy, the patients having only one or two attacks, or having very few and very mild attacks, usually achieve excellent cures regardless of which therapeutic method is used. This phenomenon conveniently bolsters every statistical claim for treatment methods. Since there is a rather high rate of spontaneous disappearance of the psychotic symptoms, naturally the psychiatrist always runs into difficulty interpreting his therapeutic results reliably. However, it is certain that therapy can cut an attack short but, if the patient is left untreated no one can predict the length of an attack. The majority of untreated manic-depressive patients, however, recover spontaneously and are usually discharged from the hospital before a year elapses. If not treated, only about 10 to 15 percent of the patients are retained in a hospital. These manic-depressive patients are diagnosed as suffering with chronic depressions or chronic manias. Many of them are actually schizophrenic but, without doubt, there is such an entity as manic-depressive chronic mania or chronic depression. An untreated chronically manic or depressed patient can, as can a patient with involutional depression, remain sick for two, three, or four years. There are also a small number of chronic patients who alternate continually between manic and depressive states and in these chronic manic-depressive individuals one attack follows another attack so closely there are practically no symptom-free intervals; these patients are never well. For example, such a patient may start out having two months of depression, then go into a manic phase, then again become depressed, and continue in this pattern. The fact remains that about 85 or 90 percent of the patients recover from each attack, regardless of whether it occurs in a manic or a depressive or classical cyclic form.

The term "recovery" requires amplification: it means

that the patient returns to the prepsychotic level of functioning. Originally, when Kraepelin described this psychosis, many investigators emphasized that manic-depressive psychotic patients are periodically "insane" and between periods they are "mentally normal." Now, these people are mentally normal between attacks in a legal sense and in the sense that they have no gross psychotic manifestations. However, if you examine manic-depressive patients during their interval periods, you discover that they are not fully well; they have mood swings. A large number of them manifest dynamics bringing to mind a psychoneurosis, and many, by the way, are diagnosed as being psychoneurotic by psychiatrists who do not know the patients have had a previous attack. Although considerable emotional instability may be demonstrated between the attacks, for all practical purposes the patient returns to his prepsychotic level of functioning after each attack and scarring of the patient does not occur. There is no deterioration of his intellect, no deterioration of his emotions, and no deterioration of his concept of reality, all of which are common occurrences in schizophrenic patients, particularly in the schizophrenic patients having recurring attacks.

16

MANIC-DEPRESSIVE PSYCHOSIS: MANIC PHASE

Manic manifestations, interestingly enough, occur much less often than the depressive; you will observe a great many depressions—the vast majority of which are not manic-depressive in type—before you will encounter a manic condition. Why that is so, is unknown. But, the manic form of mental disorder, the more pleasant form from the patient's point of view—euphoria, a state which gives the patient an exultant feeling of omnipotence—is not at all common. As mentioned before, there are three forms of mania: (1) *hypomania,* (2) *acute mania,* and (3) *delirious mania.* The three basically differ from each other quantitatively, not qualitatively.

It was pointed out by Kraepelin *(4),* and later on by a few other observers, that in both phases of the manic-depressive psychosis the cardinal deviation from the normal occurs in a basic symptom triad: in the manic phase there occurs *elation, flight of ideas,* and *increased psychomotor activity.* (In the depressive phase of the psychosis, naturally, the opposite symptom picture occurs.) First, in the manic individual the basic mood level is elevated in comparison with the emotional organization of a normal individual. This is designated as a change in mood, as a change in the basic emotional tone, which in mania is that of elation. Closely connected with the elation, there are two other alterations which are of significance; one is in the intellectual sphere, and one in the motor sphere. In the intellectual sphere there occurs a phenomenon described as "flight of ideas," a heightening and speeding up of the patient's associations. This is linked to a phenomenon of distractibility, meaning that stimuli coming from the outside are able to modify the chain of associations within the patient. Finally, in the psychomotor realm the manic patient manifests an increase of motor discharge, expressing himself by hyperactivity and restlessness.

This so-called Kraepelinian triad—elation, flight of ideas, and increased psychomotor activity—is observed in practically every manic patient in *harmonious representation.* I stress that there is harmonious representation of all three components of the triad. This is in contrast to certain other disorders, particularly schizophrenia, where the patient may display a manic picture but not the interlocking triad mechanism—influence of the emotions on the intellect and influence of the emotions on the motor behavior of the patient. For instance, the so-called "akinetic manias" described by Kraepelin are all schizophrenic disorders. Also, the extremely elated manic patient who does not show the slightest change in rate of associations, who is not distracted by outside stimuli but is distracted by ideas coming from within him, is usually schizophrenic. In the manic-depressive psychotic patient the emotional, intellectual, and psychomotor alterations are always present harmoniously.

HYPOMANIA

The mildest and most frequently observed form of mania is the state of hypomania which already presents the triad. However, (1) elation, (2) flight of ideas, and (3) increased psychomotor activities are not so marked as in the so-called acute mania and, therefore, are very often overlooked. Quite a few hypomanic individuals are considered to be normal. They have certain qualities making them popular with people and their hypomanic symptoms are, therefore, often rationalized away, not by the patient alone but also by persons in his environment.

In accord with the so-called symptom triad, first there occurs an alteration of the basic emotional mood; in the hypomanic individual it is dislocated upward. These patients are in a state of elation, are somewhat euphoric, and feel well —pathologically well. With the increased emotional tone many hypomanic patients are witty, show ability to associate quickly, have a very keen grasp of things going on around them, and can establish very successful social contact. They are most likely "the life of the party" and usually are very well liked until they become overbearing, overinterfering, domineering, or show gross lack of inhibition. It has to be pointed out that a harmony of all three cardinal symptoms may not always be obvious because often the patient's elation is masked by irritability when he is frustrated. There is usually an undercurrent of aggression and hostility and he has little patience with anything crossing his path. (The so-called psychodynamic structure of aggression has been much better clarified in the depressive phase than in the manic, as will be discussed later.) The patient in a hypomanic state is usually tactless, vain, and intolerant of criticism. He is easily provoked when he does not get his way. He tends to be demanding, and, when crossed, he often becomes fluently abusive. His aggression remains on a verbal rather than physical level and may be very obscene in content. It is extremely important to realize that practically all of the symptomatology shown, which I will discuss in detail, can be explained quite logically on the basis of the alteration of the basic mood of the patient.

Secondly, hypomanic individuals usually show a flight of ideas which expresses itself in speech. They are distractible; they are easily influenced by stimuli introduced from the environment; they jump from topic to topic and they monopolize conversation, based on excuses usually at hand. In contrast to a schizophrenic patient, this changing of topic usually follows from external environmental stimuli and not from stimuli coming from within the patient. In other words, a hypomanic patient sees something, hears something, perceives something; the new stimulus deflects his ideas, and he jumps in response to it. Manic patients are oriented outward toward stimuli; toward the environment, in contrast to schizophrenic patients who are usually oriented toward stimulation arising from within.

Formal impairment of intelligence, however, does not occur in the hypomanic individual. Memory and orientation are well preserved. Any alteration of thinking, any alteration of judgment, any alteration of other intellectual functions is due to the emotional interference. It usually fluctuates with the emotional interference and disappears when the emotional interference disappears. It is clearly observed that the flight of ideas is, therefore, not actually due to intellectual impairment but due to an emotional "speeding up." The impairment of judgment has occasionally been used as a criterion to show that an intellectual impairment is present in the hypomanic patient but that is not tenable. The lack of judgment is a logical sequence of the emotional disturbance present. The elevated mood of the hypomanic patient naturally leads to an overinflation of his ego; the patient feels that he is able to accomplish more; he feels that he is a more powerful figure; he feels that he can permit himself to do things much more and much better than before.

Although the sensory functions in the hypomanic individual are all well preserved, his performance is usually more superficial than when in a normal state. However, the flight of ideas, the speeding up of associations, the ability to establish good contact with the environment sometimes give the impression that his performance is superior or better than normal. He himself is very ready to believe that; he has little, or no, insight into his condition, except that he will often admit that thoughts are coming too fast, or admit to being nervous. Psychological tests have indicated, however, that the mental performance is below his usual level of performance, but this is markedly camouflaged by his increased sociability, good contact, wittiness, and by his ability to make quick associations. The performance, however, is rather shallow.

The third symptom described in the triad is increased psychomotor activity. These patients are usually restless, usually tense, usually "on the go," most likely using gestures when speaking. As a rule they do not like to be confined to one place and again, as in their ideation, they like to move from one area to another. They are inconsistent, changeable, and lacking in control. Certain rules and regulations, particularly social ones, are not followed by individuals in a hypomanic state. This is especially so because, in their feeling of superiority or of invulnerability, they believe they can override social rules and regulations without any contradiction. It is very often the case, therefore, that hypomanic individuals show disinhibited behavior in many ways, especially in social and sexual contacts. They often tend to indulge in alcohol and sexual promiscuity. They have heightened sexual drive and often execute it in a manipulative fashion. Many of these patients like to drink and their disinhibition with regard to alcohol often has them typed as being alcoholic, although the alcoholic patterns are purely secondary to their manic or hypomanic disinhibited states.

Now this triad of euphoria or elation, flight of ideas, and increased psychomotor activity is present in all manic patients to a varying degree. It is obvious that in hypomanic patients, in which the manic disturbance is not very marked or very pronounced, the symptoms of the triad are not necessarily very conspicuous; but usually they are. Hypomanic persons usually are individuals who are euphoric, who are mentally pressed, and who display rather increased psychomotor activity. Now, these so-called hypomanic patients are quite important as an entity. They are not rare. They are not seen in mental hospitals and, therefore, their psychotic state is often not diagnosed. Furthermore, the symptoms are often rationalized away—by patients themselves, of course. That would not be so unfortunate except that their symptoms are often rationalized away by those they contact in the environment and quite often, under the persuasion of the environment, by the psychiatrist as well. Hypomanic persons have many qualities which are stamped as social assets. Social assets are liked by people and people naturally express their likes by protecting such individuals, especially should the psychiatrist appear on the horizon. It is not rare that these individuals are stamped as very capable and aggressive persons; many actually are very capable and frequently achieve a great deal. That further complicates the situation because the moment a person is successful, or achieves something, he cannot be considered sick; this is a basic axiom not only in the minds of the general public but also in the minds of many psychiatrists. Therefore, when such a person can point to some business and social achievement or some obvious success, the symptomatology, as such, is even more likely to be neglected, and strong rationalization is given to explain the person's actions and behavior.

Now, actually from a clinical point of view the difficulty in these patients is not on a personal level or not on a level where they can injure themselves, because hypomanic patients do not commit suicide or try to harm themselves. Hypomanic patients do very well and therefore a psychiatrist would hate to interfere with this rather pleasant state of affairs because it is very nice to sometimes see a happy person! The difficulty with these people is a social one—social in the sense that they naturally get entangled in all sorts of affairs involving other people. It is because of this that we often hear the statement to the effect that the patient feels wonderful when manic, but his relatives love him more when he is depressed. For instance, they may enter into business ventures which they handle in an impulsive, flighty fashion; they lose their money; they readily go on binges; they contract all kinds of foolish marriages; and so forth. Naturally, they endanger their own or their family's security to some extent.

Although the patient usually displays memory, orientation, and intellectual functioning which are better than that of the psychiatrist, such "disinhibited" patients may be extremely dangerous from a legal point of view. Increased sexual drive and excessive drinking lead to transgression of moral codes and when such behavior causes a considerable amount of trouble to himself, in addition to others, it is finally recognized that one is dealing with a psychotic patient. Actually, whenever these people become psychiatric patients it is usually due to their behavior and not because they complain about anything or are suffering with any difficulties requiring help.

Now, as I mentioned previously, many of these patients are considered to be normal. They are not usually diagnosed as being manic-depressive psychotic or, if they are diagnosed, they are often placed in the category of other maladjustments, or other behavioral problems. Naturally, none of these diagnoses is correct. Actually hypomania is not very difficult to diagnose provided the physician understands the structure of the psychosis. However, there are many instances in the psychiatric literature stating that patients such as I have described are not psychotic; the patients do not show any symptoms of psychotic regression, such as ideation on an infantile level or behavior on a very childish level, and the patients have no hallucinations or delusions. Hypomanic patients have none of these obvious, gross psychotic symptoms but they are, nevertheless, psychotic.

Manic-depressive patients do not regress and do not manifest the schizophrenic's peculiar inability to fuse associations appropriately and form concepts properly. Hallucinations and delusions do not occur in the hypomanic state. But, we should not employ the approach that the patient is not psychotic, or that the patient is "normal," because he has no hallucinations or delusions. Many psychiatric schools are very wary about diagnosing a psychosis in an individual who does not manifest marked signs of regression, or delusions, or hallucinations. If a psychiatrist wishes to safeguard himself by diagnosing a psychosis only if gross psychotic symptoms are present, he can do so. But I am rather certain that the diagnosis of a large number of psychotic individuals is overlooked by this approach. This fact can be very easily demonstrated by means of follow-up studies on such patients. Such patients who are not followed up are usually simply considered nonpsychotic. If they are followed up, sufficient evidence is then accumulated indicating that those patients who, when first examined, did not manifest any gross psychotic disturbances probably will do so at a later time.

ACUTE MANIA

Acute mania manifests a much more impressive clinical picture than hypomania. Here everyone in the environment is convinced that the patient is quite sick and, usually, moves are made to hospitalize him. Actually, that such a person is sick is so clear, even the layman diagnoses a state of acute mania much more often and much more correctly than he does a depression. Acutely manic persons are more conspicuous than depressed persons because they frequently annoy other people very much. When they are nuisances, the diagnosis that they are sick is naturally more readily made than in the case of persons who do not annoy others.

To the psychiatrist, patients in the state of acute mania manifest the triad of symptoms much more obviously than patients who are hypomanic. In acute mania: (1) elation is extreme, impetuous, and provocative; (2) speech is rapid with marked flight of ideas and distractibility; and (3) activity is constant and these patients usually behave in a very aggravating way, becoming irritable and often aggressive or even assaultive toward the environment.

The mood of euphoria, the mood of elation is obvious; it is very strong and quite often infectious. Although in hypomanic individuals the infectious quality of the elation is somehow, I would say, completely understandable and people are able to go along with it, in acutely manic patients it has become obvious that the elation is very pathological. The acutely manic person is so elated, so euphoric, and the feeling of well-being is so marked, so exaggerated, that actually the whole phenomenon appears slightly unreal in the eyes of others. In these patients, elation and euphoria can go over at any time into a state of excitement. If manic patients do go into a state of excitement, however, they still show a certain playfulness and the elation is still tinged with good humor. This can readily be distinguished from the massive impulsive excitement of catatonic patients in which good humor is absent and in which the fervor of elation is also completely absent. Some time ago an observer differentiated the former as a so-called "warm excitement" and the latter as a "cold excitement." Even though these are naturally very schematic designations, basically they are to some extent valid. Manic excitement contains a certain amount of warmth, maintains a certain amount of direction toward the environment. (In contrast, the schizophrenic excitement state is usually cold excitement, impressing the environment with its aggressiveness and detachment so that those in the environment have very little feeling into, or sympathy for, this excited person.) However, a patient in a state of acute manic excitement may develop such marked flight of ideas and such marked psychomotor activity as to border on confusion and that may actually override any of the contagious quality of the mood.

The acutely manic patient is, of course, very euphoric

and elated, and you will often find another ingredient added to the mood admixture: irritability and aggressiveness appear when the patient is crossed. The aggression, from a dynamic point of view, is actually one of the defense mechanisms against any inferiority feelings underlying the manic self-assurance and adds to the patient's tendency to feel quite superior to the environment. There is an ego expansion to the level of self-aggrandizement in the manic patient. Naturally, going along with self-aggrandizement, the patient will display marked intolerance for any frustrations of his aggressive behavior. For example: The manic patient may start to talk to you or argue with you. As is usual, he will make many demands. For instance, he may tell you that he wants to go home, or that he wants a room in the hospital on the south side and not on the north side. Then, you probably reply that his requests cannot be fulfilled. At this point the patient flies into a terrific rage, becoming very abusive and possibly even assaultive toward you. This irritability when thwarted in aggressive demands, this aggressiveness when interfered with in any way, are very commonly observed. Occasionally, paranoid elements are also present, which will be discussed.

As mentioned before, when dealing with such a person in whom the manic excitement is strong and the euphoria or elation colors the clinical picture so markedly that the more subtle mental changes are covered, it is frequently difficult to differentiate between an irritable manic and an irritable catatonic individual having manic tinges. When I discuss in detail the differential diagnosis of manic-depressive psychosis and schizophrenia, you will see that it is possible to arrive at an early proper diagnosis in a great many patients. We do not have to wait five years, until a patient has become completely deteriorated, to know whether we are dealing with a manic-depressive or with a schizophrenic patient, even though these clinical syndromes are designated phenomenologically and are therefore much more difficult to handle than those designated in terms of etiology. (People from other branches of medicine always point out that the matter of psychiatric diagnostics is a mess; if you actually go into it carefully and statistically, you must say that, although we are not just as clear as are those in many other branches of medicine regarding diagnosis, we are still not as helpless and, I would say, not as ineffectual as some people try to make us out.) And the trouble is, especially, that certain concepts, which are probably basically sound, are not fixed in a clear-cut manner. Very often the more basic symptomatology specific for the particular disorder is over-looked, in favor of superimposed secondary symptomatology common to any number of psychiatric disorders.

The speech, of course, in the acutely manic patients also shows the typical flight of ideas, being very scattering. Often their speech is quite obscene and very profane, due to three factors: (1) They are usually under increased sexual tension; (2) they are, naturally, disinhibited; and (3) they are markedly aggressive and therefore discharge their ideas and feelings without any inhibition. Occasionally they display phenomena like the so-called "pumping," or "priming," associations. It can actually be stated that in schizophrenia there is intellectual disturbance, per se, which is not explained on the basis of emotional interference. But, intellectual disturbance which is *not* on an emotional level does not occur in manic-depressive psychosis. Conceptual alterations and distortions which are particularly observed in schizophrenia are *not* present in manic-depressive patients. The flight of ideas occasionally resembles incoherence; and if the flight of ideas becomes marked, you may not be able to clearly distinguish one from the other. In schizophrenia, both phenomena can occur simultaneously, but in acute mania there is no such actual evidence of intellectual impairment.

Now, these acutely manic patients, besides the euphoria and besides the flight of ideas, also manifest greatly increased psychomotor activity. They are very restless; they constantly move around, jump about, and are unable to remain in one spot for any length of time. These persons are actually critically disturbed. However, unlike the schizophrenic, many of these manic patients are able to control their motor activity somewhat if required of them by the environment. (On the other hand, during remissions external stimulation can lead to an exacerbation of the manic phase.) They also manifest two other symptoms which are interesting: They do not want to eat and they do not want to sleep. Usually they do not eat because they are so "busy" they do not have enough time to do so and, furthermore, they have a feeling of well-being which very often overrides hunger. The interesting thing in manic patients is the complete lack of fatigue and their seeming ability to get along with the minimum, or no, sleep. (Actually, they usually sleep very well, but tend to awaken early.) They usually appear to be quite well. Apparently all the vegetative functions are toned up (in contrast to depressions when they are toned down), and they tolerate this manic overactivity rather well. It is actually rare that a patient who is not in an older age group and who probably has some systemic disease (heart disease or other chronic physical disorder) does not stand up well under this manic state. Exhaustion in this phase of acute mania does not usually occur; the body is somehow able to comply with the manic requirements.

They rarely express any somatic complaints during the manic phase; and once in a while a patient sustains an injury or an accident and contracts some intercurrent disease, none of which he reports. He does not appear to be aware of it. He simply overrides it. (This is in marked contrast to the behavior of the depressed patient. In depression, every somatic change is watched, elaborated upon, and interpreted by the patient—so here, again, are the opposite pictures.) Vegetative changes which can be perceived subjectively and demonstrated objectively are rarely present; or, when they are present, they are not reported by the acutely manic patient. For example, menstrual disturbances are not rare in women in the manic state, but a manic patient does not pay the slightest attention to them or makes some flippant remark in connection with them. (The menstrual disturbances in depressive patients give them a great deal of material on which to elaborate.)

True delusions and hallucinations do not occur in the manic-depressive psychosis, but in acute mania they often seem to be present. Actually, they are more "expectation" phenomena; they are illusions that can easily be misconstrued as delusions and hallucinations. They are usually in the background; they are fleeting; they are not dominating over the patient, and they are not very elaborate. They are usually "topical," meaning that they are not extensive and follow the emotional state quite harmoniously. In the not so extremely acute mania the "delusion" or "hallucination" has the element of playfulness—so he plays. In other words, the terms "delusion" and "hallucination" are really figures of speech.

In acute mania the ideation is closely bound to, and erected on, the basic emotional change in the patient, indicating why it is the manic patient often has ideas of grandeur with his elation. The patient selectively exaggerates or ignores certain perceptions to fit in with his euphoric mood. When questioned, he seems quite aware of the falsity in his "bragging" and will admit he is playing. Although in very acute mania the patient appears unable to identify the reality of the matter, his pretenses are for attention and not true delusions of grandeur. They often resemble delusions observed in general paresis, but are not so bizarre, so extensive, or so inappropriate. They are simply self-aggrandizement exaggerations. The manic patient may select to regard himself as very rich or powerful. He may feel he is so powerful a man sexually that he can satisfy I do not know how many women and so forth. You will find there are many variations in the self-aggrandizement content depending on whether you are dealing with a poorly educated individual or an advanced scholar with high intelligence and high symbolization ability. They can be expressed in a rather crude form, and then again expressed in a very subtle and elaborate form, but, if the "delusions" are disregarded, that which remains constant is the idea of self-aggrandizement, being invariably a logical sequence of the emotional disorder.

It has to be emphasized that the "delusions" are topical; they are not extensive and are always in conformity with the basic mood of the patient. Therefore manic patients do not have hypochondriacal delusions—such delusions do not fit into their euphoric emotional tone. In other words, should a patient who appears to be manic tell you, "I have no pulse," or "I have no heart," you have to pause and think, because a manic-depressive patient who is manic does not do that. A schizophrenic patient with manic coloring may do so, and here there is already a splitting process. This is important because such splitting often occurs in schizophrenia; the emotional tone may be elevated but the delusional con.ent is not in harmony with the accompanying emotional and environmental tone. There is serious doubt about the existence of any so-called "mixed" manic state, any transitional state between a manic and a depressive attack having overlapping contrapuntal symptoms.

The schizophrenic individual with manic coloring suffers with a great deal of anxiety and a great deal of ambivalence; he perceives himself as both weak and powerless and, at the same time, defends himself with ideas of grandeur. The manic-depressive psychotic in a manic state can express essentially similar grandiose ideas (which are, to repeat, invariably consistent with his mood), but he does so in a different way. In contrast, should a patient, in a very systematic manner, go around stating "I am Napoleon," repeating it week after week, and giving all kinds of elaborations explaining why he is Napoleon and why he behaves like Napoleon, it is very unlikely that this patient is a truly manic patient. First of all, there is a very strong disturbance of conceptual organization. Secondly, there is a tenacity that a manic patient usually does not display. Thirdly, such delusions are bizarre; bizarre delusions do not occur in true manic patients. These, however, are only a few of the points which one has to observe.

The content of the ideations in a manic patient is, of course, usually grandiose in style. In addition, however, there is often a paranoid fringe. I deliberately use the expression paranoid "fringe" insofar as a manic patient at times expresses a few paranoid ideas on the periphery. The paranoid material is also typical in that it is closely bound with some of the behavior of the patient toward the environment. The manic patient will tell you, "Somebody is following me," or "Some people try to beat me up and will try to kill me because I am such an important person and they want to prevent me from doing this or that." In other words, a so-called logical paranoid reaction is present in relationship to the patient's grandiose behavior toward the environment. Moreover, these ideas are not sustained. Although the manic patient usually gives "logical" explanations, it is difficult for him to establish a fixed paranoid conviction that somebody is following him, or that somebody is trying to kill him, and he does not construct bizarre elaborations. Furthermore, the manic patient is never dominated by actual paranoid delusions; if the patient is dominated by paranoid delusions, one can be certain that he is dealing with a "schizo-manic" individual.

With this in mind, you can recognize the following fact: If a patient maintains his delusional ideas for a long time, if he is dominated by them, if he returns day after day to the same organized ideational misconceptions, if the delusions are bizarre with unrelated so-called primary elaborations and, what is important, if the mood of the patient alternates, the patient is not a manic-depressive psychotic but is definitely schizophrenic. For example, very often a catatonic schizophrenic whom you may admit to the hospital on Monday manifests a few manic features, being overactive, rather playful, and rather jocular. He also expresses ideas that people are after him and so forth. When you examine him on Tuesday you may find that he no longer has the jocularity and the euphoria; he is probably very solemn and he is rather, I would say, self-absorbed. However, he again expresses the same delusional ideas. You have already observed that his moods and ideas do not move in harmony with each other. These are practically the main diagnostic points. Naturally, you cannot measure precisely when a delusion is a well-organized one and when it is not, or when it is in accord with the mood and when not. These, you might say, are sensed by impression and not a matter of mathematical exactitude.

Many acutely manic patients misidentify people. This misidentification can have two sources. One is that they are playing with the environment; the other is that illusional material intrudes itself. Misidentification of people due to inattention can occur in a delirious mania, but in an acute mania this is usually not the case. Misidentification due to impairment of intellect or due to true disorientation does not occur because these patients are usually not in a confusional state; they are usually fully aware of where they are, fully aware of what is going on around them.

Actual hallucinations do not occur in an acutely manic patient, but illusions can occur in any sphere. They are experienced in connection with the emotional content and, of course, in harmony with the basic mood of the individual. If you observe a patient admitted to the hospital in an acute manic state who is preoccupied and dominated by auditory hallucinations that are not topical you are, here again, dealing with a schizophrenic patient.

Auditory hallucinations, olfactory hallucinations, tactile hallucinations, or other somatic hallucinations (all being prevalent in schizophrenia) do not occur in the true manic patient. What apparently are auditory hallucinations in mania, as I have indicated, are really illusions; they rarely obtain the dominance one observes in an hallucinating schizophrenic patient. In the true manic patient they are fleeting and are not very elaborate.

Visual illusional experiences are more likely to occur in the manic-depressive psychotic patient than are auditory or other forms. As has been mentioned, visual hallucinations stem primarily from perceptual factors and auditory hallucinations primarily from conceptual factors. Now the manic individual is actually in overcontact with the environment and that state, naturally, fosters a perceptual type of experience, such as the visual. (The schizophrenic is in undercontact with the environment, which fosters hallucinations of a conceptual type since schizophrenic patients have essentially, of course, an ideational conceptual disorder; even though schizophrenia may be based on emotional alteration, it favors an ideational derangement.) The manic-depressive patient moves on a higher level of integration than the schizophrenic.

DELIRIOUS MANIA

The extreme stage of mania, the so-called delirious mania (I would prefer the term "confusional" mania, and would reserve the term "delirious" for toxic psychoses having confusion present), presents a clinical picture which is not very difficult to differentiate from the other two manic conditions. The patient is very sick. Naturally, the patient again manifests the basic symptom triad—euphoria or elation, flight of ideas, increased psychomotor activity— which, as I described, runs through all manic conditions. These basic changes, however, are usually so markedly exaggerated as to give the appearance of an organic disorder. There occurs extreme excitement, confusion, and frenzied psychomotor activity. Delirious mania is rare—at least, this clinical entity is very rarely observed in the United States. Delirious mania has been described in a few other cultural groups, but we do not know if the manic delirium states described are really manic states or belong to other diagnostic entities. In the Malaya Peninsula and India, for instance, these states have been reported. There have been cases reported in which it was not easy to determine, according to the descriptions, what types of conditions were actually present.

Euphoria in the patient with delirious mania is not always perceived because it is not as clearly manifest as in other manic states due to the clouding of consciousness present. I would like to mention that delirious mania is the only form of the manic state in which any interference with the clarity of the patient's consciousness is observed. In hypomania and in acute mania the consciousness of the patient is completely clear and there is no interference in memory. Consciousness is impaired in delirious mania, and, as the term implies, the patient is disoriented for time and place. Furthermore, the excitement is usually so marked that the patient appears to be, and actually is, confused. The patient shows all the memory impairment observed in a delirious patient, partly due to inner tension and partly due to the confusion.

The flight of ideas in a patient who appears deliriously manic is so extreme as to be very jumbled. It is very difficult to make contact with this type of patient; he usually shouts and yells and does not pay attention to anybody's questions. He simply perceives the stimulus and answer without the relationship to it being clearly apparent. Here, the flight of ideas may resemble an actual state of incoherence, and, in speaking to such a patient, it is very difficult to determine whether he is manifesting a flight of ideas or is already in a state of incoherence. This situation often leads, naturally, to diagnostic misconception because a state of incoherence does not actually occur in manic-depressive psychosis; it does not belong in that condition. Whenever incoherence is observed in a manic or depressive setting, it is practically pathognomonic of schizophrenia.

Flight of ideas may actually be manifested as a constantly shifting, constantly changing ideational goal, expressed in speech by the patient's jumping from one topic to another, but, taking into consideration the deflection caused by the stimulus, the ideational stream is nevertheless logical. On the other hand, if there is a "mixture" of ideas manifested as a fragmented, incoherent, and scattered form of superficial verbal production without a leading goal or a leading idea binding these fragments together, incoherence is present. It is prevalent in schizophrenia. Occasionally incoherence can be demonstrated by examining, in a general way, some of the unconscious emotional motivation and the symbolism involved; you remain unable to follow the peculiar ideational shifts made by the schizophrenic patient. It is obvious that we are able to differentiate, at least theoretically, between flight of ideas and incoherence in a few cases. However, if the patient is in a state of excitement and if his speech is very rapid, it is not very easy to differentiate between these two conditions. A schizo-manic patient may have both conditions present, so to speak, in that he may manifest flight of ideas in addition to incoherence.

Patients in a state of so-called delirious mania often show an inability to care for themselves; they completely neglect themselves and do not pay attention to their personal habits. It is occasionally observed that a patient wets and soils himself, simply because the excitement is so marked. Incontinence or other very infantile regressive behavior patterns, by the way, do not belong in the manic-depressive psychosis, and are rarely observed. It is a much more common occurrence in schizophrenia and, if present in a patient, there should always be doubt regarding the diagnosis. The patient should be re-examined very carefully to determine whether or not you are dealing with a true manic-depressive psychotic person. Of course, hypomanic or acute manic patients do not show such regressive mechanisms; and, as you will note in depressions, it is also rare that the patient wets or soils or behaves in the manner so often seen in catatonic patients.

Deliriously manic patients manifest, furthermore, a state of excitement which is profound. They never rest; they never sleep; they do not eat, and their psychomotor activity is so increased that exhaustion sets in fairly rapidly. I would say that this form of mania is usually a dangerous psychotic state so far as the life of the patient is concerned. Many succumb, particularly those in the older age group, because usually the cardiovascular apparatus is unable to withstand the extreme stress. In certain instances, these profound excitement states can be quite prolonged if there is no treatment intervention. However, when the state of delirious mania is not mitigated, it usually runs its course in a comparatively short time. Delirious mania, as has been mentioned, is extremely rare and is very often confused with a form of acute catatonia, the "catatonia hyperkinesis," a condition which very rapidly ends in death—in the *hirntod* of the Germans—if not aborted by treatment.

When the differential diagnosis is discussed, it will be pointed out that the differentiation of a delirious mania from an organic state or from a schizophrenic state can be exceedingly difficult. A large number of such patients, occasionally diagnosed as belonging in the manic-depressive manic group, are actually organic cases or are schizophrenic cases with manic coloring. Differential diagnosis, paradoxically enough, became even more complicated since effective drug therapy was introduced because many hospitals do not wait for diagnosis: If the patient is in a state of marked excitement, in order to reduce it they quickly apply therapy and that, naturally, further influences the clinical picture. Therefore, it is rather difficult to decide, after the patient has had treatment and especially if he has responded to it, whether you were dealing with the so-called delirious mania or with the so-called schizo-manic patient who has responded to the treatment.

17

MANIC-DEPRESSIVE PSYCHOSIS: DEPRESSIVE PHASE

The clinical pictures of the depressive states are in direct contrast to the manic states. As was pointed out, in the manic-depressive psychosis the depressions can be subdivided into: (1) *simple retardation,* or hypodepression (the counterpart of hypomania), (2) *acute depression* (the counterpart of acute mania), and (3) the so-called *depressive stupor,* also termed "benign stupor," which is the maximum of the depressive sickness (and the opposite of manic delirium). "Benign stupor" is a term coined by August Hoch who described such an entity in a monograph *(1915).* He tried to differentiate the depressive stuporous states from the schizophrenic catatonic stuporous states and, because the prognosis of schizophrenia was considered poor, he called the manic-depressive stupors "benign," reserving the more malignant stupors for catatonic schizophrenia. How fortunate this clinical benign stupor construct was, I will discuss.

There are many other depressive clinical pictures than

471

the three just mentioned. Much more marked variations occur in the depressive pictures than in the manic, although perhaps manic pictures are not so readily interpreted. Furthermore, depressive syndromes are much more frequently observed than manic. Kraepelin *(4)* described a great many subentities of the manic-depressive psychosis, but I do not regard any of his terms useful. He described the "stuporous manias" as being the reverse of agitated depressions. He described the "immobilization manias" as being manic conditions having impairment of psychomotor activity, and so forth. It has become well recognized that these states and the many others he described, with the exception of the agitated depression, do not exist. As I have pointed out, occasionally "transitional" pictures occur, having a mixture of manic and depressive symptomatologies, but these do not present stable clinical pictures and are, as also are the "cataleptic manias," invariably cases of schizophrenia.

In a general way, patients classified as suffering from manic-depressive depression manifest the basic symptom triad which is present in the manic phase, but in the depressed patient, naturally, it occurs in the reverse manner. Instead of being elated, the patient is *depressed;* instead of having flight of ideas, usually the *speed of associations is reduced,* and instead of increased psychomotor activity, *psychomotor activity is retarded.* This slowing down of ideation can be demonstrated objectively and also is subjectively very annoying to the patient, being, by the way, a complaint voiced by a large number of mildly depressed manic-depressive patients.

Just as it is in the manic phase, the basic emotional dislocation of mood in the depressive phase is considered the most important phenomenon; practically any and every other symptom is considered to be more or less a derivative of, or secondary to, this basic emotional alteration. All symptoms are present, as they are in the manic phase, in *harmonious representation.*

SIMPLE RETARDATION

The mildest form of the depressive disorder, the so-called simple retardation, merits much more clinical attention than it has usually received. Textbooks have disposed of this mild form of depression in two or three sentences, although actually you will find it is a very important entity which we should be able to differentiate from reactive depression, involutional depression, psychoneurotic depressions, and organic states with depression. Mild depressions are a very common occurrence in the framework of any and every psychiatric disorder, and, naturally, not all belong in the diagnostic category of the manic-depressive psychosis. Differentiation depends on accessory symptoms, and they will be described when I discuss the differential diagnosis of depressions.

The number of patients suffering from this so-called light form of manic-depressive depression is very great. Obviously, these individuals never, or very rarely, enter a mental hospital, and if they do it is usually under another diagnostic category. False diagnoses are very frequently given this depressive group; many of these patients prevail under an organic diagnosis due to the presence of some impairment of the vegetative system. The number of hospital admissions of these patients under a diagnosis based on a vague headache, or constipation, or gastro-intestinal upset, or mild hypertension is quite large, although actually the underlying symptomatology is depression. From a psychiatric point of view, on the other hand, many patients are often simply treated as psychoneurotic patients and admitted to the hospital only when physical expressions (for which the psychiatrist was not prepared) of the underlying depression develop. I will discuss this issue from a diagnostic and prognostic point of view in more detail, but I must call attention again to the fact that individuals suffering with so-called hypodepression are extremely common and much more so than individuals who are hypomanic—including hypomanics who, of course, do not complain.

Now, what do we observe in a patient suffering with simple retardation or hypodepression? In this mild depression, all the symptoms of the triad described by Kraepelin are present to a varying degree. The patient's facial expression is often sad, his brow wrinkled, his eyes dull. He manifests difficulty in thinking and concentrating. He manifests a decreased psychomotor activity. However, usually the patient's main complaints are that his energy is lagging, that he has "no pep." The patient does not answer questions very elaborately, speech being slow and brief. He speaks in a low voice, but what he says is relevant. He often responds as though questions were a strain on him because all these patients report they are *thinking and performing against an inner resistance* all of the time. Their complaint about performing against inner resistance is very important. Depressed psychoneurotic patients will also complain of a lack of energy and of experiencing a strain in responding, but they rarely state that they perform against inner resistance all of the time; it is usually situational or only in the constellation of the depression in neurotic individuals. The hypodepressed patient has an everpresent, all-enveloping feeling that "No matter what I do, I am working against an inner resistance."

Most manic-depressive patients in the state of simple retardation also complain they have lost interest in everything around them. They have no initiative; they have no drive to do anything in general; they prefer to be idle but, at the same time, however, they feel restless and as though something is driving them from within. Restlessness accompanied by fatigue is a symptom hypodepressed patients have in common with many schizophrenic patients who are not necessarily depressed. It also occurs in many other depressive entities along with the feeling of being driven and yet feeling unable to perform.

In simple retardation, sensorium and intellectual functions are intact. Although a retardation is present in that thinking is slowed and attention span is poor, it is actually a "pseudoimpairment." Many patients complain of poor memory, of slipping intellectuality, and so forth, even though there is no actual memory or other intellectual defect. The patient feels as though he is retarded in his rate of thinking and performing, and many of them actually are, but in hypodepression it can happen that his feeling of retardation is greater than the actual retardation. For example, such a patient will state, "I have a great deal of difficulty attending to my work; I have to push myself very hard." And yet, people observing him will report that seemingly the patient is carrying out his achievements with the same skill, and it even appears that he is doing so with the same speed as he had done formerly.

You are probably surprised that I did not first mention, in describing the complaints of hypodepressed patients, that they feel depressed. The interesting thing is that many patients in the state of simple retardation will not complain to you that they are depressed and, therefore, the presence of depression is often overlooked. If you examine the patients carefully, you will probably be able to obtain from them sufficient material to indicate that they are actually "blue"—that they are actually depressed. However, even when questioned directly, not every patient voices it; he will tell you that he has no pep; he will tell you that he feels physically and mentally exhausted; he will tell you that he works against inner resistance; that he is unable to perform; that he is unable to make a decision, and that he has difficulty in thinking and concentrating. Finally, he will perhaps also mention, "By the way, I feel blue, I feel depressed." This phenomenon, moreover, occurs only in the depressed individuals suffering with so-called simple retardation. Even though many patients in simple retardation admit they are depressed, it must be emphasized that a large number of them do not. I emphasize this because very often the state of depression is not diagnosed.

Incidentally, many psychiatrists refer to this syndrome as being a "lurking" or "abortive" depression, which is not fully correct. However, there is such a group of patients having lurking or abortive depressions; these patients will actually state that they are not depressed and yet they have much of the symptomatology often accompanying depressive states. For example, following a period of well-being, such a person will suddenly develop marked fatigue, constipation, lack of appetite, sleep disturbance, and all the other vegetative disturbances which are difficult to categorize diagnostically since they can occur in a great number of disorders. We know there are patients with lurking depressions just as we know there are manic-depressive individuals having only one abortive attack instead of a full-fledged attack. Such patients exist and are even greater diagnostic problems than those suffering with simple retardation.

Patients belonging to the group of simple retardation definitely realize they are depressed and will probably admit it if you examine them properly and ask the question directly. In other words, there is nothing "lurking" or "abortive" about the depression even though the picture is very mild compared to the more severe depressive pictures and, actually, the usual clinical symptomatology observed in the more marked depressions can already be noted fully expressed in patients who have simple retardation.

Brooding is characteristic in patients who are in a state of simple retardation. Negative ideas develop which have to do with the person's performance, his health, his social status, his family, or, in fact, anything at all. Many of these preoccupations are dynamically important. The most important significance of the brooding is that the patient cannot divert himself from it. He cannot eliminate the negative thoughts from his mind; they are ideas which dominate him in a similar manner as observed in obsessive-compulsive individuals. The patient feels as though he is dominated by a force which he is unable to influence. This "passivity"—

the inability to direct his own thoughts—is prevalent in all depressions.

In many patients a certain *anhedonia* also develops, an anhedonia which, however, is intimately linked with depressive features. The term "anhedonia" means that the patient does not experience pleasure from anything and actually feels that he is leading a vegetative type of existence. There is no special thing which can give him pleasure. The patient will tell you that the ordinary process of eating does not gratify him, nor does sleeping. He has no sexual appetite, and his response to sexual stimuli is markedly reduced. His professional activity, which had formerly given some pleasure, no longer does so. He feels no regard for the family around him. So, whatever you suggest to the patient, he will deny that it gives him any pleasure. The state of anhedonia is a common occurrence and it is important because it envelops the patient completely. Furthermore, it is very similar to the anhedonia we will find in the framework of schizophrenia, the only difference being that in many schizophrenic patients anhedonia can be present in the absence of depressive affect, whereas in a manic-depressive depression it is closely linked to the depression and coexists with the depression. It does not have an independent existence as it does in many schizophrenic individuals who may go on for years being completely anhedonic without actually being depressed.

In a large number of hypodepressed patients there are other symptoms present which merit attention; they are symptoms which are not usually associated with depression. I would like to call this to your attention because it is rather surprising that these symptoms have not been featured and emphasized. Two of these symptoms can be observed in many depressed patients, particularly if one is able to catch the early phase of the patient's depression. First, there is the presence of an inner *tension* and considerable *anxiety*. It is interesting that many depressed patients, before the actual onset of depression, complain about feelings of great impairment of performance; about generally feeling tired, without energy, or anhedonic. Yet, often associated with this state are feelings of tension and feelings of anxiety. The tension often is rather marked. It is present, moreover, in many patients not manifesting the picture of agitated depression but manifesting the so-called simple retardation. Many hypodepressed patients are constantly tired, depressed, and at the same time are restless, which indicates the presence of an underlying constant tension.

Occasionally the anxiety so dominates the picture that the patients are diagnosed as suffering from anxiety states while actually they are depressed. The anxiety is often free-floating. In a few patients, however, it becomes channelized in the form of phobic or obsessive-compulsive pictures. When this occurs, it is often difficult to perceive whether the depression is actually superimposed on obsessive or phobic structure or whether the phobic or obsessive-compulsive manifestations are a symptomatic part of the depression. Obviously either combination can occur. A large number of patients, however, experience free-floating anxiety, which is not channelized into specific symptoms at the same time that they are having a depressive attack.

The second phenomenon frequently occurring in hypo-depressed patients is the sensation of *depersonalization,* varying in degree. These two phenomena, tension with anxiety and feelings of depersonalization, are important symptomatic features in these patients. A particularly intelligent patient is able to give fairly clear descriptions of these rather peculiar experiences that we also term "feelings of unreality," occurring with or without the feeling of anxiety. It is usually described by the patient with such statements as "Everything is hazy—things around me are not perceived as clearly as they formerly were—" and, "I have considerable difficulty keeping in touch with people." It is interesting that, although the feeling of unreality is difficult to define, when you mention the term many patients will state, "Yes, I have it." They are perfectly clear about your meaning even though they cannot verbalize very well exactly how they feel. They will tell you, "It is a very strange feeling." They cannot describe the feeling in detail, but will state, "Things are not the same as they formerly were; all has changed." Sometimes they tell you that everything happening around them seems unreal. In other words, emotionally they are unable to reach the environment. The sensation is something the patient is unable to voluntarily overcome.

Feelings of unreality never occur in a manic-depressive manic patient. If they occur in a manic state, the person is schizophrenic. Although feelings of unreality commonly occur with depression, we should not assume that they are a part of the depression. You will observe many depressed patients who have no feelings of unreality. Furthermore, feelings of unreality occur in many psychiatric entities; you will observe that feelings of unreality occur in the psychoneuroses, often in schizophrenia, and also in certain organic psychoses. Many depressive patients express these feelings by stating that they feel they have changed in relation to their environment, or that the environment is altered. Here, also, I must emphasize that elaboration on the feelings of unreality by a depressive patient does not usually extend further, whereas many schizophrenic patients—not all, but many—elaborate on the so-called feelings of unreality with all kinds of complicated ideational structures which at times are bizarre.

From the psychological point of view, we do not know the basis for this feeling of unreality although there are many descriptions of it and psychological theories about it. A few of the theories will be discussed in connection with some of the etiological concepts of the depressions. At present I would just like to emphasize that it is a very common occurrence in a depression, and the patient being examined should always be asked the question because he usually does not volunteer to tell you whether he experiences any feelings of unreality or not.

The patient suffering with simple retardation not only experiences retardation in his mood, in his thinking, and in his actions, but, as mentioned before, there is also a retardation, or depression, expressed in the form of many symptoms of *vegetative disturbances*. For instance, usually there is constipation, anorexia, and usually an interference with sleep regulation. In women there is often an interference in the menstrual cycle. Naturally, hypodepressed patients have diminished sexual interest and a low level of sexual performance.

In connection with the vegetative disturbances, hypodepressed patients often manifest hypochondriacal features. They report to you that certain bodily functions are not as they were formerly: They have no appetite; they are constipated; they are not sleeping well; a few complain about palpitation of the heart, and they sense coldness of their extremities. Originally it was thought that probably all of these ideas were hypochondriacal. I do not believe that is accurate. In these patients I think we are dealing with a mixture; there are actual changes which they recognize, and then they elaborate on those changes in a hypochondriacal manner. We are not dealing with unqualified hypochondriasis in which no actual somatic changes and no alterations of function can be demonstrated although the patient is nevertheless convinced that physical alteration has taken place. We do not know, in true hypochondriasis, whether the patient is actually evaluating an alteration or creating one in his thinking concerning a particular part of his body. However, in the manic-depressive depressed patient we definitely know and are able to demonstrate that many of the bodily changes complained about are not simply hypochondriacal preoccupations, nor are they—to use a very crude designation so often employed by laymen—"imaginary." The bodily changes are real. A depressive patient is really constipated. A depressive patient actually has no appetite.[1] A depressive patient has many peculiar sensations in the body and to some extent these sensations are based on fact because a tension is always present underneath the depression and very often emerges through the depression; an extreme awareness of visceral sensations or muscular aches and pains (as are also observed in psychoneurotic patients who are very tense) functions as a continual discharge of that tension.

The vegetative regulation, and in fact the homeostasis of the total organism, functions in exactly the same manner in a psychoneurotic depressed individual. It is irrelevant whether one perceives that there is primarily a physiological disturbance or primarily a psychological disturbance expressed as a "psychosomatic" trend through the physical apparatus; the issue concerned is that vegetative deviations are actually present in the patient. Furthermore, the patient elaborates on these disturbances, and it is that which may be termed hypochondriacal. In other words, he observes every little change; he picks up all the sensations and gives them an exaggerated importance. Therefore, this is a phenomenon which can be viewed as a mixture; there is a vegetative disturbance in the patient and he overelaborates upon it in a hypochondriacal manner. This mixture is an extremely common occurrence in depressive patients; you will observe this after you have examined a few dozen of them, and you can arrive at a diagnosis very quickly when you have heard these depressed patients relate the development of their somatic symptoms. (A psychoneurotic patient also elaborates on and relates a great many symptoms, but in quite a different manner.) It is characteristic for the depressive patient to go back again and again, in an obsessive way, to the same symptomatology without actually giving you more clues; he simply repeats the symptoms over and over. Five minutes later, he will relate the same symptoms, asking you if the "constitution" has any connection with the mental state. And so, he merely repeats his complaints in a

---

[1] Depressed housewives often project this onto their families by cooking meager portions.—*Eds.*

stereotyped fashion without actually progressing beyond them.

Hallucinations and delusions do not occur in patients suffering from this mild form of depression. Ideas indicating preoccupation with health, with their position in society, and so forth, are not so profound as to be termed delusional. They are often the so-called overvalued ideas, being vague expressions of the patient's fears. A hypodepressed patient may, however, handle the preoccupation with bodily conditions in a partially delusional manner insomuch as you cannot budge him from his preoccupation. The patient can win in any logical argument by insisting there are actual bodily changes present, and so it is rather a question of whether his insistence is completely appropriate or partially delusional. However, this is the only instance in simple retardation which could possibly be interpreted as being delusional. In all other respects, delusions and hallucinations do not occur in patients suffering with simple retardation.

The tendency for the patient to rationalize regarding his depression is great and the rationalizations take many different forms. Many patients grope for an explanation for why they are depressed and offer you all kinds of true or imaginary solutions to resolve the depression. This is important because if you do not investigate each point carefully you could often find yourself entangled in the patients' own rationalizations, which, in the treatment of these patients, could be a hindrance. The rationalization in some of these patients is interesting; sometimes it takes exactly the same form in each attack they have and appears with the same regularity as do many of the other symptoms. In a few patients, however, the same basic difficulty may return but they use different rationalizations in explaining it to themselves or to you.

There is that peculiar undercurrent of *aggression* and excitement in the hypodepressed patient which, as I have mentioned, also occurs in the manic state. This, as we will see at a later time, plays a large role in corroborating some of the dynamics of the depression. Many compliant depressed patients have it; suddenly their aggression erupts, at times directed against themselves and at times directed against individuals in the environment. Not rarely, depressive patients are quite peevish, quite demanding, and quite annoying to others. They feel helpless. They usually confess to wanting help. However, their acceptance of help is most likely only a qualified acceptance and not the convincing desire for help as is observed in persons suffering from a clear-cut organic disease.

Expectation of help is often quite interestingly paradoxical due to marked *ambivalence*. In the depressive state a patient may come to the psychiatrist and want to be treated, but, at the same time, every type of treatment proposed is met with rejection; all the patient seems to want is to prescribe what treatment he should receive. Or, when being treated, the patient will begin to complain about every move in the treatment and attribute many of the complaints which had been clearly established originally as now being due to the treatment. Hostility toward the person on whom they depend, hostility toward the person from whom they seek help, and the peculiar attitude of feeling despondent and wanting help while at the same time rejecting it, occurs. This ambivalence, which plays a role in the dynamics of depression, is also presented descriptively when you examine a patient. During the first or second interview, you are unable to recognize the ambivalence clearly in the patient; at times this makes the treatment of a depressive patient extremely difficult. Very often you must cut through the ambivalence in the patient, otherwise treatment cannot progress any further. Ambivalence can go to the extent that the patient, for example, will ask for a sedative; and, when it is given to him, he will immediately state, "No, I do not want to take it because I will probably accustom myself to this sedative," or he will ask, "Are you very sure the sedative will not do me any harm?" and so on, manipulating the situation between two poles.

It is very interesting that the depressed patient wants to die, and at the same time he watches with great anxiety everything which is being done to him. In other words, here again is a double attitude: "I want to die, but you must not do anything to harm me," or in other words, "I am very fearful that something could happen to me in treatment." This is a peculiar attitude because, naturally, if the person wants to die, this would be completely irrelevant. Many depressive patients who are being treated psychotherapeutically will even tell you it is a paradox, remarking, "I want to die, so I should not be concerned. Why should I be concerned?" But they are. It has even been possible to observe patients who, swaying with this paradox, actually commit suicide. When the anxiety or tension reaches a certain intensity they are able to break through the ambivalence and finally commit suicide, but before they finally do it, many of these patients go through a state of being completely preoccupied with what will happen to them and concerned that nothing should actually happen to them.

I once heard of a patient who contemplated suicide and finally carried it out, but half an hour before committing suicide she called for the family physician. She called for the family physician because she felt something must be wrong with her heart—it was pounding. The patient went through a very complete examination, including an electrocardiagram and so forth, and left the office only to commit suicide. One observes here again the interesting paradox; that the patient who contemplates suicide and apparently had contemplated suicide for quite a while would be so concerned about her own bodily security and her own bodily integrity. It is not rare that patients in the state of simple retardation commit suicide. Individuals in a state of mild or moderate depression (all depressions, not just the manic-depressive form) are the greatest suicidal risks, however.

Persons in the severe states of depression no longer have the initiative.

As has been mentioned, the average duration of any depressive attack is difficult to predict. As is the case with any manic-depressive depression, simple retardation episodes may last a few weeks, a few months, or perhaps a year. It may last even longer if the patient is in the involutional age group. It is not rare to observe patients suffering from these depressions for several months, or even a year, and they are often even diagnosed as suffering with some other disorder, treated for one of those disorders, and then the attack subsides of its own accord.

ACUTE DEPRESSION

Generally speaking, manic-depressive patients classified as suffering with acute depression manifest all the symptoms described in simple retardation but in a much more exaggerated fashion. Naturally, the symptom triad is present: depression of affect, retardation in the speed of association, and retardation of psychomotor activity. Just as is the case with the other manic or depressive states, all symptoms are derived from the basic alteration of the patient's level of affect.

In the acutely depressive symptom picture there is such a conspicuous and already marked emotional deviation that it is obvious not only to the patient that he is quite sick, but also to others in his environment. The person is visibly depressed. The depression is deep; the attitude of misery, dejection, or despondence is great. Associative retardation, by the way, is a complaint voiced by many acutely depressed patients; it is subjectively quite annoying to the patient and can also be demonstrated objectively. The patient speaks very rarely, or speaks only in a monosyllabic way, he does not like to be questioned, he is completely asocial and withdrawn, he usually moves slowly and may assume a hunched postural position. These patients not only lack initiative but often cannot even dress, or eat, or care for themselves properly, and every effort is made against a strong inner resistance. Tension and anxiety in the acutely depressed patient can be great. In many patients, however, the depression or feeling of dejection is so predominant that the anxiety feelings do not come to the foreground. Feelings of unreality can be marked; and occasionally the patient feels that the environment is blurred, is shadowy. This dulled perception can at times override the patient's awareness of being depressed.

In addition to these basic symptoms there are, in quite a number of acutely depressed patients, other manifestations present which are very impressive in that they resemble delusions and hallucinations. Similarly as in the manic, these are topical. In other words, the ideation which preoccupies the patient is in harmony with the basic emotional state. The affect is the source of the ideational setting for these experiences. Inappropriate delusional and hallucinatory contents which are observed so often in schizophrenia and many other psychoses do not occur in true manic-depressive psychosis. True hallucinations that dominate the symptom picture do not occur; they are only misperceptions in connection with the particular ideational formation present in the patient.

What appear to be delusions are actually intensely experienced overvalued ideas. They are obsessive ideas; the obsessiveness is mainly characterized by the fact that the patient is dominated by them and unable to dismiss them. If he has some insight into the symptomatology of his sickness, he will himself comment that, in addition to feeling blue, the most disagreeable part of his sickness is the constant reverberation of the same ideas in his mind which he is unable to shut off. We can probably reassure the patient temporarily, but we are not able to actually convince the patient that his ideation is not valid. This obsessive tendency toward dominance of his overvalued ideas is of great importance in evaluating the clinical symptomatology of the acutely depressed patient, and it also plays a very important role in the treatment of the patient.

It is obvious that the depressive patient does not have ideations of grandeur or of ego-expansion. The ideations all have preoccupational themes in harmony with the ego-reduction which usually is connected with ideas of *self-condemnation* or *self-accusation*. Self-recriminatory or self-accusatory ideas are very prevalent in depressions and, in many patients, they are not organized around recent happenings but around past happenings in his life. Often these happenings are trivial and bear no relationship to the degree of affective charge they carry. For instance, a patient who, as a child, probably stole a few pennies or who behaved in an objectionable way, will pick up one of these trivia, elaborate upon it, and exaggerate it to the level of an unpardonable sin—all of which the patient manipulates dynamically. When I discuss the dynamics of the depression, you will see why the patient does this, and for what reason he organizes such a strong affective charge around small, trivial experiences in his life.

In certain other depressive patients the ideational elaboration is organized around an actual performance of a misdeed, so considered from the point of view of the patient, or even society, which becomes at some point connected with a certain emotional need. But the patient unduly exaggerates its importance. Obsessively and repetitiously, he will continually accuse himself of "doing a wrong" without being able to dismiss such a thought from mind and without being able to accept from others any reassurance that it is not so very important. Should he be reassured, by the time the reassuring person leaves the room the patient once again returns to his preoccupations. The self-accusatory ideas that he has done something which will end in ruin to himself or to his family, that he actually is a worthless individual, that he should be killed, or that he should kill himself, are rather common preoccupations present, to at least a mild extent, in most acutely depressed patients. All kinds of wrong-doing can be the topic of these ideas; sexual and social ones are rather common. The preoccupations can be very elaborate or they can be primitive. The essential point is that the emotion-bound conviction is so strong that you are not able to convince the patient to the contrary.

Another type of ideational content which occurs mainly in a depressive patient, in addition to overvalued ideas relating to self-recrimination or self-depreciation, is elaboration of *paranoid ideation*. Basically, paranoid delusions do not, in fact, belong in the manic-depressive groups and do not ever dominate the patient in this psychosis. For instance, if a patient is dominated by paranoid delusions, we can be fairly certain the patient is not manic-depressive psychotic. However, there are quite a number of manic-depressive patients, in the depressed state particularly, who express paranoid ideation; and, here again, the paranoid content is usually closely tied in with the basic emotional charge in the patients. They develop, as we may say, paranoid ideations which are secondary to their strong feelings of inadequacy to perform.

We usually differentiate between two types of paranoid ideation: the so-called primary, and the so-called secondary paranoid ideas or elaborations. The *primary* paranoid ideas, occurring mainly in the paranoid form of schizophrenia, are not consistently concomitant with the patient's overt display of marked emotional changes, such as elation or depression. Primary paranoid elaborations, furthermore, are usually not connected, or at least not appropriately connected, with the patient's performance. This can be demonstrated if one investigates deeply into the patient's emotional life. The so-called *secondary* paranoid elaborations occur within the framework of an affective manifestation. Moreover, the elaborations are secondary in their connection with the patient's inability to cope with certain situations which the patient basically recognizes as fact but is unable to alter. They are the patient's projection of this actual deficiency of performance onto the environment. Both the primary and the secondary paranoid delusions can be observed in schizo-phrenia. In correctly diagnosed manic-depressive psychosis, usually only the secondary paranoid elaborations are found.

Here is an example to clarify how secondary paranoid mechanisms develop: A depressive patient at first has the distinct feeling that he is tired, that he is confused, that he is not able to think clearly, and that he is not able to per-form. The nonperformance then leads to ideation that he is worthless, that he is not as good as other human beings. The next idea is that the people around him are beginning to notice that he is not able to perform and is unable to cope with his environmental situations. In other words, the aware-ness of his feeling of inadequacy is projected. Around this projection, at this point, all varieties of ideas become pos-sible, and the patient is able to finally arrive at any number of unsystematized paranoid-like elaborations. Almost always these ideas are clearly connected with the basic depressive affect; most likely, one can trace them as being secondary to ideation which the depressed patient entertains about his own unworthiness and his own inability to cope with environ-mental situations.

Depressive individuals who develop self-accusatory ideas not only develop ideas that they have committed a sin and therefore will be punished, but also that their sin was committed against others and the reason they will be punished is that they have brought misfortune to others. It is then the patient states, "I am a very bad person; I should be killed." It then becomes almost logical that his next step is to anticipate happenings such as "Now they are after me; they are trying to kill me; I know the police will come and take me away." The paranoid expectations of punishment are in logical sequence from the ideas of self-accusation.

These ideations are entirely different from the para-noid ideas of the schizophrenic individual who believes that he is right and the environment is wrongly against him; that the room is wired; that certain people are after him and are trying to take away his thoughts; and that people are influencing him. In schizophrenia, as I have mentioned, mixtures of primary and secondary elaborations often occur. Paranoid ideas of the truly primary form, as observed in a paranoid schizophrenic, actually do not occur in manic-depressive psychosis.

An important group of ideational elaborations occurring in the acutely depressive patient are the so-called *hypochondriacal* ones. Hypochondriacal preoccupation and depression are very closely linked. It was originally assumed that hypochondriacal ideations occur only in the framework of a depression. At the present time we know that this is not so. Such ideation can occur in practically any form of psychiatric entity, including organic psychoses, schizophrenia, and involutional melancholia. Furthermore, hypochondriacal ideas which are not delusional, but which are overvalued or overstressed ideas—an intermediary stage of ideation between normal thought and delusional formation—are prevalent even in certain types of psychoneurotic individuals.

Hypochondriacal preoccupation with any part of the body is often interpreted in terms of whatever is considered dynamically valid. Descriptively, the only important thing to mention here is that hypochondriacal preoccupations in a depressive patient are usually elaborated around some particular organ function. A few of the patient's ideas might sound bizarre; for example, the patient may state that a part of his brain is rotting away, or his bowels are not functioning and are all stopped up. He will tell you that he has no bowels any more, that he has no mind any more, and so forth. Many of these elaborations may appear to be rather bizarre, but usually they are not so illogical and bizarre as those observed in schizophrenia. For instance, a manic-depressive patient who is acutely depressed will never tell you that his "guts" are upside down, or even that his heart has moved to the other side of his body, or that his genitals are now in his head, or his eyes are dangling, or some such obsession which can be an elaborate hypochondriacal pre-occupation in patients suffering from schizophrenia.

The idea formations such as "I have *no* bowels," "I have *no* brain," or "I have *no* mind" are designated as nihilistic ideas which then reach their height when the patient begins to deny that he exists, or deny that the whole world exists. These nihilistic ideas are present in many severe depressions, particularly severe depressions in the involutional period, and also occur in organic disorders. But the patient has to be extremely depressed to have such ideas.

Interestingly enough, all these marked hypochondriacal, nihilistic ideas, and also paranoid content, are very much more prevalent in depressions of older patients than in depressions occurring in younger individuals. We can recognize that there is probably more psychological explanation for hypochondriacal preoccupations occurring in older individuals in that their evaluation of bodily sensations and performance is, naturally, much more anxiety-tinged than it is in younger individuals in whom bodily disturbances have much less of a final import. Even in normal older individuals, and particularly in neurotic older individuals, you will find that *any* body deviations, *any* medical finding, or *any* feeling of inadequate performance is much more loaded with anxiety or elaborations around fear of what will happen to them—"Is this not a sign of deterioration, doctor?"—than in younger individuals. In depressed older individuals the anxiety is even more marked and much more emphasized.

Although hypochondriacal ideation can extend to any organ or organ system of the body, the one most often selected is the gastro-intestinal tract. In ancient Greece, "melancholia" (black bile) had already been considered somehow linked to the gastro-intestinal tract, and it is probably a correct empirical observation that it is the gastro-intestinal tract with which most depressed patients are mainly preoccupied. This phenomenon was used by Abraham and others for much of the dynamic elaborations on the depressive states. Of course, there is very often a physical basis for such preoccupation since during depression the motility of the stomach and bowels is usually interfered with; the patient's gastric motility is diminished, the secretion of gastric juices is diminished or absent and peristalsis is less active. These vegetative nervous system changes are obviously registered by patients; they are constipated, they are usually rather anorexic and dyspeptic. Whatever they eat generally remains in the stomach for a considerable period of time and they complain of feeling uncomfortable or having pain in the epigastric area.

Other than the gastro-intestinal tract, the organ system with which a depressed patient is mainly preoccupied is the cardiovascular apparatus. Concerning the cardiovascular apparatus a rather interesting phenomenon has been observed. During the first quarter of this century, most depressed persons were not especially preoccupied with the functions of the heart. Then, the general population became, I should say, "heart conscious"; quite a number of depressed patients began to deflect their tension symptoms to the chest area and would interpret a slight ache, or any pain in the chest as a sign of angina pectoris or an "impending coronary." Actual cardiac symptoms, objectively speaking, are not present, with the exception that in depression there is often a great acceleration in the person's pulse rate, stimulated by the presence of anxiety.

Furthermore, in many depressed patients, as also occurs in many patients suffering with anxiety neurosis or other anxiety states, the underlying tension is discharged into the muscles, so that frequently pains and aches are present in the neck, back, chest, and so forth. These tension symptoms in the skeletal musculature only become more extensive as they add to a patient's anxiety and it is quite certain that a number of individuals diagnosed as "rheumatic," and a number in whom some form of myositis or neuritis is postulated, are actually suffering from a tension state, the tension being discharged into the musculature producing an anxiety which the patient then, naturally, perceives and interprets as pain in a particular muscle group. Now, in many depressive patients, such muscular symptomatology develops in the chest wall. At first you will hear vague complaints, the patient will then begin to elaborate and finally he will believe he obviously has "heart trouble." The occurrence in the patient's mind of impairments of organ function are not, in every case, necessarily based on misinterpreted sensations, nor even due to altered homeostasis affecting his vegetative nervous system. Sometimes they actually are symbolic projections of the patient's ideas into a particular part of his body, there being a relationship between the physiological functioning in these patients and their psychological elaboration.

Now, a third apparatus with which depressed patients are very often preoccupied is the genito-urinary tract. There are two dysfunctions about which many patients complain: (1) frequency of urination (this is a tension symptom occurring in men especially); and, (2) loss of sexual drive and potency. This often accompanies mild depression, being invariably present in all severely depressed individuals. Again, these symptoms, naturally, give the patient basis for ideational elaborations. Many of the hypochondriacal ideas concerning sexual performance, or the functioning of their sex organs are, naturally, connected to self-recriminatory preoccupations.

Often the hypochondriacal ideas in depressed patients are mixed with phobic ideas, such as fears concerning syphilis, or going "insane." Here is an interesting observation which one will also encounter in schizophrenic individuals: A person who already manifests psychosis will fear that he is becoming mentally sick; such a phenomenon is not uncommon.

Although a few depressive patients express rather bizarre ideas, bizarre delusions do not belong in the manic-depressive psychosis. There is only one group of ideations in a manic-depressive patient which, however, could strike the examiner as being very peculiar or bizarre; these are the hypochondriacal elaborations, particularly those occurring in individuals of the involutional age group. On a descriptive level, it is frequently difficult to differentiate seemingly delusional material in the acute depressive patient from similar material in depressed delusional schizophrenics. Later I will discuss how it is possible, based on certain dynamic material, to differentiate between a schizophrenic and a manic-depressive depression. Differentiation based on the assumption that the manic-depressive person usually does not have bizarre delusions while the schizophrenic person does, is not so clear in the depressive states as it is in the manic states. Bizarre delusions in a manic person speak most strongly for a schizophrenic process, but in depressions it is much more difficult to decide what is bizarre and what is not bizarre. Often it depends on the subjective judgment of the psychiatrist whether he would consider an idea—such as wasting away of the brain—as one which fits the depressive content or as one which actually is a bizarre idea. If the psychiatrist is inclined to have a few bizarre thoughts himself, he would naturally be more lenient with the patient and would consider some of the patient's bizarre elaborations as not being bizarre. Furthermore, he might assume that some of the patient's elaborations were topical when actually they are not.

There are, to some extent, ways and means for establishing a differential diagnosis. Fortunately, in schizophrenia, much of the affective or emotional undertones are not usually maintained with the same tenacity as are the ideas; therefore, affect and ideation are not in harmony. For example, you will come upon a schizophrenic person who, at the start, is depressed and expresses bizarre ideas; a day or two later you will find him not very depressed, but rather indifferent, and at the same time continuing to express bizarre ideas. Such symptom discords are of diagnostic help only if they occur. I might add, however, that the more you are able to follow the elaborations of the patient in a depressive cycle, the more probable it is you are dealing with a manic-depressive individual. The farther these elaborations are from the affective component in the patient, the more your suspicions must be aroused that this depressed patient is suffering from schizophrenia.

I have mentioned several times, and when discussing differential diagnosis in detail I will not have to repeat, that a great amount of manic-depressive symptomatology is exceedingly prevalent in schizophrenia; this is the source of a great deal of false appraisal of patients from a therapeutic and a prognostic point of view.

In addition to seemingly delusional ideations, and in addition to the various somatic preoccupations, I must mention two other symptoms occurring rather frequently in the framework of depression. One is the presence of *anxiety* and the other is the presence of *agitation*. The *anxiety* is not always expressed completely in connection with delusional or hypochondriacal symptomatology. It can be present in a depressive patient in the form of free-floating anxiety, such as is present in certain anxiety states. It is not even rare that *because* of the presence of free-floating anxiety, and because of the nonprominence of a depressive affect, patients are diagnosed as suffering from a psychoneurotic anxiety state even though, in this case, the anxiety is a secondary symptom. Actually, every depression is preceded by a state of tension, and in certain individuals the tension continues along with the depression. In other individuals anxiety symptoms are also introduced in addition to the depression; the performance in these patients is retarded, and because they feel unable to cope they actually complain mainly that they are anxious, as do patients suffering from an anxiety state who are not depressed. However, in addition to that, they usually have the feeling of "blueness," depression, and many of the other symptom elaborations.

Secondly, *agitation* occurs in a few depressive patients. Agitation is extremely prevalent in involutional depression, but occasionally agitation is also observed in younger individuals during the onset of their depression, although retardation is the more usual form of depression in young individuals. Patients in the state of agitated depression are constantly moving about, wringing their hands, moaning, repeating certain phrases, climbing around and pacing the floor, or trying to cling to whoever is around, asking for reassurance.

As in the case of simple retardation, in the acutely depressed patient there is an undercurrent of *aggression* and excitement which can erupt and be expressed either against the patient himself, or, more likely, toward others in the environment. When aggressive, they can be very demanding of help and yet, of course, behave in a paradoxical and ambivalent manner, often expressing a great deal of hostility toward the therapist.

Now, in acutely depressed manic-depressive patients, two further issues must be emphasized: (1) The intellect of the patient remains intact; and (2) the patient does not show any alteration of consciousness. Both statements have to be amplified to some extent. You will find that many patients in a state of acute depression complain that their memory is poor, that they are unable to remember, and that they are unable to think. Objective performance in psychological tests indicates their intellectual performance is definitely slowed down, but no qualitative impairment is present. Actually, any memory impairment or any so-called thinking disorder is due to the emotional interference; it is not by any means a primary intellectual disorder as occurs in organic psychoses; it is not an intellectual disorganization (primary or secondary, whichever we may think theoretically) which, for example, is observed in schizophrenia. Moreover, even after electro-convulsive therapy the impairment of intellect is mainly on a quantitative, not a qualitative, level. If these patients have posttherapy memory impairment, it can be demonstrated that the acute state they are in follows an organic pattern. In a matter of time the memory returns more or less to the norm; an impairment remains in very few individuals and, if any impairment remains, it is purely on a quantitative level.

Actually, none of the marked progress in intellectual disorganization occurring in organic psychoses and none of the typical intellectual disorganization occurring in schizophrenia is observed in a true manic-depressive patient, even if he receives electro-convulsive therapy. However, there have been many patients, originally receiving electro-convulsive treatment under the manic-depressive diagnosis, who later developed schizophrenic disorganization; in those cases the primary diagnosis was simply wrong. I also want to remind you that a so-called deterioration which occurs in schizophrenia never occurs in manic-depressive psychosis; if symptoms of deterioration are observed, the patient is not a manic-depressive psychotic individual.

DEPRESSIVE STUPOR

The stuporous clinical picture very rarely occurs in the "pure" manic-depressive psychosis. If it occurs, it is not likely to be in the manic-depressive psychosis but it is more likely to appear in patients at the involutional age, particularly involutional patients already in the arteriosclerotic age range. Even so, such patients are not fully clear-cut cases diagnostically; and it is not quite clear which other factors, besides depression, play a determining role in the symptomatology.

Any psychiatrist having had clinical experience for many years has, on occasion, observed patients who suffered with acute depression becoming more and more retarded, who became more and more dominated by some hypochondriacal or nihilistic ideational preoccupation, and who then arrive at a state which appeared to be stuporous. I must remark, however, that although manic-depressive patients can gradually enter into a state of acute depression, or gradually enter into a stuporous state (and if such should occur, it usually would not develop rapidly), it is extremely rare that they reach a stuporous state in which they are completely out of contact with the environment.

The patient in a state of so-called depressive stupor would have extreme depression of affect, he may be tortured by ideas of death, he may be mute, inactive, and un-cooperative—all appropriate to the depressed affect. Although the retardation of associations may be great, there is no blocking and no stereotypy present. Furthermore, manic-depressive psychotic patients never display true cata-lepsy; they do not display catatonic rigidity; and they do not display the mechanisms of automatic obedience and negativism which is a characteristic form of stupor mecha-nism observed in the catatonic form of schizophrenia. This extreme depressive syndrome, if it exists at all, is very, very rare. Now, I think that I have observed only two patients whom I could possibly categorize as cases of so-called depres-sive stupor, and even these cases were doubtful in my mind.

The extreme depressive state was described by August Hoch, in one of his early papers *(1915)*, under the designa-tion "benign stupor." He observed patients in mental hospitals suffering from a so-called stuporous state which was supposedly a milder stupor than the form manifested by catatonic schizophrenic patients. These patients were confined to bed insomuch as they had to be cared for; they did not display interest in anything; they appeared to be in a cloudy state with interference of consciousness. Because, however, they manifested the picture of a "bland" and "non-productive" stupor (in other words, there were no clear-cut hallucinations and delusions as can be observed in schizo-phrenia); and, because they had displayed excitement states before they went into such a stuporous state, it was assumed these cases belonged to the manic-depressive psychotic group.

The original case material of August Hoch was followed up and it turned out that all the patients described in his monograph—without exception—were later diagnosed schizophrenic patients and remained confined in the hospital. There was nothing "benign" about these people and the original diagnosis of manic-depressive psychosis was not correct. This, again, shows that follow-up studies are extremely important, that a theoretical concept or formulation based on certain symptomatology which somebody presented on the basis of current observations can prove to be false in the light of follow-up observations. It indicates how a concept of a particular diagnostic entity can be introduced, can be accepted with all its dynamic formulations, and then later be demonstrated not to exist.

On the basis of our follow-up studies of over four hundred cases having the original diagnosis of manic-depressive psychosis *(Hoch and Rachlin, 1941)*, it appeared to me that this "benign stupor" concept actually has been dissolved into a clinical entity which is, with possibly a few clinical exceptions, nonexistent. The concept of "benign stupors" or "depressive stupors," therefore, should be evaluated only with great caution and is a diagnostic entity which has probably become of more historical than practical interest.

18

DEPRESSIONS:
DIFFERENTIAL DIAGNOSIS

Manic-depressive psychosis and schizophrenia were differentiated by Kraepelin *(4)* largely on the basis of the deterioration concept. Following that time, August Hoch became very interested in the problem of differentiation between these two disorders and wrote several papers based on his follow-up studies of a number of hospitalized patients in Boston. He found that sixty-three out of eighty-eight cases were correctly diagnosed upon admission as being cases of "dementia praecox." Only thirteen of the patients were given the initial diagnosis of manic-depressive psychosis but, later on, even they all had to be reclassified as cases of schizophrenia. On the other hand, there were very few cases in which the preliminary diagnosis of dementia praecox was changed to manic-depressive psychosis, indicating there were more mistakes made in assuming patients to be manic-depressive psychotics when they were not than

500

mistakes made the other way around. More recently, at St. Elizabeth's Hospital, Nolan D. C. Lewis and others *(Lewis and Hubbard, 1931)* followed approximately seventy-seven cases diagnosed initially as manic-depressive psychotic. More than two-thirds of these cases he later rediagnosed as patients suffering from schizophrenia. From these observations one might conclude that manic-depressive psychosis is not so prevalent as many hospitals have indicated in the past and that a great number of patients diagnosed in the category of manic-depressive psychosis, when their clinical courses are followed sufficiently, develop manifestations of schizophrenia.

In one of the New York State hospitals the 1928 ratio of admissions between patients diagnosed manic-depressive psychotic and schizophrenic was nearly equal; then ten years later the diagnosis of schizophrenia outranked manic-depressive psychosis four to one. Around this time very similar changes were observed in other parts of the country; diagnosis of schizophrenia became more and more a common practice and the diagnosis of manic-depressive psychosis less and less common, although in many state hospitals the diagnosis of manic-depressive psychosis had originally outranked the diagnosis of dementia praecox and schizophrenia. Now, this change certainly did not develop because one psychosis, for some reason or another, occurred less often than formerly. Our diagnostic approach changed. Similar changes were observed abroad where the diagnosis of manic-depressive psychosis had originally been very extensive. Practically all over the world a marked shrinkage of the diagnosis of manic-depressive psychosis became apparent, indicating again that our diagnostic observations and interpretations are subject to change.

Interestingly enough, manic-depressive psychosis as a true entity has become recognized to be a rare disorder, rare in the sense that it is not often observed, especially not observed in mental hospitals. Cases are much more likely to be encountered in private practice. Furthermore, it is more commonly encountered in certain cultural settings or groups, although it is not quite clear whether it is actually more prevalent in these particular groups or continues to be diagnosed as manic-depressive psychosis, the diagnosis of schizophrenia not being employed as often with these groups as it is in other areas.

The patient suffering from true manic-depressive psychosis usually displays the triad of symptoms in harmonious interconnection and distinction must be made from the disorders Kraepelin described which resemble this psychosis only in terms of the patient's affective picture. Manic and depressive pictures are prevalent in many psychiatric disorders, but in the manic-depressive psychosis a mixture of other psychotic features is usually not present. If other features are present, it may very well not be a manic-depressive psychosis. Furthermore, a person can be suffering from a manic-depressive psychosis but that does not mean he is not also suffering from an additional psychotic disorder which, naturally, complicates the picture diagnostically.

The great difficulty in constructing a diagnosis occurs when there are admixtures of different symptoms in patients which could be present classically in a case of general paresis, involutional melancholia, psychoneurosis, and so forth. It must be kept in mind that depression of mood is so especially prevalent as to be considered one of the *universal reaction patterns*. There are actually three or four universal reaction patterns in mental disorders. This statement is over-simplifying psychiatry, which I do not advocate, but it is useful here to demonstrate how very often the same clinical symptomatology confronts us in different constellations. The basic clinical manifestations which can occur in any mental disorder are *anxiety, depression,* and *paranoid reactions.* And at times one may want to include elation and obsessive reactions. Many observers regard the obsessive pattern as an independent one; others regard it as a special form of anxiety. Nevertheless, anxiety, depressive, or paranoid reactions, alone or in various combinations, appear so often that we are obviously dealing with rather elementary mental phenomena. These three symptoms can be observed in the framework of practically all psychiatric disorders. They occur in sociopathic conditions, in schizophrenia, in manic-depressive psychosis, in organic disorders, and in the psychoneuroses. In other words, they occur in practically every psychiatric entity mixed with, or connected with, other symptoms.

Because these basic mental phenomena appear so often, and as in each phenomenon, some of its response to therapy and some of its dynamics cut through diagnostic lines, many have suggested that we should concentrate simply on phenomenology, in terms of the presence or absence of depression, or the presence or absence of a paranoid manifestation, and so forth. In other words, they suggest we should not pay very much attention to the diagnostic grouping in which symptoms appear but should concentrate on the phenomenon itself. One should recognize that to a certain extent this is a very poor approach. Even disregarding that a depression, for instance, occurring in the framework of schizophrenia is a different thing from a manic-depressive psychotic depression or a depression occuring in the framework of an organic disorder, I still think it safer to consider a depressive manifestation itself in its direct relationship to the very entity in which it appears. Otherwise, we can be prognostically and therapeutically misled. This is not to deny that all depressions, regardless in which entity present, have certain resemblance to each other in their prognosis, or their therapy, or their dynamics.

THE IMPORTANCE OF DIFFERENTIAL DIAGNOSIS : Concerning manic-depressive reactions there are two schools of thought. One considers that manic-depressive psychosis is rare and that it is usually a reaction occurring in schizophrenia. Others do not take this view. From a clinical point of view, I think it is not so very important which theory we follow, but it is very important to know that, regardless of whether manic-depressive psychosis is an independent reaction type *or* a special form of schizophrenia, each of these disorders follows a rather different course, has a different prognosis, and responds to treatment differently. Actually, this is the reason for being concerned with diagnosis. From a prognostic and therapeutic point of view different pictures react differently. Therefore, we must differentiate manic-depressive reactions clinically whether or not we assume them to be separate entities or subentities of other disorders. Regardless of whether you consider manic-depressive depressed pictures a subgroup of schizophrenia or an independent reaction, the prognosis for these depressed patients and their response to any type of therapy is *entirely* different, for example, from those of a paranoid schizophrenic patient. This is why delineation is important clinically, despite all awareness that they are tentative and purely phenomenological.

Considering the stage of our knowledge, there can be no law against going to the other extreme and saying, "I do not make any diagnosis at all. I think that if the person is emotionally sick I shall just work out one or two of the psychodynamic factors in the case and only confine myself to that." Such a stand, however, is not at all satisfactory because the psychodynamic configurations are simply another frame of reference which actually is not very different from any other frame of reference. Therefore, I think that all factors should be viewed in conjunction with each other. It is very essential to establish just what the clinical pictures are that the patient produces. One may think that, because the clinical pictures are unclear and quite often confusing, establishing a diagnosis and prognosis will be also. One may then become convinced that the situation is so labile that any psychiatric diagnosis made will be extremely unsatisfactory. With diagnostic delineations being unclear, the psychiatrist may then feel that he cannot hope to compete with other branches of science in prognosticating anything. Nevertheless, the surprising fact is that even though well-trained psychiatrists may differ somewhat in their theoretical approaches or diagnostic appraisal of each case, they make prognostic appraisals and therapeutic recommendations that turn out to be correct in about 65 percent of their cases—provided the criteria (which I conveyed to you) of diagnosis, prognosis, and therapy are followed. This is not bad for such a supposedly confused discipline as psychiatry.

SOURCE OF ERRORS IN MAKING DIAGNOSIS: Actually, the two most common mistakes made in diagnosing are (1) misinterpreting clinical pictures and (2) mixing plain clinical factual observations with all types of theoretical conjectures which have nothing to do with the facts.

First of all, regardless of which theory you follow, if you observe a euphoric person sitting in a room, not contacting the environment and not displaying increased psychomotor activity or flight of ideas, and if you recognize that what you observe is not a true manic picture, you would then think, "This person appears to be euphoric but does not present a clear-cut manic picture; I must examine further and I shall watch for other signs." Then you would carefully watch for other clinical signs such as those of schizophrenia. If any are present, your suspicion is further supported that you are dealing with a case of schizophrenia. The moment you recognize that it is a "schizo-manic" case of schizophrenia, you realize the prognosis in this case is less favorable than that of manic-depressive psychosis but more favorable than that of the classical type of schizophrenia. In other words, you have a certain prognostic clue and then, when you begin treatment, you adapt your treatment recommendations accordingly. I do not say that such procedures are infallible and I do not say that occasionally you might not make a mistake, but, if properly employed, the diagnostic situation is not so bad as a great many psychiatrists believe it to be.

Secondly, difficulties arise when a psychiatrist has all

kinds of theoretical preconceptions which distort his clinical observations. Difficulties also arise when the psychiatrist is not an able clinician. Unfortunately, there seem to be fewer and fewer keen clinicians and more and more who fail to observe the patient adequately and who reason from a single factor. They may proceed, for example, as follows: "The patient is euphoric; therefore, the patient is manic and even though he lacks every other indication, he is a manic psychotic." Or similarly, "The patient has a short attack, and he recovers from the attack; because he recovers he is a manic-depressive psychotic individual and not schizophrenic because schizophrenia is a progressive disorder." Actually, schizophrenia is a progressive disorder in some cases but not in all, so the type of thinking I have demonstrated is single-tracked. This kind of thinking, by the way, is often reinforced by such things as psychometric tests. In other words, that symptoms are not properly evaluated is a tremendous failing in psychiatry. We have nothing like a Wassermann test for psychoses. We cannot apply a test somewhere in the so-called functional disorder and from that receive the proper diagnosis. Instead, we have to sit down with all the case material and attempt to evaluate it.

We cannot intuitively "sense" the diagnosis, nor can we go to the other extreme of basing the diagnosis on preconceived notions or overelaborating the clinical facts so that the forest is not seen for the trees. For instance, a psychiatrist may discover five or six very tempting and interesting psychodynamic factors, concentrate there, and overlook the fact that the patient is schizophrenic. It is amazing how often cases of schizophrenia—and I am not referring to borderline, or to pseudoneurotic, or to "lurking" cases, but to clear-cut cases of schizophrenia who are actually hallucinating—are diagnosed psychoneurotic because the psychiatrist simply sticks to one or two dynamic factors and overelaborates upon them instead of seeing the clinical picture as a whole.

Two factors of error made in diagnosis have now been pointed out.

If the psychiatrist safeguards himself from misinterpreting clinical pictures and mixing clinical observations with theoretical preconceptions, he can, in my opinion, diagnose fairly well. Surely the whole diagnostic procedure stands in need of a great deal of improvement, but it is not nearly so bad as many people advocate.

MANIC-DEPRESSIVE PSYCHOSIS VERSUS ORGANIC PSYCHOSES

The number of organic psychoses is very great. The number of organic psychoses that manifest manic or depressive affective coloring is also very great and, due to this, false diagnoses are frequently made. On the one hand, it occurs that many patients diagnosed as having manic-depressive psychosis later prove to be suffering from an organic psychosis, and, on the other hand, the reverse occurs. Obviously, the doctor's professional background and the clinical material he has at his disposal influence his attitude toward diagnosis to some extent. For instance, psychiatrists are much more likely to make the mistake of diagnosing an organic state as being manic-depressive psychosis. Also, neurologists are much more likely to make the reverse mistake, diagnosing a patient as suffering from a toxic state, or from a definite brain disease, although the patient is actually suffering from a condition which we do not consider organic in the narrower sense of the term. I confine the term "organic," at this time, to disorders in which the diagnosis is anatomically determined. We do not know the etiological origin of the manic-depressive psychosis and, although it may very well be an organic disorder, we cannot use the term with the same connotation until there are structural changes found in the brain.

The organic states are, generally speaking, differentiated from the manic-depressive psychosis on the basis of the presence of intellectual impairment, memory defects, and disorientation. Intellectual impairment does not occur in manic-depressive psychosis, regardless of how many attacks the patient has had. At times, the patient is so manic, or so depressed, that his intellectual functioning is interfered with by the speed or retardation of thoughts, but this is due basically to the altered emotional state. In organic psychosis the intellect is directly affected. Memory impairment in manic-depressive psychosis is usually only a subjective complaint of the patient, and clears up when the affective symptoms subside. In organic psychosis the memory impairment is often quite obvious to the observer and is stratified; remote memory is good and recent memory may be very poor. Disorientation in manic-depressive psychosis, as I have discussed, is not present as such, but in acute mania the confusion can resemble disorientation. Subjective expressions of thoughts or affect, furthermore, are of no value in differentiation.

I would like to point out a few aspects of the most common mistakes one is likely to encounter in differentiation. First, there is the mistake whereby the psychiatrist assumes the patient to be suffering from a manic-depressive psychosis when actually he is dealing with an organic condition.

In the past, one of the most common mistakes in this respect was in overlooking general paresis. For many years, general paresis held the center of the stage in psychiatry. Then it was rapidly pushed into the periphery; the incidence rate dropped, a curative treatment was discovered, and—when one stops to consider it—the diagnosis is so very simple and can be made independently from psychiatric symptomatology so that it is not necessary for psychiatry to play the major role diagnostically. A great deal of diagnostic acuity was once necessary to identify these cases, while at present the diagnosis is mainly established by serological tests. Prior to the serological era, hospital records were full of cases of patients who were diagnosed as having manic-depressive psychosis who actually were suffering from general paresis. Many such diagnostic errors are occurring even today, and I must warn you that the incidence of general paresis will periodically increase. Especially due to the effective treatments for early syphilis, doctors become careless about ordering serology tests as routinely as is desirable. Therefore, you may encounter many patients suffering with this disorder and it is important to know all its symptomatological pictures. Here, one or two general rules emerge which are not only applicable to cases of general paresis but also are valid for other organic conditions for which, unfortunately, we do not have a serological test and therefore diagnosis is not as easily established.

First of all, during the early phase of an organic disorder, manic or depressive coloring could very easily cover the real organic signs which are, of course, impairment of intellect, impairment in memory, and, at times, impairment in orientation. Furthermore, the manic or depressive coloring could possibly interfere with the intellectual functioning of the person to such an extent that clinical appraisal of intelligence, or test appraisal of intelligence, becomes very difficult. The depressive or manic coloring could be so marked, so intense, and so impressive, that the observations of the person appraising the case are also completely dominated by the affective state of the patient.

Secondly, at the onset of such an organic psychosis, the organic signs are not necessarily so pronounced as to be easily picked up by the observer.

Thirdly, it can happen—not often, but it can happen in isolated instances—that the manic or depressive affective manifestations in an organic case precede the intellectual impairment. This has been demonstrated to some extent in patients having an acute outbreak of general paresis.

Observations of these same symptom features that are applied to diagnosing general paresis can also be applied to diagnosing other organic conditions, such as atherosclerotic psychosis, multiple sclerosis, and so forth. Currently one of the greatest diagnostic pitfalls of all is in the case of brain tumors, particularly frontal lobe tumors.

The number of diagnoses of frontal lobe tumors missed by psychiatrists is, I would say, a rather gloomy story. The number of these misdiagnosed patients is very considerable, and the diagnoses usually preferred are quite surprising: depression, manic states, and psychoneuroses. Every year, one or two patients are operated upon in whom the correct diagnosis had not been made until long after it certainly could have been. I do not believe, however, that in the very early stage, brain tumors can invariably be diagnosed, but, after the disorder has progressed, the diagnosis is not made in many instances simply because the examiners had not even thought of the possibility. Is is very likely the patient was never given a complete examination, mental or physical.

When brain tumors, particularly frontal lobe tumors, manifest a manic or a depressive coloring, the manic or depressive clinical symptoms are usually not so intense as is observed in a true manic-depressive psychosis. The person with a brain tumor who presents a manic picture, furthermore, usually displays a rather bland euphoria. Bland euphoria indicates that this person lacks the mental acumen, the wittiness, the excellent relationship with the environment, and the contact with reality of the typical manic patient. He is mentally dull. His mind does not function very well. It is usually unproductive. Occasionally, a certain amount of silliness, or a certain amount of playfulness creeps into the picture, but he lacks the infectious vivacity of the true manic patient. Especially the extremely quick perception, the fast associative ability and the rapid responses of the manic patient are lacking in this person. If you then examine one of these patients more closely, you usually are able to demonstrate the presence of intellectual defects. However, it is more difficult to perceive these defects if the person should have a depressive, rather than manic, affective coloring.

Now, the question is, are we able to use more reliable

methods to differentially diagnose these patients? Many psychiatrists tried to do so using a psychodynamic base. I would like to warn against making the differential diagnosis of a brain tumor in a person with a depressive or a manic coloring based on dynamic constructs. Very often, these dynamists are profoundly misled. One of the most celebrated cases in this respect is that of George Gershwin, who underwent psychoanalysis for over two years, all his symptom reactions being definitely based on dynamic formulations, and finally he died of a once operable brain tumor. Dynamic patterns could very well appear the same, naturally, in different settings and it is by no means rare that an organic condition produces or releases all the disturbances of integration in the person, which obviously generate in him the same material that would be observed if the regression manifestations were present in the setting of a psychoneurosis or in the setting of a so-called functional psychosis. Therefore, the dynamic material cannot be used alone to differentiate reliably. Furthermore, organic conditions are prevalent and psychoneurotic conditions are also very prevalent; their symptom material may coincide and quite often blend into each other.

It is obvious that severly neurotic individuals may also develop an organic condition, and it is also very obvious that their neurotic dynamic organization would then also manifest itself, to some extent, in this organic condition. We have no safeguard preventing a psychoneurotic person, or a person predisposed to so-called functional psychosis, from also developing a severe organic disorder. Therefore, dynamic factors should be evaluated *only* in conjunction with other diagnostic methods.

At this time, I do not want to go into the matter of some of the rather complicated test situations to which we can expose a patient suffering with depression. I do not go into it because it is very rare to have such a person cooperating in these tests reliably enough to enable one to evaluate their results. The moment the patient is able to cooperate with tests (in other words, when the depressive or the manic coloring is so markedly lessened that the person can co-operate), you usually are able to make the diagnosis clinically. Naturally, if you desire to reinforce the clinical diagnosis by means of tests, you have a perfect right to do it, but no tests will give you an indication that the patient is suffering from an organic condition at the time when he is so disturbed emotionally that you are unable to examine him adequately clinically.

Obviously, the diagnosis can be obtained indirectly in many instances; for instance, the psychiatric condition is to some extent pushed into the background and, for example, if a brain tumor is suspected, the patient is submitted to neurological examination and all the ancillary tests that go along with it. The diagnosis may be established on those criteria. But at times that is also not possible to do, particularly in the case of frontal lobe tumors which very often have absent, or extremely meager, neurological signs. And many frontal lobe tumors have been known to occur, for instance, in which the patient's mental impairment preceded, for a long period of time, all the neurological and other physical impairments, during which time electro-encephalography, X-ray methods, and all the other diagnostic devices are often of no value either.

For a long time, people have tried to find a method for differentiating organic conditions from psychiatric conditions. We have as yet no absolute diagnostic methods. However, we have one method which, if applied by an experienced person, offers a certain amount of diagnostic help in many cases. This consists of intravenous sodium amytal solution given to the patient while he is in a manic or a depressive state. Sodium amytal influences preeminently the affective state in the patient. The depressed patient becomes relaxed; the patient who did not communicate now communicates; and the manic patient (who is not extremely manic) quiets down, and, here again, he is relaxed and you are better able to make contact with him. You are able to markedly reduce, or even eliminate, the manic or the depressive affective state which, incidentally, as I have mentioned before, is less pronounced in organic disorders than is usually observed in a typical manic-depressive individual. When contact is accomplished, you can observe what material he produces. If there are intellectual impairments present in the patient, many become manifest. For instance, if the patient has frontal lobe impairment, as do many patients with frontal lobe tumors, it will become obvious. This method is also useful in differentiating the atherosclerotic affective states from other disorders. Organic impairments in the patient receiving sodium amytal are usually not reduced; the organic mental manifestations usually remain the same or occasionally they even become underscored or aggravated. Therefore, by administering the drug many of the intellectual impairments present in organic cases, which had been covered by the depressive or manic affect, might be elicited. Simply with this technique, rather complicated and remote organic conditions have been diagnosed which were then diagnostically verified in surgery.

One must have personal experience in the use of sodium amytal for this diagnostic procedure; he must know the dynamics of the different disorders—manic-depressive psychosis, schizophrenia, psychoneurosis, and organic disorders. The technique with sodium amytal should never, moreover, be applied in such a manner that a maximum amount of the drug is injected which causes the patient to become befuddled and drowsy. When this is done, a toxic organic state is imposed over the possibly already existing organic state. Usually three, four, or five grains are sufficient to influence the emotional state of these patients and enable us to assess the other mental manifestations more effectively.

Please understand this aid correctly. This drug is merely a diagnostic adjunct. The work has to be done by you, not the drug. Many psychiatrists would like to reverse it and have the drug do the work, but that is not possible. The sodium amytal method for diagnosis is not infallible and the method itself has a few pitfalls. Nevertheless, if you are confronted with the question, "Is this person an organic case or a nonorganic case?" and if all the other investigations —neurological and medical—offer no clue to indicate that the patient is suffering from an organic condition, this method could at least be tried for diagnostic differentiation.

I would like to mention that there are rare organic conditions we neglect to consider which can produce manic or depressive affective coloring in a patient. These are two pitfalls: (1) rarely encountered organic conditions, and (2) certain intoxicants—both either rarely observed or not recognized.

Infrequently observed organic disorders which can be overlooked in the early stages include the presenile psychoses. Emotional changes occur in both Alzheimer's and Pick's diseases, being pronounced in Pick's disease where dullness, inactivity, lack of initiative, irritability, euphoria, or depression are usually evident. In contrast, Alzheimer cases often present a rather characteristic state of hyperactivity; long periods of restlessness may take the form of senseless activity. These affective changes may initially be more conspicuous to the psychiatrist than the neurological signs or even the memory defects which are early symptoms in both diseases. Diagnostic errors could occur if these patients (predominantly female) are not given thorough clinical examination.

I can present examples of two instances of toxic affect disorders I have observed recently, both of which are rarely encountered. One patient suffered from brucellosis and the other from scopolamine poisoning. Both demonstrated typical pictures, one of the manic and the other of the depressive state. In both individuals, the symptoms were mild, which probably added to the diagnostic confusion. If the symptoms had been pronounced, probably suspicion would have been aroused. Therefore, with certain patients, we should think that it may very well be that we are dealing with one of the innumerable organic possibilities, especially if the whole clinical picture does not click into place and especially if we are dealing with individuals having any predisposition to a given disorder with which it could be linked.

A reverse type of situation also frequently occurs, however, and this happens much less often with psychiatrists than with neurologists or other medical men who are dominated preeminently by an organic concept of disease. They consistently try to diagnose every mental condition as being based on a definite organic pathology. In this sense, it is not rare for you to find cases which a medical man or a neurologist will try very hard to convince you is a disorder due to a trauma, to an intoxication, to some other organic condition although actually the patient in this particular instance is suffering from manic-depressive psychosis. Such peculiar situations are not rare. I recall, for example, the case of a patient who had been treated for a mild infection with a sulfanilamide drug. A few of the sulfanilamide derivatives are perfectly capable of producing manic or depressive pictures as well as hypochondriacal delusions, which occur quite often in organic psychoses. This patient manifested a depressive picture with a number of hypochondriacal ideas and the physician treating him thought these symptoms due to drug intoxication. However, the patient remained depressed and in a mental hospital for several weeks after he had received small doses of the sulfanilamide. He was treated as a depressive, recovered as a depressive psychotic patient, and it was later discovered he had had a previous depressive episode of the same type years before. So errors occur, naturally, quite often on this level. Also, when somebody attempts to explain symptoms, slight deviations from the usual in the clinical picture can occasionally be misleading.

I would like to quote another case; that of a physician, a very capable physician, who developed a depression. His depression was manifested by symptoms of marked fatigue, marked drowsiness, and inability to work efficiently which often, naturally, accompanies a depression. For several reasons, one being that a mental disorder for him was intolerable, he constantly groped for an explanation on an organic basis. Because he was constipated and had a drowsy feeling he began to develop two ideas which actually were overvalued ideas and were close to being delusional. He thought he was either suffering from a neoplasm of the intestines or a brain tumor. To exclude these disorders, he underwent a number of examinations and finally received a clean bill of health so far as his abdomen was concerned. But, he consulted a neuropsychiatrist who obtained an electroencephalogram on him; the electroencephalogram disclosed vague wave formations which that particular electroencephalographer described as "abnormal." Naturally, to the physician-patient this result, combined with his overvalued ideas, gave him the certainty that he had a brain tumor, and he underwent innumerable examinations for that by I-do-not-know-how-many professional people. Now, to make a long story shorter, an additional electro- encephalogram disclosed the same abnormalities as before but, when properly evaluated, it was determined they were tension-discharges which are, of course, quite common. These tension-discharges had, naturally, nothing to do with an organic condition. The doctor-patient recovered then, after appropriate treatment, and was able himself to correct his ideas. Such events occur at times, and the final diagnostic decision has to come from the psychiatrist.

Many medical men, including neurologists, have a tendency to appoint an organic cause underlying all mental symptoms, and the case has to then be evaluated by a psychiatrist. Only the psychiatrist can evaluate the extent to which all the findings are conclusive for underlying organic conditions. For instance, in the case of a person taking a certain drug, could that drug itself be a toxic cause of the disorder? Or could that encephalographic find- ing, or could the slight change in the sedimentation rate, or could this-or-that finding which is present, indicate an organic disorder responsible for a mental manifestation?

MANIC-DEPRESSIVE PSYCHOSIS VERSUS INVOLUTIONAL DEPRESSIONS

Involutional depression is an important diagnostic entity from a prognostic and a therapeutic point of view. Historically speaking, all the involutional psychotic pictures were originally placed under the heading of manic-depressive psychosis. Then it was discovered that there are also features other than "melancholia" present in involutional psychosis. A few clinics, especially abroad, still do not differentiate between involutional psychosis and manic-depressive psychosis, particularly in dealing with the depressed form of the latter. Kraepelin himself, and to a greater extent his pupil, Dreyfus, spent considerable time and energy following up cases and classifying this psychosis; they left it in the framework of the manic-depressive psychosis, although it had already become clear to Kraepelin that there actually are melancholias occurring in the involutional age group which also manifest clinical features and prognostic features different from those observed in manic-depressive psychosis (3). (At that time, naturally, therapeutic features were not stressed since the more effective treatments had not been introduced.) Then gradually, in England and the United States under the influence of Gillespie (3), the tendency became more and more marked to differentiate involutional psychosis from manic-depressive psychosis, and we now treat involutional psychosis as a separate diagnostic entity. Although a few cases display clinical symptomatology similar to that observed in manic-depressive depression, they also manifest features which are different.

I would now like to discuss first the similarities, and then the dissimilarities which led to the differentiation. The similarities are easy to recognize: both manifest depression. (Incidentally, a clinical entity of involutional mania does not exist, which in itself is rather interesting.)

The involutional depressions clinically, furthermore, often present features which we do not often observe in patients suffering from manic-depressive psychosis, particularly those in the younger age group. That does not mean, however, that you do not occasionally observe depressed pictures in an involutional patient which are strikingly similar to those in a true manic-depressive patient, or that, conversely, you do not observe in a typical manic-depressive patient a clinical picture different from that in an involutional patient. The bulk of involutional patients, however, and the bulk of manic-depressive depressed patients, each manifest somewhat different symptomatology.

First of all, in what manner do the symptomatologies that are similar in both involutional depression and manic-depressive psychosis differ in their clinical features? Involutional depressions usually display two or three elements which are not so pronounced in the other depressive disorders, namely, (1) the *anxiety* is much more conspicuous, (2) the *agitation* is much more conspicuous, and (3) the expression of *hypochondriacal preoccupation* is much more conspicuous. Now, as I have mentioned, all of these symptoms may occur in a manic-depressive depressed patient.

Anxiety, and at times obsessive-compulsive manifestations in addition to anxiety, or phobic manifestations occurring as an expression of anxiety, can also occur in manic-depressive patients and, at times, even so markedly as to actually replace the depressive symptomatology so that such cases are diagnosed psychoneurotic. But again, in the involutional melancholias these markedly anxious, and at times phobic, pictures are much more prevalent. The symptom formation of anxiety, and the symptom formation of agitation, in involutional depression is also more diffused than is observed in psychoneurotic individuals. It is usually all-pervading, being present in every realm of activity. Anxiety in the psychoneurotic person usually remains much more focalized or, if it is not focalized, there is a fairly long history of its spreading from one area to others. Diffused distribution of anxiety, diffused distribution of noncoping, again, usually speak more for a psychotic mechanism.

Agitated depression—the second pronounced element in involutional depression—can, however, occur in any depressive setting and is not synonymous with involutional depression. In true manic-depressive psychosis, in the younger age group especially, episodes of agitated depression can occur, and for a long time, therefore, agitated depression was considered by many as one of the subgroups in the manic-depressive psychosis. However, the clinical picture of agitated depression occurs most frequently in patients suffering from an involutional depression.

As the designation implies, agitated depression is marked by the tendency of the patient who, although he is retarded in thinking and although he is depressed, manifests agitation instead of psychomotor retardation. In the ordinary depression, the whole individual is slowed down—intellectually, emotionally, vegetatively, and in psychomotor functioning. The agitated depressed patients will also manifest depression: They feel blue, they feel depressed, they express their feelings in a manner very similar to patients in ordinary depression. But, instead of being retarded they are restless, they feel driven, and, if the melancholia is rather deep, many of them are agitated. These patients usually move about; they are fidgety, they pace the floor, they groan and moan and wring their hands. In other words, they usually display increased psychomotor activity similar to that observed in manic patients. There are psychiatrists who have even tried to explain these agitated melancholias as being a mixture of a depression with certain phases of a mania, the manic feature being manifested by the increased psychomotor activity. The pictures of excitation, the marked psychomotor discharge may give the appearance of manic coloring, but they are not elated or euphoric; they are depressed. In involutional psychosis, naturally, manic pictures do not occur. If they do occur, you are most likely dealing with a case of manic-depressive psychosis.

Now, these states of agitation at times impress you as simply being a form of motor discharge of tension and anxiety. That may be the case for some individuals. However, in others the agitation is very intimately linked to delusional formation, or to hallucinations which are, naturally, linked to the delusions. If a patient hears a voice telling him that the police are about to come to take him away, or that he will be executed because of his misdeeds, it is obvious that such a patient will reactively become agitated since he regards these ideas as actuality. We must always take into consideration and accept the point of view of the patient: To him all his ideas are reality! Naturally, the patient acts just as he would in any such reality situation. It is clear that many patients having self-accusatory ideas mixed with paranoid ideas become upset and extremely agitated if they believe they are going to be killed, or will be harmed, or some other thing will be done to them in keeping with whatever ideation they have in connection with their delusional formation. So, you will realize these agitations in acutely depressed patients are not simply a form of motor discharge; such an assumption cannot be demonstrated. If you think of it as such, you may not fully know about the patient with whom you are dealing. However, it is quite possible that there are individuals who will discharge motor activity and in whom agitation is not based on an ideational level, but I must emphasize that in many patients agitation is definitely linked to the mental trend or to the content of the patient's hallucinatory and delusional experience.

Hypochondriacal preoccupations—the third pronounced element—are also very prevalent and conspicuous in involutional depressed patients. They usually feel their organs are not functioning properly, that the heart is not functioning, that the brain is decaying, and so forth. As occurs in other depressive states, preoccupation with the gastro-intestinal tract and especially with the cardiovascular apparatus, is very much in the foreground. Many of these patients are older individuals in whom fear of death or fear of suffering from a serious organic disease has much more emotional connotation than it has for a younger individual. Such fears are therefore very often elaborated upon. The interesting thing is that quite a number of depressed patients in the involutional group do not stop at simply expressing hypochondriacal ideas, or even hypochondriacal or somatic delusions. Many of the delusions become rather peculiar, rather bizarre, and at times quite nihilistic. The patient may tell you, "My bowels are gone," "I have no heart," "My brain is completely decayed," "I have no digestion anymore," and so forth. Such delusional formations may remind us of schizophrenic delusions in their organization and many observers feel that, phenomenologically, probably many of these cases are not clear-cut involutional depressions.

Actually delusional formations appear in which the individuals think they will in some way annihilate everybody and everything; they can annihilate the whole world. This is actually a paranoid delusion in reverse and falls into the same evaluation. It is basically observed much more often in schizophrenia, although it can be observed in depression. Some observers do not interpret these delusions as paranoid mechanisms, but interpret them as exaggerations of self-accusatory ideas in that, to actually relieve the guilt, the person develops ideas that he will be punished and he will even be annihilated because he is capable of annihilating everybody around him. In connection with this, the involutional patient has a very strongly sadistic attitude toward the environment and sometimes attacks others. This is often apparent in the so-called "larval" depressions observed in the involutional period and even in the noninvolutional period. Incidentally, I would like to call attention to the fact that a great deal of grandiosity, or grandiose tinge, present in this type of ideation is very similar to the grandiose tinge seen in many paranoid patients.

Ideas of self-accusation are quite prevalent and are usually very marked in these states of agitated depression, although you will also observe, particularly if the depression is mild, many cases of involutional depression in which self-accusatory ideations are not present at all. Self-accusations are usually centered around the idea of an "unpardonable sin." The patient recalls very small misdeeds from childhood, such as having disobeyed a rule, magnifies the act to the level of a sin, and expresses a great deal of extreme self-condemnation for this. This is not uncommon. However, you will observe many patients who do not have any such ideas at all, and even if you offer them ideas for self-accusation, they reject them, stating that they would prefer to select their own sins, but do not have such ideas. They are not self condemnatory and not self-accusatory.

Many of the self-condemnatory ideas, furthermore, are secondary and have to be studied in relation to the existing emotional structure. One must realize that in all mental disturbances carrying a pessimistic or negative connotation to the patient, regardless of whether they are in the setting of psychoneurosis or in the setting of manic-depressive or schizophrenic psychosis, one single issue very clearly emerges: the inability of the person to cope with certain situations or with life in general, and the feeling of a marked handicap in relation to life situations. Around this, then, a great amount of material can become organized, and quite a number of the patient's ideations are secondary, being attempts to cope with the realization of this handicap. The patient also often tries to blame himself and to rationalize his handicap and inability—a mechanism which is exactly the same as the one we are familiar with in the psychoneurotic individual. The tendency of these patients to offer explanations as to why they are sick, or why they became sick, is naturally full of these rationalizations.

I would also like to mention here that, as is similar in the manic-depressive psychosis, the sensorium of individuals suffering with involutional depression remains clear. Impairment of intellect, memory, and orientation occurs only if the person's depression is extremely profound, or if the disorder occurring in the involutional age bracket is complicated by cerebral atherosclerosis. If you perceive any impairment of intellect or memory, it is due to emotional factors and usually disappears when the emotional disorder abates. Complaints, however, about impairment of mental functioning, especially impairment of memory, are expressed very frequently by these patients. Often these are among their first complaints: They feel tired, they feel exhausted, they cannot sleep, they cannot think, they are unable to concentrate, and so forth. However, objectively speaking, an impairment is not present, or present only to the extent observed in other emotional states. Naturally, the patient's emotional preoccupation could easily lead to difficulty in thinking and could interfere with his mnemic process, but there is no such thing as deterioration occurring in involutional melancholia. From that point of view, it is classified as an affective disorder related to the manic-depressive psychosis in which such phenomena also do not occur.

The main dissimilarities observed between the involutional and the true manic-depressive psychosis are threefold in terms of (1) *prognosis,* (2) *personality structure,* and (3) *ideational content.*

Persons who develop involutional melancholia usually have only one episode of the psychosis. The duration may be one year, but more often it lasts two, three, or even four years. In other words, the involutional melancholia has a tendency to have a *more prolonged course* than an ordinary manic-depressive depression. Nevertheless, however, an episode of involutional depression has *no tendency to recur.* If it recurs, especially periodically, the psychosis is more likely to belong in the manic-depressive and not in the involutional diagnostic group.

Therefore, from a prognostic point of view, involutional psychosis is a more serious disorder than manic-depressive depression in the sense that, if the patient is not treated, the duration is much longer. On the other hand, the prognosis is much better from the point of view of fair assurance that, when the involutional patient has recovered from the psychotic depression, it will not recur. In many cases the oscillations of depression in the psychosis are mistaken for recovery although actually the patient is still in a psychotic state. Based on such cases, you occasionally read reports of involutional patients having recurrences of the psychosis two, three, or four times. Actually, however, these are patients who demonstrate a continuous psychotic course having peaks and vales. When a patient is really and truly recovered from an involutional psychosis, the possibility of recurrence is rather slim. So, that is quite naturally a point of differentiation from the manic-depressive psychosis which usually has periodic attacks. On the other hand, I must remind you of the fact that 30 to 40 percent of manic-depressive patients also have only one attack in their lives. Therefore, this is surely no differential diagnostic criterion in any absolute sense.

The second factor used in differentiating involutional psychosis from manic-depressive depression is the *previous personality make-up* of the individuals. Since the time of Kretschmer it has been felt that in manic-depressive psychosis the pyknic body build on the one hand and the cyclothymic emotional organization on the other hand are factors to be stressed. This was also linked with a few observations of Jung, Bleuler, and others on "extroversion." In other words, it was felt that manic-depressive psychosis occurs mainly in individuals having a pyknic body build, in persons having a cyclothymic personality organization, and in those who are "extroverted" and who, relatively speaking, make very good social contact.

If you examine cases of involutional melancholia—as was done extensively by Hinkley and others *(3)* a number of years ago—immediately the fact emerges that they do not follow this configuration of persons suffering from a true manic-depressive psychosis. First of all, the body build is not that of a pyknic; quite a number of asthenic, athletic, and dysplastic individuals are in this group. Secondly, they are not cyclothymic; in other words, they do not display mood swings. Thirdly, they usually manifest an obsessive-compulsive undertow which is more conspicuous than that also claimed to be present in some manic-depressive patients.

Involutional melancholia is regarded as being pre-eminently a disorder of female patients, although it occurs more frequently in males than had been formerly assumed. Usually you find that a woman who, when in the involutional age period, swings into an involutional depression, was a woman who was formerly somewhat withdrawn, who was "sensitive," "thin-skinned," rather meticulous, pedantic, and compulsive in life approach, who was very easily deranged by difficulties, indecisive, and markedly ambivalent, who was sexually inadequate and probably frigid. Very often the description of the personality make-up of these patients is much more obviously schizothymic than cyclothymic by our present classification. Therefore, we are dealing with individuals having a personality make-up closer to that of schizophrenic individuals, but who develop melancholia from which they recover eventually.

The third dissimilarity from the manic-depressive psychosis lies in the observation that quite a number of involutional melancholia patients have depressions that are not completely "pure" in a clinical sense. They have more or less *bizarre hysterical or paranoid ideational admixtures.* Paranoid admixtures were especially stressed in patients who, in addition to being depressed, display marked paranoid ideation having an organization very similar to that which you observe in the so-called "paraphrenias" or in paranoid schizophrenic individuals. The patient thinks he is being observed, being followed, being manipulated, that his bowels are not simply absent but have been removed, that his brain is not decayed but every night somebody is picking out his thoughts with some apparatus, and he is being influenced in various ways. Many of the paranoid delusions are topical in that they might still be regarded as secondary to the patient's depressive affect. In other words, the depressed

patient feels he must be annihilated because he is not functioning well, or he is not performing well, or he committed
a sin. However, a few of these paranoid delusions are outright primary, having no linkage to the depressive content.
These paranoid admixtures are present in many involutional
depressed patients and such admixtures indicate that probably these patients are actually schizophrenic.

The involutional group can be differentiated into the
following classifications: (1) The true "involutional melancholia" as that psychosis in which the preeminent picture is
depression, and where paranoid or bizarre ideational symptomatology is absent or occurs only very mildly. (2) An intermediary group is that psychosis in which the depressive
picture is mixed with paranoid symptomatology. Finally,
(3) the group in which the patient actually only expresses
paranoid delusional content, and because it appeared at the
involutional age it was designated "involutional psychosis,
paranoid trend." So far as I am concerned, those in the third
category are actually cases of paranoid schizophrenia.
Because that also occurs rather late in life, I think the
involutional designation simply indicates the age period in
which it occurs but I do not believe it has any great etiological significance. A few people, however, feel that some
of the endocrine reorganization or the mental reorganization
in the individual during involutional age warrants designating such patients "involutional, paranoid." I have never
been able to convince myself that these patients are really
clinically different from the paranoid schizophrenic.

Authorized classification systems are extremely conser-
vative and, similar to changes in law, run very far behind the
changes in attitudes and practices. We always observe many
features of classifications which are no longer considered
correct. One day, when I was working at one of the State
hospitals, the clinical director handed me a letter he had
received from the State capitol stating that we had seven
"paraphrenias" missing compared to the previous year's
statistics. So, then there was some talk about filling in the

gap by delivering the inconspicuous statistics of seven "para-phrenias" although by that time nobody cared. Recently I attended a hospital conference in which a psychiatrist presented a paper claiming excellent results with the use of electro-convulsive therapy for the psychoneuroses, contrary to observations of most people experienced in the field. Then the interesting fact emerged: In that particular hospital, 30 percent of all admissions were diagnosed "psycho-neurosis," which is simply incredible. When he read the abstracts of a few patients, he presented the following:

Case 1: A sixty-four-year-old man, who had formerly been perfectly well, developed a depression; received 4 ECT; recovered.
Diagnosis: psychoneurosis.

Case 2: A sixty-two-year-old woman, suffering with Parkinson's syndrome, developed a depression which was interpreted as reactive to Parkinson's disease; again, ECT; again recovery.
Diagnosis: psychoneurosis.

When these diagnoses were questioned by several psychiatrists present, including myself, the assistant superintendent of the particular hospital made the statement that they were made according to the manual which had been worked out by the best brains in the State hospital system, forgetting that the manual can be quite adequate but the application of it can still be wrong. So, this is the sort of thing with which one has to contend.

Of course, we must realize that as long as we are dealing with diagnosis on a phenomenonological basis and as long as we do not have any etiological basis for diagnosis, these error factors will remain because, surely, it is often difficult for people who have not had a great deal of clinical experience, to make a diagnostic differentiation between a psychoneurosis and depressive disorders. It is not easy! There are times when you have more or less of a "hunch" that the diagnosis is one disorder or another, without actually being able to supply all the scientific reasons for making your differentiation, but still any marked discrepancies could be corrected.

The prognosis of involutional melancholia, as I have indicated, is not so favorable in terms of duration but is fairly good in terms of having no repetition. Furthermore, it is a basic rule that the more the patient manifests paranoid or bizarre symptom admixtures, in addition to emotional changes, the worse the prognosis. This, again, follows along the lines of the schizophrenias; disorganization patterns, paranoid evaluation patterns, or bizarre thinking occur only in persons when their reality relationship is markedly disturbed. In such cases we are dealing with rather profound ego alterations. As August Hoch has pointed out *(1915)*, generally the more the patient manifests symptom admixtures the less the possibility for recovery.

The more the picture becomes frankly paranoid and the more the clinical picture resembles that of true paranoid schizophrenia, the more the person will follow the trend we observe in paranoid schizophrenia. It has been claimed that involutional patients with a paranoid picture are not cases of true paranoid schizophrenia because they do not deteriorate. That is not always correct; many do deteriorate. However, even in clear-cut cases of paranoid schizophrenia, deterioration is often so gradual and so inconclusive that we cannot simply state that we diagnose them as being schizophrenic only when they deteriorate. Not every schizophrenic patient, especially not every paranoid schizophrenic patient, manifests a deteriorating trend. Therefore, we usually diagnose cases of depressions occurring in the involutional period as follows: "Involutional depression" if there are no symptom admixtures, and "involutional psychosis, mixed" if there are symptom admixtures present. I, personally, do not use the designation "involutional psychosis, paranoid"; others do. I think they are cases of schizophrenia; very often the whole structure of the personality make-up in these patients could be traced back many years and the psychosis is actually only a culmination of a condition which had been profoundly wrong for a very long time. Why certain individuals manifest this form of disintegration in this particular manner so late in life and others earlier, we do not know.

Bleuler at one time acknowledged, with some reservations, the Kraepelinian ideas on "paranoia" and "paraphrenia." Now they are no longer regarded as separate entities. I think that although Bleuler viewed schizophrenia as a rather widespread disorder, he became, as did a great many other psychiatrists, somewhat afraid that we were very rapidly heading toward the concept that there is actually only one mental disorder, that being schizophrenia. This concept naturally disturbed a great many workers in the past and continues to disturb quite a number at present.

Actually, most likely the situation will take shape this way: Seemingly there are one or two universal, or collective, reaction patterns. We observe that in somatic pathology, also. Consider, for example, inflammation. The pattern in all inflammations has very similar features, and the common end paths for all inflammations is the same even though the etiological mechanisms in different cases are very different. Now, I personally visualize that the same reaction pattern principle applies to the mental disorders. Therefore, I am not at all disturbed that schizophrenia is so prevalent. To me it simply means we have a definite reaction pattern whereby some of the common end paths are similar but probably different etiological mechanisms enter into it. Those psychiatrists, however, who perceive these reaction patterns as disease entities are, naturally, very jealous of their view and constantly fear stakes are being taken away from their concepts of certain well-defined, or in their minds well-defined, disease entities.

A few of the basic ideas held by many people, which are not sharply formulated clinically, will have to be better formulated, and I think that one of these days they will be.

Actually, immediately after Kraepelin introduced his ideas of so many separate entities such as "paraphrenia," Forchet (who is not very well known here) was the first to point out that we are actually dealing with reactions, and that these reactions are probably confined to one, two, or three in number. Consider, for instance, any organ in the body; it usually has only two or three reaction patterns in response to any involvement. And most likely the nervous system, also, has only a few limited reaction patterns. Therefore, the idea that each mental disorder is a separate and different disease is not very well substantiated. Etiologically, there are probably a great many conditions which can lead to one or more of the few reaction patterns available.

MANIC-DEPRESSIVE PSYCHOSIS VERSUS SCHIZOPHRENIA

We shall now discuss the most difficult, and probably the most important, differential problem in the diagnosis of the manic-depressive psychosis: the differentiation between manic-depressive psychosis and schizophrenia. One might ask, "Why should we take all the pains to do that?" For many years that issue was actually the only content of staff meetings at a few State hospitals; at a clinical presentation some members of the staff would diagnose the case manic-depressive psychosis while the others would consider it a case of schizophrenia. Then the case would be tabled as "diagnostically inconclusive" or "undifferentiated psychosis," and the patient was discharged or retained. It was a very nice kind of acrobatics but nothing came of it.

Now, as I have mentioned, I think we do not yet know if the clinical entity manic-depressive psychosis, as we apply the term, really exists. From a clinical point of view, in my opinion, that is not even very important. The important thing is that certain clinical pictures, regardless of their etiologies and where they belong diagnostically, show certain behavior which is extremely important for our prognostication and application of therapy. If somebody should say to me that he does not recognize manic-depressive psychosis as a separate entity, that is his privilege. Nevertheless, he surely will have to admit that persons who manifest the classical manic, or the classical depressive, symptomatology without admixtures, do in fact behave differently prognostically and in therapeutic response than do, for instance, catatonic schizophrenic or paranoid schizophrenic persons. This in no way implies that the etiology for the different disorders cannot be the same.

Physical medicine in the 19th century was revolutionized by the observation that conditions based on the same etiology can clinically manifest themselves differently, and the reverse can also occur. This, naturally, is also valid in psychiatry although we cannot apply it as clearly as most other branches of medicine can. Syphilis and tuberculosis, to mention only two, manifest such varied clinical pictures that if you did not know the etiological agent of each disorder you would believe that all their different clinical manifestations are caused by a single etiological agent. In psychiatry, therefore, we do not know whether the etiological agent might not also be the same despite widely divergent clinical pictures.

The present issue is how do the manic-depressive and schizophrenic disorders behave clinically with regard to prognosis and therapy? In each disorder the clinical pictures, as we observe them at the present time, behave, to some extent, differently. This is why we differentiate; we differentiate essentially because the prognosis of manic-depressive psychosis is more favorable than that of schizophrenia (this is not a statement valid for every case, but is a generalization based on statistical averages), and because the therapeutic response in the manic-depressive psychosis is also more favorable than in schizophrenia.[1] Whether the

----

[1] Dr. Hoch's views on prognosis and therapy in these disorders remain only generally valid; considerable psychopharmacological advances have since been made.—*Eds.*

manic-depressive's response to therapy is as favorable as that of a patient with a nonnuclear form of schizophrenia is open to question. Nevertheless, clinically there are two opposite poles. At one pole are the cases of manic-depressive psychosis, which never manifest deterioration and the prognosis is rather favorable insofar as each attack is concerned. At the other pole are those schizophrenic patients having the tendency for rapid deterioration and poor prognosis, and with limited response to all the therapeutic approaches known at the present time.

Certain basic issues should be mentioned at this point. In some respects diagnostic approach has changed since the first quarter of this century, and many patients who were formerly placed in the manic-depressive group are now placed in the schizophrenic diagnostic group. The questions arise: Why has this occurred and on what principles does this change in attitude rest? Actually, the change came about based on rather simple observations. A number of hospitals began follow-up studies. As I have mentioned before, follow-up studies were introduced originally by Kraepelin and his school, then were not employed with his same regularity or to the same extent, and then later were reactivated. These reactivated follow-up studies demonstrated that a large number of patients originally diagnosed in the manic-depressive group were finally recognized to be schizophrenic individuals. When the structure of these patients was studied, both as it appeared in the follow-up and also in retrospect, it became possible to reconstruct many of the diagnostic errors, why the errors were made, and how the diagnosis probably could have been made originally. I would like to review with you a few of the major points which emerged from such studies to discern how, in retrospect, the diagnosis could have been correctly made.

It has often been stated that in psychiatry we have not shown any progress at all except for changes in the nomenclature; that patients are simply reclassified every few years in a different way, and that is then sold to the public as psychiatric progress. Now, I do not believe that to be the situation. These criticisms are always somewhat loosely made. Psychiatry has probably always been overly pre-occupied with classification schemes, but, on the other hand, the classification schemes indicate the great insecurity with regard to many of the foundations on which psychiatric appraisal of a patient rests. However, if you trace diagnostic ability or acumen of many psychiatrists, you will find their diagnostic ability is not so inadequate as it appears to those who criticize it very severely.

Provided that patients are examined by psychiatrists familiar with the dynamics as well as the descriptive pictures of manic-depressive psychosis and schizophrenia, the follow-ing points will emerge regarding their approach in assessing their patients diagnostically. First of all, they will try to avoid certain pitfalls which, to you, will probably sound extremely elementary, but which are, nevertheless, pits into which a large number of psychiatrists are falling every day even though they should know better. The main pitfalls concern the failure to assess properly a patient's (1) *clinical course,* (2) *symptomatology,* (3) *family background,* and (4) *personality structure.*

THE CLINICAL COURSE: In many hospitals it had been customary in the past to diagnose psychotic patients on the basis of the *rapidity of onset,* the *duration* of the episode, and the extent of the patient's *restitution* to the prepsychotic state following the attack. All three diagnostic criteria are invalid when applied to a particular patient.

First of all, a *sudden onset* is not more characteristic for manic-depressive psychosis than schizophrenia. There are quite a number of schizophrenic patients who display an onset that is acute, and perhaps very acute. I personally have the feeling that an extremely sudden onset is much more characteristic of schizophrenia. In manic-depressive psychosis a certain time elapses during which the patient feels somewhat blue, or somewhat manicy, before the symptoms actually erupt in full force; but neither do I mean to deny that such a phenomenon occurs whereby the person awakens with a depression, or awakens with a manic attack, or is suddenly reactive to a situation, having felt well the previous day. Nevertheless, you will observe many more acute schizophrenic reactions than acute manic-depressive reactions.

Secondly, the *duration* of a psychosis does not determine whether or not a patient is suffering from a manic-depressive psychosis; in a proper diagnostic evaluation this has absolutely nothing to do with the type of psychosis present. It is a misconception to assume that if a patient had a short-lived psychotic episode it must always be manic-depressive psychosis, and if a patient had a prolonged psychotic episode it must always be schizophrenia. We have observed in schizophrenia short-running and long-running attacks and, as we pointed out, in manic-depressive psychosis short- and long-running attacks also occur. Incidentally, when attempting to evaluate the duration of an attack to some extent, an interesting phenomenon emerged in many follow-up studies: The extremely short-lived psychotic attacks are almost invariably classified as being in the framework of schizophrenia and not manic-depressive psychosis. We observe the very acute "three-day schizophrenia" episodes, but we do not observe "three-day depressions" or "three-day manias" occurring in the manic-depressive psychosis. (I am referring here, of course, to patients having spontaneous psychotic episodes and spontaneous remissions, not those having any form of therapeutic intervention.) Such very short psychotic episodes are most likely not manic-depressive because, in this psychosis, the attack usually has a crescendo curve type of onset, then becomes more intensified and reaches a peak, and then, in a decrescendo curve, it disappears. However, we should not evaluate the diagnosis of a patient on the basis of how long or how short the attack is.

When Rachlin and I *(1941)* studied the relative structures of manic-depressive psychosis and schizophrenia, we reviewed approximately 5,000 cases, which is a rather large amount of material. We found it amazing how many of these 5,000 patients had been described correctly and, not only that, had even been diagnosed correctly upon admission. Then, certain patients recovered after a period of four or six weeks or three months, and their diagnosis of schizophrenia was thereby changed to manic-depressive psychosis on the basis of the rapid recovery. This misconception rested on two old ideas: that schizophrenic patients never recover and that manic-depressive patients always recover. That is, naturally, a very nice black-and-white concept, but it did not turn out to be true.

This leads us to the third misconception: that the *restitution* of the patient to the so-called prepsychotic level is a diagnostic criterion. It is correct that a manic-depressive patient usually recovers from the episode; at least 90 percent of them recover sooner or later from the particular episode. The reverse concept, however, that schizophrenic patients do not recover, is incorrect. Many schizophrenic patients recover, or have remissions, or whichever expression one uses. In other words, they often reintegrate very nicely, and a great many people are in society whom nobody ever suspects have had a schizophrenic episode. In fact, if you compare patients having so-called spontaneous developments and spontaneous remissions of psychosis, many more will fall into the schizophrenic diagnostic group than into the manic-depressive group because schizophrenia is far more prevalent.

You will most likely observe, however, that manic-depressive patients always return to their prepsychotic level when they recover from an attack, while schizophrenic patients, especially if the psychotic episode was of considerable duration or severity, actually will manifest some scarring, some emotional blunting, some interference with their organization in relationship to their environment. Scarring, which was described so accurately by Bleuler, is clearly demonstrable in a great many schizophrenic individuals, but not invariably. There are a number of acute catatonic patients in whom a restitution seemingly takes place during intervals between attacks, and only extremely refined methods of clinical examination demonstrate any scarring. Therefore, applying the diagnostic criterion of clinical restitution in patients following an acute psychotic state is not valid, although if they manifest positively any emotional blunting or any thinking disorganization or any behavioral patterns which may at times be bizarre, the possibility of the diagnosis being schizophrenia is, naturally, much greater.

THE SYMPTOMATOLOGY: We must always observe the complete symptomatology in order to properly evaluate a patient, as I have stressed. Unfortunately, different psychiatrists utilize different criteria in diagnosing patients. One psychiatrist may evaluate on the basis of the patient's affective symptoms and omit consideration of all other symptoms present. Another psychiatrist evaluating the same patient might take into consideration another set of symptoms. This matter is important because the type of symptom material used obviously has a great deal of influence on the studies of prognosis or studies of treatment method. Statistics on therapeutic procedures are often very confusing because not all the investigators utilized the same basic clinical material, and, depending upon which material they used, they were led to different diagnostic conclusions.

Diagnosis being based on phenomenology, a great variety exists in the approach of the psychiatrist appraising a case, and thus, naturally, the criteria are often very subjectively chosen. This is obvious, for example, when we review the marked changes in the ratio between the number of cases diagnosed manic-depressive psychosis and those diagnosed schizophrenia in the different hospitals over a period of time. Usually, when the hospital changes its superintendent or clinical director, diagnostic ratios of psychoses change markedly, indicating that apparently the criteria for making diagnoses fluctuates according to the observer and are not based on any single underlying principle for evaluating.

Therefore, to properly evaluate a patient you must try to ascertain the entire array of symptoms present. You should not be misled into thinking, for example, that because a patient displays depressive or manic symptomatology, the patient invariably belongs in the manic-depressive diagnostic category. You always must examine the patient to search for additional psychic deviations. If the manic or depressive manifestations are pure, or relatively pure, the diagnosis of manic-depressive psychosis may be justified. If, however, the manic or depressive affect appears flat and lacks emotional conviction to the observer, if the patient is feeling detached and uninvolved and having difficulty externalizing emotion to the environment, you must look further for symptoms of another psychotic disorder. The manic-depressive psychotic patient usually provokes empathy from those in his environment. Furthermore, if there are a great many admixtures of symptoms present in the patient, (to be discussed later), you must evaluate them to determine whether you are dealing with a form of mixed psychotic picture, with which you cannot decide definitely to which psychosis it belongs, or are dealing with a schizophrenic patient presenting manic or depressive coloring, as is more often the case. At this point, I would like to mention two issues that are diagnostic pitfalls if not properly interpreted: the consideration of the patient's family background and the so-called personality make-up in relation to the psychosis.

THE FAMILY BACKGROUND: The presence or absence of manic-depressive psychosis in the family tree has often been a factor utilized to determine the diagnosis in a positive or a negative sense. Manic-depressive psychosis, from genetic data, actually is prevalent in certain families. It is, however, not fully determined or agreed to what extent manic-

depressive psychosis occurs in families in which schizophrenia also occurs. The literature on this question is divided.
There are people who believe manic-depressive psychosis
and schizophrenia never occur in the same family; other
people feel there is sufficient material to indicate that in a
family a few members can suffer from manic-depressive
psychosis and others from schizophrenia. The issue is not
settled.

From the large amount of material which Rachlin and
I had studied, our impression was that if you are dealing
with a patient in whom the basic symptomatology is not fully
clear and if a member, a close member, of the patient's
family is suffering from a schizophrenic psychosis, the possibility that your patient is also a person who is schizophrenic
is rather great. The problem should always be evaluated
from this point of view because schizophrenia has a stronger
genetic penetrating power, if you want to express it this way,
than has manic-depressive psychosis. If schizophrenia is
present in other family members, it often will break through
in patients manifesting an atypical form of psychosis.

PERSONALITY STRUCTURE: An individual's personality
make-up is often utilized to argue for the diagnosis of a
psychotic picture one way or another. It is usually argued on
three levels: (1) the *body build*, (2) the personality as it
appears in the patient's *anamnesis*, and (3) the personality as
it appears in *psychological tests*. All three factors can and
should be evaluated, but I would definitely like to warn you
not to establish psychiatric diagnosis based on any one of
them without taking into full consideration the entire clinical
picture. The clinical picture, to this day, remains paramount
in the evaluation of the patient. These other factors are all
auxiliary, more or less important auxiliary, measures, but
the diagnosis should never be based on them. It should not
be based on them because many of these evaluations are not
convincingly worked out in full.

Since the time of Kretschmer, the diagnosis of an individual's emotional make-up has often been linked with the *body build*. It is not rare that when you speak to a psychiatrist he will state, "The diagnosis on this patient is manic-depressive psychosis because he has a pyknic body build." First of all, you have to ask him what his idea of "pyknic" is. Then you will discover astonishing issues: He labels dysplastic type patients pyknic; that he actually does not know how to differentiate body types well because he has never dealt with the concepts, and that he is absolutely unversed in the anthropological approach for measurements of body build. There is confusion in the differentiation between dysplastic and pyknic body structures particularly.

Manic-depressive psychosis occurs in middle-aged individuals preeminently and you must also take into consideration the alteration of body conformation taking place as persons progress through different age periods. It is often the case that an asthenic type individual becomes fat during middle age; this individual then is described as a pyknic type, although he never was in fact. Therefore, when a doctor relies on the patient's body build to support the diagnosis, he should at least apply the concept correctly. "On sight" body build determinations, especially when patients are clothed, and determinations without use of measurements are extremely unreliable for diagnostic purposes. These become completely unreliable if applied to women because the body build evaluations were elaborated on men, as were so many other physiological, psychiatric, and structural evaluations. Evaluations of women being much less clear and much less well defined creates a rather difficult issue, particularly with confusion in evaluating whether the female has a pyknic or does not have a pyknic type of body build. As you can observe, it is much easier to size up the body build of an asthenic type person than the body build of a person who has an athletic, dysplastic, or pyknic build.

Now, just because a patient has a pyknic build does not mean he must necessarily manifest a clear-cut manic-depressive psychosis. The reverse is even more likely; a person can actually be suffering from manic-depressive psychosis without any admixture of symptoms, and yet not have a pyknic type of body build. In involutional psychosis, you will observe a great many patients who are in many respects exceptions to the rules laid down in connection with manic-depressive psychosis and schizophrenia. For instance, many involutional psychotic persons are not pyknic in build but are actually asthenic, or are admixtures of asthenic and dysplastic. Emotionally they are very often "schizoid," or obsessive and phobic, and not actually cyclothymic even though they do not manifest many schizophrenic features but quite often manifest plain depressive features. Therefore, body build should always be evaluated carefully, should never be regarded as a prominent factor in differential diagnostic evaluations, but should, however, be taken into consideration. Be particularly aware of the fact that many individuals, particularly individuals considered to have a pyknic body build, on closer inspection will turn out to be dysplastic. This would mitigate against a diagnosis of manic-depressive psychosis and would actually better support the diagnosis of a schizophrenic disorder in such persons.

Now I shall discuss the emotional component of so-called personality structure based simply on the descriptions of the person's behavior or actions, the diagnosis actually being influenced by the *previous personality make-up.* For example, a psychiatrist may reason, "The patient's history shows he has a cyclothymic temperament; therefore, the psychotic picture is an exaggeration of the cyclothymic temperament; therefore, I am dealing with a manic-depressive psychotic patient." Or, "This patient has been shy, withdrawn, sensitive, and asocial; therefore, the psychosis I observe cannot possibly be a manic-depressive psychosis because this patient has a schizothymic, or at least a 'schizoid' personality make-up." Actually, the factor of the temperamental make-up is important in evaluating diagnosis. In this regard, it is much easier to assess and to diagnose a "schizoid" personality trait than a cyclothymic personality trait. If you hear a personality described who, ever since childhood, was shy, bashful, withdrawn, anxious, sensitive, asocial, and so forth, you have fairly good clues to indicate that you are not dealing with an "extroverted" individual. If, however, you have a description of a personality who has always been rather frank, rather open, sociable, and in good contact with the environment and reality, you would have to evaluate the picture still more carefully.

Studies have shown that there are many individuals described as frank, sociable, and in good contact with the environment who are not cyclothymic individuals but are what we designate as "pseudoextroverts." Pseudoextroverts have a great tendency to manipulate people and even contact people for their own ego-aggrandizement or support, and many paranoid patients belong in this group. Actually, these individuals make only very little interpersonal contact and do not have much empathy for other people. They do not manifest their anxiety by the so-called "schizoid" trait of withdrawal from people. Instead, they manifest a quite different tendency; they break through their initial anxiety and establish relationships with other people but, again, mainly for ego-manipulative purposes. You frequently observe these "pseudoextroverted" individuals developing psychotic pictures in which a manic state is present. However, the manic manifestations are very often mixed with paranoid features and it is not rare that they eventually manifest symptoms of frank paranoid schizophrenia. Therefore, the "schizoid" personality description, especially if the "schizoid" traits are fairly marked, can definitely be used in assessing the diagnosis. With the exception of patients in the involutional age group, manic-depressive psychosis actually is rarely observed in "schizoid" individuals. Involutional melancholia, however, is more prevalent; and diagnostic mistakes often occur in that these patients are actually described as manic-depressive psychotic because their personality make-up was assumed to be very adequate, especially if evaluation stressed the individual's sociability.

In appraisal of personality structure, the tendency for cyclic mood swings in an individual has frequently been regarded as conclusive for the diagnosis of manic-depressive psychosis. One thing is interesting: Manic-depressive individuals experience mood swings, but schizophrenic, or "schizoid," individuals *also* very often experience mood swings. Keep in mind that very marked and very rapid changes in mood are actually much more prevalent in "schizoid" individuals than in cyclothymic individuals. For example, if a person manifests two or three different mood levels within a day or so—perhaps feeling rather depressed in the morning, feeling very manic or being very active at night, and so forth—such fluctuation is rarely observed in manic-depressive individuals. When the manic-depressive person manifests mood swings he at least carries the particular mood deviation for a longer period of time. Therefore, simply because a person has mood swings does not place him diagnostically into the manic-depressive psychotic group.

Schizophrenia, especially in the early state of the psychosis, quite often has a periodic course. A patient, particularly if he is catatonic, may be sick for a few months, swing out of it and appear to be functioning in an adjusted manner, then the psychosis reappears, and again the patient is sick. There are schizophrenic individuals who practically always have their psychotic attacks in episodes. In the majority of schizophrenic individuals, however, the first one, two, or three appearances of the psychosis develop in attacks; then each attack becomes more prolonged and usually more pronouncedly schizophrenic in form; then the patient finally remains in a psychotic state, manifesting the schizophrenic symptomatology as we usually observe it. These cycles are of interest. There are patients who have an onset of depressive or manic symptomatology, let us say, at the age of eighteen or twenty and it is a short-lived episode. Another episode occurs perhaps three years later in which the manic-depressive features are already somewhat covered by schizophrenic manifestations—such as bizarre delusional formations, evidence of incoherence, auditory hallucinations of a special nature, and so on. An attack occurs again, a year or two later, which is more pronounced, and then finally the patient will have an attack from which he will not emerge.[1] This phenomenon of cyclic development, therefore, should not be considered always an indication of manic-depressive psychosis.

In evaluating personality structure based on *psychological tests,* the delineation of manic-depressive psychosis is, I would say, less firm than the delineation, for instance, of schizophrenia. That is obvious because in no psychological test does the diagnosis of schizophrenia ever rest alone on the evaluation of the emotional deviations which appear in the test material; diagnosis also rests to a very large extent on the evaluation of the patient's conceptual distortions that may appear in these psychological tests. Conceptual distortions do not appear in manic-depressive psychosis.

It also must be kept in mind that psychological tests are all actually based on clinical evaluation; they are derived from the clinic and they are returned to the clinic. Naturally, all the vagaries and mistakes a clinical evaluation makes on patients also can be seen in psychological tests. Therefore, in many respects the psychological tests are not more exact than the clinical evaluation of a patient. Mistakes are frequently made, and we often observe that a patient is labeled "schizophrenic" on the basis of test material alone, although clinically only a depressive or a manic picture is present and there are no signs of schizophrenia. In follow-up observations, such a patient is most likely diagnosed as suffering from manic-depressive psychosis and at no time manifests disorganization or disintegration features. Again, on the other hand, it is very often the case that a patient is labeled "manic-depressive" because somehow the disorganization features do not show up in the

[1] Dr. Hoch is here referring to a symptom course having no successful therapeutic interference.—*Eds.*

test, although clinically, in addition to the manic-depressive symptomatology, features of schizophrenia are present which would eventually prove the patient to be schizophrenic. Therefore, if psychological tests are used to determine personality organization, they should be used as auxiliaries. They should definitely be subordinated to the clinical evaluation of the patient and should never be accepted independently for evaluating patients.

Now I should like to return to the matter of symptomatology and discuss a few of the *finer symptomatologies,* first on a descriptive level and then on a dynamic level, which you will encounter when differentiating between manic-depressive psychosis and schizophrenia. Those very elementary rules which I mentioned in passing are often not put to sufficient use in appraising patients suffering from manic-depressive psychosis. Elementary mistakes continue to be made, especially in that clinical symptoms are either overlooked or are not fully evaluated.

First of all, when a patient manifests signs of *deterioration,* many psychiatrists continue to diagnose the patient manic-depressive psychotic because depressive or manic features are present. Regarding that, we can state definitely that persons manifesting deterioration are not manic-depressive patients. Naturally, you can ask what deterioration is and how it is defined, and you are entitled to do so. When we discuss schizophrenia, I shall try to clarify the concept but, at this time, I should like to mention that only deterioration is generally understood to be a state in which the patient manifests more or less permanent emotional regression, intellectual regression, or behavioral pattern regression. Manic-depressive patients never deteriorate! For example, a manic-depressive patient never manifests any emotional scarring following psychotic attacks. In other words, a shallowness of affect, the peculiar detachment from the environment, the noncontacting others emotionally, and the emotional defensiveness and withdrawal peculiar to

schizophrenia which, when permanent, is definitely interpreted as a form of emotional deterioration, does *not ever*
occur in manic-depressive psychosis.

Secondly, signs of *intellectual disorganization* must be
recognized. Intellectual disorganization in the sense that the
conceptual thinking of the patient is altered, that the patient
is unable to distinguish clearly between reality and non-
reality, that in his thinking ego-boundaries are suspended
or moved very much to the periphery, or that there are
peculiar thought processes which would indicate the thinking is markedly interfered with, never occur in manic-
depressive patients.

Thirdly, *regressive features* should be evaluated.
Markedly regressive symptoms, such as masturbation in
public, incontinence, or complete neglect of social rules and
regulations, do not occur in manic-depressive patients on a
permanent level. That, naturally, should not be confused
with an incidental presence of regressive phenomena in a
manic patient. They are never present in a depressive
patient. If you are dealing with a depressed patient and he
exposes himself, behaves in an exhibitionistic manner, or
becomes incontinent (barring the rare and not clearly recognized entity of depressive stupor), invariably the patient is
schizophrenic. Such regression does not occur in a manic-
depressive patient. In acutely manic patients it obviously
can occur because the sexual drive in a manic patient is
reinforced, is heightened, and he is, naturally, in a state of
sexual tension. However, here again, usually when the manic
attack recedes the patient reintegrates and all regression
symptoms disappear. When the patient is in a mild manic
state, we would never expect to find any of the regressive
symptoms mentioned. If they should occur, we are most
likely dealing with a schizophrenic individual.

Another mistake often made, which is also elementary,
is that of overlooking *incongruency* between the patient's
affect and the other clinical symptomatology. In a pure
manic-depressive clinical picture the manifestations are

always congruent with the mood of the patient. Incongruent behavior occurs in many schizophrenic settings but not in any manic-depressive setting. A manic-depressive depressed patient does not tell you jokes. A schizophrenic patient can be depressed and still, in one way or another, express to you a rather jocular mood; it would probably be a peculiar form of jocularity and incongruent, disharmonious, and split off from the basic mood of the patient. That does not occur in a manic-depressive patient when depressed.

There are a few further points I would like to stress. Particularly under the impact of psychodynamic insights and contributions, more and more concentration became placed on the emotional component of mental disorders, a component which was formerly ignored. Psychiatrists became more and more impressed by the extent to which many major mental disorders appeared to be primarily emotional disorders (although I would hesitate to assume this to be the case with schizophrenia, which surely has many basic disorders other than the emotional). In the minds of many, the conclusion was finally reached that in the psychoses we are actually dealing with disorders that are primarily emotional very much as is the case in the psychoneuroses. It often became completely overlooked that, in schizophrenia, definite defects in perceptual "screening" and "planning," definite alterations in thought processes and content, disturbances in vegetative homeostasis, and so forth, are present which appear to be no less primary than the emotional disorders. The issue is irrelevant whether such phenomena are secondary to primary emotional disorders or not. The main issue is that these phenomena are present in schizophrenia and are *not present in any other psychosis.*

Due to the increasing emphasis on emotional factors, the *perceptual and the conceptual operation* of patients became far less evaluated than had been the case at the start of the century. Therefore, a great amount of observation and a great deal of knowledge about the thinking disorders have had to be rediscovered. In more recent literature, you can read with astonishment about a schizophrenic person's thinking and his handling of concepts, all of which was already known in 1890 but it had been forgotten. Furthermore, with a great deal of astonishment it was again "discovered" through psychological tests that in schizophrenics we are dealing with very peculiar ideas the patient has in relation to his concept of reality. Although it has become a little more sharply defined, it is nothing new to those acquainted with the literature on schizophrenia. So, the ideation of the patient—the way in which he thinks, the way in which he operates, and the way in which he relates himself to reality, especially how autistic, how dereistic, and how bizarre his thinking is—are all evaluations which I can only state have been described decades ago.

All these perceptual and conceptual disorders must always be taken into consideration if we are to make a differential diagnosis properly. When diagnosing any patient, we cannot simply assume that we have before us an emotional machine who is now depressed or elated, and take the attitude "I don't give a damn what other symptoms the patient has; his emotional disturbance is the major symptomatology, and therefore the patient is a manic-depressive psychotic." For instance, very often schizophrenic patients make illogical remarks or their thought content and emotional tone are incongruent; this peculiar inappropriateness occurs in the schizophrenic but not in the manic-depressive patient.

Affect is never dissociated from thought content in the manic-depressive psychotic patient; even the slightest deviation is rare in this condition. If you detect such a phenomenon, it is always best to be on guard because this individual is probably presenting a *mixed psychotic picture*; most likely you are dealing with one having manifestations which, during the early stages of the disturbance, are mainly affective and then gradually the patient will display thinking disorders, incongruity between his thoughts and affect.

Many patients manifesting these mixed pictures at the

onset of their disorder were formerly diagnosed "schizo-affective" psychosis, or "schizo-manic" psychosis, depending on the affective symptomatology. It is my opinion that, for all practical purposes, it is better to designate them cases of "mixed schizophrenia," being aware that many schizophrenic mechanisms are present, a fact which from a prognostic and therapeutic point of view is important. In follow-up studies you may find that many of these patients respond quite well to the first or second treatment attempts and give the impression that, because they have the affective component, they will continue to respond well. Many of them later develop full-fledged schizophrenic pictures with bizarre delusions and hallucinations. Therefore, the favorable long-term prognosis in these cases is more the exception than the rule.

I shall now review the evaluation of hallucinatory and delusional material. In the manic-depressive psychosis, patients do not actually hallucinate. Even if you encounter a manic patient who hallucinates, immediately you must ask, "Am I really dealing with a manic-depressive psychotic patient?" Then the next move is to scrutinize the so-called hallucinations. Pure forms of hallucinations do not occur in manic patients: They are most likely illusions or expectation phenomena. They are fleeting and in the background, and are always topical and congruent with the patient's mood. However, if true hallucinations occur which are persistent, dominating, incongruent with the patient's mood, and especially if they contain any bizarre or illogical material, the patient is not an hallucinating manic patient. He is undoubtedly schizophrenic.

In the depressive setting of the manic-depressive psychosis, auditory hallucinations occur so extremely rarely that if they occur it definitely points to a schizophrenic disorder. If your patient is deeply depressed and hears voices telling him he will be killed because of his sins, you could accept that as being topical and as probably being a part of the depressive picture. If, however, your depressed patient says he hears voices talking back-and-forth to each other, either reminding him of his past or discussing something unrelated and completely irrelevant to his mood, you must realize that an incongruency is present and that the depressive affect is not dominant over hallucinatory content which is probably dissociated or fragmented away from the emotional deviation in the patient. In this instance, you are most likely dealing with a schizophrenic individual.

It has been mentioned that in the manic-depressive psychosis any "delusions" are usually grouped around hypochondriacal preoccupations, ideas of self-condemnation, and even around paranoid concepts. The ideas of self-accusation and self-condemnation are considered quite clearly depressive. I may add, however, that occasionally self-accusatory and self-condemnatory ideas occur in a depressed schizophrenic patient. Therefore, on the basis of these symptoms you cannot diagnose the patient. The presence of hypochondriacal delusional ideas is quite often observed in organic psychosis, involutional psychosis, and schizophrenia as well as in manic-depressive psychosis, and the ideational content and its formation may be very similar or even identical in each condition. This has even more validity in the case of paranoid elaborations. Diagnosis can be based only on the findings of a thorough examination of all the factors present, not just the delusional content and formation.

There are manic-depressive individuals in the older age range who develop paranoid ideations. These are interesting cases and it is not quite clear nosologically by what process it occurs. Many people in old age tend to develop paranoid elaborations; it is apparent in neurotic elderly people but is also observed up to a point in so-called normal elderly people. Naturally, it is somehow related to their lagging vitality and impairment in their adaptation to the environment. Such an individual develops an increased tendency to misinterpret that which he perceives. Now, if the person is hit by a rather severe disorder, particularly if he is hit by a depression, that would obviously reinforce his paranoid trend. (Naturally, it would not be so likely to occur in a manic state.) Obviously, depression in an older individual leads much more frequently to a paranoid elaboration than it does in a younger individual. Furthermore, you can inject here the factors of arteriosclerotic complications. Any lowering of the integrity of the psyche of a person, regardless of whether it is done by organic means or done by emotional means, could lead to misinterpretation of perceptions; and then, again, paranoid elaboration develops.

Finally, we observe quite a number of persons who at first appear to be manic-depressive individuals and wind up recognized to be schizophrenic because the schizophrenic component becomes more and more apparent with succeeding attacks. These patients may appear at the onset to be depressive individuals, let us say, in their late thirties; by the age of fifty-five or sixty you can realize they suffer with a psychosis which is actually paranoid schizophrenia having depressive features. Even in schizophrenia, paranoid pictures are more likely to develop in older individuals while catatonic and hebephrenic pictures are especially likely to develop between adolescence and, let us say, thirty-five. Then, if a person develops schizophrenic pictures after the age of forty or so, they are usually paranoid. The paranoid schizophrenic individual is actually the least schizophrenic from a developmental standpoint and obviously patients first developing schizophrenic symptoms late in life usually follow the paranoid pattern. However, occasionally you may observe a patient whose first psychotic episode is manifested by a depression at, for instance, the age of nineteen and such a patient impresses you as merely suffering from a depression. This picture is often observed among college students. The next attack, perhaps at the age of twenty-five, is defined as a depression with some paranoid admixtures. A few years later he develops a paranoid picture. You also will observe other cases in which the first attack is that of a depression, a year or so later the picture is hebephrenic or catatonic, and following that the attacks include paranoid admixtures.

Actual paranoid delusions are extremely rare in manic-depressive psychosis. When a person manifests a paranoid elaboration which is at all persistent, be suspicious that he is not suffering from manic-depressive psychosis. Often we have to determine whether the paranoid delusions are primary or secondary. Many secondary delusions, with which the depressed patient feels something will be done to him because of his misdeeds, are very clearly understood and, I would say, acceptable in terms of his affect. There are many exceptions to this rule, however, because often these topical delusions are structurally on the same level as the paranoid delusions which have no such linkage with the emotional state in the patient. There are, for instance, schizophrenic patients who display topical delusional elaborations for whom it would then be a mistake to assume that simply because their delusions are topical the diagnosis is manic-depressive psychosis. For example, frequently in a catatonic, or even a paranoid, patient who is depressed the delusions, while first being formed, are still understandable from a logical point of view and are *also* elaborated on in this manner, "Because I am ineffectual, because I am not performing, because I am not doing things correctly the environment will do something to me." Usually, however, the elaborations are quite different: The schizophrenic individual will most likely branch off with all sorts of peculiar ideas such as, "They are hypnotizing me—" "They are doping me—" or "They are knowing my thoughts and they are able to penetrate my brain." Such ideas are all symptomatic of schizophrenia and never occur in manic-depressive psychosis, with the rare exception of patients in the involutional age group.

In any differential diagnostic procedure the patient's *motor behavior* should also be evaluated in terms of its congruency to the patient's affect and ideation. Here I would like to mention only briefly a few among the many different clinical pictures that Kraepelin originally categorized as subgroupings of manic-depressive psychosis. He described certain individuals who were playful and categorized them "adolescent manias." Some observers later labeled this group "acute motility psychosis." These excited adolescents would make witty remarks, pun, rhyme, and so forth. Despite their increased psychomotor activity they did not make good contact with the environment and very often would either lapse into a catatonic stupor or display hebephrenic mechanisms such as marked regressive phenomena. Actually, these clinical pictures are easy to diagnose due to obvious discrepancy in the clinical picture, there being a split of the motor manifestations from the ideational and from the emotional manifestations.

Kraepelin also placed the "akinetic manias" and the "manic stupors," into the manic-depressive category. He described the patient who, for example, sits in a corner and does not move; the patient's psychomotor activity is markedly retarded and he is actually "turned inward." At the same time, however, the patient appears to have a certain amount of euphoria; if you approach him he may laugh, he may talk to you, make a few witty remarks, and then lapse back again into his "akinetic" state. If you observe such a patient who is in an excited state although he is not displaying any increased psychomotor activity but is lolling about, laughing, and smiling to himself without contacting the external environment, he already manifests a certain splitting in his psychic integration, there being no harmony of ideational, motor, and emotional behavior. Actually, this is a catatonic schizophrenic picture according to more recent diagnostic applications. If followed up, this patient would be found to manifest thinking disorders including memory defects, and perhaps may eventually manifest delusions and hallucinations inappropriate to his affective state.

One other question that one might ask is the very interesting matter of *memory impairment*: Does it ever occur in the manic-depressive psychosis as well as in schizophrenia and certain other mental disorders? At the time Kraepelin had described the manic-depressive psychosis, he was impressed by the experiments of Wundt, a psychologist who used experimental methods to investigate memory and thought formation. So, when Kraepelin laid the foundation for so-called experimental psychological approach, he used a few of the techniques evolved by Wundt to determine to what extent impairment of memory or impairment of thought processes occur in the different mental disorders. He found every experiment demonstrated that in the manic-depressive psychosis the mentality of the patient remained intact. This observation is valid for mild manic and mild depressive cases, but when patients are in the state of severe manic excitement, interferences of memory and thought processes occur due to the severity of the excitement and scattering of attention. These severely disturbed manic patients, as in *most* excitement cases (not only manic excitement, but the other excitement states as well) are very often partially or totally amnestic for what happened to them. In this respect, patients suffering with very severe or delirious mania behave in a manner similar to organic cases. Also, schizophrenic patients in a state of acute excitement appear and behave in a similar manner to the manic patients who are in a state of excitement; namely, following the attack they are partially or totally amnestic to what went on. They, too, behave as organic cases.

In the milder forms of mania and milder forms of depression, however, the person remembers what was going on around him during his illness and is eager to describe it to you. From an historical point of view, it is interesting that the reverse was observed in schizophrenia. Schizophrenic (particularly catatonic) patients who are *not* in a state of excitement can be observed to manifest one of two different reactions. In one group, a patient in a catatonic stupor, appearing to be absorbed and dominated by hallucinations and delusions, will nonetheless "pick up" very accurately all that is going on in the environment. When the catatonic state lifts, he is quite able to give a fairly good account of all that had occurred, at times with surprising accuracy in detail. A second group of catatonic patients have complete amnesia for what had happened around them. After the stupor has lifted, such a patient may very well state, "I do not know when I came to the hospital," and, "I do not remember how I came to be in the hospital." Therefore, it is not true that all schizophrenics are aware of what occurs around them when in a stuporous state; some do and some do not. However, with the exception of manic-depressive patients who had been in a state of extreme excitement or the rare possible cases who had been in a state of so-called depressive stupor, manic-depressive individuals always remember what had gone on.

The phenomenon of interference of consciousness is a very interesting subject, and it even occurs occasionally in so-called normal individuals, particularly when under the influence of fever, alcohol and other intoxicants, a very strong emotion, and so forth. You are able to observe all the gradations of suspension in registration of that which occurs in the external environment when a person is markedly dominated by inner psychic functions. Apparently any amount of awareness is only possible provided the person is not completely preoccupied or dominated by internal environmental experiences, and the more severe the state of excitement, regardless of its cause, the less attention is paid by the patient to the external environment.

MANIC-DEPRESSIVE PSYCHOSIS VERSUS PSYCHONEUROSIS

I now want to discuss some of the problems in distinguishing between the manic-depressive psychosis and the so-called *reactive depressions* and the *psychoneurotic depressions*. This presents problems as complicated as those in differentiating manic-depressive psychosis from schizophrenia. Differentiation cannot be made on a qualitative basis and is not even reliable on a quantitative basis.

Depression is, of course, an extremely common symptom, and, since the introduction of the concept of manic-depressive psychosis, attempts have been made to discover whether or not depressions invariably belong in the framework of manic-depressive psychosis. It was very quickly recognized that depressions occur in quite a number of organic states; these so-called "symptomatic" depressions were then removed from the category of manic-depressive psychosis and, naturally, diagnosed under the heading of the organic disorder in which they occurred. In other words, when depression occurred in general paresis, atherosclerosis, tumor, encephalitis, or what not, it was diagnosed accordingly.

It was later discovered that persons develop depressions in the involutional age period, and the question was again asked whether or not such involutional depressions belong in the category of manic-depressive psychosis. Depressions were also noticed to occur in individuals whose diagnosis certainly did not have clearly defined criteria and who, moreover, did not fit into the manic-depressive category. Furthermore, other depressions, particularly those occurring in the younger age group, were not clearly defined. It was also observed that there are persons who develop depressions seemingly without any precipitating cause. Moreover, there are depressions occurring in persons who do not have the personality make-up mainly observed in the manic-depressive psychosis. These observations led many people to feel that there actually are depressions which do not belong to the manic-depressive psychosis. Although I personally feel such depressions certainly exist, I am not clear about their diagnostic connection, and if such exists I think they are either depressions belonging in a psychoneurotic or in a schizophrenic setting. I could not accept any such proposed nomenclature as "unspecified" psychotic depression. What an "unspecified" type of depression could be, I do not know; the term expresses our dissatisfaction with existing nomenclature but does not introduce anything constructively new. Many people think that these depressions do not belong in the manic-depressive diagnostic group, and yet where they actually do belong they do not state.

As the question of diagnosis of depressions continued, it was discovered that patients suffering from psycho-neurosis—particularly in two neurotic disturbances, the hysterical and the obsessive-phobic—frequently manifested depressive features or even depressive episodes. The designation of these depressions was never very clear and, as you will observe later, is still not quite clear. They were treated as being "neurotic depressions."

It was also found that many manic-depressive patients deve oped a depression actually due to some precipitating factor. The precipitating factor was dynamically often organized around "introjection" of the love object. In other words, when the person's love object died, the loss produced a psychotic episode which was then perceived as being actually "reactive" to the loss. Incidentally, in psychiatric literature there has been a constant confusion as to what is termed reactive depression and what I have just termed neurotic depression. Many textbooks have not recognized neurotic depression but refer to depression in a psycho-neurosis as a reactive depression. And, again, all the text-books subdivided reactive depression into two groups: one being psychotic and precipitated in a manic-depressive psychosis and the other being neurotic and precipitated in a psychoneurosis. It is obvious that reactive depression itself is *not* a diagnostic entity and is not identical with neurotic depression. The term "reactive" indicates the depression occurs as a reaction to some stimulus, and such a depression can occur either in a psychotic or a neurotic setting.

I think it might be best to clarify this issue in the following manner. We observe manic-depressive depressions which occur endogenously in the sense that we are not able to demonstrate actual precipitating factors—at least any precipitating factors which are obvious. We also observe manic-depressive depressions (or manias) which occur as reactions to obvious precipitating factors. Therefore, we observe endogenous manic-depressive psychotic depression as well as reactive manic-depressive psychotic depression. On the other hand, we can observe depressions which are not at all well defined occurring in individuals having a well-defined psychoneurotic framework. Here again, neurotic depressions can occur in a reactive setting or in a seemingly nonreactive setting.

So far, this is acceptable from a descriptive point of view. As we shall observe, this differentiation which appears to be relatively clear on the surface is not so clear and is quite confusing for the following reasons. At the time manic-depressive psychosis was introduced and discussed as a clinical entity, one or two statements made by Kraepelin were considered fully valid. The first statement was that the manic-depressive patient never manifested deterioration; that is correct. The second statement was that the manic-depressive psychosis occurs in attacks, and when the attack vanishes the patient returns to a state of well-being considered to be that of a normal, or relatively normal, person. In other words, the manic-depressive individual was considered to be a relatively well-adjusted individual, especially in that his social adaptability is good, and that then, for unknown reasons, this individual periodically develops a depressive (or manic) state which lasts for a while, after which he again returns to a state of normalcy. That is *not* correct.

It was then discovered that during intervals between attacks a great many manic-depressive patients displayed neurotic structures (particularly obsessive-compulsive), which, as I shall soon describe, are often indistinguishable from the neurotic structures we observe in persons suffering from a psychoneurosis. Therefore the question immediately arose, what is so different between a neurotic depression and a psychotic depression? One individual develops a psychotic depression from which he recovers and returns to the level which appears to be neurotic, while the other individual is psychoneurotic and develops, in the framework of the neurosis, a depression which is then often repeated. To put the question very bluntly, is one actually able to distinguish between a psychotic depression and a neurotic depression? You hear this whole question being bandied around and great discussions arise on diagnostic, prognostic, therapeutic, and other points of view.

Are there features as to (1) *personality organization,* (2) *clinical course,* (3) *symptomatology,* (4) *prognosis and response to therapy,* and (5) *psychodynamic formulations* that actually distinguish a neurotic from a psychotic depression? Some people believe they are able to distinguish the differences; others will state that differences are nonexistent. Differentiation involves very difficult mental acrobatics.

PERSONALITY ORGANIZATION: If you attempt differentiation in terms of the so-called premorbid personality of the patient, you run into a great deal of difficulty. In the first place, there is no uniform characteristic premorbid personality for all depressions. As an example, persons developing involutional depressions usually have a personality structure different from the so-called cyclothymic; the really obsessive-compulsive personality—rigid, narrow, meticulous, perfectionistic, and sensitive—develops a depression usually in the involutionary period. On the other hand, these are also people who very often are treated as suffering from obsessive-compulsive neurosis, until they become depressed. Therefore, there are no clear differential features in such a case either, until psychotic manifestations actually appear. If psychosis does not appear the patient is diagnosed as obsessive-compulsive neurotic; if psychosis does appear the diagnosis is then changed to involutional psychosis.

CLINICAL COURSE: Attempts have been made to differentiate on a descriptive level in terms of the course of the depressive disorder. First of all, concerning the *severity* of the depression, if you observe a patient suffering from a depression actually the only differentiation you would probably be able to find is that a manic-depressive depression usually appears to be more profound than depression observed in psychoneurosis. As you realize, I am sure, this differential point is extremely unsatisfactory and it does not help very much. You can probably generalize statistically that psychotic depressions are deeper than neurotic depressions, but that has never been practically demonstrated in particular cases.

It has also been stated that the *duration* of attacks and the *oscillation* in the patient's depressive mood-swings are much more volatile in neurotic depression. For example, within a period of a few days the neurotic patient may be depressed, then become able to function, then become depressed again, and so on. Depressive attacks in manic-depressive psychosis, on the other hand, usually have a certain reliable duration and also a certain depth, and the oscillations are not obvious. To some extent this is valid, but again I must point out that the manic-depressive individual actually manifests mild oscillations of mood as well. And, these mild oscillations of mood are very often linked to neurotic structure deviations present just as is the case in many psychoneurotic individuals, Therefore, as a distinguishing issue, that of mood oscillation is also very, very tenuous. It is usually during the process of oscillation of the depression from severe to mild, or vice versa, when a patient is most likely to act upon his suicidal ideations, and, here again, differentiation has been attempted on a purely descriptive basis.

SYMPTOMATOLOGY: Some psychiatrists try to differentiate on the basis of suicidal behavior. If a patient commits suicide or attempts suicide because he is depressed, it is a logical sequence of his depression. If you should ask me why it is that all depressed patients do not try to commit suicide, it would be a very intelligent question because it is interesting that, even though a great many people are depressed, proportionately very few actually attempt suicide although many have suicidal ideas. When treating these patients, however, you find that suicidal notions are present in neurotic depressions as well as psychotic ones, and I have observed suicidal gestures to be just as frequent in one as in the other. A great many mistakes are made in this regard and a great many patients are lost because of the idea that the patient is suffering only from a neurotic depression and that a person in a neurotic depression only threatens suicide but does not commit it. Potentially, every patient having suicidal ideas can carry them out, and you must know your patient extremely well to be able to predict whether he will or will not. Here, I must admit, there is a predictability that in a manic-depressive depressed patient the chances of suicide are, paradoxically, greater than in a neurotic depressed patient.

Attempted suicide, in the general sense of the term used, is not a psychotic act. Suicide usually occurs in the framework of a psychosis, but to assume that every seriously attempted suicide is a psychotic act would be very similar to assuming that every anxiety attack which reaches a state of panic is a psychotic manifestation. In other words, suicide and suicidal notions are so widespread and universal that I believe it would overshoot the mark to consider the suicidal act as always being a psychotic one. Actually, you must differentiate between the numerous suicidal motivations. They are largely on a social level in certain cultures or situations, and almost entirely on an individual level in others. In some cultures suicide is very prevalent for one or another reason, and in others, as you know, it is rarely observed.

With regard to social motivations, in certain cultures suicide is practically imposed on an individual by his society as a way of allowing the individual to take his execution into his own hands, in many such cases to enable the doomed individual to "save face." Although this is not strictly suicide, it is one example to show that it is incorrect to assume that regardless of the situation a person who "suicides" is in such a marked state of emotional unbalance that he is actually psychotic. Even in terms of individual motivations there are nonpsychotic individuals who, in a dire situation, will add up the score of their survival assets and liabilities and, when there is a great disparity between the two, will decide to take the matter into their own hands and commit suicide.

Generally speaking, however, the greatest number of suicides is committed either during a state of marked depression or during a state of schizophrenic anxiety. That such a symptom is very often indicative of a total regression in the individual and thus part of a psychotic picture, and that it is surely much more prevalent in persons who are mentally unbalanced is true. However, I have observed that a great many suicides, perhaps resulting from suicidal gestures which "misfired," occur under extreme stress in psychoneurotic individuals who could not be termed psychotic. Therefore, I would be against an assumption that when a suicidal preoccupation is carried out it is automatically a sign of a psychosis, anymore than any particular obsessional preoccupation which is acted upon is automatically a sign of a psychosis.

The matter of suicide is endowed with very moral connotations and in certain countries, such as England, suicidal attempt is followed by criminal prosecution. It is regarded as a homicidal act, and basically it is. To circumvent this moral issue the idea of "temporary insanity" had to be introduced. Thus, in England those who attempt suicide are rarely prosecuted because they all plead "temporary insanity"—and it must be admitted that the majority are psychotic and have been for a long time. Neurotic persons essentially do not commit such a "crime."

It has been maintained that a neurotic depression occurs in the framework of obsessive, phobic, or hysterical manifestations, and that the presence of these symptoms determines whether the patient is to be classified as suffering with a neurotic or a psychotic depression. Frequently, however, hypochondriacal ideation could be confused with hysterical mechanisms. "Supportive" hysterical pictures, or hysterical "overlay," can be observed in a number of depressions, although I must say that massive hysterical manifestations, so designated, are not often observed in a depression. They occur more frequently in certain types of schizophrenia. What could be confused with hysterical mechanisms is the tendency for many depressed patients to dramatize. By dramatizing they can reinforce the impact on the environment of their emotions, and this can be observed in a number of depressed patients.

I have the feeling, although I do not want to commit myself 100 percent, that much of the dramatization in a depressed patient is not primary in the disorder and is not an actual hysterical mechanism but it is a reinforcement of the symptomatology in order to be believed. If you study the interrelationship of a depressed patient and his environment, it is rather interesting how extremely long it takes before the environment accepts the fact the person is sick. Then, when it accepts that fact, how long it takes before it finally accepts that depression is just as much a sickness as a clearly organic sickness is. A great many patients receive all kinds of admonitions from their relatives such as, "You should change your ways," "If you would work the whole thing would disappear," or "If you would go out and go to the movies you wouldn't be so depressed." In other words, all the "common sense," or "common nonsense" approaches to these issues are frustrations with which these patients are overwhelmed. Many patients verbalize these problems, that, "I am really unable to convince anybody that I am sick!" Incidentally, quite a number of suicide attempts are made out of the patient's inability to convey to the environment that they are sick and they are unable to function. In this situation, I think a certain amount of dramatization then prevails in those patients who may indeed have hysterical fantasies to oversell their symptomatology.

There are individuals, particularly in the involutional age group, in whom the so-called neurotic symptomatology almost fully replaces the depression and so the person does not verbalize feelings of depression—at least he does not verbalize it voluntarily. It can often be elicited from him, however, if you question him or at least explore a little deeper into the mechanisms of the patient.

There is another secondary phenomenon which is also of great interest: The way in which the patient actually feels his own symptomatology. Occasionally, you will find in depressed patients, in schizophrenic patients, and also in certain psychoneurotic patients the so-called denial of the existence of any mental symptomatology at all. For instance, as I have mentioned, there are the "lurking" depressions. Many of these patients will dwell at length on their physical disorganization or body symptoms and will not admit at all that there is any problem on an emotional level. That situation is not uncommon. Naturally, the correct diagnosis of such patients, especially if there is no clue that this person has any basic emotional disturbance, is very difficult to determine. There the differentiation is often not separated from a psychosomatic, or from a true psychoneurotic condition. I do not believe we have as yet an absolute method for diagnosing patients who deny their depression. If you analyze some of the dynamics you may occasionally pick up one or two clues indicating you are not dealing with a straight neurotic depression, although no attempts to differentiate the types of depression on the basis of psychodynamics are ever successful.

You may differentiate, to some extent, on the basis of the physiological concomitants present in the patient. Always suspect an underlying depression if you are able to demonstrate that the patient shows the following symptoms simultaneously: listlessness, weakness, feeling of being driven, agitation, sleep disturbance, and—at the same time—anorexia, constipation, weight loss, and other vegetative manifestations. Symptoms combined in this manner do not

564   DIFFERENTIAL DIAGNOSIS

usually occur in the psychoneuroses and, if present simultaneously, you should be suspicious that you are probably dealing with an individual who is depressed. However, I would not state that this is always true because, naturally, it is certainly possible for a neurotic individual who is not depressed to have such symptomatology also. With such configuration of symptoms, however, one is more likely to be dealing with a depressed individual.

PROGNOSIS AND RESPONSE TO THERAPY: It has been stated that psychotic depressions may recur, and that neurotic depressions do not recur provided the patient was properly treated. Many people assess adequacy of treatments simply on that basis. You will encounter psychoanalysts—although I must say, very, very few—who believe they are able to cure manic-depressive psychosis in so far as the patient's tendency for repeated attacks is concerned. The number of such cures reported is so few you can count them on your hands. Much of the published material is entirely unconvincing; it has not been actually demonstrated that any type of psychotherapy alone, without applying chemotherapy, can reliably prevent recurrence of a depressive psychotic attack.

The statement that the psychoneurotic patient in treatment does not have recurrence of depression depends, again, naturally, upon the extent that the neurosis was eliminated. I have known of psychoneurotic patients treated with analysis for many years whose flurries of depression cleared up completely under psychoanalysis and who functioned well. Then suddenly, two or so years later, depressive manifestations again appeared. In that event the psychoanalysts who had treated them no longer appointed them in the category of neurotic depression but in the category of psychotic depression, which is not correct. So, recurrence of depression is also not a very convincing differential factor. I must again state that, in terms of the clinical course, it is difficult to differentiate between a neurotic depression and a psychotic depression.

Incidentally, many therapists assume that reactive depression, in the framework of psychosis or psychoneurosis, usually responds very favorably to psychotherapy, the source of the "grief" being external. However, although many usually do respond favorably, quite a number of these patients respond poorly to psychotherapy in a similar manner to those suffering with endogenous depression; in fact, many cases may be more stubborn in their response to treatment.

PSYCHODYNAMIC FORMULATIONS: Differentiation on the basis of dynamics is also unreliable. In actual practice the situation appears to be the following: When you treat a patient, particularly psychoanalytically, and know the whole dynamic structure of your patient intimately, if your patient becomes depressed, you will probably assume the diagnosis to be neurotic depression. Conversely, if you are not aware of the structure of your patient, having taken only a routine history but not applied psychoanalysis, your diagnosis will tend to be psychotic depression. This is, naturally, no way to properly differentiate, but such is what I observe actually happening.

Many depressed patients—many, but not all—are unable to verbalize very well. Although manic-depressive patients are much better able to make social contact than are schizophrenic patients, they demonstrate to some extent the very same phenomenon: They have very great difficulty recalling and presenting infantile experiences and associating clearly. Many psychiatrists try to differentiate psychotic depression from neurotic depression on that level. That phenomenon, however, is also rather difficult to appraise and depends to a large extent on the impression of the therapist. One therapist would feel the patient produces an inadequate amount of material and another therapist would feel the same patient produces ample material. This is all related to the fact that many psychiatrists feel they can convincingly diagnose psychotic and neurotic depression based on dynamic formulations. You can view it the following way: Whether your patient is psychoneurotic or psychotic, if he relates to you and verbalizes well, and if you study the structure of the patient, you are likely to make elaborate dynamic formulations and explain the patient's depressive or other symptoms on the basis of your particular dynamic formulations. However, four different psychiatrists would emphasize five different dynamic elaborations—because one psychiatrist would change his mind in the course of things— and then explain symptoms accordingly. This is surely not a reliable method for arriving at a diagnosis. You should keep this in mind when I discuss dynamic concepts from the point of view of differential diagnosis. You must also keep in mind that depressions are probably multifactorial in origin and as yet we do not know etiologies.

As I have indicated, there is as yet no valid evidence for there being any qualitative difference between a psychotic and a neurotic depression—the differences are only a matter of degree. Psychodynamic research has assumed that the so-called "psychogenic" depressions can be differentiated on the basis of certain psychodynamic constellations. However, as I will discuss next, psychodynamic manifestations can be the same in both psychotic and neurotic depressions and differentiation based on dynamics is usually made arbitrarily.

Before discussing the psychodynamics of depressions, I would like to inject one remark about another diagnostic point. It is very interesting that in all these discussions about psychoneurotic depression, psychotic depression, psychoneurotic background of the manic-depressive individual, and so forth, we have been concerned only with differentiation so far as depressions are concerned. We observe no psychoneurotic mania. Nobody has ever introduced that concept. I will return to this point later.

19

DEPRESSIONS: PSYCHODYNAMIC THEORIES

Many psychiatrists feel they can convincingly diagnose a psychotic or a psychoneurotic depression based on psychodynamics. For those who are vaguely familiar with the main psychodynamic concepts of depression as formulated partly by Freud, partly by Abraham, Rado, and others, it is not necessary to recapitulate these concepts in detail but merely to mention a few of the ideas expressed regarding the dynamics of the manic-depressive psychosis and discuss them from the point of view of differential diagnosis. At the same time, I shall make a few general remarks concerning the validity of these concepts as they are applied to depression.

Historically speaking, Kraepelin's views differed basically from those of later investigators in that he held a purely objective phenomenological approach. Kraepelin assumed that depression and elation were due to organic changes.

He considered them primary phenomena that could not be further dissected. Kraepelin and Freud were on common ground in their belief that the actual basic factor in the psychoses is a disturbed, or pathological, biochemical process somewhere in the body. Kraepelin, however, did not use the concept of the unconscious and the resultant psychodynamic way of thinking as was later employed to dissect depression and elation in terms of defense mechanisms used against intolerable conflicts. However, these psychological concepts explain only the "why" regarding depressions or elations, but not the "how" question.

The dynamic mechanisms of depression were originally worked out by Freud; and based on his framework of reference, the concepts of *introjection, regression and fixation on an oral level,* and *ambivalence* were applied as being the three cardinal factors to explain the origin of depression. Freud initially believed depression to be actually some form of mourning. He believed that in ordinary mourning many features of depression can be detected but it is not so intense and the person's recovery is much quicker. He pointed out that it has a feature in common with depression: The person lost the object of his "libidinal" strivings and his "cathexis" was withdrawn. (This is his terminology.)

Freud then postulated that one of the bases of the psychodynamics of depression is the phenomenon of *introjection.* In grief the individual identifies himself with the lost object and incorporates it into himself. In a normal person, this introjection mechanism occurs in a mild form but is eliminated after a reasonable time because the individual's appraisal of reality remains intact even though a certain amount of guilt may be present in connection with the lost object.

In persons who develop depressive episodes, the introjection mechanism becomes markedly exaggerated and the introjected object is not eliminated; the introjection is modified by the patient's strong ambivalent attitude toward the introjected object. In other words, after introjection has taken place, the hating and the loving of the object continue, with the marked feelings of guilt and self-reproach connected with these feelings.

This formulation was later elaborated upon by Abraham. He accepted the fact that, naturally, in the person who mourns, a great deal of grief is present due to the loss of the love object, and he underscored Freud's observation that in very deep mourning, even in people considered to be normal, it can be discerned that the person's attitude toward the love object is an ambivalent one.

To describe it briefly, the term introjection means that the person has an identification, an ambivalent identification, with the love object; that the love object is then incorporated into the person's ego and he then applies emotional reactions to himself which he felt he had, or had wanted to, attribute to the love object. We all know the illustration of this: A child or an adolescent has an ambivalent attitude toward the mother; the mother is loved because he is dependent upon her and at the same time hated because she has introduced restrictive measures—restrictive in a Freudian sense—to this or that function of the child. Therefore, there are mechanisms present which identify him with his mother, leading him to accept the mother and to incorporate the mother's standards into his "superego"; at the same time a strong hostility is present against the mother love object because of her restrictive or punitive measures which are also incorporated into the child. Then, when the mother dies, naturally the loss of the object on whom the person was dependent causes trouble. The person is thrown into a state of ambivalence; his dependency yearnings are accentuated and, on the other hand, a marked guilt feeling is generated because of the hostile impulses present. As Abraham demonstrated, many of these persons had even verbalized death wishes against the love object with consecutive feelings of guilt. In other words, the person's actual attitude—identification with, and hostility toward, the love object—then becomes applied to the person himself after the love object has died; the love object is "introjected" into the person.

Freud described the concept as a struggle between the "ego" and the "superego" taking place in the depressed patient; the "superego" (conscience) is strong and rages against the "ego," overwhelming it. This is manifested by the patient's self-accusatory ideation and attempts toward retribution for what he assumes to be his past sins. When depressed he regards them as unpardonable sins; he needs to be punished for them; he maneuvers for self-punishment, which takes the form of a depression.

This scheme is rather interesting but, as I shall discuss, there are questions which have never been solved and have never been clarified: How does introjection actually take place? And, is this so-called introjection mechanism a general mechanism that can be applied to everybody or is it a special mechanism occurring only in a depressed individual? From what you read, you have the impression it is a general mechanism. If it is a general mechanism you must then ask, on the basis of introjection exactly how does a person who mourns differ from a person who develops a manic-depressive attack of depression? Is this a quantitative differentiation? Or, does the whole idea of introjection explain anything in terms of the etiology of the depression? Or, does it only explain the content of the depression? These questions I shall discuss later.

The formulation of introjection was later elaborated upon and a few other features were added. For instance, Abraham pointed out that a person who is in this state of ambivalent introjection usually regresses to a lower level of adaptation which he conceived as a *regression to the "oral," or the "narcissistic," level.* Actually, Freud had pointed out the observation that the manic-depressed patient becomes fixated on the oral level during depression. He differentiated between neurotic and psychotic depressions and based the differentiation on the "depth of narcissistic regression." He considered the manic-depressive psychosis (and schizophrenia) to be a "narcissistic neurosis." The only honor he gave to the manic-depressive psychosis was in his belief that, although the schizophrenic person regresses to the "auto-erotic" and "narcissistic" state, the manic-depressive actually regresses only to the "oral" or the "oral-narcissistic" state—in other words, probably half a grade higher than the state of schizophrenic regression, if you accept the regression scheme as valid.

Abraham strongly stressed the concept of regression to the oral level. He even attempted to group the symptomatology of the manic-depressive psychosis largely around the oral level: the refusal of food, fantasies of being eaten, and sadistic manifestations often directed either against the depressed patient himself or against the environment. These were all explained in terms of regression to the "oral-narcissistic" or to the "oral-sadistic" level. The "oral-sadistic" manifestations to which Abraham called attention are also present in the interval periods between depressions.

I do not wish to engage in the acrobatics of the schemes of "primary" and "secondary oral phase," "primary anal phase," and so forth, but basically the concept is that the depressed patient regresses to the "oral-anal phase," and he is preoccupied with his gastro-intestinal tract. All the tendencies to not take food, or all the patient's ideation that he will incorporate something that will harm him; all the so-called "cannibalistic" ideation observed in many patients during the involutionary period—such ideas as sadistically chewing up objects around them—are all organized around the concept of regression to the so-called "oral," "anal," "oral-sadistic," and "anal-sadistic," or, lower, to the "narcissistic" phase. In other words, it was considered that the very deep regressive manifestations were present.

I have mentioned all this rather in detail because for decades the only tendency to differentiate between a neurotic depression and a psychotic depression hinged on this regression scheme, at least in the psychoanalytic literature. For example, Fenichel stated quite clearly that it is very easy to differentiate a depression in a phobic patient from depression in a person suffering from manic-depressive psychosis. He simply stated that the depth of the regression determines whether the patient is suffering from a neurotic depression or a psychotic depression. He mentioned that if the patient regresses to the "oral" stage, or to the "oral-sadistic" stage, one is dealing with a depression which is psychotic; that if the regression is not so deep, one is dealing with a depression which is neurotic. At a later time I shall discuss the extent to which this scheme is really applicable.

So-called "oral fixation" has been demonstrated in quite a number of depressed patients. Or, to be exact, it was not so much that "oral fixation" was demonstrated as was the very strong oral *trend* present in these patients. In terms of the practical application of dynamics, the anorexia and refusal of food in many depressed patients, on the one hand, and on the other hand the rather aggressive fantasies present in the dreams and daydreams of many depressed patients were also interpreted as a so-called "oral remnant," or "regression to the oral level." The second observation is also correct; a great many depressed patients have very strong aggressive impulses toward the environment, and that can be observed particularly in the nonretarded depressed patients. For instance, the involutional depressed patient is just as much a nuisance to the environment as he is to himself. He is very strongly sadistic toward the environment, continually punishing those around him, and then having feelings of guilt about it, he turns around and punishes himself. However, straight oral manifestations, the so-called cannibalistic fantasies of chewing up the environment and incorporating the environment into himself, are not observed very often although they can be demonstrated in the dreams or associations of patients occasionally. According to statistics, it does not occur as often as Abraham had originally assumed.

Many of the aggressive fantasies can be explained, naturally, on the basis of orality, but many of them cannot.

They can also be explained in terms of "narcissistic threats" that the person perceives and elaborates upon, if you want to use this framework of reference, which will be discussed below. Abraham perceived, therefore, depression as an introjection mechanism in which a great deal of repression is present against wishes which would threaten the existence of the individual or the existence of the love object against whom the person has a great deal of hostility. According to Abraham, the hostile wishes generate a great deal of unconscious guilt feeling in the patient and the unconscious guilt feeling is then manipulated by the patient in various ways.

On one point, however, there is considerable agreement. A short time after the mechanisms of introjection and orality were discovered, the mechanism of *ambivalence* was added to the dynamic concepts of depression. From Freud's observations, Abraham tried to demonstrate that ambivalence toward the love object becomes even more markedly intensified in those persons who are actually suffering with a depression. Abraham assumed that hate and love are present in equal quantities in manic-depressive depression, both being displayed toward an object in the environment and also toward the patient himself. Abraham believed ambivalence was dynamically very important because it could also be demonstrated that during the interval between depressions the person very often shows a marked ambivalence about his performance, exaggerating it or minimizing it.

The ambivalence in depressed patients is clear-cut. They are markedly ambivalent about the wishes they have repressed; they are ambivalent about their guilt feelings; they are even ambivalent toward the introjected love object, as I have touched upon. They are extremely dependent on the introjected love object; they love the introjected object; they fear the passing away of the introjected object; but at the same time they have a very marked feeling of hostility toward this same object. They continually sway between these two poles. The ambivalence present in these depressed patients does not have to be argued at length because it is obvious. Actually making a decision, making up his mind not only regarding major issues but very often on trivialities is extremely difficult for the depressed patient and this inability to decide, this continuous vacillation between contradictory notions, is quite obvious. It does not reach the extreme of ambivalence observed in schizophrenia, and usually there is more emotion attached to it. Nevertheless, it is present and the indecisiveness of depressed patients can be clearly demonstrated.

Ambivalence in the manic patient is actually not clearly observed because usually it is covered by the euphoria or the psychomotor activity; but, when a manic patient becomes more calm, it is not rare that you hear such a patient indicate that he is quite ambivalent concerning his aims and his wishes. The ambivalence could, of course, relate to focal issues preoccupying the patient, but in depressed patients they are very often trivial matters, everyday matters, or the ambivalence may at times be so marked that practically anything and everything that the patient thinks and does is imbued with ambivalence. (I shall discuss ambivalence further in connection with schizophrenia.) Ambivalence is one of the most interesting mechanisms we encounter and occurs in the psychoneuroses as well as the psychoses, being most marked in schizophrenia. One occasionally observes manic-depressive depressed patients, however, in whom ambivalence is almost as marked, and at times it is difficult to decide whether it is operating on a schizophrenic level or not.

Other dynamic mechanisms were added somewhat later. One was a mechanism which indicated that individuals who developed manic-depressive psychosis are markedly "narcissistic." In the Freudian framework of reference, the concept of "threat to the narcissism" of the patient often appears in dynamic formulations of the manic-depressive (particularly the depressed) patient. The question of hypochondriacal or certain other delusional material expressed by many of these patients is interpreted as being an elaboration upon what is essentially a "narcissistic threat" to the patient.

Now, if that is translated into plain English, it means that the patient has a great deal of preoccupation with death and annihilation, and the death and annihilation ideation is preeminent. Ideas of death and annihilation could occur, one might say, in a general sense that the patient fears death or fears annihilation. It could also occur, however, in the form of a so-called partial death fear or partial death wish, actually being an extension of ideas of partial suicide, with which you are most likely familiar. Fearing the impairment of the function of an organ could indicate the person's fear, or wish, that he will be killed. Many of these partial suicide trends are demonstrated in patients suffering with depression.

According to the Freudian framework of reference (I do not mean to convey to you that it is the correct framework of reference; I wish to convey only the historical development), you must apply the concept in terms of "libido" being withdrawn from the environment, or "cathexis" being withdrawn from the environment onto the patient himself. This is one of the many basic mechanisms which Freud had already demonstrated in the psychoneuroses. But, he made the differentiation that in a psychosis, especially if the patient is depressed, the withdrawal is much more intense than that occurring in a psychoneurosis. In psychosis the person actually withdraws "cathexis" from the environment onto himself, onto his own body, and regresses. Again, if the developmental scheme of Freud is used, the patient regresses to the "narcissistic" level of ego development. Therefore, Freud perceived manic-depressive psychosis, and also schizophrenia, as being a so-called regressive, or "narcissistic," neurosis.

The threat to the "narcissism" of the person was considered to be one of the major dynamic issues in a depression. In other words, the depressed patient is thrown back to a lower level of libidinal development and this lower level of libidinal development activates the ideations which are connected with it. These ideas involve a fear of the environment; in such a regressed state there is an impairment of ego-boundaries in relationship to the environment, and feelings of omnipotence toward the environment. For example, the patient may think, "I have bad breath, and this breath will kill everyone in the environment, or in the whole world." Such ideas demonstrate a form of omnipotency feeling in that the person thinks that by fearing or wishing it, he can annihilate or change the whole environment, or, in reverse, that the environment is able to do that to him. These are remnants of magical thinking which are usually linked to the state whereby the person's ego-boundaries are not fully developed. Actually, this type of thinking also can occur in the psychoneuroses, but the more the disturbance approaches the psychoses, particularly schizophrenia in which thinking is preeminently magical, the more prevalent is this type of thinking.

The concept then evolved that because psychotic individuals are so extremely "narcissistic" it indicates they had never developed beyond that level; that they remained "fixated" on that low level. There were others who felt that these individuals actually had developed and moved up rather normally, but when confronted with difficulty they regressed again to a lower level. At present, the important thing is not whether the person has developmental impairment or a regression process but that he also is "fixated" on himself.

"Narcissistic" individuals manifest a phenomenon which was termed "undeveloped object love"; they have an inability to feel love toward any object. This refers to the original idea that the emotional investment of these persons is so markedly fixed within themselves—in other words, they are so "narcissistic"—that there is absolutely very little energy remaining to be invested in others. I would like to call attention to the fact that this idea is, to some extent, in contradiction to the descriptive observation that many manic-depressive persons are socially quite likable and seem to make very good contact with other people. Actually, however, it was pointed out that this is more or less a "cover" and basically they have very limited "libido investment" in other individuals or in any love object. A lack of any significant object-love is apparent in these patients, and it even goes a step further in that they actually fear very much to be in any close emotional relationship with other persons. They are afraid to give or receive any affection.

The "self-fixation" which characterizes a "narcissistic" person is, naturally, an indication that he is unsure of himself; he lacks self-esteem. The regulation of self-esteem in a narcissistic person is always derived from the external world. It is dependent a great deal on the affection or recognition he receives from others. He utilizes affection as a supply to bolster his self-esteem. He has a great need for recognition, a need for approval and acceptance. If he is rebuffed, it can precipitate an attack of depression which may or may not be obvious to others around him.

Rado clarified the connection between depression and self-esteem *(6)*. He elaborated on the concept that the impairment of self-esteem is largely due to the ambivalent attitude of the depressed individual toward the love object. He perceived the depressed phase as a process whereby the conscience mechanism ("superego") leads to the patient's ingratiation maneuvers; the individual seemingly inflicts painful depression upon himself to "pay for sins." It is as though to say, "I need to be punished—I will punish myself to avoid greater punishment [from the introjected love object] and then he [the love object] will be sorry for me and forgive me and I can depend on him." This process in the patient is punctured by episodes of coercive rage (an ego function) and transgression, again to be later replaced by further expiatory behavior periodically. Rado *(6)* believed the manic-depressive periodicity can be explained on the basis of transgression maneuvers alternating with expiatory maneuvers. He clarified Abraham's observations that in depressions patients manifest a tremendous amount of aggression—at times directed against the environment and other times directed against themselves.

The depressed person suffers with an *inability to regulate his aggression,* and this is linked with other basic dynamic features present in depressions—the *oral regression,* the *ambivalence,* and the *conscience conflicts.* As is observed in manic-depressive depression, there are intense anxiety and guilt feelings present due to the unresolved conflicts in the depressed person's ambivalent relationship to those in his environment. When the feeling of guilt becomes unbearable, depression occurs as a defense mechanism. Depression is a mechanism of defense against the anxiety; it is not a symptom based on any specific psychodynamic mechanisms.

DIAGNOSIS OF DEPRESSIONS BASED ON PSYCHODYNAMICS

I have discussed a few of the dynamic features in a superficial way, and I would like to add at this point that ever since Abraham *(6)* worked on Freud's "id-ego-super-ego" concepts and it was postulated that manic-depressive psychosis represents a conflict between the patient's primitive "superego" and his "ego," attempts have been made to differentiate neurotic depressions from psychotic depressions on the basis of this or some other dynamic observations. Oberndorf made the attempt but he did not succeed. Now, if you study the essentials of many of these dynamic factors I have mentioned, you will very quickly arrive at the conclusion that all the dynamic factors have a validity in certain patients but they do not have full validity in all patients.

Even if you should generalize and assume that the dynamic factors apply to all patients, it very soon becomes clear we are dealing here more with final symptomatological description of a depression rather than actually with any etiological explanation as to really why the patient is depressed. In other words, we can understand to some extent a few of the partial motives at work in the patient, but we are not able to clearly demonstrate that *any* of these dynamic mechanisms are actually what produces the depression. We cannot demonstrate it because, interestingly enough, we observe a great many quite similar dynamic mechanisms in the psychoneuroses.

If you should utilize a few of the dynamic mechanisms in any attempts to differentiate between a so-called neurotic depression and a psychotic depression you would have a very difficult time of it. In fact, you would not be able to do it! Therefore, the great question, "Does the patient suffer from a psychotic depression or does he have a neurotic depression?" I am sorry to say, is a very academic one. It is usually just that, because if you analyze the dynamics of the patient you will not be able to diagnostically differentiate at all well. The so-called orality, the decrease of self-esteem, the introjection, the inability to form a good relationship with love objects, the conflict between "superego" and "ego" are all as equally present in a neurotic depression as they are present in a psychotic depression.

Those who attempt to differentiate between a neurotic depression and a psychotic depression do so based on the following procedure. In the case of a neurotic depression they perceive that they know the dynamic structure of the patient's psychoneurosis and that therefore they have clues to explain why the patient develops a depression. However, as I have pointed out, if they would know equally well the dynamic structure of a psychotically depressed patient, most likely they would arrive at exactly the same conclusion. Therefore, at the present time, I do not believe diagnostic differentiation is possible on the basis of dynamics.

One or two observers have attempted to differentiate a psychotic depression from a neurotic depression based on the so-called depth of "narcissistic" regression. In my opinion, the depth of regression occurring in a patient depends to a very large extent on the subjective appraisal of the therapist. If he is a little depressed and has some regressive features he will not be so likely to recognize those features as signs of regression when present in the patient. We have no objective sign for measuring regression but must depend on our observational acumen which certainly does not reliably designate the depth of regression. A generally accepted measurement for regression does not as yet exist. You have a fairly acceptable measurement for depth of regression in those cases of schizophrenia where the patient becomes so regressed that he wets and soils and so forth. In other words, a schizophrenic patient may actually demonstrate marked regression in his behavior pattern; regression which, incidentally, does not occur in manic-depressive psychosis. In this psychosis, therefore, regression is not measured by the patient's behavior, but by the patient's ideations, the patient's associations, and the patient's dreams, all three being insufficient to afford a proper measurement of depth of regression, not to mention that these signs are continually oscillating.

I would like to challenge anybody to demonstrate to me those dynamic factors upon which he relies to differentiate whether he is dealing with a person suffering from a neurotic depression or a psychotic depression, because the same dynamic constellations can occur in both. And, there is not a single dynamic mechanism that you could demonstrate to me—qualitatively speaking, without utilizing some quantitative explanation—that occurs only in a psychotic depression and does not occur in a neurotic depression, or vice versa. In my opinion, they are all notions which have not been verified on a large sampling of patients. Actually it would therefore boil down to the following: The difference between manic-depressive psychosis and the psychoneuroses would be a *quantitative* factor which is unknown; a quantitative factor which cannot be demonstrated. Aside from that, we are dealing actually with exactly the same dynamic mechanisms present in one as in the other.

Not rarely, however, one encounters a rather interesting arrangement whereby the dynamics are discovered to explain phenomena only *after* those phenomena have been observed for the first time. For instance, let us assume you have been analyzing a patient having what you presume to be neurotic symptomatology, and you have worked out the dynamic mechanisms. You have probably worked out the introjection to some extent, it being present if the patient is depressed. You have probably worked out the patient's "narcissistic" attitude. You have worked out his extreme sadism. You have worked out the unresolved oedipal situation, which has also been accused, as have so many things, of producing depression. All these dynamic mechanisms have been worked out. Then, suddenly the patient's depression becomes much deeper and suddenly he begins to express a delusion. At the moment you observe the delusion, you can then discover a dynamic explanation for the delusion, and it then appears as though you have found the dynamic explanation for the patient's now being psychotic. But actually, the correct diagnosis had not been made before some dynamic factor was discovered which was discovered only because the patient began to produce the delusion. This occurs frequently. It is my present opinion that these are academic acrobatics and are probably very interesting from a research point of view. Clinically, however, when you are confronted with a given case of depression I do not believe you will be able to differentiate very easily.

In depression, everything points toward the probability that we are dealing with *interaction patterns*. For example, similar to the phenomenon of allergy, two factors must be present: there must be the provoking agent and there must also be a particular organization within the person to respond to it. It is obvious that in all psychotic individuals there is most likely some type of an organization that enables the person to respond in a particular manner to the environmental provocative stimulation.

Although the environmental stimulation is surely very

important, you must perceive just how it interacts with the many other factors. The only unfortunate thing is that the many studies of constitution and heredity have not progressed beyond the simple statement that interaction does exist. The interaction has not been translated, for instance, into biochemical, metabolic, neurophysiological, or whatever processes are operating there. If one were able to demonstrate that the stimulation coming from the environment is metabolized or absorbed differently in a person, let us say, having a predisposition to manic-depressive psychosis than in the general population, we would have something to go by. At present we know only that there exist constitutional and hereditary factors and it is because these factors have not been demonstrated in action—as yet they are static concepts—that they have been to a large extent neglected. In other words, these factors are present, but what does one do with them?

The psychobiological approach formulated by Adolf Meyer *(6)* discusses dynamics in terms of the adaptational framework of reference. His concept is one which is very difficult to disprove but, here again, it is also very difficult to prove valid. Actually the Meyerian approach *(3)* is based on the concept of maladaptation, viewing maladaptation patterns to some extent, if not exactly, as Pavlovian conditioning. In other words, certain environmental influences condition an individual to maladapt and then the maladaptation continues to lead to further maladaptation by means of its own gravity until the individual eventually "breaks down." That is essentially the Meyerian concept. Now, it is certain that you can condition a person or other animals to a great many forms of behavior. Most certainly you can also uncondition and recondition a person to a great many things. The main difficulty is that we do not know to what extent we are really able to condition and recondition and, what is more important, in what realms—because obviously not every behavior can be conditioned and reconditioned equally well. There are, for instance, emotional patterns which are easy to undo; there are other emotional patterns which are extremely difficult to undo. This is the problem.

So, most likely there are three or four action systems operating: First, there is the metabolic organization of the individual, which would depend on the so-called constitutional factors determining how his nervous system "digests" stimuli. Secondly, there is the complex environmental interaction. Thirdly, there is his conditioning. All these elements are valid, but unfortunately we do not know in what proportion they are actually operating in each case. To some extent, the shortcoming of the Meyerian approach was that it included every reaction of the person in the maladaptation scheme, ranging from tonsillitis to choosing tile for the kitchen, and you never knew what was what! All the beautiful schemes of all factors producing maladaptation in an individual usually became a jumbled array impossible to sort out accurately.

In any case, I think we are unable to diagnostically differentiate depressions very well at the present time. Therefore, I believe that from the point of view of prognosis and treatment we should not be too preoccupied with the question, "Does the patient suffer from a neurotic depression or does the patient suffer from a psychotic depression?" In order to decide what treatment to apply, we should attempt instead to gauge (1) how severe the depression is, and (2) the extent to which we are able to reconstruct and understand some of the mechanisms behind the depression. I would like to repeat here that suicidal ideation or suicidal attempt is not a dynamic issue essentially. It is purely a mechanism describing the behavioral attitude of a person and the consequence of his depressive suffering. To properly gauge the degree of depression— mild, medium, or severe—is *much* more important from the point of view of prognosis and from the point of view of which therapy should be selected in treating the patient, than is the academic question, "Is the patient a manic-depressive depressed psychotic or is the patient suffering from a neurotic depression?" The diagnosis of manic-depressive psychosis, naturally, can be reliable only in a few of those patients having repeated attacks. Personally, I am much more readily led by the clinical observation of the mildness or severity of the patient's depression and the presence or absence of suicidal ideas. I am not so much concerned whether it is a neurotic depression or a psychotic depression because I know I cannot differentiate on the basis of all the dynamic or other factors I have just mentioned.

The reason I have discussed these matters in considerable detail is because a great many psychiatrists spend much time and ingenuity attempting to delineate the different forms of depression. This has also led to interesting treatment approaches, to say the least. For instance, there are those who state that psychotic depressions should be approached primarily by organic means from the beginning, and that neurotic depressions should be approached primarily by psychotherapeutic means. There are others who state that these treatment differentiations do not hold true and that all depressions should be treated alike. Still others may state that all depressions should be approached by organic means, or that all depressions should be approached by psychotherapeutic means.

In order to determine the choice of any therapy for manic-depressive and other depressions, one should, naturally, be acquainted with a few of the etiological theories. The theories of etiologies of manic-depressive psychosis and schizophrenia overlap. To avoid discussing the etiologies of the psychoses twice, I shall discuss etiology in connection with schizophrenia. Following discussion of etiology from a psychological, a psychodynamic, a descriptive, and an organic point of view, I can conclude with one simple sentence: The treatment of manic-depressive psychosis is empirical to those who humbly admit they do not know the origin of the psychosis. It is, however, not at all empirical to those who indulge in psychodynamic or organic mythologies that explain to them—but only to them—the origin of the manic-depressive psychosis. The same applies regarding schizophrenia, of course.

We have had presented to us a number of hypotheses as to the etiology, and we have had many hypotheses as to treatment. They are all still hypotheses. Of course, hypotheses and theories are necessary, because obviously anybody working in any field at all wants to try and fill the vacuum of ignorance and will try to offer explanations to himself and others as to "why." That is a perfectly legitimate scientific procedure, and so I think you should feel free to formulate ideas on the "why" question. I would merely like to impress upon you the fact that any of your ideas should be treated as an hypothesis, or at best a theory. Actually, however, we do not have any theory concerning etiologies since most of the hypotheses at present have never matured sufficiently to be honored by the title of theory. Because there are no contradictions present, they are all hypotheses, and everyone is entitled to choose the one he thinks is the best.

Incidentally, in formulating nomenclature, I never would have labeled schizophrenia or manic-depressive psychosis as a "functional psychosis," or a "endogenous psychosis," or a "psychosis with unknown structural origin," to mention a few of the designations printed in many textbooks. I would simply have labeled each, "psychosis of unknown origin," and then, of course, indicated the subdivisions. It would have been much healthier and much more honest if we had not updated the issue with all varieties of organic and psychodynamic assumptions which thereby imply we know the etiologies. It is rather painful to such a discipline as psychiatry to tell people, and even to tell students in psychiatry, that we do not know the origin of the great majority of mental disorders, but I think it is much better to admit the fact and go on from there rather than to imply we do know something when we do not!

20

MANIA: DIFFERENTIAL DIAGNOSIS AND PSYCHODYNAMIC THEORIES

Differentiation between the psychoneuroses and the psychoses has been discussed from the point of view of depressions only. But, if a patient manifests manic symptomatology the diagnosis is automatically that of psychosis, which is rather interesting. No textbook from any part of the world ever contained such an entity as "neurotic mania." A person may apply the term "reactive mania," meaning the manic-depressive patient responded with a manic attack to some precipitating factor, but it has never been emphasized, or even proposed, that any of the manic deviations could be neurotic.

Before attempting to differentiate manic-depressive mania from mania occurring in other disorders, we must differentiate clearly true mania from other disorders such as excitement states on the one hand and contented euphoria or satiation on the other. The *state of excitement* is often confused with true mania and has in common with it the motor discharge, but distractibility is not present in excitement states and no euphoria is demonstrated, fear and rage being the main affective elements. *Contented euphoria*, in which feelings of satisfaction and satiation are outstanding, has in common with manic states the feeling of well-being, but it lacks the obvious tension state of the manic patient. The *satiation states* do not include exaltation but are characterized by deep relaxation rather than tension, and by the feeling of contentment which the manic patient obviously lacks. Both excitement states and states of euphoric contentment are exceedingly common while the state of mania, characterized by tension and the emotional tone of elation, euphoria, exaltation, and the feeling of exaggerated well-being, is rare. By the way, both excitement states and states of euphoric contentment can be reactive to provoking stimuli in relatively normal individuals, but I would hesitate to assume that manic states are ever simply quantitative exaggerations of normal feelings.

We can begin with one question when discussing the differential diagnosis of mania: Why is mania so rare and why is depression so prevalent? No one knows. There has absolutely never been any explanation for this on either an organic, a psychodynamic, or on any other level. In research we attempted for several years to produce various emotional states by means of different chemical compounds; not a single chemical compound was found which produced a true state of mania. We were able to produce a certain amount of elation, and a certain amount of euphoria could also be produced, but not a true manic state as defined. (Depressive states, incidentally, also are not quite so difficult to produce chemically.)

Certain drugs such as alcohol, marihuana, and hashish are able to produce atypical manic reactions in some individuals. These reactions are, however, rare. With mescaline we were able to reinforce depressions and to produce schizophrenic-like pictures in many patients, but even atypical manic states were rarely produced. ACTH and cortisone have been used in treating arthritic patients and when recovery took place a few of these patients displayed a clinical picture of hypomania which was never so marked as to be considered pathological and was not accompanied by restlessness, tension, or aggressiveness. Much of the elation could have been due to relief from pain and arthritic infirmities.

You might raise the question that perhaps the state of mania is actually not so rare, but rather is a symptom rarely recognized clinically, and, since it is overlooked, it is not classified. I do not think that this is so, because you are even able to recognize *hypo*manic states in many cases. Occasionally you encounter a neurotic person who tries to suppress and become oblivious to a great conflictual issue. He pushes the whole problem away and actually establishes a state of nonconcern. But I have never observed a patient having the state of nonconcern which would give me the impression that euphoria, increase in psychomotor activity, flight of ideas, and so forth are all actually present as occurs in hypomanic individuals. Feelings of self-euphorization, if I may use that word, can surely occur, naturally, in neurotic persons, but it is somewhat different from that which you really observe in the state of mania. Incidentally, the fully developed manic state, which is clearly recognized because its most conspicuous feature is the symptom triad, occurs also very rarely. Remember, I am not referring here to excitement states; they should not be confused with manic states. Those states mostly encountered in mental hospitals are not manic states; they are excitement states. True manic states, as I have described them, are very, very rare. We now approach another matter about which I would like to inject a certain amount of doubt. I am not so certain that in hospitals the excitement states are very frequently mistaken for being manic states. Some of the reports I have read and people with whom I have spoken were much more inclined toward classifying these states as being catatonic excitement rather than actual manic states. Furthermore, when atypical manic states occurred very often drugs were involved.

Among the Malayan people, episodes have been observed of what is termed "running amuck." These states, which are not quite clear, in our classification involve all types of mental disorders. Many of these amuck-runners suffer from epilepsy. Another group of amuck-runners are intoxicated persons. When in a state of alcohol intoxication, it is interesting that they run amuck in a manner similar to that occasionally observed in our culture. A state of rage is produced by some incident, then the person begins to drink while in a state of rage, then dissociative symptomatology occurs in the form of an hysterical fugue state, and then they run amuck. This phenomenon occurs especially in socio-pathic types of individuals.

Attempts to explain symptomatologies present us with a very complicated problem. Because we have only a phenomenological analysis of these conditions, we tend to assume the symptoms in a psychosis to be primary. It is quite possible that some unknown basic mechanism can become channelized into different forms of expression. I would not be surprised, for instance, if an American living among Malayans developed a tension state and selected as the expression of this tension symptom reactions prevalent in that particular civilization. In other words, we have here a very difficult situation regarding psychoses because many of the symptoms which are considered primary are most likely secondary to some processes which are as yet unknown. Many psychotic symptoms are already compensatory mechanisms, being attempts by the individual to solve his situation, and this symptom process is, naturally, malleable. The basic issue, causing the tension state in the individual which then becomes channelized into particular symptom pictures, is unknown.

We have to assume that there exists some primary mechanism, as yet unknown to us, which produces some form of an alteration of emotional control in these individuals. We can only observe how this is then channelized and expressed. This channelization is very often confused with etiology! The selection of channelization of symptoms, furthermore, not only varies in different cultural groups, but also changes over a period of time. For instance, there arose a tremendous difference in symptom pictures between the time of World War I and World War II.

On the grounds of clinical observations, I believe if you would review in your mind patients you have observed, you will realize that one simply does not encounter elated individuals in any diagnostic category you want to name. I very much doubt the validity of the claim that states of elation go unrecognized because the symptomatology is so pleasant that it is therefore accepted and overlooked, while the depressions are unpleasant and therefore not ignored. I do not agree! You may claim that because they are not recognized as pathological they do not come to our offices; that is probably correct. But I do not even encounter them outside the office, and surely somebody would be running across them. Apparently this type of reaction is not a very prevalent one in our civilization, which is, to a large extent, discontented. Depressions are prevalent in our culture but are rare in certain cultural groups. Among Malayan groups, for example, observations have indicated depressions rarely occur. Similar observations also were made on a Guatemalan group in which cases of depression are so extremely rare that there are no suicidal precautions taken in the hospital. The incidence of depressions occurring in different cultures needs to be further investigated.

Now, you can take another issue which is very interesting. It is a matter of opinion which I wish to mention only in passing. Take the matter of neurotic structures, or take the ideas occurring in an obsessive-phobic patient, as an example. If you show me an individual who has a pleasant phobia, or a pleasant obsession, that would be most interesting. You may be amused, but such phenomena are actually observed in certain civilizations. Unfortunately, we do not have cross-cultural studies; we have only various isolated observations.

I would emphasize the fact of its extreme rarity—I have observed it in only two cases. It occurs in the state of exaltation in individual obsessive schizophrenic patients also. I have also observed it in an epileptic patient. Although it can occur in an individual setting, apparently it is more prevalent in group settings. In our culture, it is so rare that if you observe such a phenomenon your first thought should be that you are dealing with an organic disorder. Furthermore, in urbanized and industrialized cultures you probably will not encounter groups manifesting this symptom picture. The so-called pleasant obsessions occurring in groups of people were described by Kraepelin and there have been subsequent observations. For example, among Central Americans and Javanese, phobic or obsessive symptomatology at times occurs in group situations along with manifested exaltation, and the exaltation leads to very pleasant recapitulation of a very pleasant ritual for the persons involved.

In the study of all these issues, I would very sharply differentiate between observations of independent individual pathology and abnormal behavior of individuals occurring in the framework of a group. Here, again, a great deal of confusion exists. In the same sense, it its not permissible to speak about "group paranoias," or about "hebephrenic deterioration of a civilization," as has been done in the literature. These are actually terms pertaining to individual pathology, and we do not know anything about their application to group phenomena, even though the symptoms appear to be the same or similar in both cases. If a person manifests an anxiety picture, euphoric picture, and so forth, in a group setting, that is an entirely different matter from his doing it on his own. Incidentally, I must also warn you about cultural studies: Many cultural studies have been done by anthropologists who do not know psychiatry and by psychiatrists who do not know anthropology. You can add up these two factors and then imagine, naturally, just how very reliable will be the set of data obtained by amateurs in both.

PSYCHODYNAMIC THEORIES

It has been pointed out by practically all the psychiatric schools that mania is dynamically considered to be polar opposite to depression in terms of the clinical picture, but not in terms of the actual basic symptomatology. Depression is a secondary mechanism. Mania is also a secondary mechanism. Both depression and mania are defense mechanisms and are not primary in the disorder. In certain respects depression and mania are two similar phenomena: They are symptom reactions to conflicts which may be the same in each disorder. In other words, the manic person may be faced with the same conflict that confronts the person who reacts by becoming depressed. Furthermore, in the circular type of manic-depressive psychosis the *same* person reacts by having an attack of mania alternating with an attack of depression, and his alternating attacks can occur over a period of many years. In other words, the person in a manic state merely *manipulates* the conflictual material differently than does the person in a depressed state, although in either state the conflictual material is perceived to be the same. Therefore, dynamically, it is assumed that the manic reaction is only one form of coping with the depression. The person in a state of mania is not essentially a happy person; we could describe him as a "happily depressed" person. The manic individual gives the impression of paying attention to all stimuli in a rather forced manner in order to avoid dealing directly with his conflicts. Why he does that is unknown; the euphoria and incessant activity are difficult to explain. Why the manic type of coping is infinitely more rare than the depressive also remains a question.

It remains quite unclear why some patients respond with a manic reaction and others do not. Since there are those cases where a drug (such as ACTH) may actually produce a semblance of the manic reaction, it is possible there is a defense mechanism already present in the individual which predisposes him to cope with a conflict in a manic way, but he is not able to cope with it until a new stress factor enters, namely, the introduction of a hormone which alters the homeostasis. However, it is also possible that the biochemical alteration of homeostasis also works as a primary stress and offers a predilection to defense formation. Ferenczi and Hollos (1925), in the organic interpretation of the "expansiveness" of general paresis patients, made pertinent observations in this respect. Here, we are clearly dealing with multifactorial causation of a mental state.

The ability to cut the manic attack by organic means is also important. We now know that certain drugs are able to reduce the manic attack whereas formerly electroconvulsive therapy had temporarily—and lobotomy permanently—successfully cut the manic state in a few cases. How does all this fit in concerning the dynamics of a manic patient? Why is it possible to reduce or eliminate the manic state with organic means, if it is essentially a psychogenic (goal-directed motivational) process? Obviously we can influence it by organic means because the activation of the motive mechanism takes place within the brain without which we believe there is no motivational function.

According to the dynamic formulation based on Freud's frame of reference, in the state of mania there is a regression in which the patient's superego has become fused with his ego. The functioning of the superego disappears and, when the conscience mechanisms are abolished, the individual lives out all his instinctual drives. This would indicate that the manic (as is the depressive) state is "unconsciously purposeful." The view is in contrast to Kraepelin's idea that depressive and manic states have "lack of purpose," which is correct in terms of purely objective behavior phenomenology. In other words, Kraepelin did not use the concept of the "unconscious" of Freud and his followers. What Kraepelin observed in mania were the "fugacity" of ideas and multiple goals; in depression he emphasized the inhibitions, the inability to function, and the harping expressions of guilt that were seemingly unwarranted in terms of the objective facts. Kraepelin and Freud were in common agreement in their belief that the actual basic factor in the psychoses is a biochemical pathology or disturbance somewhere in the body.

To return to the question of unconscious motivation, there is no psychodynamic pattern characteristic for a depression or for a manic state. The dynamics present may be similar to those occurring in other psychiatric disorders. Many of the psychodynamic interpretations become apparent only after the manic (or depressive) state is established, or else they are apparent in retrospect. I am quite certain that similar dynamic observations can be made in a fair number of patients who never develop a manic attack. Actually, no one has yet been able to foretell the occurrence of a manic attack based on the dynamics of a patient who is examined. It is only during and after the attack that these configurations are clear. We believe this is due to the fact that the examiner does not know what other factors play a role in the production of the manic attack, and especially how far the patient is able to withstand or regulate the tensions which are set up by the conflicts underlying the defense mechanisms. The motive of the patient to have a manic attack is only one link in the chain.

The motives perhaps explain the content of the manic state, but they do not explain the mania itself. The causation of mania is still completely obscure. More will have to be known, not only about the "why" of the patient's behavior, but also about "how" these motives release a manic reaction. Actually, the dynamics are often no more than minute descriptions of the symptomatology. Psychoanalysis may illuminate the conflicts present, but that is all.

It may explain the patient's mania (or depression) in terms of the conflict, but it does not explain *why* he developed that *particular* symptomatology. The dynamics do not give us a clue to the etiologies of the manic-depressive disorder, and the conflicts themselves also cannot be presented as being a direct cause.

The main difference between manic-depressive psychosis and psychoneurosis has been considered dynamically in terms of the extent to which the patient regresses. It has been assumed that the lower the patient regresses into the narcissistic level, the more likely the patient is psychotic rather than neurotic. Such dynamic differentiation relies on quantitative, not qualitative, descriptive features and in no way explains the etiologies of the conflicts underlying the patient's symptomatology.

I do not believe that, even though similarities exist, we can say the same dynamic mechanisms play a role in every manic state, regardless of the setting in which each occurs. A few elementary observations on the defense nature and on the type of oral regression in mania are probably valid regardless of whether or not the patient shows a schizophrenic, organic, or neurotic reaction; but the relationship of these manic manfestations to the other abnormal mental states in which framework they appear will be highly important, and a certain specificity will have to be required. If this is not done, we will not get much further than to say that all mental patients have conflicts which they wish to be rid of and that they all wish to return to the oral state of blissful tranquility.

Mental states can be released by physical and mental means and can be influenced by physical and mental means. At present it is difficult to integrate the observations made on these two different tracks of approach. If an attempt is made to do so, one can say that, broadly speaking, the organism is unable to cope with excessive stimulation. Stimulation is caused by stress or by stresses disturbing the emotional regulation. The organism has different motivational approaches to cope with conflicts, and in mania one of these is denial, a defense to ward off impulses. When the conflictual situation sets up a tension state, a second factor enters, namely, the disorganization of emotional integration. At present we may perhaps know *why* the person is conflicted, but we do *not* know *how* this disorganization takes place.

The nervous system regulates the quantity of energy discharges. After an impairment of regulation takes place, these discharges are quantitatively altered. This leads to an exaggerated stress response in which the higher regulative mechanisms are not functioning properly.

Psychoanalytic approach may disclose the origin of the conflict and motives in the patient, and the way in which he attempts to cope with the situation. This, however, does not explain why one patient responds with scarcely any emotional alteration, others with elation, and again others with a severe manic reaction. The quantity of symptoms released is not explained by means of the motivational scheme. Similarly, as in psychosomatic cases, it does not explain the selection of the organ and the quantity of organ involvement. Such states as depression and mania can be called "psychosomatic" sicknesses, and I believe that if we would study them with the same approach used in studying hypertension and colitis, we would further illuminate their obscure etiology.

I may call attention here to the now well-known observations that a peculiar reciprocal relationship exists between tension states observed in certain so-called psychosomatic disorders—such as colitis, hypertension, and asthma—and certain psychotic episodes, usually of the schizophrenic or depressive type. There are patients who alternate between discharges downward into the viscera and upward into the environment. When psychotherapeutic or other attempts are made to cure the visceral disturbances, the patient's organ function may return to normality but be followed by the appearance of a psychosis. The reverse is also often observed. The study of these phenomena will probably illuminate the different factors present in the production of emotional sickness and how it utilizes somatic channels for its expression.

We do not believe that knowing the motive on one hand, and the regulative impairment on the other of the psychic or somatic factor alone, would give us the whole picture in psychotic states. We will have to study the inter-action of both, as in the psychosomatic cases. It is possible that one stress situation is not sufficient to provoke the dis-order but that it requires several succeeding stresses. In cases of war neuroses this is quite clearly manifested; psychic motivation erupted into action when the stresses became intensified by exhaustion or deprivation of food or sleep.

When experimenting with different drugs to produce experimental psychotic states I and my associates found that with mescaline or lysergic acid it is possible to markedly intensify the emotional changes already present in the patient. For instance, if anxiety or depression is present, under the influence of the drug they become markedly exaggerated. These emotional states are not only under-scored by the drug as to form, but also as to content. Seem-ingly the drug acts here as an additional stress and the defenses of the patient which, of course, were put into operation by the motivational framework become more exaggerated and the further regression of the patient is facilitated.

In general, therefore, it can be assumed that the ability of the patient to act on his conflicts can be explained dynami-cally by understanding the motives for it. However, an additional factor enters the picture, namely, the extent to which the patient is able to regulate the emotional tension set up by the conflictual situation. This depends on the emotional regulative ability of the patient. For example, if a patient is suffering from a stomach ulcer and we cut the vagus nerve, the tension can no longer be transmitted to the stomach. If we cut the fronto-thalamic fibers in leukotomy, again, most likely the conflictual tension cannot be transmitted—in other words, the conflict still exists, but the tension created in the attempt to cope with it cannot form.

We do not actually know why that is so, and we do not even know what then happens to the conflict. We observe only that no responses occur in conflictual situations if the ego is not overwhelmed and remains able to cope with it. *How* the ego becomes overwhelmed we do not know. It remains only a fragment of knowledge if we are not able to supplement the "why" and the "how" questions with the different factors which I have tried to point out.

A very important factor is neglected in psychiatry because we have not found a way to measure the quantity of emotions. The qualitative approach is, therefore, very much in the foreground. We have tried to find out, by analyzing the psychodynamic factors of a case, what conflicts in what constellations produce the emotional disorder. The fact is overlooked that many of these conflicts can be present in a person and he still does not show an emotional disorder until the symptoms become so marked that he is dominated by his tensions and the results of his tensions. Occasionally psychotherapy is able to reduce the impact of these dominant symptoms in the patient. Drugs and psychosurgery do the same on an organic level. These latter treatments are quantitative treatments which leave the underlying conflicts untouched but somehow the patient no longer perceives them as such and is no longer disorganized by them, therefore permitting him to function. This quantitative aspect of an emotional disorder is of great importance but how it is regulated is unknown; it is surely a factor which has to be added to the qualitative aspects of the problem.

The whole problem remains to be solved; at the present time there is no theory that can completely, or even adequately, explain the manic or the depressive state.

Part V
Schizophrenia

21

HISTORY, CLASSIFICATION, AND DEFINITION OF SCHIZOPHRENIA

Schizophrenia, or the disorders which are the group of schizophrenias, has been recognized for a long time. It had already been described in ancient reports and, therefore, we cannot state that it was first described by Kraepelin. It was described innumerable times before he gave it the name dementia praecox. You also know, historically, that the subgroups of schizophrenia, and especially the hebephrenic and the catatonic forms, were also described in detail before Kraepelin by Hecker and Kahlbaum(4). Kraepelin made the great contribution of organizing the knowledge in existence at that time. He coordinated it and was able to put it into a coherent system; it was a system which—even though we all realize it has many weaknesses and has undergone a number of theoretical and practical modifications—is still the only system used the world over. Therefore, we must give Kraepelin credit because at a time when practically every symptom in a patient was described as a separate disorder, he was able to coordinate and organize apparently unrelated findings. He also had other merits; namely, the introduction of the follow-up study and the idea that some experimental approach in psychiatry would eventually elucidate some of the underlying etiologies. In the more modern psychiatry, therefore, dementia praecox is associated with the name of Kraepelin. To be historically correct, you know that even the name dementia praecox was not that of Kraepelin's. In was Morel of France who described it with the name "demence precoce" before Kraepelin. However, Kraepelin accepted this term because he believed that it expressed quite correctly the main features of the disorder as he viewed it at that time, namely, the appearance of dementia setting in at an early age.

Kraepelin was fascinated by the course of the disorder, and to some extent even more by its course than its symptomatology. It was his opinion that any mental disease of nondemonstrable anatomical origin (I here use the expression "anatomical" advisedly, because Kraepelin also considered schizophrenia to be an organic disease), and any disorder occurring around the time of puberty which led to deterioration, belonged in the dementia praecox group. On the other hand, those patients who did not show much tendency to deteriorate, and those who showed a tendency to recover, he classified in the manic-depressive group. He would often subordinate the clinical symptomatology of the disorder to the clinical course. This, however, led to the somewhat anomalous situation (of which he himself was somewhat aware) as to how to classify a schizophrenic who recovered. First of all, his scheme did not give much allowance for recovery because the disorder was naturally considered a progressive, irretrievable dementia. Secondly, there was the difficulty in classifying those patients who showed manic-depressive symptomatology and yet deteriorated— cases which later on became an increasing focus of study.

Today many are discussed as schizophrenics showing "mixed" symptomatology.

Therefore, the basic idea of Kraepelin was that what is now termed schizophrenia is a progressive disorder, with acute or insidious onset, which emerges around the time of puberty and invariably leads to deterioration of the patient. In other words, the patient becomes "de-mented." Kraepelin's description was readily accepted because the group of cases around which this idea was organized, mainly the hebephrenic group, and some patients in the catatonic group, actually followed this course. Kraepelin himself, however, acknowledged that about 8 percent of the hebephrenic patients he described showed a good remission and 26 percent of his catatonic patients showed a good remission. Therefore, he himself stated that the disorder was not quite as hopeless as it had appeared to him, although it still appeared hopeless enough.

I would like to call attention to the fact that the diagnostic approach to schizophrenia became modified. Today, if we just included in the group of what we term the schizophrenias, or dementia praecox, those hebephrenic and catatonic patients showing the massive symptomatology which Kraepelin described, his somewhat hopeless attitude would remain almost as valid. Our change in attitude about the hopelessness of schizophrenia is not so much because any of the hebephrenic patients or chronic catatonic patients behave differently than in Kraepelin's time, but because today we include a great many more conditions under the designation of schizophrenia. With this inclusion, we naturally dilute this deterioration concept. Because of the dilution by the introduction of many hopeful, or at least more hopeful, cases, it to some extent obscures the view of the outcome of these "nuclear" cases of schizophrenia—the true cases of dementia praecox.

Incidentally, when Kraepelin introduced his idea of dementia praecox he conceived it as: (1) a single disease entity, an entity to be viewed in the same manner pathologists view tuberculosis, syphilis, typhoid fever, and so forth; (2) a disease progressing to deterioration; and (3) a disease hopeless to any known therapeutic attempts. Now, immediately upon Kraepelin's introduction of this concept of dementia praecox, a reaction was set up by another group of German psychiatrists led by Alfred Hoche *(5)*. He was the first to put forth the idea that we were not dealing with a disease per se, but rather a reaction. He felt that we were dealing with a disorder not absolutely deteriorating but only relatively so; he used the analogy that in some persons a galloping tuberculosis develops, and in others it is slowly ambulating. Each is quite different in terms of outcome. Hoche, an opponent of Kraepelin, wrote a number of well thought-out papers. Quite a number of Adolf Meyer's later pronunciations *(5)* were based on Hoche's work. By maintaining that in schizophrenia we were dealing with a reaction, Meyer laid the basis for more modern ideas, rightly or wrongly, of schizophrenia. He also maintained that because it was a reaction, it was naturally not a disease in the sense of tuberculosis, syphilis, or typhoid.

The next move in actually modifying the original concept of schizophrenia came from Eugen Bleuler *(2)*, who is now considered the person who gave us the best organized and most balanced view on schizophrenia. It was considered the best balanced view in the sense that Bleuler included all the somatic and organic observations, on one hand, and psychodynamic observations on the other. The organic observations of Bleuler followed to some extent the line of Kraepelin and others. Some of the psychodynamic observations included were derived from dynamic formulations of Freud that reached him through Jung, who had worked with both Freud and Eugen Bleuler. Bleuler then evolved the concept of schizophrenia published in 1911 as *Dementia Praecox or the Group of Schizophrenias,* in which he maintained that schizophrenia is a group of disorders. In other words, he considered it a syndrome quite probably having different etiologies; however, because common features are present, as in any syndrome, he classified them together. Even in the 1911 publication, the title does not refer to schizophrenia, but in plural—the "schizophrenias." This point slowly became lost in the shuffle. Bleuler thus assumed a position acknowledging some of Kraepelin's descriptions that schizophrenia is some form of disease, but stated it as a disease having a group of syndromes. This lent itself to some of Hoche's ideas that schizophrenia is a reaction.

Bleuler, furthermore, eliminated Kraepelin's idea that the disease should or should not be diagnosed purely on the basis of deterioration. He stated that if deterioration is definitely present it is, of course, an aid in determining the diagnosis, but that in early cases of schizophrenia deterioration is usually not present, and in quite a number of even long-term chronic cases deterioration does not appear. Deterioration is, therefore, a feature which often appears, but is a facultative feature and not an absolute feature of the disorder.

Bleuler stressed that schizophrenia must be diagnosed and understood on the basis of its clinical symptomatology, especially on the psychological manifestations, later called (if one wants to) the "psychodynamic" aspects which at that time were not exactly crystallized. Nevertheless, he stressed the psychological organization of these individuals and the psychological alterations in the clinical picture, all of which he described in detail. The term he selected—schizophrenia, a split mind—also indicated that he perceived the main disturbance to be a "splitting." The psychological mechanisms of "splitting" were, according to him, actually one of the outstanding basic symptoms of the disease and present in all cases of dementia praecox. He was also the person who pointed out that this "splitting" occurs not only in puberty, but can occur earlier or much later. Although he recognized that the bulk of schizophrenias occur at an early age level, a considerable number, particularly in the so-called paranoid group—an observation which became more and more

606 DIFFERENTIAL DIAGNOSIS

n)ted—occurred at the age levels of the thirties and forties. He therefore rejected the term "dementia praecox" because these were not disorders occuring only in puberty and were not, according to him, disorders inevitably leading to deterioration. Bleuler also maintained that a number of patients show "spontaneous" or other remissions, that therefore schizophrenia is not as hopeless as it was described by Kraepelin, even though he always regarded it as a very serious mental disorder. It is!

Bleuler was the person who described the "primary" and "secondary" symptoms in schizophrenia. These observations were of great import! After Bleuler made this differentiation it became somewhat obscured, but we are again moving it into the foreground, namely, the differentiation between primary symptoms, basic to schizophrenia, and the symptomatology that stems from these basic symptoms.

Following the concepts of Bleuler, there have not been very essential changes introduced regarding the understanding and classification of schizophrenia. When I discuss some of the etiological ideas, you will find that these have somewhat changed, or the emphasis has to some extent shifted in recent years; nevertheless, the basic idea as to organization of schizophrenia today still rests on the formulations of Kraepelin and Bleuler. After Bleuler, an attempt was made—and this has always been the tendency—to divide schizophrenia into different subgroups; all kinds of arranging and rearranging took place in this respect. For instance, paranoid schizophrenia was "split off" from the schizophrenias and handled as a separate entity. "Paraphrenia" and "paranoia" were considered by a few as separate entities and by others as a part of schizophrenia. Kleist and others (3) introduced the concept of the "degeneration psychosis." These cases were all schizophrenic. He and other investigators introduced the "acute motility psychoses," which were actually schizophrenic patients in acute catatonic episodes. These were all attempts to reduce schizophrenia from a very large entity and to define other groups. We must admit that so far all these attempts have been rather unsuccessful, and even though subgroup descriptions and group descriptions of schizophrenia are sometimes treated as separate diagnostic entities, an actual separation was never very successful.

In the last decade or so, attempts were made to resurrect the old term dementia praecox and to differentiate it from schizophrenia. These attempts, I would say, were not very successful because the terms were treated practically the world over as synonymous. Along with this, an altogether new meaning was again introduced and this led to even more confusion in an already confused field. There were those who felt the nuclear forms of schizophrenia (the forms which deteriorate rather rapidly and which, phenomenologically and basically, give an organic impression just as do some early catatonic and hebephrenic schizophrenic patients) were a different group; this group should be designated as dementia praecox. It is usually characterized by a slow, insidious, progressive course with a number of somatic manifestations. It also has a bad prognosis and an inaccessibility to therapy. Accordingly, it was felt the other disorders which do not show these characteristics should be designated as schizophrenia; they should be considered as basically psychogenic disorders, as psychogenic reactions, having a relatively good prognosis and responding to certain organic and psychiatric therapies with no tendency to deterioration. Langfeldt (6) was the one who introduced this concept of a second group. He termed it the "schizophreni-form of psychosis," rather than schizophrenia. Tredgold (1945), (6), in England, however, then made the final step and called this second group "schizophrenia" and the first group "dementia praecox."

I personally feel all attempts valuable that try to delineate more closely some of the subgroups featured in schizophrenia, because schizophrenia is surely a very large entity. On the other hand, all these arrangements and rearrangements, as I mentioned, are not very successful. If I examine a patient today and this patient shows a symptomatology that is not fully developed, in most instances it would be rather difficult to say whether the patient belongs in the first or second group. All these classificatory attempts are naturally very nice if they are based on hindsight. If I am able to follow a patient for five years and reexamine him, I can then decide whether the patient belongs in the first or second group. Therefore, this is all rather vague and I think that what we should do is to diagnose a patient as schizophrenic—which is the most important—and then try to describe more closely what kind of symptoms this patient shows in the framework of the schizophrenia. Those who tried this classification have pointed out (and their objection is valid) that the findings in certain reports and statistics cannot be collated because the reporting psychiatrists simply make the diagnosis of schizophrenia and do not pay very much attention to the subgroups with which they are dealing. The subgroups are of importance because it is obvious that a patient who shows a hebephrenic picture is different from the patient showing a paranoid picture; a person with a very acute onset naturally shows a different picture than a patient showing a slow and insidious onset. Therefore, after diagnosing patients as schizophrenic, one should attempt to ascertain the subgroup in which they belong.

PRESENT CLASSIFICATION

Along with the classical divisions of the disorder, we now tend to differentiate schizophrenia into four groups. One includes the so-called *deteriorating* group, the second includes the *nondeteriorating* group. Both could show either slow and insidious or episodic courses. In both the deteriorating and nondeteriorating groups one must be able to demonstrate that the psychotic symptoms are most manifest and overt. In addition, there are the third and fourth groups, which could be termed psychotic "borderline" groups. The third shows preeminently *neurotic or sociopathic* manifestations, and the fourth group mainly shows *affective* features resembling those of the manic-depressive psychosis, or perhaps the so-called "schizo-affective" picture.

DEFINITION

The next question is to define schizophrenia. Naturally this is a legitimate question. It is very rarely asked! It is not asked because the answer is rather difficult. It is obvious that attempts have been made to find an organic, a psychological, or a psychodynamic common denominator for all cases we call schizophrenic. However, attempts in working out a common denominator upon any line have failed thus far. This is the reason why the diagnosis of schizophrenia is not as objective as, of course, the diagnosis of general paresis. No one single demonstrable organic, psychodynamic, or psychological factor defines schizophrenia; we have no such one particular criterion. In other words, to put it very plainly, we do not have a Wassermann reaction for schizophrenia. Were we to have it, everything would be very much simpler—but we do not have it. I would like to emphasize that, because recently some investigators who are markedly in love with psychological tests have tried to imply that such a particular criterion exists. It does not exist. However, in the search for a common denominator in schizophrenia we can say the following: *Most schizophrenic patients have certain deviations in thinking, in affectivity, and in behavior* which, in a certain *configuration or constellation,* could be evaluated more or less objectively as indicative of the presence of schizophrenia. I stress constellation and configuration of certain symptoms because no single symptom you can name in psychopathology can alone give you the diagnosis of schizophrenia.

There are certain symptoms which are suggestive; one example is that the patient had auditory hallucinations. Because auditory hallucinations are very common in schizophrenia, these could be a suggestive symptom. However, auditory hallucinations are not indicative of schizophrenia per se; they also occur in other states. One might say that deterioration is indicative of schizophrenia; it is, if it is a special form of deterioration. But often this cannot be differentiated very well from organic states, or from states of impaired thinking in persons under particular stress. Therefore, some symptoms are suggestive, but are not in any way pathognomonic for schizophrenia. On the other hand, if some of those symptoms which I shall soon enumerate in detail as symptoms which can be observed clinically (and also in various test situations) are present in a certain constellation and also in a certain quantity, with our present knowledge we are probably entitled to diagnose such a person as schizophrenic—whatever this diagnosis means.

Schizophrenia, because of attempts made to reduce it to one or the other of the basic phenomena, has been described as essentially a thinking disorder; it has been described by others as an affective disorder; others have described it as a personality disorder. Actually, descriptions ranging all the way from the organic through the psychodynamic, each stressing its particular aspects of the disorder, are basically correct. Some of the partial observations of different schools of thought have contributed to our knowledge. The trouble arose, however, when some of these findings were generalized. In the first phase of this effort, it was assumed that because associative difficulties are present in schizophrenia, all schizophrenics show them, and therefore schizophrenia is an associative disorder. The original idea of Bleuler, that schizophrenia is actually a disorder in which associations are loosened (partly based on some of the observations of Janet and Kraepelin) is true to a large extent, if present. First, it is not always present. I want at least to be cautious; it is not always present in a demonstrable way. Second, this is certainly not the only type of disorder that can be demonstrated in a schizophrenic, and it cannot be assumed that the emotional or affective changes are a sequence or reaction to the disorder in associations.

A second phase in the efforts to define the basis of schizophrenia emerged when more and more of the psychodynamic concepts began to develop. The picture was then turned about and a generalization was maintained that schizophrenia is essentially an emotional disorder, an affective disorder of a special kind. This idea went so far, especially under the influence of Freud's classification, that schizophrenia came to be regarded simply as a kind of neurosis. Incidentally, I would like to emphasize that Freud fully realized schizophrenia had a special role; although he grouped it under the neuroses, calling it a form of the narcissistic neuroses and was fully aware that this was just another name, he stressed that schizophrenia was something other than a neurosis. He stressed this again and again. However, semantic issues have a great influence and, because it was grouped under the neuroses, some of his followers began to treat it as if it were actually a neurosis with only some quantitative differences in relationship to the other neuroses. The basic issue was that it was considered an affective disorder, an emotional disorder; the tendency became more and more apparent to subordinate all other observations made in schizophrenia to the emotional change. Schizophrenia finally emerged as an emotional reaction whereby the organic disorders, the associative disorders, and the behavioral and action pattern disorders were all explained purely on an emotional level.

The third phase, interestingly enough, started not so much in psychiatry, but in psychology. When psychological tests became better organized and applied more intensively to schizophrenic patients, a very interesting discovery was made. This so-called discovery (which was something already known at the end of the 19th century) was that in schizophrenics not only are there emotional changes, but there are also peculiar intellectual deviations from the norm. These are especially clear in concept formations and related thinking disorders. Then, the whole business went back to where it began! *Schizophrenia is a disorder of* (1) the *intellect,* (2) the *emotions,* (3) the *regulative mechanisms* of the emotions, and to some extent also the so-called physical functions of the individual. Schizophrenia began to emerge as *a disorder of the total personality*—to use the rather trite expression which is bantered about today. Then a more or less *holistic* concept began to emerge indicating that we were dealing with a deep-rooted disorder of the whole individual in which much of the material presented was twisted, distorted, disordered, primitive, and archaic. This disorder shows itself in different aspects, in different facets, and can naturally, therefore, be interpreted and investigated from many different angles.

The tendency to subordinate some of the observations made in schizophrenia to one or the other of the current leading ideas—primarily organic or primarily psychogenic, primarily emotional or primarily intellectual—remains with us. This tendency to subordinate is perfectly legitimate and it will obviously be with us until a solution is found on one or the other levels regarding what this disorder actually means. I mention this, and wish to emphasize it, because whenever you hear or read about some new hypothesis, some new explanation, or some new diagnostic, prognostic, or therapeutic procedures, you must be aware that such a thing must satisfy us all around and not be simply a regrouping of some of the facts in attempts to subordinate some of the known things to accommodate one leading idea.

22

CLINICAL MANIFESTATIONS
OF SCHIZOPHRENIA:
BASIC CLINICAL AND
GROSS PSYCHOTIC SYMPTOMS

As it stands today, we can define schizophrenia as a deep-rooted, organically based disorder of unknown etiology. It is a disorder of the "total personality," probably based on some subcortical defects dealing with integrative and regulative processes. This disorganization in schizophrenia is a total biological affair and includes characteristic basic symptomatology on intellectual and emotional levels.

Following this assumption, I will first describe our knowledge of that which we have observed in the schizophrenic person. I will then discuss these observations in a more dynamic and interrelated way. One must keep in mind that all these observations are fragmentary: The trouble is that although we know a great deal about what is going on in schizophrenic persons, it has not as yet been possible to synthesize the observations into a basic theory and evolve a common denominator. Therefore, because we do not have a unified theory of schizophrenia that would take into consideration all the clinical observations made, I have no recourse but to describe them in this fragmentary manner.

In discussing symptomatology, I wish now to describe those schizophrenics who are overtly and manifestly psychotic. (Later I will describe patients in whom the symptoms are so subtle that they can be considered "borderline," or in the early phase of the disorder.) In dealing with a manifestly psychotic schizophrenic, you will clearly observe a basic change in the patient. This is particularly true of patients falling into the hebephrenic and catatonic groups. It is much less so in the paranoid group, because in paranoid schizophrenia some of the basic symptoms present appear in a modified form just as they do in simple schizophrenia. This basic change seemingly envelops the whole psyche of the person. Occasionally a schizophrenic patient gives the impression of having only some partial disorder. The idea mentioned originally by the old French school was that a person can have one abnormal or delusional idea, or "monomania," and be otherwise normal. And sometimes a schizophrenic will show one peculiar behavior or reaction pattern indicating to you that he is abnormal only in a circumscribed range but otherwise normal. That is never the actual case! If you investigate these patients carefully and take enough time to follow one such patient, you will find that although he appears to be impaired only in a rather circumscribed way—or if I want to borrow an expression, only shows an "abscess" formation somewhere—he is actually sick in a *diffused* way; the "abscess" formation is only the crystallization of the disorder at one point. This is very important to know for prognosticating as well as for treatment of these patients. It is too often overlooked. Now, we must first discuss the more basic symptomatology, and then the gross psychotic manifestations of schizophrenia.

BASIC CLINICAL SYMPTOMS

THINKING DISORDERS : Impairment of thinking is characterized by two or three outstanding features: the most
important is *fragmentation of thinking*; the second, *impairment of concept formation*. The person is unable to differentiate clearly between concrete and abstract concepts.
Using expressions of Gestalt psychology, which was applied
most fruitfully to schizophrenic thinking, the person is
unable to differentiate between figure and background; that
is, the so-called *Gestalt formation is impaired*. In addition
to the fragmentation in thinking and so-called categorical,
or concept, impairment, there is a tendency toward a form
of "primitive" and *"archaic" thinking* which is a mechanism
of *regression* in the realm of thinking paralleling some of the
regression tendencies in the emotional spheres.

Two other thinking disorders are not purely in the
intellectual realm in that strong emotional factors enter into
the picture. One, the thinking of a schizophrenic is dominated by complexes—the so-called *complex-bound thinking*.
Obviously, by the term "complex" we mean ideas or a group
of ideas charged with a certain emotional content. This
also implies that some repressive mechanisms are involved
by the ego in the handling of these complexes. Secondly, a
fundamental thinking disorder described by Bleuler is the
so-called *dereistic thinking*; it is a thinking away from
reality, which, with its emotional counterpart being mainly
autism or autistic behavior, is one of the basic symptomatologies in schizophrenia. Actually, autism in an emotional
sense and dereism in an intellectual sense are two fundamental manifestations in schizophrenia present in practically all patients suffering from this disorder; therefore,
they were designated by Bleuler as primary symptoms. The
turning away from reality in thinking, which you obviously
will see, also has strong emotional connotations; the domination by complexes, described as the "primitive archaic" or
the "primitive magical" forms of thinking, are all naturally

quite well known. Incidentally, all these disorders appear distinctly in the art productions of many schizophrenic people; in this respect their art is quite different from that of nonschizophrenics. Now, I shall describe these thinking disorders in more detail.

The *fragmentation of thinking* in schizophrenia has usually been described as a scattered, or incoherent, type of thinking. Incoherence or scattered thinking means that the person interconnects ideas which do not belong together, at least not in normal thinking, and the leading goal—a so-called goal-idea—is not present. This is the difference between incoherence and flight of ideas. In the case of flight of ideas, leading "goal-ideas" are present but frequently change due to the patient's distractibility. In the case of incoherency, no apparent "goal-idea" is present, and therefore the person roams around the field, connecting and interconnecting concepts which do not belong together. Now, this inappropriate connecting and interconnecting of concepts—whereby the meanings of different ideas are falsely integrated—is partly due to emotional factors. Obviously, this is not the whole explanation. Therefore, we cannot say that this peculiar thinking disorder can be explained purely on an emotional basis until we have further knowledge. Some of these peculiar interconnections are done by the patient because of falsely applied analogies and falsely applied symbolic connections whereby completely heterogeneous concepts are fused.

It is rather interesting that many schizophrenics treat symbolic connections or analogies literally in one instance and quite normally in another. The basic sequences we employ in the logical evolution of our thinking are not adhered to and are very often mixed up by schizophrenic patients. The perception of spatial or temporal relationships is sometimes impaired; then the thinking shows condensations, displacements, dissociation, and a number of other mechanisms which are very similar to those we encounter in a somewhat different way, for instance, in the dreams of the so-called normal individual or in the delirium of an intoxicated individual. Insofar as thinking and action are concerned, schizophrenia has been termed "a walking dream"; some observers even tried to explain in detail that much of this schizophrenic thinking and, to some extent, the affective mechanisms are similar to those of any person who is dreaming. Obviously we are dealing here only with analogies because there is a marked difference between schizophrenic thinking and the dream of a normal individual. The consciousness of an average schizophrenic person, provided he is not in a catatonic state, is not impaired, whereas in a normal person who is dreaming, consciousness is obviously narrowed and to some extent suspended. Therefore, we are dealing only with analogies, many of which are striking. For example, some of the telescoping of content, the confusion of complexes, and the illogical organization of sequences and events are very similar to dream phenomena.

Concept formation is impaired in schizophrenia; concepts are not dealt with in the same way as they are in normal individuals. Very often concept formation is dissolved. The concept dissolution is very interesting in that it has affective counterparts. This leads to some of the compartmentalization of thinking occurring in schizophrenic patients. For instance, a schizophrenic patient will say he is dead; he behaves to some extent as a person who is dead; and then five minutes later he complains that he does not get enough to eat. Now, if you investigate this, of course, you will see a very strong emotional charge present. On the other hand, a rather interesting intellectual impairment is present in that the person is unable to see any discrepancy in his logic. Incidentally, if you ask the patient to explain such a discrepancy to you he usually will do so by employing concepts, analogies, and symbolisms, all of which are quite strange to us. However, he of course thinks he has explained it. He will more often than not give his explanations in rather concrete terms.

With regard to confusion between the concrete and abstract and the foreground and background, as a child's ego develops and matures he becomes more and more able to differentiate between actual reality and what he had believed to be real. As you know, in very young children and in so-called primitive people, this boundary is not very well developed; the differentiation between concrete and abstract issues is actually a maturation product of the intellect. Children have it partially—primitive peoples also have it only partially, but to a varying degree—and the confusion in the child's mind or in the mind of a primitive person as to what is concrete or abstract is not always clearly delineated. The young child does not think very much in abstract terms, nor does the primitive. Furthermore, there is a tendency present in both to concretize an experience, to formulate and express it in concrete terms; their logical thinking is organized around concrete percepts and concrete concepts.

This form of thinking is often reactivated in schizophrenia when the mechanism of *regression* occurs. The individual again tends to concretize; he becomes very concrete, very literal, explains even abstract phenomena in a concrete way and—as was described by Storch *(6)*—manifests primitive *archaic form of thinking* analogous to the thinking observed in children or primitive people. When I discuss thinking disorders in more detail, however, you will be reminded that the thinking in schizophrenic individuals is not really identical with the thinking in children or in primitive people. There are significant differences. The similarities are so striking that when observations were first made the similarities were stressed. To mention just one important difference: The concretization of a primitive person or a child is usually not fragmented; it is actually logical. Even though the conclusions drawn by the individual may be nonsense, the actual operation by which he arrives at that nonsensical conclusion is logical. But in the schizophrenic individual the logic of the operation is impaired.

In schizophrenia, more must be present than simply a tendency to concretization because the execution of this concretization is quite different—it is illogical. This archaic form of thinking therefore indicates that the schizophrenic person confuses that which is abstract and that which is concrete; he will treat abstract things as concrete and concrete things as abstract, but the tendency is toward concretization. Incidentally, very often it is difficult to delineate the archaic and magical form of thinking in schizophrenia from that occurring almost invariably in obsessive-compulsive or severe phobic individuals who are still considered to be functioning in the framework of a neurosis. However, careful examination will usually disclose concretization and fragmentation in their thinking, and follow-up studies will show that actually a considerable number of these persons march on and become overtly schizophrenic.

There is also a tendency present in schizophrenia to connect markedly dissimilar things which have only one common feature. This observation was used in one psychological test for schizophrenia, namely, the sorting test, whereby the patient is asked to arrange into groups a number of objects which are different from each other but nevertheless have certain similarities. For instance, he is given spoons, knives, plates, and then again a cigarette lighter, an ash tray, or some other utensil used for smoking. If one were to ask a so-called normal individual to arrange these objects, he would arrange those used for eating in one group and those for smoking in another and so forth. The schizophrenic individual will put all those objects together that are made of the same metal, or that are red, or that are blue. He therefore employs a different type of conceptual organization. If asked why he grouped them as he did—for example, the spoons and knives with the lighter—he will say it is because they are made of the same metal. Naturally, in a severely schizophrenic individual, marked fragmentation in thinking would be obvious in his approach to any such task. Without going into detail on this rather interesting phenomenon I would just like to point out that there are, however, two sides to the issue. In the mildly disturbed schizophrenics who also have, naturally, this type of thinking capacity to some extent, it may lead to great discoveries because it is an unconventional way of thinking. They sometimes group things together which a normal individual would not think to do and thereby establish associative connections with things other people would not suspect to have any connection. In other words, when this form of thinking is extremely marked in a schizophrenic individual it obviously impairs his ability to think, but when the impairment is only slight something new may be discovered, and this is very often the case.

The *Gestalt,* as I mentioned, is also disturbed in schizophrenia. This is somewhat similar to the disturbance in concrete and abstract thinking but in a different sense; Gestalt thinking means that actually one thinks in terms of a figure. In other words, we put together all our little partial observations of things into a single whole. For instance, when you look at a landscape, you see the different details but you do not just take into your mind a tree, you do not take in just a color, you do not take in just a part of the sky; you treat each as separate and different but you fuse them all into one meaning—the particular landscape—and that is ruled a "figure." This figure is more than the sum total of all the little details perceived. As you can realize, it is important to be able to think in figures. (In disorders causing agnosia, the person is able to recognize and perceive all the details but unable to fuse these details into one coherent whole, or picture.) In order to be able to organize something into a figure, we must be able to differentiate between that which is in the foreground and that which is in the background—that which is important and that which is unimportant. Thus, by subordinating certain details in a configurational scheme we differentiate between the foreground and the background in terms of content and meaning of the figure. The schizophrenic person is unable to do so.

In being confused about foreground and background percepts, the schizophrenic person is unable to discern what is important and what is unimportant. He usually dissolves a given figure by paying inordinate attention to details. To put it another way, he is unable to see the forest for the trees. Therefore, a peculiarly jumbled-up construct results which to us is sometimes completely incomprehensible. (I am not referring to the schizophrenic constructs which have something to do with symbolism because usually that is the explanation you receive from their art productions and is called symbolization.) Schizophrenic inability to differentiate foreground from background is a Gestalt disturbance very often clinically demonstrated in their thinking as well as in a number of projective testing techniques devised, such as the Rorschach. The inability to fuse percepts or concepts into one figure, the dissolution, the paying attention to details, the inability to properly interpret form and movement, are naturally also present clinically. Here we have a peculiar thinking disorder which is obviously unexplained. It manifests itself only in schizophrenia, and therefore this distortion can contribute toward the explanation of how the schizophrenic person views the world.

In these thinking disorders, you can surely realize that strong emotional factors can further influence and alter the content of thought to a large extent. When ideas become charged with certain emotional content, the thinking can become *complex-bound*. These emotionally charged complexes may become determinants which invade perception so that immediate stimuli are perceived in a fragmented or distorted way. Furthermore, complex-bound thinking can lead to disability in the selection of past experiences appropriate to the immediate thought synthesis. The influence of this disability can be manifested by complex-determined hypermnesias or amnesias. Thus, a mass of unnecessary and minute detail is recalled from one emotionally charged experience in the past, while important recollections from another experience are not at all available. Continuity of thought may be temporarily or permanently deflected in this way. Also, all the other disorders of thinking can, in turn, be influenced by this complex-bound thinking which is, naturally, dependent on emotional factors.

Another thinking disorder also allied with strong emotional factors is, as Bleuler termed it, dereism *(2)*. The *dereistic form of thinking* (i.e., thinking away from reality) is considered basic. The only trouble is, who is to decide what is dereistic and what is not? Naturally there is a certain amount of agreement as to what can be labeled dereistic, and whenever present in a gross way not much discussion is required. For instance, it is obvious that when a person becomes increasingly dominated by fantasy life, or when events in daydreams and nightdreams are not clearly distinguished from reality experiences, he moves swiftly from fantasy experience to reality and back without clearly distinguishing between the two. In such cases, real happenings may be recognized as only fantasy, thus warranting no action. More often, fantasy experiences are interpreted as a possible reality, thus leading to untimely or inappropriate action or to confusion about reality. But, if dereism is present in only a very mild form, then considerable discussion may arise and it is open to a great deal of subjective interpretation. The difficulty in fact is this: Whenever any type of symptomatology is present in a diluted form it becomes difficult to distinguish as a symptom. Dereistic thinking in a schizophrenic may at any given moment be quantitatively so slight as to resemble the tendency to think away from reality of a so-called "introverted normal" person. Nevertheless, concept formation in schizophrenia is not only quantitatively but also qualitatively different.

Having mentioned the impairment in concrete and abstract thinking, the Gestalt impairment, and the conceptual or categorical impairment, I would like to call your attention to one fact which is probably the most interesting intellectual phenomenon in schizophrenia: *conceptual distortions*—conceptual displacements, conceptual misformations—*are not explained by the emotional disturbance.* In other words, the presence of the emotional disturbance does not explain (at least not at the present time) the peculiar conceptual impairment present in schizophrenic patients! *These conceptual impairments are unique to schizophrenia.*

Some of these conceptual impairments remind you of organic impairments, but they are not actually the same as those observed in a known organic case such as in general paresis, atherosclerosis, and so forth. On the other hand, conceptual impairments or distortions and displacements are quite different from those which you observe on a strictly psychogenic level. For instance, because there is a certain similarity between schizophrenia and hysteria, you constantly hear the statement that schizophrenic thinking is actually a neurotic form of thinking and yet, on the other hand, that schizophrenic thinking is also an organic form of thinking. Actually, neither of these assumptions is correct. Conceptual impairment of thinking is unique. It has, however, elements which might resemble both organic and psychogenic thinking.

Because the conceptual distortions and displacements are unique to schizophrenia, they are of extreme diagnostic importance (as you will observe when I discuss the early symptoms of schizophrenia). Apart from certain emotional changes, this peculiar form of thinking may be the only clue to indicate that the patient is schizophrenic. I do not speak here of the usual textbook examples of patients in whom the conceptual distortions are present so massively that they are easily picked up and give an obvious schizophrenic impression. I cannot stress enough the importance of careful clinical examination of patients to disclose these conceptual distortions. Some of these changes can be partially demonstrated in certain projective tests, but actually no psychological tests can be relied upon to demonstrate that a person has conceptual thinking disorders.

In order to emphasize what I have been discussing theoretically about certain types of conceptual distortions,

I will give you a few illustrations of these in one case: Some time ago I interviewed a girl who was in her fourth year of college. Approximately two weeks before her final college examinations, she reported herself sick. She complained of fatigue and that she was unable to concentrate. She also expressed a great deal of fear that she would not pass her examinations. All this was incomprehensible to the school because she had had an "A" average rating throughout four years of college. She did not take the examinations but went home. She begun to be preoccupied with the fact that she did not take the examinations. There then, if you wanted to look upon it as such, was a certain clue to the ambivalence in her way of treating the situation. Something was wrong. However, outwardly and clinically she did not display any sign of a psychosis. She was a somewhat shy but otherwise quite well-organized girl. The emotional relationship during the psychiatric examination was, I would say, fairly adequate. She displayed a certain amount of empathy, was able to discuss the whole situation quite logically and in detail. Therefore, the psychiatric clinical examination did not disclose any particular clue that would indicate a major mental disorder. The information obtained from the college and the mother was inconclusive. The psychological tests to which she had already been exposed in college—they usually do that routinely now—indicated a normal Rorschach and so forth.

I reexamined her, giving her some intravenous sodium amytal; during the sodium amytal interview, she associated a chain of thoughts relating to her feet. She said that very often she had the idea—which was a compelling one—to look at her feet. Nothing more than this was disclosed during this particular interview. She was accompanied by her aunt that day and I asked the aunt if there was anything conspicuous about the girl. She said no, and that the girl's behavior was perfectly normal. However, there was one thing she could not explain. In the last three weeks, rain or shine, the girl had worn her rubbers. No explanation!

Now I would like to show you here one thing which is conceptual distortion in itself—obviously I picked up this clue (I would have been inept if I had not). I discussed with the girl her wearing of her rubbers, and the following emerged: The sun is an impregnation; you protect yourself against impregnation with rubber. When I asked her if it wasn't a rather peculiar way to protect one's self against impregnation by way of one's feet, she said, "Yes, but this is more convenient." Now please follow this chain of thought: In mythology the sun is known as an impregnating force; it appears in the folklore of many people as the energy which, of course, gives growth to living things. The association then follows that it can naturally impregnate. This is the idea expressed in any number of folklore tales. If a patient in our civilization today talks to you about this and gives you a logical explanation as to how this fits, and if you understand that it is meant symbolically, the patient simply talks about it on the level of folklore. If, however, the patient treats it literally, there is a conceptual impairment present; the patient is schizophrenic.

In the second part of this chain of associations, the girl reasoned, "I am protecting myself against impregnation with rubber." Here, there are two different thoughts hooked up and linked in a very peculiar way, a way in which a normal or neurotic person does not ever do. Finally, the crowning of this was when I asked, "Now, why don't you at least apply rubber more appropriately?" She said, "No, the other method is more convenient." There also were disclosed a great many other symbolic displacements and other thinking disorders, but I do not want to digress into all of them. However, her ideas were very interesting. She was then treated; she was definitely found to be schizophrenic.

There was another thing that was most interesting. Upon giving my report, nobody believed me when I said she was schizophrenic. They believed that the girl was simply neurotic and that I had been diagnosing too many patients as schizophrenic. (You know, it is rather interesting how much is required to convince other people that someone is really mentally ill.) They found all kinds of rationalizations, stating that this was some form of normal behavior and a normal person could think as she did under certain circumstances, that anyone could behave and think this way under the influence of tomato juice or creamed spinach. Incidentally, she took her final college examinations after she had been interviewed by me, which naturally reinforced the belief of those who claimed she was all right. Six months later this girl went into a full-fledged catatonic episode, fully complete with delusions and hallucinations. Then they believed me.

The conceptual difficulty will obviously not be discernible or show up until it reaches a certain quantity. This is our greatest difficulty. Most likely when you examine an early case such as described, or a case in remission, you will not discern the conceptual disorder. This is why one examiner will state, "The patient is normal," in one interview; and forty-eight hours later another examiner will state, "He is psychotic." However, a careful examination discloses these thinking disorders in many incipient or even so-called recovered cases. A great many physicians do not even look for these symptoms. They are satisfied with the good general impression made by the patient when obvious psychotic symptoms such as hallucinations, delusions or major regression symptoms are not present.

The statements regarding conceptual disorders should be clarified. Naturally, we do not know whether this conceptual disorder is actually an intellectual disorder per se, or based on some emotional change, or if both are caused by some other unknown factors. I believe the latter to be the fact. However, I simply want to state that our present knowledge about the emotionality in schizophrenia does not explain these peculiar conceptual changes. In other words, there is a gap in our knowledge. We know a great deal about the strivings and emotions of schizophrenics but do not know how or why they express themselves in such a weird way, and why in this particular way. Here is the gap! What is the reason for these inevitable conceptual distortions? The withdrawal from reality does not alone explain it. It is a much more complicated phenomenon. There is a definite fragmentation of the mental process.

I would like to give you another example of this thinking disorder which is probably even more interesting and in some ways much more subtle than the previous example. I had to examine a psychiatrist some time ago—a young psychiatrist. The complaint was that after having started his training analysis and having had about ten or fifteen sessions, he went into a state of anxiety. This anxiety was free-floating, was quite distressing, and manifested itself in a number of psychosomatic symptoms, particularly diarrhea, although no actual colitis was present. The analyst who treated him became rather uneasy; he was unable to find very specific dynamic explanations and asked me to determine if I could find any in a different setting. I examined the patient two or three times and nothing very special emerged. Psychological test findings were normal, showing only a little anxiety and slightly depressive features, but they were not marked.

As I shifted away from these topics and began to discuss with him, in a conversational manner, some of his ideas about psychiatry and psychiatric treatment, the following ideas came up. He said he would like to treat depressed patients with hormones. I said, "Yes, this had certainly been done. What kind of hormones did you have in mind?" He had in mind sex hormones; he would like to treat male patients with female sex hormones, and female patients with male sex hormones. I asked him why, and he said it was because he thought this would have a reinforcing effect on the sexual organization of these individuals. I asked, "What do you mean—'a reinforcing effect on the sexual organization'?" He then said, "The interesting thing is that the vascular system in depressed persons is organized differently.

I read this in a book. The vascular system responds to different hormonization in different ways." Now, obviously I could not make head or tail of this explanation and asked him to write down some of his ideas on it. He wrote them out. It is very interesting that, even though he was a trained physician and psychiatrist, his account was full of the most peculiar and esoteric connections one could possibly imagine.

Naturally, this alone was insufficient to pin a diagnosis on him and I told the physician treating him I was more than suspicious that his patient was not able to evolve logical concepts and connections; that he was not able to explain to me the source of these ideas in a logical sense; that if we put all these observations together along with the anxiety created during the analysis, it is most suggestive of schizophrenia. I advised that these symptoms be followed carefully. After about six or seven months, this patient became overtly schizophrenic in a paranoid way, and the ideations he had expressed to me became the core of the delusional material.

Having mentioned these things, I also wish to mention —because I see this so often—that in cases where professional people are involved, the examiner is immediately and naturally biased when called upon to examine someone professionally trained. He forgets that conceptual impairments, sometimes of the most gross nature, occur even in those persons whose educational and professional achievements would seem to indicate such things are not possible. For instance, if you examine professional people who have become psychotic, it is very interesting that the same type of primitive hallucinatory and delusional material appearing in rather primitive and uneducated people appears in just the same way in professional people. What is even more interesting: Most often it is not even elaborated upon in a more intelligent and subtle manner as would be expected. I do not say that this is the rule, but very often you encounter persons who, even though they are physicians, relate to you the same sort of distorted ideas that people who have had no education whatsoever do. "The room is wired," "Somebody is listening in," "Last night someone injected me with something," "Someone is withdrawing my thoughts," and so forth.

Here you actually observe the small degree to which people's knowledge or education can mitigate this overwhelming experience wherein everything functioning in their minds is distorted and their perceptions are markedly altered or changed. Therefore, these conceptual changes and other thinking disorders in schizophrenia (regardless of how investigators wish to explain them theoretically) are important for diagnosis. If psychiatrists would pay more attention to these disorders than is presently done, it would be possible to accept or reject the diagnosis of the presence of schizophrenia in a greater number of individuals.

EMOTIONAL DISORDERS: Now I would like to discuss some of the basic observations we have made regarding the emotional organization of schizophrenic individuals. Naturally, here again, some of our observations are subjective. We certainly have no methods to objectively measure, for instance, the *autism,* with its withdrawal reactions and great sensitivity, and the disturbance in homeostasis with the marked *impairment of emotional regulation,* marked emotional immaturity, and so forth observed in schizophrenia.

The first to be described is the counterpart of dereistic thinking, namely, the *autistic emotional organization.* As you know, Bleuler fused these two concepts and spoke about dereistic-autistic thinking of a schizophrenic patient, or autistic-dereistic behavior, which is probably the more descriptive term. Bleuler perceived schizophrenia as essentially a disorder of association, stressing the thinking processes. Today we stress equally, and some psychiatrists stress even more, the emotional distortions present in schizophrenia.

The term autistic actually means "withdrawn" or "turned inward." Although a small amount of autistic behavior is present in a great many people, autism itself is pathological. It is a turning away from reality. The feelings of autistic individuals are somehow directed inward; their subject-object relationships are not like that of a normal individual. They usually have the tendency to withdraw from the environment. Now, is this withdrawal a withdrawal from stimulation in general, or is it a social withdrawal? This has not been fully determined. Because we know that schizophrenics have a large number of impairments in their interpersonal relationships, the social aspect of this impairment has been markedly stressed. However, we do not know whether the autistic part of the schizophrenic disorder is actually produced by the social situation or is intrinsic in the disorder itself. Very bluntly, if you put a schizophrenic individual down on an island where there are no people, would he be as withdrawn there by himself or would he be withdrawn only if other people were also dropped on that island? This is a fundamental issue. If schizophrenic autism is a disease process having some organic implications in the background, obviously he would be as withdrawn when alone on an island—just as a paretic person would be paretic alone on an island or with other people; in some social situations his symptoms would be more obvious, but he would be sick in any case. The question remains whether or not a schizophrenic would be as sick without his social environment. Both views could be argued.

The assumption that withdrawal in a schizophrenic is primary was first ventilated in the belief that the withdrawal or apathy is a part of the disease process per se. This is possible because we do not know the etiology. I personally feel, however, that this so-called autistic mechanism in schizophrenia is already secondary to the handicap many patients feel when dealing with stimulation, physiological and psychological. That, naturally, only pushes the question further into the background because it is still not known why schizophrenics are unable to cope with stimulation. In my opinion, rightly or wrongly, the dereistic and autistic manifestations are phenomena secondary to the handicaps in which the organism finds itself.

This autistic emotional organization and withdrawal behavior is observed in many shapes and forms and to varying degrees. The individual usually withdraws from reality, from society, and from the environment in general. This occurs very early in many schizophrenics and is easily diagnosed; the person is constantly by himself, loses contact with others more and more, and socially withdraws. The autistic tendency usually shows up in the Rorschach test, but there are no reliable quantitative tests of it to better enable us to diagnose schizophrenia in its early phase. Furthermore, if we observe a child of seven or eight who is somewhat shy, withdrawn, and socially inadequate, what could we determine to be the child's prognosis? Will he develop into an "introverted normal," a "schizoid-neurotic," or an overt schizophrenic? We do not even know whether these so-called autistic manifestations are the same in all three conditions and only differ quantitatively, or are qualitatively different and only appear alike phenomenologically. No psychological tests offer more than a very crude quantitative measure: The patient is mildly, moderately, or severely autistic.

The situation becomes more complicated in that occasionally individuals who are only mildly autistic develop schizophrenia, and occasionally those who are severely autistic remain able to live out their lives in their autistic way, never developing a full-fledged psychosis. Therefore, although there is a background relationship between the autism and schizophrenia, there is no absolute relationship in the sense that one can predict that someone who is markedly autistic will become overtly schizophrenic and that someone who is mildly autistic will not. However, I think that you would be able to demonstrate that at least 60 to 70 percent of persons diagnosed as schizophrenic had a previous history of autistic behavior. Naturally, you must realize one thing: The descriptions you obtain from a patient about his past life are naturally not very accurate, and very often several members of his family must be interviewed before you can determine just what is what.

There is also another matter of great importance. Many patients' families, including professional people and psychiatrists, make mistakes when they describe the person as non-autistic who is actually a so-called pseudoextrovert. In withdrawn schizophrenic ones, the autism is uncompensated; in pseudoextroverted individuals, it is compensated. These compensating people often cause a great deal of trouble, especially the group that seems very prone to developing the paranoid form of schizophrenia. Pseudoextroverts are constantly with people; they are constantly manipulating people, but make very little emotional contact with people. Actually, they are cold, distant persons with a tremendous power drive and ambition along with a strong paranoid streak. Invariably, when I hear an account of such people, they are described as sociable and "the life of the party." This makes it appear as though they are not at all autistic because they run from one social group to another, expounding their ideas and emotional convictions. Many "reformers" belong in this group. If you question them, however, they will tell you they do not really like the social contacts, and then if you go into this in more detail, you get the impression they are emotionally cold and have very little empathy. Very soon you realize that actually their entire social behavior is organized on a strong ego compensatory drive in order to cover their sensitivities and feelings of inferiority. They are actually autistic individuals even though they appear to be so very sociable that they are never alone. This differs from a description of uncompensated autism whereby the person prefers to be alone and withdraws from social stimulation.

Along with the autistic behavior pattern, schizophrenic individuals show quite a number of other emotional changes which I will discuss one by one. Some of these emotional disorders are subentities of the basic autism and others are secondary to it.

In connection with autism, most schizophrenics display a great *sensitivity*. This great sensitivity is particularly interesting because these individuals are unable to externalize their emotions very well and, therefore, quite often appear to be bland, cold, distant, and even nonresponsive. Nevertheless, within them there is a great deal of turmoil. When Kretschmer first described the temperament of a "schizoid" or schizophrenic individual, he said that the most astonishing thing is that they are cold, but sensitive. In more marked cases of schizophrenic psychosis, you will find descriptions of persons who have no emotion at all, emotions that are flattened or blunted, or who are unable to express their emotions, and so forth. Actually, I do not believe that any of these statements are correct. I do not believe it correct that, even in the case of deteriorated schizophrenia, the patient has no emotions. One can always observe a small percentage of chronic schizophrenic patients who, with or without treatment, suddenly swing back and again begin to display emotion. Seemingly, their difficulty is in externalizing emotion in terms of responding to stimuli with the appropriate emotion at the proper time. The schizophrenic has peculiarly poor timing in displaying his emotion; he is aware of that but he does not even know how to correct it. Many patients admit this is so. They will state, "I never know how to respond emotionally to another person." They overrespond; they underrespond. They respond paradoxically. Their response is often "too little, too late" or "too much, too soon." They may appear completely impassive when something of highly emotional content is communicated to them, and yet can "blow up" over some triviality which would arouse no emotion, or very little, in a nonschizophrenic individual. In my opinion, instead of speaking about the lack of emotion in schizophrenia, we should speak about the impairment of emotional regulation.

Impairment of emotional regulation is basic. Similarly, the homeostasis of schizophrenic individuals is markedly disturbed; this involves their total personality as well as their physiology. Naturally, there is homeostatic disturbance manifested in their emotional dysregulation. We observe emotions—tremendous emotions—displayed, and a tremendous overreaction to stimuli. On the other hand, we observe patients who lack any display of emotion and they give us the appearance of being flat, blunted, and unemotional. You can see now that this emotional rigidity, inflexibility, dullness, and flatness of affect is *not* basic, even though many textbooks describe it that way. It is no more basic than paralysis in general paresis. The texts referred to chronic deteriorated patients who show these ultimate manifestations. But, dysregulation of emotion—lack of modulation of affect and in inappropriateness of affect—actually is a basic condition and is, to some extent, part of the autism.

The great sensitivity linked with autistic behavior comes to view again and again in the form of dysregulation. The sensitivity is especially obvious when the individual is in social situations; he demonstrates innumerable sensitivity reactions, usually trying to avoid response to all sorts of social situations, or else trying to push himself through and make contact. In this, he is alternately passive and aggressive, submissive and negativistic. Many of the more gross emotional symptoms, especially those observed in the catatonic-like automatic obedience and excitement states, actually go back to this peculiar emotional dysregulation.

An important feature in the affective dysregulation is the inability of the schizophrenic to regulate *aggression*. This is very outstanding! It has become common news to hear or read of a person who suddenly became enraged and killed someone who provoked him in a minor and unimportant situation. Such reactions very often occur in persons with organic brain disorder or a sociopathic personality. However, it is not rare to observe these rage-dyscontrol reactions in a schizophrenic person. Conversely, quite often a schizophrenic is unable to mobilize his anger and unable to react with aggression when it is appropriate to do so. For example, I know of a patient who went to a physician complaining that she had a great deal of anxiety and felt somewhat depressed. The physician wrote a note. He sealed the letter and gave it to her with instructions she was to deliver it (obviously not a good idea) to a psychiatrist at Bellevue. In the taxi, the woman opened and read the letter which stated that she was suicidal and should be hospitalized at once. She had the idea to go back to the physician and explain to him that she had no inclination at all to kill herself. However, she continued on her way, delivered the letter at Bellevue and allowed herself to be admitted. This shows dependency, perseveration, ambivalence, and a lot of other symptoms, but I want to stress here that with this inability to regulate proper assertion, or even aggression, you often see such a schizophrenic person reacting with abnormal compliance and passive submission in situations calling for defiance. Naturally, the reverse is frequently observed, and the same person who is overly compliant in one situation, at other times will be abnormally defiant.

These emotional responses in schizophrenia are notoriously "infantile." This is described in the literature. I believe a better expression would be *emotional immaturity*. Many schizophrenics appear emotionally as persons with an arrested emotional development. Their immature behavior expresses itself particularly in the tendency to be dependent; this dependency is linked with the desire for protection. Here you already have a very interesting paradox: The individual who desires protection and desires dependency at the same time has a strong desire to withdraw from persons upon whom he can depend to give this protection. Every schizophrenic invariably hates the person upon whom he is dependent. In analyzing the dynamics of this in schizophrenia, the issue usually comes out very quickly and very beautifully. They attach themselves to one or the other parent, or one or the other sibling; at the same time, they display tremendous hostility toward these people upon whom they are dependent. The only probable explanation for this could be that, as they themselves feel inadequate and unable to function, they resent the person who helps them for obviously having a good idea as to just how inadequate and nonfunctioning they are. The desire for protection and the rejection of protection, the desire to be loved and the rejection of the love object, are very pronounced. This emotional ambivalence is obviously discernible in cases of early schizophrenia. In deteriorated cases those mechanisms could be so blunted, or so little expressed, that they are not easily discernible.

The *ambivalence* of the schizophrenic person is very important to observe. Ambivalence is a basic mechanism. Unfortunately, we also observe this mechanism in the neuroses and, here again, in concentrating just on ambivalence itself, it is sometimes very difficult to distinguish the neurotic from the psychotic mechanisms because qualitatively they may appear to be the same. But, a qualitative difference may be observed in many cases. The schizophrenic lacks clinical insight; he accepts his ambivalence as a part of reality. His all-or-none vacillations are often in response to his delusions or to what his "voices" dictate and contradictate. For example, a patient will sit down to eat; he will pick up his fork and then hear a voice telling him to put it down; immediately he will hear a voice telling him to pick it up and eat, and he will accordingly maneuver back and forth in a repetitive manner. The neurotic, on the other hand, will certainly not have this experience; he has complete insight into the fact his ambivalence is unrealistic. Psychotherapy reveals the difference at once. He will describe it as a distressing "indecisiveness" which causes his compulsive doing-and-undoing behavior, and he wants to fight against it.

Quantitatively, ambivalence in a schizophrenic is much more marked, much more diffuse and all-pervasive, usually involving many more issues than in the neurotic individual wherein ambivalence is usually circumscribed, channelized, and organized around some specific dynamic material. (We will discuss the comparison more fully in connection with the pseudoneurotic form of schizophrenia.) In the schizophrenic, ambivalence is not reserved for important decisive issues, and it is surprising how many trivial issues are connoted in an ambivalent way. Naturally, these quantitative differentiations are not very strict; quantitative points of differentiation are never as clear-cut as qualitative ones. But if you should observe ambivalence to be quantitatively marked or all-pervading, you should be most suspicious that you are dealing with a psychotic individual.

Two other emotional phenomena in schizophrenia are of importance: One is the so-called *low-frustration index,* and the other (often emphasized) is the so-called *lack of empathy.*

The *low frustration index* is an observation made in a great many schizophrenic individuals, especially during the early stages while the defenses continue to be more strongly mobilized than in advanced chronic schizophrenic patients. It is well known that schizophrenics respond very strongly not only to stimulation coming from the outside, but also that stemming from within. The most important source of external stimulation is, naturally, that of interpersonal relationships. The social anxieties of schizophrenic persons are very great. Now, usually any happening in the environment which does not fit the mood or the emotional organization of these persons causes a certain amount of frustration. The schizophrenic has an urgent need to have wishes and expectations fulfilled immediately, his tolerance for coping with frustration being very low. In other words, he is unable to adapt himself; he is too rigid, too inflexible. This is probably because he is so constantly using his emotional life for a defense against these frustrations as to be unable to adapt himself by swinging more easily with changes in the environment. This low frustration index can be observed in a great many schizophrenic (as well as "schizoid") individuals and is part and parcel of their particular emotional disorganization. It naturally causes them a great deal of trouble.

Empathy actually indicates the ability of a person to feel into, or "with," another person. You must realize that a great deal of our ability to estimate—or, perhaps better expressed, to guess—what is going on in another person emotionally is due to the fact that we are to some extent able to identify ourselves emotionally with that person. This process of emotional identification, this ability to feel what is going on in the other person, is represented by the word empathy. Now, schizophrenics seemingly have a certain lack of empathy. This so-called lack of empathy is a two-sided issue: The schizophrenic individual does not understand very well what is emotionally going on in other persons, and other persons have great difficulty understanding what is going on in the mind of the schizophrenic individual.

Such an expression as lack of empathy is actually too broad a term to really cover the facts: It is not true that we are entirely unable to understand a schizophrenic person because we can, up to a point. The more we recognize some of the dynamic mechanisms in the patient, the more we are able to understand how he feels. Therefore, it is not a basic inability to understand a schizophrenic patient but probably a relative inability, resting to a large extent on the fact that we simply lack all the knowledge required to understand what is going on in him. Conversely, it is not true that a schizophrenic is entirely unable to feel into another person. In many respects he is able to do so. A great many of them, particularly those who are not deteriorated, have an extremely acute awareness of what is going on in another person, and with a certain sensitivity which is sometimes uncanny. Therefore, this whole issue of lack of empathy in schizophrenia should be taken with a grain of salt and obviously should be revised.

It is also true that schizophrenics have a feeling into each other and a sensitivity enabling them to pick up certain emotions and ideas in other patients. Sometimes, if you ask one schizophrenic patient about another patient who has similar symptoms, his empathy will cause him to completely override his own symptoms and state that he is all right, that there is nothing wrong; and then he will talk on and give you an excellent description of what is happening in the other person. In addition, anybody who has intensively treated schizophrenic people knows, for instance, that it is not necessary to give explanations of symbols to many intelligent schizophrenics. They have a good feeling for symbolism and will often give you penetrating explanations.

There is another side to this matter of so-called empathy. First of all, you have to understand that the emotional organization in schizophrenia is such that sometimes patients are able to carry out very complicated intellectual, emotional, or social performances without any difficulty. On the other hand, sometimes they just cannot carry through in simple or even trivial matters. This peculiar "stopper" performance, as it is called on certain psychological tests, is of course quite significant. You can confront a schizophrenic patient with a complicated intellectual problem, and he solves it; the next moment, if a rather simple problem is presented to him, he is unable to solve it. Similarly, you will find the schizophrenic able to give a very intelligent, elaborate discussion of why another person does this or that, and yet some extremely simple emotional relationship is misinterpreted, not perceived, or simply ignored. The same schizophrenic patient who at one moment displays empathy and insight into other persons will in the next moment behave in such an extremely tactless and primitive manner that any observer would immediately recognize it should not have been done. Since this peculiar inability to regulate and to organize behavior patterns is also present, there is no contradiction in stating that the schizophrenic understands to a large extent that which is going on in another person, and, at the same time, he does not. This certainly contributes to the schizophrenic person's many difficulties in relationship to his environment and I would like to mention that it also contributes to the strong feeling of the sense of failure present in a great many of these patients. This sense of failure is present in every area of functioning and, naturally, is accompanied by great anxiety.

The *anxiety mechanisms* are also, naturally, of great importance. Interestingly enough, the presence of anxiety in schizophrenia is a comparatively recent discovery which shows how certain preoccupations with certain concepts cause obvious clinical observations to be ignored, and how often fundamental clinical observations are not registered, or are completely ignored because they do not fit into some theoretical preconception. You will find that the majority of older psychiatric textbooks do not mention anxiety. It is probably due to the fact that these textbooks focused on the so-called deteriorated schizophrenic cases, and early cases displaying anxiety were not discussed or well handled. Today we know that anxiety plays a very great role in schizophrenia; anxiety (especially in early schizophrenic forms such as those showing many neurotic mechanisms) is an outstanding feature of the disorder.

However, there is already a discernible tendency in psychiatric thinking to fall over to the opposite direction. The former idea was that, because schizophrenia is a deteriorating disorder, the anxiety need not be dealt with as important. More recently, ideas have slowly emerged which focus so much attention on anxiety that the anxiety is actually pushed forward as an etiological mechanism. We do not have the slightest indication for this assumption. It can just as well be assumed that the anxiety is not an etiological mechanism but simply the expression of the person's inability to cope with internal or external environmental situations, in which case the presence of anxiety in schizophrenia is very important and leads to many secondary mechanisms. But we have no evidence for assuming that schizophrenia is "caused" by anxiety or that schizophrenia is only a special mechanism for coping with the anxiety. These theories which are emerging will most likely lead to exactly the same inconclusiveness as the first, in that many other observations which contradict this concept will not be registered because they will not fit into whichever new pre-concept is being organized today.

Confronted with diffuse and overwhelming anxiety, naturally, there is the tendency for the schizophrenic individual toward *regression*—in the emotional sense. Here, regression is described as the person's stepping back to a more immature level of emotional organization, a stepping back to that well-established level at which he felt better able to cope with environmental stimulation. You must realize that this whole regression theory of schizophrenia and the whole regression theory of the neuroses are very shaky. I do not want to veer off into a theoretical discussion at this point, but a great deal of "nibbling" is being done on this concept and it is questionable how much of it will finally remain. In a general way, we can use the term regression here because it is useful, but you must realize that it is one of the terms borrowed from neurology. We observe that the person recedes to a lower level of adaptation in his emotional organization or reactivity to the environment. Is this just a lower level of adaptation or does it correspond to the regression on an actual neurological level? It is all, naturally, hypothetical. There are, of course, the many regression hypotheses of Freud which were all intimately linked with the "libidinal" development of a person and conveyed the notion that the person steps back to a lower level of libidinal organization also. This was particularly used in describing the sexual organization of schizophrenia and can be interpreted that way if one wishes to do so. However, when applied in relationship to the sexual organization of a schizophrenic it is rather vague.

I would like to spend a few words on that issue. The *sexual organization* of the schizophrenic individual is a peculiar one. Of course, if we use the Freudian scheme, the basic interpretation is that in schizophrenia a regression takes place to the earliest level of libidinal development. In other words, the autoerotic and narcissistic phase of libidinal development reappears in the foreground and all the other developments indicating pregenital drives—the oral, anal, and so forth—predominate. Now, there is no question that in schizophrenia all these fragments of sexual manifestation are present. However, in most schizophrenic patients it is very difficult to put this whole scheme into order, and I personally feel it is much more appropriate to describe the sexual organization in schizophrenia as "chaotic," rather than to believe that very definite and clear phases of active libidinal development can be discerned. That a schizophrenic is an individual who is markedly preoccupied with himself and with his body, that he shows trends described as narcissistic—whatever that means—is obvious. If you examine him, you will also find that a great many oral, anal, and other drives are present, and in addition you also find a strong tendency to homosexual as well as heterosexual drives. Now, which drive you select to organize this whole regression scheme around is more or less dependent on your preconception, your preoccupation, or your preference for certain fragmented sexual performances. A great deal has been written, for instance, on the homosexuality of schizophrenics. You can write a great deal about the orality or about anality of a schizophrenic person. You can also write a great deal about the exhibitionistic tendencies, about their fetishistic tendencies, and many other sexual disorders.

Actually, schizophrenic patients show a markedly disorganized sexual patternization, a disorganization very similar to that in their intellectual or emotional make-up. In other words, somehow and somewhere a leading pattern, or a fusion of these fragments into a whole, is lacking. Whether this is a regression, an underdevelopment, or is some other form of disorganization, we do not know. Actually, we must be aware of the fact that it is present and can be clinically demonstrated in a great many schizophrenic patients. It is present, naturally, to different degrees in different schizophrenic persons—that is obvious. There are patients who are completely fragmented in their sexuality, just as there are patients who are completely fragmented in their intellectual performances or emotional performances. Again, there are others in whom the sexual organization, or performance, appears to be relatively adequate.

Having discussed the more basic intellectual and emotional symptomatology of schizophrenia, I should like to remind you that, because we have no unified theory of schizophrenia today, these observations are presented in a fragmentary way. No single symptom mentioned can be viewed as identical to any other symptom, but they are interrelated functions. Please be aware that in the intellectual sphere probably the only symptom pathognomonic of schizophrenia is the peculiar conceptual impairment, and in the emotional sphere no single emotional change is in itself pathognomonic. However, if a configuration of alterations is present you should suspect that the matrix on which the disorder rests spells out the diagnosis of schizophrenia.

GROSS PSYCHOTIC SYMPTOMS

In addition to the more basic symptomatology present in the intellectual and emotional spheres, we usually observe symptoms in schizophrenia that are considered representative of the disorder, but which actually develop secondarily when the basic mechanisms so overwhelm the individual that he is unable to function in the reality setting. Among these symptoms it is very important to mention the *hallucinations* and *delusions*. I would like to repeat—hallucinations and delusions do not have to be present in a schizophrenic individual in order to establish the diagnosis. This is especially the fact in the simple form of schizophrenia, and in some of the other forms such as the pseudoneurotic. The person can have an unmistakably schizophrenic organization but nevertheless have no hallucinations or delusions. It is true, of course, that the diagnosis is much more easily determined if actually present, but hallucinations and delusions, and also the very clear regression or deterioration symptoms, need not be present in order to establish the diagnosis.

The *hallucinations* in schizophrenia are very interesting in that they are so-called conceptual hallucinations; they usually stem from an idea. When this idea becomes very strong, it is then projected onto the environment. Then the idea returns and the patient experiences it as if it were actually perceived. But essentially these hallucinations are conceptual experiences, usually auditory in nature. It can be demonstrated in most schizophrenic persons that what they hear is usually a fairly complex issue. Usually, they do not simply hear a sound; they do not, in other words, have primitive, unorganized auditory experiences. Sometimes they interpret actual sounds as words (akoasms), but usually they hear voices, and, of course, the voices always say something. What the voices say is usually in very close relationship to whatever conceptual issues are going on in the patient's mind.

Auditory hallucinations are preeminent in schizophrenia. The second most common are the somatic hallucinations. Hallucinations of taste, smell, vision, and so forth occur but are comparatively rare in contrast to the extremely common auditory type. Any hallucinations occurring may be more or less permanent, but more often they are transitory. In addition, schizophrenic patients very often also have pseudohallucinations and illusions, these quite often all occurring simultaneously with actual hallucinations.

The somatic hallucinations are rather interesting. A great many schizophrenic patients will report to you that they were burned, that they were stabbed, split open, or that they were blown up! Some of these descriptions are fairly understandable; others are very weird and most peculiar. It is unclear whether certain of these hallucinations stem from actual somatic sensations or peculiar feelings and that these experiences are then interpreted similarly as in their delusions, or whether they are actual hallucinations in that no sensory stimulus is present. Both ideas have been advocated by investigators working in this field. That sometimes these very peculiar experiences are probably based on certain sensory experience might be supported by the following example: A patient complained, "I keep feeling a little machine running in my right side." X-ray of the patient disclosed an area of density in the right upper quadrant and surgery disclosed an adrenal tumor. In this case, the auditory hallucination and the delusion of a "little machine" were the patient's interpretations of sensations based on an actual lesion. Similar observations have been made by those who have experimented with various drugs capable of producing schizophrenic-like symptoms in so-called normal subjects. While these subjects retain a clear sensorium, they experience peculiar sensory manifestations. Interestingly enough, they often interpret these sensations very similar to the way schizophrenics would; control subjects, too, may experience the sensation, for instance, that one part of the body is missing, or that the head is split open, and so forth.

You have to realize, however, that many of the reports given by schizophrenics of the sensations they experience are markedly distorted by the fact that these patients actually utilize their hallucinations in the service of delusional formation. Thus, their reports of what is going on tell not alone what they feel, but their interpretation of what they feel. Thereby, also, a great deal of their bizarre and peculiar interpretive material can be uncovered. And sometimes their descriptions of what they feel are further filled with symbolization. So it is very difficult to get an accurate description from schizophrenic patients of their actual hallucinatory experiences because they usually distort the validity of these feelings by including their interpretations. Obviously, it is not clearly known whether these so-called somatic hallucinations are true hallucinations, illusions, or delusional misinterpretations of certain sensory experiences.

In a great many schizophrenic patients the peculiar

sensations are immediately interpreted in such a way as to reveal their feeling that something is being done *to* them. For instance, they may feel that some telepathic force is in action, that somebody has put electricity into them, or that someone is drawing their thoughts away. This feeling of passivity—the feeling that they are actually subjected to forces from somebody on the outside—is very characteristic of many of their ideations. Ideas of reference are occasionally built on some delusionary or hallucinatory material which may arise. In this conceptual sphere it is always very difficult to differentiate between hallucinations and delusions because many schizophrenic patients actually deal with them in combination.

With regard to the *delusions* in schizophrenia, ideas of reference and ideas of persecution are the most common. Ideas of wish fulfillment and ideas of defense are also quite common, as are hypochondriacal preoccupations. The organization of delusions in schizophrenia is a very complex and involved matter and I will not go into detail at this time. I only want to call your attention to the fact—which is very important and very interesting—that in the schizophrenic, as in all persons who form delusions, usually two basic components are present before a delusional formation occurs: (1) *the ability to form a conviction which cannot be shaken,* and (2) *a certain tension "readiness" to form such a conviction.*

The first component mentioned is the peculiar ability of a schizophrenic person *to be firmly convinced that the conclusions which he draws are correct.* This is in marked opposition to the vacillating, ambivalent emotional reactions in connection with marked feelings of inferiority otherwise present in many of these patients. Furthermore, I would like to call your attention to the fact that often the conclusions which the patient draws are so peculiarly bizarre and illogical that he, also, is unable to give you an explanation as to why he is convinced of them.

To give an example: A patient reads a book in Spanish;

first of all, he will think and tell you that there is a difference between Spanish and Portuguese; the next moment he will state that Spain and Portugal are waging a war. If you then ask him why he is convinced that Spain and Portugal are waging a war, he will say, "I don't know." If you ask him how he arrived at this conclusion on the basis of the fact that the two languages are different, he will tell you, "They are different, and differences lead to war." This is a typical form of schizophrenic thinking. I am not so concerned here with the type of thinking displayed as I am in pointing out that the patient has an absolute conviction he is right and that with this type of thinking he is able to fill in all the logical gaps which are obviously present—and that you are unable to shake him from this conviction. Naturally, a great many such delusional ideations can be collected and interpreted, this being only one example to demonstrate that a schizophrenic person not only employs conclusions falsely but, as is any delusional person, is completely convinced that his idea is correct without, of course, being able to give you valid reasons.

The second component, which is of importance in many schizophrenic patients, is that before they form an hallucinatory or delusional content they are in a peculiar frame of mind which is described as a *certain "readiness" to form delusions.* In other words, they are perplexed, they are uneasy, they express all kinds of ideas that something is wrong, that something will happen to them, or that something will happen to others. This frame of mind usually precedes the crystallization of the ideas into some concrete delusion. It compares emotionally with the suspicious feelings some schizophrenics have that something is going on around them having implications to themselves. This feeling is vague at first and they cannot explain why it is that people somehow appear peculiar, that people are behaving in a peculiar way; then eventually this crystallizes into the idea, "They are watching me! They are following me!" and then perhaps, "They are actually trying to kill me!" The very pronounced and very elaborate delusional ideations that develop in schizophrenics can usually be traced back to initial indescribably vague feelings of "something happening" around them—all in connection with the alterations and distortions of their relationship to the environment—which eventually crystallizes into an explanatory delusion.

In schizophrenic individuals it is frequently observed that when an emotional tension state becomes sufficiently strong, due to endogenous and/or exogenous stresses, the more subtle basic symptomatology becomes exaggerated. At some point, the patient is no longer able to defend himself against this overwhelming experience and a disintegration process occurs. The patient develops gross psychotic symptoms. Schizophrenic psychosis can take many forms and is classified into different groups according to phenomenology. I shall discuss these groups next.

23

SUBGROUPS OF SCHIZOPHRENIA: HEBEPHRENIC AND CATATONIC

First I shall discuss considerations concerning classification of the schizophrenic entities. I will describe the symptomatology of the classical subgroups of schizophrenia and then go on to some of the lesser known entities. In particular, I will point out the relationship of schizophrenia to other conditions, especially the paranoid states.

CLASSIFICATION

Textbooks have subdivided schizophrenia into four classical groups: *hebephrenic, catatonic, simple,* and *paranoid.* Historically—long before the introduction of Kraepelin's concept of dementia praecox and, later on, Bleuler's concept of schizophrenia—these so-called subentities now described as part of the same disorder were already recognized and categorized. For instance, catatonia had been delineated long before Kraepelin. The same is true of the hebephrenic form of schizophrenia. Later on, when the organized description of the disease entity of dementia praecox was taken into consideration, these different factors were naturally organized into the dementia praecox group.

Today we must realize *there are more than these four classified subgroups of schizophrenia.* Moreover, some of the lesser known forms are presently as important as the so-called classical groups of schizophrenia. Because their symptomatology is not so clearly delineated as the other four, obviously they are not as well recognized.

Classification of the subgroups is definitely based on descriptive symptomatological observations. The basic psychological organization of the schizophrenic individual and some of the psychodynamic factors observed in schizophrenia are the same in all subgroups, with some variations, particularly in the paranoid group. This group is the only one where doubts have been expressed. There is a constant movement back and forth to determine whether or not this paranoid mental condition is really a form of schizophrenia or something else. Since the inception of the so-called paranoid form of schizophrenia, there has been this shuffling, this detaching of the paranoid form from schizophenia and then reattaching it. I will consider that in more detail when discussing this particular form of schizophrenia. I will also point out that some of the psychodynamic observations, especially the relationship of the paranoid ideation to homosexuality, tried to indicate that the paranoid form is most likely something other than schizophrenia, but very little has remained of all attempts to separate it from schizophrenia. This group responds differently in clinical symptomatology, in prognosis, and also in treatment; nevertheless, from the basic psychological observations we are able to make on most schizophrenic patients, it is clear we are also dealing here with individuals whose basic approach to the life concept is very similar to that of other schizophrenic patients even though they handle it somewhat differently.

When I discuss some of the etiological concepts of schizophrenia, I will again return to the idea of whether or not
the paranoid form as a whole is a disease or a reaction, and
how far the schizophrenic subgroups fit into such an idea.

In general, the symptomatology of schizophrenia is
changing to some extent, just as is the symptomatology of
the neuroses. In the neuroses this is probably due to changing cultural patterns or the increasing knowledge of people
in general about some of the symptomatology of various
emotional disturbances. Therefore, neuroses are manifested
more and more as so-called psychosomatic disorders. In
other words, tensions are now discharged more internally
than formerly and fewer hysterical and overtly marked
anxiety reactions are observed.

Although in schizophrenia the same basic symptomatology continues to be present, changes are taking place in the
subgroup symptomatologies. I would attribute the changes
primarily to the increasingly adequate care schizophrenic
patients receive. Even though our therapeutic procedures
for schizophrenia are still limited, one thing has been gained
in the last few decades; schizophrenic patients receive
decidedly more attention and have much more contact with
the environment in the treatment situation. This has had a
definite influence on schizophrenia, particularly with regard
to deterioration. Many of the patients formerly observed
sitting around in a completely catatonic or hebephrenic
state are now seen only in those hospitals where the therapeutic approach was very limited.[1] Those other schizophrenic patients who are less prone to deterioration usually
move on a higher level than they were formerly able to do.
Incidentally, this gain should not be confused with the
"cure" of schizophrenia. These are actually two different

---

[1] Since these lectures, great changes in progress and prognosis of schizophrenic patients have been due to the use of the various symptom-
ameliorating drugs, especially the tranquilizers. Dr. Paul H. Hoch
was one of the earliest investigators in the use of these drugs.—*Eds.*

issues—even though they are constantly being confused. That a schizophrenic patient operates on a higher level, or a schizophrenic patient is less deteriorated and obviously functions better, is naturally a gain. It is the same as in the case of a person suffering from polio who has had rehabilitation therapy and becomes able to move more easily. It is definitely a gain, but it is not an improvement of, or a clue to, the underlying disorder.

This influence on the symptomatology is also apparent when one examines schizophrenic patients who are so markedly deteriorated as to be described as "vegetative." Because of the various stimulations and therapies to which patients are now exposed, this is not as common today as once observed even in well-conducted mental hospitals. Incidentally, the introduction of shock treatment also contributed because it was able to cut through some of the overt symptoms and prevent the eruption of marked hebephrenic or catatonic symptom displays.

Many investigators of schizophrenia found that the older a person is before developing an acute schizophrenic disorder, the less the possibility for him to show marked deterioration. Basically this is a correct observation, although one finds many exceptions to this rule. Occasionally we see a person in his forties showing a rather typical hebephrenic symptomatology; we also see schizophrenic patients in their forties showing a more or less rapid tendency to deterioration. The converse is also true: Sometimes the patient who shows a hebephrenic symptomatology in his teens does not show deterioration later. There are innumerable exceptions in schizophrenia, and you must consider all these classificatory attempts mainly as indicators for grouping individuals who appear to be somewhat similar or behave somewhat similarly. One should not attempt to classify them with the same exactitude as one would for a somatic diagnosis.

I would also like to reemphasize something because it is very often forgotten: It is a fact that a great many patients show a mixed symptomatology. This would make it difficult to group them. Moreover, sometimes in the course of the disorder the clinical symptomatology changes. For instance, a patient we may have judged to be suffering from a hebephrenic form of schizophrenia may appear catatonic a few months later. To repeat, these classifications are only general indicators.

The general indications of the grouping, however, even though some psychiatrists want to disregard them, are still of great importance because the prognostic aspects of schizophrenia and the therapeutic responses of schizophrenic patients are, to a large extent, still tied to the kind of symptomatology they show. At least so far, no other method has been found to interpret prognosis and response to therapy; we have to remain with these old classificatory attempts, regardless of their inadequacies. If a patient develops a schizophrenia at the age of seventeen or eighteen, shows a classic hebephrenic picture, shows a catatonic picture, shows a neurotic picture, or shows an acute confusional picture, by grouping them symptomatically, in the majority of the cases the correct prognostication actually can be made by those who know the disorder well. I once made a follow-up study in an attempt to ascertain and judge the accuracy of the diagnoses and prognoses made by different physicians and found that, if the clinical signs are interpreted properly, one is able to judge the outcome correctly in about 60 to 70 percent of schizophrenic patients. Although these figures vary somewhat with different clinical experiences, prognostication is not as hopeless as it often appears or is described. This holds true for prognostication in all forms of schizophrenia. The response to therapy can also be foretold to some degree in a few cases, but unfortunately not in a great many. Therefore, the subgrouping of cases is very important, regardless of how these groups are formed, of how many exceptions there are to this rule, and how often patients show a mixed symptomatology or a change in their clinical picture.

The classical forms of schizophrenia described here will

be the hebephrenic and catatonic forms—these two forms both belonging in the more "organic" class of schizophrenias. They fall into the older classification of dementia praecox, or so-called nuclear forms of schizophrenia, being the two forms most prone to regression and deterioration.

HEBEPHRENIC FORM OF SCHIZOPHRENIA

As the name implies, hebephrenic schizophrenia was originally observed in *adolescent* persons. The term "hebephrenia" actually means an adolescent impairment of the mind. These cases were described before Kraepelin by Hecker, Kahlbaum, and others to be persons in their middle teens, usually between the ages of fifteen and eighteen, who developed a psychosis, sometimes insidiously but most often in a more or less acute manner. The basic idea that the hebephrenic form of schizophrenia occurs only in adolescence was discarded just as the idea that the schizophrenias are specifically an adolescent disorder as the term dementia praecox indicated. It is nevertheless true that the hebephrenic form of schizophrenia rarely develops after the age of twenty-five. The older the person is when he develops a schizophrenic psychosis, the less hebephrenic the symptomatology and the less tendency for deterioration, although there are exceptions to this rule.

This psychosis, which disorganizes the personality nearly completely, shows a rapid progression and usually ends in more or less profound deterioration. Originally it was thought the hebephrenic form of schizophrenia was actually a form of organic brain disease in which an inflammatory or severe metabolic disturbance of the brain led to the dementia. This idea was later revised, but certain similarities were consistently and constantly pointed out. If one observes some of these deteriorated hebephrenic patients, a certain similarity to the organic type of patient can be striking.

Thus, the hebephrenic form of schizophrenia is characterized not only by its usual occurrence in adolescence, but also by *two main clinical features:* First of all there is usually a *rapid downward course,* which can obviously be ascertained when the patient is followed for a period of time. This is the most pernicious form of schizophrenia in that it shows the greatest tendency to *deterioration,* deterioration occurring rather frequently. A number of these adolescent schizophrenic patients are mentally "finished up" in two or three years, having reached the deteriorated state. Secondly, during the early acute symptomatology, irrespective of follow-up studies, the outstanding feature is the gross disorganization of the intellectual and emotional life of the person. In fact, *the most massive disorganization of the total personality occurs in the hebephrenic form of schizophrenia.*

These are the patients intellectually showing a gross incoherence, a great deal of scattering with "word salad," and a marked impairment of the associative powers. Actually the older ideas, especially those of Bleuler, about the impairment of association are clearly demonstrated in these patients. As I have pointed out before, this associative impairment, along with marked incoherence, inability of the person to concentrate, and inability to formulate any leading ideas and to express ideas coherently, naturally gave earlier psychiatrists the impression they were no doubt dealing with an organic disorder.

The disorganization of thought, disorganization of concept formation, and fragmentation of the intellectual power of the patient are not the sole impairments of the hebephrenic individual. The same disorganization is observed in his emotional life. This individual's emotional life usually becomes inappropriate; it is inappropriate to his own intellectual performance and, along with it, is also inappropriate in his relationship to the environment. These persons are usually markedly withdrawn, the withdrawal very often being punctuated with states of overactivity and overexcitement. This is rarely so massive as that seen in the catatonic form of schizophrenia. Nevertheless, it is most definite. Of course, irritability and asocial behavior are also common with this picture.

Massive mood changes are almost always characteristic. Many of these persons, particularly in the initial phase when often the actual psychosis fully erupts, demonstrate this syndrome. They run the gamut of emotions in a comparatively short time: They are depressed; they are elated; they are discontent; they feel very inferior; they feel very superior. In other words, in the early phase of the hebephrenic psychosis, many patients show this rapid shift from one emotional pole to another. Naturally, when deterioration finally sets in, they very often show the typical schizophrenic emotional deteriorated picture of withdrawal, emotional rigidity, flatness, and a general blunting of emotional contact with the environment. However, this can be observed only in the later phase of either the hebephrenic or catatonic disorder.

Concerning the emotional life of these persons, there is one very interesting observation which, by the way, was never actually clarified from a psychodynamic point of view. A number of theories have been offered. In practically all adolescent hebephrenic patients, you will see a form of *marked silliness*; this silly behavior is so conspicuous that formerly the diagnosis was often based upon that particular clinical picture. You observed a person who was incoherent, someone behaving in a very silly manner, and you made the diagnosis of schizophrenia. This silliness is of importance in many respects. Originally it was considered nothing more than the silly behavior of an adolescent. (I personally never thought that adolescents behave in a silly way, and especially not in the silly way of a schizophrenic. Therefore, I never was very keen on this analysis.)

Later on, when concepts of regression were introduced, particularly under the influence of Freud, this silly behavior was assumed to be, and interpreted as, a part of regression. Here again, it is very difficult to believe that this behavior is simply a regression symptom. Should you ask hebephrenic patients who have made a form of recovery to give you some idea as to what went on during the psychosis and why they behaved this particular way, they usually give an explanation. One patient might say he behaved in a silly way as a form of defense, namely, that he was very anxious, upset. In other words, his behavior resembled that of persons who adopt a somewhat silly attitude when anxious and embarrassed, except that seemingly there is an exaggeration of this behavior in the hebephrenic person. Another patient, interestingly enough, might interpret this silliness as an obsessive-compulsive phenomenon: He might say, "I couldn't help it; I felt forced to do this," but offers no further explanation for it, and the whole phenomenon is handled as a kind of forced laughter, forced crying, or forced silly behavior. We do not know if forced laughter or forced crying is always an organic symptom. Up to a point, behaving in a silly way could be a habit with which the patient is stuck, and therefore would not be exactly in the organic category. I only want to indicate that the subjective experience of many hebephrenic patients is that they feel forced to behave in this silly manner and are unable to interfere with it. We have no other adequate explanations for this very common and outstanding clinical feature. Silly and usually bizarre behavior is expressed especially often in their speech patterns. The very peculiar and bizarre ideas brought up in their conversation are expressed in a definitely silly fashion, usually intermingled with silly laughter or completely inappropriate affect.

Interesting motor phenomena also occur in many anxious hebephrenic patients. Grimacing, posturing, and peculiar perseverational movements remind us of tics, and sometimes are much more complex. These stereotyped movements, or stereotypies, are very common. Many patients are profoundly sick before these symptoms are noticed. Always look for one or two stereotyped bizarre behavior patterns which cannot be explained by the patient. In other words, a neurotic patient with a tic would never say, "I don't know why I do this," but will offer some explanation. It is the schizophrenic person who, having more or less broken his relationship with the environment, will find it unnecessary to give an explanation. Nevertheless, many of these patients know they are profoundly sick.

In addition to the massive intellectual and emotional disorganization and bizarre behavior, many hebephrenic patients show marked regressive phenomena. (Actually, the hebephrenic and the catatonic forms of schizophrenia are the two forms showing regressive tendencies in a massive way.) Not only does their thinking, their concept formation, or their feeling regress, but actually regression includes the whole behavior pattern toward their environment. Although the most massive regression phenomena can be observed in catatonic patients, hebephrenic regression is much more disorderly and dissolved than catatonic regression which retains a certain organization. Regression in hebephrenic patients is fragmented, just as the whole personality is fragmented. Many hebephrenic patients show very childish, playful, mischievous behavior; others display temper tantrums as very young children do. Many show infantile sexual behavior. Very often they speak in "baby talk" and frequently revert to a childish level in many habits.

One common symptom of regression observed in hebephrenic patients is the markedly "narcissistic" behavior. (The original observations on "narcissism" were made on hebephrenic patients; if there is such a thing as a "narcissistic patient," you can see it here.) These patients are body-conscious to an extremely exaggerated degree; they will do such things as standing nude before a mirror, admiring and analyzing themselves. This behavior rarely occurs in a neurotic person. Many other ramifications of "narcissism" should be looked for in hebephrenic patients.

I would like to mention one point here which will, of course, come up again and again. In schizophrenia it is always difficult to know when so-called regression merges or crosses over into deterioration. Actually, deterioration is nothing less than a fixed or permanent regression; there is no other difference between deterioration and regression. In an acute form of schizophrenia one can observe mild, medium, or massive regression manifestations, and in the acting-out stage we are aware it does not matter very much how far the person has regressed, provided he once again bounces back. A number of schizophrenic patients do this. For instance, sometimes catatonic patients manifest marked regressive symptoms, but it nevertheless does not have very much influence on the ultimate outcome. They usually show a good remission tendency. Generally speaking, however, the hebephrenic patients do not!

Actually, in most cases intravenous sodium amytal, or similarly acting drugs, can be used as a form of test to determine the extent of the deterioration in a schizophrenic patient. In conducting such an interview, especially when the patient is in an acute phase, or even in a chronic phase before any deterioration has occurred, you are able to bring about a little more order in the patient's thinking. In other words, you "lift" the patient's level of functioning. Incoherence very rarely completely disappears but he is able to carry on a decidedly more intelligent conversation. The more deteriorated the patient, the less effect this procedure has. If you inject sodium amytal and the patient does not show any "lifting," is not better organized, and remains on the same level of regression, this is a fairly reliable indication he is deteriorated. It is also a fairly good prognostic sign that he will not respond to forms of treatment.

Prognosis in the hebephrenic form of schizophrenia is worse than that for all other forms because of the marked mental disorganization and regression in these patients, and especially because of the tendency for them to remain in the regressed state—the state of deterioration. The importance of these prognostic features should be emphasized. However, in the hebephrenic patient as in any form of schizophrenia, it is to a considerable extent possible to prognosticate by viewing the following signs: the premorbid personality organization and adjustment, the type of clinical onset, the precipitating factors, and the clinical picture.

In general, the *previous personality make-up* and the previous adjustment of the person are extremely important. If a patient had shown poor personality adjustment and inability to adapt effectively prior to his illness, the outcome will not be as favorable as that of a patient who had a good premorbid personality organization.

Another very important point of which we must be aware is the *type of onset* of the psychosis. The more insidious the onset, the less favorable the prognosis; and, the more acute the disorder, the better the prognosis. This seemingly peculiar paradox is also apparent in other forms of schizophrenia, especially the pseudoneurotic. If a person goes into an acute episode, regardless of what subtype of schizophrenia, regardless of how massive this acute episode is and how upsetting it appears, the better the prognosis. The more insidious, slow, and mild the disorganization, the less favorable the prognosis. Prognosis in acute cases is better because the weakness is a more quantitative rather than a qualitative one. Those schizophrenic patients admitted to the disturbed ward in a mental hospital usually have a much better prognosis than those who have slowly developing symptoms and are admitted to the chronic ward of well-behaved psychotic patients. These chronic patients will probably never return to the physicians who saw them originally. Later on I will discuss the acute confusional states of schizophrenia. These patients definitely show that the more clouding of consciousness and the more organic the picture, the better the prognosis. The more psychological the picture appears, the less favorable is the prognosis. Naturally there are many other factors which must be taken into consideration.

An important indicator in prognosis is also the extent to which *precipitating factors* influence the attack. The more precipitating factors or, to put it this way, the more psychogenic trigger mechanisms present, the better the prognosis—provided, of course, that these psychogenic trigger mechanisms do not involve completely unalterable and impossible life situations. The less you are able to point out trigger mechanisms, the less favorable the prognosis. Naturally, I am not referring to the psychogenic trigger mechanisms discovered only after you have followed the patient psychotherapeutically for a long time, but to the immediately obvious ones. The more obvious the trigger mechanisms, the more favorable is the possibility of the patient's adjustment.

In viewing these factors mentioned, the worst prognosis is given the patients showing gradual onset without any discernible cause. You will encounter persons whose history indicates that they were rather sensitive, cranky, already withdrawn by the age of two or three, and who, according to their parents, behaved differently from other children. They showed a marked sensitivity, a tendency to withdraw themselves from stimulation; they did not like to play with other children; and they usually had all kinds of eating and sleeping difficulties. They had many complaints that were not often serious; they were sickly with all kinds of troubles such as frequent colds. When such children began school, these difficulties became even more aggravated; the sensitivities became more apparent, their adjustment to the school situation and to the other children remained poor.

When they reached adolescence they became more and more peculiar, more and more withdrawn, and more and more maladjusted to their environment. However, no one observing them would be able to give you any adequate idea as to what produced this. Then, insidiously, at the age of fifteen or sixteen, such a person might begin to express ideas that people are watching him; he invariably goes over and looks at himself in the mirror every few minutes and tries to see how his body is constructed. Most often a great deal of masturbation is involved, usually connected with all kinds of bizarre ideas. Fragmentation of ideas slowly begins to appear. If intelligent, the person might begin to be interested in all kinds of peculiar philosophies and some of his mental productions are often very interesting, although inappropriate and expressed in a fragmented and silly way. It is then that you finally realize you are dealing with a full-fledged psychosis. Sometimes it appears as if it were a sudden outbreak even though you can trace it very far back. Nonetheless, within a year or two these persons may become practically useless and sit in a hospital in a vegetative state. Even with present therapies, these insidious cases have a bad prognosis, regardless of any type of treatment applied. I personally believe there is absolutely no sense in fooling ourselves.

[Not many decades ago there was a tendency in psychiatry, especially in the United States, to regard these serious disorders as similar to ordinary neuroses. A tremendous amount of overoptimism was enthusiastically put forward by the psychiatric and medical professions. If you read these reports, which are usually based on isolated cases and unsupported by good general statistics, you very soon get the impression that schizophrenia and hay fever are about on the same level, and it would appear that if we do this or that, we are able to prevent the occurrence of either one; if we do this or that we are able to treat them both very effectively without any effort, and 90 percent of the patients will recover. A rather recent release reported about a 90 percent recovery rate in schizophrenia. This was stated in a popular lecture by a very prominent psychiatrist. I believe this to be not only foolish but downright dishonest. Any psychiatrist who sees a large number of these patients and is honest enough to appraise his own work and the work of others will state that schizophrenia is still a very serious disorder, and our ability to treat it is still severely limited. This does not imply that the opposite extreme view is valid.]

It has been joked that psychiatrists are divided into two groups: the psychiatric optimists and the psychiatric pessimists. The psychiatric optimists claim they can cure every patient they see; the pessimists claim that psychiatry has no effective treatment at all. Naturally, both extremes are wrong. However, that extreme which believes a hebephrenic schizophrenic patient who has had a few shock treatments, a little insulin, some psychotherapy, or one thing or another, and is able to show an 80 to 90 percent recovery rate is naturally foolish.

The hebephrenic form of schizophrenia has a spontaneous recovery rate of a possible 15 percent and not more. You have an additional 15 percent improvement rate. All the other hebephrenic patients who were said to be recovering with the different treatments are exhibited in state hospitals. There are psychiatrists who believe no recovery occurs in schizophrenia; I do not believe that. Naturally there are recoveries. Obviously, by recovery we mean the person returns to his prepsychotic level of adjustment. You cannot expect the patient to be a perfectly normal individual in every respect, but about 10 or 15 percent of these hebephrenic patients show a very good remission whereby no further attacks occur. In other words, a patient has one attack, recovers after a year or so, and remains well. These figures and observations are based on extensive and long follow-up studies.

The overall average of spontaneous recovery in schizophrenia, disregarding the subgroupings, is a little more than 30 percent. In other words, approximately one-third of the nonhospitalized and nontreated cases of schizophrenia recover. However, from this general statistic of one-third, about a half show psychotic manifestations at a later date. In other words, you may say that of those patients diagnosed as schizophrenic about 15 percent recover and remain well, and in the other 15 percent the improvement is not complete but the person is able to navigate to some extent. The remaining 70 percent or more will have trouble: either they do not come out of the psychosis, or, if the psychosis is of a remittant nature, a new attack will occur later on. In other words, we can say that slightly less than one-third of untreated schizophrenic persons, in general, recover or have a good remission.

If you apply shock treatment, for instance, the acute remission rate doubles; it goes up to about 60 percent. However, if you do follow-up studies, you find that after a period of five years the shock-treated patients' recovery rate and the spontaneous recovery rate differ only about 5 percent in favor of the shock-treated patients. I do not have to remind you that 5 percent statistical deviations up or down are still in the framework of statistical error and cannot be considered very valid. Today shock treatment has certainly improved the prognosis in the acute phases but is unable to maintain it in the majority of schizophrenic patients.[1]

There are very few statistics on recoveries with the use of various psychotherapies. Unfortunately, psychotherapeutic efforts in schizophrenia, or in any other mental disorder, have no statistics. Therefore, only impressions remain. Impressions are naturally interpreted in a positive or negative manner depending upon the idealogical biases of the interpreter. Some physicians believe psychotherapy can cure a large number of patients; others feel that only when the patients are seen after a long follow-up period can they be regarded as relatively cured cases.

It is not always easy to *differentiate* the hebephrenic from the other forms of schizophrenia. Of all available statistics on recovery, the hebephrenic form of schizophrenia has the worst prognosis; the possibility for reintegration is less than in the other forms of schizophrenia. I say this with some reservation because of two clinical entities at one time described as "acute motility psychosis" and the "puberty reaction." The so-called acute motility psychosis actually belongs in the catatonic group, but sometimes these patients show hebephrenic features; an adolescent boy or girl sud-

---

[1] Since the widespread use of phenothiazines and more recent psychotropic drugs, these figures on long-term prognosis are subject to favorable reevaluation.—*Eds.*

denly develops a tremendous motor excitement with thrashing about and running about, all with a great motor discharge. This should not be confused with a manic excitement because these patients show no relationship to mania; it is only an occasional passing episode and usually all sorts of emotions are mixed in with it. Most of these acute schizophrenic cases have a fairly good prognosis.

I would like to mention that occasionally hebephrenic patients, especially in the early phase of the illness, show manic features, and sometimes their "silliness" is overlaid with elation. When these patients show an elation and a motor discharge, one cannot easily differentiate between flight of ideas versus incoherence; you will have the impression you are dealing with a manic patient. There is one general rule to aid us: Manic-depressive psychosis is extremely rare in teenage persons. It is a disorder of older people. If you observe the patient a little longer, invariably you find the manic features disappear but a great deal of silliness remains.

The other entity was once described as the so-called puberty reaction. (This term is as unspecific as was the term "catarrhal disorder of the lungs" which at one time was usually an indication of pulmonary tuberculosis.) The so-called puberty reaction is invariably schizophrenia. Nevertheless, as a form of schizophrenia this acute hebephrenic picture has a relatively good prognosis. Therefore, if you see a patient with an acute onset in adolescence, showing regressive emotional and behavioral symptoms without significant intellectual regression, and with the intellectual impairment probably more on a confusional level, you must follow this case for a few weeks or months in order to be sure whether you are dealing here with a more "benign" hebephrenic reaction or with the more classical form of hebephrenic schizophrenia. There is no way of determining this difference in one examination. Unfortunately, in many instances you will find the patient belongs in the second group.

Many persons show an exaggeration of attitudes and behavior during puberty. There is swiftly changing affect and uncontrolled emotional display. These things make one think of it as a puberty reaction. It is generally considered normal pubertal behavior. Some individuals display this and never become schizophrenic. In hebephrenic schizophrenia, however, this pubertal behavior becomes more and more marked. Consistent display of inappropriate behavior is surely very, very suspect of a schizophrenia.

If an adolescent person develops an acute confusional episode while under a great emotional stress, even should he appear grossly psychotic, the prognosis is not poor and the patient usually responds to treatment. If, however, he does not show an acute motility or confusional picture, if this picture comes on more or less insidiously and if the precipitating factors are not clearly discernible, if you see a gradual disintegration with intellectual regression, this is probably a chronic form of hebephrenia, and the prognosis is poor.

I would like to especially emphasize the intellectual regression. The schizophrenic patient displays so much disorder of the emotions it is more and more forgotten that he also shows profound intellectual alterations. Our present concern is not whether the intellectual alterations are primary or secondary to the emotional changes, but in actually noting that they are present! In my experience, many psychiatrists give the wrong prognosis in cases of schizophrenia because they completely overlook the intellectual changes. They do not wish to see them! In some patients rather profound intellectual changes take place, changes which can often even be demonstrated with the use of projective tests such as the Rorschach. The more pronounced the intellectual changes in the patients, particularly if they persist, the less encouraging is the prognosis. In other words, those patients who show a profound disorganization of their intellect are the ones who show the least tendency to recover.

We do not know why the intellect is so profoundly invaded in some patients and not in others. At least mild intellectual changes are shown by all schizophrenic individuals. It is most surprising, especially when treating patients psychotherapeutically and seeing them very often month after month, how frequently an individual who appears to be quite capable and even brilliantly intellectual will suddenly show staggering intellectual alterations. I will return to this perceptive view when discussing the pseudoneurotic form of schizophrenia in detail. Nevertheless, if you see gross intellectual changes in a patient, namely, incoherence and inability to formulate concepts, these are much more important than the delusions and hallucinations which are usually fleeting and very often less impressive than this basic disorganization of the personality.

Of course, in the hebephrenic form of schizophrenia, delusions and hallucinations often appear. However, these hallucinations are usually auditory, and the delusions usually bizarre, fantastic, and badly elaborated delusions dealing most commonly with sex and performance. The patient has the delusion he is a great inventor, a great musician, a writer, and so forth, or he has hypochondriacal delusions dealing mainly with the body. The appearance of his body is closely watched by this "narcissistic" person and invariably he expresses hypochondriacal ideas, many of which are naturally concerned with sex. Very often he reveals really very bizarre delusions, as when he verbalizes such ideas as, "My stomach is upside down," "I am turning into a woman," or "into a man," "My eyes are changing," or "The shape of my nose is assuming a different form." All types of delusions will be expressed which you will recognize as being of pernicious significance and particularly so if they occur in a "clear setting."

Unfortunately in some hospitals many hebephrenic patients are diagnosed as paranoid. Actually the paranoid form of schizophrenia is not a schizophrenia of adolescence. I do not believe a single diagnosis of paranoid schizophrenia made in a person of eighteen or nineteen years of age is correct. Paranoid schizophrenia is a schizophrenia of older age groups, usually developing in the late thirties and forties, and the main characteristic is that the personality in these persons is very well preserved. In many instances you sense that paranoid schizophrenia can be excluded when you examine these patients. The regression, incoherence, and silliness is not seen in paranoid schizophrenia. However, the fact that every schizophrenic person can have paranoid ideas is true, but this is a different issue. This is often confusing. Some hebephrenic patients actually believe they are being followed on the street or that remarks are being made about them (usually sexual), but these projective ideas do not determine them to be paranoid schizophrenic.

Paranoid schizophrenia should be diagnosed definitely only in a person who is well preserved, who shows no disintegration of intellect, and no regression. It is a delusional disorder. The paranoid form of schizophrenia and schizophrenia with paranoid ideation are two different things. This is important because the hebephrenic patient with paranoid ideas will respond differently, prognostically and therapeutically, from the person with a paranoid form of schizophrenia. Paranoid ideas are not the essential issue in hebephrenia. Paranoid schizophrenic and the hebephrenic schizophrenic patients can both have delusions which are very bizarre and fantastic, but in paranoid schizophrenia the delusions are consistent; in hebephrenic schizophrenia they are not. Moreover, the ideational system in the paranoid schizophrenic is much better elaborated and is logically better evolved than in the hebephrenic patient. The hebephrenic patient handles them in a peculiarly unrealistic, bizarre, and fragmented manner. In other words, we base the diagnosis on the type of delusions, how they are organized, and especially whether or not disintegrative symptoms are present, particularly intellectual fragmentation and fragmented regressive patterns.

Paranoid patients also can deteriorate (this being one reason why the paranoid form of schizophrenia was kept in the schizophrenic group), but the deterioration is slow and never so profound as that seen in the other groups. However, I am not now discussing the patients one observes when ten years' sickness has more or less diluted, or "washed away," these differential signs; I am speaking of those patients in an acute state. For example, if you see an eighteen-year-old person with paranoid ideas, you would know that, even if the symptomatology appears to be paranoid, paranoid schizophrenia is practically nonexistent at this age. Suppose you see a twenty-five-year-old person who expresses paranoid ideas, it is then you ask yourself the following: Are these paranoid ideas well organized or are they vague, not so well organized, not very logical, and so forth? If they are well organized and appear to follow logically, then you can have the suspicion that the person is paranoid schizophrenic. If the ideas are not very well organized, most likely it is something else. Then you look for additional symptoms. You determine whether the person has symptoms of intellectual fragmentation—say, of incoherence or scattering. If you cannot establish very good contact with the patient, if he shows regressive symptoms such as talking like a baby, if he makes stereotyped movements, or if he displays catatonic manifestations, then again you would not diagnose him as paranoid. You keep in mind that although it appears to be primarily a delusional disorder, hebephrenic and disintegration symptoms are also present. If you see this same patient ten years later, regardless of whether he had started out with paranoid or other features of schizophrenia, you would then see a deteriorated schizophrenic. Eventually they all appear somewhat similar. It is not always easy to delineate in which subgrouping any deteriorated schizophrenic person belongs—unless from the history. I hope this is clear to you.

As I mentioned, some of these patients recover and although many who recover are able to make fairly adequate adjustment it is usually on a lower level than their prepsychotic level. For instance, a patient begins high school; he does not progress very well; in the second year he fails; and in the third year the psychosis breaks out and he withdraws from school. After recovery from this psychotic break, there is no tendency to return to school or to his so-called normal existence. He accepts a job somewhere—perhaps as a messenger. Incidentally, this very often occurs even in persons who had formerly been functioning on a very high academic and social level. I know messenger boys who have university degrees. They were unable to adjust on a higher level of performance but adjust reasonably well on this lower level.

This applies to many other types of schizophrenia. I know a lawyer who developed an overt schizophrenia and was treated by quite a number of physicians with different methods, without demonstrable success. One day I learned he was operating a gas station in the far West somewhere. Mind you, this gas station was very isolated; I believe only two cars passed through each day. He leads a harmonious life and appears perfectly happy. This type of adjustment can occur. The merchant marine, for instance, is also a great reservoir where you will find all kinds of schizophrenic individuals. They seem perfectly happy away from land, touching it only occasionally. They live in such a way that they do not have to act on any mobilized sexual drive, or it is fulfilled on the ship, usually in a homosexual way. They go to sea, and then become markedly disturbed each time the ship comes close to port; when in port they get drunk, usually spend all their wages within a few days, and then return to sea. The number of schizophrenic seamen who establish this level of adjustment is very great.

The degree of adjustment depends largely on the character of the environmental stress intrinsic in the life position. For example, there is the very interesting case of a certain employee, a clerk at one of the largest state hospitals, and this very intelligent man practically ran all the administrative work on one of the services. This man had been admitted to the hospital as an adolescent almost twenty years before. The diagnosis was that of an obsessive-compulsive neurosis, and it was this patient's idea he could not leave the hospital building because something would then immediately happen to him. He was "analyzed" by two psychiatrists, sine facto, maintained his obsessional trend throughout and continued to do outstanding clerical work. Then an interesting thing occurred. He suddenly went into a psychotic episode—typically schizophrenic. This episode lasted a few weeks and apparently he came out of it and once again resumed his job. Incidentally, I think the episode was precipitated by paranoid ideas concerning money withdrawn for tax purposes, the state paying him five dollars less than the two hundred and fifty per month he had been receiving. That shows his level of performance and adjustment. In a number of state hospitals you will find people doing very good work, including doctors, who also belong in this group.

I may add here that not only is the prognosis poor in hebephrenic patients, but also their therapeutic response, regardless of any organic or psychotherapy used, is still not good. This form of schizophrenia is still a very serious disorder and when the diagnosis is made, one must be aware of the prognostic implications and the therapeutic resistance.

CATATONIC FORM OF SCHIZOPHRENIA

The catatonic form is considered to be the second of importance in the group of schizophrenias in terms of proneness to marked regression and deterioration. Although the most pronounced deterioration usually occurs among the hebephrenic patients, *catatonic patients often manifest the most marked regression.* In many instances the regression, which can be very profound, is confused with deterioration. Some catatonic patients show a definite tendency to deteriorate; others, however, do not.

It is rather characteristic for this form of schizophrenia to *occur in episodes*; it is the form most prone to appearing in attacks with good remission between them. There are even persons who have only one attack and then reintegrate well; often the reintegration is seemingly spontaneous. Many patients, however, have repeated attacks, reintegration becoming less and less clear-cut over the years.

The catatonic manifestations in this form of schizophrenia appear to be partly on both a psychological level and an organic level; the catatonic is the more *organic-appearing* group because the neuromuscular and vegetative systems are very much involved. This catatonic group is characterized by four clinical phenomena: (1) alternation between *negativism and automatic obedience*; (2) *stupor and excitement* behavior; (3) *muscular phenomena,* namely, catalepsy and flexibilitas cerea; and (4) *profound regressive manifestations.*

The alternation between *negativism and automatic obedience* is a very interesting basic emotional behavior phenomenon. We have already discussed this as mildly discernible in most schizophrenic patients, including those who do not show catatonic manifestations. Many paranoid, hebephrenic, and even pseudoneurotic schizophrenic patients show this alternating behavior. This is a schizophrenic tendency, but it becomes most pointed in the catatonic state, naturally. Here you see ambivalence become so extreme that the marked alternation between negativism and obedience is automatic. These patients show a stubborn negation of certain issues, and a stubborn negation in many of their relationships to the environment, including the transference situation when under treatment. Suddenly, they turn around and become completely dependent and compliant to the environment or persons treating them. Incidentally, one of the difficulties in the psychotherapy of schizophrenic patients is in their dodging transference relationship. In catatonic patients, however, not only is the transference relationship very brittle and tenuous, but the therapist also has to deal constantly with this peculiar pattern of alternating polarity—this compliant or opposing, dependent or independent, ambivalent attitude—and especially the automatic negativism and automatic obedience. These people can be very negativistic! If you ask to shake hands with them, they pull their hand away. When you ask a question of these patients, they are often evasive or do not trouble to reply. Blocking is very common. Then, if you begin talking about some neutral matter, the patient will suddenly begin answering the question you asked him ten minutes before. Negativism suddenly turns to automatic obedience, the so-called echo phenomenon being most commonly observed. Echopraxia and echolalia occur whereby the person actually follows everything you do or repeats fragments of what you say, just like an automaton. The ambivalence expresses the catatonic person's profound impairment in regulation of passivity, aggression, and his emotions.

Actually, based on this principle of impaired regulation and ambivalence is the second outstanding clinical feature of catatonia: *stupor and excitement*. Each is at the maximum ends of the ambivalence scale. In stupor, the tendency to withdraw from stimulation has reached such an extent that the person withdraws from the environment completely. He responds only to inner stimulation. The excitement reaction is naturally the opposite; the person tries to break through to the external environment and becomes markedly excited. A considerable number of catatonic patients alternate between stupor and excitement. However, many catatonic patients experience only stupors; a few experience only excitements. Some cases show mild stuporific manifestations or mild types of excitement manifestations. In other words, you do not have to assume every catatonic patient shows every symptom in a nice, clear-cut manner. If you are perceptive, you can discern these manifestations in quite a number of catatonic patients who do not show massive symptomatology.

Catatonic patients who are kept active in some occupation and with therapy can be prevented from sinking into a stupor. During full-fledged stupor, catatonic patients are mute, idle, and remain in one position for long periods of time. Their facial expression is vacant; they show no interest in the environment; they cannot take care of their bodily functions; they are insensitive to pain and often operate on themselves. Amputation of the sexual organs or enucleation of the eye is commonly done by the patient himself—without pain. Here we have evidence to indicate that sensation of pain depends on how much is perceived; it must be perceived cortically before it can be felt. In many ways schizophrenic individuals are more sensitive than normal individuals in perceiving sensations, and yet they are also able to selectively include, exclude, alter, or distort sensory perceptions.

A catatonic excitement episode sometimes begins with a sudden outburst of impulsive wild behavior. It can last for days, or months, if not treated. It may be preceded by a period of restlessness but sometimes occurs without warning in the presence or absence of obvious precipitating factors. Efforts to relate to the patient are futile. His uncontrolled behavior can be extremely dangerous to others; he is usually very aggressive and negativistic. The patient accepts his hyperactive behavior as justified, but in many other respects the mannerisms and stereotypies usually present remind us of an organic disorder of subcortical origin. Very large doses of sedation are required to influence patients who are in such a state.

A third characteristic clinical feature is the obvious *muscular phenomena,* namely, catalepsy and flexibilitas cerea occurring in catatonic patients. However, it usually develops when the patient is in a marked stupor, and therefore it is not necessarily present in each catatonic schizophrenic.

A fourth clinical phenomenon observed is the *very pronounced regressive manifestations* such as drooling, incontinence, the so-called fetal-like posturing, and so forth.

This is usually observed in the stupor phenomenon, but also appears in other catatonic pictures.

Please be aware of the fact that all these catatonic symptoms are only secondarily superimposed on many of the basic schizophrenic manifestations that are present in all forms of schizophrenia. This is important to know! A number of mistakes are made with patients in failing to realize that their catatonic symptoms are not basic. For instance, with some form of treatment these characteristic catatonic manifestations are removed, it also then being interpreted that all the schizophrenic symptoms are removed. That is not the case! In a number of catatonic patients a few electro-convulsive treatments enable one to remove the negativism, the stupor, and muscular manifestations such as rigidity, flexibilitas cerea, and so forth. Nevertheless, the basic schizophrenic manifestations remain below the surface. We must always pay attention to that fact because a large number of these catatonic patients are very "slippery," especially in response to treatment. In other words, it is not difficult to remove catatonic manifestations with the combined use of organic, drug, and psychotherapeutic methods at our disposal, but it does not follow that the basic schizophrenic manifestations are eliminated. Actually, we must always satisfy ourselves as to how far any delusional or hallucinatory material is removed, and how far the more basic schizophrenic mechanisms, especially the ambivalence, are actually influenced by our treatments. Otherwise, we are merely treating the catatonia as a surface phenomenon, but are not treating the schizophrenic patient who manifests these catatonic features. And, later on, many patients show a return of the catatonic picture.

The neuromuscular phenomena in catatonic patients are of great interest; naturally they have been studied by every means and been a source of controversy in many papers. The question remains, is this catatonic syndrome psychological and due to the patient's reaction to extra-neural factors, or is it due to an organic disease process in the nervous system? In other words, is it primarily a psychological disorder manifested somatically, or a somatic disorder which we then interpret psychologically?

Actually, there are two diametrically opposed ideas on the subject. One view is that catatonic manifestations are based on organic pathology. Those who claim this, point out that catatonic pictures are present in different neurological disorders due to impairment of the basal ganglia. They also point to the experimental production of catatonia with the use of certain drugs, bulbocapnine being one of the most important for producing catatonia in human and other animals. These investigators actually believe that in schizophrenic catatonia some organic impairment of the basal ganglia is present, probably due to some metabolic alteration which produces catatonic manifestation.

On the other hand, some observers offer the psychogenic interpretations of catatonia; that catatonia is actually a regression phenomena; that the muscular manifestations, especially the form catatonic patients show, are actually a regressive return to a lower level of functioning. They explain these catatonic manifestations as being partly dependent on the ideation of the patient, and even more dependent on unconscious emotional forces which force the patient to return to what has even been interpreted as the "intra-uterine level" of regression.

In my opinion, the difficulty with both approaches is that they work with analogies. One approach analogizes catatonia in relationship to organic syndromes; the other analogizes catatonia with the behavior of a fetus *in utero*. Of course, you could even establish a bridge of analogies from either direction. I nevertheless feel that, although there are some existing similarities, true catatonic phenomena are not identical to the organic or behavioral phenomena with which the analogies are made. As to the organic analogy, in the nonschizophrenic person certain drugs can simulate the catalepsy but do not produce the alteration of mental content observed in catatonic schizophrenia. Catalepsy produced by bulbocapnine or urethrane, especially in the experimental work on animals, has shown without doubt that a catatonic-like picture can be produced. The trouble is that this so-called catatonia in animals is not true catatonia; these are cases of catalepsy, and these were very often confused with catatonia. As to the behavioral analogy, the infantile muscular posturing of a fetus is far from that of so-called regressive behavior of a catatonic schizophrenic, provided you take into consideration other components and not merely the position of the legs.

Today I believe probably the best approach toward explaining catatonia is to assume that we are dealing with emotional mechanisms which relay through, and obviously trigger off, neuromuscular alterations which are very similar to extrapyramidal manifestations. Therefore, it is a combination of organic reactions with psychogenic factors. If one wants to label it, one might call it a psychosomatic disorder. Why some individuals, and especially some schizophrenic individuals, are able to produce catatonic manifestations whereas others do not, is completely obscure. Only a small group of schizophrenics are able to do so.

I would like to call attention to the fact of the intimate relationship between narrowing of consciousness and catatonic manifestations. It is not invariably so, but the majority of patients wherein profound catatonic manifestations are observed are usually individuals who are self-absorbed, quite hallucinatory, and show a narrowing of consciousness. In many of these patients, narrowing of consciousness goes so far that when they come out of the catatonic episode they retain a complete amnesia for it. I must remind you that, according to most textbooks, the difference between an organic and a schizophrenic case is that the schizophrenic patient, and in this case a catatonic patient, always observes the environment and is able to give you a good account of what had occurred during the episode. This assumption, used as a criterion for a differential diagnosis, is one of many fairy tales we find in the texts. A few schizophrenic patients showing catatonia phenomena undoubtedly behave this way. They lie in bed; they are stiff; they would probably show resistance if you tried to move them, and even show flexibilitas cerea. At the same time, they observe very carefully what is going on around them. After they come out of it, they are able to give you an excellent account of what went on. Therefore, there was no interference with consciousness—at least not noticeably—and, therefore, no amnesia is present. These are usually the rather chronic catatonic cases.

On the other hand, just the opposite occurs in many of the relatively acute catatonic cases; here the patient in a state of stupor actually is so dominated by voices and other hallucinations, or so dominated by somatic sensations and other such phenomena, he is constantly too preoccupied to follow anything that is going on in the environment. Then, after the patient comes out of the stupor, he claims complete amnesia for what had gone on and does not even know how he came to be in the hospital. With the aid of drugs such as sodium amytal, it is possible for a few of these patients, *but not all,* to regain a portion of their memory. Sometimes it is possible to elicit from such a patient that, while in the stupor, he had been so preoccupied with certain compelling ideas or voices and strange sensations within himself that he was unaware of what went on around him, and therefore he cannot remember. Many of these patients are unable to regain amnestic material despite all the psychological or drug methods at our disposal; they behave as do organic cases and, in a similar manner to individuals following a brain concussion, they actually do not know what had transpired during the time periods of their attack because, most likely, the registration of stimuli coming from the external environment had been suspended.

We once ran a series of studies *(Hoch, 1948)* on catatonic patients who had claimed amnesia. We examined them with "lie detectors." Those who had complete recall but tried to suppress it gave a "lie response." Those, however, who claimed they did not remember anything and were unable to regain memory material with methods described, behaved as did organic individuals in the test; in other words, they simply gave no "lie response" when stating they did not know what had occurred during their attack.

So, one will observe many variations in catatonic schizophrenic patients: those who are completely amnestic, those who are partially amnestic, and those patients who fully remember what had occurred although they had been in a state of so-called stupor. A schizophrenic person's memory depends to some extent on the state of excitement he is in, and to some extent on mechanisms which are partly psychodynamic, partly environmental, partly neurochemical, and partly as yet unknown determinants—all playing a role so that the schizophrenic person at times remembers and at times does not.

The main thing to realize is that many of these catatonic patients do manifest a narrowing of consciousness, but it is unlike the narrowing of consciousness in an organic case in which it is primary. The narrowing of consciousness in catatonic patients is secondary to the domination by hallucinations or other sensations. It is similar to the reaction of a person dominated by anxiety or by some very intense emotion who consequently becomes unobservant of the environment. Naturally, this person begins to "listen" only to that which is going on within him. The maximum of the "listening inward" is reached in a catatonic patient who so completely cuts himself off from the environment that he is in a state of stupor.

Catatonia is an extremely interesting phenomenon in that most likely many organic and psychogenic mechanisms occur in an interwoven way. This has been only partially studied. It is very interesting that catatonia can be precipitated by both organic tools and psychological means. Conversely, catatonia can be broken through by psychotherapeutic and also by organic means (the Kempf method). This all indicates we are probably dealing with what could be called a junction disorder in which some somatic manifestations are linked with psychogenic manifestations. I have stated it this way only as a form of illustration because personally I am very far from being a dualist who believes that the body is one separate entity and the so-called spirit is another—that the body moves the spirit, or the spirit moves the body. I simply use it to illustrate that catatonic manifestations can be precipitated and removed by approaching them primarily from the physical and primarily from the emotional viewpoints. If you attempt to establish contact with a catatonic patient and succeed, the catatonic manifestations will vanish before your eyes. In another patient you can inject sodium amytal and the catatonic manifestations will vanish within a few minutes. Or, you can give a patient one or two electro-convulsive treatments and the catatonic manifestations will vanish under their influence.

This working phenomenon of manipulating an emotional state by organic means and manipulating an emotional state by psychotherapeutic means is, in my opinion, one of the most important facts in clinical psychiatry and also from the point of view of research: Only by these procedures will it eventually be established what mechanisms play which roles and what therapies should be applied in which case condition. The role of mechanisms varies in degree in each case. Some catatonic patients are completely refractory to any attempts to make contact and it is absolutely necessary to use organic means first in order to break through and thereby establish contact. Other catatonic patients readily establish contact, and naturally the psychotherapeutic approach is attempted before relying on organic measures.

24

SUBGROUPS OF SCHIZOPHRENIA: SIMPLE AND PARANOID

I have discussed the hebephrenic and the catatonic classical forms of schizophrenia. The two other most well-known classical forms to be discussed are the simple and the paranoid forms. These two forms of schizophrenia do not appear to be as "organic" as the hebephrenic and catatonic forms; regression and deterioration are not as pronounced.

SIMPLE FORM OF SCHIZOPHRENIA

This form of schizophrenia has been markedly neglected—probably because it seems so simple. The simple form of schizophrenia is much more common than assumed. Actually you do not see this simple form in your psychiatric practice very often, nor do you see it very often in an average hospital practice. Simple schizophrenia is encountered mostly in prisons and wherever persons are admitted or committed who show asocial or antisocial tendencies. A great many of these persons are suffering from so-called simple schizophrenia. Occasionally we do see them in office practice, but they are usually diagnosed incorrectly, and only after they have been treated for a time is it discovered that in all probability they are suffering from schizophrenia.

The label "simple" does not really accurately apply to this form of schizophrenia because its structure is by no means simple. The term "simple" merely alludes to the fact these patients have no hallucinations or delusions. In other words, they show *no trend reactions,* as compared to other forms of schizophrenia in which trend reactions are present, such as hallucinations and delusions and other so-called productive symptoms.

I must emphasize that the basic structure of the simple form of schizophrenia rests on exactly those same observations we have seen in the other forms. There is an impairment of the associations, impairment of affect, autistic-dereistic approaches, and some of the other criteria I have already discussed. All are present in such patients the same way as in the other forms of schizophrenia. You could actually formulate it this way: In simple schizophrenia, there are no symptoms present "on top" of the existing basic manifestations of the schizophrenia to distort or obscure them, and therefore these basic symptoms are sometimes more easily discerned. On the other hand, the diagnosis in these cases is obviously much more difficult to determine and much more uncertain. Actually, diagnosing any psychosis, including a schizophrenic psychosis, becomes increasingly easier the more we are able to limit ourselves to relying on just the trend reactions present. It is obvious that a schizophrenic psychosis in a patient who has hallucinations and delusions is not too difficult to diagnose and, as Bleuler formulated, you do not need psychiatric training to make such a diagnosis—anyone, even the janitor of the hospital, is able to do it. In simple schizophrenia the diagnosis is mainly determined by the patient's behavior patterns, and (if you wish to use them) there are some psychological tests which may give you some assistance.

The simple type of schizophrenia may occur at any age. However, it usually *appears rather early in life* and is usually present by the time of adolescence. It is rare to find an apparently normal and well-adjusted individual who, in his forties, then develops manifestations of a simple form of schizophrenia. I have never seen this. There are cases in which it was suspected to be present in such people; as it turned out, they were either organic cases, or the previous anamneses contained errors and the so-called normalcy of the patients' previous adjustment and personality organization was just not the fact.

Therefore, simple schizophrenia develops rather early in life. The patients show a gradual *withdrawal* from the environment and display all the autistic and dereistic mechanisms observed within the framework of a withdrawal. In addition to the withdrawal, there is an *impairment of energy* in these individuals. They usually do not do much, or if they do anything at all it is to concentrate on some one issue or another, discarding an overall display of energy output. *Emotional apathy* and dulling, apparent in so many schizophrenic persons, are very conspicuous in these patients and sometimes you are able to diagnose them by their peculiar apathetic behavior. They are emotionally dull, they are emotionally blunted, and they usually display a rather indifferent attitude toward the environment which is often punctuated by states of aggression. This aggressive punctuation often puts them into the antisocial category. Very often they are apathetic and at the same time irritable, moody, and asocial.

They have a strong tendency to withdraw and remain alone. They are actually living a very solitary existence without contacting others. Many simple schizophrenics are hoboes or persons who work at odd jobs and move around a great deal. Even when they move around, their inability to establish contact is always very conspicuous. They actually fear human contact and try to shut out any such stimulation which would lead to an interpersonal relationship. In many cases the migration of some of these people, their moving from one place to another, is to some extent based on vague paranoid ideas; they cannot tolerate the same environment any longer because they feel it is full of something hostile or is cruel to them.

A number of simple schizophrenic patients have paranoid ideas, usually based on some constellation in their human contacts, but they lack the ability to evolve a paranoid system; they do not respond to these ideas in a sustained way. There is a very similar relationship here to the type of paranoid ideation seen in some hebephrenic or catatonic patients. However, in simple schizophrenics the paranoid ideation frequently has a strong environmental precipitated quality. For instance, if a stress situation occurs and the patient is unable to cope with it, he may develop some paranoid ideation. This rarely crystallizes into a clear-cut delusion. There is only a feeling of uneasiness, of concern, and of surveillance, but it does not manifest itself with very clear-cut and organized delusional ideas. These patients then move away and later reappear, slowly becoming more uneasy, more suspicious and more irritable; then they may suddenly display aggression.

Basically, there is a tendency for withdrawal, especially from interpersonal stimulation, and there is also a tendency to turn around and attempt to press through. Actually, these are basic psychological maneuvers which are executed by so-called normal and neurotic persons but, I would say, in a much more diluted way. In other words, there are two ways of coping with excessive stress: You simply take flight or you fight. Now, we all do both one and the other. In many schizophrenics you often see some difficulty in this. A patient attempts to withdraw more and more; sometimes the patient suddenly feels he has to make a stand; he then turns around and begins to crash through. A temporary state of excitement follows, during which he may make a suicidal or homicidal attempt by turning his aggression inward or outward. Following that, he may again return to a catatonic-like withdrawal state which, of course, is what we observe in simple schizophrenia.

There are two schools of thought concerning the withdrawal and the emotional dulling in schizophrenia: One assumption is that the withdrawal of the schizophrenic is primary and—on a level with the memory impairment of a paretic—is due to the disease process per se. However, I feel that the autistic mechanism in schizophrenia is already secondary to the handicap many patients feel due to their inability to cope with stimulation.

In addition to the withdrawal, the emotional blunting, and apathetic behavior, simple schizophrenic patients very often manifest the *intellectual impairment* which is present in every form of schizophrenia. The thinking is very often schizophrenic. In other words, they have a thinking disorder peculiar to schizophrenia whereby the thinking is illogical compared to what is considered normal logic. It is not completely illogical in itself; these persons have their own logic. Distortions are seen in their logic. Their concept formation and concept evaluations are usually disturbed and very often rigid. There are no sensorial defects. Memory and basic intellectual functionings, insofar as formal intelligence goes, are well preserved. Deterioration is usually mainly on an emotional level.

Some simple schizophrenics, however, deteriorate intellectually, similarly as do other forms of schizophrenia. *The deterioration is rather slow, slowly progressive.* Sometimes this is not easy to diagnose because in the bland, apathetic, nonproductive individual it is rather difficult to demonstrate the progress of a gradual intellectual decline. We do not see the marked regressive symptoms observed in hebephrenic or catatonic patients. Regression symptoms develop so slowly in the simple form of schizophrenia that they become apparent only when the patient deteriorates to such a considerable extent that it becomes most obvious. By then, as I have pointed out, markedly deteriorated schizophrenics look very much alike regardless of their original subgroup designation.

The gradual deterioration going on in these patients, their nonparticipation in contacting others, and their complete "I don't care" attitude toward performance often put them into the diagnostic designation of mental deficiency by inexperienced psychiatrists. This is particularly so if the psychiatrists deal with younger persons—say, sixteen or seventeen years of age. It is rather common for these persons to be diagnosed simply as morons, or as persons with mental defects combined with sociopathic traits, particularly if they do something antisocial. All so-called dull-normal, mentally deficient, sociopathic patients should be carefully examined if one is to determine whether or not the patient actually is suffering from the simple form of schizophrenia. If a patient is carefully examined and properly tested, the diagnosis can be made without too much difficulty in the majority of cases. In the same respect, it is also possible to differentiate simple schizophrenia from sociopathic behavior, even though sometimes it is seemingly a much more complicated issue.

One of the interesting features in these patients—which is diagnostically very helpful to know about—is that some of them are people who had originally performed quite well in childhood. In fact, very often you are unable to determine the presence of schizophrenic symptoms in a patient's childhood, because there are no rules or regulations as to when these difficulties become manifest. It is even not rare to find in a patient's history that, when a child, he appeared to be rather bright, that he performed quite well in school, and then suddenly, at the age of fourteen or sixteen, he began to change. He showed a marked withdrawal from the environment, a great slump occurred in his school performance, and, finally, instead of continuing to be rather alert and bright, he displayed a withdrawn and apathetic demeanor, lounging around the house all day, doing nothing. Any scurrying attempts of those concerned to force him to do more was rejected with an "I don't care" attitude; if pressed hard, he would assume a definitely negative state which occasionally even went into a state of excitement. His behavior would often be punctuated with all kinds of peculiar acts which are difficult to explain, illogical, and sometimes bizarre. All these combined symptoms at that age usually spell schizophrenia, and quite often the simple form.

The diagnosis is based on clinical observations and, what is more important, a good anamnesis. A rather good anamnesis, I might say, would be the average anamnesis obtained from relatives. Upon sifting very carefully through the historical data when examining the childhood of a schizophrenic patient, you become more and more impressed by the fact that deviations were present at a very early age. These deviations are not always easy to interpret. Sometimes they are even difficult to find because the environment has to be unusually alert to be able to give this information. The histories obtained are very much transmuted by the environment; relatives will simply deny the patient is abnormal, peculiar, and so forth. Furthermore, there are variations as to the symptomatology in every case, and sometimes this variability factor makes diagnosing difficult. For instance, you probably could assume a patient's diagnosis on the basis of his behaving emotionally and socially just like a simple schizophrenic, but intellectually he might maintain his ability and even continue to be rather brilliant. Personally, I would rather place such a schizophrenic case in the unclassified group, or some might belong in the pseudoneurotic group.

In the typical case of simple schizophrenia, however, intellectual impairment is present and, of course, in a typically schizophrenic way. Interestingly enough, these patients usually drop to simple levels of adaptation, and some of them, in whom the process is apparently not "burning" as intensely as is observed in hebephrenia, somehow maintain themselves in simple occupations. It is not rare to have these people hanging around as unskilled laborers or, if they formerly had a better intellectual standard, they may be able to perform the same duties year in and year out with relative reliability. They do not bother anyone and maintain a solitary existence. It is only if you discuss various subjects with them that you notice this complete barrier, this complete inability to cope with anything having to do with their social environment.

Very often, simple schizophrenics are overly concerned with their bodies and self-imposed health regulations are observed to be on a hypochondriacal level. Many complain of various aches and pains and about stomach symptoms. Their interpretations of these complaints are often typically schizophrenic. Some of them have a medicine chest full of different pills, and you will find that they go on or off medications seemingly without any rhyme or reason.

Actually, a symptom triangle is observed: *emotional withdrawal, or an autistic and dereistic approach to life; hypochondriacal preoccupation; and inclination to paranoid interpretations.* This "narcissistic triangle" is present in the same way as in all other forms of schizophrenia. In other words, these people, too, are extremely preoccupied with their own security on every level.

One interesting thing that comes to mind is the question of cultural influence on symptom manifestations. Environments must be considered. For instance, in so-called primitive civilizations it is common to find hysterical manifestations superimposed on the basic symptoms in these patients. Actually the schizophrenic patient has a great tendency to fragmentation, and hysterical symptom formation is naturally a form of fragmentation. However, hysterical symptom formation is much more massive in neurotic than in schizophrenic patients; in schizophrenics the fragmentation is more molecular. Incidentally, in our civilization, hysteric symptomatology is displayed less and less in recent years. On the other hand, psychosomatic manifestations have become more prevalent in many of these cases.

Simple schizophrenia is similar to the hebephrenic

group in that the *prognosis is not very favorable.* Usually the disorder continues creeping along its insidious way and, as I have mentioned, some patients deteriorate and some do not to any great extent. Just as in any form of schizophrenia, this tendency to a downgrade course could stop at any level, reverse itself temporarily, and again become active. In other words, there are many variations in the course of the disorder. Many simple schizophrenics unfortunately become criminals or, if not criminals, at least asocial. A large number of them withdraw with the use of alcohol or other drugs. Many of the drug addicts belong in this group. Naturally, rehabilitation of all such patients presents quite a problem.

I would like to call to your attention, however, the fact that some simple schizophrenic patients actually are able to adjust, even though on a precarious level and often on a lower level than would be appropriate to their intellectual ability. Therefore, in many instances their condition is not hopeless and attempts should always be made to rehabilitate such patients and help them make this adjustment.

Nevertheless, the prognosis is definitely not good, and simple schizophrenia is very *resistant to any presently applied form of treatment.* This is valid with regard to organic treatments as well as psychotherapeutic attempts. These patients, for instance, do not respond to either electroconvulsive or insulin therapy; some patients achieve a temporary amelioration with these forms of therapy but do not sustain the response for very long. Certain psychotropic drugs may alleviate tension and the frequency of aggressive states, but as yet there are none which will prevent the downward course of this disorder.

Psychotherapy is usually attempted in treating these patients; this requires the use of environmental manipulation and adaptational measures to a much larger extent than is used for other patients. This approach is superior to any attempt at conventional organized psychotherapy—which simple schizophrenic patients usually reject or defeat by their extremely indifferent, bland, and nonparticipating behavior. Treating such a patient is extremely difficult, and it taxes the psychiatrist's emotional structure to a very large extent. I think it is realized that to treat a patient who has a simple form of schizophrenia is most exhausting and not very rewarding. On the other hand, the psychiatrist, by astute and clever evaluation of the patients' adaptive ability to the environment, can sometimes help a considerable number of them.

They usually do not respond to organized psychotherapy on any deep level. There is one reservation here which occasionally gives rise to some question in the mind of the therapist. Many of these patients, as do most schizophrenics, have a great deal of difficulty (1) regulating their aggression and (2) regulating their anxiety. As a resultant of these regulatory impairments, they have (3) an inability to make a decision between dependence and independence. Practically speaking, in many schizophrenic patients the conflict rages as to how dependent and how independent they should be in relationship to the social environment, and especially with respect to people they regard as being there to help or hinder them.

If you treat such persons in whom this conflict is very marked, you could, of course, probably ameliorate this conflict temporarily. This can be done more easily if the patient becomes dependent upon you. You are then able to manipulate the transference situation in such a way that the patient's aggression (which is naturally present simultaneously with dependency feelings in his ambivalent approach to you) is not so strong that he then becomes very rejective of you because he is so dependent on you. Therefore, quite frequently, at least in the first phase of such a psychotherapeutic attempt, an amelioration of the symptomatology occurs. Sometimes it is very impressive. The patient appears to function much better; he adapts himself much better, and he naturally tries to play up to the therapist for the pleasant dependency by behaving better. Then, after a few months, the situation begins to turn and the seemingly positive results of treatment begin to disappear. By this time (if you think yourself very clever), the patient has already been dismissed from treatment, and you have put down in your record "schizophrenic patient very much improved." By now the patient has another therapist (but, of course, you know nothing about this). These cases are very common. Occasionally, however, simple schizophrenic patients do respond to a form of such treatment more or less permanently, but the majority simply lead a very precarious existence. And as I have mentioned, a few may adjust in some occupation with which they are able to cope and can lead a life of splendid isolation.

PARANOID FORM OF SCHIZOPHRENIA

This is one of the most interesting forms of schizophrenia. It is not only very interesting from the point of view of schizophrenia, but is extremely so because of the delusional formation, the relationship of normal psychological defense mechanisms versus the paranoid defense mechanisms, and that of the paranoid form of schizophrenia to the other paranoid states. Unfortunately, I can only touch upon it rather superficially because I must discuss the other forms of schizophrenia. There is a very great deal of literature on paranoid schizophrenia. You can find all this data in many textbooks and in a number of other compilations. *Research in Dementia Praecox,* by Dr. Nolan D. C. Lewis *(1936),* for example, contains the whole literature on dementia praecox. This subject was further discussed and published by Bellak. (Some descriptions of the clinical entities must be read in other languages because they all have not been translated.)

Although the paranoid form of schizophrenia was recognized before his time, Kraepelin described it as a psychosis *developing at an older age* than the other dementia praecox disorders, but he classified it as a dementia praecox because deterioration can occur, although usually it is very slow—if observed at all. The paranoid form occurs almost equally in men and women. It very rarely occurs in young people; it is exceptionally rare, even in the early twenties. From then on the number of these patients grows rapidly and the majority suffering from this disorder are in their late thirties and forties. Of course, paranoid ideation may occur in young people who have other forms of schizophrenia or in people who are markedly depressed. Also, fleeting paranoid thinking can occur at any age in so-called normal people under certain stress, and so forth. However, I am now talking about the paranoid schizophrenic disorder. The fact remains it is actually a psychosis of an older age group and is the psychosis of individuals who, up to a point, were apparently able to cope with their environment—or able to cope with it in a compensatory manner. Generally speaking, patients with the paranoid form of schizophrenia seem, on a physiological as well as on a psychological level, to possess more ability to compensate than do those with the other forms of schizophrenia. How far this contributes to its late appearance in life is naturally a question open for discussion.

You know that some investigators, particularly those who consider schizophrenia essentially a constitutional disorder, tied·in schizophrenia with the so-called schizoid temperament and with the so-called asthenic and dysplastic constitutional types. This involves some of the theoretical issues on the etiology of schizophrenia. I wish to mention here only that usually those schizophrenic persons who develop the paranoid form of schizophrenia do not belong in the asthenic category, but are usually individuals having athletic, mixed athletic-asthenic, or mixed dysplastic body forms. That would indicate the presence of so-called *physiological compensatory mechanisms*.

Furthermore, autopsies performed on schizophrenic patients, reported many years ago by two or three investigators—one among them being Dr. Nolan D. C. Lewis *(1923)*—demonstrated that many schizophrenics have a relatively small heart and a small vascular system. In other words, the asthenic component expressing itself in general body build is also expressed in some of the internal organs, and especially in the build of the cardiovascular apparatus. It was also assumed that in these individuals the reticulo-endothelial system does not function in the same way as in nonschizophrenics, but in my opinion this is subject to much doubt. However, the observation of body form is correct for a rather large group of schizophrenics. Dr. Lewis *(1923)* pointed out that the hebephrenic and catatonic types have the hypoplastic cardiovascular constitutional factor but, in comparing these physical findings with physical findings in patients suffering from the paranoid form of schizophrenia, he observed that bodily they are not asthenic and that their cardiovascular system is very well developed. It is practically normal; in many ways it is even somewhat over-developed. Therefore, the paranoid has a different somatic organization than have other schizophrenic types,

If we now switch over to the so-called temperamental background, individuals with the so-called schizoid personality show a tendency for withdrawal from stimulation into an autistic and dereistic approach to life. They are usually sensitive individuals with a cold exterior. The paranoid schizophrenic is also an individual who withdraws. He, too, is unable to cope with interpersonal stimulation. At the same time, he has in his body organization a so-called athletic component in contrast to the asthenic manifestations in the other schizophrenias. This indicates he is able to overcome this withdrawal tendency to some extent—or at least has the ability to try to manipulate the environment for his own purposes.

Therefore, we often observe such an individual compensating for his tendency to withdraw from interpersonal stimulation by means of a partial reaction formation; his behavior is outgoing and he may even be aggressive in influencing other people, although he remains emotionally detached from them. Some of the so-called *pseudoextroverts* belong in this group. These are persons who constantly attempt to manipulate those in their environment, yet make very little emotional contact. In some way they use this device for their own advancement, and more often to overcome their feelings of inferiority. Therefore, paranoid individuals in general, and paranoid schizophrenic patients in particular, have at their disposal certain compensatory mechanisms not ordinarily present in other forms of schizophrenia.

Again I wish to mention the fact that paranoid mechanisms appear in all forms of schizophrenia. The presence of one or two paranoid ideas and vague delusions does not mean the patient is suffering from the paranoid form. But, the paranoid form of schizophrenia has all the basic clinical manifestations of schizophrenia previously described and, in addition, the so-called athletic component. This compensatory element is characterized by the fact that the *delusional formation is in the foreground*. Actually the clinical picture is dominated by paranoid delusions based on the fantasies of these individuals which they project onto the environment. This is a peculiar reaction formation, and one which has been interpreted in detail in psychoanalytic studies. Generally speaking, we know as little about it today as we did fifty or sixty years ago, psychodynamically and otherwise. I do not want to attempt to trace the paranoid form of schizophrenia in relationship to the other paranoid states, but naturally all paranoid persons have a similar tendency to project.

This projection has been used in various attempts to explain the whole paranoid process. Projection has explained some of the content of these patients' delusions. It has not at all explained how the process of projection comes about. In other words, the content of delusions was somewhat illuminated by our psychodynamic knowledge, yet why it is that this person chose the delusional way to solve conflicts is completely unknown. Throughout the literature, and more often the psychoanalytic literature, constant confusion prevails between the motivation of these persons' ideas and behavior versus the etiology of the behavior. The motivation is very often treated as if it would be etiological. It is not.

The problem of the *classification* of different paranoid groups has been the cause of a great deal of confusion. When psychiatry consisted essentially of classifying the different clinical pictures observed, many subdivisions were made of paranoid manifestations. According to the old classificatory attempts, not all the paranoid groupings were considered schizophrenic. The more logical, the better organized, and the less fantastic the delusional system, the more frequently the diagnosis of paranoia was made. Furthermore, delusions in paranoia always occurred in a clear setting and no hallucinations occurred, whereas other paranoid groups displayed them. On the other end of the scale, paranoid schizophrenia has delusional formations which were bizarre, fantastic, and not too well elaborated upon compared to those in paranoia, and hallucinations could occur. In the group termed paraphrenia (a synonym for paranoid condition) the delusional pictures were somewhere in between.

Now, in my opinion, the observation of these different clinical pictures is probably still important and should perhaps be studied further on a dynamic level. It is interesting why a so-called paranoiac develops a delusional system while his mental integration is otherwise left intact (although the mentality of patients having delusions is, of course, not fully integrated but only relatively so), and yet on the other end of the scale a paranoid schizophrenic person can have the most bizarre and most fantastic delusions and impress you as a person whose mentality is far from highly integrated. So far as I know, nobody understands why it is some individuals go around having only one or two delusional ideas, but otherwise appear to be all right. When we compare such a person to one who has fantastic delusions— that he is influenced by moonbeams, that the whole room is wired, that all his thoughts are being recorded—there is naturally quite a gap which we are as yet unable to understand fully.

However, if you investigate the personality structure of persons who have a so-called true paranoia, what would emerge? Again you would see the same type of structural features observed in the other paranoid states, only with differences in gradation. But, I am not too sure the differences in gradation are just quantitative. I am not convinced that this "paranoia" entity exists. Practically speaking, paranoia was such a rare disease that many psychiatrists lived for fifty years and never saw a case. Moreover, no one has ever been able to differentiate very well between paraphrenia and paranoid schizophrenia because differentiation was usually not based so much on the quality of the delusional system seen as on the quantity of the symptom.

Follow-up studies have strongly indicated that these entities such as paranoia and paraphrenia do not exist. Even the newer German psychiatry which mainly, you might say, hoarded these special diagnostic entities, is giving them up—although at one time they were very proud of this, you know? Only recently have they admitted all these syndromes are more or less well-preserved cases of schizophrenia. I never saw a true case of paranoia or paraphrenia which did not have a schizophrenic background.

A number of psychiatrists would flatly contradict me. They would say they realize there is such a thing as paranoid schizophrenia, but that the cases of paranoia and paranoid condition have nothing to do with schizophrenia. These psychiatrists maintain this because these patients are usually outgoing, make a much better contact, are pseudo-extroverted, and so forth. This symptom feature can surely be stressed. I admit there are variations in the symptomatology, but I do not see basic differences. I believe there is a great deal of hairsplitting going on. I do not presently believe that it matters very greatly whether a patient is diagnosed a case of paranoia, paranoid condition, or paranoid schizophrenia; to me, they are all schizophrenias despite variations in the clinical picture.

The question as to whether or not there are paranoid

reactions, paranoid states, or paranoid psychoses not belonging in the schizophrenic group has not been settled. Occasionally we see individuals developing paranoid episodes—particularly in certain life situations with which they are unable to cope. The episodes may last for a few weeks or a few months and then disappear. These paranoid reactions are often benign versus the paranoid schizophrenic delusions which are not at all benign. Some psychiatrists feel these cases should be separated from schizophrenia and designated as a paranoid reaction, or a paranoid state.

The *predominant symptomatology* in the paranoid form of schizophrenia is, naturally, the *delusional system*: It is both organized and consistent. It usually develops gradually.

Prodromal symptoms vary. Before the development of the full, consistent delusional ideation, many of these patients show characteristics of circumstantiality during the interview. In other words, they behave as do many obsessive-compulsive patients. They begin by explaining to you their entire story in minute detail; then they lose themselves completely in the detail and forget the actual main issue. When treating such a patient, you will observe him to "fill in" with fantasies, which he constantly organizes in his thinking, to adapt everything to fit his delusional views. This process describes the "readiness" to formulate delusions. In other words, every experience or happening the person observes in the environment is given all forms of translation while being transmuted and adapted to the main idea of reference uppermost in his mind. As you follow the patient along, it is extremely interesting to see how neutral and indifferent issues will suddenly become loaded with affect, and then to see how the transmutation occurs. A completely unimportant and unrelated issue will, in time, become crucial and significant to the particular form of delusion developing in the patient.

In paranoid schizophrenia, as in other forms of schizophrenia, the delusions can be seemingly primary, but often they are secondary to these affective deviations or to situations with which the person is unable to cope. While in depressive disorders such as manic-depressive or involutional psychosis, paranoid delusions are usually secondary to strong guilt feelings and are self-accusatory in nature, in paranoid schizophrenia there is more massive projection and no self-recrimination.

The ideas these patients can have may be manifold; the paranoid delusions are usually those of reference or persecution, but ideas of grandeur may also develop. Some paranoid schizophrenic patients, as was pointed out many years ago, express their ideations of grandeur in combination with their ideas of reference and persecution. Actually, the delusional formation in these patients usually begins with ideas of persecution—with or without accompanying hallucinations—and these ideas spread until finally the individual is dominated by his delusions.

The delusions are very often perplexing, subject to changes and to becoming bizarre. They are usually somewhat systematized, but are not fully logical. Quite a number of paranoid schizophrenic patients are unable to explain an important part of their delusional mechanism in a completely logical way. (This was used as a point of differentiation from paranoia, where the delusional system was conceived to be logical, very well knit, very well organized, and fully understandable to whomever the patient related those ideas.)

The delusional content in paranoid schizophrenia is usually described in textbooks as illogical, fantastic, and so bizarre that you are not able to "feel" yourself into these things. This is true for some patients; it is not true, however, for a number of them. In the first place, many of these patients possess an ability to put across even not too logical ideas partly because they are very aggressive and very domineering, and partly because they are pseudoextroverts who bring their delusions forward with a great deal of conviction. Their ideation, therefore, often carries a great deal of weight. In the second place, you will even find that in the early phase of such a psychosis many of the ideas expressed by the patient actually are perfectly understandable and quite logical. If they are not logical, at least the patient makes an attempt to justify the claims and statements he has about his delusions. He may succeed in this because it is commonly observed that paranoid delusions have a basis of truth behind the elaborations, such as true guilt feelings, true rejections, and so forth. This leads many physicians to cast aside the idea that the patient is delusional. For instance, a man who cheated on his wife may develop a fear, which then becomes a conviction he is being followed by detectives sent by his wife. In another case, a patient may develop delusions of jealousy; he may be right in that there are reasons for his jealousy, but that does not mean he is not delusional even though the core of his delusion is based on truth.

Paranoid ideas organized around jealousy, especially, and paranoid ideas organized around ideas of reference can sometimes be quite convincing. To give you an example, I recently saw a forty-eight-year-old wife of a doctor who was very tense, very apprehensive, and beginning to express ideas about her husband's infidelity. She had all kinds of ideas which she related in a perfectly logical and well-organized manner. She was seen by the family physician, and he believed her story. When I saw her a few weeks later she related the same story to me, and by then she already began to express ideas that were not quite logical. For instance, she said that while sitting in the living room, her husband would receive messages. When he received a message, he would pick up his hat and coat and go out to see "the other woman." When asked what these messages were, she said they were some sounds in the radiator. Another time she added she was convinced he saw another woman because his pocket handkerchief had spots on it which she interpreted to be seminal fluid. This went on for about six or seven weeks, and then she began to express ideas that the room was wired and her husband was receiving messages through all kinds of rays; her delusions became manifestly very bizarre.

So you see, in paranoid schizophrenia sometimes the delusional ideas originally are related most logically, and then they may gradually deteriorate and become more fantastic and more peculiar. The delusions can become bizarre and fantastic, but they are consistent! For example, in Freud's description of Schreber, the patient was obviously a paranoid schizophrenic and, even though his delusions were bizarre, Schreber consistently interpreted an alliance with God and his father; he consistently interpreted what God did to him, including all the sexual approaches from behind, and so forth.

Occasionally delusional systems are "encapsulated" or circumscribed apart from the person's other performances and, therefore, do not appear very conspicuous on superficial examination. These observations have led to the occasionally expressed idea that one is dealing with a person with a "fixed idea," or as you might have read in the psychiatric texts some time ago, a "monomania." (In French literature "mani" is equivalent to a psychosis and has no implication in our terminology.) Such a thing as a circumscribed singular delusion, a fixed idea, or a monomania does not exist. All these individuals usually have many other distortions and other peculiar notions. However, we must admit that although some individuals are dominated by delusions and are disorganized by them, others are relatively well organized and function fairly well, sometimes disclosing peculiar ideas on only one or another level. This latter group is obviously much more difficult to diagnose; at times these individuals are not diagnosed as paranoid schizophrenic at all until the symptoms become more massive, and they behave in a considerably more disorganized manner.

Of course, in the paranoid form of schizophrenia, the more clear-cut the delusional elaboration is, the better the patient's adjustment. Quite a number of them always remain in the community; they never get into psychiatric hospitals, and often you see these persons suddenly reveal their delusional system. I think it was about fifteen years ago at a university that suddenly a laboratory technician shot two professors of the dental school. He had been examined for some little injury by a physician in the department of psychiatry who had given him a clean bill of health a few days before. Now, this man was about fifty years of age who had been wandering around for years, living in one room, never talking to anyone. He came to work in the dental laboratory and was considered very outstanding in his work. He never bothered anyone and never socialized with anyone. In other words, he lived a completely isolated existence. Then this thing occurred! After the shooting he was naturally arrested and examined. Then he told the examiners that for years the two professors had tried to do something to him; they were plotting against him; they were trying to get him out of his job; he presented a large array of logical evidence to show how they did it, and why they did it. He told it so convincingly that he almost persuaded the police it was true. Well, as it turned out, he went to a state hospital and remained there. But never did he show any deterioration.

It also happens, and I have seen it in every variation, that some of these patients have phases during which their ideations lack emotional charge, and there is nothing to push the delusional ideas. In other words, a patient will perhaps tell you that in the office where he works they do not like him, that there is one man who is always bothering him. He tells you all this in a matter-of-fact way, but does not act upon it. The whole thing sounds very much like some of the remarks anyone is likely to make about persons or places wherever they work. Then, a few years later, due to some change in the constellation or sometimes even apparently without one, this man will suddenly tell you they are trying to get him out of his office, and that one man in particular yesterday went to the police and complained about him. Then again a year later the delusion goes back to the original emotionally uncharged state. It is interesting that environmental changes can have some influence on diminishing the intensity of the delusion in some persons, and in others the delusional phase is maintained.

As you know, there are plenty of such individuals and sometimes it is very difficult to see at what point an overvalued idea stops—in religious, political, scientific areas, and so forth—and at what point delusion begins. Actually, you would be astonished to know how many people are going around with delusions who otherwise appear to be all right—and the number of paranoid schizophrenic persons is very great. Naturally, many of these are well-preserved delusional individuals and walk around unnoticed, or if noticed it is only by accident. They are sometimes described as odd individuals with very strong convictions, with extremely strong ideas, and who sometimes behave in a rather peculiar way. Occasionally you run across such persons indirectly when treating other members of his family. Then you receive all kinds of reports that make you wonder if you are dealing with a well-preserved psychotic individual—and more often than not, you are.

Naturally, the correct diagnosis may be overlooked in paranoid schizophrenics due to their rather good personality integration. Not only their personality but very often their intellectual functioning is surprisingly well preserved, even though they may have been delusional for many years. After a period of ten or more years, a certain amount of deterioration may have occurred in many cases. However, deterioration is much less frequent in the paranoid than in other forms of schizophrenia. Sometimes there is no evidence of deterioration at all.

If you take on some of these delusional patients and treat them with organic methods and in some cases with psychotherapy, the interesting fact is that *the more elaborated and clear-cut the delusions* in these patients, *the less they yield to therapy.* But, the more there are symptom-atological mixtures present, the more these patients are apt to give up their delusions. It is especially for these reasons that patients diagnosed as so-called pure paranoia were never really cured. There is one exception in the literature— Paul Bjerre's famous case example *(1922)*. The patient had a very elaborate paranoid content, and the psychoanalyst who treated him claimed the patient was cured by his analytic efforts. Later on there was a follow-up on this case in which the patient claimed that someone had pushed him from a horse; that this caused him to suffer a concussion, and that following the concussion he was well—he no longer had the paranoid ideas. Now, I do not know who is right— the patient, the horse, or the analyst. But, from this you must be aware of one thing, even though it appears a little far afield: It would be most interesting to someday deter-mine just how far the influence of therapies in general, and psychotherapies in particular, can be assessed. In other words, what functions are being performed and what is actually being accomplished by the various therapies.

The paranoid form of schizophrenia has many clinical details. However, we cannot go into all of them here and now. I would only like to say that it is a serious disorder. Formerly, it was considered so serious that some of the feel-ings of hopelessness in the treating of schizophrenia were based partly on the treatment of cases of hebephrenic dementia praecox with rapid deterioration, on one hand, and on these paranoid cases on the other. If someone was diagnosed as having a paranoid psychosis, it was assumed he would have it forever. Since these paranoid cases have been given much more careful study, we now know that a certain percentage recovers. Nevertheless, the majority remain delu-sional and therefore the paranoid form of schizophrenia, just as any other form of schizophrenia, is a serious and very complicated disorder, both prognostically and therapeu-tically.

A great many therapies have been used—drugs, somatic, and others. Various therapies most likely help a few patients, but from a statistical point of view the therapeutic results are not impressive. Many patients relapse. On the other hand, since we have been applying more intensive psychotherapy in some cases, insulin and psychosurgery in others, I believe the number of patients we are able to help is greater than it was fifty years ago. Nevertheless, I freely admit that all the therapeutic methods used today must be improved in manifold proportions before we can state we are able to help the majority of these patients.

Paranoid schizophrenics naturally could be very disturbing, and actually my experience has been that the environment suffers much more from this kind of schizophrenia than from the other forms. These are individuals who are relatively well preserved; if the delusional ideas do not dominate them completely, they maintain themselves and carry on fairly adequately. However, some of these people are in such a condition that they must be hospitalized only because of the dangerousness of their delusional ideas, if for nothing else. Obviously their relatives can suffer very much from such patients, and if any relatives or people in the community are in those patients' delusional system it can be very difficult to live with them. What is more, you can never be certain those persons will not act upon their delusions and occasionally, as I have described, it does happen. If it occurs outside of a hospital setting it can naturally lead to a great deal of trouble and can cause legal problems as well as direct harm to others.

I believe I should discuss very briefly the question of *homosexuality in relation to paranoid schizophrenia*. Homosexuality has been dealt with in psychiatric literature as either a psychodynamic entity, or the basis of some neurotic or psychotic disorders. Neither is true. *Homosexuality is a symptom.* It is a symptom which must be appraised within the constellation of other symptoms where it appears. *It is not an entity; it is not a cause.*

The symptom of homosexuality may have the following relationship to the psychodynamics of a neurotic or psychotic disease entity: (1) *It can cause emotional disorder in reaction to the person's feelings of isolation,* of being different, and the social stigma involved; (2) *it can be a part of the psychodynamic pattern* existing in some cases of the disease entity, but it is not a part of the disease nor present in every case; and (3) *it can occur coincidentally* in some other disease entity but be unrelated to it. Again, the homosexual symptom is not a disease entity and is not a "cause" of one.

As I have previously discussed, the sexual life of schizophrenic individuals contains a myriad of sexual activity, including homosexual. These are all signs of developmental abnormality, with its irregular maturation and impressive infantilism. The schizophrenic has a peculiar approach to sex; he wants it and at the same time he rejects it. He is ambivalent to sex as in every aspect of life striving. Since he withdraws from intimate relationships in his environment and is even fearful about talking to another person, he is naturally markedly disorganized if he must have some kind of sexual ideas or involvement. This is more often the conflict in schizophrenia underlying any homosexuality symptoms. All types of perversion can occur simultaneously in schizophrenic thinking. The so-called paragenital sexual behavior based on the theory of regression is theoretically correct in some cases, but homosexuality is only a *part* of the chaotic sexuality seen in schizophrenia.

It stands to reason that one cannot agree with Ferenczi or Abraham, who practically stated paranoid conditions are nothing else than repressed homosexuality *(1)*. This is a distortion and oversimplification of what actually goes on in schizophrenic persons; their sexuality is disturbed in many more ways than simply homosexuality. I personally do not deny the observation of homosexuality in some paranoid patients, nor the importance of the dynamics of patients in their struggle with the homosexual conflict, but it should be mentioned that so-called latent or manifest homosexuality is commonly observed in all forms of schizophrenia—not just the paranoid form.

I would like to state that in a great many patients homosexuality is not the source of the paranoid ideation and paranoid psychosis, contrary to what Ferenczi believed. Such an assumption, in my opinion, is only a fantasy and not a theory; it is not correct, as is borne out by studies of the dynamics of persons living in different cultures and in different environments. It cannot even be assumed correct in our own cultures if you compare, for instance, the paranoid delusional system of men versus women. Female paranoid patients are very rarely preoccupied with homosexuality; they are often preoccupied with heterosexuality—that they will be raped, they will be overpowered by a man, or that they feel an irresistible urge toward some man, and so forth. In male paranoid patients, preoccupation with homosexuality often prevails, but we must question very seriously if this is based on the original ideas of Ferenczi and Freud. In other words, does it have something to do with the libidinal organization of the patient, or is it rather a matter of cultural overevaluation of homosexuality in certain civilizations? Might not the factor of physical inferiority also be involved?

It is very interesting that in the delusions and hallucinations of a paranoid schizophrenic man the idea emerges that he is a sissy or a homosexual; he hears it commented upon with all the related four-letter words. Of course, these individuals do not perform well sexually. This is correct. They do not perform well, not because they are homosexual but because they are schizophrenic; their sexual disorganization is much more complicated than simple regression or developmental fixation at the homosexual level. Women having paranoid delusions and hallucinations rarely hear comments about, or accusations of, homosexuality. Furthermore, if they are accused, our society is much more tolerant of them than it is with men. These two factors were never fully or separately investigated. Therefore, what is actually the cultural element in the homosexual ideation and (if you wish to formulate it in the orthodox Freudian way) what is actually the libidinal element involved?

There is another cultural issue. As you know, in some countries homosexuality is handled differently than in the United States. For instance, homosexuality is tolerated in Italy, and it is even an accepted form of sexual manifestation in some parts of the Orient. Unfortunately, we do not have reliable psychodynamic investigations on patients from these countries. Superficial observations, however, indicate interestingly that in these countries the paranoid ideation does not have homosexual content, but is based on other paranoid elaborations. Today we can formulate that in some paranoid individuals an actual sexual inadequacy and probably the preoccupation with homosexuality is no doubt an important part of the dynamics of the delusional formation. However, that still does not explain the cause of the delusional formation; there are plenty of homosexual individuals who never have a paranoid psychosis, and there are many paranoid schizophrenic individuals who are not even "latently" homosexual. Therefore, we cannot state that homosexuality is the cause of the psychosis. We have to assume there are other ways and means of becoming paranoid; there is not just one road, through repressed homosexuality, to paranoid delusional formation. Furthermore, if some of the homosexual features are resolved in treatment of a paranoid schizophrenic patient, one cannot expect the schizophrenia to thereby be cured. In my opinion, the whole issue is ready to be reviewed and revised.

25

SPECIAL SUBGROUPS
OF SCHIZOPHRENIA:
ACUTE PSYCHOTIC FORMS

It has become well recognized that it is not always possible to classify schizophrenic cases according to the four classical forms described by Kraepelin and Eugen Bleuler. Before discussing the special subgroups I should remind you that "mixed" forms of schizophrenia are encountered whereby patients manifest predominant symptomatology of two or more main forms of schizophrenia. Many of these patients initially manifest one type of symptomatology which later changes to that of another and there is not only a mixture of symptoms during the transition but these chronic cases often remain undifferentiated and must be classified as such. An increasing number of patients, however, are observed who do not present this "mixed" picture and who present symptomatology which does not fit into the hebephrenic, catatonic, simple, or paranoid groups. These patients must

708

therefore be classified into special subgroups. Since the publication of Bleuler's *Dementia Praecox or The Group of Schizophrenias* in 1911 (it is still a "modern" book, by the way) there has been an increasing awareness of the incidence of these patients.

Schizophrenic patients are classified according to a special subgroup on the basis of the dominant clinical features manifested. Naturally, patients classified into one subgroup will show clinical features similar to those of another group during the course of illness, but those additional features do not dominate the clinical picture and are only variations in the clinical picture to be expected in any schizophrenic group. The basic clinical symptoms of schizophrenia are, naturally, present in these special subgroups just as they are in every schizophrenic patient regardless of which group he belongs in, but it is the dominant symptom patterns and elaborations that determine the classification. Now, various classification schemes for the many special clinical forms of schizophrenia have been suggested, but it would be impractical to attempt to classify all the possible clinical variations. I shall, instead, describe a few of the rather prevalent forms observed in our present cultural settings.

Certain subgroups manifest acute psychotic pictures, namely, the *acute confusional,* the *hysterical,* the *schizoaffective,* and the *cyclic* forms of schizophrenia. I might add brief mention of the ill-defined *"symptomatic"* subgroup in which symptoms of schizophrenia develop in the course of certain chronic disorders—which usually leads to diagnostic confusion because underlying schizophrenia is present in some cases and not in others. Of these prevalent subgroups mentioned, the acute confusional form is extremely important to discuss because it presents considerable difficulty in terms of diagnosis: The psychotic picture is often confused with that of an acute organic reaction, or that of a manic attack.

There are other special subgroups that manifest a

chronic course having nonpsychotic symptomatology dominating over the underlying schizophrenic process: These are mainly the *pseudoneurotic* form which usually presents a clinical picture difficult to differentiate from a psychoneurosis; and, the *pseudosociopathic* form in which the schizophrenic symptomatology is usually overshadowed by acting-out symptom behavior. In fact, because these two chronic forms present considerable diagnostic difficulties, and because they are so extremely prevalent today, they deserve special emphasis (and therefore shall be discussed separately later).

ACUTE CONFUSIONAL FORM OF SCHIZOPHRENIA

The so-called acute confusional form of schizophrenia has also been referred to in the psychiatric literature as "Acute Turmoil Schizophrenia" (Campbell) and as the acute hallucinatory form, or the acute delirious form ("delire schizophrenique" of the French school). Many years ago the Viennese school termed these cases the "amentia" form of schizophrenia. More recently McCullock and Meduna *(6)* in Chicago derived the term "Oneirophrenia," indicating that this acute disorder occurs as "dream states." The essential issue is that marked alterations of consciousness occur in the setting of acute psychotic episodes.

The symptom onset in these cases is very acute and resembles an acute catatonic episode in which the patient may appear excited or stuporous. However, prior to the attack it is interesting that the patient appears quite well; he manifests no overt signs of any chronic psychosis or other disorder.

There are a number of variations possible in this acute clinical picture. However, a narrowing of consciousness always occurs; the patient appears disorientated, confused, dazed, and bewildered. With this markedly impaired sensorium he appears delirious although there is no evidence of toxemia or other organic disease present. The patient gives a dream-like appearance. He is usually dominated by auditory (rarely visual) hallucinations. Memory impairment and paralogical ideation occur with these other symptoms.

The course is rather fulminating. The duration of such an attack varies. In some cases the attack continues for a few weeks before a very sudden remission takes place; in others the attack is extremely brief and subsides within a few hours or days—the so-called three day schizophrenia syndrome.

Remission is complete for the acute episode. Many patients show a very strong tendency for a seemingly spontaneous recovery from the attack; others respond very readily to electro-convulsive, insulin, or drug therapy. A complete amnesia for the attack follows the episode, but some amount of recall can be elicited when the patient is interviewed under the influence of sodium amytal or hypnosis.

Precipitating factors play a role in many of these cases. For instance, such acute confusional psychotic states have been observed in connection with wartime combat stress, or the "convoy fatigue" cases. And similar acute episodes occur as the so-called postpartum psychosis, formerly referred to as the "toxic-exhaustive psychosis of childbirth." A variety of psychological and physiological stress factors may precipitate acute confusional psychotic states. Actually, so-called schizoid individuals appear to be especially prone to the development of a schizophrenic symptomatology in connection with emotional stress situations, or organic stress such as toxicity. In such events the stress probably acts as a mechanism which releases the psychotic process. Naturally, when the stress-releasing factors are organic it adds to the diagnostic confusion, and at best this disorder is often difficult to diagnose correctly. There are no absolute criteria for diagnosis.

The theory that this acute form of schizophrenia occurs

as a protective mechanism, in that the patient unconsciously utilizes this seemingly organic means of reacting to overwhelming stress (as might an hysterical patient), is questionable. If that is so, it is not purely so. More likely these episodes are manifestations of a disorganization process in which there is a physiological and psychological "breakdown" of the individual's homeostatic defense mechanisms, and it occurs in those individuals who are susceptible due to underlying schizoid personality configuration. Actually, many of these people later develop schizophrenic symptomatology in the absence of any apparent stress situation.

Prognosis for the acute confusional form of schizophrenia is more favorable than for that of all the other groups, at least with regard to recovery from the episodes themselves. The recovered individual seemingly returns to his previous level of functioning. However, there should not be so much optimism regarding the long-term prognosis. To apply Bleuler's terminology, there are two types of prognostications for schizophrenia: (1) *prognosis for a given "stretch" of time,* or short-term prognosis, and (2) *the "directional" prognosis,* or ultimate prognosis. According to these terms, probably cases of acute confusional schizophrenia have a very favorable "stretch" prognosis. Now, in some cases no recurrences of acute psychotic episodes occur, but in other cases there may be several recurrences. Follow-up studies have indicated that many of those patients who do experience recurrences eventually develop a more classical picture of schizophrenia. In other words, in many cases the direction of the ultimate prognosis is toward the gradual development of a chronic form of schizophrenia over a period of years, during which time the person may experience several acute attacks.

This acute confusional form should be differentiated, however, from the chronic form of schizophrenia in which acute episodes of agitation and confusion occur in the framework of the chronic symptomatology. For instance, in the chronic catatonic group especially, there can occur an abrupt onset, a brief duration, and a good remission of acute psychotic symptomatology per se. However, the difference in these cases is apparent in the quite different history: They do not appear well prior to an attack, and following an attack they continue to appear obviously psychotic and to suffer from their chronic form of schizophrenia. As I have mentioned, the acute confusional form of schizophrenia can eventually develop into a more chronic form, but otherwise it remains in a separate group classification.

Differential diagnosis further presents a difficult problem because acute confusional states can occur in disorders other than schizophrenia. They can occur in acute organic reactions, in the framework of chronic organic disorders, and similar states are even confused in some instances with psychoneurotic "dream states." This acute confusional form of schizophrenia, with its sudden onset and delirious picture, has puzzled many observers.

Some time ago, McCullock and Meduna *(6)* provoked a great deal of discussion by attempting to differentiate the acute confusional group from the schizophrenias. They considered the disorder a separate entity—or if not a separate entity then at least a separate subentity—from schizophrenia. They reasoned that according to Bleuler's classification scheme schizophrenia is characterized by disturbances of associations and affectivity and that both these disturbances are present in connection with a clear sensorium, while these acute cases not only manifest disturbances of associations and affectivity but they manifest profound disturbances of the sensory system as well. In other words, these acutely psychotic patients are confused and therefore their sensorium is impaired. Although this differentiation appears very nice on paper, I personally do not believe it is at all valid. As I have previously pointed out, quite a number of catatonic patients—who surely nobody doubts belong in the group of schizophrenias—are observed to have impairment of their sensorium. To assume that simply the clarity or nonclarity of the sensorium should determine the presence or absence of schizophrenia is rather tenuous.

An additional observation made by these investigators, and probably the most important, was that when these patients manifest a mild psychosis, a sugar tolerance test shows a pseudodiabetic reaction curve. This observation, if valid, would prove of interest even though immediately the question arises: Are not these metabolic alterations the result of the excitement state in the patient rather than having any causal relationship? Actually, temperature increase, leukocytosis, and carbohydrate metabolic alterations can be observed in any severely disturbed individuals who are suffering from a delirium, whether it is based on schizophrenia or on something else. That the carbohydrate metabolism does not function very well in schizophrenic individuals is an established fact. Whether this is *post hoc* or *pro hoc* remains unknown, but it is common knowledge that in many cases of schizophrenia the carbohydrate metabolism is impaired, and tests often show paradoxical sugar tolerance curves. This is not only true in cases of so-called oneirophrenia but in certain other types of schizophrenia also. A few of Meduna's theoretical speculations relating these findings to the anti-insulin factor are interesting but, as Gillies suggested *(6),* these endocrine factors are probably the effect rather than a cause; they may be a part of what Selye *(1950)* termed "adaptation syndrome," and a response to the acute psychotic disturbance.

In my opinion, the so-called oneirophrenia group is a subentity of schizophrenia. These cases are quite interesting: They have an acute onset; they are acute catatonic episodes; they have a rather fulminating course, and they have a good prognosis. Those that do not recover spontaneously respond well to organic therapies. But, it seems to me that Meduna and McCullock failed to supply sufficient evidence to set this syndrome definitely apart from other forms of schizophrenia, or even that on the basis of their observations it would be possible to split off from schizophrenia.

Incidentally, in investigating schizophrenia or any other disorder, when examining some small newly disclosed fact there is always the tendency to split that disorder off into a separate diagnostic category. I might consider this tendency justifiable. For example, in investigating mental deficiency, a similar procedure occurred and the phenyl-ketonuria form of mental deficiency was discovered to be a specific enzymatic metabolic disorder producing that particular symptomatology. The same tendency, naturally, is taking place in investigating schizophrenia: Attempts are continually made to discover a physiological or psychological factor which would be a definite characteristic for a group. I consider all these attempts justifiable from a research point of view. Clinically, on the other hand, we must be cautious about accepting the research findings. None of these findings to date have been very impressive.

The acute confusional form of schizophrenia with its sudden onset of delirium has been regarded by some observers as an acute organic reaction identical to that of an infectious or toxic delirium. However, in a typical acute organic reaction the hallucinations are predominantly visual, while in the acute confusional state, as in ecstasy states, visual hallucinations are rarely reported. This disorder resembles other forms of schizophrenia in that auditory hallucinations are more characteristic than visual ones. However, this is not an absolute differential point. At one time attempts were made to classify these acute confusional states as cases of acute encephalomyelitis. But the demyelination and hemorrhages found on autopsy of patients who suffered acute encephalomyelitis were rarely present in those who died during an acute confusional state—although few such cases have been reported because, of course, 95 to 98 percent of these patients recover.

It has been speculated that the acute confusional state has a relationship to epilepsy, that it is actually an epileptic dream state identical with that following an epileptic convulsion. However, dream states do not invariably follow epileptic convulsions, nor are dream states necessarily in any way connected with epilepsy. Furthermore, an epileptic patient usually does not have a complete amnesia for the dream state; in fact, in his recall of the dream state he continues for quite some time to believe the experiences he had in that state were actual events and not delusions and hallucinations. Here again, a careful history of the patient together with electroencephalographic findings is important for diagnostic evaluation.

This acute form of schizophrenia should also be differentiated from other types of chronic organic disorders having brain involvement leading to acute psychosis being "released" by the chronic organic process (as I have discussed in connection with the various organic disorders). It should also be emphasized again that the acute confusional form of schizophrenia does not belong in the subgroup with the chronic forms of overtly psychotic schizophrenia in the framework of which acute episodes occur.

It should be rather easy to differentiate cases of acute confusional form of schizophrenia from the actual psychoneurotic hysterical dream states. In most cases of so-called hysterical dream states there is no confusion and disorientation during the episode and the contents are usually organized dynamically as to be meaningful to the patient on the basis of emotional, rather than organic, factors.

HYSTERICAL FORM OF SCHIZOPHRENIA

In the hysterical subgroup of schizophrenia any type of hysterical symptomatology may appear. It is interesting that in these patients the hysterical symptoms do not appear in response to any gross precipitating factors. This is a very important differential point! Whenever gross hysterical symptoms are present and no gross precipitating factors can be discovered, the case should be carefully reevaluated to ascertain whether or not underlying symptoms of schizophrenia are present. Hysterical manifestations are extremely prevalent in schizophrenia, as you know. They may appear in many patients who have no previous history of overt schizophrenic symptomatology. When such a patient initially develops hysterical symptoms or enters into an hysterical state, the symptom picture is often that of a true hysteria. After a period of two or three months, however, the picture may merge more and more with that of an overt schizophrenic psychosis. Early recognition of the presence of underlying schizophrenia is therefore very important from the standpoint of prognosis and therapy of these cases.

SCHIZO-AFFECTIVE FORM OF SCHIZOPHRENIA

The symptomatology in schizo-affective cases is seemingly in between that of schizophrenia and manic-depressive psychosis. The patient may initially present a pure manic, or a pure depressive, symptom picture. Then, in a period of a few days or weeks, symptoms such as auditory hallucinations or paranoid delusions may appear as well as other definite symptoms of schizophrenia. Course and outcome vary in different individuals according to one of several possibilities: (1) the patient's affective symptomatology may disappear and definite schizophrenic symptomatology characteristic for some major group may remain; (2) the symptomatology may remain mixed, a manic or depressive picture being present along with the schizophrenic; (3) the patient may apparently completely recover but within a year or two schizophrenic symptomatology recurs from which he might again recover, but following several more attacks he may remain overtly schizophrenic; and (4) the patient may have just one attack and recover without recurrences or sequellae.

Differential diagnosis is often problematic. Careful reexamination of a patient will often reveal the basic schizophrenic symptoms that had been previously overlooked. If these basic symptoms are not clearly demonstrated they become apparent when the patient is interviewed under the influence of sodium amytal. Otherwise, secondary schizophrenic symptoms must be relied upon to make the diagnosis. For instance, should any hallucinations or delusions appear in a manic or depressive setting, the suspicion of schizophrenia is, of course, verified.

The quality of affect in the patient is also a differential feature. In the schizo-manic patient the affect is subjectively evolved; in other words, it stems from stimuli within the individual and is unrelated, and often inappropriate, to any external stimuli. And, it is not particularly stimulated by the environment, as it is in the elated phase of the manic-depressive psychosis. The affect may be manic, but somehow it lacks actual empathic quality; it is cold; it is not contagious to others.

Prognosis for this group of schizophrenic individuals differs from that in manic-depressive psychosis in that deterioration may occur. However, the prognosis is usually more favorable than that in many of the common forms of schizophrenia in that these patients do not deteriorate readily; their recuperative powers are great. As in the acute confusional group, many schizo-affective patients recover "spontaneously," others tend to respond well to routine therapies. Follow-up observations have nevertheless indicated that the long-range prognosis is not always favorable, in that some of these patients become chronic schizophrenics and may eventually deteriorate.

Formerly, a few psychiatrists attempted to correlate the schizo-affective group of patients with the "pyknic" body build assumed to be characteristic of the manic-depressive psychotic group—they attempted to establish a "mixed psychosis" entity. No such genetic group exists. Even schizophrenic patients who show a manic-depressive variation in outcome are different in terms of their basic symptomatology.

It should be kept in mind that the symptom of depression often ushers in a schizophrenic process. This form of onset very often occurs early in life—especially during adolescence. The depression, naturally, usually lifts and the patient frequently is diagnosed as suffering from manic-depressive psychosis (which, as you know, rarely has a sudden onset and rarely occurs at such an early age), only to develop a definite schizophrenic psychosis at a later time.

PERIODIC OR CYCLIC FORMS OF SCHIZOPHRENIA

Kraepelin pointed out that the course of manic-depressive psychosis is cyclic with complete recovery between attacks, while in schizophrenia the course is steady and continuous, progressing downward to deterioration. Actually, however, quite a number of schizophrenic patients are observed to manifest periodic psychotic attacks. Some cases manifest cyclic attacks with manic or depressive symptomatology. The so-called cyclic forms of schizophrenia can be differentiated from manic-depressive psychosis upon careful evaluation. First of all, in periods of remission between attacks, schizophrenic patients show indications that an alteration—a "scarring"—has occurred. The "scarring" may be very slight and not discovered by the psychiatrist until several attacks have occurred. Secondly, following a second or perhaps third attack, schizophrenic patients display more and more personality disintegration. As the disorder progresses the remission intervals become less clearly delineated with an increasing tendency for patients to remain in the period of overt psychosis.

Periodic attacks are frequently observed in the catatonic form of schizophrenia. Periodic and occasionally cyclic attacks may also occur in patients suffering from the pseudoneurotic form of schizophrenia (as I shall discuss). The attacks are actually overt psychotic symptoms of schizophrenia superimposed on the more subtle schizophrenic processes already present in these individuals. In many instances, the attacks are observed to be "reactive" to some undue psychological or physiological stress situation, and when the etiology of the precipitating stress is recognized and the problem resolved, the patient usually recovers from the psychotic episode. Patients suffering from such "reactive" attacks are frequently misdiagnosed and the underlying schizophrenia is very often overlooked.

Psychological stress—such as war stress—leading to an attack of acute paranoia may in certain patients be interpreted as a "homosexual panic" occurring in the framework of a neurosis. Certain other patients may be diagnosed as suffering from an "acute hysteria" reaction, and in these cases the schizophrenia is very likely to be overlooked when psychodynamic conflicts are assumed to be obviously the cause of the attack. Follow-up studies of these cases, however, often disclose that within a few years a full-fledged psychosis develops, or at least some basic clinical symptoms of schizophrenia become clearly apparent. Physiological stress situations, such as those due to an infection or alcohol and other toxic drugs, often lead to the psychotic state being diagnosed as an "acute organic reaction." This diagnosis may be valid for some cases but, particularly if the physiological stress is only slight, it is important to reevaluate these patients for evidence of a so-called schizoid personality structure with a history of a predisposition to having toxic delirious reactions.

"SYMPTOMATIC" (ORGANIC DISEASE)

"Symptomatic" schizophrenia continues to be a very ill-defined group wherein symptoms of schizophrenia occur in an organic setting. In other words, a patient suffering from an organic disease then develops an organic psychosis but the organic psychosis resembles schizophrenia. The number of such cases that are actually not schizophrenic remains a question, but it might very well be a much larger group than was formerly recognized. The psychotic attacks could occur in the framework of general paresis, alcoholism, brain tumors, and other degenerative neurological disorders.

Quite often the organic disorders are overlooked. An explanation for the production of the symptoms remains unknown; it is not based on any concept of localized cerebral lesions such as lesions in the temporal or parietal lobes. Depending on the basic personality make-up of the individual, the symptom picture may be that of an organic, a schizophrenic, or manic-depressive reaction. In some patients the symptomatology may be mixed. But, any valid correlation between the organic disorder and the psychotic symptomatology is difficult to determine.

Symptoms resembling schizophrenia may be varied. One prevalent picture is difficult to diagnostically differentiate from acute confusional forms of schizophrenia and cases of "reactive" schizophrenia. These are the patients who experience acute delirious episodes without its even being recognized that they are suffering from an underlying chronic vascular disorder. For example, persons suffering from a cerebral form of Buerger's disease can develop episodic attacks of acute delirium. One time I examined such a patient who had been misdiagnosed as a case of schizophrenia. Now, in Buerger's disease the symptomatology develops differently from that observed in the acute forms of schizophrenia (6). Careful examination often discloses that focal changes—indicated by vague symptoms of weakness, fatigue, vague parasthesias, and other signs of neuropathy—usually make their appearance several years prior to the onset of an acute delirious episode. Furthermore, these patients often show a history of hypertension and evidence of peripheral vascular pathology. Therefore, whenever one deals with a patient who manifests an acute seemingly schizophrenic episode, the patient should be investigated for the presence of organic disorders such as hypertensive encephalopathy, alcoholic or luetic encephalopathy, brain tumor, and so forth. The patient's age, type of clinical onset, and history of the development of his particular symptom picture should be taken into thorough consideration.

It is especially difficult to differentiate so-called symptomatic schizophrenia from an organic psychotic reaction during the early stages of the symptomatology, but in the event that marked intellectual impairment develops, differentiation is usually clear-cut. However, even in the early stages of the disorder a careful history of symptom development in addition to neurological, serological, and other tests at our disposal often clarifies the diagnosis. The question nevertheless arises in many cases: To what extent is the acute psychotic process actually organic and to what extent is it a schizophrenic psychosis released by some mechanism operating in the underlying organic disorder?

26

PSEUDONEUROTIC FORM
OF SCHIZOPHRENIA

The pseudoneurotic form of schizophrenia does not show overt manifestations of the psychosis, and its dominant clinical symptomatology is that of the neuroses. These neurotic symptoms do not, however, indicate the presence of a true neurosis; therefore we *(Hoch and Polatin, 1949)* term it a "pseudo" neurosis. This interesting form of schizophrenia is extremely prevalent in our culture and (as in the simple form of schizophrenia) the diagnosis is often missed because gross symptoms of overt schizophrenia are absent.

Although there are no obviously psychotic manifestations, certain deviations from the norm are present which indicate these patients to be psychotic nonetheless. One may refer to it as a "diluted" or an "attenuated" psychosis, but they are psychotic. In this pseudoneurotic form, early symptoms are overlaid by those of neuroses and many cases never progress further. A few cases will "break" into a full-fledged psychotic episode and many of them seemingly fully reintegrate to their former level while others may remain in an overt psychotic state.

Before outlining the major features of this disorder, I would like to remark that some of my publications and discussions on this topic have perhaps inadvertently led to confusion in differentiating the pseudoneurotic form from "early" schizophrenia, and many psychiatrists have regarded these two schizophrenic conditions as being the same.

The term "early" schizophrenia simply refers to those cases in which the psychotic symptomatology has not "perforated." To carry the analogy further, schizophrenia should no longer be diagnosed in the crude way that appendicitis was diagnosed in 1850—after the appendix "perforated" and produced symptoms of peritonitis. Some psychiatrists make the diagnosis of schizophrenia only when massive symptomatology is present—when the personality is "perforated" by gross psychotic symptoms indicative of personality disintegration. In the pseudoneurotic form the psychotic manifestations also remain "latent," or "larval," for an indefinite period. Although my objection to the terminology "latent" and "larval" schizophrenia is that these pseudoneurotic cases are observed to be suffering from schizophrenia quite discernibly if one looks for the basic symptoms present. To put it another way, a snake in the grass is not a "latent" snake nor a "larval" snake; it is a snake. And it is not concealed by the grass if one looks for it.

Actually, the early phase of schizophrenia resembles the pseudoneurotic form only in this one aspect: The schizophrenic symptoms are probably not as yet crystallized into a gross psychotic picture. The early phase, however, generally refers to those patients who display some of the very mild symptoms, and if this early picture merges into a full-fledged picture of schizophrenia it occurs within a brief period of a few weeks or months. The pseudoneurotic form of schizophrenia is something else entirely; it does not have such a sudden course, with very few exceptions.

It is, however, quite true that occasionally a patient suffering from an early phase of schizophrenia might manifest a so-called pseudoneurotic picture in transition before developing the full-fledged psychotic picture. Here is an example: Let us assume you examine a patient, and his history discloses a lifelong pattern of being somewhat shy, somewhat withdrawn, perhaps even somewhat peculiar in his ways. You then observe this person begin to profess a great fear of traveling on the subway, of being in elevators, and he may also become so upset about being at home alone that somebody must be with him at all times. In other words, the patient suddenly develops phobias. Moreover, obsessive-compulsive manifestations probably also develop in addition to the phobias. You examine the patient further and detect an anxiety structure along with these neurotic manifestations. You already suspect by the peculiar manner in which the patient handles this material, by the manner in which he relates his ideations and by his massive ambivalence, that he is probably not a case of psychoneurosis despite the neurotic symptomatology. The rather sudden onset of this symptomatology also adds to your suspicions; the majority of neurotic patients do *not* develop obsessive-compulsive and phobic symptoms *suddenly*. Now, you continue observing the patient; four weeks later he suddenly becomes very excited and demonstrates a true catatonic picture. In such a case, it can be stated that during the initial phase of observations this patient demonstrated an early schizophrenic symptom picture.

Actually, when describing the pseudoneurotic form of schizophrenia we did not have exactly such patients in mind. We had more in mind those patients who gradually, over many years, develop an emotional disorder which resembles a neurosis; the neurotic-like picture continues for a number of years. The patient is treated for the so-called neurosis for a number of years, and eventually he may perhaps arrive at the point of becoming overtly schizophrenic. If one wants to be exacting, it could be stated that this, too, is a case of early schizophrenia but one in which the early phase lasts as many as five, ten, or fifteen years before the patient becomes overtly psychotic. Nevertheless, it is these very *chronic* cases we placed in the pseudoneurotic group, not those in which a neurotic picture develops from an early phase and lasts for just a few weeks or so before an outbreak of a full-fledged psychosis. The symptomatology, meanwhile, can be similar and overlap.

In some cases there will be considerable doubt for quite some time that the patient is schizophrenic, especially since these pseudoneurotic patients usually make a good impression and seemingly good contact with the examiner. In many cases the emotional, intellectual, and other homeostatic disturbances usually observed in frank schizophrenia are not obvious to the examiner. It must always be kept in mind, however, that the person may give outward appearance of a neurosis and yet be suffering from schizophrenia. Usually, pseudoneurotic schizophrenics do manifest many of the basic mechanisms observed in an early phase of schizophrenia, perhaps not very conspicuously or clearly, but they are discernible nevertheless. In other words, the diagnosis of pseudoneurotic schizophrenia rests on the same basic criteria as in the other forms of schizophrenia.

Therefore, before discussing the superimposed neurotic symptomatology, I should first like to review the main aspects of the criteria for diagnosing the early phase of schizophrenia.

BASIC DIAGNOSTIC CRITERIA

There are two main diagnostic criteria to be considered: (1) The relationship of the schizophrenic psychosis to the *previous personality organization,* the so-called "schizoid" make-up of the individual (This will include a brief discussion of the *problem of predictability,* about which we know very little); and (2) a review of the *early symptoms of schizophrenia,* even though it has been previously stressed, because this serves as the intricate basis for diagnostics. The ability to diagnose an impending schizophrenic psychosis is a very important clinical problem. For instance, if you examine today a hundred men at the draft board, would you be able to predict how many of these persons will develop a schizophrenic psychosis eventually, and how soon? In answer to this question one might reply that there are no diagnostic criteria to do so; occasionally there are hunches, some are good and frequently they are very poor. If these persons do develop a psychosis, we can usually predict which type will be developed, but I state flatly that we are unable to foretell which individuals will develop the psychosis and which ones will not.

THE PERSONALITY ORGANIZATION: Proper evaluation of this criterion is diagnostically helpful. There are certain personality traits often observed in the background of so-called schizoid individuals: As children or young adolescents they are usually shy, withdrawn, prefer to play by themselves, and show marked mood fluctuations (this is rarely mentioned), which indicates the presence of apprehensiveness and anxiety, and often is precipitated by small or apparently irrelevant events. Sensitivity is very marked; they interpret everything personally, as being directed toward them. Furthermore, they show a variable and usually diminished energy output—they are "born tired." Linked with this feeling of tiredness there is often a tendency for sleep inversion and other subtle forms of anxiety perhaps manifested by phobias and hypochondriacal symptoms, particularly vegetative forms. From childhood on, many of these individuals complain of gastro-intestinal disturbances and, the second most common, cardiovascular disturbances.

Incidentally, August Hoch indicated in a lecture that about 60 percent of persons suffering from schizophrenia showed a "good" personality background. This was later supported by a few other investigators in special reference to those schizophrenics who developed the sudden "three-day schizophrenia" attack. I tend to be quite skeptical of how intensively these personalities were examined. Moreover, I would like to offer a somewhat different explanation that Meyerson gave some years ago: In a lecture he made a rather happy notation that, "You do not know if a person is allergic to roses before he smells them." In other words, there are innumerable individuals walking around with a personality organization such that the moment they are confronted with the impact of certain internal or external stimulation, a reaction is evoked and they "break." Therefore, why could it not be possible that the "schizoid" individual is, to use a figure of speech, "allergic" to certain life situations due to an endogenous predisposition which is as yet undefined. Internal and external stresses play a role: Even though the causation is basically intrinsic, precipitating factors may be extrinsic.

Innumerable individuals have this so-called schizoid personality structure. There are whole nations wherein 60 to 70 percent of the population is schizoid, but I have never seen any book terming a whole nation schizophrenic, because of course that is not so. But, what is the relationship, if any, between a so-called schizoid, or "schizothymic," personality make-up and the possibility of developing a psychosis? The relationship is very tenuous. Although it is true that most, if not all, schizophrenic individuals show a so-called schizoid personality pattern—a certain reaction pattern in their manner of dealing with internal and external environmental stimuli—this does not necessarily mean that such an individual will eventually become overtly psychotic. Which schizoid individuals will become psychotic and which will not cannot be predicted. In investigating children having a somewhat schizoid behavior pattern, it is a rather interesting observation that in many cases the schizoid pattern remains; in some it changes; in others it becomes so malignant that a psychosis can be expected, and in these cases some develop the psychosis and others do not.

Attempts have been made to find physiological, psychological, psychodynamic, and clinical psychiatric clues to *predict* the development of schizophrenic psychosis. I assure you that after investigating such material on the subject, I have found prognostications by reliable physicians made in a negative sense on patients who, twenty-four hours later, developed a full-blown psychosis. Such is the reliability of our present diagnostic instruments.

With regard to physiological observations, no single physiological clue indicates which individuals will develop schizophrenia. On a physiological level one actual thing is known: Just as the individual's emotional and intellectual regulation is impaired in schizophrenia, the vegetative and metabolic regulation is also impaired. It is impaired in a very peculiar way. Seemingly the balancing, or homeostatic, mechanism is not functioning normally and such an imbalance can be observed in a great many individuals who later develop overt schizophrenia. However, similar imbalance can be observed in many schizoid individuals who later develop psychoneuroses. I might point out that the great difficulty in this regard is that the schizoid temperamental organization not only fosters schizophrenia, but it is also present in practically all the major psychoneurotic developments in a considerable number of individuals. Here again, of course, the uncertainty of differentiation creeps in.

Not one single psychodynamic factor described in the psychoanalytic literature could be applied for predicting whether or not an individual will ever develop a schizophrenic psychosis. Certain psychodynamic observations have been offered and certain clinical observations have been offered, all of which are illuminating after the person already develops a psychosis. I refer to this as "hindsight psychoanalysis" (or psychiatry) because once the patient begins to develop ideas of reference, or catastrophic anxiety, and so forth, a few of the psychodynamic factors picked up, naturally, could then be tied in with this newly arisen symptomatology. However, before these symptoms arise they usually cannot be predicted. In other words, do not confuse "motivology" with etiology; we have some hindsight information into some of the motivology in schizophrenic patients, not etiology.

Clinical psychiatric observations enable us to make guesses but not predictions. A great deal has been made of psychological tests to predict the development of schizophrenia. The psychological tests are just as adequate and as inadequate as the clinical observations; tests are never independent but are derivatives of the clinical observations and subject to the same faults and errors. Psychological tests could indicate the presence of a schizoid personality organization in an individual, and in a schizophrenic individual might indicate the presence of the psychosis. However, no tests presently used disclose that an overt psychosis is impending in the prepsychotic, or has occurred in the postpsychotic, phases of the sickness. They merely show the schizoid organization similar to that present in individuals who never will and never had developed a psychosis. Therefore, to rely on this tool as a prognosticating instrument is, in my opinion, quite dangerous.

At the present time the diagnostic predictability in terms of who will and who will not develop an overt schizophrenic psychosis is on a very low level. On the other hand, the moment a person develops a schizophrenic psychosis we are in a much better situation than some years ago. At the time I assisted in Bleuler's clinic (1928-29), it was probably the only clinic in the world which recognized the large number of schizophrenic cases among individuals not so diagnosed when examined in other clinics because different diagnostic criteria were applied. But even in Bleuler's clinic at that time, the diagnosis of schizophrenia relied largely on four main criteria: *(a) gross disorganization of thinking,* incoherence, bizarre thought formations, and marked impairment of the patient's associative ability; *(b) gross affective changes,* dullness, stiffness, and blunting of affect; *(c) delusions, hallucinations,* or *bizarre conduct;* and *(d)* more or less *gross regression phenomena.* Since that time, our whole diagnostic approach to schizophrenia has become more refined and the diagnosis no longer need rest on those criteria mentioned. Because the diagnostic approach has become more refined it has thereby, to some extent, become more insecure; this is particularly so with regard to differentiating schizophrenia from the neuroses. Nevertheless, we are now able to discern the presence of schizophrenia in more individuals than formerly, and follow-up studies have clearly indicated that our present diagnostic approach, regardless of etiological and other speculations, is more fruitful.

Actually, present diagnostic criteria for schizophrenia focus attention not alone on the importance of the presenting clinical symptomatology, but also on the great importance of the many *impairments of adaptive mechanisms* present. These important mechanisms are now also included in the present-day diagnostic approach to schizophrenia. Upon examination of an individual in the chronic early phase, the maladaptive mechanisms disclosed appear in a much more subtle form than in the gross clinical picture of schizophrenia, but basically these mechanisms are in fact identical. Quantitatively, they are less manifest, but because the mechanisms are qualitatively identical we classify them with the schizophrenias rather than attempting to establish a separate entity of disorders floating between the neuroses and schizophrenia. Furthermore, a very large number of individuals having these identical mechanisms, as is often observed in the pseudoneurotic group, later develop a psychosis fitting all the demanded criteria of gross schizophrenic psychosis.

Kraepelin's greatest contribution to psychiatry, in my opinion, was his painstaking ability to do follow-up studies; this ability should be resurrected. The whole face of psychiatry, including psychoanalysis, would appear different were follow-up studies made of the progression of adaptive development, particularly on those patients who appear to be neurotic.

In studying these individuals in detail, realize the

following: Whenever a person comes to the office and presents a set of symptoms, our investigation must run through a great many criteria before we are able to establish the diagnosis. It should be emphasized that the diagnosis of schizophrenia is, of course, purely phenomenological because no etiological diagnostic tools are available. Because it is purely phenomenological, I would like to warn against making the diagnosis on the basis of just one or two of the many criteria which I shall describe. Diagnosis of pseudo-neurotic schizophrenia, as in any form of schizophrenia, must be arrived at by putting together the different presenting criteria and attempting to establish a *constellation* among those various fragmentary observations. You must also bear with our present diagnostic model; it is not erected on any unified system or unified theory of schizophrenia, but actually it empirically picks up all the valid observations that have been tracked down on these individuals. Therefore, most of the observations from which one arrives at the conclusion that a person is most likely schizophrenic are descriptive phenomena; a few are perhaps more easily clarified by means of certain psychological tests; others are picked up as a result of psychodynamic interpretations.

There is another matter regarding the diagnosis of schizophrenia which is often sinned against: The diagnosis in these early or dubious cases should not be made merely on the basis of symptom contents present in the patient but should be based on the patient's *reaction to* those contents, and the manner in which he handles the material he brought forth. The inability of a schizophrenic person to act appropriately—the blocking, confusion, or lack of integration of his actions from the lowest to the highest level—is actually one of the most characteristic symptoms in schizophrenia. There is a "scatter" action on the physiological, psychological, and even psychodynamic levels. Those who become familiar with it acquire a rather reliable ability to spot schizophrenia in patients, although it is occasionally considered quite difficult to detect.

EARLY CLINICAL SYMPTOMATOLOGY: This is the second criterion upon which the diagnosis of schizophrenia rests at the present time. These patients do not have hallucinations or delusions, do not wet and soil themselves, are not in a state of stupor, and so forth. Their behavior often resembles that of individuals who present a neurotic disturbance. Upon careful investigation, however, certain more subtle symptom features often become apparent. Without implying whether they are secondary mechanisms and compensatory derivatives of the anxiety structure, or are primary and basic to the anxiety, I am now simply going to review some of these symptoms as features on which one should focus attention when making a diagnosis.

Markedly underdeveloped emotional regulation is usually apparent. Often there is a rather striking contrast between the individual's intellectual maturity and his inability to handle even simple emotional problems. Incidentally, many of them are fully aware of this, and I have observed quite a number of patients make the diagnosis themselves, which was disparaged by the psychiatrists or psychoanalysts treating them. The patients are invariably correct. They feel unable to handle emotional problems well; they feel better able to handle intellectual problems, although, as you shall see, even the intellectual functioning of these individuals is below par, and they know that, too. They also show a marked impairment of regulation of affect, manifested especially in their inability to regulate passivity or aggression. This regulation is markedly impaired since early childhood; patients will state that they were never able to decide when, in which situation, and to what extent they should be passive or aggressive, obedient or defiant. Automatic obedience and negativism are essential features in the catatonic disorder, but actually the same swaying between the two extremes is observed in early schizophrenia, although, of course, in a diluted fashion.

Emotional sensitivity is a complaint made by practically all patients. This sensitivity is much greater, much more all-embracing, and much more easily mobilized in every life situation than is observed in neurotic individuals. Whether the difference is merely quantitative, as some observers imply, or also qualitative, remains to be determined. In my opinion, schizophrenia differs from the neuroses in many qualitative as well as quantitative ways. That there are marked quantitative differences is obvious. Sensitivity reactions are present at all times and in every life situation, particularly every interpersonal situation. These schizophrenics seem "allergic" to people, and whenever thrown into contact with others their extreme sensitivity comes to the fore. Another sensitivity feature in these individuals—clearly indicating a very diluted psychosis—is their subtle way of interpreting every happening around them as being of significance to the ego. In this, their proneness to evaluate issues as signifying a threat to themselves is tremendous. This sensitivity is usually universal.

Obviously, these individuals all crave security; they all crave ego support. If one knows the patient's structure well, within two or three interviews one will definitely feel the presence of a strong craving for support of the nonfunctioning ego, and at the same time a rejection of the one who should supply this support because they resent their need for it. Many of them continually make great demands for protection while simultaneously rejecting it. This ambivalence phenomenon, characteristic in children and well described *(Despert, 1947)* as being marked in many schizophrenic children, is identical to that observed in schizophrenic adolescents and adults. Their craving for protection and security and their rejection of the person who gives it to them are often pronounced. Some patients express it very openly even during the first interview. A patient will explain that he goes to his mother for everything, that she does everything for him, and that each time she does so he resents it, stating, "I hate her, I hate her because I have to go to her to do these things for me." This game is played, of course, by neurotic persons, but in schizophrenics it is a very much more marked and basic a pattern.

In practically every one of these individuals it is about all they can do to figure out their position in relationship to others. Their *self-assertion, self-confidence,* and *self-esteem problems* are tremendous. These issues are usually not focalized, as in neurotic individuals, around a certain nonperformance area, but are generalized. Every issue is included. They go about as though with a little scale continually weighing whether they are being accepted or rejected, whether their self-esteem should be up or down, whether to be confident or not! In treating such patients and going through these evaluation peregrinations with them, one could collect within a few hours fine details of what I refer to as their self-esteem struggle. It is so pronounced that Hoskins—in his *Biology of Schizophrenia (1946),* which mainly deals with the physiology of schizophrenia—gave the opinion that schizophrenia is actually a disorder of self-esteem. This struggle with regard to self-confidence and self-esteem, inferiority versus superiority, is, in a broad and generalized way, very indicative of schizophrenia and should always be inquired into and investigated.

It has been correctly pointed out in many publications that in attempts to simplify schizophrenia and find some common denominator for the many different clinical pictures, one thing emerges quite clearly: There is an intolerance of tension and a very low frustration index in schizophrenic individuals. There are two main sources of tension: Tension created by stimuli within the individual and tension stemming from the outer environment. Incidentally, many schizophrenics are aware of that, too, and may even state, "I am unable to cope with the simplest stimulation coming from without or arising from within me." Along with this there is a very interesting paradoxical mechanism operating on the surface: The same individual who withdraws from stimulation and shuns it, craves and seeks it.

This peculiar tendency to crave and expose themselves to stimulation and then withdraw from it is a very important characteristic.

They crave tension; it is essential in order to contact reality because reality boundaries are impaired, just as they are in a full-fledged schizophrenic person. However, the moment they contact reality they become tense and recoil from it because it creates a great deal of anxiety. This ambivalent play—contacting and then withdrawing, withdrawing and then breaking through—is, here again, very characteristic and quite clearly discerned. Those who manifest tendencies to withdraw from reality, and most of them do, handle it in exactly the same manner as do full-fledged schizophrenics. In fact, all the mechanisms of autism and dereistic thinking occur in them, in a much more subtle fashion, as that observed in the full-fledged schizophrenic individual.

There are several other features of great importance. One is the so-called contact impairment. Practically all these individuals complain that they are unable to establish contact with other people, or, if they do, it breaks down very rapidly because they do not know how to deal with other people emotionally. In some cases they can camouflage this, but it leads to their strange and often inappropriate social responses: They underestimate or overestimate others; they give in to or fight others, and so forth. This emotional incoordination Stransky (2) referred to as "intrapsychic ataxia," and it leads to what could be termed the "extrapsychic ataxia." It gives these patients the feeling of isolation they often express. This is rarely observed in the neuroses, and when it does occur it is confined specifically to one or a few particular persons, not to all people. In schizophrenia these isolation phenomena may be very volatile due to the patient's marked ambivalence leading to emotional swings from moment-to-moment or day-to-day; often these shifts are so swift that other people find it very difficult to empathize with him.

The complete inability to handle themselves emotionally and to understand the inner experiences of other people at a given moment is rather interesting in that, here again, a peculiar paradox is present: The empathy of the schizophrenic is very great in some respects, but very poor in others. His capacity for empathy is good insofar as negative feelings are concerned. The schizophrenic individual is constantly picking up from the environment any, even the slightest, signs of hostility or uncertainty in other persons. But he does not pick up anything that involves pleasant feelings or which perhaps could contribute to his pleasure. Since the schizophrenic person is geared to protect himself, in that regard he is very perceptive of the feelings of others with an excellent empathy. This explains the contradictory statements floating about in the psychiatric literature: That, for instance, the schizophrenic patient is unable to understand what emotionally takes place in other persons, yet he has excellent insight into their unconscious. Insight is present only insofar as it represents a threat to his ego, but in any other issue he seems incapable of being interested.

Another feature, so-called anhedonia, is observed in some patients suffering from early schizophrenia, although in many cases not. However, a feeling of discontent, of not being able to function, of being unable to provide pleasure, and the feeling that they are somehow misplaced in this world is present in most cases. In my opinion, it is extremely important to investigate this incapacity for pleasure experiences. Rado (1969) implies that this is basic in schizophrenia, but in my opinion so-called anhedonia is not a basic issue. However, it is important to mention that if the individual is unable to derive pleasure from anything his compensatory ability to deal with vicissitudes of life is, naturally, much more impaired than in an individual who is able to draw upon some pleasure reserves in at least some areas. Here again, however, the underlying anxiety in connection with faulty ego integration is probably basic to any anhedonia present.

It has long been known that, because of poorly integrated ego organization, schizophrenic persons seek to "borrow" the integration present in others, and therefore living through others is a common pattern. This is to some extent a normalization pattern in that it enables them to "bypass" ambivalence mechanisms (sometimes this is very clearly the case) and force themselves into situations with which they cannot cope. And they think they must cope, that because other people are able to do it, they must, too. However, a more basic issue is probably involved: It is *because* these individuals are unable to integrate that they try to integrate through the emotional life of others, and therefore very often live a vicarious form of existence. Incidentally, it is interesting that many patients are aware of that, also, and verbalize it: "I'm not able to reach people," "I don't have a feel of what they are doing," "I have to be with someone who somehow directs me emotionally," "I have to be with someone who is stronger than I to show me the way." That is observed again and again in their verbalization.

Ambivalence, as I have often mentioned, is a mechanism very much in the foreground in schizophrenic individuals. It was pointed out by Bleuler *(2)* as one of the basic symptoms. In the early phase of schizophrenia the ambivalence is so very great that frequently the diagnosis can actually be made by studying these mechanisms. It should be kept in mind that ambivalence in schizophrenia is quantitatively much more marked than is observed in psychoneurosis, and also that in schizophrenia the ambivalence pervades every area. These patients could toss about the simplest decision, back and forth, back and forth, similarly as might a depressed patient, or somewhat similarly as does an obsessive-compulsive patient. However, the important thing is that, although schizophrenics feel this ambivalence as disagreeable to some extent, they accept it much more readily than do obsessive-compulsive or depressed patients. Schizophrenics actually fight along with, rather than against, this ambivalence and do not fully reject it.

The differentiation point must be stressed that ambivalent behavior in the psychoneuroses is especially common in the obsessive-compulsive and phobic groups, and since many obsessive and phobic patients show similarities to the psychoses in their dynamic structures they could actually be cases of diluted psychosis rather than neuroses phenomenologically resembling a psychosis. One fact remains: All the basic mechanisms observed in schizophrenia (including so-called narcissism as well as ambivalence) are usually observed in those neuroses assumed to have some similarity or some relationship to schizophrenia. Therefore, if marked ambivalent behavior can be demonstrated in a neurotic person, his dynamic structure most likely also bears some resemblance or similarity to schizophrenia. This would indicate that some neurotic patterns are closer to schizophrenia than others. At any rate, ambivalence occurs in certain neuroses as well as in schizophrenia and is not pathognomic for one or the other.

Disorders of thinking in early schizophrenia are also definitely present. As you know, schizophrenia was originally perceived as being a disorder of thinking; even Bleuler's idea was that the basic disturbance in schizophrenia is the impairment of associations. Since it has become increasingly recognized that schizophrenia is a disorder in which the emotional life of the individual is markedly impaired, thinking disorders became so very much relegated to the background that a considerable number of psychiatrists do not even realize they exist in schizophrenia. However, the thinking disorders present are important. Although in the pseudoneurotic or other early forms of schizophrenia they may not be manifested in a gross way, quite a number of patients are observed to make formulations and handle ideational material exactly as do full-fledged schizophrenic patients.

Concept formations, concept condensations, inability

to distinguish between abstract and concrete, telescoping of concepts are all commonly observed. Actually, the conceptual disorder that appears in some of the psychological tests can also be clinically demonstrated in many cases. Although a few of these patients do not show gross thinking disorders, the more one studies them the more one is impressed by the fact that they are really unable to employ highly intellectualized concepts properly. These individuals are not only impaired emotionally, but the fact is that on the intellectual level also, some integrative mechanism is not functioning adequately. It so often expresses itself in the actions of these individuals that sometimes one is completely flabbergasted: How could an individual with such a high intellectual ability show such an error in judgment, or handle conceptual material so queerly! A scattered performance is another very significant feature. You will encounter this in many patients; they were outstanding scholars one year, but the next year they were unable to follow through.

The interrelating of fantasy and reality, a magical form of thinking and a magical doing-and-undoing behavior, is quite characteristic. This is handled differently from the same type of magical thinking occurring in the obsessive-compulsive neurotic patient. For instance, some early schizophrenic patients complain they feel "doped" or "dazed," but they never seek to explain it, as would a neurotic patient. It is not treated as a delusion, but the schizophrenic patient will state, "It is *as if* I am doped," or "I know I am not being poisoned but it *feels* as though it is so." This already indicates such a heightened feeling of the environment *doing* something *to* them as is rarely observed in a neurotic individual. There are exceptions: In serious anxiety states a block can occur in the neurotic's ability to think objectively or put thoughts together, but this is temporary. In the schizophrenic it is permanent and occurs regardless of the degree of anxiety. Incidentally, feelings of depersonalization are common in schizophrenics, but can occur mildly and briefly in depressions, anxiety neurosis, or in obsessive-compulsive neurosis.

These and other thinking disorders in schizophrenia have been discussed in other lectures, but it should be emphasized that it is a good plan to follow the thinking process and content in every patient and investigate it much more closely than is usually done. A patient's thinking difficulty often reveals a rather profound disturbance that would otherwise be overlooked.

Finally, after all these various aspects of the patient's personality have been thoroughly studied and all the symptomatology has been evaluated, one must also concentrate a great deal of attention on *the manner in which the person relates* the material and the manner in which he communicates in interview. Actually, the patient's transference relationship and the way he handles the material during the first interview is of very great significance. It is essential that a few papers be written about the interview behavior of these schizophrenic individuals and how it differs from that of other patients—or, if some form of analytic treatment is being applied, how the patient behaves in the initial phase of the treatment—because these patients do behave differently from nonschizophrenics, and if one is aware of the significant differences they can easily be recognized. I will mention only one or two features here.

Many patients make a rather good impression on the examiner. They appear to make good contact and lack the emotional or intellectual alteration usually observed in frankly psychotic schizophrenic individuals. However, it is rather interesting to note that intellectually well-endowed schizophrenic individuals often relate their difficulties in a very vague and unorganized fashion. This vagueness is so characteristic that one can readily recognize it as being different from what is observed in psychoneurotic patients. The latter usually offer a very clear, very elaborate, and rationalized account of the development and status of their complaints. But individuals in the early phase of schizophrenia remain comfortably vague and seem unable to relate their problems concisely.

The manner in which the early schizophrenic patient relates material is often characterized as being either "too little, too late," or "too much, too soon." In the first instance, the patient discloses an extremely scant amount of historical and psychodynamic material about himself and is very delayed in bringing it forth. In other words, it is difficult for him to associate freely; he is blocked. It is very interesting to note that a great many patients who are blocked associatively are especially blocked in associating material dealing with their past lives. When they eventually do, a tremendous amount of anxiety is usually unleashed and such patients can become very panicky.

In the second instance, the patient walks into the office and verbalizes by the hour, in great detail, on matters such as ideas of incest with a parent, or other ideations which are usually relegated to the unconscious in neurotic individuals. In the neurotic, the similar type of material would be gathered only after the patient had had at least six months or a year of therapy, but the schizophrenic can deliver it on a platter immediately. This is positively diagnostic, *unless* the patient has had previous psychoanalytic therapy. Therefore, do not be favorably impressed by the ability of patients who initially verbalize a great amount of material.

Many early schizophrenic patients relate material in a stereotyped manner. In other words, over a period of three or four interviews they will always relate the exact same material; nothing else is added. Such stereotypy can be very startling and can occur initially, with overwhelming richness. However, the "oil well" peters out very rapidly and no new material follows. The same ideation simply moves along in a stereotyped pattern, and in a perseveratory manner—also quite characteristic for these patients. Should the therapist attempt to elicit further elaborations, these patients will then become vague, blocked, and unable to formulate emotional and conceptual material.

There are many additional issues which could be discussed concerning schizophrenia in its early phase, but I have given you a general review of how diagnosis can be made by evaluating all the factors mentioned, and that diagnosis cannot be made on the basis of just one or two of these factors; rather, that all the clinical features described, when present in some constellation, are diagnostic criteria for an underlying schizophrenia.

NEUROTIC DEFENSE MECHANISMS

In the pseudoneurotic form, certain additional symptoms in the patient provide further evidence for the presence of schizophrenia: *pan-anxiety, pan-neurosis,* and a *chaotic organization of sexuality. These are the dominant symptoms* in the pseudoneurotic form of schizophrenia. To some extent, however, they also appear in the pseudosociopathic and other forms, and are often found to fluctuate in any case of early schizophrenia.

PAN-ANXIETY: Pseudoneurotic individuals are constantly living in a state of catastrophic anxiety. Actually, not a single patient in the acute phase of the schizophrenic disorder, nor a single patient belonging in the chronic early phase, especially the pseudoneurotic group, is without the feeling of anxiety. Pseudoneurotic schizophrenics are practically always fear-ridden even though some may be able to give an exterior impression of being calm and collected. The lack of anxiety is mainly in those schizophrenics who are already "dulled" by some amount of deterioration. Because formerly the schizophrenias were always studied in deteriorated patients, all the early textbooks described the schizophrenic as not showing anxiety. Actually, the schizophrenic patient is the most anxious individual we encounter!

The pan-anxiety in these patients is so tremendous that they are unable to cope with it despite attempts to master it with every possible means of defense at their disposal. The source of this anxiety is not determined; it could be primarily on an organic basis, or secondary to a psychological factor, or due to some interaction. The fact remains that these patients do suffer a great amount of anxiety which is manifested in varying ways. Observations indicate it is usually present rather early in childhood, often increases during adolescence, and becomes more sustained as the individual is required to cope with a greater number of ordinary life situations, all of which these individuals experience as stress. Generally speaking, attempts at performance in social, sexual, occupational, or in any life area produce profound feelings of anxiety and often long periods of panic.

The fact that it is a *pan*-anxiety differentiates these cases from the ordinary psychoneuroses. Furthermore, overt or covert anxiety in neurotics may be very intense at times, but it is not so intense as that occurring in pseudoneurotic schizophrenic individuals. Anxiety is the common feature in all neuroses, and the various dynamic mechanisms represent the neurotic patient's means for coping with it. It becomes organized around some strategic conflictual material and, thus becoming localized, is not so generalized as in the pseudoneurotic patient. Whenever a neurotic maneuvers away from the anxiety-creating situation his anxiety subsides and is not carried over into all other areas of his life. Therefore, the patient suffering from an anxiety neurosis is able to cope with his anxiety for a period of time because, regardless to what extent he is handicapped, certain areas remain anxiety-free in which he can function and perform rather satisfactorily. This is not the situation for the pseudoneurotic schizophrenic; an intense anxiety is so all-pervading that the whole individual is actually one bundle of anxiety!

It could be immediately argued that there are a number of patients who are diagnosed, for instance, as "anxiety hysteria" or "phobic" neurotics in whom the anxiety is as all-pervading, as intense, as strickening as the anxiety just mentioned in the pseudoneurotic group. Actually, this issue is probably the main point of deviation from the psychoanalytic classification of these cases. Re-examination and follow-up studies on these very severe phobic or obsessive-compulsive "neurotic" patients would disclose that the great majority are schizophrenic.

PAN-NEUROSIS: This is the most outstanding symptom in the pseudoneurotic group. Here again, I would like to emphasize that unless the neurotic symptomatology dominates the clinical picture the schizophrenic patient should not be classified in the pseudoneurotic group. He may be a case of chronic early schizophrenia or belong in some other group, depending on the predominant symptomatology present. The pan-neurosis actually represents the attempts made by these tremendously anxious and tense individuals to cope with all their diverse conflictual situations. They thereby utilize all the known—and probably even a few unknown—neurotic defense mechanisms for coping with anxiety, various ones being tried and discarded. These patients may display an extremely broad, extremely ramified, neurotic picture which is very rarely observed in a neurotic individual. For instance, the patient will show symptoms of anxiety neurosis, anxiety hysteria, or obsessive-compulsive manifestations; several or all of these symptoms can appear in succession or simultaneously. The patient is a walking textbook of the neuroses and every known neurotic configuration exists, due mainly to the extreme severity of the anxiety.

One must not be tempted to make a diagnosis on the basis of superficial dynamic configurations. The psychodynamics may seem very convincing, for instance, in conversion hysterical symptomatology. Keep in mind that gross conversion symptoms are very prevalent in early schizophrenia. Actually, gross hysterical symptoms rarely occur in a psychoneurosis, except perhaps in the framework of acute traumatic situations—such as is observed in war stress—or in feebleminded persons. Otherwise, gross hysterical manifestations will, upon deep examination, reveal an underlying schizophrenia with macro- and micro-fragmentation of the personality. Therefore, do not be easily misled when psychodynamic formulations appear to explain the symptomatology quite well.

It might be argued that of course there exists such a group as the "mixed neurosis," that the classification of the neuroses must be taken with a great grain of salt because a large number of neurotic individuals show mixed symptomatology. Nevertheless, in a true neurosis very rarely is there such a widely ramified picture that the patient actually presents a pan-neurosis. A neurotic patient usually presents one major type of symptomatology, although other mild neurotic symptoms may occasionally be present. In other words, a neurotic patient's symptomatology will usually be either predominantly obsessive-compulsive or predominantly hysterical, or else free-floating anxiety may predominate for a while until some major symptom pattern acts as a mechanism to successfully "bind" the anxiety. In the pseudoneurotic schizophrenic, on the other hand, innumerable neurotic symptoms occur and shift in their predominance, none of which do "bind" the anxiety successfully—and the anxiety is not just free-floating but invades all areas of functioning; it is a pan-anxiety. This offers some clue as to why the neurotic symptoms shift in these schizophrenic patients; each symptom fails to absorb the tremendous amount of anxiety. This phenomenon may not be quite so extensive or pronounced in mild cases and therefore the underlying schizophrenia is often overlooked.

I would not go so far as to state that every case which manifests pan-anxiety and pan-neurosis is invariably schizophrenic, but one should suspect that such a patient is probably suffering from more than a neurosis. He should be examined by every clinical or other method at our disposal, whereupon very often auxilliary clues are picked up to indicate the patient is suffering from schizophrenia. In following up such patients for a considerable period of time, it will be noticed that many develop overt schizophrenia. When first interested in these cases, I traced back the history of a great number of patients who had undergone various types of therapy. Many of them had remained fairly well integrated, but during the course of treatment began to manifest a clinical picture of schizophrenia. In reviewing their history, I invariably found that these patients had been diagnosed as neurotic and were treated as neurotic. Upon following the symptomatology further back, we concluded that a great many of these so-called severe neurotics who had initially presented a picture of pan-anxiety and pan-neurosis eventually "blew up" and developed an overt psychosis, following which some fully reintegrated and others remained overtly psychotic *(Hoch et al., 1962).*

CHAOTIC SEXUALITY: This clinical component, present in all forms of schizophrenia, originally called our attention to the pseudoneurotic group. It is of extreme diagnostic importance to investigate in detail the psychosexual organization of patients. Those appearing to be neurotic may actually have a chaotic concept of sexuality rather than the so-called regression phenomenon observed in the neuroses. In some cases this is in startling contrast to an emotional, social, or intellectual organization that somehow may continue to function rather well in a number of pseudoneurotic patients. The presence of chaotic sexuality, therefore, is in itself a fair indication these patients are not simply neurotic. In the pseudoneurotic patient, some or all possible sexual patterns may be present simultaneously—a pan-sexuality. And, along with heterosexual behavior, the patient may represent a walking textbook of sexual malfunctions. Every possible source of gratification may be attempted; one after another they are utilized, discarded, utilized, and discarded—none give the person fundamental gratification, so he continues to seek and chase after various and peculiar sexual experiences. The patient might state, "No matter what I do sexually, it gives me no pleasure and I am always tense and fearful about it." Incidentally, do not be misled by the fact that in some cases the heterosexual act may be performed normally—often more so than in neurotic cases—but one will find that these individuals do so with lack of pleasure, lack of empathy, and feelings of isolation. It is startling to find that the greatest impairment lies in an absence of pleasure where the area of greatest pleasure should be. The anxiety in their lives obviously prevents pleasure.

I would like to mention that, in my opinion, psychoanalytic literature has unjustly concentrated mainly on the homosexual aspect of this problem and has frequently provided seemingly valid psychodynamic explanations. But the true explanation is that the homosexual behavior in schizophrenia is actually only one portion of the fragmentation present in the psychosexual organization. The inability to arrive at sexual pleasure by seeking it in all directions is much more characteristic for these individuals than is any partial mechanism they might display. In all schizophrenic "homosexual" individuals, one usually finds not just one, but many deviations from the norm. The sexual malfunctions are often a clue in diagnostic evaluation, just as is the presence of pan-anxiety and pan-neurosis.

Naturally, underlying symptoms of schizophrenia—thinking disorders, emotional dysregulation, and many other disturbances in homeostatic mechanisms—are present in the pseudoneurotic as well as in the other forms of schizophrenia. Although many of these basic symptoms may be quite apparent in pseudoneurotic individuals, they usually appear in a very diluted form. Therefore, they are often overlooked due to the predominating overlay of neurotic symptomatology, which is absent in the other groups of schizophrenia or present only in a more subtle manner.

Taking into consideration all clinical observations described, it is not surprising that the method of treatment, the response to treatment, and the prognosis for the pseudo-neurotic schizophrenic patient differs from that in either the neurotic patient or the patient suffering from any other form of schizophrenia.

PROGNOSIS

The outcome in pseudoneurotic schizophrenia of non-treated, or inappropriately treated, patients usually takes one of three forms. Approximately one-third of these patients remain in a pseudoneurotic state. In another third the symptomatology remains more or less stationary, but radical short-lived psychotic episodes occur. The episodes have no single pattern but usually are paranoid or catatonic in their manifestations and are usually reactive to some physical or emotional environmental stress. In some cases they are precipitated by the influence of drugs—such as barbiturates, amphetamines, alcohol, or psychotropic drugs —and hallucinatory episodes suddenly develop, last for perhaps a few weeks or a month, disappear, and then the patient returns to the original pseudoneurotic level. A third group of patients develop a rather mild schizophrenic psy-chosis and remain in that state. Beginning usually with their phobic symptoms, such patients may gradually develop hallucinations with either catatonic or paranoid manifesta-tions, or may develop a severe depression. Never are there any hebephrenic manifestations in these patients; never is there any significant tendency for deterioration. In other words, they behave as do many schizophrenics who have strong phobic and obsessive-compulsive components in their symptom structure; their reality testing and reality contact remain more or less intact.

Now, the prognosis with regard to the development of a chronic schizophrenic psychosis, and surely with regard to deterioration, is much better in the pseudoneurotic group than in main groups of schizophrenia. Nevertheless, in this group of patients the pseudoneurotic symptomatology is very tenacious and the treatment is difficult; the tendency to "snap out" of the pseudoneurotic symptomatology is much less than that in cases of frank schizophrenic psychosis.

THERAPEUTIC APPROACH

The pseudoneurotic form of schizophrenia is also quite interesting because the response to treatment differs from that observed in the neuroses, and to some extent from that observed in the other forms of schizophrenia. As in most schizophrenias, this group is very refractory to any present treatment methods, although the response is better than in the simple form of schizophrenia. It is not unusual for pseudoneurotic patients to enter into psychotherapy or psychoanalysis and to continue with either form of treatment for a number of years—in some cases not by just one but by two or three therapists in succession—without showing improvement. By this time they are usually very chronic patients. After psychotherapy or analysis has failed to improve their condition, many patients are then exposed to electro-convulsive therapy and undergo one, two, or three series of treatments. But I can tell you now that I have never encountered a single pseudoneurotic person who ever responded to this therapy! In a few cases the procedure is in reverse: The patients first receive electro-convulsive therapy and then go through the entire gamut of psychotherapeutic procedures, to which they are completely refractory. Incidentally, some patients have responded very well to psychosurgery.[1] Some also respond rather well to psychotherapy which, however, has to be applied with a markedly different technique than that for treating the neuroses on the one hand or the psychotic forms of schizophrenia on the other.

----

[1] Dr. Hoch directed research on a series of pseudoneurotic schizophrenic patients at the New York State Psychiatric Institute Department of Experimental Psychiatry. See Hoch, 1951a, 1951b.—*Eds.*

Treatment of these patients should essentially be based on the following procedures: (1) *initial exploration of the dynamic mechanisms* (as in any other type of patient), (2) *influencing the anxiety structure,* and (3) *actual psychotherapy.* Of course this is somewhat schematic and actually all three procedures simultaneously interact.

In terms of *dynamic mechanisms,* naturally, the basis for treating pseudoneurotic schizophrenic patients differently from neurotics relies, of course, on *the great differences in the basic disturbances* present in each diagnostic group. We postulate that in all schizophrenic individuals there is an inherent deficiency of integrative capacity. This manifests itself in many ways: There is a hypersensitive reaction to stimuli from the external and internal environment, and stimuli are most likely screened differently in schizophrenics than in neurotics. But the most outstanding feature in schizophrenic persons is the dysregulation of any ability to fuse, in a homeostatic fashion, external environmental stimuli with stimuli arising from within themselves, as normal and neurotic individuals are able to do. This impairment of integrative capacity is aggravated by every environmental happening so that the environment in which the schizophrenic lives continually adds insult to injury.

Because the integrative impairment varies in configuration in each patient, any number of symptom patterns is possible. For instance, the neurotic symptoms in a patient may be influenced mainly by his thinking disorders, while his emotional disorders may be subtle and in the background, or vice versa. Therefore, one must explore those dynamic mechanisms which obviously influence the patient's ability to utilize his integrative capacity most effectively. This initial exploration does not require deep probing or deep interpretation.

As mentioned, pseudoneurotic patients suffer from a *much more marked and an all-pervading anxiety* than do neurotic individuals. The therapist constantly has to cope with the patient's pan-anxiety, and surely many psychiatrists who have treated such patients agree that *no constructive treatment is possible until the therapist is able to reduce the pan-anxiety these patients suffer* to the extent that the patient becomes better able to regulate his reactions to stimuli—and can relate to the therapist. This makes it possible for him to contemplate changing certain patterns of behavior—patterns which had become rigid, frozen, due to the intensity of anxiety produced by any previous suggestions of changing them. Anxiety can be reduced by two methods: special psychotherapeutic maneuvers, and appropriate medication. Combined psycho- and pharmaco-therapy is particularly important in this group of patients because their pan-anxiety cannot otherwise be reduced. In rare instances psychotherapy alone might reduce this anxiety, but there it would take a very long time. Obviously, a therapist would be unable to treat these patients constructively for as long a time as it takes to reduce the anxiety structure; only then can actual psychotherapy commence.

Concerning *actual psychotherapy* of the pseudoneurotic schizophrenic patient, there are a *few important facets of treatment that make it differ from those techniques used in dealing with either neurotic individuals or other types of schizophrenics.*

In comparing the treatment technique applied in pseudoneurotic schizophrenia to that in the neuroses, two issues can be stressed. First of all, the therapist must not remain a silent auditor; he must be far more active than is usually the case in treating a neurotic patient. He must interfere more actively, especially with regard to the patient's life because these patients usually need advice on concrete matters that are predicated on conflicts and great ambivalence. The conflicts should be interpreted to the patient, and when some of the ambivalence is thereby reduced, he will be greatly helped in his learning how to make simple decisions. Initially, it is important to determine the patient's ambivalence structure before attempting to

direct him. In fact, because the therapist must be appropriately active, he must be keenly aware of the actual type of
individual with whom he is dealing. If the therapist is too
inactive, the patient becomes unable to verbalize and unable
to relate; if the therapist is too active, he may precipitate a
frank psychosis in the patient. Therefore, the therapist must
walk a tightrope, and to learn how this is done is probably
one of the most important aspects of therapy.

The second issue in technique, clearly important to most
psychiatrists experienced in treating these individuals, is
that, regardless which treatment approach is applied, it is
necessary to practically reeducate the patient in relation
to many life situations. The therapist cannot simply assume,
as he could in treating a neurotic, that it is sufficient to interpret the patient's difficulties to him, or to interpret a few
of the dynamic mechanisms underlying his actions and
expect him to draw conclusions about their application to his
daily life. The therapist must go further: he must point out
why the interpretation is given; how it has been derived;
and, what remedial measures are indicated in reference to
the patient's current situation. Incidentally, these individuals
are extremely sensitive and perceptive; many of them have
a rather keen insight into their dynamics but remain unable
to behave in a constructive way despite this insight. It is
particularly in this situation that a reeducation process must
take place. Here again, therefore, the therapist must be
more active than in the treatment of a neurotic individual.

Treatment of the pseudoneurotic schizophrenic differs
in technique also from that applied to patients suffering from
other forms of schizophrenia. Although obviously many
approaches apply in the general treatment of all types of
schizophrenic patients, there are specific differences. In
other forms of schizophrenia the therapist is not coping with
predominating neurotic mechanisms, and therefore manipulation of these neurotic mechanisms is, of course, not in the
treatment picture. The general rule applies in the pseudoneurotic as in all forms of schizophrenia that the therapist

should not allow the patient to become very close emotionally because he would become too dependent, nor should
the therapist express a great deal of emotion in a positive
or negative sense toward the patient because he wants to be
careful not to frighten him. Be aware that in any schizophrenic person a marked emotional immaturity is present
and one cannot discuss with them emotional material as one
could with a neurotic. But, in other respects, in treating the
pseudoneurotic schizophrenic there are a few specific
differences in technique.

To begin with, in applying psychotherapy to other
types of schizophrenic patients the therapist can, in many
ways, be far more blunt and far more active than is possible
to do in treating this delicately balanced pseudoneurotic
individual. In other words, a schizophrenic patient who is
already in an uncompensated psychotic condition either
comes out of his psychotic state or he does not, and in any
event the therapist does not precipitate one condition on
top of another. But, should the therapist be overly blunt
and overly active in applying therapy to the pseudoneurotic
type of schizophrenic, he can precipitate a psychotic state
and this, naturally, is what he would very much like to
avoid.

Now, the neurotic mechanisms should be unraveled
rather cautiously, rather gingerly, especially during the early
part of therapy. Then, if the patient responds favorably to
this, more of it can be done. However, *the therapist must
not directly aim at the removal of the neurotic "target"
symptoms as he might do in treating a neurotic individual.*
If the therapist's primary efforts in treatment are aimed at
removing one or two of the pseudoneurotic patient's neurotic
mechanisms, and should the therapist fail to recognize that
these neurotic mechanisms are defenses utilized by the patient
as attempts to cope with a pan-anxiety, one of several results
can take place. The patient either does not progress in treatment, he develops a gross psychotic picture, he enters into a
severe depression, or—and, fortunately, this commonly

occurs—the patient defends himself against intolerable anxiety by a shifting of his neurotic symptomatology. In this case, for instance, a patient manifesting obsessive-compulsive symptomatology may, in the course of therapy, discard that symptomatology and at the same time develop hysteric or phobic symptomatology. What is often observed is the concurrence of many neurotic mechanisms manifested simultaneously, alternately waxing and waning during the course of therapeutic manipulation and other environmental changes in stress. This occurrence is not observed in the neuroses. The phenomenon is comparable to that of a partially deflated rubber ball having a concavity on one side and when that indented portion is manipulated out to a normal position a new concavity develops on another area of the ball.

The aims and goals of treatment should be very carefully considered and kept clearly in mind by the therapist treating a pseudoneurotic schizophrenic patient. Most psychiatrists experienced in treating this form of schizophrenia fully realize that, due to limitations in our present knowledge, the treatment "cure" is essentially an orthopedic one, not a surgical one. The therapeutic goal is that of enabling the patient to overcome some of the symptom manifestations of his integrative impairment. This point should be greatly stressed because fundamental mistakes are made by therapists who fail to consider the schizophrenic process in these patients and thereby attempt to shoot for very high therapeutic goals. In such a case, the patient is unable to attain those goals, which then creates an even greater anxiety than that which was initially present. The disappointment feeling within the patient becomes very great! Many psychotic "breaks" precipitated during treatment were based either on injudicious dealing with the psychodynamic material too early, or on the fact that the patient felt the therapist was pushing him, forcing him into some type of position wherein he is unable to cope. It is important for every therapist to acquire certain methods for gauging just how far he can push each patient; he should push, but he should recognize when, how, in which direction, and to what extent it is appropriate to do so.

In conclusion, it is obvious that because these patients are actually schizophrenic there is a certain cardinal approach to them which is, of course, the same as that in treating any other form of schizophrenia. Nevertheless, in the actual treatment of pseudoneurotic schizophrenics the therapist should probably steer a course somewhere in between the treatment of an overt schizophrenic and a neurotic patient. We must be aware of the difference in treatment technique and it is this difference which should be particularly stressed in the treatment of the pseudoneurotic schizophrenic patient.

It may again be stated that, in treating the pseudoneurotic group of schizophrenic patients, in many respects the therapist cannot be as blunt, as aggressive, or as active as he may often be with patients suffering from other forms of schizophrenia. Furthermore, he also must take into consideration that in this form of schizophrenia the neurotic mechanisms are actually only a facade. The person may appear to be functioning with this facade, but surely a great amount of disturbance is occurring behind it which undoubtedly is not so very healthy. Nevertheless, the unique ability to form a facade and to function through a facade, an ability which many other schizophrenic patients lack, is a very important point of differentiation. The technique applied in treating these patients basically differs from techniques applied in treating those schizophrenic patients who do not have the neurotic facade.

Further questions remain to be answered concerning the treatment of pseudoneurotic schizophrenia. For instance, is it better to treat these patients in individual therapy or in group therapy? I have encountered patients who have been treated individually, those who have been treated in group therapy, and those who have experienced both. Many patients who initially received individual therapy thereby became better able to socialize when placed in a therapy group. On the other hand, I have encountered many patients for whom the therapeutic approach was just the reverse. It has been my observation that many pseudoneurotic patients probably gain more when therapy is initially on an individual basis, and then as their anxiety is somewhat reduced they often benefit when switched to group therapy. Then later, if necessary, they can again return to individual therapy. It should be realized, of course, that because of the anxiety structure present, *a priori,* many of these patients feel uncomfortable in a group situation; it immediately arouses and aggravates much of their anxiety, especially when something is expected from them even though this expectation is probably not more than a certain amount of relating to other members of the group. It is certain that group treatment experiments will be continued with these particular patients and probably it will eventually be recognized which treatment procedures are best for them.

Schizophrenia is a very common disorder, probably the most common of all mental disorders, and the pseudoneurotic is only one form of it. It is a fact that a tremendous number of people suffer intensely from schizophrenia, but that does not mean that the very large number of patients suffering from the form of schizophrenia manifested by the pseudoneurotic structure must, by definition, continue to suffer, since the prescribed treatment, which is very unique, can be applied.

27

SOCIOPATHIC PERSONALITY AND PSEUDOSOCIOPATHIC SCHIZOPHRENIA

In order to discuss the pseudosociopathic form of schizophrenia we must first attempt to *define* the so-called *nuclear sociopathic personality* (also termed the psychopathic personality). This is the diagnostic "waste basket" grouping in psychiatry. It deals with that group of poorly integrated individuals who display no conflict within themselves but who are in continual conflict with the environment due to their antisocial acts. These people live from day-to-day or week-to-week on a very self-indulgent level. They act out for their immediate gratifications or to discharge the enormous tension that accumulates when they are frustrated. This behavior, naturally, causes a great deal of trouble to the environment as well as for the individual. The number of these sociopathic individuals is very large; they are prevalent in every society and are encountered in every socioeconomic and intellectual level.

As with all psychiatric disorders, the question must first be asked: Is the disorder an entity per se or is it a relative disorder depending upon the environment? (In the schizophrenias, one deals with an actual process existing within the individual but which has a strongly reactive element in relation to the environment. And, in the psychoneuroses it is difficult to separate the disorder from its relationship to the environment; it is apparently a relative disorder in the simple cases but this becomes unclear to us in the more complicated cases.) In attempting to define the so-called sociopathic personality group we are immediately confronted with this difficult question. The symptoms are organized around antisocial behavior, but many psychiatrists believe this to be a relative issue and dependent upon the particular society in which the person lives. Others, however, believe the disorder an entity per se, that the antisocial behavior is based on an underlying emotional difficulty. These observers make the diagnosis on the basis of the individual's repeated violations of the law or social rules. In other words, they diagnose every person who behaves in an antisocial manner as being a sociopathic personality—which is not the case! Therefore, we must define the disorder not alone on the basis of the patient's antisocial behavior but on other grounds as well. We must investigate the underlying personality structure.

In reviewing history, the so-called sociopaths were the group at one time referred to as "moral imbeciles," meaning that they are mentally deficient on the ethical level, that they congenitally lack moral sense just as a color-blind person congenitally lacks color-sense. Many in this group, however, never violated laws and yet were labeled sociopathic personalities because they did lack moral sense. This term "moral imbecility" remains valid to some extent but not in implying that the sense of morality is constitutionally lacking. For instance, there are people who acquire sociopathic traits in the framework of other disorders. There are many apparent sociopathic personalities in whom the disorder is actually organic, or in whom the disorder is psychotic (although there are also many sociopathic individuals who have episodes of psychosis). For example, sociopathic syndromes can be the result of organic disorders such as encephalitis. This is especially true in certain cases that occur in childhood or early adolescence. There are certain sociopathic individuals labeled in the "acting out psychoneurosis" category, which made the delineation between "sociopathic" and "neurotic" vague and diagnosis became confusing. Therefore, it may appear easy to make a diagnosis of so-called "nuclear" sociopathic personality but because sociopathic behavior occurs in the framework of a variety of etiological disorders the issue has been confused.

Until rather recently, the definition of sociopathic personality was tied in with antisocial behavior. But, because that which is considered antisocial behavior varies with each particular society, the question arose as to which types of antisocial behavior are to be accepted as the criteria for the so-called sociopathic entity. People having antisocial behavior can fall into the following categories: criminals, those having the tendency for impulsive violence, pathological liars, pathological swindlers, kleptomaniacs, drug addicts, and "pushers," sexual perverts—particularly those who are sado-masochistic—and to this list could be included all people in general who are called thieves, gamblers, forgers, or whatever. Obviously, however, these groups are very unrelated to each other. Assuming the absence of psychosis or organic disorder, their one feature in common is that the behavior of these people offends the moral code of the environment. It is this lability of diagnostic criteria that makes the sociopathic personality a diagnostic "waste basket" into which are dumped all those individuals who cannot be defined in the category of the neuroses or psychoses.

It follows naturally that the *etiology* of the sociopathic

personality disorder is as yet unknown. Most likely genetic factors are involved but the role they play is not fully determined. The tendency seemingly runs in families, and identical twin studies *(Lange, 1930)* indicate the likelihood of strong genetic influences. The role played by environmental factors is unclear. Incidentally, approximately 65 percent of aggressive sociopathic personalities show an abnormal electroencephalographic picture. Abnormal pictures are also found to be more prevalent in the passive sociopathic individuals than in the average population. Just what this signifies is not as yet determined. The electroencephalogram resembles that observed in immature individuals. This could indicate that in the sociopathic individual some factor of immaturity is combined with the tension present which easily becomes intolerable to him and needs release. The discharge of tension is then channelized into a particular form of behavior depending on the personality of the individual and his environmental situation. The channelization of the tension can be understood to some extent, but the primary basis for the tension is difficult to explain.

In describing the *symptomatology* of the so-called "nuclear" sociopathic personality it must be kept in mind that we are dealing with a phenomenological syndrome which may have one or more etiological bases.

There are several characteristic behavioral patterns that can be observed in these people. One very common pattern is that of rather passive exploitation of the environment by means of charm and ingratiation whereby they manipulate others for their own emotional gratifications. These are the "con artists" who are soft-spoken, likable, and appealing. Their behavior can fool even those with whom they live because their persuasive ways make it easy to overlook their past antisocial and exploitative acts. Another common pattern observed is that of aggressive exploitation of the environment. These are the "tough" characters who are generally flamboyant, bragging, demanding, and noisy in social situations. Such behavior usually becomes exaggerated whenever these people are frustrated. Frustrations are poorly tolerated and aggravate their tension which, when it becomes intolerable, leads to belligerent and "blackmailing" acting-out behavior. They can be dangerous. Actually, the sociopathic individuals who are predominantly ingratiating in their acting-out behavior often switch to an aggressive role when frustrated and then become hostile toward anybody who stands in their way. It is not rare to observe sociopathic patients shifting from one behavioral pattern to another, depending upon the situations in which they find themselves. In all these people genuine empathy is superficial or lacking. In relating to other people, however, their display of affection can be quite convincing and they are known to be very seductive manipulators. They view people simply as objects—to be used.

The so-called nuclear sociopathic individuals are often viewed as being moronic due to the fact that they yield to their emotional drives and the emotions are divorced from their intellect. These individuals continue displaying unregulated emotional behavior beyond the period of childhood. They are neither neurotic nor psychotic; they are sane. Even though sane, these people are more disorganized than are psychotic individuals—and more dangerous. They are unable to distinguish between that which is generally considered "good" or "bad," "right" or "wrong." Because they are legally regarded as "sane," no constructive measures can be taken in dealing with sociopathic individuals. Their antisocial behavior often lands them in jail or in a mental hospital, but they are subsequently discharged unimproved and continue to behave in an unstable manner emotionally, occupationally, socially, and sexually. Instability is often expressed in their use of drugs such as alcohol and narcotics, and this only aggravates the underlying condition. These "nuclear" sociopathic individuals do not usually suffer with neurotic symptoms; they will tell you that they feel quite well.

Character deformity is basic. Ordinarily, the superego organization in an individual has three convenient subchapters: guilt, anxiety, and moral structure. The sociopathic individual, however, shows no guilt for the antisocial acts he performs, the apparent exception being that he often professes guilt in order to ingratiate the authorities. In fact, he is unable to grasp the concept of guilt and cannot understand why other people do react with guilt for their antisocial acts. In a few cases there is a stratified type of guilt. In other words, the sociopathic person might consider it all right to forge, but not to murder. Among gangsters, for instance, there is a strict moral code employed in an inverted manner; accordingly, they would never permit "squealing" on a rival but would endorse murdering him. The sociopathic individual is "color blind" to actual moral issues. Unlike the neurotic or psychotic person, he suffers no conflictual anxiety in connection with his antisocial acts. Therefore, his superego structure differs from that observed in the normal or neurotic individual. Either it is weak or it is differently organized and easily overridden by strong emotional tensions.

The peculiar intellectual impairment in these individuals should not be overlooked. There is a sort of "semantic dementia" (the word "semantic" here referring to "significance"), meaning that, although the patient is able to understand concrete situations, he fails to grasp their moral implications and is unable to attach appropriate significance to the acts he has performed. In his superficial view of issues the sociopathic individual would state, "Stealing is not right." Then when asked why that is so, he would be unable to give a satisfactory answer; if pressed he might reply, "Because one could get caught." This semantic dementia is present in practically all cases of "nuclear" sociopathic personality.

These individuals consistently show emotional instability. It is endogenous. Tension and mood swings are generated from within the individual but are often precipitated by external events. Because sociopathic behavior is at times intimately linked with an environmental change, the environment is often erroneously labeled the cause of the acting out behavior. However, when analyzing these situations one observes that the environment simply has triggered the release of tension already existing within the individual. The emotional instability often leads sociopathic individuals to perform acts which are antisocial. However, this is not necessarily so because many individuals having a similar emotional structure do not commit antisocial acts, or just commit borderline antisocial acts. The emotional instability, however, is an outstanding feature in these people.

These unstable persons lack emotional perseverance. They withdraw emotionally very readily in the majority of situations requiring sustained emotion. (Many such individuals therefore belong in the schizophrenic group.)

One of the most disagreeable features encountered when attempting to treat sociopathic personalities is their persistent failure to profit from experience. For that reason they were labeled "constitutional inferiors." This failure in learning persists despite treating them with punishment or reward systems. It is based on an habitual lack of foresight. In this regard the emotions are clearly divorced from the intellect; rudimentary planning and short-circuited foresight operate on an emotional here-and-now basis and long-term cause-and-effect are not weighed intellectually. Antisocial behavior is often unpremeditated and resembles a reflex set into motion by a trigger mechanism. However, many acts are premeditated but are performed with a peculiar short-circuit type of foresight. In other words, there is a peculiar compulsive need requiring the sociopathic person to perform the act, just as a drug addict cannot resist taking his drug.

All acting-out patients should be examined for these clinical features of instability before making the diagnosis of so-called sociopathic personality. Other factors of instability may also be present and all such factors should be taken into consideration from a diagnostic point of view, regardless of psychodynamic factors. In these cases the diagnosis is especially important from the point of view of prognosis and treatment. However, no form of therapy yet devised influences the basic sociopathic disorder. The prognosis remains poor although usually the acting out behavior tends to diminish with age. Incidentally, one rarely encounters such a person having an onset of antisocial behavior after the age of, let us say, thirty—except when it develops in the framework of some underlying organic or psychotic disorder. Possibly pharmacological research will at a future time discover drugs which will somehow influence the maturation process in these individuals.

Treatment of the sociopathic personality is the most difficult problem in psychiatry. Therapy is mainly a matter of management. Maturation also plays a large role and to stimulate this process benefits many patients. As in dealing with a small child, therapy involves explaining very basic cause-and-effect issues to the patient, relating for him his acting out behavior and the environment's reactions to it. The patient is, naturally, unable to grasp the significance of the acts he has performed and therefore the therapist usually finds he must explain them again and again to the patient in each new situation and attempt to teach him how to generalize from past experiences. Moralizing with the patient makes matters worse; being "color blind" to moral values, the patient feels he is being "preached" to, and he becomes resentful, increasingly tense, and then probably acts out even more than ever.

Naturally, the patient behaves in an antisocial manner not only toward his environment but also in relationship to his therapist, especially by means of lying and clever distortion of facts. And, as the saying goes, "The lie is the handle of all misdemeanors." Therefore, during the initial interview it should be clearly stated to the patient that therapy cannot be conducted unless the psychiatrist is enabled to maintain some form of contact with a reliable member of the family or other person with whom the person lives. Unless the patient agrees to this—and he probably will not—any treatment attempts are futile because the therapist will not be able to distinguish between the patient's lies and the actual facts in his daily life. Many psychiatrists have been outwitted by sociopathic patients who can convincingly demonstrate improvements in their assumed "neurotic" condition while they are actually using the treatment situation as a license to practice their antisocial acts at the expense of someone who is subsidizing the "analysis."

Supportive drugs should be prescribed with caution. The so-called "nuclear" sociopathic person does not usually complain of depression and stimulants should generally be avoided because they tend to increase the patient's tension and aggravate his acting out behavior. Mild doses of barbiturates or tranquilizing drugs diminish tension in many patients but the use of such drugs can lead to their abuse, and, furthermore, they do not influence the underlying pathology.

Although the so-called sociopathic personality has long been a psychiatric as well as a medico-legal problem it is questionable that the "nuclear" group described exists as an entity. Sociopathic behavioral patterns are observed in the framework of quite a number of organic disorders, as I have mentioned. These include postencephalitis, chronic alcoholism, general paresis, and many others. There are also epileptic sociopathic individuals; these people accumulate a tremendous tension—then they "explode." There is the group of acting-out individuals in whom psychoneurotic dynamic mechanisms are present; these people suffer with fears, guilt, and, in addition, an irresistible urge to commit antisocial acts either in spite of their guilt or predicated on it. One point remains unclear with regard to the differentiation between the neurotic and the sociopathic individual: How does the neurotic individual who is able to resist acting out differ from the individual with similar dynamic structure who cannot resist? Until the differences are made known, the differentiation in the diagnosis should be maintained.

In addition to these sociopathic personality syndromes, there is the large group of patients in whom antisocial behavior is the outstanding feature but who also manifest symptoms which remind us of schizophrenia. Many of these patients actually are schizophrenic individuals; for this group we have advanced the term "pseudosociopathic schizophrenia."

PSEUDOSOCIOPATHIC FORM OF SCHIZOPHRENIA

The term pseudosociopathic schizophrenia we *(Dunaif and Hoch, 1955)* have applied to that group of schizophrenic individuals who resemble the sociopathic personality in that the outstanding clinical features revolve around their antisocial behavior. Actually, the antisocial behavior is intimately linked with an underlying schizophrenic process in these cases. Unfortunately, the underlying psychosis is frequently overlooked. When apprehended for criminal acts these individuals are often diagnosed, "Sociopathic personality, without psychosis." Careful examination would have disclosed that many of the basic clinical symptoms of schizophrenia had always been present, namely, a disorganization of the personality with peculiar thinking disorders, emotional dysregulation, and other features of impaired homeostasis. Too often, if these features are observed they are simply dismissed as "schizoid tendencies." The secondary clinical symptoms of schizophrenia observed in the pseudoneurotic form of schizophrenia are also frequently present in the pseudosociopathic patient, particularly pan-neurosis and signs of chaotic sexuality. Pan-anxiety may appear absent on the surface in some cases but is most likely expressed in the form of the antisocial behavior; in other cases anxiety is insufficiently absorbed by the acting-out behavior but is expressed by obsessional and phobic symptomatology, often related to guilty fear of bodily disintegration.

Clinical pictures are varied, as in the sociopathic personality. They may be roughly divided into three major descriptive groupings. First, there is the so-called "typical psychopath"; he is usually the hostile, sneering, and aggressive individual who appears "tough" or nonchalant on the surface. This group in particular may show no evidence of surface anxiety. These individuals usually rationalize that their actions are not "wrong," that their current offense is misjudged by the particular society accusing them. When they do admit criminal acts, the guilt they express is often superficial and aroused mainly by the fact of having been apprehended. Many of these individuals, however, actually do have strong guilty fear which seemingly drives them to commit offenses in order to satisfy an unconscious need for punishment. In such cases, an overwhelming guilt is bound in with the personality structure and may manifest itself dynamically as a diffuse obsessional, phobic, and hypochondriacal picture which underlies their overt show of toughness and defiance. For instance, a patient may be obsessed for years with the fear of having contracted syphilis or some other destructive disease due to his past sexual misbehavior; this may lead not only to many phobic behavioral patterns regarding personal hygiene but also to his again committing further antisocial sexual acts in such a way as to unconsciously invite being apprehended and punished.

A second group consists of individuals who present a surface picture of passive-aggressive dependency and coy ingratiation. Rather than appearing "tough," they may be "smooth" and persuasive. This group usually displays a full-blown pan-neurotic and pan-anxiety picture along with their chaotic and antisocial sexual behavior. Anxiety is not absorbed by the acting-out behavior and they are usually obsessed with fearful fantasies of disintegration and death.

A third grouping consists of individuals who are withdrawn and remain rather isolated—the "loners." They also use the mechanism of denial of their antisocial acts. As in other groupings, obsessional and hypochondriacal symptoms predominate. They often lead alcoholic lives and during psychotic episodes frequently manifest regressive and bizarre behavior.

In most cases there is a mixed clinical picture, as in the so-called "nuclear" sociopathic personality. In other words, depending upon the environmental circumstances, he shifts from one to another pattern of acting-out behavior. For instance, the withdrawal or ingratiation pattern can be punctuated by outbursts of aggression especially when tension is aggravated by frustrations.

The life history of antisocial behavior in these individuals is similar to that observed in the nonschizophrenic sociopathic individual in many and more exaggerated respects. Early behavior often includes repeated truancy, juvenile delinquency, aggression, and destructive behavior. In the pseudosociopathic schizophrenic individual these patterns are often bizarre in quality. When adult, the behavior often includes bizarre aggressive outbursts, alcoholism, drug addiction, vagrancy, and various criminal offenses which lead to repeated imprisonment.

The emotional instability is present throughout their lives and is markedly exaggerated by the underlying schizophrenic process. Affect is very shallow: these people are "cold." Furthermore, the affect displayed is often inappropriate. Mood swings commonly occur. There may be periods of apparent euphoria which usually alternate with periods of depression. Depression may be mild but is often severe and at times agitated. Intellectual impairments are always present and should be recognized. In addition to the so-called "semantic dementia" characteristic of the sociopathic individual, typically schizophrenic concretization, paralogical thinking and circumstantiality are present. Usually these people are suspicious and have ideas of reference. Many cases have outbursts of unsystematized paranoid delusions. Delusions are usually grandiose and linked with the ideas of persecution.

Hypochondriacal fears are often connected with the paranoid ideation. These fears are usually inappropriate to the patients' actual physical status and indications of the great underlying anxiety concerning disintegration and annihilation. Therefore, many of these people are fanatically cautious regarding matters of health and safety. Paradoxically, this phobic behavior can be suddenly punctuated by a recklessness whereby they seemingly act out their obsessional fantasies of violence and destruction. Incidentally, these features commonly earn such individuals a wartime reputation for being "good combat soldiers"; when called upon to kill they can be ruthless. However, in other respects their adjustment in military service is usually very poor. They are belligerent and refractory to discipline. Many of these soldiers go "AWOL" or in other ways win "dishonorable discharge" from the armed forces.

In civilian life their work record is one of extreme instability. Their work is unreliable, irregular, and sporadic with frequent job changes. Many of these people attempt to support themselves through gambling, robberies, dealing in drugs, and other illegal activities. Quite a number of them spend portions of their lives in prison. Socially their behavior is erratic, impulsive, and irresponsible. They relate to others on a superficial and exploitative level. They usually make very poor marital adjustments and are often sexually promiscuous.

These patients have a very poorly integrated concept of sexuality. All varieties of perversions are practiced in keeping with bizarre aggressive and sado-masochistic sexual fantasies. Behavior includes sexual assaults on children and adults, exhibitionism, incest, homosexual acts, transvestitism, fetishism, and so forth. Often the perverted sexual acts are performed while the individual is under the influence of some drug. As in the "nuclear" sociopathic personalities, there is a tendency to rely heavily on the use of drugs in attempting to relieve tension states which these people are unable to tolerate. In many cases full-blown psychotic states occur while under the influence of drugs which, naturally, further aggravate the acting-out behavior in these individuals.

There is an interesting alcoholic group which is not so likely to be encountered if one is in a specialized form of practice. This is the group of sociopathic personality types who are periodic drinkers and who, when under the influence of alcohol, develop psychotic reactions. They are heavy drinkers—unlike those sociopathic individuals in the pathological intoxication group which I have discussed—in whom psychotic episodes are released under the influence of alcohol. They periodically go on alcoholic bouts that may last for days or, in rare instances, for several weeks. Some of these individuals then develop an atypical psychotic reaction. It may consist of a rage reaction, hallucinations, short-lived paranoid delusions, and, occasionally, depressive or manic states. Usually the psychotic episode is brief, following which the person returns to his prepsychotic state, which is that of a sociopathic type of individual.

In following the life history of pseudosociopathic schizophrenic individuals it has been observed that many develop full-blown psychotic episodes at some time or other. The episodes may be of brief or prolonged duration. These psychotic states are often confused with the Ganzer syndrome, or "prison psychosis," particularly when occurring in a prison setting. The psychotic episodes differ from the Ganzer syndrome, however, in that they do not occur as a reaction to environmental situations but seem to develop spontaneously. Close examination discloses that the reactive elements stem from stimuli within the individuals which exacerbate the continuous schizophrenic process. The psychotic episodes vary in symptomatology. There is an aggravation of their underlying clinical symptoms of schizophrenia, namely, thinking disorders, marked emotional dysregulation, regression, stereotyped behavior, and so forth. Some of these patients develop auditory or visual hallucinations, others develop poorly elaborated paranoid delusions. The patients usually act out their psychotic experiences. When hospitalized during such episodes and on the basis of the patient's previous history of antisocial behavior, the diagnosis often made is that of "Psychopathic personality, with acute psychosis." Nevertheless, these psychotic episodes differ in no way, qualitatively or quantitatively, from a schizophrenic psychosis.

In those cases of pseudosociopathic schizophrenia which did not have a psychotic break sufficiently apparent to require the attention of a psychiatrist, the underlying schizophrenic disorder is nonetheless evidenced in the basically autistic and dereistic life approach, the varying degrees of disturbances of affect and interpersonal relationships, and usually in the profusion of pseudoneurotic and antisocial symptomatology present. This particular group of patients often experiences "micropsychotic" episodes which do not necessitate hospitalization. They may return rather quickly to a relatively compensated psychotic level, or they may adjust on a lower level of functioning than they were formerly able to do. Actually, even those schizophrenic individuals who have repeated overt psychotic episodes do not usually deteriorate but manage to continue to function on the so-called criminal fringe of society.

Why it is some schizophrenic patients act out and others do not, remains unclear. There is no reliable information to explain the origin of acting-out behavior. There is considerable data to explain the acting-out behavior when it does occur, however, because it points up some of the motives behind the antisocial acts. But the motivations do not give us any explanation as to why an individual seeks a solution for his problems by means of acting-out behavior. It is also quite unclear why the so-called *ego functioning* is faulty in these individuals. Generalizations, such as "lack of ego strength," "weak" and "impaired superego structure," and so forth merely indicate the general areas of pathology but offer no detailed information as to the actual mechanisms involved.

28

ETIOLOGICAL CONCEPTS
OF SCHIZOPHRENIA

Many concepts concerning the origin of schizophrenia have been proposed, a few of which I shall review because they relate to ongoing research. The widely divergent opinions expressed have contributed to our knowledge of schizophrenia, but no clear understanding of the etiological factors has as yet emerged. Should we strip our etiological knowledge of all the verbiage covering our ignorance, it becomes clear that actually the etiology of most mental disorders remains unknown, and that practically none of the present theories—organic, heredito-constitutional, psychodynamic, and so forth—are really new. Most of the ideas were already expressed in the 19th century and are now simply being reformulated with refinements due to the progress made in various scientific disciplines. However, despite methodological refinements and rather impressive research

774

constructs, many of the fundamental problems remain the same as they were in the past century.

HISTORICAL BACKGROUND

Before the time of Kraepelin, the approach to schizophrenia consisted mainly of many partial descriptions of the clinical phenomena—hebephrenic, catatonic, and so forth—as discussed by Hecker and Kahlbaum *(6)*, but with the assumption that each of the pictures described was a separate disease entity.

Kraepelin *(2)*, Eugen Bleuler *(4)*, and others offered unifying concepts; they grouped the different clinical syndromes together into one and separated them from other forms of mental disorder. Some of the etiological ideas were at that time already implied. Kraepelin assumed schizophrenia to be due to some hereditary and/or chemical dyscrasia and formulated the idea that schizophrenia is a disease entity. He compared it to typhoid fever, syphilis, tuberculosis, and others, in that although the symptomatology is very ramified it is all produced by a specific etiological agent. He described the extremely varied manifestations of schizophrenia with the hope that soon there would be pathological and neuropathological confirmations for them as there were for disease entities such as general paresis. The idea that schizophrenic individuals are suffering from a disease in which the process leads to deterioration was the essence of Kraepelin's classification (and is to some extent still retained).

Bleuler then modified this view; he pointed out that schizophrenia should not be diagnosed on the basis of the clinical outcome. Bleuler had a very logical mind, and he pointed out quite clearly that in other disorders it is not the outcome that determines the diagnosis. For instance, one does not diagnose a patient as suffering from tuberculosis because he has cavity formations and will die, or diagnose another patient as suffering from tuberculosis because he has only an indurating process and will live happily ever after. Therefore, Bleuler dropped the idea that schizophrenia is a deteriorating disorder. We now know, naturally, that deterioration is preventable, and therefore it is not an intrinsic component of schizophrenia as Kraepelin had viewed it. Although Bleuler discarded the deterioration concept, he retained the idea that schizophrenia is a disease process because he also recognized that we are dealing with more than just a reaction. He believed that we are here dealing with a disorder, but a disorder which probably cannot be treated in exactly the same fashion as a single disease entity. For a time he termed schizophrenia a group of diseases, referring to it as a *processe psychose,* and described the variative manifestations of this process.

I would like to remind you that at the same time Kraepelin and Bleuler introduced the disease concept of schizophrenia, a German psychiatrist, Hoche, made the statement that he believed schizophrenia to be a reaction— a maladaptive reaction based on heredito-constitutional and psychogenic influences but not a disease or a group of diseases. He was actually the instigator of the movement later to be carried on by Adolf Meyer, the so-called psychobiological reaction concept of schizophrenia (which I shall discuss later).

ETIOLOGICAL CONCEPTS

Actually, the questions as to whether schizophrenia is a reaction, a disorder, a disease entity, or a group of diseases, and whether it is based on a single etiology or multiple etiologies, are as yet unsolved. This classificatory game will continue to be played until these matters become known. Meanwhile, attempts continue to be made to determine the extent to which the *organic, psychogenic,* or *combined* factors contribute to the development of schizophrenia. Two extreme positions could be assumed: One extreme would be to consider schizophrenia a single organic disease comparable to a physical disease whereby the diversified symptomatology could be explained as either ramifications of the disease or as due to various compensatory mechanisms established to cope with it. The other extreme would be to assume that schizophrenia is purely psychogenic whereby the diversified symptomatology could be explained dynamically on the basis of the person's interaction with his environment. Between these extremes, naturally, there are various etiological appraisals of schizophrenia. It is obvious that all organismic functioning, including psychic function, is biological in nature, but an understanding of the proper relationship between organic and psychic factors and their relative importance in schizophrenia is not at all clear. In other words, our present situation is comparable to that before the causative agent of, for instance, general paresis became known; everything under the sun was accused of being the cause, and when the etiological factor became known the various assumed factors became unscrambled and placed in their proper perspective. This, of course, will also happen in schizophrenia.

We cannot discuss all the etiological concepts that have been postulated, but shall discuss briefly those which are, in my opinion, important.

Kraepelin assumed that dementia praecox is an *organic disease entity* due to some hereditary and/or some chemical dyscrasia having some *anatomical substrate* for the manifold symptomatology. In terms of *physiology,* practically every metabolic system, every organ, and the endocrine glands in particular, were thought to be involved. Many research attempts were made to find histopathological changes in the different organs of the body, particularly in the brain, but none of the findings were specific for schizophrenia. Of course, it is possible that newer techniques may disclose specific alterations of cell structure and metabolism. Very possibly systematic investigations of the subcortical brain areas may eventually disclose pathological changes that have not been found in the cortex. You must remember that many investigators assumed Parkinson's disease to be a psychogenic disorder until studies eventually disclosed definite changes in the subcortical gray matter.

Actually, the unitary disease concept of schizophrenia is still under consideration because most of the *biochemical* research is now attempting to find chemical deviations which will be universally present in schizophrenic individuals and absent in other disorders, thus setting schizophrenia apart. In reviewing the biochemical research being carried out at the present time, however, the findings are, in my opinion, quite inconclusive. The findings of a special enzyme or metabolic substance and labeling it specific for schizophrenia is most often speculative and all are inconclusive so far. No specific biochemical factor for schizophrenia has been demonstrated to be etiological. It has been demonstrated, however, that in schizophrenia the regulation of metabolism is not quite normal, that the functioning of the homeostatic mechanisms differ from normal and do not operate very smoothly. Naturally, homeostasis is disturbed in mental functioning as well as in many other physiological ways—particularly noticeable in the catatonic form of schizophrenia—but these alterations shift and take various forms in each case, so that homeostatic disturbance per se is not specific and cannot be employed as a diagnostic test. Even should certain biochemical or metabolic alterations be discovered which are specific for schizophrenia, these findings would not indicate whether the disorder is actually caused by these changes or whether the disorder produces these changes secondarily, and therefore would not indicate to us whether the disorder is a disease entity or a reaction.

The matter of *hereditary* mechanisms operating in schizophrenia has been under investigation by quite a number of geneticists, especially Kallmann. For instance, it was demonstrated that in one-egg twins the incidence of schizophrenia is 86 percent, whereas in fraternal twins it is only 7 percent. This enormous discrepancy cannot be entirely explained by pointing out that they were raised in the same environment, or that there is a special pattern of interaction between one-egg twins which would therefore account for this very high concordance rate. In my opinion, much more interesting and much more convincing evidence that there is an hereditary background in schizophrenia is the existence of a so-called cluster-pattern, or dilution-pattern: For instance, in the siblings of schizophrenic patients the incidence of schizophrenia is seven times higher than that of the general population; in the children of schizophrenic patients it is between ten and twenty times higher than that in the general population; in the grandchildren and in nephews and cousins of schizophrenic individuals it is about three times greater than in the average population. This would indicate that the disorder has a certain tendency to cluster around some families and quite possibly something is being genetically transmitted in those families. The question is, exactly what is transmitted? Is it the disposition to schizophrenia, which then must be triggered by other factors, or is it that—as Kallman postulated (6)—schizophrenia is actually inherited as such but that its manifestations are capable of being suppressed to varying degrees by equally inherited defense mechanisms? Most likely, schizophrenia as such is not transmitted, but what is probably transmitted is a certain nervous system organization for coping with stimulation—the way in which this individual reacts when under stress. What is probably also transmitted is the rate of speed and extent to which the nervous system and corresponding psyche are capable of developing in an individual. That, of course, would indicate that a certain group of individuals have the propensity to respond to stimulation according to a special disorganization pattern, and that these individuals, when under environmental pressure, more readily display this type of disorganization than do other individuals. In other words, we are dealing here with a situation very similar to that of, for instance, an allergy whereby the person has an inherited disposition to it; if not confronted with the allergen, nothing happens, but if so confronted a certain allergic reaction then occurs, its severity depending on the strength of the allergen as well as the proneness of the individual.

The modality of genetic inheritance will surely be determined, but the question remains: Are all types of schizophrenia inherited, and if not, in what way do they differ and why do they have so much similarity? For example, psychoses in amphetamine intoxication sometimes appear indistinguishable from a schizophrenic psychosis, and differential diagnosis cannot be made without our knowing beforehand that the person was under the influence of amphetamine. But, in the so-called spontaneously occurring schizophrenic psychosis there is sufficient evidence to indicate it is surely an hereditary disorder.

The manner by which the mechanism of inheritance translates itself into function in schizophrenia is being investigated. The biochemist must keep in mind the possibility that the genetic factors operate to determine inappropriate reactions or interconnections between certain normal chemical components of the brain. In my opinion, it is some form of regulatory inefficiency in schizophrenia that is inherited, this dysregulation based on some aberrant functional organization of the diencephalon, mesencephalon, and reticular system which, in turn, influences the cortex. Biochemical genetic studies will, hopefully, give us a clue as to the type of chromosomal defect or influence that is transmitted and causes the impairment.

Turning now to the question of the relationship between the so-called schizoid *constitutional* make-up of an individual and schizophrenia, some psychiatrists consider it a quantitative issue, that the schizoid individual is a potential schizophrenic; others take the stand that the *schizoid personality organization* of the individual has nothing to do with the actual schizophrenic disorder. One interesting observation has been made: A history of schizoid personality organization is observed to be fifty times more prevalent in schizophrenic persons than in nonschizophrenic persons. Therefore, some relationship between the schizoid organization and schizophrenia must exist. But then the question arises, could not many so-called schizoid individuals simply be temperamental variants within the norm, or are they always attenuated cases of schizophrenia? To answer this question we need to have much more extensive studies of family members of schizophrenic patients than is usually done today. Probably you would find that if you carefully examined the relatives of a schizophrenic patient psychiatrically, many of them would be found to be as psychotic as the patient, but perhaps because they were not admitted to a hospital they were not labeled schizophrenic. Or, you might find that many of the relatives are not so overtly psychotic as the patient but manifest an attenuated form of the disorder with all the basic mechanisms present even though they continue to have sufficient hold on reality and are able to cope with everyday life.

Studies of the constitutional organization in relation to schizophrenia have included observations concerning various body types. Here again, it has been demonstrated that, as Kretschmer postulated (6), there is some correlation between certain body types and certain personality organizations which seemingly has some influence on the development of schizophrenia. For instance, the relationship of the so-called asthenic type to schizophrenia indicated that probably some definite metabolic factors are involved. Dr. Nolan D. C. Lewis (1923) found that in the hebephrenic and catatonic groups there is some cardiovascular aplasia, but that this was not observed in the paranoid group. Schizophrenic individuals usually show many more endocrine disturbances than do neurotic individuals. Males are seemingly less masculine in appearance and a dysplastic or eunichoid intersex make-up is much more prevalent in schizophrenia. Many female schizophrenic patients have a rather infantile sexual apparatus which probably corresponds to the infantile characteristics otherwise present. Therefore, probably some of the underdevelopment, or hypoplasia, is somehow correlated with schizophrenia. The psychosexual underdevelopment is not so well defined as is the mental underdevelopment, but usually it is there. Let me remind you, however, that many people having a so-called asthenic habitus, or having a schizoid personality structure, do not ever develop schizophrenia.

Most likely, we need biochemical evidence to demonstrate how one so-called constitutional type functions differently from another, how this relates to mental functioning, and how it is linked to a schizoid personality make-up. The relationship between constitutional type and predisposition to develop schizophrenia explains some of the mechanisms of schizophrenia and indicates some of the metabolic defenses in coping with it, but it of course does not explain the actual schizophrenic process itself etiologically.

It can presently be assumed, however, that schizophrenia is a disorder rooted in a special organization of the individual; that it is an organismic response, of a special sort, to stimulation. If the individual does not have this particular organization, he will not respond in a schizophrenic manner. However, occasionally individuals are encountered who show mental manifestations which have certain resemblance to those of schizophrenia, and it is not quite clear whether or not these individuals are actually schizophrenic. But essentially it should be assumed that if a person responds with a schizophrenic psychosis, some crucial organismic difference is present in him. You have to expect that quite a number of psychiatrists have an opposite viewpoint; they think that schizophrenia is actually nothing more than a reaction pattern in an individual—a disorganized one, if you wish, but a pattern similar to an anxiety reaction, an hysterical reaction, and so forth. In other words, they deny the specificity of this predispositional organization which many of us believe to be basic. On the other hand, if that is correct, the question arises: What determines and differentiates the schizophrenic reaction from those of other mental or emotional disorders? In other words, why do schizophrenic individuals respond in a schizophrenic manner and not in an organic psychotic, a manic-depressive psychotic, or a psychoneurotic manner? Does it differ qualitatively as well as quantitatively from other such disorders?

Nevertheless, keep in mind that all our diagnostic classifications of schizophrenia are phenomenological. They are all empirical. Nobody knows whether symptoms which appear alike are actually on the same basis or not, and therefore we do not know whether an individual who shows one sort of symptom picture actually belongs etiologically in the same group with another individual who shows the same sort of symptom picture. This issue is further complicated by the fact that schizophrenia most likely is not a disorder having a single etiology. There could be various etiological agents involved, and what we view as schizophrenia might be just a common form of *reaction* of individuals responding to different etiological stresses in the same way. As an analogy, there are many different types of bacteria which can produce fever; the fever is similar in its manifestations, but the microorganisms that produce it could be quite different.

To take up another point in this connection, attempts are being made to find the basis of schizophrenic symptomatology on an *experimental level,* and data are accumulating which are very interesting. We are finding that there are quite a number of compounds with which we can produce schizophrenic-like psychotic pictures. By administering these drugs to a so-called normal individual, within a half an hour this person will, for all practical purposes, appear schizophrenic. These drugs indicate that a physically produced disturbance of homeostasis leads to a lowering of mental integration and, in turn, leads to many different emotional symptoms and disorganization patterns very similar to those observed in schizophrenia. The question arises, to what extent are these experimentally produced conditions the same as the mental changes observed in schizophrenia? Phenomenologically, they appear to be very similar, if not identical, to the acute schizophrenic symptom-atology. Some investigators may therefore assume that in schizophrenic persons similar toxic substances in the body are somehow produced which have the same effect on the nervous system as the drug intoxicants used experimentally, but this has not been verified biochemically. At present, we can only speculate about how these mental changes are linked to the chemical changes. It is unclear whether the mental changes are due to the chemical action of the drug per se or occur secondary to an alteration of reality percep-tion and other changes. Perhaps some of the symptoms are due to the ego's attempting to evolve defenses against the altered reality feelings. It is a fact, however, that the influ-ence of these drugs disrupts mental integration and releases unconscious forces in the person, many of which can then be explained in psychodynamic terms. The fact still remains that these symptoms are produced by somatic means.

The ability to handle the stimulation caused by these drugs is closely related to the intensity of its stimulation in the organism; small doses produce relatively mild deviations of psychic functioning, but when the drug dose is so intense that the person is overwhelmed by its impact, the clinical symptoms become massive and he is unable to defensively cope with them. Not only can disruption of homeostasis in the organism be achieved by these physical means, but also by confronting the organism with adaptational tasks with which it is unable to cope, thus creating a great amount of tension. This tension state then leads to alteration in homeo-stasis similar to that produced by chemical means. And the more vulnerable, the more immature the organism con-fronted with this stress, the more the disruption of homeo-stasis.

Therefore, the disorganizational reaction that occurs in schizophrenia is a very universal human propensity. It can be provoked by chemical stress, it can be provoked by emo-tional stress, and can probably be provoked by several other

forms of stress. But, should you inject one of the experimental psychogenic drugs into a schizophrenic individual,
whether he is just potentially psychotic or overtly psychotic,
you would be able to blow up the symptomatology very
rapidly into a marked schizophrenic reaction—a much more
marked reaction than would be observed in a so-called
normal subject—indicating that the homeostatic mechanism
in schizophrenic individuals is under some strain to begin
with and, of course, when additional strain is added there
is aggravation of the existing psychosis.

This points to the still valid Bleulerian concept that
what he termed the primary symptoms of schizophrenia are
physiogenic, and the secondary symptoms psychogenic. In
other words, in schizophrenia and in other mental disorders
we are able to explain the content of hallucinations and
delusions in psychological terms, but we are unable to
explain their physiological processes by the content. As I
have mentioned, experimental production of hallucinations
and delusions can be done by means of certain drugs but the
content of these psychotic symptoms is seemingly unrelated
to the etiological agents. Systematic studies in this area have
not as yet been done because everybody is fascinated by the
content, regardless of the fact that these organic psychoses
clearly indicate that understanding the content of an hallucination or a delusion does not explain the process by which
it originates. Parallel to this, the physiological basis of
normal dreaming is not readily open to psychological
explanations although the contents of dreams are. In schizophrenia, then, to what extent are the distorted perceptions,
the feelings of depersonalization, the anxiety, and the disintegration on an organic basis, and to what extent are they
psychogenic? In other words, we do not know at what point
symptoms cease to be organic and begin to be so-called
psychogenic. To overcome this difficulty and evade controversy of the disease-versus-reaction concepts of schizophrenia, the rather noncommital designation of a

"syndrome" was introduced. This equivocation is justified clinically for as long as the etiology of schizophrenia remains unknown.

According to the hypothesis of Adolf Meyer *(5, 6)*, who founded the psychobiological school of thought, schizophrenia was considered to be a form of *maladaptation*. According to his concept of the origin of schizophrenia, everything was included—organic, hereditary, and constitution, as well as psychogenic factors. He believed that the constitutional predisposition of the individual manifested itself in disease when environmental experiences caused a series of maladaptational patterns to develop until the accumulation finally "broke the camel's back." He pointed out that the defective organism did not function in a vacuum, but functioned in response to interrelationship with the environment. Up to a point, this view explains the ground upon which schizophrenia develops more than it explains anything about the actual psychosis. The concept, furthermore, is so all-inclusive as to be rather vague. Obviously, conditioned maladaptation is cumulative, but this does not explain the actual relationship between personality and schizophrenia, or between constitution and schizophrenia. Surely the past history of schizophrenic patients discloses cumulative maladaptations in all areas, especially in their distorted interpersonal relationships, but why is it that so many persons with similar personality organization and maladaptive patterns never become psychotic and are regarded by their environment as being so-called normal introverts?

Now I should like to mention briefly a few of the mainly *psychogenic* approaches to the understanding of schizophrenia, namely, psychoanalytic theory, the newer Gestalt and the existentialistic views of the etiology of schizophrenia.

The contributions of many *psychoanalytic* investigators are important in illuminating some of the motivations in schizophrenic patients' feelings, thinking, and particularly in their interactions with the environment. They also have demonstrated the importance of early life experiences and parental pathological influences on these schizophrenic individuals. Here again, contributions have explained much about the content of schizophrenic thinking with all its condensations, displacements, symbolization, and so on, but none of this has enabled us to understand the basis for the loosening of associations, the bizarre and incongruous ideations and feelings, or so-called intrapsychic ataxia (Stransky). In other words, the symptom superstructure was dynamically understood in more detail without insight being gained regarding the basic schizophrenic structure itself *(2)*.

The linkage between thinking and emotionality and the loss of reality boundaries in schizophrenia has been explained to quite an extent by Jung *(2)*. And if you accept the libidinal fixation and regression theories of Freud in relationship to schizophrenia, or if you accept the concepts of disturbance of object relationships and ego boundaries offered by Melanie Klein *(3)*, the development of many schizophrenic symptoms can be somewhat explained. But, these are rather far from explaining schizophrenia as a whole. We may be able to explain partial mechanisms once they have occurred, but we cannot understand exactly how and why these mechanisms operate in schizophrenia. For instance, assuming Freud's regression concepts to be correct, why is it that only schizophrenic patients and not neurotic patients regress so deeply to an infantile developmental stage? Freud and others attempted to answer this question by establishing the category of narcissistic neurosis. This tended to blur the boundaries between psychosis and neurosis which led to an assumption that a neurotic person could become progressively disturbed and eventually become schizophrenic and, conversely, that a schizophrenic patient could progressively improve and then become neurotic— that, in short, similar psychodynamic mechanisms could be constructed and applied to both. Therefore, schizophrenia seemingly differed from the neuroses only quantitatively.

Some modifications of this idea led to the optimistic attitude that the conflicts in both can be understood and the symptoms in both could be removed psychotherapeutically. (Freud disagreed; he did not claim that schizophrenics are "cured" by analysis, but patients "learn" from it.) This idea was supported by many psychoanalysts who felt that schizophrenia is almost as psychogenic in origin as the neuroses. When the etiology of schizophrenia becomes known, the validity of such an assumption will be settled.

Actually, a neurotic person under great stress does not become schizophrenic but becomes more neurotic; a schizophrenic person when relieved of some stress does not become neurotic, but his psychotic symptomatology becomes more subtle and he may even develop a few so-called neurotic defense mechanisms. In other words, even should we assume these neurotic symptoms to be the same as those observed in the neuroses, schizophrenic individuals have many thinking and emotional mechanisms present which do not occur in neurotic individuals. In mild cases of schizophrenia it is not always easy to recognize these emotional and thinking disorganizational patterns, especially because these patients often are not properly evaluated. There are several reasons for this.

First of all, many psychiatrists have felt that schizophrenia was too large an entity to be valid and attempted to split it into several disorders independent of schizophrenia. For example, attempts were made to split the paranoid form from it, and some forms of acute catatonic or confusional states, such as the "sensitive reference psychosis" (Kretschmer), "acute motility psychosis" (Kleist), "acute catatonia" (Gjessing), "oneirophrenia" (Meduna), and a number of others (3, 6). Another view held was that schizophrenia should be split into two groups: those of organic origin and those of psychic origin—the "schizophreni-form psychosis" of Langfeldt (3). Then a group of investigators emphasized the common features present in these separate disorders and again placed them into the single category of schizophrenia.

A second reason schizophrenia is not clearly recognized is that there has been some difficulty in describing the primary symptoms of schizophrenia as postulated by Bleuler. Actually, although some of these so-called primary symptoms I believe to be secondary, this is not very important from a clinical point of view because schizophrenia is not diagnosed merely on the basis of these so-called primary symptoms, but rather on the basis of a constellation, or configuration, of more secondary clinical symptoms. However, many psychiatrists hesitate to diagnose all patients schizophrenic who manifest any of these clinical symptom constellations since they are so very prevalent. The actual issue involved is that many psychiatrists wish to avoid making the diagnosis of schizophrenia on their patients because of prognostic, legal, social, personal, or any number of other troublesome complications that this diagnosis may provoke in the mind of the psychiatrist. However, palatable diagnostic substitutes are hard to find, and so these patients are usually classified as neurotic or, at best, as suffering from some psychosis other than schizophrenia. Unfortunately, in most instances the actual fact of schizophrenia overtakes the therapist as well as the patient. Moreover, while the therapist must now admit that schizophrenia is a very large entity, somehow it still does not seem to concern him that the neuroses are an even larger entity. This is presumably because the neurotic individual is generally regarded as a normal variant, it even being stated that everybody is neurotic.

Here I might add that another factor influencing diagnostics rests on the assumption that schizophrenic patients do not respond to psychotherapy and, if they do, then the difference between the neuroses and schizophrenia must not be very great. This duplicity overlooks the fact that psychotherapy may eliminate many of the symptoms present in schizophrenia while leaving the actual matrix unchanged.

Obviously, any preferential attitudes concerning schizophrenia will influence the investigator's diagnostic appraisal of a patient. Psychiatrists have too often been biased, rigid, and confused, all of which can compound the issue by leading to a subjectively ordered selection of case material as well as faulty diagnostic appraisal. This, in turn, has frequently led either to unwarranted nihilism because the etiology of schizophrenia is unknown, or to unjustifiable optimism due to lack of recognition that the patient is schizophrenic.

Now I should just like to mention briefly a few other approaches to the concept of schizophrenia—the contributions from the schools of *Gestalt* and *existentialism*. These more recent views have contributed to a better understanding of schizophrenic symptomatology, but do not lead to disclosure of the etiology.

The *Gestalt* school attempts to explain schizophrenia on the basis of disordered perceptions. Although perceptual alterations were demonstrated in schizophrenia, they are not specific, any more than are the alterations of conscious awareness specific in organic reactions. It was postulated that the ideations and feeling in schizophrenic individuals could be explained in terms of their altered perceptual Gestalt. Actually, the Gestalt is important in relation to delusional formations and also in connection with the peculiar feelings experienced in schizophrenia. For instance, it begins to explain somewhat why it is a schizophrenic individual will feel himself fused with omnipotence and at the same time feel himself a passive inferior victim of the environment. Here again, however, partial manifestations are explained by the Gestalt concepts but not completely so. In many instances, the Gestalt explanations seemingly are constructs; sometimes even unknown constructs are being used to explain other unknown phenomena. This takes place frequently in research in schizophrenia.

The Gestalt school also introduced the concept of disturbance of energy potential in schizophrenia. Some pro-

ponents viewed schizophrenia as a disorder in which biological energy is abnormally controlled, being channelized
inward and expressed in terms of self-related abstract ideations; insufficient energy thereby is available for contacting
and relating meaningfully to other people. Until we know
more about the energy mechanisms in even the normal person, we cannot appraise the value of this hypothesis and, as
is probably also true of Freud's libidinal energy concepts,
these speculations will have to be relegated to the realm of
philosophy.

Existentialism in relation to psychiatry originated from
the work of Heidegger in Germany and Sartre in France.
Sartre and his followers attempted to explain schizophrenia
in terms of existential anxiety. Actually, every phenomenon
in psychiatry could be considered based on anxiety, on
"Dasein" existence, and all else could be ignored. These
speculations are also philosophical and probably will not
throw light on the etiology of schizophrenia even though
some schizophrenics think they will. However, existentialism
has contributed a very important point in that it focused
attention on the role played by anxiety in schizophrenia.
Many schizophrenic symptoms relate back to this "Dasein-
Angst," with which they all suffer. Thus, the role of anxiety
has become recognized as being a powerful motivating force
for schizophrenic withdrawal from reality with which he
cannot cope and constructing a substitute, both being pathological attempts made by the schizophrenic person to allay
this overwhelming anxiety. As I have said, the role of
anxiety can also be observed when schizophrenic individuals
are under the influence of psychotropic drugs, but, here
again, this so-called existential anxiety does not in itself
explain schizophrenia as a whole.

Most of these psychiatric views suffer from one common difficulty: One or more aspects of schizophrenic psychopathology are unduly selected as all-important, while
other aspects are relegated to a subordinate role or disregarded. Furthermore, the interpretations given of schizo-

phrenia deal mainly with the more secondary symptomatology which are actually unimportant in terms of understanding the disorder. The disorder is a much deeper one—the secondary symptoms are very often simply defense elaborations of that particular patient due to his incapacity to cope in an adaptive way because of the underlying disturbance.

Having touched on some of the approaches made in attempts to throw light on the etiology of schizophrenia, I would now like to summarize briefly a few of my own ideas—which are perhaps neither better nor worse than those already mentioned.

In my opinion, schizophrenia is basically an *organic disorder*. Probably schizophrenia should not be regarded as a single disease, like diabetes, but because of the tremendous variations in the clinical picture and because the number of people afflicted is so enormous, we are dealing with a disorder probably based on a disintegrative process. Clinical and experimental evidence largely indicates that what is presently termed schizophrenia is a *special form of integrative impairment*. The widespread integrative disorganization pattern present in schizophrenia is as characteristic a pattern as is that, for instance, in the organic types of reaction. Schizophrenia is prevalent in every social group and can be precipitated by all sorts of stress-producing factors. It occurs in predisposed individuals; this predisposition is inherited.

The organic matrix of schizophrenia is still a matter of speculation. There is increasing evidence to show that when we excite the subcortical gray matter in a person, psychotic symptoms will occur; conversely, when we inhibit the activity of the subcortex, as can be done with such drugs as phenothiazine, psychotic symptoms diminish or disappear. This is also observed when we disconnect the cortex from the subcortical gray matter, as is done by means of prefrontal or frontal lobotomy. Therefore, rather than there being a preeminently cortical impairment as in the typical organic reaction psychoses, the impairment in schizophrenia probably is preeminently a *subcortical impairment,* or more likely a *disruption of the normal relationship between cortex and subcortex.*

The disturbance of integrative functioning in schizophrenia leads to an inability to regulate functions in an organized manner. This regulatory disorganization in schizophrenia is a *total biological affair.* It involves the mental process as well as the vegetative nervous system and there is *impaired homeostasis* in many physiological areas.

In the mental area of functioning this disorganization leads to *an inability to cope, in an integrative and regulative manner, with stimulation coming from within and without.* With better understanding of this regulatory inability, the so-called primary symptoms described by Bleuler—autism, dereism, loosening of associations, and so forth—will probably be recognized as secondary to the primary symptoms of dysregulation. For instance, autism is withdrawal from overwhelming stimulation; dereism is preoccupation with the unreal based on impairment in the process of integrating reality perceptions. In other words, they are probably secondary mechanisms utilized by the schizophrenic individual in his attempts to cope with his poorly integrated and regulated reaction to stimulation. These secondary symptoms would also include the other subtle clinical symptoms present in every schizophrenic individual: Impairment of thinking processes, impairment of emotional regulation, and impairment of action processes. With these impairments present, the schizophrenic individual, naturally, is unable to utilize adequate adaptive processes in relating to the environment and is overwhelmed by anxiety in all areas, the poorly regulated attempts further compounding this anxiety.

The struggle to allay the massive anxiety may contribute to many of the psychic mechanisms observed in schizophrenic individuals. Some individuals are able to construct a defensive façade, the pseudoneurotic mechanisms being one form, the pseudosociopathic and the paranoid mechanisms being others. For some unknown reason, however, many schizophrenic individuals are unable to construct such defense mechanisms and in these cases the subtle symptoms become more pronounced under stresses—physical or emotional—and gross psychotic clinical pictures then develop. Delusions, hallucinations, regressive phenomena, and, in fact, the whole gamut of psychotic symptoms can appear which are mainly quantitative exaggerations of the more subtle symptoms. It is not clear whether these massive psychotic symptoms are direct expressions of the lack of integration and inability of the person to cope with sensory stimulation, or are the person's secondary interpretations of his own anxieties and his difficulties in relating to the environment. Most likely both are factors. These massive symptoms are open to psychodynamic interpretation and influence, and, as I have said, this explains the motivology to some extent but does not disclose anything about the etiology. The intensity of inner and outer stress and other factors can influence many schizophrenic patients to oscillate in their display of symptoms. They may show disintegrative reactions and then may reintegrate and work themselves back toward the reality line. However, we do not know why it is that one schizophrenic patient who has conflicts remains fairly well integrated and yet another person having similar conflicts becomes overwhelmed and will suddenly manifest the disorganizational reaction.

It is important to realize that schizophrenia is far more than just an emotional disorder. It is a disorder of the total personality. Emotional factors have been recently overemphasized, just as were the intellectual factors in the past. But in assessing any disorder in terms of its being emotional in origin, it is important to ascertain whether the emotional state is causative, or contributory, or simply an emotional reaction to the patient's illness. Actually, in schizophrenia the involvement of the cognitive and conative aspects of the psyche should both be emphasized, keeping in mind that schizophrenia affects multiple facets and influences the total psyche of the individual.

Finally, I would like to indicate that, *because the regulative deficiency in schizophrenia involves the total organism, it probably would be fruitful to investigate very carefully the many regulative dysfunctions* which lead to the mental and physiological manifestations. I believe this theoretical approach to be more important than to proceed on an assumption that schizophrenia is due to one single chemical alteration or one single metabolic disturbance (just as we should not assume that it is due to some psychodynamic or social force alone). This is not to state, however, that the regulative deficiency may have no biochemical implications; quite possibly the chemical ingredients in schizophrenic metabolism are the same as those in normal individuals, but due to faulty regulative processes they are perhaps balanced differently, thus leading to homeostatic disruptions. At the present time, I therefore feel that investigation into the regulative inefficiency is the only approach which could bring under a common denominator the known organic and the known psychological mechanisms operating in schizophrenia. It is imperative that these regulative mechanisms be investigated intensively and become better understood.

In conclusion, I would like to emphasize again that there is no etiological common denominator known for schizophrenia. The basic symptoms cannot be determined by the presence of any single clinical, psychological, psychodynamic, neurophysiological, biochemical, or other factor at our disposal at the present time. We psychiatrists have a great many partial fragments of knowledge—and we play with these fragments as do schizophrenics play with their fragments of knowledge. In my opinion, research in schizophrenia was not furthered, but retarded, by the introduction of so-called unification concepts in attempting to mold and subordinate the tremendous amount of partial observations into some integrated whole. Please do not misunderstand me: Integration attempts are necessary in every field of science, but we should always be aware of the extent of success and failure of such attempts.

Due to the fact that the bases of research in the biochemical, epidemiological, psychodynamic, and social fields are each so different, I believe these different approaches should continue to work separately. Of course, investigators should take cognizance of each other's methodologies and findings; they should integrate established facts; they should compare the results based on each of the different frames of reference. But the search for the etiology of schizophrenia must be done by investigators having singleminded pursuits based on clearly defined, clearly distinguishable methodologies. As in conducting treatment, research cannot be conducted profitably by committees.

REFERENCES

Alexander, L. (1940), Wernicke's disease: identity of lesions produced by B-avitaminosis in pigeons with hemorrhagic polioencephalitis occurring in chronic alcoholism in man. *Amer. J. Path.,* 16:61.

Arnold, E., Cutler, J., Wright, R., and Levitan, S. (1952), Studies in penicillin treatment of syphilis. *Public Health Report,* 67:78-89.

Bjerre, P. (1922), Delusions and obsessions and their treatment. *Hygiea,* 84:1009. Stockholm, Sweden.

Cleckley, H., Sydenstricker, V., and Geeslin, L. (1939), Nicotinic acid in the treatment of atypical psychotic states. *J. Amer. Med. Assoc.,* 112:2107.

Despert, J. (1947), The early recognition of childhood schizophrenia. *M. Clin. North. Amer.,* 680-687.

797

Deutsch, F. (1949), *Applied Psychoanalysis: Selected Objectives of Therapy*. New York: Grune & Stratton.

Dunaif, S. and Hoch, P. (1955), Pseudoneurotic schizophrenia. In *Psychiatry and the Law,* eds. P. Hoch and J. Zubin. New York: Grune.

Faris, R. and Dunham, H. (1939), *Mental Disorders in Urban Areas*. Chicago: Univ. of Chicago Press.

Fenichel, O. (1945), *Psychoanalytic Theory of Neurosis*. New York: Norton.

———— (1963), *Collected Papers*. New York: Norton.

Haslam, J. (1798), *Observations on Insanity, with Practical Remarks on the Disease and an Account of the Morbid Appearances on Dissection*. London.

Hoch, A. (1915), A study of the benign psychoses. *Johns Hopkins Hospital Bulletin,* vol. 26. Baltimore: Johns Hopkins.

Hoch, P. and Davidoff, E. (1939), Preliminary observations on the course of the traumatic neuroses. *J. Nerv. and Ment. Dis.,* 90:3.

———— and Rachlin, H. (1941), An evaluation of manic-depressive psychosis in the light of follow-up studies. *Amer. J. Psychiat.,* 97:4.

———— (1948), The effects of electro-convulsive therapy on the functioning of mental patients. *J. Personality,* 17:48.

———— and Polatin, P. (1949), Pseudoneurotic forms of schizophrenia. *Psychiat. Quart.,* 23:248.

——— Cattell, J., Pennes, H., and Glaser, G. (1951a), Evaluations of the results of topectomy operations. *Surgery, Gynecology, and Obstetrics,* 92 : 601.

——— (1951b), Personality changes after topectomy. *Psychiat. Quart.,* 25 : 402-408.

——— Cattell, J., and Pennes, H. (1952), Effect of drugs: theoretical considerations from a psychological viewpoint. *Amer. J. Psychiat.,* 108 : 585-589.

——— Cattell, J., and Pennes, H. (1935), Psychoses produced by administration of drugs. In *Metabolic and Toxic Diseases of the Nervous System,* eds. H. Merritt and C. Hare. Baltimore: Williams & Wilkins.

Hollos, I. and Ferenczi, S. (1925), *Psycho-analysis and the Psychic Disorders of General Paresis.* Washington, D.C.: *Nerv. and Ment. Disease.*

Hoskins, R. (1946), *The Biology of Schizophrenia.* New York: Norton.

Knight, R. (1937), Psychodynamics of chronic alcoholism. *J. Nerv. and Ment. Dis.,* 86 : 538-548.

Lange, J. (1930), *Crime and Destiny.* New York: Charles Boni Paperbacks.

Lewis, N. D. C. and Hubbard, L. (1931), The mechanism and prognostic aspects of the manic-depressive-schizophrenic combinations. In *Ass'n Res. Nerv. and Ment. Dis. Proc.,* ch. 27.

——— (1936), *Research in Dementia Praecox.* Washington: Nat'l. Comm. Ment. Hyg.

―――― (1937), An anatomical study contrasting the dementia praecox constitution with that of paranoid developments. *So. Med. J.*, 16:325.

―――― and Strahl, M. (1968), *The Complete Psychiatrist: The Achievements of Paul H. Hoch, M.D.* Albany: State Univ. New York Press.

Menninger, K. (1919), Psychoses associated with influenza. *Arch. Neurol. and Psychiat.*, 2:291-337.

Rado, S. (1969), *Adaptational Psychodynamics: Motivation and Control.* New York: Science House.

Ross, T. (1937), *The Common Neuroses.* Baltimore: W. Wood.

Selye, H. and Fortier, C. (1950), Adaptive reaction to stress. *Psychosomatic Med.*, 12:3:149-157.

Tredgold, A. (1945), *Manual of Psychological Medicine.* Baltimore: Williams & Wilkins.

Williams, R. (1947), The etiology of alcoholism; a working hypothesis involving the interplay of hereditary and environmental factors. *Quart. J. Stud. Alcohol.*, 7:567.

GENERAL READINGS IN PSYCHIATRY AND NEUROLOGY

1. Arieti, S., ed. (1959), *American Handbook of Psychiatry.* New York: Basic Books, 1950.

2. Bleuler, E. (1911), *Dementia Praecox or the Group of Schizophrenias.* New York: International Universities Press, 1950.

3. Freedman, A. and Kaplan, H., eds. (1967), *Comprehensive Textbook of Psychiatry.* Baltimore: Williams & Wilkins.

4. Kraepelin, E. (1913), *Lectures on Clinical Psychiatry.* London: Bailliere, Tindall, and Cox.

5. Lewis, N. D. C. (1941), *A Short History of Psychiatric Achievement.* New York: Norton.

6. Mayer-Gross, W., Slater, E., and Roth, M. (1954), *Clinical Psychiatry.* London: Cassell.

7. Wechsler, I. (1932), *A Textbook of Clinical Neurology*. Philadelphia and London: W. B. Saunders.

8. Weil, A. (1945), *A Textbook of Neuropathology*. New York: Grune & Stratton.

Index

AA (Alcoholics Anonymous), 346-51, 353
ACTH (adrenocorticotropic hormone), 139
mania simulated by, 588, 593
Acting out, 96, 762-64, 766
in pathological intoxication, 266, 352
in pseudosociopathic schizophrenia, 767, 771-72
in sociopathic personalities, 762, 764
Acute confusional schizophrenia, 710-16
course of, 711
definition of, 710
differential diagnosis of, 712-16
physiological factors in, 714-16
symptomatology of, 710-12, 714-16
Acute organic reaction states, 145-77, 192, 193-96, 206, 218
acute delirium reaction phase, 145, 147-77
coma, 149-50
delusions, fleeting and primitive, 148, 153, 156-57
dream states, 148, 153
emotional liability, 148, 157-58
hallucinations, 148, 153
illusions, 153
oscillating state of consciousness, 148-50

stratified disorientation, 150-51
stratified memory impairment, 151-52
definition of, 194-95
differential diagnosis of, 152, 169-77, 587-88
etiological agents in, 157-77
allergies, 145
avitaminosis, 163-64
drugs, 159-60, 193
emotions, 168
infections, 161-63
intoxicants, 159-61
metabolic disorders, 165-67
organic disorders of the brain, 167-68, 225, 226
trauma, 167, 225
initial delirium reaction phase, 145-47, 176
fluctuations of consciousness, 146-47
impaired anamnestic functions, 147
subjective complaints, 146
"mixed" with chronic organic reaction states, 194, 226-27, 249-50, 302, 371-72
postdelirium reaction phase, 145, 148, 175-77
diminishing symptomatology, 148
emotional weakness, 175-76
postpartum, 177, 218

803

in treatment of alcoholic psychoses, 308
in treatment of depression, 131
in treatment of epilepsy, 417
Anamnesis, 540-43
Anamnestic orientative functions,
53-57, 64, 69-70, 153
in acute organic reaction states,
147
and consciousness, 64, 69
in depression, 70
and dream states, 56-57
in hysteria, 58, 69-70
in organic psychoses, 70
in schizophrenia, 69
in state of rage, 55
See also Consciousness, alterations of
Anoxemia, 139
Anoxia, 227
Anxiety, 518-19
in delirium tremens, 278, 279-80
etiological agent, 640-41
homosexual, 278
in neurosis, 54
in schizophrenia, 640-41, 743-48,
751
in universal reaction pattern, 437-
38, 442, 502-3
Arteriosclerosis, 225, 253, 363-64,
321, 373-74
Atherosclerosis, 196, 201, 222, 224,
227, 293
Atherosclerotic psychosis, 361-62,
363, 366-85
age factor in, 363-64, 374
and depression, 379-81
differential diagnosis of, 367,
373-85, 436-37
and metabolic disorder, 373
paranoid aspects of, 381-82
treatment of, 380-84
See also Senile psychosis

Autism, 615, 629-33, 634
childhood, and prognosis of
schizophrenia, 631
Automized acts, 55, 56, 58
See also Sociopathic personality
Avitaminosis, 163-64, 262, 306-7,
308-10, 338, 340, 382

Bang's disease, 162
Barbiturates, 87, 159
and alcoholic psychoses, 308
and chronic alcoholism, 356
and delirium tremens, 247
and epilepsy, 396
in treatment, 308
Body type, 435, 524-25
in differential diagnosis, 539-40
Borderline schizophrenic, 319, 325-
26, 608-9
See also Schizoid personality
organization; Sociopathic
personality
Brain tumor, 167-68, 201
differential diagnosis of, 386, 436-
37, 510-13
Bromides, 159, 193, 225
in epilepsy, 412

Carbon monoxide poisoning, 225,
232
Catatonic schizophrenia, 649, 671-
80
ambivalence, 671-74, 679
course of, 673-75, 677-78
definition of, 671, 677
deterioration in, 671, 675
prognosis of, 671, 675
symptomatology of, 671-80
muscular phenomena, 672,
674, 675-77
narrowing of consciousness,
677-79
regression, 272, 274-75

treatment of, 675, 678-80
See also Schizophrenia
"Chaotic" sexuality, 335-37, 641-43
Chronic alcoholism, 313-60
    definition of, 313-15
    history of, 325-26, 339-40, 343
    physiological, psychological, and
        social aspects, 315, 316-17,
        341, 346-51, 358
        environment, 338, 341, 346-51,
        360
        physiology, 315, 316-18, 358
        psychological organization,
        315, 318-37
    problem drinkers, 319-29
    psychodynamic mechanisms, 325,
        327-37, 352
    sexual behaviour of, 332-37
    social drinkers, 319-20
    treatment, 337-60 *passim*
        physiological, 338-46
        psychiatric, 338, 351-53
        sociological, 338, 346-52
Chronic organic reaction states
    (Korsakoff syndrome), 192-227,
    297-98
    definition of, 195-96
    diagnosis of, 205
        age of onset, 223, 224
    general paresis, 220-57 *passim*
    "mixed" chronic and acute or-
        ganic reaction states, 194, 226-
        27, 249-50, 302, 371-72
    occurrence in "clear setting", 195-
        96
    prognosis of, 225-27
    symptomatology of, 196-227
        alteration of affective state,
        196, 206-20
        See also Emotional "tilting"
        alteration of personality, 196,
        220-25

impaired intellectual function,
    196-206
neurological alterations, 224-
    25
Coma
    definition of, 149
    differentiated from stupor, 149
    in traumatic mental disorders,
    181-82
Conceptual disorders, 104-33 *passim*
    See also Delusions, Hallucina-
    tions; Overvalued ideas; Schi-
    zophrenia
Consciousness, 49-70 *passim*
    alterations of, 49-70, 53-54, 59,
        80, 146-50
    affectivity and, 50-51, 68, 75
    in dream states, 55-59
    drug experiments, 75
    examination for, direct and
        indirect, 59-69
    in intoxication, 56-57, 61, 65,
        67, 75
    in normal individuals, 51, 53-
        54, 67-69, 146-47
    in organic disorders, 50, 51-55,
        65-67, 70, 146-50
    in psychoneuroses, 51, 53, 55-
        59, 67, 69-70
    in schizophrenia, 51, 55, 56
        See also Schizophrenia;
        specific schizophrenic dis-
        orders
    in sociopathic states, 53, 55
    spontaneous, 58, 59
    in state of rage, 54-55
    and anamnestic orientative func-
        tions, 53, 55, 57, 64, 69-70
    clarity aspect of, 51-55
    components of, 60-63
    and criminal acts, 54
    definition of, 49, 51
    "double attention", 79

ego functions in, 49-50, 60-63
field aspect of, 51-55
fluctuating, 146-50
impairment of, *See* specific disorders
Convulsive states, *See* epilepsy
Countertransference in interviews,
38-39, 43-44
Cultural factors, 58, 61, 62, 427
in alcoholic psychoses, 261, 271
in chronic alcoholism, 313-15
in delusions, 105, 110-12, 126,
127-28
in general paresis, 237-39
in hallucinations, 276
in homosexuality, 336, 706-7
in manic-depressive psychosis,
441-42, 467-68, 501-2, 589-92
and recent memory impairment,
203
in schizophrenia, 441
in suicide, 560-61
Cyclic schizophrenia, 709, 719-20
differential diagnosis of, 119-20
scarring, 711
Cyclothymic temperament, 433,
435, 524-25, 539-40

Delirious states, 89
See also Acute organic reactions
states
Delirium tremens, 161, 259-60, 262-
63, 270-84, 291, 298, 300, 302,
309, 311
diagnostic criteria for, 271
history of, 270
incidence of, 270-71
onset of, 273-74
precipitating factors in, 272-73
prognosis of, 282-84
symptomatology of, 274-82
anxiety about sexual integrity,
278

cardiovascular impairments,
281-82
emotional changes, 279-80
illusions and hallucinations,
275-77
intellectual impairment, 274
labile attention, 274
neurological impairment, 274-
76, 281-82
psychomotor hyperactivity, 280
suggestibility, 279
vegetative impairment, 281,
282
See also Alcoholism
Delusions, 91-92, 101-2, 104-33,
148, 175
in acute delirium reaction states,
153, 156-57
in alcoholic hallucinosis, 295
definition of, 105-10
depersonalization in, 130-31
in depressions, 114, 129-30, 131-
32
descriptive symptomatology of,
112-20
primary type ("clear setting"),
113
secondary type (interpretive),
113-14
differential diagnosis of, 108-9,
493-95
dynamic content of, 83, 123-30
direct wish, 123-24, 126
fear, 123, 126-30
dynamics of, 120-33
congruence, 120-21
mental impairment, 121
wahnbereitschaft ("readiness to
form delusion"), 119, 120
emotional factors in, 114, 116-18,
120-22
in epilepsy, 119, 407

etiological theories of, 115-19, 124-28

emotional demand, 116-18, 126-28

Freudian "regression continuum", 116-17

intellectual impairment, 117-18

multiple intrinsic and extrinsic mechanisms, 124-28

in general paresis, 247, 249

homosexual, 127-28

See also Homosexuality in mania, 120, 123, 132, 463-64

in paranoid group, 106-7, 108, 109-10, 113, 115, 118-19, 121, 123, 125, 127-29, 131-32

reaction states, 110-11, 113-14, 133

in schizophrenia, 107, 110, 118-19, 121-33 *passim*

See also Schizophrenia; specific forms of schizophrenia

and self-preservation, 126

and somatic sensations, 130-31

in traumatic mental disorders, 182, 185

Dementia *See* Deterioration

Depressions, 201, 212, 218, 437-38, 442, 500-66, *passim,* 567-85

cultural factors in, 501-2, 581-82

differential diagnosis of, 503-6, 507-66

in manic-depressive psychosis and involutional depression, 517-30

in manic-depressive psychosis and organic psychoses, 507-17

in manic-depressive psychosis and psychoneuroses, 554-66

in manic-depressive psychosis and schizophrenia, 530-54

in senile and presenile psychoses, 379-80

follow-up studies of, 500-1

history of, 500-1, 517, 530-31, 555-58

involutional *See* Involutional depression

psychodynamic configurations in, 504, 511, 546, 555, 558, 565-66

psychodynamic diagnosis of, 578-85

psychodynamic theories of, 567-85

reactive, 554-57, 565-66

treatment of, psychobiological approach, 582-83

Dereistic thinking, 615, 622

See also Schizophrenia

Deterioration (dimentia), 197-98, 199

Dilantin, 213, 412, 417

Dipsomania, 260, 355-56

Dissociation, *See* Dream states

Dreams, 74, 85-86, 89-94, 101

of the blind, 86

content of, 227-28

of the deaf, 86

and hallucinations, 90-92

as pictorial report, 154

and schizophrenia, 616-17

Dream states (twilight states), 55-59, 80, 89-90, 148, 153-54, 179, 183-84, 392-409 *passim*

in acute delirium, 153-54

and amnesia, 57, 265

diagnosis of, 57

and emotional stress, 58-59

in hysteria, 55, 58

in organic disorders, 55

in pathological intoxication, 56-57

in primitive cultures, 58

in psychomotor epilepsy, 392, 394, 403, 407-09
in schizophrenia, 55
in traumatic psychoses, 183-84

Ego boundaries, 61-62, 95
altered by intoxication, 61
in children, 61, 95
in feebleminded, 62-63
in normal individuals, 62
in primitive cultures, 61-62
in schizophrenia, 61
Ego functioning, 49-50, 60-63, 157
Eidetic imagery, 74-76, 84, 86, 101
and affectivity, 75
in children, 76
definition of, 74-76
and hypnagogic experiences, 86
and impairment of consciousness, 75
and intoxication, 75, 84
and metabolic processes, 76
and pseudohallucinations, 86
Electro-convulsive therapy, 257, 496-97
in alcoholic psychoses, 309
in depressions, 380-81
in manic-depressive psychosis, 447
in paranoid group, 382
in senile and atherosclerotic psychoses, 380
Electroencephalography, 393, 394, 395, 408-9, 410-11, 416
Emotion
as organic force, 359
See also specific disorders
"Emotional incontinence", 207-8
Emotional "tilting" in chronic organic reaction states, 211-20
Empathy, 467, 632, 637-39, 683, 762
Encephalitis, 97, 168
Environment, *See* Cultural factors
Epilepsy, 225, 391-418, 589, 591

clinical forms of, 405-18
grand mal, 403-13
narcolepsy, 395, 416-18
petit mal, 403, 404-5
psychomotor, 268, 392, 394, 403, 405, 407-11, 414
pyknolepsy, 395, 416-18
symptomatic, 391
definition of, 392-94
deterioration in, 405-7
determining factors of, 394-403
electroencephalography, 393-94
"epileptic character", 397-401
fugue states, 407-9
idiopathic, 391-400
legal aspects of, 408-9
and pathological intoxication, 266, 268
psychodynamic configurations of, 401-403
psychotic pictures, 405, 407-11
rebirth fantasies, 402-3
and schizophrenia, 394, 395-97, 416
treatment of, 411-18
trigger mechanisms of, 392, 394, 395-97, 416
Euphoria, 586-87
Excitement states, 250-51, 586-87, 588

Fixation, 568-72, 577, 579
See also Psychodynamic theories
Follow-up studies, 425-27, 444, 458, 498-99, 500-1, 532, 602, 619, 653, 655, 664, 696, 720
Free association in interviewing, 27, 28, 37
Fugue state (frenzy), 396, 407-9
Functional (idiopathic) mental disorders, 421-28
definition of, 421, 422-24
diagnostic approach to, 421-28

809

etiology of, 421-25
history of, 424-28
universal pathological phenomena, 427
See also Involutional psychosis;
Manic-depressive psychosis;
Psychoneuroses; Schizophrenia; Sociopath

General paresis, 196, 217, 220, 222,
223, 224-25, 228-57
age factor, 240, 246
differential diagnosis of, 249, 253,
255, 386, 436, 508-9
epidemiology, 237-39
history of, 228-31
immunology, 234-36
incidence of, 231-32
incubation, 236-37
onset of, 239-44
pathology of, 233-34
prognosis of, 256-57
symptomatology of, 239-53
onset phase, 239-44
full blown phase, 239, 242, 244-
52
terminal phase, 239, 242, 252-
53
treatment of, 255-56

Hallucinations, 72-103 *passim,* 110,
148, 159, 174-75, 177
in acute delirium reactions, 153-
54
in alcoholic hallucinosis, 294, 295-
96
attributes of, 77-82
disagreeability, 80
dominant, 78-79
involuntary, 81-83
irresistible, 77-78
sustained, 80
auditory, preeminent in schizophrenia, 77, 295, 644

in children, 94-95
conceptual, 77, 295, 644
content of, 99-100
culturally determined, 99-100
definition, 73
descriptive symptomatology, 76-
83
differential symptomatology, 88-
103
dreams, 88-94
fantasy, 88-89
illusions, 73
See also Pseudohallucinations
drug induced, 78, 82, 83-84, 85,
94, 97-98, 100, 159
dynamic mechanisms in, 82-83,
90-92, 95-96
in epilepsy, 407
in general paresis, 247, 249
in organic psychoses, 73, 77, 79,
95, 153-54
and psychogalvanic experiments,
81
in schizophrenia, 73, 77, 79, 81,
86, 95-96, 100-1, 102
in traumatic psychoses, 182, 183
visual, 85-86, 102
See also specific disorders
Hashish, 587-88
Head injury, *See* Traumatic mental
disorders
Hebephrenic schizophrenia, 654-71
course of, 654-55, 660-62
definition of, 654
deterioration, 652, 668-70
differential diagnosis of, 664-69
onset of, 660, 661-62
prognosis of, 659, 660-66
symptomatology of, 655-62, 664-
67
marked silliness, 656, 658-59
motor phenomena, 657-58

narcissistic behavior, 658, 667
regression, 656, 658-59
trigger mechanisms, 660-61
Herxheimer reaction, 226-27, 250
Histamine liberation, 168
History taking, 19-44
evolution of, 20-26
importance of patient's conscious
motivation, 24-25
unitary approach, 25-26
constitutional, hereditary, and
physical factors, 21
experiential factors, 21, 24
socioeconomic factors, 21, 25,
42
Homosexuality
in alcoholic hallucinosis, 296-97
in chronic alcoholism, 332-37
and culture, 336, 706-7
in delirium tremens, 278
and paranoid schizophrenia, 704-
7
and psychodynamics of psychoneuroses and psychoses, 704-5
in schizophrenia, 642, 748
See also "Chaotic" sexuality
Hyperinsulinism, 138
Hypertension, 596
Hyperthyroidism, 76, 138, 139, 166-
67
Hysterical schizophrenia, 709, 716-
17

Ideation, continuum of, 104-5
Idiopathic mental disorders, See
Functional mental disorders
Illusions, 72-73, 84, 89, 148, 174
in acute delirium reaction states,
153-54
definition of, 72-73
differentiated from hallucinations, 73

in manic-depressive psychosis,
463-64
Incoherence
in delirious mania, 468
pathognomonic of schizophrenia,
468-69
See also Acute organic reaction
states; Chronic organic reaction states; Epilepsy;
General paresis
Interviews, 19-46
drug induced, 27, 29
form of, 29-34
history taking, 19-27
hostility during, 37-38, 41, 43
privacy during, 37-38, 41, 43
with psychotic patients, 26, 42-45
somatic complaints, 39-40
technique, 27-46
Introjection, 568-70, 573, 577, 579-
80
Involutional depression, 200-1 212,
218, 517-30
classification of, 526-27
course of, 523
differentiated from manic-depressive psychosis, 503-7, 517-30
prognosis of, 517, 523-24, 528
symptomatology of, 517-29

Korsakoff psychosis, 259, 260, 261,
263, 282-83, 284-93, 302, 304,
306-8, 309-11
age factor, 292-93
course of, 291-93
definition of, 284
euphoria, 290
onset of, 284-85
and polyneuritis, 290-91
prognosis of, 291-93
symptomatology of, 285-91
confabulation, 287-89
emotional liability, 289-90

812

classification of, 137-44
    acute organic reactions (acute hallucinatory reactions), 142-44
    chronic organic reactions (Korsakoff syndrome), 142-44
    definition of, 137
    differential diagnosis of, 139, 507-17
    histology of, 138
    history of, 137-44
    "mixed" acute and chronic organic reactions, 249-50, 302, 371-72
    stereotyped pattern in, 141
    See also Acute organic reaction states; Chronic organic reaction states
Overvalued ideas, 104, 116-17, 124
    in continuum of ideation, 104-5
    See also Delusions

Paranoid ideation
    admixtures of, 525-26, 528, 529
    age and hypochondrical, 491
    in alcoholic hallucinosis, 296
    in manic-depressive psychosis, 488-90
        in schizophrenia, 488-90
        See also Paranoid schizophrenia
Paranoid group, 106-7, 108, 109-10, 113, 115, 118-19, 121, 123, 125, 127-29, 131-32, 212, 213, 216-17
    intellectual preservation in, 248-49
    pseudofacts in, 106-7
    See also Homosexuality, Paranoid schizophrenia; Paranoid senile psychosis
Paranoid litigants, 109, 110
Paranoid reactions, as component

of universal reaction pattern, 502-3, 529-30
Paranoid schizophrenia, 691-707
    age factor, 667-68, 691-92
    body type, 692-93
    classification of, 695-97
    delusional system, 697-703, 706
    diagnosis of, 668
    differential diagnosis of, 244-45, 693-94, 698, 702, 703
    and gender, 692
    history of, 691, 695-97
    and homosexuality, 704-7
    prognosis of, 702-3
    psychoanalytic interpretation of, 705-6
    symptomatology of, 697-707
    treatment of, 703-4
Paranoid senile psychosis, 371, 372-73, 381-82
    See also Senile psychosis
Paresis, general, *See* General paresis
Pathological intoxication, 56-57, 170, 259, 260, 263, 270
    automization in, 269-70
    constellative release, 269-70
    course of, 265-66
    diagnosis of, 266-70
    incidence of, 263-64
    legal aspects of, 267
    See also Alcoholism
Pellagra, 164-65, 382
    See also Avitaminosis
Perception, alterations of, 71-103
    See also Illusions, Hallucinations, Pseudohallucinosis
Periodic schizophrenia, *See* Cyclic schizophrenia
Personality inventories, 27
Personality organization, 42-44, 45, 183, 185, 214-15, 220-24, 399-400, 523, 524-25, 528-29, 533, 538-44, 726-32

differential diagnosis of, 201, 221, 223, 224, 239-40, 319, 327, 328, 350, 352-53, 473, 495, 554-66

See also Pseudoneurotic schizophrenia; Psychodynamic theories

Psychopath See Sociopathic personality

Psychotherapy, See Psychodynamic theories; specific disorders, treatment and therapy of

Pyknic body type, 435, 524-25, 539-40

Pyknolepsy, 395, 416, 417-8 See Epilepsy

Questionnaires, in interviews, 27

Regression, 198-99, 568-80 passim, 593, 595, 597, 641
in chronic organic reaction, 198-99, 221
definition of, 198-99
in schizophrenia, 656, 658-59, 672, 674-75
See also Psychodynamic theories; specific disorders

"Release" mechanisms, 209, 215-19, 250
in alcoholic hallucinosis, 300
in organic reaction states, 262, 268, 269-70, 416
in postpartum psychosis, 218
in traumatic mental disorders, 184-86

Repression, of hallucinations, 90
See also Psychodynamic theories; Psychoneuroses

Retardation, 131, 471-85 passim

Rorschach test, 27, 398, 631

Schizo-affective schizophrenia, 709, 717-19

age factors, 718-19
differential diagnosis of, 717-18
onset of, 718-19
prognosis of, 718

Schizoid personality organization, 185-88, 319-57 passim, 558, 726-32
and alcohol, 319, 323-25, 328, 329, 330, 335, 336, 340, 350, 352, 356-57
See also Personality organization

Schizophrenia, 166, 172, 186-88, 198, 203-4, 209-10, 213, 214-15, 216-17, 218-20, 311-12, 432, 446, 468, 531-32, 533-36, 548-51, 601-43, 649-54, 708-10, 726-43, 744-96
and alcoholic hallucinosis, 298-301, 311-12
anamnesis, 533, 538-44
classification of, 532-33, 601-12, 649-54, 708-10, 788-90
history of, 601-609
conceptual organization in, 546-47, 615-29
course of, 533-36
reintegration under stress, 173-74
cultural aspects of, 441-42
definition of, 609-13, 782, 792-96
"disorder of the total personality", 794
diagnosis of, 301, 726-43
early symptoms, 733-43
differential diagnosis of, 446, 465-66, 530-54
etiological concepts, 774-82
constitutional, 774, 780-82
body type, 538-40, 692-93
eunichoid intersex make-up, 781
hypoplasia, 188, 692-93, 781

815

hereditary, 774, 778-80
organic, 774, 777, 792
  biochemical factors, 778
  electroencephalograph patterns, 394
psychoanalytic, 786-88
psychodynamic, 729, 774, 786-92
  existential, 786, 790, 791
  Gestalt, 786, 790-91
  reaction, 782-85
  environment, 440, 533, 537-38
  experimentally induced with drugs, 783-85
follow-up studies of, 602
in general paresis, 256-57
history of, 530-31, 601-8, 610-12, 775-76
incidence of, 756-57, 779
onset of, 533-34
paranoid mechanisms in, 694
and pathological intoxication, 266-68
personality factors, 726-32, 794
predictability of, 728-30
prognosis of, 311-12, 531-32
  See also specific subgroups of schizophrenia
psychological tests for, 538, 543-44, 609, 617-20, 730
psychotherapy of, 690-91
"release" of, *See* "Release" mechanisms
subgroups of, 649-773
  See also Acute confusional schizophrenia; Catatonic schizophrenia; Hebephrenic schizophrenia; Hysterical schizophrenia; Paranoid schizophrenia; Periodic schizophrenia; Pseudoneurotic schizophrenia;

Pseudosociopathic schizophrenia; Schizo-affective schizophrenia; Simple schizophrenia; Symptomatic schizophrenia
symptomatology of, 464, 533, 536-37, 544-54, 613-43, 651-54
  basic clinical symptoms, 613-43
    emotional disorders, 629-43
    thinking disorders, 615-29, 739-41
  gross psychotic symptoms, 643-48
  biological impairment, total, 793
  delusions, 493-95, 548-51, 643, 646-48
  deterioration, 544-45, 652
  hallucinations, 548-51, 643-46
Senile psychosis (Senile dementia), 197n, 225, 361-85
age factors in, 363, 374
classification of, 362-65
course of, 375-76
  suicide, 372
depression in, 379-81
differential diagnosis of, 367, 374-78
organic and acute reaction mixtures in, 371-72
paranoid type, 371-73, 381-82
symptomatology of, 366-73
treatment of, 380-84
  electro-convulsive, 380-81
  metabolic alterations, 382-83
  psychotherapy, 383-84
Sexual anxiety, 278, 296-97
  See also Homosexuality
Sexual pathology, 33, 271
  See also "Chaotic" sexuality; specific mental disorders

Simple schizophrenia, 649, 681-91
  age factors in, 683, 686-87
  cultural factors in, 688
  diagnosis of, 681-83, 687
  differential diagnosis of, 686
  incidence of, 681-82
  prognosis of, 688-89
  symptomatology of, 683-89
  treatment of, 689-91
Society, *See* Cultural factors
Sociopathic personality, 53, 55, 56-
    57, 96, 203-4, 210, 221, 222,
    223, 224, 319, 326-27, 394, 758-
    67
  and chronic alcoholism, 319, 326-
    27, 328, 351-52
  definition of, 759-60
  diagnosis of, 764-65
  differential diagnosis of, 766-67
  electroencephalograph patterns
    in, 394
  etiology of, 760-61
  and head trauma, 179
  history of, 759-60
  incidence of, 758
  onset of, 765
  prognosis of, 765
  symptomatology of, 761-64
  treatment of, 765-66
    See also Pseudosociopathic
      schizophrenia
Sodium amytal, 27, 55, 659
  decorticating effect of, 158
  in differential diagnosis, 190, 512-
    14
  in psychiatric interviews, 624-25
Stupor, 52, 64-65, 79, 149
  differentiated from coma, 149
  hallucinatory "double attention",
    result of, 79
  in hysteria, 55, 57
  in organic reaction states, 53
  in schizophrenia, 52-53

Suicide, 150, 264-65, 484-85, 559-61
  in acute delirius reaction, 150
  in mild depression, 484-85
  in pathological intoxication, 265
Symptomatic schizophrenia, 720-22
  differential diagnosis of, 721
Syphilis, 228-57 *passim*, 292
  rising curve of in U.S., 232n
    See also General paresis

Tension
  intolerance to, in chronic alcohol-
    ism, 324-25
    See also Anxiety; Epilepsy;
      Psychoneuroses; Schizo-
      phrenia
  and psychosurgery, 597-98
Thinking disorders, *See* Schizo-
    phrenia, symptomatology of
"Toxic exhaustive states", 165-66
Toxic reactions, 67-68, 169-71
  elaborate, 169-70
  simple, 169
Tranquilizers, in treatment of alco-
    holic psychoses, 274, 308, 340, 356
Transference, in initial interviews,
    28, 32, 33, 38, 40
Traumatic mental disorders, 178-
    91, 218-19, 266-68, 293
  definition of, 178-79
    as aftermath of concussion,
      contusion, compression, or
      fat embolism, 178
  and Korsakoff psychosis, 293
  "mixed" symptomatology in, 178
  and pathological intoxication,
    266, 267-68
  subgroups of, 178-90
    posttraumatic amentia, 179-80
    traumatic neuroses, 179-80,
      188-91

818